THE
SPECTATOR

Oxford University Press, Amen House, London E.C.4

GLASGOW NEW YORK TORONTO MELBOURNE WELLINGTON
BOMBAY CALCUTTA MADRAS KARACHI LAHORE DACCA
CAPE TOWN SALISBURY NAIROBI IBADAN ACCRA
KUALA LUMPUR HONG KONG

JOSEPH ADDISON
From the Kit-cat painting by Sir Godfrey Kneller in the National Portrait Gallery, London

THE
SPECTATOR

EDITED
WITH AN INTRODUCTION
AND NOTES BY
DONALD F. BOND

VOLUME I

OXFORD
AT THE CLARENDON PRESS
1965

© *Oxford University Press 1965*

PRINTED IN GREAT BRITAIN
AT THE UNIVERSITY PRESS, OXFORD
BY VIVIAN RIDLER
PRINTER TO THE UNIVERSITY

TO

MY WIFE

PREFACE

IT is likely that no single collection of eighteenth-century prose has been oftener reprinted than the *Spectator*, at least during its own century and the nineteenth. By 1729, the year of Steele's death, at least twelve 'editions' had been published by Tonson, and throughout the century a stream of reprints emanated from the presses of London, Edinburgh, and Dublin. It has fared less well from the standpoint of critical editing. Well-merited attention has been given to the texts of Swift, Pope, Gay, and others, but in the 250 years since its first publication there has been no edition of the *Spectator* affording either a reliable text or adequate annotation. The present edition attempts to supply this lack.

Thomas Percy was the first who sought 'to rectify whatever mistakes are crept into the modern copies, by collating them with old original papers', i.e. with the original folio sheets. 'In this work', he wrote to Thomas Birch on 26 April 1764, 'I have made a considerable progress, and in the course of it have been tempted to give now and then a short marginal note, where an Anecdote has occurred to me that threw light upon a passage; and have subjoined the names of some of the occasional writers, which I have happened to discover.'[1] Percy eventually gave up the work when he became chaplain to the Duke of Northumberland, and his materials were turned over to John Calder, who made further annotations. The edition was finally brought out in 1788–9 by John Nichols, with lengthy and often discursive footnotes (those retained from Percy being marked 'P', and those by 'the annotator', i.e. John Calder, marked 'A'). The chief value of this edition, it is perhaps needless to say, lies not in its text but in the scraps of tradition as to authorship, identifications of allusions, reminiscences of customs and personalities, &c., to be found scattered throughout the notes—many of them reprinted by Nichols from the correspondence columns of the *Gentleman's Magazine*. The same is true of the two editions which followed at a short interval of time: by Robert Bisset in 1793, 'with notes and lives of authors', and by Alexander Chalmers in 1806.

It was not until 1868, with the appearance of Henry Morley's

[1] Add. MS. 4316, f. 200; Nichols, *Lit. Illus.* vii (1848), 373.

edition, that any serious endeavour was made to clear the text of the corruptions and 'improvements' which the frequent reprintings of the essays had inevitably introduced. Although he is vague as to the copy-text used, Morley seems to have looked at some of the original sheets as well as the first two reprints (in octavo and duodecimo), and he gives, though not consistently, variant readings in his footnotes. His edition contained many errors, and its annotation was scanty, but it deserves high praise as a pioneer effort to establish an accurate text.

The only other editions with any pretensions to a critical text are the two which appeared almost simultaneously in 1897-8—those of George A. Aitken and G. Gregory Smith. Both are based on the text of the first octavo reprint, and both are equipped with notes. Those of Aitken are richer in quoting contemporary documents, while Gregory Smith's are more extensive, particularly in pointing out sources. Both editions are far from satisfactory, however, either in annotation or in text. Aitken offers a modernized text, while Gregory Smith professes to reproduce exactly 'the antique manner of the original in regard to spelling, punctuation, italics, and capital letters', even to the insertion of new catchwords at the foot of the page. Neither edition, however, does more than approximately represent the text of the first octavo reprint—which itself had introduced many erroneous readings.

In the present edition the text has been based, not on the first octavo or duodecimo volumes, but on the original folio sheets, collated with these two earliest reprints, and incorporating into the text the revisions which may fairly be claimed as authorial. By thus returning to the original sheets for its copy-text, it represents a consistent effort—for the first time in the 250 years since the essays were initially printed—to remove all the normalizations, 'improvements', and corruptions accumulated in the numerous reprintings of the essays. It is too much to hope that this ideal has been completely realized, but the editor may claim with some confidence that the present text is less inaccurate than any hitherto offered and that the introduction and notes supply a fuller commentary than are to be found elsewhere.

The authors of the *Spectator* deal with almost every aspect of life in the reign of Queen Anne and, in one way or another, touch upon most of the intellectual and religious topics of the age. Much of the learning derives from the pages of Bayle's *Historical and Critical*

Dictionary, the first English translation of which appeared in 1710, in four volumes, folio. Addison's indebtedness to Bayle has long been known, but it has now been possible to document in much greater detail the borrowings from the great *Dictionary*. The sources of the *Spectator* extend, of course, far beyond Bayle, and the documentation of the present edition will indicate the extent of the reading engaged in by Addison and others to enliven the seriousness of these daily 'speculations'. An effort has been made to avoid overloading the annotation with contemporary illustrative material, but the notes will probably seem too extensive to some readers— and perhaps inadequate to others. In view of the decline in classical learning in the twentieth century it has seemed desirable to provide translations for all the Greek and Latin quotations, both in the mottoes and in the text of the essays. These, whenever possible, are taken from seventeenth- or early eighteenth-century versions—many from the collection of Thomas Broughton, *The Mottoes of the Spectators, Tatlers, and Guardians translated into English* (1735). It has not been practicable to reproduce the advertisements of the original sheets, but many have been quoted in the annotation; and the titles of all books advertised as 'this day published' are given in Appendix III. Since the *Spectator* served throughout its century as a virtual library of readings for every well-educated person, the present edition is accompanied by a full and analytical index, not only of names but of ideas, allusions, anecdotes, proverbs, references to authors, and so on.

In the many years devoted to the preparation of this edition I have received friendly assistance from more persons than I can name. The three to whom this edition owes most—R. W. Chapman, George Sherburn, and D. Nichol Smith—are unhappily no longer here to receive my thanks. My colleagues and students, past and present, have helped me in countless ways. In particular I must express my gratitude to Professor R. S. Crane, in whose seminar I first attempted any scholarly work on the *Spectator*; to Professor Arthur Friedman, who has discussed with me many of the problems encountered here; to Professor Hannibal Noce, who identified for me the author of the letter in No. 545; and to Professors Edward L. Bassett and Benedict Einarson, who have been unfailingly generous in assisting me to track down the numerous Latin and Greek references in the essays. To Professor Fredson Bowers I am greatly indebted for advice and assistance in working out the relationship of the earliest editions and for allowing me to read in manuscript Greg's now classic essay on 'The Rationale of Copy Text' at a decisive period in the preparation of this edition.

Others who have given me assistance on specific points are Professor Emmett Avery, of Washington State University; Professor Richmond P. Bond, of the University of North Carolina; Miss Elizabeth Burton, of Grass Ground Farm, Haley, near Witney, Oxfordshire; Professor John Butt, of the University of Edinburgh; Dr. Robert D. Chambers, of the University of Saskatchewan; Professor Herbert Davis, of the University of Oxford; Professor Allen Hazen, of Columbia University; Mr. M. J. C. Hodgart, of Pembroke College, Cambridge; the Very Rev. W. R. Matthews, Dean of St. Paul's, London; Dr. Lois G. Morrison, of San Antonio, Texas; Mr. James M. Osborn, of New Haven, Connecticut; Peter Smithers, M.P., of Winchester; the late Very Rev. Norman Sykes; Professor Geoffrey Tillotson, of Birkbeck College, University of London; and Professor William D. Todd, of the University of Texas.

For permission to use material I am indebted to the Duke of Marlborough, for allowing me to quote from the papers at Blenheim Palace; to Major-General Sir Eustace F. Tickell, who generously lent me the collection of manuscripts formerly in the possession of his ancestor Thomas Tickell; to the Houghton Library for permission to use the manuscript now at Harvard (first printed by J. Dykes Campbell) containing an early draft of several essays; and to the Newberry Library for allowing me to photograph the rare original folio sheets of *Spectators* 556–635.

Any person working on Steele must benefit from the labours of Miss Rae Blanchard; my indebtedness to her, as well as to others who have published on Steele and Addison, will be apparent throughout these volumes.

I have many acknowledgements to make to members of the staff of my own University library, as well as to those in the libraries of the British Museum, the Bodleian, the New York Public Library, and the Newberry Library, all of whom have afforded me uniformly courteous and generous assistance. I am indebted also to the Delegates of the Press at Oxford and their staff for many helpful suggestions and advice during the long period in which these volumes were passing through the press.

To the Division of the Humanities in the University of Chicago and to its former Dean, Professor Napier Wilt, I owe thanks for a

Grant in Aid for Research in 1954; and to the John Simon Guggenheim Memorial Foundation for a Fellowship in 1958-9, which allowed me to complete work on the present edition.

My debt to my wife, whose unfailing confidence has sustained me throughout the many years devoted to this labour of love, can never be adequately expressed.

D. F. B.

Chicago
April 1964

CONTENTS

VOLUME I

Joseph Addison. From the Kit-cat painting by Sir Godfrey Kneller in the National Portrait Gallery, London.
By permission of the Trustees   *Frontispiece*

INTRODUCTION
Beginnings of the *Spectator*   xiii
The Character of the New Journal   xviii
Publishing, Distribution, and Circulation   xx
Contents; *Dramatis Personae*   xxix
Letters from Correspondents   xxxvi
Authorship   xliii
Content and Style: The Relative Contributions of
    Steele and Addison   lix
Success of the *Spectator*: Publication in Volume Form   lxix
The Second Series   lxxiii
Contemporary Readers   lxxxiii
Reputation in the Eighteenth Century—and after   xcvi

THE TEXT   cvi

ABBREVIATED TITLES   cxi

ERRATA   cxiii

NUMBERS I–125   I

VOLUME II

Sir Richard Steele. From the painting by Jonathan
Richardson in the National Portrait Gallery, London.
By permission of the Trustees   *Frontispiece*

NUMBERS 126–282   I

CONTENTS

VOLUME III

Eustace Budgell. From the engraving by Knight after the portrait by D. Firmin. British Museum, Add. MS. 37232. By permission of the Trustees   *Frontispiece*

NUMBERS 283–426   I

VOLUME IV

John Hughes. From the engraving by G. Van der Gucht after the portrait by Sir Godfrey Kneller (Hughes's *Poems on Several Occasions*, 1735)   *Frontispiece*

NUMBERS 427–584   I

VOLUME V

Thomas Tickell. From the painting by Sir Godfrey Kneller in The Queen's College, Oxford. By permission of the Provost and Fellows   *Frontispiece*

NUMBERS 585–635   I

DEDICATIONS   174

APPENDIXES
    I. Emendation of Accidentals   189
    II. Collation of Textual Variants   196
    III. Advertisements of Books   205
    IV. Sources of Mottoes   225
    V. Documents   233

INDEX   241

INTRODUCTION

If one wishes to know what the eighteenth-century Londoner
and his environment looked like, the best source of information is the paintings and engravings of William Hogarth; if
one wishes to know what the eighteenth-century Londoner
thought about, one can do no better than to read *The Spectator*:
it both conditioned and freshened the minds of its readers, and
it was read throughout the century. GEORGE SHERBURN

THE periodical essay was a unique genre of the eighteenth
century: there was nothing quite like it before, and there has
been nothing exactly like it since, in length, in scope, and in point
of view. In ancestry it looks back to the essays of Montaigne and
Bacon, to the 'characters' and table-talk of the seventeenth century,
and above all to the journalistic and pamphlet literature of the
Restoration. In the nineteenth century its place was partly taken by
the *feuilleton* and the literary essay of Hazlitt, Lamb, and Stevenson;
to be succeeded in our own day by the work of the newspaper
'columnist' and the featured contribution to the weekly review. In
subject-matter the periodical essay ranged from reflection on the
latest happening in London or Paris to contemplation of the universe
and man's place in it. Because of the many letters from readers which
it received and published, it combined the voice of the author with
the widest form of 'audience participation'. It numbered among its
distinguished conductors not only Addison and Steele but writers
of such diverse talents and background as Defoe, Swift, Fielding,
Johnson, and Goldsmith. Of the hundreds of periodical essays which
flourished in the eighteenth century the *Spectator* was one of the
first in time, as it was also—in the opinion of competent judges—the
most widely read and the best.

I. *Beginnings of the* Spectator

The polite world of London, which had been so pleasantly diverted
by the 'Lucubrations of Isaac Bickerstaff' thrice weekly through the
greater part of 1709 and 1710, seems to have been unaware when
Steele published the final number of the *Tatler*, on the second day
of the new year in 1711, that this famous periodical was to have an
even more brilliant successor. Although Steele hinted that his own

renown as a reporter tended to make his friends and acquaintances chary of talking freely in his presence, the prevailing opinion apparently was that Esquire Bickerstaff had at last exhausted his fund of invention. A pity, for Steele had scored a real success with 'the grave and facetious Squire Bickerstaff, who hath drawn Mankind in every Dress, and every Disguise of Nature, in a Style ever varying with the Humours, Fancies, and Follies, he describes'.[1]

'We were Surpriz'd all at once', writes John Gay in May 1711, 'by a Paper called *The Spectator*, which was promised to be continued every day, and was writ in so excellent a Stile, with so nice a Judgment, and such a noble profusion of Wit and Humour, that it was not difficult to determine it could come from no other hands but those which had penn'd the *Lucubrations*.'[2]

The statement of Gay—who cannot be accused of excessive partiality for the Whigs—appears in a pamphlet written as a letter to a friend in the country, dated from 'Westminster, May 3. 1711', and published early in the same month[3] under the title *The Present State of Wit*. The letter, signed J. G., is designed to acquaint the country friend with the names and characters of contemporary periodical papers, 'whether Monthly, Weekly, or Diurnal'. It begins on a gloomy note. The town has grown weary of Dr. King's *Philosophical Transactions*, Mr. Ozell's *Monthly Amusement* turns out generally to be some French novel or play indifferently translated, Defoe's *Review* is exhausted and grown contemptible, while the *Observator* would be in much the same state but for a revival of party-struggles. As for the political papers, all allow the *Examiner* to be well written, but though its reputed author is Dr. S—t, it has become little more than an official mouthpiece of the new Tory government.

I presume I need not tell you that the *Examiner* carries much the more Sail, as 'tis supposed to be writ by the Direction, and under the Eye of some Great Persons who sit at the helm of Affairs, and is consequently look'd on as a sort of publick Notice which way they are steering us.[4]

Its adversary the *Medley* does not count for much, but the five issues of the *Whig Examiner*, which had appeared in the autumn of

---

[1] Henry Felton, *A Dissertation on Reading the Classics, and Forming a Just Style* (1713), p. 207 (written 1709).
[2] *The Present State of Wit* (1711), p. 19.
[3] Swift in the *Journal to Stella* mentions having seen it on the 14th.
[4] P. 9.

were born within a few weeks of each other in 1672—they had studied together at the Charterhouse and had both gone then to Oxford, after which their paths had diverged.

Steele—Captain Steele as he continued to be known after his period of service with the Coldstream Guards—was perhaps the better known of the two, at least in the world of the London coffee-houses. As the author of three moderately successful comedies—two of which, *The Funeral* and *The Tender Husband*, were still being regularly produced each year—Steele could be considered one of the major playwrights of the day. His *Christian Hero*, written, as he himself said later, 'principally to fix upon his own Mind a strong Impression of Virtue and Religion, in Opposition to a stronger Propensity towards unwarrantable Pleasures',[1] was often cited by his enemies as proof of his wavering principles, and it is true that he had not only, in Johnson's phrase, practised the lighter vices but had more than once laid himself open to legal action. But—however belittled for political reasons by the Tories—he seems to have been generally regarded with affection as a warm-hearted and generous wit and man about town.

Addison's reputation had been made with his poem, *The Campaign*, written in 1704 to celebrate the victory of the Duke of Marlborough at Blenheim, but he had also written a respectable amount of Latin and English poetry earlier, poems which, to quote Gay's grandiose words, had 'long since convinc'd the World, that he was the greatest Master in *Europe* of those Two Languages'.[2] He had without question a solid reputation for learning at Oxford—he continued to hold his Fellowship at Magdalen until 1711—and by government-sponsored travel on the Continent had fitted himself for the responsible series of government positions with which he had been rewarded by the powerful Whig leaders—Commissioner of Appeals in Excise, then Under-Secretary of State (first under Sir Charles Hedges and later under the Earl of Sunderland), and finally in 1709–10 Secretary to the influential Earl of Wharton, Lord Lieutenant of Ireland.

Both Addison and Steele in fact had profited by the dominance of the Whigs in the first years of Anne's reign, as both in turn suffered, after 1710, during the four lean years when the Tories were in

1 Steele's *Apology for Himself and his Writings*, in *Tracts and Pamphlets*, ed. Rae Blanchard (Baltimore, 1944), p. 339.
2 *The Present State of Wit*, p. 15.

1710, were 'writ with so much Fire, and in so excellent a Stile, as put the *Tories* in no small pain for their favourite Hero'.[1]

The greater part of his letter, however, Gay devotes to the success of the *Tatler* and the town's surprise when on 2 January 1711 'Mr. *Steele* flung up *His Tatler*, and instead of *Isaac Bickerstaff* Esq; Subscrib'd himself *Richard Steele* to the last of those Papers'. Not only were individual readers disappointed but 'the Coffee-houses began to be sensible that the Esquires Lucubrations alone, had brought them more Customers than all their other News Papers put together'.[2]

After speculating on the reasons which had caused Steele to bring the *Tatler* to a close and listing a few of its imitators, Gay goes on to describe the amazement and delight of London when the *Spectator* appeared—not thrice a week but every day. Mr. Spectator had 'come on like a Torrent and swept away all before him'. After a threatened deluge of would-be imitators of Squire Bickerstaff the new paper had become 'our shelter from that Flood of False Wit and Impertinence which was breaking in upon us'. Now it is 'in every ones Hand, and a constant Topick for our Morning Conversation at Tea-Tables, and Coffee-houses'. The only fear was that it could not keep going every day.

> We had at first indeed no manner of Notion, how a *Diurnal Paper* could be continu'd in the Spirit and Stile of our present *Spectators*; but to our no small Surprize, we find them still rising upon us, and can only wonder from whence so Prodigious a Run of Wit and Learning can proceed; since some of our best Judges seem to think that they have hitherto, in general, out-shone even the Esquires first *Tatlers*.[3]

The *Tatler* itself had contained such excellent variety that it seemed impossible for one person to be responsible for it. 'This set every one upon guessing who was the Esquires Friend, and most people at first fancied it must be Dr. *Swift*; but it is now no longer a Secret, that his only great and constant assistant was Mr. *Addison*.'[4] For a daily paper like the *Spectator* a whole society of writers would surely be necessary? Gay can confidently announce, however, that the bulk of the writing is the work of 'Mr. *Steele* and *His Friend*'.[5]

The two friends, so alike in many ways and yet so different in temperament, were ideally suited for collaboration on a daily periodical of general appeal. Just thirty-nine years of age—they

---

[1] Pp. 8–9. Swift's annoyance at reading these passages is understandable.
[2] Pp. 10–11.   [3] P. 20.   [4] P. 15.   [5] P. 20.

control. Steele had held the office of Gentleman Usher to Prince George of Denmark, and in 1707 was appointed writer of the *Gazette*, the official government newspaper, at an annual salary of £300. The turn of events in 1710, beginning in June with the Queen's dismissal of Sunderland and followed in October by the overwhelming Tory victory at the polls, removed their patrons from office and power, leaving Steele and Addison with time on their hands and freedom to write more or less as they pleased.

During this period of transition from a Whig to a Tory government—the latter half of 1710—Steele was continuing the *Tatler*, and in the summer published the first two volumes of the collected edition, dedicated to Arthur Maynwaring and Edward Wortley Montagu, both of them personal friends and staunch Whigs. Addison, who had returned from Ireland in August, accepted Maynwaring's invitation to write the series of weekly *Whig Examiners* during September and October—five essays in all, which, as we have seen, Gay praised so highly—to rebut the violent attacks on the Whigs in the weekly *Examiner*, mainly from the hand of Matthew Prior. He was also busy campaigning at this time for his election at Malmesbury, which returned him to Parliament in October, in spite of the general Tory victory.

In the absence of diaries or personal letters our most intimate glimpses of Steele and Addison at this period come from the increasingly unfriendly pen of Swift, who had also just come over from Ireland (in September 1710); in the *Journal to Stella* there are frequent references, especially at first—he goes with Addison to see the drawing of the lottery, he dines at the Chelsea retreat 'where Mr. Addison often retires', and he spends an evening occasionally with Steele and others. Early in October Swift had an interview with Harley, soon to be the most powerful figure in the new government, and shifted his allegiance to the rising Tory leaders, Harley and St. John. At the beginning of November he took over the conduct of the Tory *Examiner*, and the allusions in the *Journal to Stella* henceforth are mainly of growing coldness or irritation toward his former friends. 'Mr. Addison and I', he writes on 12 December, 'hardly meet once a fortnight; his Parliament and my different friendships keep us asunder.'

Towards the close of the year Addison, whose eyes were continually troubling him, seems to have thought of going to Bath for his health and to have arranged to leave London on 3 January. Did he know that Steele was bringing the *Tatler* to a close? 'In a joint enterprise in which he was so intimately concerned', writes Addison's latest biographer, 'it is incredible that it should be stopped without his knowledge, particularly in view of the fact that he had arranged to leave town the day following the publication of the last number.'[1] Although it is impossible to be certain, it seems likely that the two men had come to the decision together, particularly when one considers the short time elapsing between the publication of the last number of the *Tatler* (2 January) and the first number of the *Spectator* (1 March). Addison remained in London, and during the months of January and February doubtless planned with Steele the character and organization of the new periodical.

II. *The Character of the New Journal*

Whereas its predecessor (despite the grave character of Isaac Bickerstaff) had been a frequenter of coffee-houses and a tattler in ladies' assemblies, the new paper will record the more sober reflections of a silent and even diffident man, withdrawn from the strife of the market-place, an observer of life—in short, a Spectator.

In keeping with the detached reflective point of view of the new paper, there will be a total avoidance of politics. With the founding of the weekly *Examiner* in the preceding August the Tories had opened a relentless attack upon the Whig party, a campaign in which both the *Tatler* and Steele personally came in for much abuse. Since November even heavier artillery had been brought in, as Swift took over the journal and began his very effective campaign of propaganda in defence of Harley's policies. For Steele the temptation to counter-attack must have been great. Nevertheless the temptation was resisted: the new paper would not be just a rebuttal of the *Examiner*—that could be left to the *Medley*. In the very first number Mr. Spectator declares his resolution 'to observe an exact Neutrality between the Whigs and Tories, unless I shall be forc'd to declare my self by the Hostilities of either side'.

The new paper is to differ from the *Tatler* in another significant respect. The earlier journal had begun by presenting in each issue a variety of separate topics: accounts of 'Gallantry, Pleasure, and Entertainment' supposedly emanated from White's Chocolate House; poetry was written at Will's Coffee-house in Covent-Garden; 'learning' came under the article of the Grecian Coffee-house in Devereux

[1] Peter Smithers, *Life of Joseph Addison* (Oxford, 1954), p. 198.

Court in the Strand; 'Foreign and Domestick News, you will have from St. *James's* Coffee-house; and what else I have to offer on any other Subject, shall be dated from my own Apartment'. In place of this medley of topics Steele and Addison designed the new paper as a single unified essay, and in no sense a sheet of news, though successive issues might afford as much variety as had been suggested by the names of the different places of resort in the *Tatler*. Mr. Spectator in fact claims acquaintance with all the important coffee-houses. He often joins the 'Round of Politicians at *Will's*', and sometimes smokes a pipe at Child's, while he overhears the conversation of every table in the room. He occasionally joins 'the little Committee of Politicks' in the inner room at St. James's Coffee-house, and his face is very well known at the Grecian and the Cocoa-Tree.

I have been taken for a Merchant upon the *Exchange* for above these ten Years, and sometimes pass for a *Jew* in the Assembly of Stock-Jobbers at *Jonathan's*. In short, where-ever I see a Cluster of People I always mix with them, tho' I never open my Lips but in my own Club.

Mr. Spectator and his Club—these will form the organizing machinery of the new paper. The members of the club are sketched in the second number, a paper written by Steele, but certainly in conjunction with Addison. They include an old-fashioned country squire, a member of the Inner Temple and amateur of the stage, a successful merchant in the City of London, a retired army officer, an elderly beau and man of the world, and a 'very philosophick' clergyman. These, says Mr. Spectator, 'are my ordinary Companions'.

Finally, the new paper announces no definite 'programme'. Mr. Spectator has lived so long in the world, has seen so much and reflected so widely, that he only designs to 'publish a Sheet-full of Thoughts every Morning, for the Benefit of my Contemporaries'. Nor are these contemporaries limited to the male sex. In No. 4 Steele notes that he will take it 'for the greatest Glory of my Work, if among reasonable Women this Paper may furnish *Tea-Table Talk*'. Readers familiar with the *Tatler* might guess that there would be a continuation of the reforms advocated in the earlier paper—the campaigns against gambling, against duelling, against immorality on the stage. These do appear in the *Spectator*, but they are incidental to a larger aim, that of softening the rough edges of life, of raising the general standards of morality, and at the same time of providing interesting material for thought and conversation—in short, to make instruction agreeable and diversion useful.

For which Reasons [Addison writes in No. 10] I shall endeavour to enliven Morality with Wit, and to temper Wit with Morality, that my Readers may, if possible, both Ways find their Account in the Speculation of the Day. . . . It was said of *Socrates*, that he brought Philosophy down from Heaven, to inhabit among Men; and I shall be ambitious to have it said of me, that I have brought Philosophy out of Closets and Libraries, Schools and Colleges, to dwell in Clubs and Assemblies, at Tea-Tables, and in Coffee-Houses.

III. *Publishing, Distribution, and Circulation*

The first number appeared on Thursday, 1 March 1711. A small handbill preserved in the Bagford collection in the British Museum[1] contains the announcement:

> *Wednesday, February* 28. 1711
> TO Morrow will be publish'd,
> A Paper intitled,
> The S P E C T A T O R;
> which will be continued every
> Day. Printed for *Sam. Buckley* at
> the *Dolphin* in *Little-Britain,* and
> sold by *A. Baldwin* in *Warwick-Lane.*

It is also advertised in the *Daily Courant* for 1 March, 'This Day is Publish'd'.

Samuel Buckley, whose name appears as publisher of the new paper, was a man of considerable experience with books and periodicals. In 1699 he had removed from Fleet Street to St. Paul's Churchyard, and shortly thereafter to Little Britain, where, at the sign of the Dolphin, he followed his dual trade of printer and bookseller. John Dunton describes him as 'Originally a Bookseller, but follows Printing—He is an excellent *Linguist,* understands the *Latin, French, Dutch* and *Italian* Tongues; and is Master of a great deal of Wit. He prints *The Dayly Courant,* and *Monthly Register,* (which I hear he Translates out of the Foreign Papers himself).'[2] As the successful publisher of the first daily newspaper in England, the *Daily Courant,*[3]

---

[1] Harl. MS. 5996, No. 72.
[2] *Life and Errors of John Dunton* (1705), p. 314.
[3] The first number (11 Mar. 1702) bore the imprint 'Sold by E. Mallet, next Door to the King's Arms Tavern at Fleet-Bridge', but about a month later (20 Apr.) it began to appear under Buckley's imprint. By 1711 the familiar words 'Printed for

he was well equipped to place the production and circulation of the *Spectator* on a sound footing.

In format the new paper looked very much like the *Daily Courant*, a folio half-sheet, printed on both sides, two columns to the page, with advertisements taking up a part of the second page.

In addition to Buckley's name, the colophon of the *Spectator* also read: 'And sold by A. Baldwin in Warwick-Lane; where Advertisements are taken in.' Anne Baldwin was the widow of Richard Baldwin, who had begun publishing about 1681 and had died in 1698. The Baldwins had had experience with another popular newspaper, the *Post-Man*, which they published from 1694 to 1700, when it was sold to Francis Leach. After her husband's death Mrs. Baldwin continued to publish books and pamphlets, particularly those with a strong Whig and anti-French character.[1] Dunton praises her good business sense, saying that she 'might Vye with all the Women in *Europe*, for *Accuracy and Justice* in keeping Accounts'.[2] She had been earlier associated with Buckley in a news-digest called *The Monthly Register*, beginning in 1703. Other publications in which she had a hand were the *Female Tatler* (1709) and the Whig periodical essay, the *Medley*. Soon after the *Spectator* had started she appeared (October 1711) at the Queen's Bench Bar along with several other booksellers accused of 'printing, publishing, vending, and dispersing several scandalous Pamphlets and Libels' and described by the Tory *Post Boy* as persons 'of Anabaptistical, Heteredoxical, Antimonarchical, &c. Principles'.[3] Her connexion with Buckley had been renewed just the week before the *Spectator* began to appear. The imprint of the *Daily Courant* had read:

LONDON, Printed and Sold by *Sam. Buckley*, at the *Dolphin* in *Little-Britain*.

Beginning with the issue of Monday, 26 February, this was changed to read:

LONDON, Printed by *Sam. Buckley*, at the *Dolphin* in *Little Britain*; and Sold by *A. Baldwin* in *Warwick-Lane*.

The *Spectator*, appearing a week later, bears this identical imprint, so that the new paper might almost seem to its readers a literary

---

Sam. Buckley at the Dolphin in Little Britain' at the bottom of the *Spectator* would augur well for its success.

[1] Leona Rostenberg, 'Richard and Anne Baldwin, Whig Patriot Publishers', *Papers of the Bibliographical Society of America*, xlvii (1953), 1-42.

[2] *Life and Errors*, p. 343.   [3] 25 Oct. 1711.

supplement to the old-established newspaper. Mrs. Baldwin's name appears as the official agent for the *Spectator* throughout its original run of 555 numbers, and she was a frequent advertiser in its columns.[1] Her bookselling business was conducted at a shop near the Oxford Arms in Warwick Lane, between Newgate Street and Ludgate Hill, not far from Buckley's shop in Little Britain. She died in November 1713.[2]

Mrs. Baldwin's shop is named in the imprint as the place where the *Spectator* is sold and also 'where Advertisements are taken in'; within a few days another name is added: 'as also by *Charles Lillie*, Perfumer, at the Corner of *Beauford-Buildings* in the *Strand*'.[3] Lillie was not, of course, a professional bookseller, but he had taken a prominent part with John Morphew in the publication of the *Tatler*.[4] In the spurious continuation of the *Tatler* early in 1711 the writer alludes vaguely to difficulties with Lillie and to the latter's 'ingratitude'. By the middle of March 1711 Lillie seems to have realized that Steele was now the editor of the *Spectator*; his letter appears in No. 16 (19 March) asking for the appointment 'to take in Letters and Advertisements for the City of *Westminster* and the Dutchy of *Lancaster*'. The allusions to him in the *Spectator* suggest personal friendship with Steele. A mock advertisement for instruction in the exercise of the snuff-box at Charles Lillie's appears in No. 138. He is referred to in Nos. 140, 258, and 310 (all by Steele), and his engraving of a mosaic design 'lately discovered at *Stunsfeild* near *Woodstock*' is given free publicity by Steele at the beginning of No. 358.[5] Lillie's 'collection of choice receipts and observations, proved in an extensive practice of thirty years', was published in 1822, under the title *The British Perfumer, Snuff-Manufacturer, and Colourman's Guide*. In 1725 Lillie brought out a collection of unused letters from the *Tatler* and *Spectator*, with a prefatory note by Steele authorizing their publication:

[1] There are fifty advertisements of books 'Printed for A. Baldwin' and ninety-eight of books 'Sold by A. Baldwin'.
[2] An advertisement in the *Post Boy* of 26 Nov. announces that 'Books, Pamphlets, &c. are publish'd as usual, at the late Dwelling-House of A. Baldwin deceas'd, in Warwick-Lane, by her Son-in-Law, JAMES ROBERTS'.
[3] First in No. 16 (19 Mar. 1711), then in No. 18, and thereafter through No. 499.
[4] The imprint of the first collected edition of *The Lucubrations of Isaac Bickerstaff* reads: '*LONDON*, Printed: And to be deliver'd to Subscribers, by *Charles Lillie*, Perfumer, at the Corner of *Beauford-Buildings* in the *Strand*; and *John Morphew* near *Stationers-Hall*.'
[5] This engraving, 'Imprinted on a large Elephant Sheet of Paper', is advertised by Lillie in Nos. 351, 353, 355, 361, and 365.

Original and Genuine Letters sent to the Tatler and Spectator, during the Time those Works were publishing: none of which have been before printed. Printed by R. Harbin, for Charles Lillie, Perfumer, at the Corner of Beauford-Buildings in the Strand; and John Morphew near Stationers-Hall, 1725. 2 volumes.

In No. 499 (2 October 1712) the imprint of the *Spectator* was changed to read: '*LONDON:* Printed for *S. Buckley,* and *J. Tonson:* And Sold by *A. Baldwin* in *Warwick-lane.*' A notice in this issue, however, informs readers that advertisements continue to be taken in by S. Buckley, J. Tonson, C. Lillie, and A. Baldwin, information which is repeated ('Advertisements and Letters continue to be taken in') in Nos. 500, 505, 506, 507, 511, and 512.

Jacob Tonson (the younger), nephew of the first Jacob Tonson, who is named as co-publisher beginning with No. 499, was the second member of the well-known publishing firm. The elder Tonson had long known Addison and had published, among other things, *The Campaign, Remarks on Italy,* and *Rosamond.* The younger Tonson seems also to have taken over the publishing of the *Tatler* volumes by the middle of 1711;[1] in November and December he advertises in the *Spectator* that volumes III and IV of *The Lucubrations of Isaac Bickerstaff, Esq.* are ready to be delivered at his shop in the Strand, adding:

N.B. The Author desires that such Gentlemen who have not received their Books for which they have Subscribed, would be pleased to signifie the same to Mr. Tonson.[2]

It seems likely, as we shall see later, that Tonson shared with Buckley in the printing of the folio sheets; his publications are consistently advertised in the *Spectator* from the beginning; and from No. 499 his name appears, as we have noted, in the colophon as co-publisher with Buckley.

The four persons, then, who may be considered primarily responsible for the business side of the new periodical were Samuel Buckley and Jacob Tonson as printers, with Mrs. Baldwin and Charles Lillie as distributors, so to speak. We have little other evidence of how the paper was circulated. Although the price is not given on the original sheets we know from a letter printed in No. 134 that it sold for a penny—until the stamp tax which was imposed in August

---

[1] See the letter in Steele's *Correspondence,* ed. Rae Blanchard (1941), p. 50 and note.
[2] Nos. 227–34, 237, 247, 248.

1712, when it raised its price to twopence. We may infer from statements in other periodicals that it could be delivered to subscribers at their homes[1] for a quarterly fee, that it could also be obtained on the streets at the hands of hawkers, and that single copies as well as 'monthly sets' could be bought from booksellers and 'news-shops' throughout London.

Before the first month was out, readers of the *Spectator* were advised that 'Compleat Setts of this Paper, for the Month of March, are to be sold by Mr. Graves in St. James's Street; Mr. Lillie, Perfumer, at the Corner of Beaufort-Buildings; Mr. Sanger at the Temple Gate, Mr. Knapton in St. Paul's Church-Yard, Mr. Round in Exchange Ally, and Mrs. Baldwin in Warwick-Lane'.[2] This advertisement, which is repeated in later numbers,[3] is followed by similar notices of sets cumulatively for succeeding months, through May, June, July, August, September, October, and November, with an increasing number of distributing agents. 'Mr. Lewis under Tom's Coffee House, Covent Garden' is added in No. 39; Mr. Lloyd near the Church in the Temple in No. 69; Mrs. Boulter next the Rose Tavern at Temple Bar in No. 125; Mrs. Treganey near Essex-Street in No. 135; Mrs. Bond at the Old Vine at Charing-Cross in No. 145; and Mrs. Dodd at the Peacock without Temple Bar in No. 221— a total of twelve agents by mid-November. Thomas Graves, Egbert Sanger, James Knapton, James Round, William Lewis, O. Lloyd, Ann Dodd, and Anne Baldwin were all recognized booksellers of the day.[4] Mrs. Boulter, Mrs. Treganey, and Mrs. Bond operated 'news-shops', where books and pamphlets, newspapers, patent medicines, &c., were sold. In October 1711 all three (as well as Mrs. Baldwin) were in trouble with the Tory government under charges of 'printing, publishing, vending, and dispersing several

---

[1] The *British Apollo* (9 July 1708) informs subscribers 'who were serv'd by the Boy in the Blew Livery' and had not received their papers on Wednesday, that 'the reason was, that the said Boy run away from his Service the Day before'. The following week (16 July) the following notice appears: 'Whereas the Lad who carryed the Papers to part of our Subscribers (mention'd in our Paper last Week) is return'd to his Service, we having not found him unjust in his Accounts, desire that they who have not paid in his Walk, will pay their Quarteridge to him.' On 3 Apr. 1710 the same journal announces: 'Any Persons in Town may have these Papers brought to their Houses at 3*s. per* Quarter, by directing to Mr. *Carter*, at the *Rose* and *Crown* in St. *Paul's Church-yard*, Mr. *Bickerton* at the *Rose* and *Crown* in *Little Britain*, or to 'the Printer hereof, superscrib'd to the *British Apollo*. N.B. All that begin within the Quarter to pay on Quarter-day a Penny for each Paper they have had.' This journal was 'Printed for, and Sold by J. Mayo, at the Printing Press against Water-Lane in Fleet-Street'.
[2] No. 29.
[3] Nos. 31, 35, 37, 39, 41, 43, 45, 47, 49, and 53.
[4] Henry R. Plomer, *Dictionary of Printers and Booksellers . . . 1668–1725* (1922).

scandalous Pamphlets and Libels, highly reflecting on the Government and Church of England, by Law Establish'd',[1] and Mrs. Boulter had to appear again at the Queen's Bench in February and April 1713.[2]

With such a well-organized system of publication and distribution behind them, Steele and Addison could proceed with confidence. In less than a fortnight Addison records (in No. 10) his satisfaction in hearing 'this great City inquiring Day by Day after these my Papers, and receiving my Morning Lectures with a becoming Seriousness and Attention. My Publisher tells me, that there are already Three Thousand of them distributed every Day.' This is indeed an excellent record for a new literary paper. The well-established *Post-Man* and *Post Boy* a few years earlier had reached circulations of 4,000 and 3,000 respectively, but they were newspapers and were published but three days a week.[3] Four months later, on 23 July 1711, 'my Bookseller tells me,' Addison writes in No. 124, 'the Demand for these my Papers increases daily'; and in retrospective mood at the end of the year (31 December 1711) he finds gratification in the thought that 'notwithstanding I have rejected every thing that savours of Party, every thing that is loose and immoral, and every thing that might create Uneasiness in the Minds of particular Persons, I find that the Demand for my Papers has encreased every Month since their first Appearance in the World' (No. 262). The growth in the number of distributing agents for the monthly sets, from six in early April to twelve by the middle of November, is also indicative of steadily increasing popularity.

The stamp tax of August 1712 certainly decreased the sales of the *Spectator*. 'It at first reduced it to less than half the number that was usually Printed before this Tax was laid', writes Steele in No. 555; but, even so, 'the Tax on each half Sheet has brought into the Stamp-Office one Week with another above 20 *l*. a Week arising from this single Paper'. If Steele's statement is correct, this would

---

[1] *Post Boy*, 25 Oct. 1711.

[2] *Evening Post*, 12 Feb.; *Post Boy*, 23 Apr. Mrs. Bond, who was selling the *Daily Courant* in 1702, 'next Door to Old Man's Coffee-House at Charing-Cross' (*Daily Courant*, 13 May), and 'Wasse's Elixir for the Gout and Rheumatism' in 1704 (Tutchin's *Observator*, 20 May), had moved by 1706 to 'the Sign of the Old Vine over against the Blue Post[s] and Rummer', still near Charing-Cross (*Post-Man*, 14 Feb.). By 1716 a certain Thomas and Elizabeth Griffiths 'keep the great old publick News-Shop (commonly known by the Name of Mrs. Bond's News-Shop) over-against the Blue Posts and Rummer Eating House at Charing-Cross' (*Daily Courant*, 11 Sept.).

[3] James R. Sutherland, 'The Circulation of Newspapers and Literary Periodicals, 1700–30', *The Library*, 4th ser., xv (1934), 110–24.

mean a printing of between 1,600 and 1,700 after the imposition of the tax. 'I once heard it observed', wrote Johnson in 1781, 'that the sale may be calculated by the product of the tax, related in the last number to produce more than twenty pounds a week, and therefore stated at one and twenty pounds, or three pounds ten shillings a day; this, at a halfpenny a paper, will give sixteen hundred and eighty for the daily number.'[1] If this is 'less than half the number' of those printed before 1 August 1712, the circulation had reached a figure between 3,000 and 4,000 in the second year of publication.[2] Moreover, if the stamp duty was evaded, as it certainly was by other newspapers, the circulation figures would be even greater; and there is evidence that this was sometimes the case with the *Spectator*.[3]

The sales of certain numbers have been said to be much higher. William Fleetwood, Bishop of St. Asaph, wrote to Bishop Burnet on 17 June 1712 that No. 384 had reached a figure of 'above 14,000',[4] and there is also the statement in the *Biographia Britannica*,[5] repeated by Thomas Tyers[6] and the author of *Addisoniana*,[7] that 20,000 were sometimes sold in a day. Later scholars have been sceptical of such figures because of the physical difficulties of printing so many copies of a daily paper. Professor Nichol Smith shows, from the rate of working estimated in Timperley's *Printer's Manual*, that eight hours of steady work would be required to print 2,000 sheets, and that 'if the circulation rose to 3,000, twelve hours' printing at top speed would be required'.[8] 'These figures have only to be stated', he continues, 'to show that in the printing-house of a popular paper at least four presses had to be used—two for each side of the sheet, and

---

[1] 'Life of Addison', *Lives of the Poets* ('World's Classics' ed.), i. 426. All further references are to this edition.

[2] Aitken (*Life of Steele*, i. 319-20) makes much the same computation. 'A payment of over £20 a week for stamp duty represents a daily circulation of more than 1600 copies, or 10,000 a week, from the 1st August to the 6th December 1712, and the daily circulation before the 1st August would therefore be, according to Steele's statement, nearly 4000.'

[3] Sutherland, p. 121. 'It would be interesting to learn if unstamped copies of the *Spectator*—after the stamp duty came into force—are in existence. If so, an estimate based on Steele's statement would have to be revised.' I have a copy of Nos. 535 and 555 without the stamp, and two copies of No. 530, one with the stamp and one without.

[4] Printed in *Mr. Pope's Literary Correspondence* (Curll, 1736), iv. 107, and in *A Compleat Collection of the Sermons, Tracts, and Pieces of all Kinds, that were written by the Right Reverend Dr. William Fleetwood* (1737), p. vi.

[5] (2d ed., 1778), i. 49. Kippis gives Tickell as authority for this figure, but Tickell actually says nothing of the circulation of the *Spectator*.

[6] *An Historical Essay on Mr. Addison* (1783), p. 42.

[7] *Addisoniana* (1803), ii. 52.

[8] D. Nichol Smith 'The Newspaper', *Johnson's England* (Oxford, 1933), ii. 334.

that, in these days before stereotyping, the whole paper had therefore to be set at least twice.'

We should be forced to the conclusion, therefore, that, if the circulation of the *Spectator* rose to 3,000 and if the original numbers were set up in one printing-house from day to day, there would have to be duplicate printings, as was certainly the case with the *Tatler*.[1] If, however, Buckley—already busy with the printing of the *Daily Courant*—shared the work with another printing-house, Buckley doing the work on one day and the other printer on the alternate day, the time available for preparing 3,000 copies would be exactly doubled. In such a case there would be two days, not one, for setting up type and running off the copies, and the difficulty of issuing 3,000 copies a day would be obviated.

An examination of the original sheets shows that this was, in fact, the procedure followed in the printing of the *Spectator*,[2] that not one printing-house but two were employed and that these two —for the greater part of the original run of 555 numbers—worked in exact alternation. For the first 132 numbers (1 March–1 August 1711) Printer A is responsible for all the odd-numbered papers— 1, 3, 5, 7, &c.—and Printer B for all the even-numbered—2, 4, 6, 8, &c. There is a break in the alternation in Nos. 133–62, with Nos. 133–47 all done by Printer A, and Nos. 148–62 by Printer B. The exact alternation is resumed with No. 163 (6 September 1711) and continues as far as No. 410 (20 June 1712). Another break occurs in Nos. 411–21 (the series by Addison on 'the pleasures of the imagination'), which are all done by Printer A, followed by Nos. 422–32 by Printer B. From this point to the conclusion of the series there is a different pattern of printing—not alternately, but in groups of three, Nos. 433, 434, 435 by Printer A; Nos. 436, 437, 438 by Printer B; and so on to the end, with Nos. 553, 554, and 555 done by Printer A.

Evidence for two distinct printings is to be found in the recurring features which were kept standing in type—the letters forming the heading, the rules separating the date from the body of the paper, the broken or bent rules recurring in papers printed by one or the other of the shops, and the various misprints in the colophon which occur only in alternate issues. It is also observable if one compares the width of the type-line, the size of type, and the physical

---

[1] F. W. Bateson, 'The *Errata* in *The Tatler*', *Review of English Studies*, v (1929), 156.
[2] The material presented here is condensed from my article, 'The First Printing of the *Spectator*', *Modern Philology*, xlvii (1950), 164–77.

characteristics of certain letters in the text. Typographical pecu-
liarities, including misprints, in the hundreds of advertisements of
books and patent medicines provide additional confirmation.

It is clear also from advertisements left in standing type and used
both in the *Spectator* and in the *Daily Courant* that the printer of the
B papers is Samuel Buckley, and it seems likely that Printer A can
be identified with Jacob Tonson the younger. Buckley and Tonson
also shared between them the printing of the *Spectators* in collected
volumes, in both octavo and duodecimo.[1]

Such an arrangement, with two printing-houses responsible for
alternate numbers, might be awkward for a paper of news, where
daily supervision would be necessary, but for a species of periodical
essays like the *Spectator* it would offer a very convenient method of
working. It explains how 3,000 copies and more could be produced
every day, since each printer had two days instead of one for his
work. And when enough material had accumulated, there was
nothing to prevent the papers being run off in advance and properly
dated ahead.

The first break in the regular alternation of papers occurs in
August 1711, with numbers from 2 to 18 August (Nos. 133–47)
done by Tonson, and numbers from 20 August to 5 September (Nos.
148–62) done by Buckley. With the exception of six papers,[2] these
thirty numbers are all by Steele. We know that Addison was at
Bath during the greater part of August 1711,[3] and Steele may have
found it more convenient to have these papers done in two large
consecutive batches. The only other break in the alternating series
occurs from 21 June to 16 July 1712, with numbers from 21 June to
3 July (Nos. 411–21, the series on the pleasures of the imagination)
done by Tonson, and numbers from 4 to 16 July (Nos. 422–32) done
by Buckley. The tradition that the essays on the pleasures of the
imagination had been written earlier and were adapted for the
Spectator is confirmed by this explanation of the printing. Tickell,
in the preface to the *Works* of 1721, observed that Addison could

---

[1] In an article, 'The Text of the *Spectator*', *Studies in Bibliography*, v (1953), 109–28,
I have attempted, on the basis of textual variants and spelling differences, to assign
particular volumes in 8vo and 12mo to their respective printers.

[2] Nos. 135, 159, 160, and 162 by Addison, and Nos. 150 and 161 by Budgell.

[3] Smithers, p. 226. Addison's letter to Joshua Dawson, dated from Bath, 18 Aug.
1711, was first printed by Graham (p. 264). The preponderance of essays by Steele
at this point puzzled G. Gregory Smith, who asks, 'Was Addison on holiday, or
indisposed, or was he in Ireland looking after his threatened interests?' (Note to
No. 132.)

not have contributed so largely to the *Spectator* 'if he had not in-grafted into it many pieces, that had lain by him in little hints and minutes, which he from time to time collected, and ranged in order, and moulded into the form in which they now appear'.[1] It would be much simpler for Addison at this point to turn over the whole manuscript to one printer than to divide it between two. While Tonson was occupied with these eleven papers, Buckley would be entrusted with the material for Nos. 422–32, which would then follow with proper dates. The remaining essays in the original series (Nos. 433–555) were done, as we have seen, alternately in groups of three. It seems reasonable to infer that, by this time, Addison and Steele were a little weary with daily concern over a paper which had occupied their energies for some sixteen months, and that they found it easier to prepare material at once for three numbers, each group of three to be turned over to the appropriate printer. By this scheme Steele became responsible for the numbers appearing on Mondays, Tuesdays, and Wednesdays, while Addison would pro-duce the essays for the latter half of the week, including the more serious paper customarily written for Saturdays. Moreover, by this time a great deal of material, in the form of letters and contributed essays, had accumulated, which could be rapidly prepared for the printer. Many of these later numbers as a matter of fact consist mainly or entirely of letters, from a great variety of correspondents.

IV. *Contents*; Dramatis Personae

At the beginning, however, letters could not be counted on. Addison and Steele, in undertaking the production of a 'sheet-full of thoughts every morning', had to depend on themselves alone for the daily writing of a paper which, they hoped, would catch the fancy of the public. There had been earlier papers produced once or twice a week—at most, three times a week—but no one had hitherto attempted the writing of a daily essay, one which would appear with the regularity of the *Daily Courant* (resembling it in size and format) but which should not depend on news or political propa-ganda for its subject-matter. These daily observations or 'specula-tions', striking just the right balance between affairs of everyday life and more serious matters of universal concern, needed the kind of collaboration which these two friends were able to give.

This at any rate was the opinion of Gay, who speaks of 'those two

---

[1] Addison's *Works* (1721), vol. i, p. xiii.

Great Genius's' (in the pamphlet referred to above) as men 'who seem to stand in a Class by themselves, so high above all our other Wits'. Their contrasting temperaments remind him of 'two famous States-men in a late Reign', Lord Somers and Lord Halifax. 'The first was continually at work behind the Curtain, drew up and prepared all those Schemes and Designs, which the latter Still drove on, and stood out exposed to the World to receive its Praises or Censures.'

Mean time, all our unbyassed well-wishers to Learning, are in hopes, that the known Temper and Prudence of one of these Gentlemen, will hinder the other from ever lashing out into Party, and rend'ring that wit which is at present a Common Good, Odious and Ungrateful to the better part of the Nation.[1]

The performance of the new paper fulfilled all the expectations to which Gay had given voice. The essays produced during the opening months (March, April, and May) reveal a diversity of theme and a unified point of view which enable us easily to understand why, from the first, the new paper caught on. There are lively articles on such current institutions as the Bank of England, the Italian Opera, the masquerade, the theatre, sign-boards, coffee-houses, and the Royal Exchange. Interspersed with these, from the beginning, are more serious discussions on such topics as the conduct of life, consideration for others, envy, impudence, the reform of life, ugliness, the proper use of time, &c. Curiously enough, these moralizing essays are not all by Addison, nor the more topical ones by Steele. It is as if the two men consciously tried their hands, at the outset, in the production of papers which were not to be, in the long run, their 'specialities'. It is Addison who leads off, in No. 3, with a rather daring paper on the Bank of England, showing the dangers which it might expect from Tory control; and it is Addison, again, who is responsible for a series during the first month on the absurdities of Italian opera. Steele's essays on envy (No. 19) and on reform of life (No. 27), on the other hand, are among his most serious and studied efforts and in a vein which is more generally characteristic of Addison.

The first month sees also the appearance of a full-length tale, 'Inkle and Yarico', in No. 11, the first of many such in the *Spectator*. The story is introduced in a very personal way, in the course of a visit to 'Arietta', and this tone of intimacy characterizes most of the

[1] P. 21.

essays during the first month of the *Spectator*. In April, with the appearance of the paper on True and False Humour, by Addison, we have the first example of the impersonal and more formal essay— the kind of paper which Addison later describes as the 'methodical discourse'—followed almost immediately by a series of four on English tragedy, which, though referring to contemporary conventions in the theatre, are written in a serious and impersonal vein. The most striking example of this more formal discourse during the early months is the week's series on True and False Wit, though even these six essays are introduced in the half-jocular, half-serious style which Addison was fond of assuming—a style more to the taste of the eighteenth century than of our own.

I intend to lay aside a whole Week for this Undertaking, that the Scheme of my Thoughts may not be broken and interrupted; and I dare promise my self, if my Readers will give me a Week's Attention, that this great City will be very much changed for the better by next *Saturday* Night.

Except in a few instances, however, the *Spectators* do not fall into the category of the personal essay.[1] It is true that the personality of Mr. Spectator gives unity of tone to the papers. His early life is sketched in the first number, by Addison, but various bits of information about his past emerge in subsequent essays, so that the reader comes to recognize the fictional Mr. Spectator as an individual person with background and character. His visit to Grand Cairo is frequently referred to: it was there, for example, that he picked up several Oriental manuscripts, including the 'Vision of Mirza' (No. 159), and it was there that he met the good-natured Mussulman, who promised him so many favours (No. 604). He has also travelled in France, where he delighted in listening to the songs of the people; in Rome he saw the Pope officiate at St. Peter's, and he speaks, apparently at first hand, of a fragment of a statue 'still to be seen at Rome' (No. 229). He recalls a certain counsellor from the days when he was a young man 'and used to frequent *Westminster Hall*' (No. 407), as well as other characters from his past (Nos. 493, 497). He remembers the remarkable year of Blenheim, when England was 'raised to the greatest height of Gladness it had ever felt since it was a Nation' (No. 165), and he recalls the poems addressed to Louis XIV after he had lost the battle of Ramillies (No. 306). He

---

[1] Cf. Melvin R. Watson, 'The *Spectator* Tradition and the Development of the Familiar Essay', *ELH* ,xiii (1946), 189–215.

remembers the period, some thirty years before, 'when Dr. *Titus Oates* was in all his Glory' (No. 57); it was at this time of the Popish Plot that Mr. Spectator, because of his taciturnity, was suspected of being a Jesuit (Nos. 4, 77, 131). 'When the four *Indian* Kings were in this Country about a Twelve-month ago, I often mix'd with the Rabble and followed them a whole Day together' (No. 50); and there are many other references to recent events, such as going to the theatre, which help to give the author of the essays more than a nominal personality. He recounts in No. 12 his recent efforts to find a suitable lodging in London, first with 'an officious Land-lady', then with a jolly Landlord (this was R. B., Fishmonger in the Strand), and finally with 'a Widow-woman, who has a great many Children, and complies with my Humour in every thing'.

On a more personal note he reveals, at the beginning of No. 261, the story of his unsuccessful courtship:

> My Father . . . has very frequently talked to me upon the Subject of Marriage. I was in my younger Years engaged, partly by his Advice, and partly by my own Inclinations, in the Courtship of a Person who had a great deal of Beauty, and did not at my first Approaches seem to have any Aversion to me; but as my Natural Taciturnity hindered me from shewing my self to the best Advantage, she by degrees began to look upon me as a very silly Fellow, and being resolved to regard Merit more than any thing else in the Persons who made their Applications to her, she married a Captain of Dragoons who happened to be beating up for Recruits in those Parts.

Such is the man who, years later, after a lifetime of travel and reading, settles down in lodgings in London, where he can indulge his fondness for mingling anonymously with the crowd, observing much and saying little, and publishing for the instruction and diversion of his fellow creatures the results of his reflections on men and manners.

The other six members of the Club, to whom Steele, doubtless with Addison's collaboration, gives in the second number an elaborate introduction, fail to play any very lively role as contributors or stimulants to discussion in subsequent numbers. It seems likely that Steele and Addison thought of using this varied company as mouthpieces for different points of view, yet of them all only Sir Roger de Coverley functions completely as an independent fictitious creation. Just why the others failed to develop we do not know: possibly there was little 'reader response' among the letters received, possibly the original plan was lost or altered during the course of serial publication, as was sometimes the case later in the work of Dickens and Trollope.

The Templar, who might have been an obvious choice for the expression of opinions about the drama and other literary matters, has little to do. He ridicules Will Honeycomb for his poor spelling in No. 105 and expresses an opinion about Will's marriage in No. 530; he is mentioned briefly in four or five other papers. He is seen one evening at the theatre, where he looked 'very little pleased with the Representation of the mad Scene of the *Pilgrim*' (No. 22). But the only paper directly attributed to him is the 'farewell Essay' on pronunciation and action in the drama, by Hughes (No. 541).

The Clergyman plays a slightly larger part. He gives Mr. Spectator some letters in No. 27, he discourses on dissimulation and compliment in No. 103, he submits an essay on atheism in No. 186; and Addison's 'thought in sickness' (No. 513) is attributed to 'that Excellent Man in Holy Orders, whom I have mentioned more than once as one of that Society who assist me in my Speculations'. Beyond a brief reference in No. 34 and an allusion to his death in Nos. 542 and 553, that is all.

Sir Andrew Freeport, as a spokesman for the Whig view of the importance of trade and commerce, receives more attention. Readers are reminded more frequently of him throughout the course of the *Spectator*; he often smiles upon Mr. Spectator at the Royal Exchange (No. 69), and although there are good-natured references to his strong anti-Tory bias, there is no doubt of the general approval in which he is held by Mr. Spectator and the rest of the Club. His discourse on the economic aspects of charity (No. 232) is one of the well-argued set-pieces in the *Spectator*, and he ably defends (in No. 174) the cause of the commercial interests against the Tory arguments of Sir Roger de Coverley.

Captain Sentry, who recalls (in No. 152) stories of army life such as those which may have remained in Steele's memory, was obviously created as a vehicle for defence of the military profession, then under violent attack by Tory party writers. Yet he actually appears very little in the *Spectator*, in spite of the frequency with which military matters and military language are discussed. He accompanies Sir Roger to the play (No. 335), wearing the sword he had used in the battle of Steenkirk, and as nephew and next heir to Sir Roger he inherits Coverley Hall and the entire estate after

Sir Roger's death (No. 517), after which he retires from London and the Club (No. 542).

The two most fully individualized members are unquestionably Will Honeycomb and Sir Roger de Coverley, both type characters yet with sufficient individuality to rank among the great characters of English fiction. Both embody attitudes and points of view under attack by the *Spectator*: the one representing the fashionable gallantry of the Restoration, the other typifying the Tory landowner who resists all that is to make England prosperous in the coming century. It is also significant that while both men are disapproved of, they are more interesting and attractive than some of the others who are held up as models.

Will Honeycomb is frequently mentioned as a companion to Mr. Spectator; his opinions, especially in matters relating to the fair sex, are often quoted; and he is responsible for several interesting pieces—his translation (from the French) of an epigram of Martial (No. 490), his account of the modern women of Hensberg (No. 499), his description of the auction of women at fairs (No. 511), and finally the much admired letter (No. 530) in which he announces his own marriage to a poor but virtuous country maiden.

The natural Sweetness and Innocence of her Behaviour, the Freshness of her Complection, the unaffected Turn of her Shape and Person, shot me through and through every time I saw her, and did more Execution upon me in Grogram, than the greatest Beauty in Town or Court had ever done in Brocade.

The figure of Sir Roger de Coverley, one of the permanent characters in the gallery of English 'humourists', was early recognized as a supreme example of the eighteenth-century country squire. In the preliminary sketch by Steele (in No. 2) he is depicted as a cheerful, gay, and hearty bachelor in his fifty-sixth year, with a rather full experience of Restoration gallantry behind him, a mixture of sense and folly, but one whose 'Singularities proceed from his good Sense, and are Contradictions to the Manners of the World, only as he thinks the World is in the wrong'. It is not until the *Spectator* had run for some four months that much is done with him, apart from brief mentions in No. 6 and No. 34. But in June 1711 appears the long series of papers by Addison, describing Mr. Spectator's visit to the country; and it is here, in Nos. 106–31, that the character of Sir Roger is fully sketched out, along quite different lines from Steele's initial portrait. The extravagance and eccen-

INTRODUCTION

tricity of Sir Roger are emphasized, but, more significantly, his *naïveté* and rather unintelligent conservatism—manifested in his half-credulous attitude toward Moll White, in his behaviour with the gipsy fortune-teller, and in his actions at the assizes—and it is Addison who develops Sir Roger's character in this quite different direction.[1] The only new aspect of Sir Roger developed by Steele is the story of his love for the perverse widow (Nos. 113, 118), charming in itself but too self-critical and self-possessed[2] to be consistent with the fully outlined portrait by Addison.

It is Nos. 106–31 which form the series of 'De Coverley papers' proper; but in later numbers, most of them by Addison, we get further glimpses of Sir Roger—coming to London for a view of Prince Eugene (No. 269), displaying his learning out of Baker's *Chronicle* in the visit to Westminster Abbey (No. 329), going to the theatre and to Vauxhall (Nos. 335, 383)—and throughout he is presented as the ineffective and quixotic Tory squire, not the vigorous gentleman whose singularities 'proceed from his good sense'. The inconsistency between the two conceptions of Sir Roger was sensed by Johnson and others in the eighteenth century, but it was John Aikin, writing in the *Monthly Magazine* in 1800, who seems to have first pointed out the extent to which Addison employed the figure of Sir Roger as 'a covert for throwing ridicule upon that class of society which he has more openly satirized in his country-gentleman in the Freeholder' [No. 22].

Both have the same national and party prejudices, and exhibit an equal inferiority to the more cultured inhabitant of the town. As the papers in which Sir Roger appears have ever been among the most popular in the Spectator, I cannot but think they have done much in fixing on the public mind the abstract idea of a country gentleman, and attaching to it that sort of contempt with which, whether justly or otherwise, it has usually been treated; and I should no more hesitate to term Addison a *satirist* in this piece of pleasantry, than the author of the celebrated 'Lettres Provinciales' . . .[3]

It was the work of Cervantes, rather than that of Pascal, with which the figure of Sir Roger was most often compared in the eighteenth century, and it was as a great fictional creation that this character

[1] Émile Legouis, 'Les deux "Sir Roger de Coverley", celui de Steele et celui d'Addison', *Revue germanique*, ii (1906), 453–71; reprinted in Legouis's *Dernière Gerbe* (1940), pp. 85–104.
[2] Cf. the final paragraph in No. 118.
[3] *Monthly Magazine*, ix (Feb. 1800), 2–3.

achieved the enormous popularity which it attained, particularly in the nineteenth century, a popularity which can be measured by the great number of school editions and cheap reprints of the 'Sir Roger de Coverley papers' issued both in England and America. It was a creation which Joseph Warton held worthy to rank with the masterpieces of Cervantes and Shakespeare.

The great art of Cervantes consists in having painted his mad hero with such a number of amiable qualities, as to make it impossible for us totally to despise him. This light and shade in drawing characters, shews the master. It is thus Addison has represented his Sir Roger, and Shakespeare his Falstaff.[1]

The satire is there, and all the more effective for being unobtrusive. Whatever Sir Roger may have meant to later generations there can be little doubt of Addison's intention: this combination of personal charm and political ineptitude represented an obsolete and wrongheaded type in English society—attractive and companionable, but not the sort to be entrusted with the management of the country's affairs!

V. *Letters from Correspondents*

Although the various De Coverley papers can be assigned to their respective authors with reasonable certainty, the question of authorship of the *Spectator* essays in their entirety is difficult to solve satisfactorily. The use of 'signature letters'—C, L, I, O for Addison, R and T for Steele, and X for Budgell—is clear enough, but many of the numbers bearing these signatures are made up in part, or entirely, of letters. It will perhaps be best to say something of these before going on to consider the complicated question of the authorship of the essays as a whole.

In the first issue Addison invited correspondents to address their letters to him in care of his publisher, Mr. Buckley in Little Britain. In the following week, in No. 8, he printed two, on the subject of the midnight masquerade. A week later, in No. 16, Charles Lillie offered to take in letters and advertisements for the *Spectator*—an offer which was readily accepted—and within the first month of the new paper's existence the policy of publishing correspondents' letters was well established and over a score of letters were printed.

In this policy Addison and Steele were following an already recognized procedure. Except for more serious journals, like the

[1] *Essay on the Genius and Writings of Pope* (1782), ii. 404 n.

History of the Works of the Learned, every periodical has to a certain extent depended on the co-operation of its readers for a part of its material. De la Croze, in starting his monthly *Memoirs for the Ingenious* (1693), hopes 'the Learned will supply him with Materials to make so great an Undertaking the more easie to him'. Peter Motteux, whose *Gentleman's Journal* (1692–4) may be considered the first English magazine, includes a variety of correspondence and contributed material interspersed with Motteux's own essays, translations, reviews, &c., and frequently advertises that 'the Ingenious who are willing to have any thing in *Verse* or *Prose* inserted in this *Miscellany*, are desir'd to direct it' to him at specified places.

Even more dependent on contributions from readers were the papers which took the form of question and answer entirely. The two best known of these were the *Athenian Mercury* (1691–7), conducted by the eccentric and enterprising John Dunton, with the announced purpose of 'resolving the nice and curious questions proposed by the Ingenious', and the *British Apollo, or Curious Amusements for the Ingenious*, 'performed by a Society of Gentlemen' from 1708 to 1711. Both journals, appearing twice a week at the start, offer a curious medley of queries and answers on all kinds of subjects, religious, scientific, philosophical, and literary, a large proportion dealing with interpretation of Biblical texts and explanations of words.

Very few questions of this sort are to be found in the *Spectator*, since the whole approach was on an avowedly loftier and more serious plane, but there are numerous letters propounding questions of conduct ('Which lover shall I marry?') which show some similarity to the queries in the *Athenian Mercury* and the *British Apollo*. The true predecessors of the *Tatler* and *Spectator* are Motteux's *Gentleman's Journal* and those supplements to Defoe's *Review* which he called 'Advice from the Scandal Club' and 'The Little Review, or an Inquisition of Scandal', plus the French journals which served as their prototype. Typical of these, and in many ways the most important, is the *Mercure Galant*, established in 1672 by Donneau de Visé and conducted at this time (1710–13) by Charles Rivière Du Fresny.[1] This journal (Addison quotes from it in No. 60) is, like the

[1] It was published at The Hague by Thomas Johnson, whom Addison knew. In 1724 it became the *Mercure de France*. For its history see Eugène Hatin, *Histoire politique et littéraire de la Presse en France* (1859), i. 378–462. For Johnson see Addison's letter to George Stepney dated 3 Sept. 1706 (*Letters*, ed. Graham, p. 57; Aitken, *Life of Steele*, i. 186).

Spectator, addressed in part to women and contains a judicious mixture of fiction, serious essays, comment on current affairs, verse, competitions, and letters from readers—a successful blending of amusement with agreeable and not too heavy learning.

Like these earlier journals the *Spectator* profited from its readers' fondness for seeing if not their names at any rate their literary efforts in print, and it is clear that they responded readily to the editor's invitation for letters. Twenty-one letters are printed in the first month of publication, and in succeeding months the number mounts, especially in the following winter.[1] Steele as editor made especial use of them, and as time went on he tended to depend on them more and more. In the original series of 555 numbers nearly 250, almost half, contain letters, the greater part of them in papers signed by Steele. Did he write some of them himself? It seems not unlikely, though we cannot be sure. Defoe, in the *Review* of 4 October 1711, refers to the charge made against editors 'of first Writing Letters to themselves, and then answering them in Print', and denies that he has had to have recourse to this practice: 'I have been so far from having occasion to do so, that I have thrown by a monstrous Heap of such Letters, wholly un-answer'd. . . .' Addison alludes to this in No. 271:

Some will have it, that I often write to my self, and am the only punctual Correspondent I have. This Objection would indeed be material, were the Letters I communicate to the Publick stuffed with my own Commendations, and if, instead of endeavouring to divert or instruct my Readers, I admired in them the Beauty of my own Performances.

Sometimes the letters serve to link several numbers together, as in the series on the Ugly Club early in the course of the journal. Occasionally they comment on an earlier number, and at times they propound problems which serve as a starting-point for the day's speculation. Too frequently, however, they are rather pointless, and badly written. There is more than a suspicion that the editor—Steele especially, since he depends on them more than does Addison—uses them to eke out the required space for a number.[2] On one occasion (No. 310) an anonymous petitioner requests that 'such Letters of your Correspondents as seem to be of no Use but to the

[1] The figures are: November, 27; December, 30; January, 35; February, 44; March, 25.

[2] See, for example, Abraham Dapperwit's note in No. 534, with Mr. Spectator's reply.

Printer' be discarded in favour of advertisements, which will serve better to communicate knowledge to readers. In July 1712, when correspondence was apparently dropping off, Steele devotes an entire number (No. 428) to a general invitation to 'all Persons who have any thing to say for the profitable Information of the Publick, to take their Turns in my Paper'. He particularly urges practical contributions on business topics.

Is it possible that a young Man at present could pass his Time better, than in reading the History of Stocks, and knowing by what secret Springs they have such sudden Ascents and Falls in the same Day?

Later in the same month (No. 442) Steele defends his use of letters and again requests contributions, this time on the subject of 'money'.

In this number he admits that he has at times altered some of the letters received, 'by dressing them in my own Stile, by leaving out what wou'd not appear like mine, and by adding whatever might be proper to adapt them to the Character and Genius of my Paper'. Addison, writing near the close of the original series (in No. 542), is more specific. Many, he says, have thought him to be the writer of letters which were actually sent in by correspondents; many more have taken for original letters some which he has himself composed or recast into better Spectatorial form. He then cites five reasons for casting his thoughts into the form of a letter.

First, out of the Policy of those who try their Jest upon another, before they own it themselves. Secondly, because I would extort a little Praise from such who will never applaud any thing whose Author is known and certain. Thirdly, because it gave me an Opportunity of introducing a great variety of Characters into my Work, which could not have been done, had I always written in the Person of the *Spectator*. Fourthly, because the Dignity Spectatorial would have suffered, had I published as from my self those several ludicrous Compositions which I have ascribed to fictitious Names and Characters. And lastly, because they often serve to bring in, more naturally, such additional Reflections as have been placed at the End of them.

It is clear, however, from the number of unused letters which have survived that a large proportion of the correspondence was genuine. In No. 304 a petitioner signing himself Anthony Title-Page, 'Stationer, in the Centre of *Lincolns-Inn-Fields*', writes that he 'has certain Intelligence that you receive great Numbers of defamatory Letters design'd by their Authors to be publish'd, which you throw aside and totally neglect.

Your Petitioner therefore prays, that you would please to bestow on him those Refuse Letters, and he hopes by printing them to get a more plentiful Provision for his Family; or at the worst, he may be allowed to sell them by the Pound Weight to his good Customers the Pastry-Cooks of *London* and *Westminster*.'

Whatever the outcome of Title-Page's petition, we know that several years later, in 1725, Charles Lillie brought out, with Steele's approval, a two-volume collection of unused letters which had been sent in to the *Tatler* and the *Spectator*. Lillie's volumes read like a rather poor continuation of the *Spectator*, except that there are fewer letters on the subject of love (perhaps Steele had used most of the love-letters already?). Many attack particular papers in the *Spectator*; some propose new subjects for treatment; and many contain verses which their authors would like to see published. They are on the whole less interesting than the contributions already printed in the journal and are valuable chiefly for the light which they throw on the material actually published in the *Spectator*.

In addition to these, other letters survive in private collections—in the archives at Blenheim Palace,[1] the home of the Duke of Marlborough, and among the Tickell family papers.[2] Fifteen of those in the Blenheim collection were published by Aitken in his edition of the *Spectator* (1898), in a bowdlerized and otherwise not very accurate text; and more recently fifteen more from the Blenheim collection, together with eleven from the Tickell papers, have appeared.[3] Like the scraps printed by Lillie these are of interest in showing the variety of topics elicited by the *Tatler* and *Spectator*. The letters which Steele printed, as well as the vast quantity which he did not find suitable, also give a hint of the widespread popularity of the *Spectator*. Cheapside and Cornhill, the Strand and Piccadilly, Red Lion Square and Cripplegate, Vinegar Yard and Wapping—letters from these and many more sections of London and its environs are represented. Correspondents write from Oxford and Cambridge, from Exeter, from Norwich, as well as from Glasgow and Dublin.

Even from the other side of the world readers were moved to send in contributions. In Boston the Rev. Cotton Mather noted in

---

[1] Described in the eighth report (1881) of the Historical Manuscripts Commission. Cf. John Loftis, 'The Blenheim Papers and Steele's Journalism, 1715-18', *PMLA*, lxvi (1951), 197-210.

[2] Now in the possession of Major-General Sir Eustace F. Tickell, a lineal descendant of Thomas Tickell.

[3] *New Letters to the Tatler and Spectator*, ed. by Richmond P. Bond (Austin, Texas: University of Texas Press, 1959).

his diary (6 August 1713) his intention of perhaps 'sending some agreeable things' to the author of the *Spectator*, that 'there may be brought forward some Services to the best Interests in the Nation'.[1] From far-away Sumatra the deputy governor of the East India Company station at York Fort, Joseph Collet, relates (1 March 1713/14) to a friend in England a story which he has had from one of his slaves, 'a true Story Applicable to any Man in Love', which he is sending 'to the reviv'd Tatler as an Instance of Heroic Love'.

> The Spectator's Improvements on this theme may raise the young amorous Brittains to a pitch yet unknown; and by the warmth of his Spirit supply to them the absence of our Neighbouring Sun.[2]

These contributions from New England and Sumatra—if they were in fact sent to the *Spectator*—are not, so far as is known, extant; and there must have been many other contributions for which Steele did not find a place in the journal.[3] In his diary (17 February 1715/16) Dudley Ryder describes a visit to his friend Oliver Horseman, who 'showed me some letters that were sent to Mr. Steele when he wrote the *Spectators* which he had not made use of, that came to him by Mr. Harris who was Steele's secretary and had all his letters that he did not use'.[4]

Fortunately in a few instances the original texts of printed letters survive, so that we are able to see some of the ways in which Steele used them. A striking instance is the letter on the death of a wife, written from Norwich and signed F. J., which Steele prints (No. 520) without editorial comment, as if it had been received in this form. The text of the original, preserved at Blenheim Palace, shows that the version printed by Steele is in fact a rewriting of the letter.[5] And evidently F. J. expected this, for the original letter ends with what is virtually a request that his thoughts be put into better language than he can command.

> 'Tis true the memory of this departed Creature will most certainly bee ever most deare and valueable to me—But inasmuch as your truely valued advice will live and flourish in your happy papers to many generations, and may make others equally happy with myself, I intreat you in their names alsoe, that you will give us some few and speedy

---

[1] *Diary of Cotton Mather, 1704-1724*, Massachusetts Historical Society Collections, 7th ser., viii (Boston, 1912), p. 227.

[2] *Private Letter Books of Joseph Collet*, ed. by H. H. Dodwell (1933), pp. 74-75.

[3] Sloane MS. 4067, f. 85, contains another letter addressed to 'Mr Spectatour' and signed Philast[or].

[4] *Diary of Dudley Ryder*, ed. by William Matthews (1939), p. 183.

[5] See Appendix V.

directions how to make the memory of such a wife not only deare but delightfull. And you will thereby not only obleige me and the World I hope, but add to the just veneration you have always had. . . .

This letter is dated 7 October 1712. That F. J. was pleased with Steele's use of his contribution is indicated by another letter (also in the collection at Blenheim) in the same hand, dated 'Norwich, November 22d, 1712', and concluding 'Your most (and very lately) obleiged humble Servant, F. J.'

A second example which allows us to see Steele's editorial hand at work is afforded by No. 404, the original of which is in the same collection. In this case the manuscript consists not of a letter but a completed 'essay' designed for the *Spectator* and headed by an appropriate motto from Cicero. A comparison between the texts of the original and the printed version[1] reveals that on this occasion Steele keeps the main structure of the essay and makes only a few verbal changes. He removes the Ciceronian motto and uses it—in an English paraphrase—as a concluding sentence for the paper, substituting a new line from Virgil as a motto. Otherwise little is altered.

The Blenheim archives also contain a short letter written from 'Tom's' and signed Eustace, which was printed by Steele in No. 539. In the published version Steele has completely rewritten the rather confused epistle in a slightly shorter form and with some improvement in syntax,[2] though in its revised version the letter is not one of the brighter passages in the *Spectator*.[3]

Of the three examples cited above, the letters from F. J. and Eustace were, as we have seen, completely rewritten before they appeared in the *Spectator*. The contribution which was published as No. 404, on the other hand, appeared with little change. Obviously, if a manuscript came to Steele of about the right length for a *Spectator*, on a suitable topic, and decently written, he might accept it and send it on to the printer with little or no change. As a general rule, however, it seems that letters were considerably modified if not completely rewritten before appearing in print. Steele's statement at the beginning of No. 268, 'I am of Opinion that I ought sometimes to lay before the World the plain Letters of my Correspondents in the artless Dress in which they hastily send them',

---

[1] See Appendix V.   [2] See Appendix V.
[3] An earlier form of Eustace's letter will be found in Lillie (i. 32–33). It was only after a second appeal that Steele obliged by taking notice of this love-problem.

seems to imply that such procedure would be the exception rather than the rule.[1]

VI. *Authorship*

In considering the authorship of the *Spectator* one must not only estimate the proportion of letters to original material but also distinguish between the first series (Nos. 1–555), the joint work of Steele and Addison, published in sheets daily from March 1711 to December 1712 and later in seven volumes; and the continuation (Nos. 556–635), conducted by Addison, with the assistance of Budgell and Tickell, published three times a week from June to December 1714 and later as Volume VIII of the completed *Spectator*. A certain amount of confusion in the past has resulted from the failure to distinguish between the two series.

When Thomas Tickell, Addison's literary executor, brought out his edition of Addison's *Works* in 1721 he reprinted—presumably with authority—all the *Spectators* which his friend had written, 274 in all. (This figure, however, includes No. 2, Steele's paper giving an account of the Club, reprinted by Tickell partly for completeness and partly because, as he says, it was planned jointly by the two men. The figure for Addison's essays in the *Spectator*, as identified by Tickell, should therefore stand at 273.) Later authorities, alike the biographers of Steele and Addison and editors of the *Spectator*, have generally repeated, without qualification, the figure 274 to represent Addison's contributions, without considering whether this applies to the original 555 numbers or to the total 635 of both series. In itself this is not so important, but when joined with a relative estimate of Steele's contributions it gives a completely misleading impression.[2] Nathan Drake in 1805 gives a table of authorship (for both series), assigning 274 papers to Addison and 240 to Steele.[3] In his study of Addison in the English Men of Letters series (1884)

[1] For No. 635, the last number of the second series, the original manuscript by Henry Grove survives among the Tickell papers. Evidence that this manuscript was itself sent to the printer and used by him as copy is afforded by the fact that he has marked the point at which the printed column two ends, in the word 'laboured' (labour-/ed). Yet the essay as printed in the folio sheets differs in several places from the manuscript: words and phrases are added and omitted, and there is considerable revision of style. The letter is postmarked 17 Dec. (Friday), and the essay appeared on the following Monday, 20 Dec. Evidently the changes were made in proof.

[2] On this point see Fritz Rau, 'Texte, Ausgaben und Verfasser des "Tatler" und "Spectator":Forschungsbericht', *Germanisch-Romanische Monatsschrift*, N.F., viii (1958), 139–40. Dr. Rau gives full evidence from both English and German scholarship.

[3] *Essays biographical, critical, and historical, illustrative of the Tatler, Spectator, and Guardian*, iii. 377.

Courthope, who discusses only the original run of the *Spectator* and says nothing of the second series, observes that 'Addison's own papers were 274 in number, as against 236 contributed by Steele'— where the figure 274 refers, of course, to the two series and the figure 236 only to the first.[1] These figures are repeated in the following year by Austin Dobson, in his *Selections* from Steele, but he carries the error a step farther by specifically confining his tabulation to the original series:

> Out of a total of 555, [Addison's] papers numbered 274 to Steele's 236, leaving only 45 for Budgell, Hughes, and (with exception of Pope) the other comparatively undistinguished occasional assistants.[2]

This unfortunate statement appears also in Dobson's little book on Steele in the English Worthies series,[3] and it received a kind of official imprimatur by Aitken in his two-volume biography three years later.

> Addison was certainly at his best in the *Spectator*. He wrote 274 out of the 555 numbers, while Steele contributed 236, leaving only 45 for Budgell, Hughes, Pope, and other occasional contributors.[4]

It is repeated in the two *DNB* articles—on Addison, by Leslie Stephen, and on Steele, by Dobson himself—and by almost every succeeding writer on the subject. The formula 'Addison 274, Steele 236, others 45', becomes a familiar cliché in literary history, demonstrably incomplete and false.

The principal evidence for authorship in the original series—to which we confine ourselves at this point—is Steele's statement concerning the initial letters used as signatures in the folio sheets and in the octavo and duodecimo reprints. All the papers marked with C, L, I, or O, he says, 'were given me by the Gentleman, of whose Assistance I formerly boasted in the Preface and concluding Leaf of my *Tatlers*'—in other words, Addison. For the papers marked X, Steele continues, he is obliged 'to the Ingenious Gentleman who diverted the Town with the Epilogue to the *Distressed Mother*', i.e. Eustace Budgell. He says nothing of the letters R and T, but since R was used from the beginning (No. 2) and T shortly thereafter (No. 95) in papers unmistakably by Steele we can be certain that papers marked R or T are by him. There are, in addition, ten papers

[1] W. J. Courthope, *Addison* (1884), p. 112.
[2] *Steele: Selections*, ed. Austin Dobson (Oxford, 1885), p. xxxi.
[3] *Richard Steele* (1886), pp. 142–3.
[4] G. A. Aitken, *Life of Richard Steele* (1889), i. 312.

signed Z and one (No. 250) marked Q. Steele does not tell us what these signatures stand for. Finally, there are fifteen papers without signature letters at all, in any of the three editions. Placed in tabular form, the figures read:

Papers signed R or T	251
Signed C, L, I, or O	249
Signed X . .	29
Signed Z . .	10
Signed Q . .	1
Unsigned . .	15
Total . .	555

Two of the unsigned papers, however, may be attributed to Addison (Nos. 237 and 538), since they were included by Tickell in the 1721 edition of the *Works*. We learn also, from statements by Steele in Nos. 537 and 554, that five papers of the unsigned group (Nos. 375, 525, 537, 541, and 554) are by John Hughes, and that one of the papers signed Z (No. 210) is also by Hughes. The table may then be revised to read:

Papers by Steele .	251
Papers by Addison .	251
Papers by Budgell .	29
Papers by Hughes .	6
Other papers signed Z	9
Other papers unsigned	8
Paper signed Q .	1
Total . .	555

All but eighteen papers, then, in the original series may be assigned with some confidence to Steele, Addison, Budgell, and Hughes, although, as we have seen, the papers bearing Steele's signature are frequently made up of letters or other contributions, which can be identified as the work of other writers. As to the authorship of these eighteen papers, various surmises have been offered in the past, but most of these guesses have had to be made on the basis of internal evidence alone. In No. 555 (the paper discussing signature letters) Steele speaks of 'other Assistances which I have had'. These, he says, 'have been conveyed by Letter, sometimes by whole Papers, and other times by short Hints from unknown Hands.'

I have not been able to trace Favours of this kind, with any Certainty, but to the following Names, which I place in the Order wherein I received the Obligation, tho' the first I am going to Name can hardly be mentioned in a List wherein he would not deserve the Precedence. The Persons to whom I am to make these Acknowledgments are Mr. *Henry Martyn*, Mr. *Pope*, Mr. *Hughs*, Mr. *Carey* of *New-College* in *Oxford*, Mr. *Tickell* of *Queen's* in the same University, Mr. *Parnelle*, and Mr. *Eusden* of *Trinity* in *Cambridge*.

To this acknowledgement Steele added, as a postscript, in the 8vo and 12mo editions:

It had not come to my Knowledge, when I left off the *Spectator*, that I owe several excellent Sentiments and agreeable Pieces in this Work to Mr. *Ince* of *Grey's-Inn*.

A striking feature of this pronouncement is the order of the eight names, since even in Steele's own day few readers would be likely to place the name of Henry Martyn first. It is probable that in his first draft Steele intended to begin with Addison's name, to be followed by that of Budgell, and then by those of Martyn and the rest. He may well have concluded that Addison obviously deserved greater attention and consequently devoted a whole paragraph to his work and another shorter paragraph to Budgell, and then placed both of these just before the statement regarding 'other Assistances' quoted above.

Most of the contributions made by these writers seem to have been in the form of letters or 'short hints' which Steele used in papers over his own signature letters (R or T), at times perhaps printing them as they stood, at times rewriting them. They do not afford much help, therefore, in clearing up the mystery of the eighteen papers of unknown authorship. It may be convenient to have a list of these eighteen, with dates, signature letters (if any) in the three editions, and a brief notation of contents.

1711

No. 224 (16 November) Z— On Love of Fame.

No. 232 (26 November) XZ– On Charity and Beggars.

No. 250 (17 December) QQQ (1) A letter on optics, signed T. B.
(2) A letter on perspective glasses, signed Abraham Spy.

1712

No. 286 (28 January)	ZZZ	(1) A letter urging greater severity towards vice, dated from York, 18 January. (2) A letter in praise of brunettes, signed Philobrune.
No. 292 (4 February)	Z–Z	(1) On Additional Graces. (2) A note signed Jezebel.
No. 316 (3 March)	ZZZ	(1) A letter on the use of time, signed Samuel Slack. (2) A note from Clytander to Cleone.
No. 338 (28 March)	——	(1) An introductory paragraph. (2) A letter attacking facetious epilogues, signed Physibulus.
No. 396 (4 June)	——	(1) An introductory paragraph. (2) A letter on punning, signed Peter de Quir, St. John's College, Cambridge, 3 February.
No. 404 (13 June)	ZZZ	On Following Nature.
No. 408 (18 June)	ZZZ	A letter on the use of the passions, signed T. B.
No. 425 (8 July)	ZZZ	A letter, unsigned, containing an Allegory of the Seasons.
No. 467 (26 August)	ZZZ	On the Love of Praise; the character of Manilius.
No. 518 (24 October)	——	(1) A brief introduction. (2) A letter with three epitaphs. (3) A letter on physiognomy, signed Tom Tweer, Cambridge.
No. 524 (31 October)	——	(1) A long introductory paragraph. (2) A letter, with an Allegory of Heavenly and Worldly Wisdom, dated 'Glascow, Sept. 29'.
No. 527 (4 November)	——	(1) A brief introduction. (2) A letter on jealousy, signed Philagnotes. (3) A letter with verses on Procris and Cephalus.

No. 539 (18 November) —— (1) A letter from a young widow, signed Relicta Lovely.
(2) A letter signed Eustace.
(3) A letter describing a tedious preacher.

No. 548 (28 November) —— A letter on poetic justice, dated 27 November, unsigned.

No. 551 (2 December) —— (1) A letter with epitaphs from the Greek Anthology.
(2) A letter on legal jargon, signed Philonicus.[1]

Of the above scattered pieces only one, the third item in No. 527, can be immediately identified. This is by Pope, since the verses, translated from Ovid, were reprinted in Pope's *Works* of 1717, under the title 'On a Fan'. Guesses have been made about the other items, but we can be sure of this.

What other contributions by Pope did Steele have in mind when he named him among the assistants in No. 555? Certainly Pope's poem *Messiah*, which occupies almost the whole of No. 378, introduced by Steele as 'written by a great Genius, a Friend of mine, in the Country'. There are also two letters, one on city and country life (in No. 406) and the other on the last words of the Emperor Hadrian (in No. 532), which Pope reprinted in his correspondence. Another letter (in No. 457), proposing two new burlesque journals, has been suggested by Professor Sherburn as the work of Pope,[2] since its language parallels other letters of Pope written at the same time. Acceptance of this automatically identifies Pope as the writer of a similar letter in No. 452, since No. 457 is 'written by the same Hand with that of last *Friday*'. These six pieces are all that can with much certainty be assigned to Pope—and only one of these is from our 'mystery group' of eighteen papers. Since Nos. 404 and 408 from this group repeat some of the ideas and phrases found later in Pope's poetry, Nichols in 1789 thought it 'not unreasonable to suppose that Pope might be the writer' not only of these but of all the papers bearing the signature letter Z. One would like to think of Pope as an important contributor to the *Spectator*, and Norman Ault actually included seven essays from this group—Nos. 224,

[1] In the 8vo and 12mo reprints of No. 551 a third letter with an epitaph on Homer is added.
[2] George Sherburn, *The Early Career of Alexander Pope* (Oxford, 1934), pp. 74–75.

292, 316, 404, 408, 425, and 467—in the first volume of his edition of the *Prose Works* of Pope (Oxford, 1936). But the parallels with Pope's other writings which he offers as evidence are so general that they cannot be entitled to much consideration. Equally good and even better 'parallels' can be found among *Spectators* which we know are not from Pope's pen.[1] It should be noted, too, that the manuscript of No. 404, the essay which is perhaps closest to Pope's in phrasing, is still extant and that the handwriting is not that of Pope.

If the papers signed Z are not by Pope, can any other contributor be named? Since No. 210, which consists of a letter on immortality signed T. D. and which bears the initial signature Z in the octavo edition, is known to be by John Hughes,[2] the suggestion has been made by Nichols and other editors that Hughes was the author of *all* the Z papers. There are nine of these among the eighteen papers of unknown authorship.[3] But Z cannot be a uniform symbol for Hughes, since No. 286, which consists of letters from York and from Trinity College, Cambridge, is obviously not by him; and No. 404, also signed Z in all editions, the manuscript of which is extant, is not in his hand. We must infer that Steele used the signature as a general symbol for contributed matter of some importance (other things he printed under his own initial R or T), perhaps for contributions which he thought he might identify later.

So far as Hughes is concerned, we have other important external evidence. His *Poems on Several Occasions: with some select Essays in Prose* appeared in two volumes in 1735, after the death of Hughes, edited by his brother-in-law William Duncombe; and in the preface (pp. xxxiv–xxxv) Duncombe gives a list of Hughes's contributions to the *Spectator*. In addition to the six numbers (210, 375, 525, 537, 541, and 554) which Steele had named as the work of Hughes, Duncombe also claims for him Nos. 91, 237, and 302. The first two of these attributions can hardly be correct: No. 91 is almost certainly by Steele,[4] and No. 237 was reprinted by Tickell in Addison's

[1] For a fuller discussion of this point see my article, 'Pope's Contributions to the *Spectator*', *Modern Language Quarterly*, v (1944), 69–78.

[2] According to Steele's statement at the end of No. 537. It appeared over Steele's own initial letter T in the folio sheets, and also in the (unrevised) 12mo edition, but in looking over the papers for publication in book form Steele evidently knew then who the author was and gave it another signature.

[3] Of these, No. 224 is signed Z only in the folio sheets and unsigned in the reprints; No. 232 is signed X in the folio, signed Z in 8vo, and unsigned in 12mo; and No. 292 is signed Z in folio and 12mo, but unsigned in 8vo.

[4] See notes to this number.

Works in 1721.[1] No. 302, however, appears as a contributed piece, which Steele says he 'publishes just as it came to my Hands'. In view of Steele's practice with contributed matter editors have hesitated to take this statement literally, and there have been several vague and contradictory efforts to identify the author. There seems no reason in this case, however, to doubt Duncombe's statement, and No. 302 may be assigned to Hughes. In addition to the whole papers which Duncombe claimed for his brother-in-law, he specifies the following portions of essays as the work of Hughes. These too have been generally accepted, and there is no conflicting evidence against the ascriptions.

No. 33.   A letter, signed R. B., on the art of improving beauty.
No. 53.   A second letter, signed R. B., on the same subject.
No. 66.   Two letters, the first signed Celimene, on fine breeding.
No. 104. A letter, unsigned, on ladies' riding-habits.
No. 141. A letter, unsigned, criticizing the comedy, *The Lancashire Witches*.
No. 220. A letter, unsigned, concerning expedients for wit.
No. 230. 'All, except the last letter.'
No. 231. A letter, unsigned, on the awe of appearing before public assemblies.
No. 252. A letter, unsigned, 'on the eloquence of tears and fainting fits'.
No. 311. A letter, signed Tim Watchwell, from the father of a great fortune.

Other essays have been claimed for Hughes outside the group marked Z, notably No. 306[2] and No. 540,[3] but these are not in Duncombe's list and cannot be identified with any certainty. In sum, we may reasonably claim for Hughes the authorship of seven papers (Nos. 210, 302, 375, 525, 537, 541, 554) and of contributed material in ten others (Nos. 33, 53, 66, 104, 141, 220, 230, 231, 252, and 311).

---

[1] The fact that No. 237 bears (through an oversight?) no initial signature in folio, 8vo, or 12mo, suggests the possibility that Duncombe is correct. In the present edition it is assigned to Addison, with the realization that there remains a shadow of doubt.

[2] Duncombe's son, the Rev. John Duncombe, writing many years later in the *Gentleman's Magazine* (Apr. 1780, pp. 174–5), claimed for Hughes the authorship of No. 306, an essay on Parthenissa and her loss of beauty by small-pox. Since there is no indication that this is a contributed piece (it is signed T in all three editions), the ascription to Hughes must be considered doubtful.

[3] The only basis for attributing the letter which makes up this entire number to Hughes is the fact that Hughes published an edition of Spenser three years later.

There can be little doubt as to the contributions of Eustace Budgell to the first series; there are twenty-nine papers bearing the signature letter X in the three early editions.[1] All but three were published on Tuesday or Thursday—Addison's customary 'days' from September 1711 to the middle of June 1712—and Budgell's contributions are clearly written by way of assistance to Addison, or even perhaps with his collaboration.[2] Budgell's mother was a first cousin to Addison: her father, William Gulston, Bishop of Bristol, and Addison's mother Jane Gulston were brother and sister. Budgell, who was born in 1686 and was thus fourteen years younger than Addison, matriculated in 1705 at Trinity College, Oxford; he afterwards entered the Inner Temple and was called to the Bar. Like the Templar of the Spectator Club, Budgell seems to have cared very little for legal studies: instead, according to his earliest biographer, 'he followed his own inclinations, which carried him to the study of polite literature, and to the company of the genteelest people in town'.[3] Early in 1710 he went to Ireland with Addison as one of the clerks in his office, and during the time that the first series of the *Spectator* was published seems to have been an intimate friend and companion of Addison's. During 1711 he contributed eight papers, beginning with No. 67 on 17 May, on modern dancing, followed in No. 77 with a 'character study', in the manner of La Bruyère, of the Absent-minded Man. He has two lively papers on country sports, including the account (in No. 116) of the hunt at Sir Roger's. Beginning with No. 301 (14 February 1712) Budgell contributed one paper regularly a week to the *Spectator* down to the middle of June—in February and March on Thursdays, in April on Tuesdays, and in May and June on one or other of these days. Four of these (Nos. 307, 313, 337, and 353) form a connected series on the subject of education. Others deal with such varied topics as beards, the Mohocks, women's vanity, Will Honeycomb's amours, friendship, dangers in the month of May, and the belief in God among the heathens. His essays are characterized by rather short paragraphs

---

[1] Budgell's first paper (No. 67) is signed R in the folio sheets, but X in the 8vo and 12mo editions.

[2] No. 197, an essay on contention and argument, consists in part of a few rules which 'I gave in Writing to a young Kinsman of mine who had made so great a Proficiency in the Law, that he began to plead in Company upon every Subject that was started'. These remarks would apply perfectly to Addison and Budgell. The final paragraph of this number begins with a characteristic locution of Addison, 'I shall close this Subject . . .'.

[3] *Cibber's Lives of the Poets* (1753), v. 2.

and a liberal sprinkling of out-of-the-way learning, much of it derived from Bayle's *Dictionary*. Boswell (26–29 April 1776) reports Johnson as saying that 'Addison wrote Budgell's papers in the Spectator, at least mended them so much, that he made them almost his own'.[1] This was hinted at in Budgell's own day by an anonymous translator of Aristaenetus:

Permit me to mention the *Spectators* with the Letter *X*, which were writ with so much Spirit, that unless you had inform'd us to whom they had belong'd, we might have mistook them for another great Author's. So that we may justly say, that the same Genius runs through the whole Scale of Relations.[2]

Budgell's twenty-nine papers in the original series are Nos. 67, 77, 116, 150, 161, 175, 197, 217, 277, 283, 301, 307, 313, 319, 325, 331, 337, 341, 347, 353, 359, 365, 373, 379, 385, 389, 395, 401, and 506. No. 232, which is signed X in folio, is signed Z in 8vo and unsigned in 12mo; it cannot be assigned to Budgell.

Of the other contributors mentioned by Steele in No. 555, Henry Martyn is best remembered today as one of the principal writers in the periodical *The British Merchant, or Commerce preserv'd*, published twice a week from 7 August 1713 to 30 July 1714 ('Sold by A. Baldwin next the Oxford Arms in Warwick-lane'), and written in opposition to Defoe's *Mercator, or Commerce retrieved*. It was largely due to Martyn's writing that the treaty of commerce with France at the Peace of Utrecht was ultimately rejected. The government thereupon made Martyn Inspector-General of Imports and Exports of Customs. He died at Blackheath on 25 March 1721, according to the *DNB*. Nichols in 1789 identified Martyn as the author of the long letter signed Philarithmus in No. 180. A later essay on the subject of 'political arithmetic' (No. 200) is introduced by Steele as based on a hint from Philarithmus and has accordingly been assigned to Martyn by most editors. Nichols (in a note to No. 555) goes a step farther: 'Mr. H. Martyn was probably thought of, and alluded to by his intimate friend Steele in all the Papers of the *Spectator* where Sir Andrew Freeport is mentioned, or makes any figure; and in those Papers especially Mr. Martyn himself might have had some hand.' This would apply particularly to No. 232, which contains

---

[1] *Life of Johnson*, ed. Hill–Powell, iii. 46.
[2] Dedication 'to Eustatius Budgel, Esq.' of *Letters of Love and Gallantry: Written in Greek by Aristaenetus* (London: Printed for Bernard Lintot, 1715?), sig. A4.

Sir Andrew's observations on beggars and the economic aspects of charity. Since Martyn's contributions were never reprinted, we cannot be sure of what assistance he provided; Nos. 180, 200, and 232 were probably at least suggested by him, and possibly he was entirely responsible for them.[1]

Steele's allusion to 'Mr. Carey of New-College in Oxford' has generally been taken to refer to Henry Carey, author of 'Sally in our Alley,' and the only contemporary poet of any consequence bearing this name. His first book, *Poems on Several Occasions*, appeared as early as 1713.[2] He is not known to have been one of the circle at Button's Coffee-house and does not appear in the correspondence of either Addison or Steele, but he mentions twice in print the fact that he had received encouragement from Addison.[3] The chief objection to this identification is that Henry Carey had not studied at either university. There was, however, at this time a 'Mr. Carey of New College': Walter Carey (1685–1757), of West Sheen, Surrey, and St. James's, Westminster, who entered New College 14 December 1704, graduated B.A. 1708, and became M.P. for Helston 1722–7 and for Dartmouth 1737 until his death in 1757. Appointed Warden of the Mint in 1725, he became later one of the four clerks comptrollers of the Board of Green Cloth and a member of the Board of Trade and Plantations.[4] He represents exactly the type of 'rising' young man who saw a future in the reviving fortunes of the Whigs after 1714, one of several young men encouraged by Addison. That he was known to the circle of Addison and Steele is indicated by a passage in a letter from Tickell to George Bubb (20 June 1717):

Mr Carey, who is just returned to Town from a Survey of his Lady's Jointure in Wales, tells me that Mr Young has promised to pass part

---

[1] Cf. also E. A. J. Johnson, *Predecessors of Adam Smith* (1937), chap. viii (on Charles King, one of Martyn's collaborators on the *British Merchant*). 'No. 180 is certainly [Martyn's] essay and probably No. 200 and No. 232' (p. 348).

[2] It is advertised in the *Daily Courant* of 20 January as published 'yesterday'.

[3] In his verse epistle to Lord Chesterfield, *Of Stage Tyrants* (1735), Carey writes:

> So when, long since, in simple Sonnet Lays,
> I made the 'Prentice Sing his *Sally*'s Praise,
> Tho' rude the Numbers, yet the Subject mov'd;
> Immortal ADDISON the Song approv'd.

In the 'Argument' prefixed to the poem Carey states that in spite of ridicule the ballad 'made its way into the polite World, and amply recompenced him by the Applause of the divine *Addison*, who was pleased (more than once) to mention it with Approbation' (*Poems on Several Occasions* [3rd ed., 1729], p.128).

[4] *Daily Post*, 2 June 1725; Foster, *Alumni Oxonienses*, early ser. i (1891).

of the Summer with him at Sheen where Sir William Temple was our Friend's Predecesser.[1]

A decade later the anonymous pamphlet, *Characters of the Times* (1728), defending 'Umbra' and other victims of the Swift–Pope *Miscellanies*, identifies 'Umbra' as Walter Carey and dwells on his friendship with Steele and Addison. Whether Carey was in fact the original of 'Umbra' is doubtful,[2] but the account in *Characters of the Times* affords further evidence that Walter Carey was indeed the person named by Steele as a contributor to the *Spectator*. Pope told Spence on 28 July 1739 that

Cary had scarce anything in ye S[pectato]rs, &c.[3] Perhaps a little Song or Copy of Verses or two. Steele (wm he always flatter'd greatly) mention'd him to do him a service: & has said so himself to Mr. P. It had its effect & gave him w[t] Rep[utatio]n he Ever had.

Pope's statement that in mentioning Carey Steele 'gave him what reputation he ever had' also applies with more cogency to Walter than to Henry Carey, whose poetic reputation, such as it was, had a more substantial basis. It is not known what 'little Song or Copy of Verses or Two' Walter Carey may have contributed. There are two or three things of this nature which he may have written (in Nos. 208, 473—and in No. 591, of the second series), but none has been identified. Steele's acknowledgement may well have been intended mainly as a gesture of friendly publicity for this young recruit to the Whig forces.

'Mr. Tickell of Queen's in the same University' is, of course, Thomas Tickell (1685–1740), who while at Queen's had commended himself by 'a beautiful copy of verses addressed to Addison, on his opera of Rosamond',[4] and who assisted Addison in bringing out the

---

[1] Egerton MS. 2174, f. 311.

[2] Pope used the name 'Umbra' in three later poems—the 'Epistle to Cobham', the *Satires of Donne* (iv. 177), and the *Essay on Man*—and some editors have assumed that the name was meant in every case for Walter Carey. Croker, however, thought it 'doubtful whether Pope had any particular parasite in view' (Elwin–Courthope, iii. 58), and the latest editors of Pope's minor poems, the late Norman Ault and Professor John Butt, incline to the view that the 'Umbra' of the *Miscellanies* is more probably to be identified with Budgell (Twickenham ed., vi. 141). For a full account of Carey see James M. Osborn, 'Addison's Tavern Companion and Pope's "Umbra"', *Philological Quarterly*, xlii (1963). I am grateful to Mr. Osborn for giving me much of the above information on Walter Carey.

[3] Another MS reads 'and Guardians'. Mr. Osborn has kindly provided me with this text from Spence.

[4] *Cibber's Lives of the Poets* (1753), v. 17.

second series of the *Spectator* in 1714. There is nothing to indicate what contributions Tickell may have made to the earlier series. According to Nichols[1] some attempts had been made to associate Steele's signature letter T with Tickell as author or 'transcriber', but Nichols is sceptical of this theory, and there is no evidence to substantiate it. It seems likely that these guesses, made late in the eighteenth century, arose from Tickell's known association with Addison after 1714. All that can be said of his share in the original series is that Addison publicly praises his *Poem on the Prospect of Peace* in No. 523 and that a fortnight later Steele prints (in No. 532) Tickell's 'excellent Paper of Verses', entitled 'To the supposed Author of the *Spectator*'.

The next name in Steele's list is that of the Rev. Thomas Parnell (1679–1718), Archdeacon of Clogher and one of the members of the Scriblerus Club. Although intimate with Swift and other Tories, he seems to have kept on good terms with Addison and Steele as well. He contributed two allegories or dream-visions to the *Spectator*, one on 'The Paradise of Fools', printed by Steele in No. 460, and the other, 'The Grotto of Grief', printed by Addison in No. 501. In the introductory paragraph in No. 501 Addison identifies the 'very ingenious Gentleman' who contributes the present allegory with the author of the dream-vision in No. 460. Both pieces were reprinted in Parnell's posthumously published *Poems on Several Occasions* (1722), and there can be no doubt of their authorship.

Laurence Eusden (1688–1730), named by Steele as another contributor, was admitted pensioner at Trinity College, Cambridge, in 1705, and graduated B.A. 1708, M.A. 1712. He later became a member of the Whig circle under Lord Halifax and in due time was appointed Poet Laureate (24 December 1718).[2] Nichols attributes the letters in Nos. 54 and 78 to Eusden, apparently because they are dated from Cambridge. He also names him as author of the letter signed T. T. in No. 87. No evidence is given for any of these attributions, which have been followed by most later editors. Since Steele names Eusden as a contributor, these identifications, probably based on oral tradition, may be correct, but no external evidence has so far been found to substantiate them.

The last name in Steele's list refers, apparently, to Richard Ince of Christ Church, Oxford (B.A. 1707, M.A. 1710), a barrister of the Middle Temple (1711), and Secretary to the Comptrollers of Army

---

[1] Notes to Nos. 324 and 328.　　　　　　　　[2] W. P. Courtney in *DNB*.

Accounts (1740).[1] When he died in 1758 he left instructions to his executors 'to burn all his papers', and Mr. Clare (one of his executors) 'could not positively say that he was acquainted with any one Paper of his writing in the *Spectator*'.[2] A few years later Boswell (10 April 1776) reported a conversation with Johnson touching on this.

> Mr. Murphy said, he remembered when there were several people alive in London, who enjoyed a considerable reputation merely from having written a paper in 'The Spectator.' He mentioned particularly Mr. Ince, who used to frequent Tom's coffee-house. 'But (said Johnson) you must consider how highly Steele speaks of Mr. Ince.'[3]

These, then, are the persons named by Steele, in his role as editor, as having afforded him various 'assistances', beginning with Addison and Budgell, and followed by Henry Martyn, Pope, Hughes, Carey, Tickell, Parnell, Eusden, and Ince. He might have included William Fleetwood, Bishop of St. Asaph, whose Preface to his *Four Sermons* Steele had published as No. 384. He might have named Peter Motteux, whose letter had appeared in No. 288; or the three musicians Clayton, Haym, and Dieupart, whose names occur at the end of petitions in Nos. 258 and 278; or even John Sly, whose reports Steele had published in Nos. 532, 534, and 545.

Other contributors are now known. The paraphrase of Psalm cxiv in No. 461 is by Isaac Watts and was reprinted in his *Psalms of David* (1719); the letter accompanying it is accordingly also from the pen of Watts. One James Heywood contributed the letter in No. 268 signed 'James Easy'; it is reprinted in Heywood's *Poems and Letters on Several Subjects* (1722). The letter signed A. B. and the accompanying paraphrase of 'the 7th Chapter of the *Proverbs*' are by the Rev. James Ward, later Dean of Cloyne; the paraphrase was later reprinted under his own name. The letter in No. 334 may be assigned with reasonable certainty to John Weaver, whose *Essay towards an History of Dancing* (mentioned in the letter as in preparation) was published a few months later.

Other contributors who have been suggested from time to time are Swift, not only for having given the hint for No. 50 but as the author of a paragraph in No. 575, in the second series; John ('Orator') Henley, as the writer of the letters signed Peter de Quir (No. 396)

[1] Foster, *Alumni Oxonienses* (early series), where he is called 'one of the writers to the "Spectator" '.
[2] Nichols, note to No. 555.   [3] *Life of Johnson*, ed. Hill–Powell, iii. 33.

and Tom Tweer (No. 518); one Golding as the 'T. B.' of No. 250; Robert Harper as the writer of the letter signed M. D. in No. 480; Philip Yorke, afterwards Earl of Hardwicke, as the author of the letter on travelling in No. 364; John Francham of Norwich as the contributor of No. 520; and Professor Alexander Dunlop and a Mr. Montgomery as the joint authors of the dream vision in No. 524.[1]

These are the principal names which have been proposed as additional 'authors' of the *Spectator*. Arthur Murphy remembered, as we have seen, more than sixty years after the paper had ceased to appear, 'when there were several people alive in London, who enjoyed a considerable reputation merely from having written a paper in "The Spectator" '. Books occasionally turn up which profess to be written by contributors to the *Spectator*. One such was published in 1723, with the title *The History of Providence, or the Six Days Work of the Creation: in a Dissertation upon the Sacred Writings*, and described on the title-page as 'by the Author of several Spectators'. The book itself gives no clue to what contributions the author had made, if any, to the *Spectator*, nor does his style suggest that he would have been accepted as a contributor.[2]

To list even men like Peter Motteux and Isaac Watts, however, among the authors of the *Spectator* and to draw up a list of contributors on the basis of single letters or hints would be to give an unrealistic picture of the authorship. Steele and Addison— and to a much smaller degree Budgell and Hughes—are the men responsible for practically the whole of the first series, Nos. 1 to 555.[3]

---

[1] Most of these proposed attributions depend only on tradition. See notes to the respective essays.

[2] As for *God, a Poem* (1724), 'revised and recommended by the late Joseph Addison, Esq. and wrote by the Rev. John Lloyd, M.A. &c. Author, also of several of the Spectators', my only information concerning this comes from an article in the *Gentleman's Magazine*, lxi (1791), 502, by one T. B.

[3] It is possible that one of the papers in the group of 'unknowns' (No. 548) should be assigned to Addison. It offers 'additional arguments' in defence of No. 40 against the objections of 'some eminent criticks' (almost certainly Dennis, in particular). It is in the form of a letter, purported to be written on the day preceding the publication of this number. If the date is authentic, little time would be allowed for conveying the letter to the printer and setting it up in type by the following morning. Morley and Aitken both attribute it in fact to Addison, and the position it takes on poetic justice is consistent with Addison's views on the subject. In the 8vo and 12mo reprints the letter contains an additional paragraph elucidating further the position of the *Spectator* on poetic justice—a natural procedure, if one assumes that Addison had written the original letter. No. 548 may be a genuine contribution, but it is quite possible that Addison composed the letter himself, in reply to Dennis, and was unwilling at the time to attach his initials to it—'willing to wound', as Pope would

Finally, in attempting to clear up the mystery of uncertain authorship, we may consider the further point of Steele's association with Buckley and Addison's with Tonson in the publication of the *Spectator*. If we look at the numbers printed after 1 November 1711, when the rhythm of publication had been fairly well established, it will be seen that—omitting consideration of papers of doubtful authorship—Steele's papers are almost without exception printed by Buckley and Addison's quite as uniformly by Tonson.

In this period 156 papers can be assigned without question to Steele and 142 to Addison. Distributed by printers they fall into the following pattern:

	Steele	Addison
Tonson	4	139
Buckley	152	3

Taking the eight papers without signatures (Nos. 338, 396, 518, 524, 527, 539, 548, and 551) and noting that five of these are from the shop of Buckley and three from that of Tonson, we may provisionally say that for the five produced by Buckley—Nos. 338, 396, 527, 539, and 551—Steele was responsible, whoever the actual contributor may have been; and that for the remaining three—Nos. 518, 524, and 548—Addison may similarly take responsibility. The absence of signature letters towards the end of the original run of the *Spectator* is probably more a matter of carelessness or accident than anything else. Earlier, Steele's 'copy' when delivered to the printer would regularly bear the signature letter R or T—even, as was often the case, for a paper made up entirely of letters. Too much significance should not be placed upon the absence of signature letters in these papers printed during the final weeks of the original series.

Of the 555 papers in the first series Steele and Addison may take credit for over 500, i.e. for about nine-tenths. But to assign 251 to Steele and 251 to Addison is to give a misleading impression, since, as we have seen, the greater part of Steele's papers consist of letters, many of which we have every reason to believe were actual contributions. The majority of papers bearing Addison's signature letters, on the other hand, are independent essays and give no

have said, 'and yet afraid to strike'. At best, however, this is speculation, and too much weight cannot be attached to it, without better evidence.

indication of having been sent in by correspondents. Put in tabular form, the figures stand as follows:

	Addison	Steele
Independent essays, with no contributed matter	202	89
Papers made up wholly or in part of letters or contributed matter	49	162

In other words, about two out of every three papers with Steele's signature letters are made up of contributed matter, sometimes with a sentence or two by way of introduction, at other times with no editorial comment whatever. Hence, while it is true to say that the two men shared equal responsibility for the 555 numbers, Addison's contribution in the form of original essays looms much larger. One can appreciate the force of Macaulay's verdict, that 'Addison is the Spectator'.[1]

VII. *Content and Style: the Relative Contributions of Steele and Addison*

By contemporary readers, however, Steele—who had but recently laid down the *Tatler*—was generally credited with the direction and main authorship of the paper. And it is true that the strong ethical purpose of old Isaac Bickerstaff is again to the fore in many of the solid papers on such topics as envy (19), beauty (144), old age (153), true *v.* seeming worth (172, 188, 206), and the art of pleasing (248, 280, 294), written by Steele, especially in the early months of the *Spectator*, as well as the attack on such particular problems as the behaviour of servants (88, 137), the right choice in marriage (320, 437, 479, &c.), the relationship between parents and children (192, &c.), or between patron and client (193, 214). Steele's earnest efforts against the prevalent low standards of sexual morality find expression in vigorous papers on immorality in plays (51, 208), loose and immodest conversation (155), and prostitution (266, 274, &c.). His attitude towards women, if one may generalize, is a rather tender, somewhat old-fashioned solicitude for their position in society. And he leaves his reader in no doubt what this position is.

The utmost of a Woman's Character is contained in Domestick Life; she is Blameable or Praise-worthy according as her carriage affects the House of her Father or her Husband. All she has to do in this World, is contained within the Duties of a Daughter, a Sister, a Wife, and a Mother. . . .[2]

---

[1] *Edinburgh Review*, July 1843, p. 237.   [2] No. 342.

Addison shares Steele's concern for moral uplift, with essays on such standard topics as honour (99), virtue (243), good-nature (169, 177), and love of fame (255–7). Like Steele he deals with problems of courtship and married life (128, 261, 475, &c.), but in general his attitude towards the other sex is less sentimental and more detached. He is likely to concentrate on their foibles—their love of show (15) or of French fopperies (45), their fondness for extravagant clothes (98, 127, 265, &c.), their love of praise (73), and their meddling in politics (57, 81), to name but a few. In noting the failings of either sex Addison is likely to adopt an original framework for driving home his meaning: thus the dissection of a beau's head (275) and its companion dissection of a coquette's heart (281) combine a telling analysis of fashionable frivolity with a neat and graphic incident. Two of his best treatments of courtship and married life are characteristically presented as imaginative tales—the modern women of Hensberg (499) and the auction of women (511).

Both writers are in earnest and both are satirists, but Steele's point of view is generally more serious and straightforward, Addison's marked by greater variety and a spirit of comedy. The difference can be seen if one compares Steele's De Coverley papers— on Sir Roger and his servants (107), on the family portraits (109), and on Sir Roger and the perverse widow (113 and 118)—with those of Addison. Steele's series of fictional papers centring on the figure of Pharamond (76, 84, 97, and 480) illustrate the serious-ness and the limitations of his approach. Or again, the high ethical purpose of Steele's four critical papers on the drama—on 'Sir Fopling Flutter' (65), 'The Scornful Lady' (270), 'The Distressed Mother' (290), and Terence's 'Self-Tormentor' (502)—may be contrasted with Addison's high-spirited series on the absurdities of Italian opera (5, 13, 18, 29, and 31).

Some of Steele's best papers are in the tradition of La Bruyère— the character of the fine gentleman (75), the pert and talkative (148), the man of wit and pleasure (151, 156), the soldier (152), the in-quisitive man (228), and so on; sometimes with invented epithets such as the 'Picts' (41) or 'Friblers' (288), at other times under the guise of fictitious names such as Irus (264) or Fidelia (449). Many of the most effective stories in the *Spectator* are from the pen of Steele—Inkle and Yarico (11), Laetitia and Daphne (33), the cor-respondence of James and Elizabeth (71), the 'History of the Rival Mother' (91), Brunetta and Phillis (80), Cynthio and Flavia (398),

Basilius and his son (426), Will Trap and Jack Stint (448), and Rhynsault and Sapphira (491).

This interest in the variety of human nature is shared, of course, by Addison, who contributes notable papers on witchcraft (117) and gipsies (130), on the three learned professions (21), on the Londoner's fondness for clubs (9, 72, &c.), and on 'men in great place' (469). He usually vitalizes such topics by creating an imaginary character such as 'the Trunk-maker in the Upper Gallery' (235), or inventing a fictitious history of the cat-call (361), or playing on the idea of an Academy for Politicians (305), or devising the 'Journal of a Citizen' (317) to reveal the emptiness of the idle life, with its pendant, 'Clarinda's Journal' (323). Like Steele, he enlivens his pages with tales, real or imaginary: some of the more admired in this category are Marraton's Visit to the World of Spirits (56), Eudoxus and Leontine (123), Theodosius and Constantia (164), the Castilian and his Faithless Wife (198), the Rival Negroes (215), the Incarnations of Pugg (343), and the Commonwealth of Amazons (433, 434). Above all, of course, there are the essays portraying Sir Roger de Coverley, at home (106, 107, 110, 112, 122, 131) and in London (269, 329, 335, 383), together with the fine papers on his death (517), on Will Honeycomb's marriage (530), and Sir Andrew Freeport's disposal of his own estate (549), which represent perhaps the finest achievement in English fiction before Richardson.

Present-day interest in the *Spectator* derives to a great extent, of course, from the vivid picture which it gives of ordinary daily life, and for this both Steele and Addison are responsible. Like Pepys's *Diary* and Boswell's *Life of Johnson*, it provides an inexhaustible source of information on the way people lived—their dress, their food and drink, their homes, their amusements, their reading, and a thousand other details. The increased size of the hoop-petticoat and the proper way of handling the fan, the fashions in hair-dress and methods of colouring and powdering, the 'pinch of Barcelona' and the ounce of right Virginia; the gentleman's red coat 'to go a wooing in', his laced and knotted cravat, the beaver hat edged with silver, the little silver hasps instead of buttons down the front of the coat—these are the bits which help to re-create the world of Queen Anne's day before our eyes. We read of the domestic décor—the walls covered with tapestry and hangings, or sometimes decorated with 'printed papers', the chimney-pieces glazed with looking-glasses—and glimpse the lady of fashion as she receives morning visitors in bed. Now there will be a reference to a recipe for hasty-pudding, now an allusion to hams and Portugal onions; now to the various kinds of tea, now to Burton ale. The 'gluttony of a modern meal' is detailed in one essay (No. 195), where the diners

devour Fowl, Fish and Flesh; swallow Oyl and Vinegar, Wines and Spices; throw down Sallads of twenty different Herbs, Sauces of an hundred Ingredients, Confections and Fruits of numberless Sweets and Flavours.

We read of chocolate as an inflamer of passion, and catch a glimpse of the Christmas feast, where there is always 'a Piece of cold Beef and a Mince-Pye upon the Table' (269). Health with its relation to temperance (195), or to exercise (115), or to cheerfulness (387), naturally follows; and there are sobering accounts of the numerous distempers—from 'the lingering hectick' to the deep-seated hypo-chondria—which lie in wait, as well as 'Envy, Avarice, Superstition, Despair, Love, with the like Cares and Passions that infest humane Life' (159).

The world of eighteenth-century London passes before our eyes —the hackney coachmen and the street hawkers, the knife-grinders and the sow-gelders, the lacemen and the bellows-menders, the pastry-men and the street jugglers. We hear the bellman's voice and witness the 'eloquence of beggars', we read the outrageous advertisements of the quack doctors and hear the complaint of the woman bar-keeper at the coffee-house against the 'Gentleman who besieges me as close as the *French* did *Bouchain*' (534). The descrip-tions of the 'how-d'ye servants' or the *homme de ruelle* recall now obsolete customs, and we are introduced to such colourful oddities as Nicholas Hart the fabulous 'sleeper' (184), Moll Hinton, the woman of the town (77), or Isaac Hedgeditch, a poacher (168), to say nothing of such popular actors as William Penkethman, who mounts the back of an elephant at Bartholomew Fair (455), and Clench of Barnet, who imitates flute, bells, and organ by his natural voice (31). Graphic scenes are brought before our eyes—between the young Templar and his father in a coffee-house (150), between the bawd and the young girl from the country (266), or between bookseller and customer, 'which happen'd while I was yet Writing, and I over-heard as I sat in the Back-room at a *French* Booksellers' (438). We witness the clash of interests at a great man's levee (193) or the manner of 'demolishing a Prude' at a Club of She-Romps (217),

see a would-be seducer outwitted by a shopkeeper (182), and witness a trial of skill between two gladiators at Hockley in the
Hole (436).

The wealth of such detail is endless, and this is but a fraction of
the subject-matter. Natural science, classical learning, the theatre,
the world of books, philosophy, religion, art, and music—these and
many other subjects form a part of the learning which the *Spectator*
sought to bring out of schools and colleges, 'to dwell in Clubs and
Assemblies, at Tea-Tables, and in Coffee-Houses'. In the process it
is surprising how much recondite lore and curious learning came to
be served up at the morning tea-table—now a statement of Diodorus
Siculus on the ichneumon, now an observation on the Emperor
Leopold's skill in handicrafts, a comment on the *diverticula* of Lucan,
a translation of a Lapland love-poem, or a speculation on why beards
have flourished at particular ages in history. The variety of subject-
matter and the freshness of its treatment help us to understand why
the *Spectator* was such a tremendous success in its day and why it
continued to be read throughout the century.

The critical papers proper—which proved at the time to be one
of the most popular features of the journal—were mainly the work
of Addison. There are nearly sixty of these, including the four large
groups—the papers on English tragedy (39, 40, 42, 44, and 548), on
true and false wit (58–63), on the pleasures of the imagination (411–
21), and on *Paradise Lost* (beginning with No. 267 and continuing
on Saturdays, eighteen in all). Individual critical essays are those on
the ballads (70, 74, 85), on Sappho (223, 229), on Pope's *Essay on
Criticism* (254), on humour (35, 47, 249), on the language (135, 165),
on genius (160), on authors and writing (166), on the fable (183,
512), on taste (409), on method in writing and speaking (476), and
on modern poetry (523). By modern standards many of these seem
unnecessarily simplified and 'unphilosophical', but to the contemporary reader they provided just the right amount of critical learning,
amply supported with illustrative quotation and without the
pedantry of the schools.

Of all Addison's contributions, however, the series on philosophical and religious topics were beyond question the most highly
valued. In the pattern of alternating days which established itself
between Addison and Steele (corresponding to the alternating
printers Tonson and Buckley), it fell to Addison's lot to provide the
Saturday paper, and he soon adopted the habit of providing a more

serious discourse for the occasion, a kind of lay sermon appropriate to week-end meditation. Such serious discourses as those on immortality (111), enthusiasm and superstition (201), prayer (207), good intentions (213), God in nature (393), trust in God (441), gratitude (453), faith (459, 465), hope (471), and the idea of God (531), all appeared in the series of Saturday papers. These and many more, such as the essays on death (26, 349), on zealotry (185), on atheism (186), on the animal economy (120, 121), on dreams and fortune-telling (487, 505), and on the scale of beings (519), seemed appropriate to the nature of the fictitious author, and gave a more serious and solid tone to the paper. The five hymns composed by Addison, including the very popular *The Spacious Firmament on High*, all appeared among the Saturday essays (441, 453, 465, 489, 513).

Of the personal relationship between Addison and Steele during the publication of the original series of the *Spectator* we have little direct information. Tickell implies that the two men worked more or less independently and that Steele in his role of editor did not supervise all the material in the way we should expect of an editor today. The essays written by the two, he says, 'were never or seldom shown to each other by their respective authors'.[1] Contemporary readers would be likely to regard the new paper as a sequel to the *Tatler* and to look upon it therefore primarily as a project of Steele's.

> When first the *Tatler* to a Mute was turn'd,
> *Great Britain* for her Censor's Silence mourn'd.
> Robb'd of his sprightly Beams she wept the Night,
> Till the *Spectator* rose, and blaz'd as bright.[2]

From the first, however, Addison seems to have taken a leading share in the direction of the *Spectator*. The most important statements of policy in the early papers occur in Nos. 1, 4, 10, and 16, of which three are by him. Later on it is in essays by Addison that we find the really significant statements as to the direction and purpose of the paper—on the reception of the *Spectator* (124 and 448), on its two classes of readers (179 and 598), on the kinds of papers attempted (124, 435, and 476), on the choice of mottoes and signatures (221), and on the increased stature of Mr. Spectator when the daily papers will be collected into handsome octavos (529).

---

[1] Preface to Addison's *Works* (1721), vol. i, p. xiii. Tickell and Steele, of course, were not on good terms.

[2] 'On the *Spectator*. By Mr. Tate.' (Printed in No. 488.)

On three separate occasions—at the end of the year 1711 (No. 262), at the end of July 1712, just before the new stamp tax went into effect (No. 445), and as the paper was drawing to a close in November 1712 (No. 542)—Addison pauses for a serious review of the policies of the *Spectator*, with an important summing-up of what he feels has been accomplished in the new venture. Perhaps the most important point, stressed in each of these, is that he has 'new-pointed all the Batteries of Ridicule' and 'set up the Immoral Man as the Object of Derision' (445). On this fundamental issue Addison and Steele were completely united.

The two friends, so different in temperament, were apparently equally divergent in their methods of composition. Steele, so far as we know, wrote with rapidity and ease, consciously tried to give his writing 'an air of common speech',[1] and was not greatly inclined to revising. Nathan Drake, summing up opinion at the end of the century, notes that Steele contributed little to the development of the art of composition. 'He found it incorrect, and left it so.'

Nothing has contributed so much to depreciate him in the estimation of the public as the evident inferiority of his style, when compared with that of his friend and coadjutor.[2]

Addison, on the other hand, while he 'wrote very fluently', was sometimes 'very slow and scrupulous in correcting'. So Pope recalled (talking to Spence of Addison's efforts in poetry). 'He would show his verses to several friends; and would alter almost every thing that any of them hinted at as wrong.'[3] On another occasion Pope observed to Spence:

Mr. Addison would never alter any thing after a poem was once printed; and was ready to alter almost every thing that was found fault with before.—I believe he did not leave a word unchanged, that I made any scruple against in his *Cato*.[4]

All this suggests a painstaking care in the choice of diction and polishing of expression quite different from the freer method of Steele. According to Joseph Warton, Addison was equally scrupulous in the composition of his essays.

Addison was so extremely nice in polishing his prose compositions, that when almost a whole impression of a Spectator was worked off, he would stop the press to insert a new preposition or conjunction.[5]

---

[1] *Tatler*, no. 5.   [2] *Essays* (1805), i. 186–7.
[3] Joseph Spence, *Anecdotes*, ed. S. W. Singer (1820), p. 49.
[4] Ibid., p. 151.   [5] *Essay on the Genius and Writings of Pope* (1782), i. 152.

Nichols, in a note to *Tatler* 77, recalls a conversation with 'old Mr. Richard Nutt', who had been employed with his father John Nutt in the printing of the *Tatler*.

Mr. *Richard Nutt* remembered that the press was stopped, and not seldom, but not by *Addison*, or for the sake of inserting new prepositions or conjunctions; it was stopped, he said, *for want of copy*. In these cases, he had often a hard task to find out *Steele*, who frequently furnished him with the needful supply, written hastily, in a room belonging to the printing-office. This merry old man, who died but lately, mentioned upon recollection a particular paper, which he saw rapidly written by *Steele*, at midnight, and in bed, whilst he waited to carry it to the press.[1]

Nutt is recalling the days of the *Tatler*, not the *Spectator*, but the anecdote is not inherently improbable. The evidence provided by the revisions in the *Spectator* bears out contemporary opinion that the ease and gracefulness of style which so pleased eighteenth-century readers was primarily due to the attention given to such matters by Addison.

The first of these revisions are those marked in the errata lists (in the folio sheets): by far the greater part of them are due to Addison. There are nearly a hundred errata in the first series—93, to be exact—of which 66 are by Addison, 26 by Steele, and 1 by Budgell. A number of them are simply alterations of spelling or correction of fact—words which have been misunderstood by the printer—but a great many of Addison's, notably in the Milton papers, are careful revisions and improvements of style.[2] Steele's, on the other hand, are for the most part simply the correction of misprints; only five out of the twenty-seven in his papers are anything more.[3]

When the *Spectator* was reprinted in 8vo and 12mo the papers underwent a thoroughgoing revision of style—there are over 1,500 authorial changes—and here too it is in the essays of Addison that we find a greater proportion of stylistic revisions. More than two-thirds of the total number are due to him. Many of these are made to avoid inadvertent repetition of a word, and with fairly regular consistency he drops the relative pronoun 'that' and replaces it by 'which' or 'who'. The number of revisions in single papers is also much higher in Addison's than in Steele's. Addison's papers will

[1] *The Tatler*, ed. Nichols (1786), iii. 21.

[2] Cf. F. W. Bateson, 'The *Errata* in *The Tatler*', *Review of English Studies*, v (1929), 155–66.

[3] To complete the record: there are six errata in the second series of the *Spectator*. Five of these are in essays by Addison.

contain as many as twelve or fifteen stylistic revisions within a single essay: Steele's revisions run to a much lower figure; a few papers contain as many as seven, but the figure is generally lower. Steele's inattention may be illustrated by the manner in which he allows reproduction of his own earlier writings to stand in the *Spectator*. On two occasions he quotes long extracts from *The Christian Hero*, in texts which are palpably careless and inexact. The phrase 'the Machiavilian Scheme' appears in the folio text of No. 516 as 'the Machiavilian Scene', an error which was allowed to stand when the paper was reprinted in 8vo and 12mo. Again, the phrase 'Their proud and disdainful Hearts, which were putrified with the Love and Pride of this World' appears in No. 356 (all three texts) with the reading 'petrifyed'. One might argue that this change was Steele's own revision but for the fact that he continues to use 'putrified' in editions of *The Christian Hero* after 1712.[1]

Finally, it will be evident to every reader of the *Spectator* that it is Addison who is not only responsible for most of the essays dealing with style (the Milton papers, among others) but also acutely aware of stylistic matters in his own compositions. In No. 124 he comments on the advantages which the writer of books has over 'those who publish their Thoughts in distinct Sheets, and as it were by Piece-meal'.

We must immediately fall into our Subject and treat every Part of it in a lively Manner, or our Papers are thrown by as dull and insipid: Our Matter must lie close together, and either be wholly new in itself, or in the Turn it receives from our Expressions. Were the Books of our best Authors thus to be retailed to the Publick, and every Page submitted to the Taste of forty or fifty thousand Readers, I am afraid we should complain of many flat Expressions, trivial Observations, beaten Topicks, and common Thoughts, which go off very well in the Lump.

For a few of Addison's essays we have early drafts which throw considerable light on his methods of composition and the pains he took to avoid 'flat Expressions' and other vices inherent in rapid composition. One group of these is contained in the manuscript volume discovered by J. Dykes Campbell in 1858 and published by him in a limited edition under the title, *Some Portions of Essays contributed to the Spectator by Mr. Joseph Addison: Now first printed from*

---

[1] Further details are given in my article, 'The Text of the *Spectator*', *Studies in Bibliography*, v (1953), 109–28.

his MS. Note-Book (Glasgow, 1864). He announced his discovery in *Notes & Queries*, 22 August 1863:

I possess a note book which contains a number of Addison's contributions to the *Spectator*, in his handwriting. Originally the book has been written on only the right hand page, in a very plain but almost print-like hand; and afterwards amended and added to, on the blank pages, in the author's ordinary handwriting. Even in the amended state, the text differs considerably from the printed *Spectator*. My theory is that the Essays were written for College exercises, or the like, at least to be read to an audience (this I draw from the very distinct characters which are as easily read as type); and that they were afterwards expanded by Addison, and touched up for his darling paper.[1]

This manuscript volume, now in the Harvard Library, contains early versions of the texts of the two papers on jealousy (Nos. 170, 171), the three on fame (Nos. 255–7), and a part of the series on the pleasures of the imagination (Nos. 411–21). The earlier history of the manuscript is obscure,[2] but it contains corrections unmistakably in Addison's hand, and of the same kind which we see Addison making in the revisions for the 8vo and 12mo texts. It thus supports the view of Dykes Campbell that the manuscript represents an early draft of some of the more serious papers in the *Spectator*.[3]

Another manuscript containing early versions of *Spectator* material, now in the Bodleian Library,[4] is apparently a copy made by an amanuensis, with corrections in Addison's hand, of twenty-four essays. Since it contains the bookplate of Richard Tickell, it probably once belonged to his grandfather, Addison's friend, though it is not in the handwriting of Thomas Tickell. The material in these twenty-four essays was utilized by Addison in twenty-eight of the published papers, all but three of them printed during the early months of the *Spectator*'s history. Like the contents of the Harvard notebook, the Bodleian essays are on serious topics, fifteen of them being used for the Saturday papers in the *Spectator*. The Bodleian manuscript has been made the subject of two detailed studies which show the extent to which Addison revised the material to make it

[1] *Notes & Queries*, 3 ser., iv. 146. See also the *Athenaeum*, 27 Aug. 1864, p. 274; 3 Sept., p. 308; 19 Nov., p. 674.

[2] See the later article by Campbell, 'Addison's "Spectator" MSS.', *Athenaeum*, 1 Nov. 1890, p. 586, in which he conjectures that the manuscript must have remained at Bilton Hall after the sale of Addison's library in 1799.

[3] Nichols, as early as 1789, had suggested that Addison's essays on the pleasures of the imagination were 'perhaps composed from sketches in his *Common-Place Book* written when at *Oxford*' (note to No. 411).   [4] MS. Don. d. 112.

suitable for publication.[1] Of particular interest is the fact that the long essay 'Of Fame' in the Bodleian manuscript (Nos. 255–7 in the *Spectator*) is also to be found in an earlier version in the Harvard notebook, so that the consecutive steps in the revision of material can be followed.[2]

The materials provided in these early manuscripts, as well as the revisions made for the 8vo and 12mo reprints, afford concrete evidence of Addison's efforts to achieve perfection of style, and confirm the testimony of contemporary witnesses to the almost unique position which he held in the eighteenth century.[3] Steele, in the angry letter to Congreve written after Addison's death, comments on 'the Elegance, Purity, and Correctness which appear'd in his Writings', contrasted with his own less ambitious aims.[4] It is this unceasing labour of the file and conscious seeking after perfection which has caused Addison's writing, in the eyes of some twentieth-century critics, to appear too contrived and lacking in vigour. In his own day and throughout his century he seemed to have attained the goal to which all classical writing strives, the perfect adaptation of language to subject-matter without too obvious effect—'on grave subjects not formal, on light occasions not groveling; pure without scrupulosity, and exact without apparent elaboration'.[5]

VIII. *Success of the* Spectator: *Publication in Volume Form*

When the *Spectator* ceased publication on Saturday, 6 December 1712, it had been running for twenty-one months, and no doubt could have continued much longer, so far as public response was concerned. How much profit it made for its authors and publishers is unknown, but it had an extremely large circulation for a literary paper and it was one of the few periodicals to survive the stamp tax

---

[1] M. C. Crum, 'A Manuscript of Essays by Addison', *Bodleian Library Record*, v (1954), 98–103; Robert D. Chambers, 'Addison at Work on the *Spectator*', *Modern Philology*, lvi (1959), 145–53.

[2] Miss Crum's conclusion is that the Bodleian manuscript 'derives from the corrected notebook, but that there was an intermediate copy containing minor corrections' (p. 100).

[3] The best analyses of Addison's style are those by Zilpha E. Chandler, *An Analysis of the Stylistic Technique of Addison, Johnson, Hazlitt, and Pater* (University of Iowa Studies, Humanistic Studies, IV, no. 3, 1928); and Jan Lannering, *Studies in the Prose Style of Joseph Addison* (Essays and Studies on English Language and Literature, ed. S. B. Liljegren, IX, Uppsala, 1951). With the materials now available it is to be hoped that more complete studies of the subject will be undertaken.

[4] Dedication prefixed to the second edition (1722) of Addison's *Drummer* (*Correspondence of Steele*, ed. Blanchard, p. 510).

[5] Johnson, *Life of Addison* (World's Classics edition), i. 466.

imposed at the beginning of August 1712. From the beginning Buckley seems to have thought of it as a medium for advertising, along with the *Daily Courant*, and the rising 'curve' in number of advertisements provides evidence of its success from a business point of view.

Although each number announced that advertisements would be 'taken in' by Mrs. Baldwin and Charles Lillie, no hint is given as to the charge made. Possibly it varied according to the length or position of the advertisement, or according to the kind of goods advertised. A few years earlier the *Observator Reformed* (1704) offered to take in notices of eight lines for a shilling, and the *Country Gentleman's Courant* in 1706 made a charge of 2*d.* per line.[1] The *British Apollo* (1708) accepted advertisements at 2*s.* 6*d.* each, with no reference to size or position, and this seems to have been the normal rate at the time the *Spectator* was being published.[2] It seems likely that an extra charge might be made for an unusually long advertisement, or for the notice of the play at Drury Lane Theatre (which usually headed the column of advertisements in the *Spectator*), but there is little direct evidence. In No. 336 a notice of a forthcoming sale of pictures to be held on 27 March 1712 'at the Corner of the Little-Piazza in Russel-street, Covent-Garden', is placed first among the advertisements for the day, preceded by the following statement (in italics):

The Proprietor of the Pictures exposed to Sale according to the following Advertisement, being a Person of an excellent Taste in Paintings and great Probity in his own Character, for the Benefit of the Curious the said Advertisement is preferred to all others in the present Paper.

Whatever the rate charged for advertisements, there can be no doubt that the *Spectator* quickly established itself as a reliable and popular medium in the new and as yet little explored art of advertising. The first issues contain only advertisements of books, but

[1] Nichols, *Literary Anecdotes*, iv. 80, 82.

[2] The *Guardian*, 'Printed for J. Tonson in the Strand; and Sold by A. Baldwin in Warwick-Lane', announces in No. 169 (24 Sept. 1713) that 'Advertisements will for the future be inserted in this Paper for 2s. 6d. each, notwithstanding the Duty of 1s.' As late as 1738 the *London Daily Post* receives advertisements 'of a moderate length' at 2s. each, and the *Daily Post* of the same year announces (7 April 1738) that advertisements 'of a moderate Length, that require no Preference of *Place* or *Character*, are taken in at Two Shillings each'. Since the official newspaper, the *London Gazette*, charged 10s. for each advertisement in 1710, it has been suggested that five shillings 'would seem by comparison just about the proper tariff for the *Spectator*' (Richmond P. Bond, 'The Business of the *Spectator*', *University of North Carolina Extension Bulletin*, vol. xxxii, no. 3 (1953), p. 12), but direct evidence is lacking.

beginning with No. 10 the field is widened: in this issue appear advertisements for silk gowns ('at Mrs. Rogers's in Exchange-Ally'), for 'Plain Spanish Snuff', for wines (two notices), and for a house to be let, 'at Sutton in Surrey, on the Edge of Bansted-Downes'. The number of advertisements shows a steady increase (with a seasonal drop in the summer months) up to August 1712, when the Tory government imposed a tax of one shilling on each advertisement, as well as a halfpenny on each copy of a paper. Throughout, it is papers printed in Buckley's own shop which contain most advertisements, frequently in the same standing type used for advertisements in the *Daily Courant*, also printed by Buckley.[1] The popularity of the *Spectator* as an advertising medium is shown by the table.

	Month (and number of issues)	Advertisements			
		(Tonson)	(Buckley)	Total	Average
1711	March (27)	100	130	230	8·51
	April (25)	74	104	178	7·12
	May (27)	87	97	184	6·81
	June (26)	87	111	198	7·61
	July (26)	67	108	175	6·73
	August (27)	72	64	136	5·03
	September (25)	61	91	152	6·08
	October (27)	108	136	244	9·29
	November (26)	126	117	243	9·34
	December (26)	138	140	278	10·69
1712	January (27)	137	145	282	10·44
	February (25)	109	148	257	10·28
	March (26)	115	176	291	11·09
	April (26)	142	160	302	11·61
	May (27)	134	160	294	10·89
	June (25)	149	95	244	9·76
	July (27)	76	184	260	9·63
	August (26)	40	54	94	3·61
	September (26)	42	49	91	3·50
	October (27)	76	81	157	5·81
	November (25)	86	85	171	7·00
	December (6)	17	16	33	5·50
	Total	2,043	2,451	4,494	8·01

It is interesting to note the remarkable 'recovery' made in the number of advertisements after the sharp decline precipitated in August 1712 by the heavy tax on advertisements. By November 1712 the number had begun again to climb, and if the paper had continued it seems likely that it would have reached the high totals it had attained in the early months of 1712.

[1] For details see my article, 'The First Printing of the *Spectator*', *Modern Philology*, xlvii (1950), 168–72.

Before the original series had run half its course a subscription edition was undertaken by Tonson, advertised in No. 227 of the folio sheets, on 20 November 1711:

There is now Printing by Subscription two Volumes of the SPECTATORS on a large Character in Octavo; the Price of the two Vols. well Bound and Gilt two Guineas. Those who are inclined to Subscribe, are desired to make their first Payments to Jacob Tonson, Bookseller in the Strand; the Books being so near finished, that they will be ready for the Subscribers at or before Christmas next.

This notice (with the reading 'will certainly be ready') was repeated in Nos. 228–34, again in No. 237, and finally in No. 248 (14 December). After that it evidently was realized that the books would not be ready for delivery by Christmas. The next advertisement appears in No. 269 (8 January 1712):

The First and Second Volumes of the SPECTATOR *in 8vo are now ready to be delivered to the Subscribers, by* J. Tonson *at* Shakespear's *Head over-against* Catherine-street *in the* Strand.

Although Tonson handled the subscriptions to this edition, the imprint carries the names of both Buckley and Tonson as publishers, and from typographical evidence it looks as if volume i was issued from the shop of Tonson and volume ii from that of Buckley.[1] Ten days later, in No. 278, an advertisement appears for 'a neat pocket edition' (volumes i and ii) issued also by Buckley and Tonson. In both formats these first two volumes reprinted *Spectators* 1–169.

Volumes iii and iv (Nos. 170–321) were published in 8vo and 12mo towards the end of 1712. The 12mo edition is advertised in No. 533 (11 November):

This Day is publish'd,

A very neat Pocket Edition of the 3d and 4th Volumes of the Spectator *in 12°. To which is added a compleat Index to the whole 4 Volumes. Printed for* S. Buckley *at the Dolphin in* Little Britain, *and* J. Tonson *at* Shakespear's *Head over-against* Catherine-street *in the* Strand.

The third volume is dated 1712, the fourth 1713. The octavo edition was probably published about the same time, or a few days earlier, but no advertisements for it have been found. In this edition volume iii is dated 1713 and volume iv 1712.

---

[1] *Studies in Bibliography*, v (1953), 121.

With the publication of the first four volumes Addison and Steele sold their rights to the work, one half to Tonson and one half to Buckley, each of whom paid £575. The assignment to Buckley,[1] dated 10 November 1712, 'at the Fountain tavern in the Strand', recites that whereas four volumes are already printed and two volumes more are now printing (which would carry the number of essays to No. 480 'or thereabouts') and whereas the authors intend 'to Continue writing the said Spectator to the end of this present month of November which will make a Seventh volume', Joseph Addison, 'of St. James's Westminster', and Richard Steele, 'of St. Giles's in the fields', assign their right and title to a half-share in the seven volumes to Samuel Buckley. (The document is witnessed by Richard Thwaites and David Verdon.) A similar assignment of a half-share to Tonson was made at the same time.[2] (Two years later, on 13 October 1714, Buckley sold his half-share in the *Spectator* for £500.) Actually it was found necessary to continue publication through the first week of December 1712 in order to fill a seventh volume. Volumes v, vi, and vii were advertised in *Guardian* 27 (11 April 1713):

This Day is Publish'd,

The Fifth, Sixth, and Seventh Volumes of the Spectator in 8vo *and* 12mo. *Printed for S. Buckley at the Dolphin in Little-Britain: and J. Tonson at Shakespear's Head against Catherine-street in the Strand.*

IX. *The Second Series*

The history of the second series, or the continuation, or 'Spectator II', as it is sometimes called, may be dealt with more briefly. It comprises Nos. 556–635, published later as volume viii. It was after an interval of a year and a half that Addison decided to revive the paper, in the summer of 1714. The *Daily Courant* of 18 June carried the following advertisement:

This present Friday, the 18th of June, is revived, and will be published every Monday, Wednesday and Friday,

The SPECTATOR

Printed by S. Buckley in Amen-Corner, and J. Tonson in the Strand, where Advertisements will be taken in.

---

[1] Now in the British Museum (Add. MS. 21,110, f. 41).
[2] Now in the Henry E. Huntington Library (MS. H.M. 20052). See Steele's *Correspondence*, ed. Blanchard, p. 462.

In the eighteen months since the last number of the original series had appeared Addison had witnessed the successful production of his tragedy *Cato* at Drury Lane Theatre on 14 April 1713 and had contributed several essays to the new periodical, the *Guardian*, which Steele had carried on from 12 March to 1 October 1713. Shortly thereafter, on 6 October, Steele began a new journal, the *Englishman*, solely devoted to politics, the first series of which (57 numbers) ran to 15 February 1714. Politics in fact occupied Steele increasingly during this time. He had been elected Member of Parliament for Stockbridge, Hampshire, in August 1713, and his strenuous attachment to Whig interests made him increasingly unpopular with the ruling Tory government. The culmination came in his expulsion from the House of Commons on 18 March 1714. His *Apology for himself and his Writings*, published the following October, shows Steele too busily engaged in politics at this time to think of working with Addison in a revival of the *Spectator*. The summer of 1714, however, marked a turning-point in the political fortunes of both Steele and Addison, for on 1 August the Queen died, and with the accession of the Hanoverian line and the return to power of the Whigs both men could expect substantial rewards from the incoming government.

When, in October 1713, John Hughes suggested to Addison that they collaborate on a new paper, Addison declined on the ground that he was 'written out'.

I have been so taken up with thoughts of that nature for these two or three years last past, that I must now take some time *pour me délasser*, and lay in fewel for a future work.[1]

At the time of reviving the *Spectator*, eight months later, Addison had evidently accumulated sufficient material to carry on for several numbers. There are twenty-five papers in the new series by Addison himself, the last of which (No. 600) appeared at the end of September. Since the beginning of August, however, with the death of the Queen and his appointment as Secretary to the Lords Justices (the Regents), Addison would certainly have been too busy to take an active personal part in the conduct of the new paper. His two assistants were Budgell and Tickell.

Eustace Budgell, who, as we have seen, had contributed twenty-nine papers to the original series and who had been closely con-

---

[1] Addison to Hughes, 12 Oct. 1713 (*Letters*, ed. Graham, pp. 279-80).

nected with Addison both in Ireland and in London, was probably associated with the continuation of the *Spectator* from the beginning. His own contributions begin at the end of June or early in July; and by 3 August, when Addison was appointed Secretary to the Lords Justices, Budgell probably assumed acting editorship of the journal.[1] His own papers, either original essays or material worked over from contributions, appeared mainly in July, August, and September; and in addition he seems to have recast two or three numbers which Addison had left for him. Towards the end of September Addison was able to secure for him the lucrative post of Secretary to the Lords Justices of Ireland, in the place of Joshua Dawson.

Mr. Budgell set out for Ireland the 8th of October, 1714, officiated in his place in the privy council the 14th, took possession of the secretary's office, and was immediately admitted secretary to the Lords Justices.[2]

With the departure of Budgell the work of editing material, sorting out contributions, and arranging the essays for publication fell to another disciple of Addison, Thomas Tickell. Tickell is named by Steele as one of the contributors to the original series, but his association with Addison, which had begun with his complimentary verses on *Rosamond*, did not become close until 1714, when the translation of Homer was in active preparation. By the summer of 1714 he was in London; in September, when Addison became Secretary to the Lord Lieutenant of Ireland, he appointed Tickell his personal secretary.[3] Like Budgell, Tickell in some cases reworked material which Addison turned over to him, but from the beginning of October until the paper was finished in December he produced several essays of his own.

When the eighty numbers (556–635) were reprinted as volume viii (in both octavo and duodecimo) on 1 September 1715,[4] 'printed on a Royal and Demy Paper in Octavo, that Subscribers to the former Volumes may compleat their Setts', the following notice was prefixed:

The Bookseller to the Reader.

In the Six hundred and thirty second *Spectator*, the Reader will find an Account of the Rise of this Eighth and Last Volume.

---

[1] For the reconstruction of events and evidence of authorship of this second series, I am indebted to Mr. M. J. C. Hodgart's excellent article, 'The Eighth Volume of the *Spectator*', *Review of English Studies*, N.S., v (1954), 367–87.
[2] *Cibber's Lives of the Poets* (1753), v. 5.
[3] See R. Eustace Tickell, *Thomas Tickell* (1932), pp. 34–51.
[4] Advertised in the *Daily Courant* of this date.

I have not been able to prevail upon the several Gentlemen who were concerned in this Work to let me acquaint the World with their Names.

Perhaps it will be unnecessary to inform the Reader, that no other Papers, which have appeared under the Title of *Spectator*, since the closing of this Eighth Volume, were written by any of those Gentlemen who had a Hand in this or the former Volumes.

The warning in the last sentence was occasioned by a spurious 'Volume IX' which had been published twice a week from 3 January to 3 August 1715 (61 numbers) under the direction of William Bond and published as 'Vol. Ninth and Last' by J. Roberts. And there were other attempted continuations.[1] Budgell, writing several years later in the *Bee*, recalled the vain efforts made to capitalize on the magic name of *Spectator*.

When the *Old Spectator* was laid down, by those Hands which at first composed it, the Paper was immediately set on foot again by some of the greatest *Wits* in *England*, several of whose Writings, of different Kinds, had been received with the utmost Applause by the Publick; yet even these Gentlemen, to their great Surprize, found the Thing would not do; and had the good Sense not only to drop their *Design*, but to *conceal* their *Names*: The late Mr. *Addison* said upon this Occasion, that *he looked upon the Undertaking to write SPECTATORS to be like the Attempt of* Penelope's *Lovers to shoot in the* Bow *of* Ulysses; *who soon found that no Body could shoot* well *in that* Bow *but the* Hand *which used to* draw *it.*[2]

The statement of the Bookseller regarding authorship was prompted by the fact that, unlike the original series, no signature letters were used for the essays in Nos. 556–635. Evidence for authorship of these eighty numbers rests in part—as in the first series—on material later reprinted and acknowledged by their several authors. Tickell, for instance, in his edition of Addison's *Works* in 1721, reprinted twenty-four of the essays from this volume, and there can be no doubt about these. More recently new evidence of authorship has been brought to light by the discovery of the manuscript draft of 'The Bookseller to the Reader' among the Tickell papers, now in the possession of Major-General Sir Eustace F.

[1] The library catalogue of Edinburgh University lists a copy of *Spectator* No. 54, dated 22 July 1715, apparently not one of Bond's continuation. In the following year Morphew attempted to bring out another continuation: No. 1 ('London: Printed and Given Gratis') is dated Wednesday, 13 June 1716, and announces that it will be published every Wednesday.

[2] No. 1 (Feb. 1733), p. 27.

Tickell.[1] This manuscript draft, a full account of which will be found in Mr. Hodgart's article,[2] assigns authors to all but twelve of the eighty numbers. Although not many new names are offered, the list is of the greatest value in assigning authorship to the eighty papers, and in the following account its evidence has been accepted when not in direct contradiction to better-authenticated testimony.

In addition to the twenty-four essays of Addison reprinted in the *Works* of 1721, the Tickell manuscript includes another paper (No. 594) as by Addison. His contributions may be listed as follows:

556 (18 June)	The talkative Spectator.
557 (21 June)	Integrity: the Ambassador of Bantam.
558 (23 June)	Griefs and Calamities.
559 (25 June)	Griefs and Calamities: Patience.
561 (30 June)	Letter describing the Widow Club.
562 (2 July)	Egotism.
565 (9 July)	The Omnipresence & Omnipotence of God.
567 (14 July)	Satiric Pamphlets.
568 (16 July)	Satiric Pamphlets.
569 (19 July)	Drunkenness.
571 (23 July)	Letter, with prefatory sentence; 'founded on a former Spectator' (i.e. 565), and 'sent me by a particular Friend'.
574 (30 July)	Contentment.
575 (2 August)	Immortality.
576 (4 August)	Singularity.
579 (11 August)	Chastity.
580 (13 August)	Letter: 'Sir, I considered in my two last Letters . . . the Ubiquity or Omnipresence of the Divine Being' (i.e. 565, 571).
582 (18 August)	The Itch of Writing.
583 (20 August)	The Obligation to Plant.
584 (23 August)	Hilpa and Shalum.
585 (25 August)	Hilpa and Shalum.
590 (6 September)	Eternity. 'The following Discourse comes from the same Hand with the Essays upon Infinitude' (i.e. 565, 571, 580).
592 (10 September)	Genius and the Rules.
594 (15 September)	Gossip and Slander.
598 (24 September)	Levity and Seriousness.
600 (29 September)	Immortality.

[1] I am greatly indebted to Major-General Tickell for allowing me to use this material. Mr. Hodgart, in the article cited above as well as in personal correspondence, has also been very generous with help.   [2] See above, p. lxxv, n. 1.

Four of these (561, 571, 580, 590) are made up of letters, and of these only 561 could possibly be doubted as Addison's; the other three continue the subject of No. 565, which is certainly his. No. 571 is in letter form, with introductory sentence (by Budgell?), as is No. 580. No. 590, however, appears as a 'Discourse', with a sentence of introduction (again by Budgell?). All four are reprinted in Addison's *Works*.

Ten papers can be assigned, in whole or in part, to Budgell:

560 (28 June)	Four letters, with introduction and editorial notes.
564 (7 July)	Human Nature a Mixture.
566 (12 July)	Three letters, with an introduction.
570 (21 July)	Amateur Music Makers.
577 (6 August)	Letter from an Eccentric; with the petition from John a Nokes, &c.
578 (9 August)	Personal Identity: Fadlallah and the Dervish.
581 (16 August)	Replies to letters; with two short notes.
589 (3 September)	Letter on planting trees.
591 (8 September)	Letter from the Love Casuist, and contributed verses.
596 (20 September)	Letter from Jeremy Lovemore.

Much of this material is obviously contributed, and it is difficult to say how much is original with Budgell. Tentatively it may be analysed as follows:

$$
\begin{array}{lr}
\text{Independent essays (564, 578)} & = 2 \\
\text{Partly contributed (566, 581, 591)} & = 3 \\
\text{Wholly contributed (589, 596)} & = 2 \\
\text{Material from Addison worked} & \\
\text{over by Budgell (560, 570, 577)} & = \underline{3} \\
\text{Total} & 10
\end{array}
$$

Tickell's contributions are more numerous, consisting of twenty-six numbers, some of them based on Addison's notes and some utilizing letters and other contributed material. There are, first of all, seven papers (595, 604, 615, 619, 620, 629, and 634) which may be assigned wholly to him, one of which (No. 620) is taken up with his poem, 'The Royal Progress'. Tickell is also responsible for three additional essays (610, 624, and 631), which are apparently based on Addison's notes.

In addition to these ten papers, Tickell is responsible for six numbers which are made up in part of letters:

606 (13 October)	On Needlework (contains a short letter).
612 (27 October)	A letter on Pride in Ancestry, with a brief introduction.
616 (5 November)	On Ridiculous Phraseology.
617 (8 November)	On Pedantic Phraseology, with a translation of Strada.
618 (10 November)	A letter (by Ambrose Philips) on Epistolary Verse, with comment.
632 (13 December)	On Whimsical Fancies, with a letter and poem by James Ward.

There is, finally, a third group containing ten numbers made up entirely of letters:

605 (11 October)	Report from the Love Casuist.
607 (15 October)	Letter on Married Happiness: the Flitch at Whichenovre.
608 (18 October)	Another letter on the Flitch.
614 (1 November)	Report from the Love Casuist.
621 (17 November)	Letter on 'Toys and Trifles'.
622 (19 November)	Letter with the Memoirs of a Country Gentleman.
623 (22 November)	Report from the Love Casuist.
625 (26 November)	Report from the Love Casuist, and a letter from Thomas Quidnunc.
627 (1 December)	Letter on a friend, with a copy of his letter to Zelinda.
628 (3 December)	Letter on Eternity, with a Latin version of Cato's Soliloquy.

Three of the letters in this last group (607, 621, and 622) were apparently left by Addison for Tickell's use.

The other authors (of whole papers) in volume viii are Henry Grove, John Byrom, Zachary Pearce, and Lady Mary Wortley Montagu. The Rev. Henry Grove (1684–1738) was a popular nonconformist minister at Taunton, Somerset, where he also conducted a dissenters' academy. He had studied in London under the Rev. Thomas Rowe (a relative), where he had come to know Isaac Watts, Elisabeth Singer Rowe, and others in dissenting circles. Four *Spectator* essays have long been known to be his (588, 601, 626, and 635); they are reprinted in his *Miscellanies in Prose and Verse* (1739), in his *Sermons and Tracts* (1740), and in his *Discourses, Tracts and Poems* (1747). In the preface (vol. i, p. xxix) to the 1740 collection Grove's nephew Thomas Amory (not the author of *John Buncle*) says of these contributions to the *Spectator*:

Their finding a place in that celebrated work is a sufficient proof of their worth. By these papers Mr. *Grove* showed himself well acquainted with the lovely and generous affections of the human soul, as well as its surprizing dignity and large capacities for happiness, which he hath represented in a manner fit to inspire his readers with a strong concern to act a part answerably generous and noble.

Grove also submitted an essay, on the necessity of charity and tolerance in religious matters, soon after the *Spectator* had resumed publication in June 1714. This was not used, but the manuscript survives among the Tickell papers.[1] One of Grove's essays (No. 626) was highly praised by Johnson (10 April 1776).[2] This seems to be also the paper referred to by Johnson in the Notes from Langton (1780):

He mentioned with an air of satisfaction what Baretti had told him; that, meeting, in the course of his studying English, with an excellent paper in the Spectator, one of four that were written by the respectable Dissenting Minister, Mr. Grove of Taunton, and observing the genius and energy of mind that it exhibits, it greatly quickened his curiosity to visit our country; as he thought if such were the lighter periodical essays of our authors, their productions on more weighty occasions must be wonderful indeed![3]

The contributions of John Byrom (1692–1763), the poet and shorthand writer, consist of a poem and two or three letters. At the time of his death the *London Evening Post* of 29 September 1763 wrote of Byrom:

During his residence in College [Trinity College, Cambridge], he held literary correspondence with several great men of the age, wrote several letters, signed John Shadow, in the Spectators, and many excellent poems: was the author of that justly admired pastoral in the Spectators, beginning,

My Time, O ye Muses, was happily spent.

The pastoral poem occupies almost the whole of No. 603; the papers on dreams in volume viii are Nos. 586, 587, 593, and 597.

---

[1] *New Letters to the Tatler and Spectator*, ed. Richmond P. Bond (No. 86).
[2] *Life*, ed. Hill–Powell, iii. 33.
[3] Ibid., iv. 32.

Of these, Nos. 586 and 593, signed 'John Shadow', may be attributed to Byrom. No. 587 cannot be assigned to him, since we are told (in No. 593) that it is not by 'Mr. Shadow'. No. 597, often attributed to Byrom, is actually made up of editorial comments on dream experiences sent in by a number of correspondents, and is more likely to be from the pen of Addison or Budgell. At most, then, Byrom can be credited with three papers (586, 593, and 603), all three in the form of contributions, with an introductory sentence by the editor.

The papers of Zachary Pearce (1690–1774), later Bishop of Rochester, are also in the form of contributions. These are acknowledged in a letter (5 June 1764) from Pearce, among the Birch manuscripts in the British Museum, addressed either to Birch or to Bishop Percy, who was at that time preparing his edition of the *Spectator*. He names two papers (Nos. 572 and 633) as his, as well as one in the *Guardian*.[1] No. 572 is prefaced by a sentence on the part of the editor (Addison, or Budgell), apologizing 'for those Additions and Retrenchments which I have made in it'. The other paper, No. 633, 'is printed, as it came to my Hands, without Variation'. Since No. 572 is entered under Budgell's contributions in the Tickell manuscript, it is probable that the 'additions and retrenchments' referred to are by Budgell.

As for Lady Mary Wortley Montagu, the Tickell manuscript names her as the author of the long letter which makes up the whole of No. 573, a letter beginning 'Smart Sir', and purporting to be from the President of the Club of Widows. This attribution is accepted by Lady Mary's latest biographer,[2] who suggests that 'the honourable Edward Waitfort', the most important character mentioned in the paper, may refer to her husband, Edward Wortley Montagu, whose long courtship had culminated in their marriage only two years previously.

In addition to these authors of whole papers—Addison, Budgell, Tickell, Grove, Byrom, Pearce, and Lady Mary Wortley Montagu —the Tickell manuscript also names Ambrose Philips as the author of the letter in No. 618 and James Ward, of Trinity College, Dublin, as the author of the poem in No. 632.[3] Addison had printed two of Philips's translations from Sappho in the original series of the

[1] Add. MS. 4316, ff. 179–80.
[2] Robert Halsband, *Lady Mary Wortley Montagu* (Oxford, 1956), pp. 35–36.
[3] Both 618 and 632 are now assigned to Tickell, among his six papers made up in part of contributed matter.

Spectator (Nos. 223, 229), and he and Steele had given several friendly notices both to *The Distressed Mother* and to Philips's *Pastorals*. During this period Philips was one of Addison's closest friends, if not actually his amanuensis. The poem, 'To Mrs. —— on her Grotto', is reprinted under Ward's name in the *Miscellaneous Poems, Original and Translated, by several hands*, brought out in 1724 by Matthew Concanen (pp. 347–9). Ward, who later (1726) became Dean of Cloyne and died in 1736, was also the author of the paraphrase from Proverbs published in No. 410.

There are nine remaining papers (563, 587, 597, 599, 602, 609, 611, 613, and 630) which are of uncertain authorship. Most of these consist almost entirely of letters, the chief exceptions being Nos. 597, 599, 611, and 613. No. 597 comments on letters which have been sent in with accounts of dreams; No. 599 is a separate essay on the Cave of Trophonius; No. 611 consists of a letter with a long comment on it; No. 613 is made up of three letters, with a paragraph introduction. Tempting as it is to assign No. 599, particularly, to Addison, the four papers are unmarked in the Tickell manuscript and are not reprinted in the *Works* of Addison, so that there is no positive clue to authorship. Possibly 597 and 599 were prepared by Budgell, and 611 and 613 by Tickell, in their respective roles as editors in charge of providing material for the journal.

Except for the twenty-five essays which Addison wrote for it, the second series is generally regarded as inferior to the original *Spectator*. Certainly its tone is more sombre, though there are exceptions. Macaulay is almost alone in not regretting the absence of Steele in this new venture. 'Nothing can be more striking', writes Macaulay, 'than the contrast between the "Englishman" and the eighth volume of the "Spectator"—between Steele without Addison, and Addison without Steele. The "Englishman" is forgotten; the eighth volume of the "Spectator" contains, perhaps, the finest Essays, both serious and playful, in the English language.'[1] The eighth volume seems to have been mainly a commercial venture, probably suggested by Tonson, and since Addison became involved in government affairs soon after the new series started he did not have much time or energy to devote to the paper. Boswell (10 April 1776) reports Johnson's comment on the *Spectator*:

It is wonderful that there is such a proportion of bad papers, in the

---

[1] *Edinburgh Review*, July 1843, p. 244.

half of the work which was not written by Addison; for there was all the world to write that half, yet not a half of that half is good.[1]

These words of Johnson's, though not applied specifically to the continuation, provide an appropriate comment upon it. The absence of Steele in these last eighty numbers makes itself felt in the somewhat over-prominent moral tone. His papers, in the first series, especially those on contemporary manners, had provided an effective balance to some of the more serious essays of Addison. Both men were undoubtedly at their best when working together, and the first 400 numbers of the paper, before Steele came to depend too much upon contributed matter, could hardly be equalled for the variety of interest, unity of tone, and happy balance between the informative and the merely diverting which marked this early and best of the periodical essays of the century.

X. *Contemporary Readers*

There is abundant testimony to the astonishing success which the *Spectator* achieved in contemporary London, and elsewhere. Whatever the circulation of the daily issues was, 4,000 perhaps, many of the essays were certainly read aloud to frequenters of the numerous coffee-houses which were then a prominent feature of London, so that there was an even wider reading public for the paper. Addison himself, in No. 10, had estimated twenty readers to every paper, at a 'modest computation'. That the paper was popular we may infer from the quantity of letters which came in to the editor, and from the rising number of advertisements. The 'personal' advertisements, which were a feature of the *Spectator*, indicate in themselves that the paper had wide circulation. Two typical ones may be quoted, the first from No. 94, the other from No. 297.

Whereas a Letter dated Friday Noon, signed A. B. directed to a Gentleman in the City, desiring a Place of Meeting; the Person desired will meet the said A. B. at the Bell Tavern in King-street, Westminster, at 2 a Clock this present Monday. Enquire for No. 2.

A Person in a white Cloth Suit, laced with Silver, who handed two Ladies out of the Box in the Gallery of the Play-house in Drury-lane, on Wednesday last, is desired to come this Day, without fail, to the Abby Church in Westminster, betwixt 3 and 4 in the Afternoon.

[1] *Life of Johnson*, ed. Hill–Powell, iii. 33.

Whatever the occasion, whether for arranging meetings or offering a reward for lost articles, the *Spectator* was a natural medium for communication, and one of the first periodicals in the history of journalism to make use of the art of advertising on a large and varied scale.

The *Spectator* appears frequently in advertisements of the news-papers. In the *Evening Post* of 29 January 1712 we read:

> At the Old News-Shop at Essex-street End in the Strand, near St. Clement's Church, liveth B. Berington, who selleth all sorts of Pamphlets, News-Papers, Votes, Spectators, &c.

In the *Daily Courant* of 24 April 1712 a reward is offered for the contents of 'a little Paste-board Band-Box', left in a boat plying between Arundel Stairs and St. Mary Overy's; the lost items are 'A Black Hood all of Lace, an 8 Square small Silver Tea Canister with a Coat of Arms on it, 3 Black Caps for Children, and 3 Spectators'.

The topics treated in the *Spectator*—true and false wit, the relationship between parents and children, Sir Roger de Coverley's affairs—are often referred to in other papers. Thus the *Plain Dealer* of 12 April 1712 (a paper not friendly to Steele) ends its account of a scuffle in the lobby of the House of Commons and a dispute regarding a certain noble lord: 'For, according to Sir *Roger*, *Much may be said on both Sides.*' In the same month (4 April) the *Medley*, the Whig counterpart to the *Examiner*, writes:

> I heard t'other Day some sowr-fac'd Criticks complain, that the *Spectator* writes about *Nothing*; and yet who is there so remarkable in any sort of Learning, that would not be content to part with all his past Reputation, to be able for the future to write like the *Spectator*?

Even the writer of an anonymous attack upon *The Distressed Mother*, that favourite play of the *Spectator*, acknowledges the power of Steele and Addison's periodical in influencing contemporary taste:

> And here, though I must be forc'd to bear a little hard upon the Spectators too violent Passion express'd for the *Distrest Mother*, however I have some hopes of not so highly incurring his Displeasure in that Boldness with his Favourite, when this Publication shall appear not so much an Affront to his *Judgment*, as a Congratulation of his POWER, when a Stroke of his Ingenious Pen could carry so Universal a Sway o'er the Town in Favour to that Play.[1]

[1] *A Modest Survey of that celebrated Tragedy The Distrest Mother, so often and so highly applauded by the Ingenious Spectator* (Redmayne and Morphew, 1712), pp. 6–7.

We get an interesting glimpse of Mr. Spectator's position in the minds of the extreme Tories, from a notice in the *Flying-Post* of 2 December 1712 that Papists and Jacobites were stealing from coffee-houses the papers 'writ in Defence of the Constitution and Protestant Succession' and that from Mr. Blacknell's Coffee-house in Hatton Garden 'they lately stole the Elector of Hanover's Memorial, and the Bishop of St. Asaph's Preface, put up in Frames; a Volume of Spectators, and other Papers . . .'.

The multitude of letters received, as we have seen, not only from London but from places as diverse as Exeter, Norwich, Bath, Edinburgh, and Dublin, indicates that the *Spectator* was read throughout the United Kingdom and Ireland. At Spalding, in Lincolnshire, we are told, the *Tatlers* were read 'every post day, generally aloud to the company, who could sit and talk over the subject afterwards. . . . In March, 1711, the Spectator came out, which was received and read here as the Tatler had been; and next year these gentlemen formed themselves into a voluntary society' which eventually became the Spalding Society (of antiquaries).[1] In the Highlands of Scotland the papers were read aloud on Sundays.

Rare as the intercourse was between the capital and the Highlands of Scotland, yet did the Spectator find its way regularly to that part of the kingdom. Mr. Steuart of Dalguise, a gentleman of Perthshire, of very great respectability, who died near ninety, about twelve or fourteen years ago, has informed us, that when, as usual in that country, the gentlemen met after church on Sunday, to discuss the news of the week, the Spectators were read as regularly as the journal. He informed us also, that he knew the perusal of them to be general through the country.[2]

In the American colonies too it was read and admired. In Boston the Rev. Cotton Mather was reading it in 1713.[3] In the same city Benjamin Franklin, then a youth in his teens and an apprentice in his brother's printing shop, happened upon an odd volume (the third) of the *Spectator*, which so delighted him with its excellent writing that he used it as a means of learning to write effective prose.

With that view, I took some of the papers, and making short hints of the sentiment in each sentence, laid them by a few days, and then without looking at the book, tried to complete the papers again by expressing each hinted sentiment at length and as fully as it had been

[1] Maurice Johnson, 'Introduction to the Minute Books of the Spalding Society', *Bibliotheca Topographica Britannica*, ed. John Nichols, iii (1790), 23–24.
[2] Bisset (1793), i. 36.   [3] See above, p. xli, note 1.

expressed before, in any suitable words that should occur to me. Then I compared my *Spectator* with the original, discovered some of my faults, and corrected them.[1]

He also tried turning some of the tales in the *Spectator* into verse and reducing them to prose again; at other times he would jumble his 'collections of hints' into confusion and then attempt to reduce them into order, 'to teach me method in the arrangement of the thoughts'.[2]

Mention has already been made of Joseph Collet, the Deputy Governor of York Fort in Sumatra, as a possible correspondent of the *Spectator*.[3] In a letter which he wrote to Steele on 24 August 1714 we get an interesting insight into the position held by the *Spectator* in the mind of a serious, hard-working Englishman (of nonconformist background):

> The Spectator has visited me in this Side the Globe; his conversation relieves me from the fatigue of business; by him I am always entertain'd and often improv'd. The Bible has the first place in our Study as teaching me the whole compass of my Duty to God and Man; Mr. Lock who first taught me to distinguish between Words and things has the next place; Mr. Steele who had taught me a more easy and agreeable manner of practising Vertue it self, precedes all Others.[4]

The Bible, Locke, and Mr. Spectator—there must have been many young men of the time who found this triad a source of strength in becoming more virtuous and more agreeable members of society.

Another such was Dudley Ryder,[5] later the Attorney-General, in 1715–16 a young man in his twenties, seriously devoting himself to reading and self-improvement. His diary contains many references to books which fit a man for conversation, or give an agreeable insight into human nature, or afford a model of good style; and high among these is the *Spectator*. In it 'you see the different manners of men set in a very clear and distinguishing light'.[6] *Spectator* No. 38 attacks 'the fault that I find myself extremely guilty of, and that is

---

[1] *The Autobiography of Benjamin Franklin*, ed. Max Farrand (Berkeley, 1949), pp. 18–19.
[2] P. 19. Franklin does not name the year in which he made these experiments, but it was before he left for Philadelphia at the age of seventeen.
[3] See above, p. xli, note 2.
[4] *Private Letter Books of Joseph Collet*, ed. H. H. Dodwell (1933), p. 99.
[5] See above, p. xli, note 4.
[6] *The Diary of Dudley Ryder 1715–1716*, ed. William Matthews (Methuen, 1939), p. 46.

a too great desire and love of applause in things which are in themselves the least commendable'.[1] There are many entries like the
following:

> Wed., Aug. 1, 1716. Rose at past 7; took my physic. Read law till
> past 11 when read some *Spectators*. There are abundance of very just
> remarks upon human nature and the customs and manners of people.
>
> Sat., Oct. 13, 1716. Read some *Spectators* at night. Have resolved to
> read them over with very great care and attention in order to observe
> the peculiar thoughts upon gallant subjects such as are proper to enter-
> tain the ladies with.[2]

A decade later, when Voltaire came to England (1726), it was
from the *Spectator* that he improved his knowledge of English.
In Wandsworth he 'boarded a while with a scarlet dyer nigh the
[Friends'] School', and here, wrote one of his acquaintances at the
time, 'I had to wait on him several times, and hear him read, in
the *Spectators* chiefly'.[3] His later writings, notably the correspondence, show how well Voltaire recalls many of the ideas and stories
from the English periodical.

If it is hard to find a common denominator for such diverse
figures—Cotton Mather, Franklin, Joseph Collet, Dudley Ryder,
and Voltaire—one thing is clear: they are not drawn from the class
which had but a short time before provided the chief support for
the man of letters. They are representative of a new social stratum
of readers which is rapidly coming to the fore. The letters printed
in the *Spectator* reveal the same diversity among those who read (and
wrote to) the journal—ladies of fashion, business men, clergymen,
players, perplexed parents, footmen and ladies' maids, lovers, and
schoolboys—persons with a multiplicity of interests and back-
grounds. A new reading public is emerging in England, not confined
to the aristocracy or to the learned. The transition from the Restoration period, when writers were dependent on the patronage of the
aristocratic and the wealthy or were forced to write for the fashionable world which went to the theatre, to the time of the first
Georges—when Pope could claim complete literary independence
and live by the earnings of his pen—is the theme of the classic work
of Alexandre Beljame, *Le Public et les hommes de lettres en Angleterre au*

---

[1] 20 Dec. 1715 (p. 121). [2] Ibid., pp. 287, 346.
[3] 'Edward Higginson's Account of a Conversation with Voltaire', quoted in *Lettres
philosophiques*, ed. G. Lanson (1909), i. 19–21.

dix-huitième siècle, 1660–1744.[1] It was the success of the *Spectator*, as Beljame points out in his third chapter, 'Joseph Addison', which formed a new reading public in England and helped to create a taste for books among many persons who had hitherto taken little heed of 'literature'.

Stout volumes and lengthy treatises would have rebuffed readers so lacking in self-confidence as those of Addison's day. They would not even have been opened. . . . The paper that consisted of short essays tempted the timorous by its brevity and variety, and held them by never overtiring them. Its unambitious modesty won their confidence. People who would otherwise never have read at all, unconsciously acquired the habit, and the taste for reading thus became widespread.[2]

Additional information as to the kind of reading public to which the *Spectator* appealed may be gained from the list of subscribers to the collected octavo edition of 1712–13. A subscription edition, of course, always elicits a certain amount of aristocratic support— members of the peerage who automatically lend their names to such enterprises as a matter of policy, or politics—and it is not surprising to find a representative number (47, to be exact) from the peerage among the 402 subscribers. The greater number of these come from the great Whig families, as one would expect, but there is a respect- able number of Tories as well.[3] Other prominent names in the list are those of the Archbishop of Canterbury,[4] Lord Chancellor Har-

[1] Published in 1881. Now best read in the translation by E. O. Lorimer (Kegan Paul, 1948), with an introduction and notes by Bonamy Dobrée, who corrects some errors of fact, supplements the bibliography—and takes issue with Beljame when he 'overpraises' Addison.

[2] Page 314. Beljame's words provide the obvious reply to the critic who laments that Addison 'had not the least design of tackling those problems which are the brute material of philosophy, of dealing with those puzzling questions of reality, or of the validity of the ego' (Bonamy Dobrée, *Essays in Biography* [1925], p. 276).

[3] Three of the peers to whom separate volumes of this subscription edition were dedicated—the Earl of Wharton and Lords Halifax and Somers—are represented. The names of the other four patrons are missing, though the Earl of Burlington (brother to one of them, Henry Boyle) is there, as are a number of Marlborough's connexions—the Duke of Montagu, Lord Rialton, Brigadier Francis Godfrey, Hugh Boscawen, and Adam Cardonnel, his secretary and close personal friend. Other peers perhaps worthy of mention are the Marquis of Dorchester, father of Lady Mary Wortley Montagu; the Duchess of Somerset, Swift's great enemy; Lord Foley, the Earl of Oxford's brother-in-law; Sir Thomas Parker, later Whig Lord Chancellor and Earl of Macclesfield; the Earl of Warwick and Holland, Addison's future stepson; and the Duchess of Hamilton, who though the wife of a Tory peer seems to have been a patroness of both Steele and John Hughes.

[4] Thomas Tenison. There are also in the list two bishops—of Ely (Dr. John Moore) and Winchester (Sir Jonathan Trelawny)—as well as Dr. Gibson, later Bishop of London, and Dr. Smalbroke, later Bishop successively of St. David's and of Coventry and Lichfield.

court, General William Stewart,[1] Robert Walpole, Sir Isaac Newton, Sir Godfrey Kneller, John Vanbrugh, James Craggs, Dr. Samuel Garth, Sir William Wyndham, and Dr. J. C. Pepusch. Eustace Budgell and Henry Martyn—two of the known contributors to the *Spectator*—are here, as well as a number of the personal friends of Steele and Addison, some of them from the Kit Cat Club— Arthur Maynwaring, Sir Matthew Dudley, Edward Ashe, Charles Mein, John Warner, Henry Furnese and his son-in-law Richard Edgcumbe, Sir Richard Temple, and Edward Wortley Montagu.

Not all the persons in the list of subscribers can be identified with certainty,[2] but one is impressed immediately by the number of names drawn from the financial and mercantile world of London. A 'profile' of the average subscriber is scarcely possible, but its features would undoubtedly be closer to those of Sir Andrew Freeport than to those of Will Honeycomb. Here are such men as Sir Gilbert Heathcote, member of the Vintners' Company, who built up a fortune of over £700,000 trading as a Spanish wine merchant to Jamaica and the East Indies; Matthew Decker, the great philanthropist and trader, the first in England to develop 'the East and West India plant called the *Annanas*, or Pine Apple, so famous for its incomparable taste and beauty';[3] Edmund Halsey, M.P., the wealthy brewer of Southwark and Governor of St. Thomas's Hospital, whose only daughter married Viscount Cobham; Nathaniel Gould, active in the Mediterranean and Turkey trade, and 'Contractor for Pitch and Tar for the Navy'; and Micaiah Perry, described at the time of his death as 'the greatest Virginia Merchant in England'[4]—to name but a few of these wealthy 'cits' whom Addison astutely recognized as by far the most useful members of the Commonwealth. 'They knit Mankind together', he writes in No. 69, 'in a mutual Intercourse of good Offices, distribute the Gifts of Nature, find Work for the Poor, add Wealth to the Rich, and Magnificence to the Great. Our *English* Merchant converts the Tin of his own Country into Gold, and exchanges his Wooll for Rubies.'

[1] The list includes also four lieutenant-generals (Palmes, Seymour, Stanhope, and Wade), and such well-known figures as Brigadier Phineas Bowles and Brigadier Dormer (both in the *DNB*), and Colonel Henry Disney, or Desaulnais, the friend of Swift and Pope and member of the Tory 'Brothers Club'.
[2] It does not seem very profitable to attempt to trace 'Mr. Clark' or 'Mr. Smith' —or 'Mrs. Ann Admirer'!
[3] Wotton's *Baronetage* (1741), quoted in G. E. C., *The Complete Peerage*.
[4] *Political State of Great Britain*, xxii (1721), 232.

Many of them are Directors of the Bank of England,[1] others are goldsmiths or private bankers and money-lenders,[2] some are directors of companies, and others are promoters and speculators, or 'projectors', to use the contemporary term. Eight are East India Company directors,[3] one of whom, Francis Eyles, was also a Director of the South Sea Company. Created a Baronet in 1714, 'in consideration of his firm Adherence to the Protestant Succession',[4] he left a fortune to his two sons, who were equally active in City financial and mercantile affairs—Sir John Eyles, Bart., Lord Mayor of London in 1726–7, and Sir Joseph Eyles, Kt., Alderman and Member of Parliament. According to a tradition recorded by Percy, this was the family of the *Cornelii*, the 'eminent Traders' described by Steele in No. 192:

where the Father lives with his Sons like their eldest Brother, and the Sons converse with him as if they did it for no other Reason but that he is the wisest Man of their Acquaintance.

In addition to Francis Eyles the list contains the names of twenty others who were directors of the South Sea Company,[5] eleven of whom were involved after the bursting of the South Sea Bubble, when the House of Commons instituted an investigation. The estates of many of these reached very high figures, especially when we consider the relative value of money at that time, those of Sir Theodore Janssen and John Fellowes being well over £243,000.[6]

[1] In 1711, the year the *Spectator* was launched, the Governor of the Bank was Nathaniel Gould, and the Deputy-Governor John Rudge. Both are in the list of subscribers, as well as twenty-six others who at one time or another were Directors—Sir Thomas Abney, Sir William Ashurst, James Bateman, Justus Beck, Brook Bridges, Robert Bristow, Gerard Conyers, Sir John Cope, William Henry Cornelison, Peter Delme, Josiah Diston, Francis Eyles, John Francis Fauquier, Sir Henry Furnese, John Gore, John Hanger, Sir Gilbert Heathcote, Philip Jackson, Theodore Janssen, Charles Peers, Jeremiah Powell, Thomas Scawen, Samuel Shepherd, John Shipman, John Smith, and John Ward. For their terms of office see W. Marston Acres, *The Bank of England from within, 1694–1900* (1931), appendix i.
[2] Examples are Moses Hart, Charles Shales, John Mead, Conrade de Gols, Jacob Sawbridge, John Warner, George Caswall and his son, and Benjamin Tudman.
[3] Matthew Decker, John Drummond, Francis Eyles, Sir Henry Furnese, William Gosselin, Nathaniel Gould, John Styleman, and John Ward.
[4] *Political State of Great Britain*, May 1716, p. 642.
[5] Lambert Blackwell, Charles Blunt, John Blunt, George Caswall, Sir Samuel Clark, James Craggs, Henry Durley, John Fellowes, Edward Gibbon, John Gore, Edmund Halsey, Edward Harley, Francis Hawes, Jacob Jacobson, Theodore Janssen, Sir John Lambert, Harcourt Masters, John Rudge, Jacob Sawbridge, and John Williams.
[6] Sir John Blunt—he had been created baronet in 1720—was the chief object of public indignation; in the debate Walpole showed that he 'was a Projector of many Years standing; and had been the Author of several fallacious Schemes, by which

James Craggs the Elder, though not actually a director, was involved in the transactions of the Company; when he died in March
1721, just a month after the death of his only son (Addison's friend
and literary executor), he left an estate valued at a million and a half
pounds. When Sir Theodore Janssen's case was being considered in
the House of Commons, 'Horatio Walpole and Sir Richard Steele
having spoken in his favour', he was finally allowed £50,000 out of
his estate.[1] Sir George Caswall in his defence spoke of 'the Extraordinary Zeal and Affection he had shewn for the Support of the
present happy Settlement, having assisted the Government with
vast Sums of Money, at Three *per Cent.* when they could get it no
where else'.[2] Sir John Lambert, a French refugee merchant, who had
been created baronet in 1711 upon the recommendation of Harley
for advancing to the government 'upwards of £400,000', also defended himself before the House on the grounds of his services
in the national interest. He had, he said, been a trader thirty-six
years, 'during which Time, few private Men have exported more
of theWoolen Manufacture and Products of these Kingdoms, or
have been greater Encouragers of the *British Navigation*', his
exportations in the past eight years having amounted to more
than £500,000.[3]

Many of the traders and financiers in the list had made money by
supplying stores of clothing and food to the armed forces, both in
the time of William III and in the long series of campaigns during
the War of the Spanish Succession.[4] The best known of these was
Sir Solomon de Medina, who with Moses de Medina had contracts
'for supplying bread and bread waggons to the Army in Flanders'.[5]
In 1712, after the Tories had succeeded in removing the Duke of

unwary People had been drawn in to their utter Ruin' (*Political State*, xxi [1721],
616). Blunt died a disgraced and ruined man in 1733. His nephew Charles had committed suicide on 4 Sept. 1720, leaving an estate variously estimated at from £100,000
to £250,000. Some of the other estates: Edward Gibbon, £106,543; Sir Lambert
Blackwell, £83,529; Jacob Sawbridge, £77,254; John Lambert, £72,508; Francis
Hawes, £40,031; John Gore, £38,936; Harcourt Masters, £11,814; Jacob Jacobson,
£11,031.

[1] *Political State of Great Britain*, xxi (1721), 629.
[2] Ibid., p. 315.
[3] Ibid., p. 603.
[4] See the *Calendars of Treasury Books*, under the names of David Campbell, Robert
Findley, Robert Gardner, Charles Le Bas, Moses de Medina, Sir Solomon de Medina,
Thomas Scot, William Sloper, James Taylor, Benjamin Tudman, William Wallis, and
John Wilkes.
[5] He had followed William III to England as his banker and was knighted by him
in 1700. Cf. Werner Sombart, *The Jews and Modern Capitalism*, trans. by M. Epstein
(1913), pp. 51, 55.

Marlborough from his offices, the contracts of the Medinas were the subject of extended investigation by Parliament.[1]

The largest single group of subscribers, however, includes the great body of secretaries, commissioners, clerks, and agents in the various branches of government, civil and military, required to carry on the war abroad and manage affairs at home. Here are the commissioners of appeals in excise, the auditors of crown land revenues, the deputy paymasters of the marine regiments, the clerks of petitions in the treasury, the keepers of the privy council chamber, the solicitors to the commissioners for salt duties, the grooms of the bedchamber—and so the list goes on. Their duties are specified and their quarterly salaries entered in the *Calendars of Treasury Books* throughout the reign of Queen Anne. Some, like William Lowndes, Secretary of the Treasury, are wealthy and distinguished men of the time, but for the most part they come from the humbler ranks of the bureaucracy, men like Charles Mein, 'Wine Examiner in the Customs', or Thomas Dummer, 'Deputy Master of the Great Wardrobe'. They provide tangible evidence of the great and increasing middle-class body of readers, a public which is to grow immeasurably in numbers and importance as the century proceeds.

Finally, in view of the *Spectator*'s avowed appeal to the fair sex, it is interesting to note that there are thirty-six women among the list of subscribers, about equally divided between the aristocracy and the middle classes. The presence of women in this connexion who are neither titled ladies nor blue-stockings but apparently ordinary citizens' wives and daughters is perhaps the most revealing aspect of all, in view of the subordinate position of women in earlier times. Particularly interesting are what seem to be the six representatives of one family, headed by 'Mr. Richard Bull', and including Mrs. Elizabeth Bull, Mrs. Mary Bull, Mrs. Jane Bull, Mrs. Sarah Bull, and Mr. Richard Bull, jnr. Is Richard Bull the Whig haberdasher on Ludgate Hill whom Swift called upon in September 1710?[2] One

---

[1] 'This day the commons considered the report of the commissioners of accounts, relating to the duke of Marlboroughs taking 5000 *l*. per ann. of sir Solomon Medina, who provided bread and waggons for the army in Flanders, which the duke claims as a perquisite belonging to him as commander in chief, towards the charges for private intelligence, &c., prince Waldeck, king William, and lord Overkirk, having had it before' (Luttrell, 24 Jan. 1711/12; vi. 718–19).

[2] He carried Swift on the 13th 'to his house at Hampstead to dinner among a great deal of ill company; among the rest Mr. Hoadley, the whig clergyman, so famous for acting the contrary part to Sacheverell' (*Journal to Stella*, ed. Harold Williams, p. 16).

'Richard Bull, Merchant', was a member of the Society for the Propagation of the Gospel in Foreign Parts,[1] and 'Mr. Richard Bull,
Druggist', was one of the subscribers to the collected edition of the
Tatler. He removed from the Golden Lion upon Ludgate Hill to the
King's Arms at the West End of St. Paul's Church in Ludgate Street
in 1716, where instead of coffee, tea, chocolate, or drugs, he now
advertises 'fine Hollands, Printed Callicoes, Chints, &c.'[2] Whoever
Richard Bull and his family were, they suggest the middle-class
(nonconformist?) family of comfortable means and adequate education, whose tastes are increasingly to determine the course of
popular literature in years to come.

To such readers the *Spectator* essays provided a form of recreation
and diversion at once instructive and innocent. Like Matthew
Arnold in the nineteenth century they offered a glimpse of the best
that had been thought and said in the past, through a medium
which managed to combine high seriousness with freshness and
variety of style. 'They diverted Raillery from improper Objects',
Addison himself said of them a few years later, 'and gave a new
Turn to Ridicule, which for many Years had been exerted on
Persons and Things of a sacred and serious Nature'. Most important
of all, perhaps, such writings 'refute the common Objection against
Religion, which represents it as only fit for gloomy and melancholy
Tempers'.[3] Steele's objection to Restoration comedy rests mainly
on the grounds of its immorality, and Addison's praise of *Paradise
Lost* derives in part from his conviction that the poem has a noble
and important theme.

The principal Actors in this Poem are not only our Progenitors, but
our Representatives. We have an actual Interest in every thing they
do, and no less than our utmost Happiness is concerned, and lies at
Stake in all their Behaviour.[4]

The quotations from Milton, from the Bible, from Cicero and
Seneca, which are so frequent in the *Spectator*, all help to give it an

---

[1] E. Chamberlayne, *Magnae Britanniae Notitia* (edit. 1708), p. 670.
[2] *London Gazette*, 15 Dec. 1716. 'A House, known by the Sign of the Golden Lyon,
on Ludgate-Hill, late Mr. Bull's, a Druggist, with or without the Houshold and
Shop Goods', is advertised to be let in the *Daily Courant*, 18 Nov. 1721.
[3] *Free-Holder* 45 (25 May 1716).
[4] No. 273. H. V. Routh has remarked that Addison's discussion of the similes in
Paradise Lost emphasizes their superiority to the artifices of contemporary wits and
that his comments on the purity and modesty of Eve are meant to point a contrast
to contemporary looseness of morals (*Cambridge History of English Literature*, ix.
60–61).

infusion of culture and a tone of seriousness which no doubt made a special appeal to the rising generation of middle-class readers.

The testimonials[1] in praise of the *Spectator*'s campaign of reform, as well as hints of individual benefits received,[2] indicate that readers welcomed a paper which could successfully combat the once fashionable vices of Restoration days and effectively temper wit with morality. Not only has learning become 'a more necessary Part of good Breeding than it was before you appear'd', writes one reader in August 1712, but

Modesty is become fashionable, and Impudence stands in need of some Wit, since you have put them both in their proper Lights. Prophaneness, Lewdness, and Debauchery are not now Qualifications, and a Man may be a very fine Gentleman, tho' he is neither a Keeper nor an Infidel.[3]

Epithets such as 'Spectator General', 'the Lowndes of the Learned World', 'the British Censor', are from time to time bestowed upon this new critic of morals and manners. There are also gibes by some disgruntled readers who call for 'less Tully' in the essays or urge Mr. Spectator to burn his Seneca. One correspondent, who is 'now between fifty and sixty, and had the Honour to be well with the first Men of Taste and Gallantry in the joyous Reign of *Charles* the Second', writes dolefully on the new values which are being introduced by Mr. Spectator.

You seem with the utmost Arrogance to undermine the very Fundamentals upon which we conducted our selves. It is monstrous to set up for a Man of Wit, and yet deny that Honour in a Woman is any thing else but Peevishness. . . . We had no more to do but to put a Lady in good Humour, and all we could wish followed of Course. Then again, your *Tully*, and your Discourses of another Life, are the very Bane of Mirth and good Humour.[4]

---

[1] Particularly the letter signed George Trusty in No. 134, the praise of individual papers in No. 205, the letter signed D. G. in No. 300, the praise of Addison's hymns in No. 461 (a letter by Isaac Watts), and the testimonials to particular papers in No. 547, to cite only a few.

[2] See the letter in No. 53 from 'a reformed Starer', who has 'conceived a Detestation for that Practice from what you have writ upon the Subject'. Mr. Spectator's ridicule of the 'grinning contest' at Coles-Hill, Warwickshire, in No. 173 caused the contest to be dropped, we learn from a letter printed in Lillie (ii. 72–73); when the races at Coles-Hill were advertised the following year no mention was made of the grinning-match. (See note to No. 173.) A reader in No. 208 writes that he so admires *Spectator* 182 that he has 'put it in a Frame and Glass, and hung it behind my Counter', so that his young ones may read it every morning.

[3] No. 461.

[4] No. 158.

If some of these letters, whether of praise or otherwise, may be suspect, we have evidence from outside the paper of approval for its position in morals. Dudley Ryder, we have seen, frequently took to heart the faults which the *Spectator* saw fit to warn against, and his regular and careful reading of the essays suggests that he took them seriously, not merely as examples of good literary style but as useful sermons on the conduct of life. Another striking example occurs in a letter from Joseph Collet, the East India agent,[1] writing from Marlborough Fort in Sumatra to his eldest daughter Elizabeth in London (26 August 1714), with suggestions for her reading:

> Instead of enlarging on the instructions I have already given for your conduct, I enjoyn you to study the Spectators, especially those which relate to Religion and Domestick Life. Next to the Bible you cannot read any writings so much to your purpose for the improvement of your mind and the conduct of your Actions.[2]

Collet's advice to his daughter—next to the Bible, the *Spectator*—would doubtless be endorsed by most considering parents throughout the century. It is hard to think of any other work except the *Pilgrim's Progress* which enjoyed such a position. It was a wholesome antidote against the immoral and the irreverent which could be safely taken by persons of either sex and any age.

> Nor harsh thy Precepts, but infus'd by Stealth,
> Please while they cure, and cheat us into Health.[3]

So Tickell had written before the first series had been completed. Edward Young, another personal friend and admirer of Addison, contrasted the 'wholesome and pleasant regimen' of the *Spectator*, 'which was universally relished, and did much good', with the more violent medicines of his contemporaries. Might it not be said, he asks,

> that *Pope* preferred a purgative of satire, which, tho' wholesome, was too painful in its operation; and that *Swift* insisted on a large dose of ipecacuanha, which, tho' readily swallowed from the fame of the physician, yet, if the patient had any delicacy of taste, he threw up the remedy, instead of the disease?[4]

Dr. Johnson, in his appraisal of Addison's benefits to his countrymen, expresses the verdict of the century:

---

[1] See above, p. xli, note 2.　　　　[2] *Letter Books* (1933), p. 100.
[3] 'To the supposed Author of the *Spectator*' (in No. 532).
[4] *Conjectures on Original Composition* (1759), ed. by Edith J. Morley (Manchester, 1918), p. 43.

No greater felicity can genius attain than that of having purified intellectual pleasure, separated mirth from indecency, and wit from licentiousness; of having taught a succession of writers to bring elegance
and gaiety to the aid of goodness; and, if I may use expressions yet more
awful, of having *turned many to righteousness*.[1]

XI. *Reputation in the eighteenth century—and after*

To trace the reputation and influence of the *Spectator*—in England,
on the Continent, and in America—does not fall within the scope
of the present work; to attempt this would be to write the inter-
national history of a distinctively eighteenth-century genre.[2] The
number of reprints and editions, the many imitations, the translations
into French, Dutch, and German, and the countless adaptations
and reworkings of individual essays—all testify to the world-wide
success of this most popular of all eighteenth-century periodical
essays. The *Journal littéraire de la Haye* acknowledged that the
French had nothing to equal the writing in the *Tatler* and *Spectator*.
These papers

sont si beaux & si achevez de toutes les manieres, ils sont si variez du
côté du stile & du côté des sujets, qu'on peut avancer que les François
n'ont rien à opposer à cette production qui puisse la valoir en tout.[3]

Sir Roger and the other members of the Club, the perverse Widow,
Will Wimble, Abraham Froth, 'the Trunk-maker in the Upper-
Gallery'—all are as well known to the eighteenth-century reader as
any characters in fiction or drama, if we may judge from allusions
to them in the journals and correspondence of the period. And so
with such themes as the Vision of Mirza, the Cave of Trophonius,
or the Everlasting Club; such stories as Inkle and Yarico, Constantia
and Theodosius, or Hilpa and Shalum. Books are advertised as
having been 'recommended by the *Spectator*', its praise of Milton
and criticism of the ballads continue to be cited and imitated, and a
long line of periodical essays continue the *Spectator* tradition.[4] 'A
Poem, from a Story in the *Spectator*', 'The humble Petition of . . .,

---

[1] *Life of Addison* (World's Classics ed.), i. 444.
[2] 'On pourrait maintenant, je crois, écrire une histoire des périodiques du type
Spectator en Europe; beau sujet de littérature générale, dont l'unité est évidente et
dont l'intérêt est très grand' (Paul Van Tieghem, *Revue de Synthèse historique*, l [1930],
127).
[3] Vol. ix (1717), p. 160.
[4] The list of periodical essays down to 1800 occupies twelve columns in *CBEL*
(ii. 661–7).

in imitation of the *Spectator*'—how often one encounters these in the pages of the magazines and newspapers of the eighteenth century!

Young James Boswell in the London of the 1760's, like Dudley Ryder a half-century earlier, shows admirably the power which the *Spectator* still exerted as an ideal of conduct. It is astonishing how frequently Boswell, in the pages of the *London Journal*[1] and elsewhere, attempts to put himself in an 'Addisonian' frame of mind or to conduct himself in a way which Mr. Spectator would have approved. His feelings upon attending Evensong will illustrate:

> At three o'clock I went to Westminster Abbey and the verger politely showed me into one of the prebend's stalls, where I sat in great state with a purple silk cushion before me. I heard service with much devotion in this magnificent and venerable temple. I recalled the ideas of it which I had from *The Spectator*.[2]

He has an affection for Child's coffee-house because it had been frequented by Mr. Spectator; ideas suggested by the *Spectator*, 'and such as I could not explain to most people', fill his mind as he drives through the city. 'As the Spectator observes, one end of London is like a different country from the other in look and in manners.'[3] Journeying to Oxford, he imagines himself 'the Spectator taking one of his rural excursions', and when he and his friend Temple are in the gallery of Drury Lane Theatre watching *Macbeth* they try to live up to the occasion. 'We endeavoured to work our minds into the frame of the Spectator's, but we could not. We were both too dissipated.'[4] Throughout the period covered by the *London Journal* Boswell seems in fact to waver between two conflicting images of conduct—on the one hand, the gallant and dashing Macheath of the *Beggar's Opera*, and on the other, the sober and dignified figure (a 'father-image' in twentieth-century parlance) of Mr. Spectator. That we come to hear more and more of the latter is perhaps owing to his subsequent association with Dr. Johnson.

Johnson himself, we know from his conversations with Boswell, thought highly of Addison, and wrote a brief advertisement for an edition in 1776, which does not exaggerate the general opinion held of the *Spectator* at the time.

The Book thus offered to the Public is too well known to be praised

---

[1] *Boswell's London Journal*, ed. F. A. Pottle (Heinemann, 1950).
[2] 29 May 1763 (p. 270).   [3] Ibid., pp. 76, 130, 153.
[4] Ibid., pp. 244, 240.

It comprizes precepts of criticism, sallies of invention, descriptions of life, and lectures of virtue: It employs wit in the cause of truth, and makes elegance subservient to piety: It has now for more than half a century supplied the English nation, in a great measure, with principles of speculation, and rules of practice; and given Addison a claim to be numbered among the benefactors of mankind.[1]

Johnson's reference to Addison as the author of the *Spectator* is echoed by nearly every writer of the time.[2] As the essays quickly established themselves among the classics of English prose, and writers on rhetoric began to attempt a 'historical view' of the development of English style, Addison's writings early assumed a commanding position. William Melmoth, writing in 1748, suggests Sir William Temple as possibly 'the first of our prose authors, who introduced a graceful *manner* into our language'.

But wheresoever we may look for its origin, it is certainly to be found in its highest perfection in the late essays of a gentleman whose writings will be distinguished so long as politeness and good sense have any admirers.[3]

This gentleman was Addison. 'I never read him', wrote Young in 1759, 'but I am struck with such a disheartening idea of perfection, that I drop my pen'; and Joseph Warton, no great admirer of Addison's poetry, owned that 'in various parts of his prose-essays, are to be found many strokes of genuine and sublime poetry; many marks of a vigorous and exuberant imagination'—the highest kind of praise from Warton.[4] Richard Hurd, who was later to edit Addison's works, thought that such purity of taste, clothed in such exquisite language, was nowhere else to be found.[5] Vicesimus Knox, whose series of 'elegant extracts' included generous selections from Addison, wrote in 1779:

Thus extensively useful and entertaining, no wonder Essays are

[1] *Public Advertiser*, 14 Dec. 1776, quoted in Boswell's *Life*, ed. Hill–Powell, ii. 503.
[2] The attribution of the *Spectator* to Addison is still generally made today, even by those who are not fond of Addison. In 1711–12 the average reader would be more likely to assume that Mr. Spectator—as the successor of Isaac Bickerstaff—was Steele.
[3] *Letters on Several Subjects by the late Sir Thomas Fitzosborne, Bart.*, i. 78. Melmoth's praise of Addison attained wide circulation, especially among the young, after David Irving borrowed it—without acknowledgement—in his *Elements of English Composition* in 1801 (pp. 170–1), a book which went through many editions.
[4] Young, *Conjectures*, ed. E. J. Morley, p. 43; Warton, *Essay on the Writings and Genius of Pope*, i (1756), 270.
[5] Letter to William Mason, 26 Oct. 1770 (*Correspondence of Richard Hurd & William Mason*, ed. by E. H. Pearce, Cambridge, 1932, p. 76).

more universally read than any other productions extant. The names and works of Montaigne, of Bacon, of Temple, of Addison, of Steele, and of their successful followers, are held in a degree of esteem, which neither the lapse of time nor the caprice of fashion has been able to diminish. There is scarcely an individual, not only of those who profess learning, but of those who devote any of their time to reading, who has not digested the Spectators.[1]

The two eighteenth-century critics who probably did more than anyone else, however, to set a seal of approval for many years to come were Hugh Blair and Dr. Johnson. Blair, in a series of lectures delivered in the University of Edinburgh in the 1760's and 1770's, not only praised Addison as the perfection of English style but set his students the task of analysing the essays and himself delivered 'critical examinations' of four of them (Nos. 411–14); Addison, he felt, 'though one of the most beautiful writers in the Language', was not always the most correct, and the 'minute imperfections' which might be discovered, like 'spots in the sun', would be of use in assisting beginners to avoid mistakes and set off the corresponding graces.[2] Addison's style, according to Blair, was 'natural and un-affected, easy and polite, and full of those graces which a flowery imagination diffuses over writing'; his chief talent, Blair thought, lay in 'describing and painting'.[3] His general verdict could scarcely be higher.

The Spectator, of which his papers are the chief ornament, is a book which is in the hands of every one, and which cannot be praised too highly. The good sense, and good writing, the useful morality, and the admirable vein of humour which abound in it, render it one of those standard books which have done the greatest honour to the English nation.[4]

Blair did not, of course, introduce Addison to his countrymen but he paid him the compliment of treating him as a classic and began the tradition, so popular in the nineteenth century, of serious exa-mination of Addison's prose style.[5]

Johnson's praise has no doubt been oftener quoted than anything

[1] *Essays Moral and Literary* (1778–9), ii. 10–11.
[2] *Lectures on Rhetoric and Belles Lettres* (1783), i. 408–9.
[3] Ibid. i. 408, 447.
[4] Ibid., pp. 408–9.
[5] On Blair's critical method and Johnson's conception of Addison as the model of 'the middle style' see Morley J. Mays, 'Johnson and Blair on Addison's Prose Style', *Studies in Philology*, xxxix (1942), 638–49.

else ever written of Addison, but it must be repeated here, not only because of its influence on later judgements but because, as the most balanced and most intelligent appraisal of Addison's style ever made, it deserves reading today.

His prose is the model of the middle style; on grave subjects not formal, on light occasions not groveling; pure without scrupulosity, and exact without apparent elaboration; always equable, and always easy, without glowing words or pointed sentences. Addison never deviates from his track to snatch a grace; he seeks no ambitious ornaments, and tries no hazardous innovations. His page is always luminous, but never blazes in unexpected splendour.

It was apparently his principal endeavour to avoid all harshness and severity of diction; he is therefore sometimes verbose in his transitions and connexions, and sometimes descends too much to the language of conversation; yet if his language had been less idiomatical, it might have lost somewhat of its genuine Anglicism. What he attempted, he performed; he is never feeble, and he did not wish to be energetick; he is never rapid, and he never stagnates. His sentences have neither studied amplitude, nor affected brevity: his periods, though not diligently rounded, are voluble and easy. Whoever wishes to attain an English style, familiar but not coarse, and elegant but not ostentatious, must give his days and nights to the volumes of Addison.[1]

Even at the height of Addison's reputation as prose essayist and critic, however, a few dissenting voices are raised. John Pinkerton's *Letters of Literature*, published in 1785 under the pseudonym of Robert Heron, includes an examination of 'the critical errors of Mr. Addison',[2] but it is concerned mainly with details and is largely motivated by Pinkerton's anti-French bias. The tone is apologetic (Addison 'is one of my most favorite writers'), and the real animus is against Boileau. William Godwin, who thought English prose reached its high point in his own day, devotes one section of his long essay 'Of English Style' in the *Enquirer* (1797) to Addison, taking issue with Johnson's verdict. Godwin finds Addison 'eminently enervated', and his prose 'strikingly loose and unsystematical'. He quotes parts of *Spectators* 70, 107 (which is by Steele), and 126, marking with asterisks the 'most glaringly offensive' phrases; and then passes on to an attack upon the style of Swift. More good-natured is the digression at the end of chapter v of *Northanger Abbey*

---

[1] *Life of Addison* (World's Classics ed.), i. 466.
[2] Letter xlix (pp. 420–8).

(published in 1818), where Jane Austen describes a young woman as ashamed of reading novels.

Now, had the same young lady been engaged with a volume of *The Spectator*, instead of such a work, how proudly would she have produced the book, and told its name!

Yet, she continues, it is filled with 'improbable circumstances, unnatural characters, and topics of conversation which no longer concern any one living', and its language frequently is so coarse 'as to give no very favourable idea of the age that could endure it'. De Quincey, too, in a number of his essays, and particularly in his article on Shakespeare in the seventh edition of the *Encyclopaedia Britannica* (1838–9), ridicules Addison for his lack of appreciation of mountain scenery, his plagiarisms of Bayle, and his 'indifference' to Shakespeare.[1]

The most important analysis of Addison's style after Hugh Blair occurs in 'An Essay on the Variations of English Prose, from the Revolution to the Present Time', read by Thomas Wallace before the Royal Irish Academy on 18 June 1796, and awarded the Gold Medal of the Academy.[2] Wallace specifies certain faults in 'the loose, inaccurate and clumsy style' of Addison's predecessors, notably Atterbury, Burnet, Tillotson, Petty, and Temple.

The forced metaphor, the dragging clause, the harsh cadence, and the abrupt close, are all of them strangers to the works of Addison. In the structure of his sentences, though we may sometimes meet marks of negligence, yet we can seldom find the unity of a sentence violated by ideas crowded together, or the sense obscured by an improper connection of clauses. Though, like his predecessors, he frequently uses two words to express one idea, yet, in this instance, he is less faulty than they; and, among the variations introduced by him, we must reckon a more strict attention to the choice of words, and more precision in the use of them.[3]

The best writers before 1700, in Wallace's view, are Hooker, Dryden, and Sprat; but it is Addison who has accomplished a revolution in prose style and achieved a degree of excellence 'which constitutes him a model for imitation'.

It was, indeed, from the productions of that classic and copious mind

---

[1] *Works* (Edinburgh, 1862–3), vii. 51–52; xv. 9–13. De Quincey professes to believe that Addison 'never in one instance quoted or made any reference to Shakespeare'.
[2] *Transactions of the Royal Irish Academy*, vi (1797), part ii, pp. 41–70.
[3] Pp. 56–57.

that the public seems to have caught the taste for fine writing which has operated from that time to the present, and which has given to our language perhaps the greatest degree of elegance and accuracy of which it is susceptible.[1]

Wallace has an interesting analysis of Addison's use of figurative language, and concludes with a comparison between Addison and Swift, the one achieving correctness, the other precision and purity. 'Swift hewed the stones, and fitted the materials for those who built after him; Addison left the neatest and most finished models of ornamental architecture.'[2]

Addison's prose, under the influence of Blair's lectures, long continued to furnish models for analysis in the schools. David Irving's *Elements of English Composition* (1801), which became a popular textbook of rhetoric, includes a sentence-by-sentence analysis of No. 39,[3] done in the manner of Blair, but with no general appraisal. An examination of similar nineteenth-century textbooks would no doubt show that many students learned a part of the technique of writing by giving their days and nights to the volumes of Addison. When Edward Maltby, later Bishop of Durham, sat for the Chancellor's Medals at Cambridge (in 1792) he was given a number of the *Spectator*, different parts of which were to be turned, at one sitting, into Latin prose, Greek prose, Latin verse, and Greek verse.[4]

The most complete survey, down to its time, of all that was known and thought about Addison's work is that of Dr. Nathan Drake in 1805, who devotes a long passage to consideration of his style, 'a medium between the dry and unornamented language of Swift, and the pompous and elaborated diction of Shaftesbury'.[5] Those who object to his style as too 'feeble and relaxed' should consider the subjects which employed his pen, which demanded a style easy and familiar, yet simply elegant. 'Even in this subdued and middle style he was singularly attentive, . . . not only to grammatical purity, but to the modulation of his sentences. . . .'[6] Drake quotes from *Spectators* 26, 413, 421, 477 and others to illustrate the virtuosity of Addison's style, and he also devotes some space to a list of 'what would now

---

[1] P. 58. [2] P. 59.
[3] Chap. xxvi, 'Critical Examination of a Passage in the Writings of Addison' (pp. 189–99).
[4] M. L. Clarke, *Greek Studies in England 1700–1830* (Cambridge, 1945), p. 27. Cf. also George C. Brauer, jr., 'Recommendations of the "Spectator" for students during the eighteenth century', *N & Q*, May 1955, pp. 207–8.
[5] *Essays biographical, critical, and historical, illustrative of the Tatler, Spectator, and Guardian* (1805, 3 vols.), ii. 92. [6] ii. 95.

be termed inelegancies or vulgarisms'.[1] He concludes that, although with regard to the minutiae of grammar and composition Addison may be found less accurate than the best writers of the present day,—in all the great qualities of style, in perspicuity, simplicity, and ease, in harmony, elegance, and amenity, he has been surpassed by none and equalled but by few.[2]

Drake devotes several pages to discussion of Addison's criticism, his gift of humour,[3] and above all the moral tendency of his writings. 'Perhaps to the writings of no individual,' he concludes, 'of any age or nation, if we except the result of inspiration, have morality and rational piety been more indebted than to those which form the periodical labours of our author.'[4]

These words, which do not exaggerate the majority opinion of the eighteenth century, also presage to the nineteenth, when the reputation of the *Spectator*, and of Addison as its chief architect, no doubt reached its highest point. The most eloquent statement comes from Macaulay, whose own tastes and abilities made him an able advocate of all that the *Spectator* stood for. The famous essay on Addison, resounding in tone and splendidly final in judgement, is the voice of the nineteenth century as surely as Johnson's *Life of Addison* had been that of the eighteenth. It appeared in the *Edinburgh Review* for July 1843, occasioned by the publication of Lucy Aikin's two-volume biography. The epithets bestowed on his subject are in Macaulay's grandest style: Addison is an essayist without equal in his field, the forerunner of the great English novelists, a writer worthy of comparison only with Shakespeare and Cervantes. 'His best essays approach near to absolute perfection.' Just before Macaulay wrote, a monument to Addison had been erected in Westminster Abbey, the full-length marble statue still to be seen in Poets' Corner. 'It represents him, as we can conceive him', writes Macaulay, 'clad in his dressing-gown, and freed from his wig, stepping from his parlour at Chelsea into his trim little garden, with the account of the Everlasting Club, or the Loves of Hilpa and Shalum, just finished for the next day's Spectator, in his hand.'

Such a mark of national respect was due to the unsullied statesman, to the accomplished scholar, to the master of pure English eloquence, to the consummate painter of life and manners. It was due, above all, to

---

[1] ii. 106-8.   [2] ii. 116.
[3] 'In humour, no man in this country, save Shakspeare, has excelled him' (ii. 351).
[4] ii. 319-20.

the great satirist, who alone knew how to use ridicule without abusing it, who, without inflicting a wound, effected a great social reform, and who reconciled wit and virtue, after a long and disastrous separation, during which wit had been led astray by profligacy, and virtue by fanaticism.[1]

Macaulay's panegyric, which illustrates perfectly the esteem in which the nineteenth century held the *Spectator*, practically identifies Addison as its sole author. It is easy to see why the qualities usually associated with Addison—charm, dignity, calm rationality, serenity, control—should prove congenial to the Victorian mind, in contrast to the impulsiveness, the extravagance, the dissipation of Steele. (The Victorians seem to have regarded Steele much as they did Boswell, and for the same reasons.) Addison's moderation and good sense, expressed at their best in the *Spectator*, made an irresistible appeal to an age in which—though awkward questions, it is true, were beginning to be raised—prosperity and a settled order of society seemed to point the way to 'Utopia, Unlimited'. A passage in Courthope's *Addison*, published as late as 1884, reminds us of the comfortable vantage-point from which the Victorians looked back upon earlier days:

We have to reflect on the ease with which, even in these days when the foundations of all authority are called in question, we form judgments on questions of morals, breeding, and taste, and then to dwell in imagination on the state of conflict in all matters religious, moral, and artistic, which prevailed in the period between the Restoration and the succession of the House of Hanover. To whom do we owe the comparative harmony we enjoy? Undoubtedly to the authors of the *Spectator*, and first among these by universal consent to Addison.[2]

The 'ease with which we form judgments on questions of morals, breeding, and taste' is less apparent to us than it was to our Victorian forefathers; a world which has drifted away from many of the religious certainties of the past does not so readily appreciate the moral reforms of a Steele or the essays on faith and religion of an Addison. Writers whose beliefs are fundamentally optimistic seem less congenial than those who question or doubt—or deny; and the secure belief in progress exhibited by the Whigs is less exhilarating and less popular than 'the gloom of the Tory satirists'. It is easy to forget, or to discount, the revolution in morals and manners which Addison and Steele helped to bring about, a reform which has

[1] P. 260. [2] P. 162.

become, it is to be hoped, a permanent part of our civilization. We need to remind ourselves of the point well stated by Professor C. S. Lewis:

That sober code of manners under which we still live to-day, in so far as we have any code at all, and which foreigners call hypocrisy, is in some important degree a legacy from the *Tatler* and the *Spectator*.[1]

The personality of Addison was also more readily appreciated by the Victorians than by us. His personality and character in fact received such extreme praise that—as with Aristides the just—a reaction was bound to come. The story, first related by Young in 1759, of his calling in his graceless stepson to see 'in what peace a Christian can die', as well as rumours of excessive drinking (a weakness readily excused in other men of the eighteenth century!), led easily to suggestions of self-righteousness, or worse. To his contemporaries, however, Addison was a man of great personal modesty and charm. Swift was a lifelong friend, and even Pope found him a delightful companion—until political differences (and wounded vanity?) began to cause difficulties. Steele compared an evening spent with Addison to 'the Pleasure of conversing with an intimate Acquaintance of *Terence* and *Catullus*, who had all their Wit and Nature heighten'd with Humour, more exquisite and delightful than any other Man ever possessed'.[2] In the reaction to such universal praise, it is not surprising that many critics have professed to discover self-righteousness in place of rectitude, and underhand malice beneath the personal charm. Pope's satiric 'Atticus' lines, published after Addison's death, have been defended as a truthful portrait of a literary dictator, 'willing to wound and yet afraid to strike'. Even twentieth-century praise of Steele has frequently taken the form of disparagement of his friend. 'Better to err with Steele than shine in rectitude with Addison.'[3] Our admiration or disapproval of an author's character, however, is not the soundest basis for a critical judgement; and it is best to concentrate on the writings of Steele and Addison, without regard to the lapses from virtue of the one, or the unswerving rectitude of the other.

Their writings belong to a literary genre which has scarcely ever

[1] C. S. Lewis, 'Addison', *Essays on the Eighteenth Century presented to David Nichol Smith in honour of his Seventieth Birthday* (Oxford, 1945), p. 7.
[2] Steele's Dedication to Congreve of *The Drummer* (*Correspondence*, ed. Blanchard, p. 514).
[3] Bonamy Dobrée, *Variety of Ways* (1932), p. 87.

been more popular than at the present time. The essay has gone through a great many mutations of form since the days of Addison and Steele, but it is doubtful whether it will ever lack readers, since it deals with a subject of perennial interest—human nature—and can claim with justice that nothing concerning humanity is foreign to it. The constantly varied essays produced each day by the authors of the *Spectator* have their counterpart in the more specialized articles of modern journalism—the weekly 'column' or sketch devoted to travel, gardening, home decoration, cosmetics, fashions, music, new books, art, the theatre, and what not. To the modern reader of the newspaper, the weekly review, or the monthly magazine these articles appeal in much the same way as the 'speculations' of Addison and Steele did to the reader in the days of Queen Anne. The *Spectator* papers are a part of the times in which they were written—to a degree scarcely paralleled by any other productions of that age—but they also deal with problems and tastes and interests common to men and women of every century. They are still worth reading.

THE TEXT

The folio sheets of the *Spectator* have been used as copy-text for the present edition.[1] Editors in the past—who have been almost exclusively concerned with annotation—have based their texts on one of the two early reprints (octavo or duodecimo), or have used some later reprint of one of these reprints as copy-text. The result has generally been to multiply error upon error.

Of the six important editions before the present—by Nichols, Bisset, Chalmers, Morley, Gregory Smith, and Aitken—only Henry Morley's, in 1868, showed any real concern with the text. Morley was conscious of the bad state of the text and the reasons for it; he estimated, on the basis of a sampling of forty numbers, some 3,000 textual corruptions in the 635 numbers. He alone seems to have checked with any thoroughness the folio sheets and the two reprints, and he often, though not consistently, indicates variant readings in his footnotes.[2]

[1] For the Dedications to the eight collected volumes I have used the 8vo edition as copy-text.

[2] The Nichols edition had been begun by Thomas Percy in 1764, continued by John Calder, and finally brought out by John Nichols in 1789. A few of Percy's notes, signed P, are retained, while Calder's materials are usually designated those of 'the annotator'. Percy's edition of the *Tatler* was also brought out by Nichols (in 1786), with fuller annotation. Neither edition deals more than sporadically with

The 8vo and 12mo editions contain many authorial revisions and therefore have to be consulted for textual changes made, particularly by Addison. (On the other hand, they are full of errors, some of them obvious and others misleadingly plausible. This is especially true of the octavo edition, which has served more often than any other as a copy-text.) These authorial revisions are numerous and obviously have to be taken into account. In the essays in which they occur I have followed the advice of W. W. Greg and the practice of modern textual critics, retaining the 'accidentals' (spelling, punctuation, and capitalization) of the folio sheets and introducing into this fabric the changes for which the authors, and not the compositors, seem to have been responsible.

The remaining essays, which contain no substantive alterations, are printed without change, apart from correction of misprints (discussed below), from the folio sheets. Many of these—over half, in fact—consist of letters or other contributed materials, sometimes with a short introductory or concluding paragraph. Such documents were, of course, far less likely to be revised by Addison or Steele when the *Spectator* came to be reprinted in volume form; and to print them now directly from the folio sheets, before the colloquialisms and contractions had been 'corrected' in the printing-shop, is to recapture some of the freshness and vitality of these pieces as they first appeared at the breakfast-tables of contemporary readers.

Collation of the folio, 8vo, and 12mo texts shows unmistakably that the reprints introduced a great many errors into the text. It also indicates that Steele and Addison did not greatly concern themselves with matters of spelling and punctuation, even in essays which underwent stylistic revision. Very likely they were content to leave such matters to the discretion of the printing house, and since both Buckley and Tonson were involved in the publication of the *Spectator* it is true that many of the typographical variants, such as differences in spelling, are due to the practice of the printing houses rather than to that of the authors. Nevertheless, when it comes to a choice between the folio sheets and the 8vo or 12mo reprints as copy-text, there can be little hesitation. By printing from the earliest text we

textual matters. The edition by Robert Bisset (1793), 'with notes and lives of authors', and that by Alexander Chalmers (1806) are of no value textually and repeat much of the annotation from Nichols. The editions by Gregory Smith and G. A. Aitken appeared almost simultaneously in 1897–8, the first in old-style spelling and the second modernized. In both of these the notes are better than the text. For a fuller account see my article, 'The Text of the *Spectator*', *Studies in Bibliography*, v (1953), 109–28.

come as close to the authors' manuscripts as possible and reduce the possibilities of textual corruption.

In the necessary correction of typographical errors I have tried to follow the rule of altering only those which seem due primarily to the compositor, including his failure to read the author's hand. These have not been given as footnote variant readings but have been collected into a list headed 'Emendation of Accidentals' and placed in an appendix. They include duplications of words, inadvertent reversals of words, mistakes in numbering or dating particular essays, and the like. They also include such obvious spelling errors as 'procedeed' for 'proceeded' (No. 257) and 'cilvil' for 'civil' (No. 313). But I have not corrected errors in spelling or grammar when these seem due to the writer, particularly when they occur in letters. 'Redicule', for example, in No. 244, has not been corrected to 'Ridicule', nor 'Sparrow-grass' in No. 371 to 'Asparagus'.[1] Mistakes due to similar forms of words, such as 'wig' and 'Whig', 'heirs' and 'hairs', 'words' and 'worlds', &c., have been corrected, as well as misprints in Latin words, especially in the mottoes (*amabiter* for *amabitur*, e.g., in No. 552). Proper names have usually been corrected, particularly if the correct form appears in other portions of the *Spectator* or in the 8vo and 12mo reprints: thus *Cataline* has been changed to *Catiline* (No. 55), *Sidenam* to *Sydenham* (No. 25), and *Le Conte* to *Le Comte* (No. 189). But I have not modernized the contemporary spellings of *Shakespear*, *Johnson*, or *Lock*. Punctuation has been changed only when obviously erroneous, as in the omission of a full stop at the end of a sentence or in the insertion of a mark of punctuation where it could not possibly be intended (e.g. 'Dear, Sir,' in No. 311). I can hardly expect to have achieved consistency in dealing with these matters, but I have not altered such things silently, and the reader will be able to see for himself what the original form was in the copy-text.

The only silent changes made have been in italicizing, chiefly of proper names, the substitution of the modern for the long *s*, and the expansion of certain abbreviated forms (such as 'y^e' to 'the', and 'neq;' to 'neque'), except in quotations from manuscripts.

The footnotes have been confined to the recording of substantive changes from the copy-text. The rejected readings from the 8vo and 12mo editions are not given as footnote variants but have been

---

[1] Even Morley silently corrects this.

placed in a separate appendix, under the title 'Textual Notes', to which the reader is also referred in a few cases where doubtful readings are discussed. By keeping the footnotes to a minimum I hope to enhance the ordinary reader's pleasure and to escape the censure which Addison in No. 470 bestowed upon the textual critics of his own day:

Indeed, when a different Reading gives us a different Sense, or a new Elegance in an Author, the Editor does very well in taking Notice of it; but when he only entertains us with the several ways of Spelling the same Word, and gathers together the various Blunders and Mistakes of twenty or thirty different Transcribers, they only take up the Time of the learned Reader, and puzzle the Minds of the Ignorant.

The footnote gives first the emended reading of the text and then after the square bracket the original reading which it replaces. Unless otherwise indicated, the emended reading is that of *both* the 8vo and 12mo editions. Thus if 'runs' is the reading in the 8vo and 12mo editions, replacing 'goes' in the folio text, the footnote reads:

runs] goes *Fol.*

If only the 8vo edition has made the change, the footnote reads:

runs] *8vo*; goes *Fol., 12mo.*

Similarly, if the emendation has been made only in the 12mo edition, the footnote reads:

runs] *12mo*; goes *Fol., 8vo.*

If the emendation comes from a later edition, I have tried to give credit to the earliest making the change, using the following symbols: M = Henry Morley; *1721* = Addison's *Works*, ed. Tickell, 1721; *1723* = *Spectator*, 1723 (12mo); *1724* = *Spectator*, 1724 (12mo). If no source is given for the revised reading, the emendation is my own.[1]

The Dedications for the separate eight volumes are here printed at the end of the text.

[1] In the eighteen *Paradise Lost* papers an additional symbol is used: *19* = *Notes on Paradise Lost*, an edition of these eighteen papers with revisions by Addison, and published in 1719, shortly after his death.

ABBREVIATED TITLES

Aitken   *The Life of Richard Steele.* By George A. Aitken. London, 1889. 2 vols.
                The Spectator. With Introduction and Notes by George A. Aitken. London and New York, 1898–9. 8 vols.

Apperson   *English Proverbs and Proverbial Phrases: A Historical Dictionary.* By G. L. Apperson. London, 1929.

Arnold   *Addison: Selections from Addison's Papers contributed to the Spectator.* Ed., with Introduction and Notes, by Thomas Arnold. Oxford, 1875.

Ascoli   Georges Ascoli, *La Grande-Bretagne devant l'opinion française au XVIIe siècle.* Paris, 1930. 2 vols.

Ashton   *Social Life in the Reign of Queen Anne. Taken from Original Sources.* By John Ashton. London, 1882. 2 vols.

Bayle   *An Historical and Critical Dictionary. By Monsieur [Pierre] Bayle. Translated into English, with many Additions and Corrections, made by the Author himself, that are not in the French editions.* London, 1710. 4 vols.

Bisset   *The Spectator. A New Edition . . . with Illustrative Notes. To which are prefixed the Lives of the Authors.* By Robert Bisset. London and Edinburgh, 1793–4. 8 vols.

Chalmers   *The Spectator.* Corrected from the Originals, with a Preface historical and biographical, by A. Chalmers. London, 1806. 8 vols.

Danet   *A Complete Dictionary of the Greek and Roman Antiquities. . . . Compiled originally in French . . . for the use of the Dauphin, the Dukes of Burgundy, Anjou and Berry: By Monsieur [Pierre] Danet. Made English, with the addition of very useful mapps.* London, 1700.

Dobson   *Steele: Selections from the Tatler, Spectator and Guardian.* Ed. with Introduction and Notes by Austin Dobson. Oxford, 1885.

Drake   *Essays, biographical, critical, and historical, illustrative of the Tatler, Spectator, and Guardian.* By Nathan Drake, M.D. London, 1805. 3 vols.

Guthkelch   *The Miscellaneous Works of Joseph Addison.* Ed. by A. C. Guthkelch. London, 1914. 2 vols.

Hatton   *A New View of London. . . .* By Edward Hatton. London, 1708. 2 vols.

Hodgart   M. J. C. Hodgart, 'The Eighth Volume of the *Spectator*', *RES*, N.S. v (1954), 367–87.

Hurd   *The Works of the Right Honourable Joseph Addison.* A New Edition, with Notes by Richard Hurd, D.D., Lord Bishop of Worcester. London, 1811. 6 vols.

Koenig   *A Royal Compleat Grammar, English and High-German . . . durch John King, englischen Sprach-Meister in Londen.* London, 1715. (Pp. 217–62: 'London Guide . . . .')

Le Bossu   *Monsieur Bossu's Treatise of the Epick Poem. . . . Made English, with a Preface upon the same Subject, by W. J.* 2nd ed. London, 1719. 2 vols.

Lillie   *Original and Genuine Letters sent to the Tatler and Spectator, during the Time those Works were publishing. None of which have been before Printed.* London: Printed by R. Harbin, for Charles Lillie, Perfumer, at the Corner of Beauford Buildings in the Strand, 1725. 2 vols.

Miege   *The Present State of Great Britain.* By Guy Miege. London, 1707.

Misson   *Mémoires et observations faites par un voyageur en Angleterre* [Henri Misson de Valberg]. La Haye, 1698.

Morley   *The Spectator. A New Edition, reproducing the Original Texts, both as first issued, and as corrected by its Authors.* With Introduction, Notes, and Index. By Henry Morley. London, 1868.

Nichols   *The Spectator.* London, 1788–9. 8 vols. (This edition was originally undertaken by Thomas Percy, continued by John Calder, and finally brought out by John Nichols. In this edition Percy's notes are marked 'P' and Calder's 'A' [for Annotator].)

Nicoll   *A History of Early Eighteenth Century Drama, 1700–1750.* By Allardyce Nicoll. Cambridge, 1929.

Percy   *See* Nichols.

Smith   *The Spectator.* The Text edited and annotated by G. Gregory Smith. With an Introductory Essay by Austin Dobson. London and New York, 1897–8. 8 vols. (Reprinted, without Dobson's essay, in 'Everyman's Library', 1907 [8 vols. in 4]; revised ed., 1945.)

Spingarn *Critical Essays of the Seventeenth Century.* Ed. by J. E. Spingarn. Oxford, 1908–9. 3 vols.

Tilley   *A Dictionary of the Proverbs in England in the Sixteenth and Seventeenth Centuries. . . .* By Morris Palmer Tilley. Ann Arbor, Mich., 1950.

Trevelyan *England under Queen Anne.* By George Macaulay Trevelyan. London, 1930–4. 3 vols.

ERRATA

VOLUME I

P. 144, line 16: *for* HONEYCOMBE *read* HONEYCOMB
P. 233, line 10: for *quo* read *quò*

VOLUME II

P. 15, line 22: *Justice of the Peace* (italics added in *Fol.*)
P. 20, line 4: *White* (italics added in *Fol.*)
P. 46, note 2: A proverb (Tilley, R27).
P. 64, note a: *for* of Misfortune *read* of Misfortune,
P. 120, line 38: for *World* read *Sun*
P. 207, note 4: See also British *Apollo*, 8 June 1709.
P. 258, note d: *read* Bounteous,] *1723*; Beauteous, *Fol., 8vo, 12mo*
P. 310, motto: for *multum* read *multùm*
P. 365, note 1: *for* 3. 1–5 *read* 3. 1. 5–6
P. 505, line 29: *for* shortly, *read* shorter,

VOLUME III

P. 42, note 1: The motto from Winterton = Menander, *Monostichoi* 462.
P. 149, note 4: *read* Cf. No. 624 (vol. v).
P. 163, note 1: The reference is to No. 129, not 128.
P. 167, note a: *read* Scenes] *8vo*; Science *Fol., 12mo*
P. 309, note c: *add square bracket after* casts
P. 347, note 1: The reference is to a character in Horace (*Epist.* I. 18. 31–36).
P. 349, note 4: *The Humorous Lieutenant* is by Fletcher.
P. 352, note a: add *Fol.*
P. 413, note 1: for *Pythagorea* read *Pythagoreo*.
P. 416, motto: *add* Hor.
P. 462, note 2; line 4: *read* Mathurin Veyssière de Lacroze
P. 499, lines 1–2: These lines should not be indented.
P. 499, note a: *read* successively] *1723*; successfully, *Fol., 8vo, 12mo*
Pp. 505–6, note 1: *read* see Appendix V.
P. 511, note a: *read* Fathers,] *1723*; Fathers *Fol., 8vo, 12mo*
P. 511, note b: *read* Physician,] *1723*; Physician; *Fol., 8vo, 12mo*

APPENDIX I

Volume I, add: 144. 16: HONEYCOMB] HONEYCOMBE
Volume II, add: 73. 11: comes to,] comes,

[ADDISON]

Non fumum ex fulgore, sed ex fumo dare lucem
Cogitat, ut speciosa dehinc miracula promat.
Hor.[a]

I HAVE observed, that a Reader seldom peruses a Book with
Pleasure 'till he knows whether the Writer of it be a black or a
fair Man, of a mild or cholerick Disposition, Married or a Batchelor,
with other Particulars of the like nature, that conduce very much to
the right Understanding of an Author. To gratify this Curiosity,
which is so natural to a Reader, I design this Paper, and my next,
as Prefatory Discourses to my following Writings, and shall give
some Account in them of the several Persons that are engaged in
this Work. As the chief Trouble of Compiling, Digesting and
Correcting will fall to my Share, I must do my self the Justice to
open the Work with my own History.[2]

I was born to a small Hereditary Estate, which, according to the
Tradition of the Village where it lies,[b] was bounded by the same
Hedges and Ditches in *William* the Conqueror's Time that it is at
present, and has been delivered down from Father to Son whole and
entire, without the Loss or Acquisition of a single Field or Meadow,

---

[a] *After motto*: To be Continued every Day. *Fol.*   [b] which . . . lies,] which I
find, by the Writings of the Family, *Fol.*

---

[1] *Motto*. Horace, *Ars Poetica*, 143–4: Not smoke after flame does he plan to give,
but after smoke the light, that then he may set forth striking and wondrous tales.
[2] The character of 'Mr. Spectator', sketched in by Addison in this opening number,
is maintained with fair consistency throughout the original series. As a spectator of
men and manners he is above all a 'silent man' rather than a tatler; and allusions to
his 'profound', 'invincible', and 'natural' taciturnity abound, particularly through
the first 150 numbers. In early life he had travelled, in France and 'to Grand Cairo';
now, after a disappointment in love, he is a bachelor of retired habits, whose pleasures
consist chiefly in reading and conversation at the coffee-house. Most of these biographical details are to be found in papers written by Addison, and the portrait which
emerges is consistent with what we know of Addison's tastes and temperament. One
additional important trait, however, is introduced by Steele in No. 17 ('I am a little
unhappy in the Mold of my Face, which is not quite so long as it is broad'), and
the frequent references to Mr. Spectator's 'short face' contribute to the vitality of the
composite portrait and prevent readers of the essays from taking some of the lay
sermons too seriously. In contrast to the self-portrait of Isaac Bickerstaff in *Tatler* 89
this sketch of Mr. Spectator remains astonishingly vivid and calculated to maintain interest in the daily 'speculations' which diverted the readers of London throughout 1711 and 1712.

during the Space of six hundred Years. There runs[a] a Story in the Family, that when my Mother was gone with Child of me about three Months, she dreamt that she was brought to Bed of a Judge: Whether this might proceed from a Law-Suit which was then depending in the Family, or my Father's being a Justice of the Peace, I cannot determine; for I am not so vain as to think it presaged any Dignity that I should arrive at in my future Life, though that was the Interpretation which the Neighbourhood put upon it. The Gravity of my Behaviour at my very first Appearance in the World, and all the Time that I sucked, seemed to favour my Mother's Dream: For, as she has often told me, I threw away my Rattle before I was two Months old, and would not make use of my Coral 'till they had taken away the Bells from it.

As for the rest of my Infancy, there being nothing in it remarkable, I shall pass it over in Silence. I find, that, during my Nonage, I had the Reputation of a very sullen Youth, but was always a Favourite of my School-Master, who used to say, *that my Parts were solid and would wear well*. I had not been long at the University, before I distinguished my self by a most profound Silence: For, during the Space of eight Years, excepting in the publick Exercises of the College, I scarce uttered the Quantity of an hundred Words; and indeed do not remember that I ever spoke three Sentences together in my whole Life. Whilst I was in this Learned Body I applied my self with so much Diligence to my Studies, that there are very few celebrated Books, either in the Learned or the Modern Tongues, which I am not acquainted with.

Upon the Death of my Father I was resolved to travel into Foreign Countries, and therefore left the University, with the Character of an odd unaccountable Fellow, that had a great deal of Learning, if I would but show it. An insatiable Thirst after Knowledge carried me into all the Countries of *Europe*, in which[b] there was any thing new or strange to be seen; nay, to such a Degree was my Curiosity raised, that having read the Controversies of some great Men concerning the Antiquities of *Egypt*, I made a Voyage to *Grand Cairo*,[1]

[a] runs] goes *Fol*.   [b] in which] where *Fol*.

---

[1] The visit is again referred to in Nos. 8, 17, 46, 69, 101, 159, and 604. Nichols, followed by all editors, considers this as 'a sarcasm on Mr. Greaves and his book intitled *Pyramidographia . . .*'. John Greaves, the Professor of Astronomy at Oxford, had taken measurements of the pyramids in 1638–9: '*I twice went to Grand Cairo from Alexandria*, and from thence into the deserts, for the greater certainty, to view them: carrying with me a *radius* of ten feet most accurately divided, besides some other

on purpose to take the Measure of a Pyramid; and as soon as I had set my self right in that Particular, returned to my Native Country with great Satisfaction.

I have passed my latter Years in this City, where I am frequently seen in most publick Places,[1] tho' there are not above half a dozen of my select Friends that know me; of whom my next Paper shall give a more particular Account. There is no Place of general[a] Resort,[2] wherein I do not often make my Appearance; sometimes I am seen thrusting my Head into a Round of Politicians at *Will's*,[3] and listning with great Attention to the Narratives that are made in those little Circular Audiences. Sometimes I smoak a Pipe at *Child's*;[4]

---

[a] general] publick *Fol.*

---

instruments, for the fuller discovery of the truth' (Preface to *Pyramidographia: or a Description of the Pyramids in Ægypt*, 1646). Interest in the subject had been recently revived by the appearance (19 Jan. 1706) of a pamphlet, *The Origine and Antiquity of our English Weights and Measures Discover'd, by their near Agreement with such Standards that are now found in one of the Egyptian Pyramides . . . by Mr. John Greaves, Astronomy Professor at Oxford*. In spite of the title-page, this is not by Greaves; it is a series of 'Answers' to three letters dealing with measurements made by Greaves on the pyramids and with the origins of English weights and measures. It is not necessary, however, to assume that Mr. Spectator's visit to Grand Cairo alludes to Greaves, since the subject was a favourite one with travellers. Jean de Thévenot took dimensions of the pyramids, 'and having compared them with the Measures of the Reverend Father *Elzear* the *Capucin*, I found him to have bene as exact as one possibly could be, there not being the third part of a Barley-corn difference betwixt him and me . . .' (*Travels into the Levant*, 1687, pt. i, p. 130). Mr. Spectator's interest in these matters places him in the company of antiquarians and 'pedants', favourite butts of the Queen Anne wits.

[1] The opening number of the *Tatler* had announced that 'all Accounts of Gallantry, Pleasure, and Entertainment shall be under the Article of White's Chocolate-house; Poetry, under that of Will's Coffee-house; Learning, under the title of the Grecian; Foreign and Domestic News you will have from Saint James's Coffee-House'.

[2] Coffee-houses. Miège in 1707 reckons 200 taverns, 5,000 ale-houses, and 1,000 coffee-houses in London. 'The *Coffee-houses* particularly are very commodious for a *free Conversation*, and for reading at an easie Rate all manner of *printed News*, the *Votes* of *Parliament* when sitting, and other *Prints* that come out Weekly, or casually' (p. 137). Misson had also described them as 'extreamly convenient. You have all Manner of News there: You have a good Fire, which you may sit by as long as you please: You have a Dish of Coffee; you meet your Friends for the Transaction of Business, and all for a Penny, if you don't care to spend more' (pp. 39–40). For a list of contemporary pamphlets see Hermann Westerfrölke, *Englische Kaffeehäuser als Sammelpunkte der literarischen Welt im Zeitalter von Dryden und Addison* (Jena, 1924), chap. xii.

[3] Will's Coffee-House, named after Will Urwin, its proprietor, stood at the north-west corner of Russell Street and Bow Street, Covent Garden. It had formerly been the resort of wits rather than politicians, and it was here that Dryden had presided in his last years. 'This Place', writes Steele in *Tatler* 1, 'is very much alter'd since Mr. *Dryden* frequented it, where you us'd to see *Songs*, *Epigrams*, and *Satyrs*, in the Hands of every Man you met, you have now only a Pack of Cards. . . .'

[4] Child's Coffee-House, in St. Paul's Churchyard, was a favourite rendezvous for authors and booksellers, as well as for physicians and the clergy. It had a predominantly Tory atmosphere, if we may accept Addison's hint in No. 556.

and whilst I seem attentive to nothing but the *Post-Man*,[1] over-hear the Conversation of every Table in the Room.[I appear] on *Sunday* Nights at St. *James*'s Coffee-House,[2] and sometimes join the little Committee of Politicks in the Inner-Room, as one who comes there to hear and improve. My Face is likewise very well known at the *Grecian*,[3] the *Cocoa-Tree*,[4] and in the Theaters[5] both of *Drury-Lane*, and the *Hay-Market*. I have been taken for a Merchant upon the *Exchange*[6] for above these ten Years, and sometimes pass for a *Jew* in the Assembly of Stock-Jobbers at *Jonathan*'s.[7] In short, where-ever I see a Cluster of People I always mix with them, tho' I never open my Lips but in my own Club.

Thus I live in the World, rather as a Spectator of Mankind, than as one of the Species; by which means I have made my self a Specu-lative Statesman, Soldier, Merchant and Artizan, without ever medling with any Practical Part in Life. I am very well versed in

[1] The *Post-Man*, established in 1695 and appearing thrice a week, was one of the important newspapers of the day. At this period it was written by Jean de Fonvive, a French Protestant, and printed by Swift's 'cousin' Dryden Leach (*Journal to Stella*, 26 Oct. 1710). It had an excellent news coverage, but was recognized as a 'Whig paper' by the Tories (*Examiner*, 24 Apr. 1712).

[2] St. James's Coffee-House, on the west side of St. James's Street, near St. James's Palace, was frequented by Whig guardsmen and men of fashion. It was the house 'most favoured by Whig statesmen and members of Parliament, who could there privately discuss their party tactics' (Morley). Some of its servants are named in No. 24.

[3] The Grecian, in Devereux Court in the Strand, near the Temple, was one of the oldest coffee-houses in London, said to have been founded about 1652 by the Greek servant of an English merchant returned from the Levant. It was a place of resort for lawyers and Greek scholars, as well as 'learned Professors and Fellows of the Royal Society' (Morley).

[4] The Cocoa-Tree, in Pall Mall, was a chocolate-house frequented by the extreme Tories. Charles Ford, the friend of Swift, had his letters regularly addressed there (*Letters of Jonathan Swift to Charles Ford*, ed. D. Nichol Smith, Oxford, 1935, *passim*). Koenig notes that 'the Parties have their different Places' and that 'a *Whig* will no more go to the *Cocoa-Tree*, then a *Tory* will be seen at the Coffee-House of St. *James*'s' (p. 220).

[5] Drury Lane Theatre after the fire of 1672 had been rebuilt by Sir Christopher Wren and opened in 1674; the Haymarket, built under the direction of Vanbrugh and Congreve, had opened in 1705. During the period of the *Spectator* (since 23 Nov. 1709) plays were presented at Drury Lane and operas at the Haymarket.

[6] There were three buildings with this name in 1711—the Royal Exchange, the New Exchange, and Exeter Exchange. The reference here is probably to the Royal Exchange, for which see No. 69. For the New Exchange see No. 96. Exeter Exchange was on the north side of the Strand, on the former site of Exeter House. 'Here are about 48 Shops let to Milleners, and room for as many above, where much is in the Occupation of the Company of *Upholsters*' (Hatton, p. 604). It had been built in 1676, but after the erection of the New Exchange (also in the Strand) its popularity decreased.

[7] Jonathan's coffee-house, in Exchange Alley near the Royal Exchange, is referred to in *Tatler* 38 as 'that General Mart of Stock-Jobbers.' Jonathan's and Garroway's (also in Exchange Alley) were the principal resorts of merchants.

the Theory of an Husband, or a Father, and can discern the Errors in the Oeconomy, Business, and Diversion of others, better than those who are engaged in them; as Standers-by discover Blots,[1] which are apt to escape those who are in the Game. I never espoused any Party with Violence, and am resolved to observe an exact Neutrality[2] between the Whigs and Tories, unless I shall be forc'd to declare my self by the Hostilities of either side. In short, I have acted in all the parts of my Life as a Looker-on, which is the Character I intend to preserve in this Paper.

I have given the Reader just so much of my History and Character, as to let him see I am not altogether unqualified for the Business I have undertaken. As for other Particulars in my Life and Adventures, I shall insert them in following Papers, as I shall see occasion. In the mean time, when I consider how much I have seen, read and heard, I begin to blame my own Taciturnity; and since I have neither Time nor Inclination to communicate the Fulness of my Heart in Speech, I am resolved to do it in Writing; and to Print my self out, if possible, before I Die. I have been often told by my Friends, that it is Pity so many useful Discoveries which I have made, should be in the Possession of a Silent Man. For this Reason therefore, I shall publish a Sheet-full of Thoughts every Morning, for the Benefit of my Contemporaries; and if I can any way contribute to the Diversion or Improvement of the Country in which I live, I shall leave it, when I am summoned out of it, with the secret Satisfaction of thinking that I have not Lived in vain.

There are three very material Points which I have not spoken to in this Paper, and which, for several important Reasons, I must keep to my self, at least for some Time: I mean, an Account of my Name, my Age, and my Lodgings. I must confess I would gratify my Reader in any thing that is reasonable; but as for these three Particulars, though I am sensible they might tend very much to the Embellishment of my Paper, I cannot yet come to a Resolution of communicating them to the Publick. They would indeed draw me out of that Obscurity which I have enjoy'd for many Years,

[1] In backgammon a blot is an exposed piece, liable to be taken (*OED*). For this proverbial phrase cf. Swift, *Tritical Essay*, 1711: 'A Stander-by may sometimes, perhaps, see more of the Game than he that plays it' (*Prose Works*, ed. Herbert Davis, i. 247) and for earlier examples Tilley (S822) and Apperson (s.v. 'Lookers on').

[2] With some striking exceptions (notably No. 384) the *Spectator*, in contrast to the *Tatler*, preserved throughout its career an attitude of aloofness from party quarrels and a concern not 'to encrease the Number either of Whigs or Tories, but of wise and good Men' (No. 556).

and expose me in publick Places to several Salutes and Civilities, which have been always very disagreeable to me; for the greatest Pain I can suffer, is[a] the being talked to, and being stared at. It is for this Reason likewise, that I keep my Complexion and Dress, as very great Secrets; tho' it is not impossible, but I may make Discoveries of both in the Progress of the Work I have undertaken.

After having been thus particular upon my self, I shall in to-Morrow's Paper give an Account of those Gentlemen who are concerned with me in this Work. For, as I have before intimated, a Plan of it is laid and concerted (as all other Matters of Importance are) in a Club. However, as my Friends have engaged me to stand in the Front, those who have a mind to correspond with me, may direct their Letters *To the Spectator*, at Mr. *Buckley*'s[1] in *Little Britain*. For I must further acquaint the Reader, that tho' our Club meets only on *Tuesdays* and *Thursdays*, we have appointed a Committee to sit every Night, for the Inspection of all such Papers[2] as may contribute to the Advancement of the Publick Weal. C[b]

[a] Pain . . . is] Pains I can suffer, are *Fol.*   [b] *Signature om. in Fol*

---

[1] Samuel Buckley was already a successful printer and bookseller, best known perhaps for the *Daily Courant*, the first daily newspaper to be published in England, which since 1702 had been issued from Buckley's shop (he continued to print it until 24 Sept. 1714). His association with Mrs. Baldwin is marked by the imprint of *The Monthly Register, or Memoirs of the Affairs of Europe, &c.* (first issued 12 Feb. 1705) which reads, 'Printed for Sam. Buckley in Little-Brittain, and Sold by A. Baldwin in Warwick-Lane'. Buckley occupied this shop in Little Britain, off Aldersgate Street, until February 1714, when he removed 'to Amen-Corner at the End of Pater-Noster-Row' (*Daily Courant*, 27 Feb.). In 1719 he was appointed Gazetteer for life, at a salary of £300 a year (*Applebee's Weekly Journal*, 6 June 1719), a post which he held until his death on 8 Sept. 1741. The inscription on his tomb in Hornsey Church, Middlesex, is given in Nichols, *Literary Anecdotes* (1812), ii. 27. For Buckley's connexion with the Whigs see John J. Murray, 'An Eighteenth-century Whitebook', *Huntington Library Quarterly*, xiii (1950), 371–82.
[2] Letters from correspondents occupy an important position in the *Spectator*, and many of the later numbers, particularly those by Steele, are made up entirely of such contributions. In No. 271 Addison suggests some of the ways in which letters are used and replies to questions raised as to their genuineness. Charles Lillie's *Original and Genuine Letters sent to the Tatler and Spectator . . .* (2 vols., 1725) contains some of the unused correspondence, and there are other letters, not printed by Lillie, in the British Museum, at Blenheim Palace, and elsewhere.

> ... *Ast Alii sex*
> *Et plures uno conclamant ore.*
>
> Juv.

THE first of our Society[2] is a Gentleman of *Worcestershire*, of antient Descent, a Baronet, his Name Sir ROGER DE COVERLY.[3] His great Grandfather was Inventor of that famous Country-Dance which is call'd after him. All who know that Shire, are very well acquainted with the Parts and Merits of Sir ROGER. He is a Gentleman that is very singular in his Behaviour, but his Singularities proceed from his good Sense, and are Contradictions to the Manners of the World, only as he thinks the World is in the wrong. However, this Humour creates him no Enemies, for he does nothing with Sowrness or Obstinacy; and his being unconfined to Modes and Forms, makes him but the readier and more capable to please and oblige all who know him. When he is in Town he lives in *Soho-*

[1] *Motto.* Juvenal, *Satires*, 7. 167–8: Six and more cry with one voice.

[2] The Club, meeting on Tuesdays and Thursdays (No. 1), with its 'committee', sitting nightly for the inspection of papers submitted, occupies a less prominent position in the *Spectator* than would be expected from this description of its members —six in addition to Mr. Spectator. They are admirably diversified to represent various points of view and interests in contemporary society, but only Sir Roger is developed to any extent in later essays. It is a tribute to the liveliness of Steele's pen that originals have been sought for most of the club members.

[3] The 'famous Country-Dance' (and tune), which Steele suggests was derived from the De Coverley family, dates from about 1685 (*OED*) in the form 'Roger of Coverly' (it is called 'Roger de Caubly' in *Tatler* 34); the later form 'Sir Roger de Coverley' is due to the *Spectator*. 'Roger' is also an appropriate name for a person of old-fashioned and somewhat rustic character. Actually, only a few years earlier, John Tutchin had used the same name for the Countryman who is one of the interlocutors in his *Observator* (vol. iii, no. 1, 25 Mar. 1704). The Countryman explains himself thus to Observator: 'You know my Family are good Honest Yeomen, and my Name is plain *Roger* of *Coverly*, my Father, *Gods Peace be with his Soul*, Died you know but two years ago, there he lies in our Church-Yard, with a good Post and Rail over him to tell who he was, and how Old he was, and I think that's Decent enough for us Poor Folks. . . . I am of the Family of the *Honest-Ones*, I am Honest *Roger*, and my Father was Honest *Roger*, and my Grand-Father was Honest *Some-Body* or *Other*, I don't know who.' Various attempts have been made to establish an original prototype for Sir Roger, the most popular guess being that of Sir John Packington, the Tory squire of Worcestershire (*Gent. Mag.*, Oct. 1779, pp. 494–5; see also *DNB*). William Walsh has also been proposed: see *N & Q*, 2nd ser., iii (1857), 46, &c., and more recently by Phyllis Freeman, 'Who was Sir Roger de Coverley?', *Quarterly Review*, Oct. 1947, pp. 592–604. The best general discussion of the development of Sir Roger's character throughout the *Spectator* remains that of Émile Legouis, 'Les deux "Sir Roger de Coverley", celui de Steele et celui d'Addison', published in the *Revue germanique* in July 1906 and reprinted in Legouis's *Dernière Gerbe* (Paris, 1940), pp. 85–104.

Square:[1] It is said he keeps himself a Batchelour by reason he was crossed in Love, by a perverse beautiful Widow[2] of the next County to him. Before this Disappointment, Sir ROGER was what you call a fine Gentleman, had often supped with my Lord *Rochester*[3] and Sir *George Etherege*, fought a Duel upon his first coming to Town, and kick'd Bully *Dawson*[4] in a publick Coffee-house for calling him Youngster. But being ill used by the abovementioned Widow, he was very serious for a Year and a half; and tho' his Temper being naturally jovial, he at last got over it, he grew careless of himself and never dressed afterwards; he continues to wear a Coat and Doublet of the same Cut that were in Fashion at the Time of his Repulse, which, in his merry Humours, he tells us, has been in and out twelve Times since he first wore it. 'Tis said Sir ROGER grew humble in his Desires after he had forgot this cruel Beauty, insomuch that it is reported he has frequently offended in Point of Chastity with Beggars and Gypsies: But this is look'd upon by his Friends rather as Matter of Raillery than Truth. He is now in his Fifty sixth Year, cheerful, gay, and hearty, keeps a good House both in Town and Country; a great Lover of Mankind; but there is such a mirthful Cast in his Behaviour, that he is rather beloved than esteemed: His Tenants grow rich, his Servants look satisfied, all

[1] This fashionable residential district, south-west of the junction of Oxford Street and Tottenham Court Road, dates from about 1680 and was in Queen Anne's time 'the genteelest part of the town' (Nichols). Koenig describes it as 'larger, and more regular' than Leicester and Golden Squares, and notes that 'Persons of the first Quality have their Hostels here' (p. 223). It seems to have been originally known as King's Square. Other town residences for Sir Roger are given in Nos. 335 and 410.

[2] See No. 113.

[3] John Wilmot, Earl of Rochester (1647–80), and Sir George Etherege (1635?–91) as Sir Roger's supper-companions would represent to contemporary readers the two most celebrated rakes of the past generation. Rochester's poem *On Nothing* is referred to by Addison in No. 305, and his lines on Sedley are twice quoted by Steele (Nos. 91, 400). Rochester was thought to be the original of Dorimant in Etherege's *Man of Mode*, which Steele criticizes in Nos. 65 and 75.

[4] Tom Brown has a letter 'From Bully Dawson to Bully W——' in *Letters from the Dead to the Living* (*Works*, 1715, ii. 215–30) which gives a lively idea of this Restoration rake (see also Brown's *Works*, i. 81, 162; ii. 230–41). Tutchin's *Observator* (5 Apr. 1704), speaking of Jessamy Tom, remarks, 'Oh I know that Fellow, he's a perfect *Beau*, and serv'd some part of his Time to Bully *Dawson*, and learnt of him to Huff and Hector . . .'. According to William Oldys, 'The character of Capt. Hackum, in Thomas Shadwell's comedy *The Squire of Alsatia*, was drawn (as I have been told by old John Bowman the player) to expose Bully Dawson, a noted sharper, swaggerer, and debauchee, about town, especially Blackfriars and its infamous purlieus' (*N & Q*, 2nd ser., xi [1861], 182). Sir Roger's kicking Bully Dawson seems to refer to a well-known jest; in *The Weekly Comedy, or, The Humours of the Age* (5 Dec. 1707) we read: 'Then I find a Man in the Middle Station is in the Condition of a Famous Fellow, call'd *Bully Dawson*, who being upbraided by a Gentleman for suffering himself to be Kick'd by all the World, reply'd, *You are much mistaken, Sir, I am only Kick'd by one half of the World, and the other half I Kick.*'

the young Women profess Love to him, and the young Men are glad of his Company: When he comes into a House he calls the Servants by their Names, and talks all the way up Stairs to a Visit. I must not omit that Sir ROGER is a Justice of the *Quorum*;[1] that he fills the Chair at a Quarter-Session with great Abilities, and three Months ago gain'd universal Applause by explaining a Passage in the Game-Act.[2]

The Gentleman next in Esteem and Authority among us, is another Batchelour, who is a Member of the *Inner-Temple*;[3] a Man of great Probity, Wit, and Understanding; but he has chosen his Place of Residence rather to obey the Direction of an old humoursome Father than in Pursuit of his own Inclinations. He was plac'd there to study the Laws of the Land, and is the most learned of any of the House in those of the Stage. *Aristotle* and *Longinus* are much better understood by him than *Littleton* or *Cooke*.[4] The Father sends up every Post Questions relating to Marriage-Articles, Leases, and Tenures, in the Neighbourhood; all which Questions he agrees with an Attorney to answer and take care of in the Lump: He is studying the Passions themselves, when he should be inquiring into the Debates among Men which arise from them. He knows the Argument of each of the Orations of *Demosthenes* and *Tully*, but not one Case in the Reports of our own Courts. No one ever took him for a Fool, but none, except his intimate Friends, know he has a great deal of Wit. This Turn makes him at once both disinterested and agreeable: As few of his Thoughts are drawn from Business, they are most of them fit for Conversation. His Taste of Books is a

[1] At this period the term had apparently come to mean simply Justice of the Peace (see *OED*). For the increasing power of these magistrates in the reign of Queen Anne see Trevelyan, i. 100–2.

[2] Game-laws restricted the right of shooting game-birds to landowners, but only if they were worth £100 a year or more. See G. N. Clark, *The Later Stuarts* (Oxford, 1934), p. 391. In No. 122 Sir Roger mentions a yeoman who 'is just within the Game-Act, and qualified to kill an Hare or a Pheasant'.

[3] The Templar, though playing no very important part in the Club, is designed to represent the young men of the day ostensibly studying the law but mainly interested in the theatrical and fashionable life of the town—those, in Pope's phrase, 'who study Shakespeare at the Inns of Court' (*Dunciad*, iv. 568). Congreve and Budgell were members of the Temple before becoming known as professional authors. Fielding's *Temple Beau* (1730) gives an interesting picture of the type. The Templar in the Spectator Club recalls Young Maggot in Shadwell's *True Widow*, who is described as 'An Inns-of-Court Man, who neglects his Law, and runs mad after Wit'. Old Maggot says of him: 'My roguy Nephew must leave *Cook* upon *Littleton*, for *Beaumont* and *Fletcher*!' (I. i.).

[4] Sir Edward Coke's *First Part of the Institutes of the Lawes of England: or Commentarie upon Littleton* was published in 1628. The 10th edition is advertised in the *Term Catalogues* for Easter 1703 (Arber, iii. 350).

little too just for the Age he lives in; he has read all, but approves of very few. His Familiarity with the Customs, Manners, Actions, and Writings of the Antients, makes him a very delicate Observer of what occurs to him in the present World. He is an excellent Critick, and the Time of the Play, is his Hour of Business; exactly at five he passes through *New-Inn*,[1] crosses through *Russel-Court*, and takes a Turn at *Will*'s till the Play begins;[2] he has his Shooes rubb'd and his Perriwig powder'd at the Barber's as you go into the *Rose*.[3] It is for the Good of the Audience when he is at a Play, for the Actors have an Ambition to please him.

The Person of next Consideration is Sir ANDREW FREEPORT,[4] a Merchant of great Eminence in the City of *London*: A Person of indefatigable Industry, strong Reason, and great Experience. His Notions of Trade are noble and generous, and (as every rich Man has usually some sly Way of Jesting, which would make no great Figure were he not a rich Man) he calls the Sea the *British Common*. He is acquainted with Commerce in all its Parts, and will tell you that it is a stupid and barbarous Way to extend Dominion by Arms; for true Power is to be got by Arts and Industry. He will often argue, that if this Part of our Trade were well cultivated, we should gain from one Nation; and if another, from another. I have heard him prove, that Diligence makes more lasting Acquisitions than Valour, and that Sloth has ruin'd more Nations than the Sword. He abounds in several frugal Maxims, among which the greatest Favourite is, 'A Penny saved is a Penny got.' A General Trader of good Sense, is pleasanter Company than a general Scholar; and Sir ANDREW having a natural unaffected Eloquence, the Perspicuity of his Dis-

[1] An inn of Chancery belonging to the Middle Temple, situated in Wych Street, just north of Norfolk Street. Russel Court was a narrow passage leading from Drury Lane to Bridges Street.

[2] i.e. about six in the evening. (Cf. Charles Povey, *The Visions of Sir Heister Ryley*, 11 Sept. 1710.)

[3] The Rose Tavern, in Russell Street, Covent Garden, near the Drury Lane Theatre, was 'much favoured by the looser sort of play-goers' (Morley).

[4] As a representative of the rising Whig merchant class Sir Andrew stands next to Sir Roger de Coverley among the memorable creations of the *Spectator*. His 'noble and generous' notions of trade are often contrasted with Sir Roger's old-fashioned and somewhat crotchety views of the importance of the landed interests. Since the merchant class was at this moment the target of a campaign of vilification by the Tory party writers, the creation of Sir Andrew affords a convenient method of reply and yet allows the *Spectator* to avoid violating its professed neutrality in politics. Both William Paterson, the Founder of the Bank of England, and Sir Gilbert Heathcote, Lord Mayor of London in 1711, have been suggested as 'originals' for Sir Andrew. The name is frequently used later in the eighteenth century as a pseudonym by economic writers. The earliest I have noted is *A Dialogue between Sir Andrew Freeport and Timothy Squat, Esq; on the Subject of Excises . . .* (1733).

course gives the same Pleasure that Wit would in another Man. He has made his Fortunes himself; and says that *England* may be richer than other Kingdoms, by as plain Methods as he himself is richer than other Men; tho' at the same Time I can say this of him, that there is not a Point in the Compass but blows home a Ship in which he is an Owner.

Next to Sir ANDREW in the Club-room sits Captain SENTRY,[1] a Gentleman of great Courage, good Understanding, but invincible Modesty. He is one of those that deserve very well, but are very awkard at putting their Talents within the Observation of such as should take notice of them. He was some Years a Captain, and behaved himself with great Gallantry in several Engagements and at several Sieges; but having a small Estate of his own, and being next Heir to Sir ROGER, he has quitted a Way of Life in which no Man can rise suitably to his Merit, who is not something of a Courtier as well as a Souldier. I have heard him often lament, that in a Profession where Merit is placed in so conspicuous a View, Impudence should get the Better of Modesty. When he has talked to this Purpose I never heard him make a sower Expression, but frankly confess that he left the World because he was not fit for it. A strict Honesty and an even regular Behaviour, are in themselves Obstacles to him that must press through Crowds who endeavour at the same End with himself, the Favour of a Commander. He will however in this Way of Talk excuse Generals for not disposing according to Mens Desert, or enquiring into it: For, says he, that great Man who has a Mind to help me, has as many to break through to come at me, as I have to come at him: Therefore he will conclude, that the Man who would make a Figure, especially in a military Way, must get over all false Modesty, and assist his Patron against the Importunity of other Pretenders by a proper Assurance in his own Vindication. He says it is a civil Cowardice to be backward in asserting what you ought to expect, as it is a military Fear to be slow in attacking when it is your Duty. With this Candour does the Gentleman speak of himself and others. The same Frankness runs

---

[1] Editors have, with some justice, assumed that this portrait of the military man, 'never over-bearing, . . . nor ever too obsequious', derives from Steele's own experiences in the army. From a mention of 'Collonel Camperfelt' in No. 544 the tradition grew that Camperfelt, or Magnus Kempenfelt (1665–c. 1727), was the original of Captain Sentry. A native of Sweden, 'he followed the fortunes of King James the Second, and was afterwards invited by Q. Anne to accept a commission in her service, and in the reign of George the First died lieutenant-governor of [New] Jersey' (*Gent. Mag.*, Oct. 1782, p. 476).

through all his Conversation. The military Part of his Life has furnish'd him with many Adventures, in the Relation of which he is very agreeable to the Company; for he is never over-bearing, tho' accustomed to command Men in the utmost Degree below him; nor ever too obsequious, from an Habit of obeying Men highly above him.

But that our Society may not appear a Set of Humourists[1] unacquainted with the Gallantries and Pleasures of the Age, we have among us the gallant WILL. HONEYCOMB,[2] a Gentleman who according to his Years should be in the Decline of his Life, but having ever been very careful of his Person, and always had a very easy Fortune, Time has made but very little Impression, either by Wrinkles on his Forehead, or Traces in his Brain. His Person is well turn'd, of a good Height. He is very ready at that Sort of Discourse with which Men usually entertain Women. He has all his Life dressed very well, and remembers Habits as others do Men. He can smile when one speaks to him, and laughs easily. He knows the History of every Mode, and can inform you from which of the *French* King's Wenches our Wives and Daughters had this Manner of curling their Hair, that Way of placing their Hoods; whose Frailty was covered by such a Sort of Petticoat, and whose Vanity to shew her Foot made that Part of the Dress so short in such a Year. In a Word, all his Conversation and Knowledge has been in the female World: As other Men of his Age will take Notice to you what such a Minister said upon such and such an Occasion, he will tell you when the Duke of *Monmouth* danced at Court such a Woman was then smitten, another was taken with him at the Head of his Troop in the *Park*. In all these important Relations, he has

[1] It is hardly necessary to point out that this word, occurring frequently in the *Spectator*, is used in the obsolete sense of 'persons subject to "humours" or fancies; fantastical or whimsical persons; faddists' (*OED*).

[2] In attacking the Restoration concept of the 'fine gentleman' the *Spectator* adopts the method of ridicule rather than direct attack. Just as Sir Roger is portrayed as a harmless, eccentric, and decidedly outmoded Tory, so Will Honeycomb—a kind of Dorimant born too late—is represented as a vain and affected 'ladies' man', whose 'Conversation and Knowledge has been in the female World'—and of a past generation. His conversation is of the age of Charles II: 'the French King's Wenches' would be the mistresses of Louis XIV, long before the time of Madame de Maintenon, and the gallantries of the Duke of Monmouth go back to the 1670's. It is difficult to account for the tradition which saw 'Colonel' William Cleland (*c.* 1674–1741), the Scottish friend of Swift and Pope, as the prototype of Will Honeycomb. Swift, writing to Pope on 15 Jan. 1730/1, describes him as 'a tall Scots gentleman, walking perpetually in the Mall, and fastening upon everybody he meets'. The facts of his life are summarized by Miss Blanchard as a footnote to the one existing letter from Steele to Cleland (*Correspondence*, pp. 119–20).

ever about the same Time received a kind Glance or a Blow of a Fan from some celebrated Beauty, Mother of the present Lord such-a-one. If you speak of a young Commoner[1] that said a lively thing in the House, he starts up, 'He has good Blood in his Veins, *Tom Mirabell* begot him, the Rogue cheated me in that Affair; that young Fellow's Mother used me more like a Dog than any Woman I ever made Advances to.' This Way of Talking of his very much enlivens the Conversation among us of a more sedate Turn; and I find there is not one of the Company but my self, who rarely speak at all, but speaks of him as of that Sort of Man who is usually called a well-bred fine Gentleman. To conclude his Character, where Women are not concerned, he is an honest worthy Man.

I cannot tell whether I am to account him whom I am next to speak of, as one of our Company; for he visits us but seldom, but when he does it adds to every Man else a new Enjoyment of himself. He is a Clergyman,[2] a very philosophick Man, of general Learning, great Sanctity of Life, and the most exact good Breeding. He has the Misfortune to be of a very weak Constitution, and consequently cannot accept of such Cares and Business as Preferments in his Function would oblige him to: He is therefore among Divines what a Chamber-Councellor is among Lawyers. The Probity of his Mind, and the Integrity of his Life, create him Followers, as being eloquent or loud advances others. He seldom introduces the Subject he speaks upon; but we are so far gone in Years, that he observes, when he is among us, an Earnestness to have him fall on some divine Topick, which he always treats with much Authority, as one who has no Interests in this World, as one who is hastening to the Object of all his Wishes, and conceives Hope from his Decays and Infirmities. These are my ordinary Companions. R[3]

---

[1] A member of the House of Commons. Now rare (*OED*).

[2] This sixth member of the Club, unnamed and not very vividly characterized, becomes a useful means of introducing some of the more serious moral themes of the *Spectator*.

[3] Although this essay has Steele's signature letter, it seems unlikely that it was drafted without consultation with Addison. Following Tickell's example in 1721, editors of Addison have included the essay in his works, and writers on the *Spectator* have usually considered it a result of collaboration between Addison and Steele. Nichols, however, remarks that it 'is disfigured by a piece of careless bad taste which makes it more than probable that Addison never saw it until it was published. The passage concerning beggars and gipsies in the description of Sir Roger, is one which Steele's rapid pen may conceivably have thrown off in a hurry; but it is also one to which Addison . . . could hardly have given his *imprimatur*.'

No. 3   *Saturday, March 3, 1711*[1]
[ADDISON]

Quoi quisque ferè studio devinctus adhæret:
Aut quibus in rebus multùm sumus antè morati:
Atque in quâ ratione fuit contenta magis mens;
In somnis eadem plerumque videmur obire.

                                        Lucr. L. 4.

IN one of my late Rambles, or rather Speculations, I looked into
the great Hall where the Bank is kept,[2] and was not a little
pleased to see the Directors, Secretaries, and Clerks, with all the
other Members of that wealthy Corporation, ranged in their several
Stations, according to the Parts they act in that just and regular
Oeconomy. This revived in my Memory the many Discourses
which I had both read and heard concerning the Decay of Publick
Credit,[3] with the Methods of restoring it, and which, in my
Opinion, have always been defective, because they have always
been made with an Eye to separate Interests, and Party Principles.

The Thoughts of the Day gave my Mind Employment for the
whole Night, so that I fell insensibly into a kind of Methodical
Dream, which dispos'd all my Contemplations into a Vision or
Allegory, or what else the Reader shall please to call it.

Methoughts[4] I returned to the Great Hall, where I had been the

---

[1] *Motto.* Lucretius, 4. 962–5:
... What studies please, what most delight,
And fill men's thoughts, they dream them o'er at night. CREECH.
This essay is quoted by Trevelyan to illustrate the fears of the Whigs that in the
coming Bank Election (in April) a Tory majority among the Directors would be
likely to bring on a Jacobite restoration and a corresponding decline in public credit.
'This was no mere poetic fancy of Addison's', writes Dr. Trevelyan. 'The most solid
men in the City believed that the Restoration of James III would mean the repudia-
tion of government debts contracted since the Revolution, and it was not a little
this fear that kept the members of the Bank of England faithful to the Whig cause in
the hour of its deepest depression' (iii. 105).
[2] The great Hall where the Bank is kept. The room known as the Hall in Grocer's
Hall, at the upper end of Grocer's Alley, just north of the Poultry and east of Old
Jewry, had been let to the Governors and Directors of the Bank of England since its
establishment in 1694. Strype in 1720 (iii. 51) describes Grocer's Hall as 'a large
building, with a spacious court before it, and a garden behind'.
[3] Addison has in mind such things as Defoe's *Essay upon Publick Credit*, published
during the preceding summer, on 23 Aug. (*Daily Courant*). In the same newspaper
(23 Dec. 1710) is advertised as 'just publish'd' *The Vindication and Advancement of our
National Constitution and Credit attempted in several Tracts*, the fourth of which is entitled
'An Essay on our National Credit'.
[4] 'The curious form *methoughts*, used in the 17th and the first half of the 18th c.,
probably owes its *s* to the analogy of the present tense *methinks*' (*OED*).

Morning before, but, to my Surprize, instead of the Company that I left there, I saw towards the Upper-end of the Hall, a beautiful Virgin,[1] seated on a Throne of Gold. Her Name (as they told me) was *Publick Credit*. The Walls, instead of being adorned with Pictures and Maps, were hung with many Acts of Parliament written in Golden Letters. At the Upper-end of the Hall was the *Magna Charta*, with the Act of Uniformity[2] on the right Hand, and the Act of Toleration on the left. At the Lower-end of the Hall was the Act of Settlement,[3] which was placed full in the Eye of the Virgin that sat upon the Throne. Both the Sides of the Hall were covered with such Acts of Parliament as had been made for the Establishment of publick Funds. The Lady seemed to set an unspeakable Value upon these several Pieces of Furniture, insomuch that she often refreshed her Eye with them, and often smiled with a Secret Pleasure, as she looked upon them; but, at the same time, showed a very particular Uneasiness, if she saw any thing approaching that might hurt them. She appeared indeed infinitely timorous in all her Behaviour: And, whether it was from the Delicacy of her Constitution, or that she was troubled with Vapours,[4] as I was afterwards told by one who I found was none of her Well-wishers, she changed Colour, and startled at every thing she heard. She was likewise (as I afterwards found) a greater Valetudinarian than any I had ever met with, even in her own Sex, and subject to such Momentary Consumptions, that in the twinkling of an Eye, she would fall away from the most florid Complexion, and the most healthful State of Body, and wither into a Skeleton. Her Recoveries were often as sudden as her Decays, insomuch that she would revive in a Moment

[1] *The Moderator* of 25 Aug. 1710 had used the same figure to support the Tory position, in an essay entitled 'The False Fits of Whiggish Credit Discovered; or, An Account of the Turns and Returns, Comings and Goings, Visits and Departings of that Subtle Pharisaical Lady call'd Whiggish Phanatical Credit'. Here the writer depicts 'this Hypocritical Lady Credit' as flourishing and declining according to the outward fortunes of the Whigs.
[2] By balancing the Act of Uniformity (of 1662) with the Act of Toleration (of 1689) Addison emphasizes the middle-of-the-road policy which the Whigs thought of themselves as practising with respect to persons outside the Church of England.
[3] This Act, passed in 1701, guaranteed the Protestant Succession, in the person of the Electress Sophia and her descendants.
[4] The vapours, the hypo, the spleen—all three terms are used to describe a morbid condition ranging from depression and 'nerves' to melancholia. Pope's Cave of the Spleen in Book IV of the *Rape of the Lock* gives a contemporary description of some of the manifestations of the disorder. No. 52 advertises as 'Just publish'd' Mandeville's *Treatise of the Hypochondriack and Hysterick Passions, vulgarly call'd the HYPO in Men and VAPOURS in Women; in which the Symptoms, Causes and Cure of those Diseases are set forth after a Method intirely new.*

out of a wasting Distemper, into a Habit of the highest Health and Vigour.

I had very soon an Opportunity of observing these quick Turns and Changes in her Constitution. There sat at her Feet a Couple of Secretaries, who received every Hour Letters from all Parts of the World, which the one or the other of them was perpetually reading to her; and, according to the News she heard, to which she was exceedingly attentive, she changed Colour, and discovered many Symptoms of Health or Sickness.

Behind the Throne was a prodigious Heap of Bags of Mony, which were piled upon one another so high that they touched the Ceiling. The Floor, on her right Hand, and on her left, was covered with vast Sums of Gold that rose up in Pyramids on either side of her: But this I did not so much wonder at, when I heard, upon Enquiry, that she had the same Virtue in her Touch, which the Poets tell us a *Lydian* King[1] was formerly possess'd of; and that she could convert whatever she pleas'd into that precious Metal.

After a little Dizziness, and confused Hurry of Thought, which a Man often meets with in a Dream, methoughts the Hall was alarm'd, the Doors flew open, and there entered half a dozen of the most hideous Phantoms that I had ever seen (even in a Dream) before that Time. They came in two by two, though match'd in the most dissociable Manner, and mingled together in a kind of Dance. It would be tedious to describe their Habits and Persons, for which Reason I shall only inform my Reader that the first Couple were Tyranny and Anarchy, the second were Bigotry and Atheism, the third the Genius of a Common-Wealth, and a young Man of about twenty two Years of Age,[2] whose Name I could not learn. He had a Sword in his right Hand, which in the Dance he often brandished at the Act of Settlement; and a Citizen, who stood by me, whisper'd in my Ear, that he saw a Spunge in his left Hand. The Dance of so many jarring Natures put me in Mind of the Sun, Moon and Earth, in the *Rehearsal*,[3] that danced together for no other end but to eclipse one another.

[1] Midas, the legendary king of Phrygia.

[2] The Pretender, James Francis Edward, was born on 10 June 1688. Swift in *Examiner* 15 (16 Nov. 1710) had referred sarcastically to the mnaœuvres of the Whigs in using the word 'Pretender' to frighten their countrymen. 'Half a Score Stock-Jobbers are playing the Knave in *Exchange-Alley*, and there goes the *Pretender* with a *Sponge*' (*Prose Works*, ed. Herbert Davis, iii. 17). It will be noted that Addison points out as dangers to public credit both extremes of Jacobitism and republicanism, in the hideous phantoms which come in 'two by two'.

[3] In the final act of Buckingham's play Bayes, who has the Moon, the Earth, and

The Reader will easily suppose, by what has been before said, that the Lady on the Throne would have been almost frighted to Distraction, had she seen but any one of these Spectres; what then must have been her Condition when she saw them all in a Body? She fainted and dyed away at the Sight.

Et neque jam color est misto candore rubori;
Nec Vigor, & Vires & quæ modo visa placebant;
Nec Corpus remanet . . .[1]   Ov. *Met.*, Lib. 3.

There was as great a Change in the Hill of Mony Bags, and the Heaps of Mony, the former shrinking, and falling into so many empty Bags, that I now found not above a tenth Part of them had been filled with Mony. The rest that took up the same Space, and made the same Figure as the Bags that were really filled with Mony, had been blown up with Air, and called into my Memory the Bags full of Wind, which *Homer* tells us his Hero receiv'd as a Present from *Æolus*.[2] The great Heaps of Gold, on either side the Throne, now appeared to be only Heaps of Paper, or little Piles of notched Sticks, bound up together in Bundles, like *Bath*-Faggots.

Whilst I was lamenting this sudden Desolation that had been made before me, the whole Scene vanished: In the Room of the frightful Spectres, there now entered a second Dance of Apparitions very agreeably matched together, and made up of very amiable Phantoms. The first Pair was Liberty, with Monarchy at her right Hand: The second was Moderation leading in Religion; and the third a Person whom I had never seen,[3] with the Genius of *Great Britain*. At their first Entrance the Lady reviv'd, the Bags swell'd to their former Bulk, the Piles of Faggots and Heaps of Paper changed into Pyramids of Guineas: And for my own Part I was so transported with Joy, that I awaked, tho' I must confess I would fain have fallen asleep again to have closed my Vision, if I could have done it.[4]   C

the Sun perform a dance together, remarks: 'And of necessity by the very nature of this dance, the earth must be sometimes between the sun and the moon, and the moon between the earth and sun; and there you have both your eclipses.'

[1] 'No longer has [she] that ruddy colour mixing with the white, no longer that vigour and strength, and all that lately was so pleasing to behold; hardly does [her] body remain . . .' Ovid, *Metamorphoses*, 3. 491–3.

[2] *Odyssey*, 10. 19.

[3] A standing complaint of the Whigs was that Prince George, son of the Electress, had so far never been invited to visit Britain. Liberty and Monarchy, Moderation and Religion, with the Genius of Great Britain, contrast effectively with the figures of excess who accompany the Pretender.

[4] This essay of Addison, which contrasts rather surprisingly with the statement of political neutrality in the opening number, seems to be referred to in *Examiner* 37

No. 4   *Monday, March 5, 1711*[1]
[STEELE]

. . . Egregii Mortalem, altique silenti!
                                                          Hor.

A N Author, when he first appears in the World, is very apt to
believe it has nothing to think of but his Performances. With
a good Share of this Vanity in my Heart, I made it my Business these
three Days to listen after my own Fame; and as I have sometimes
met with Circumstances which did not displease me, I have been[a]
encountered by others which gave me as much Mortification. It is
incredible to think how empty I have in this Time observ'd some
Part of the Species to be, what mere Blanks[2] they are when they
first come abroad in the Morning, how utterly they are at a Stand
till they are set a going by some Paragraph in a News-Paper: Such
Persons are very acceptable to a young Author, for they desire no
more in any thing[b] but to be new to be agreeable. If I found Consolation among such, I was as much disquieted by the Incapacity of
others. These are Mortals who have a certain Curiosity without
Power of Reflection, and perused my Papers like Spectators rather
than Readers. But there is so little Pleasure in Enquiries that so
nearly concern our selves, (it being the worst Way in the World to
Fame, to be too anxious about it), that upon the whole I resolv'd for
the future to go on in my ordinary Way; and without too much
Fear or Hope about the Business of Reputation, to be very careful of
the Design of my Actions, but very negligent of the Consequences
of them.

It is an endless and frivolous Pursuit to act by any other Rule
than the Care of satisfying our own Minds in what we do. One
would think a silent Man who concerned himself with no one
breathing, should be very little liable to misinterpretations; and yet

---

[a] have been] was *Fol.*   [b] in any thing] *om. Fol.*

(19 Apr. 1711) by his friend Swift, who apparently thought Steele was the author:
'To hear some of these worthy Reasoners talking of *Credit*; that she is so nice, so
squeamish, so capricious; you would think they were describing a Lady troubled
with Vapours or the Cholick, to be only removed by a *Course of Steel*, or *swallowing
a Bullet.*' (*Prose Works*, ed. H. Davis, iii. 134.)

[1] *Motto.* Horace, *Satires*, 2. 6. 58:
                    Of all men a man of profound taciturnity!

These are referred to again in No. 10. A letter from T. Blank, 'descended from
the ancient Family of the *Blanks*', is printed in No. 563.

I remember I was once taken up for a Jesuit,[1] for no other Reason but my profound Taciturnity. It is from this Misfortune, that to be out of Harm's Way, I have ever since affected Crowds. He who comes into Assemblies only to gratify his Curiosity, and not to make a Figure, enjoys the Pleasures of Retirement in a more exquisite Degree, than he possibly could in his Closet; the Lover, the Ambitious, and the Miser, are follow'd thither by a worse Crowd than any they can withdraw from. To be exempt from the Passions with which others are tormented, is the only pleasing Solitude. I can very justly say with the antient Sage, *I am never less alone than when alone*.[2] As I am insignificant to the Company in publick Places, and as it is visible I do not come thither as most do, to shew my self; I gratify the Vanity of all who pretend to make an Appearance, and have often as kind Looks from well dressed Gentlemen and Ladies, as a Poet would bestow upon one of his Audience. There are so many Gratifications attend this publick sort of Obscurity, that some little Distastes I daily receive have lost their Anguish; and I did the other Day, without the least Displeasure, over-hear[a] one say of me, *That strange Fellow*, and another answer, *I have known the Fellow's Face these twelve Years, and so must you; but I believe you are the first ever asked who he was*. There are, I must confess, many to whom my Person is as well known as that of their nearest Relations, who give themselves no further Trouble about calling me by my Name or Quality, but speak of me very currently by Mr. *what-d'ye-call-him*.

To make up for these trivial Disadvantages, I have the high Satisfaction of beholding all Nature with an unprejudic'd Eye; and having nothing to do with Mens Passions or Interests, I can with the greater Sagacity consider their Talents, Manners, Failings, and Merits.

It is remarkable, that those who want any one Sense,[3] possess the

[a] I did . . . over-hear] I can without the least Displeasure over-hear *Fol*.

---

[1] 'In the whole range of Addison's wit, is there anything more perfect than Steele's making the Spectator remember that he was once taken up for a Jesuit, for no other reason than his profound taciturnity?' (Forster, *Hist. & Biog. Essays*, 1858, ii. 188, quoted by Dobson.)
[2] Cicero, *De Officiis*, 3. 1. 1. Cowley's essay 'Of Solitude' opens with the words: '*Nunquam minus solus, quam cum solus*, is now become a very vulgar saying. Every Man and almost every Boy for these seventeen hundred years, has had it in his mouth. But it was at first spoken by the Excellent *Scipio* . . .' (*Essays*, ed. Waller, p. 392). Swift also quotes it in this form in the *Tritical Essay*, 1711 (*Prose Works*, ed. H. Davis, i. 249).
[3] Cf. Sir William Temple's *Essay upon the Ancient and Modern Learning* (1690): 'Besides, few men or none excel in all Faculties of Mind. A great Memory may fail

others with greater Force and Vivacity. Thus my Want of, or rather Resignation of Speech, gives me all the Advantages of a dumb Man. I have, methinks, a more than ordinary Penetration in Seeing; and flatter my self that I have looked into the Highest and Lowest of Mankind, and make shrewd Guesses, without being admitted to their Conversation, at the inmost Thoughts and Reflections of all whom I behold. It is from hence that good or ill Fortune has no manner of Force towards affecting my Judgment. I see Men flourishing in Courts and languishing in Jayls, without being prejudiced from their Circumstances to their Favour or Disadvantage; but from their inward Manner of bearing their Condition, often pity the Prosperous and admire the Unhappy.

Those who converse with the Dumb, know from the Turn of their Eyes and the Changes of their Countenance their Sentiments of the Objects before them. I have indulged my Silence to such an Extravagance, that the few who are intimate with me, answer my Smiles with concurrent Sentences, and argue to the very Point I shak'd my Head at without my speaking. WILL. HONEYCOMB was very entertaining the other Night at a Play to a Gentleman who sat on his right Hand, while I was at his Left. The Gentleman believed WILL. was talking to himself, when upon my looking with great Approbation at a young thing[a] in a Box before us, he said, 'I am quite of another Opinion: She has, I will allow, a very pleasing Aspect, but methinks that Simplicity in her Countenance is rather childish than innocent.' When I observed her a second time, he said, 'I grant her Dress is very becoming, but perhaps the Merit of that Choice is owing to her Mother; for though, continued he, I allow a Beauty to be as much to be commended for the Elegance of her Dress, as a Wit for that of his Language; yet if she has stolen the Colour of her Ribbands from another, or had Advice about her Trimmings, I shall not allow her the Praise of Dress, any more than I would call a Plagiary an Author.' When I threw my Eye towards the next Woman to her, WILL. spoke what I looked, according to his Romantick Imagination,[b] in the following Manner.

'Behold, you who dare, that charming Virgin. Behold the Beauty of her Person chastised by the Innocence of her Thoughts. Chastity,

[a] young thing] blooming Beauty *Fol.*　　　　[b] according . . . Imagination,] *om. Fol.*

of Invention, both may want Judgment to Digest or Apply what they Remember or Invent' (Spingarn, iii. 61). Pope also uses the idea in the *Essay on Criticism*, 52–67.

Good-Nature, and Affability are the Graces that play in her Countenance; she knows she is handsome, but she knows she is good. Conscious Beauty adorn'd with conscious Virtue! What a Spirit is there in those Eyes! What a Bloom in that Person! How is the whole Woman expressed in her Appearance! Her Air has the Beauty of Motion, and her Look the Force of Language.'

It was Prudence to turn away my Eyes from this Object, and therefore I turned them to the thoughtless Creatures who make up the Lump of that Sex, and move a knowing Eye no more than the Portraitures of insignificant People by ordinary Painters, which are but Pictures of Pictures.

Thus the working of my own Mind, is the general Entertainment of my Life; I never enter into the Commerce of Discourse with any but my particular Friends, and not in Publick even with them. Such an Habit has perhaps raised in me uncommon Reflections; but this Effect I cannot communicate but by my Writings. As my Pleasures are almost wholly confin'd to those of the Sight, I take it for a peculiar Happiness that I have always had an easy and familiar Admittance to the fair Sex.[1] If I never praised or flatter'd, I never belyed or contradicted them. As these compose half the World, and are by the just Complaisance and Gallantry of our Nation[2] the more powerful Part of our People, I shall dedicate a considerable Share of these my Speculations to their Service, and shall lead the Young through all the becoming Duties of Virginity, Marriage, and Widowhood. When it is a Woman's Day, in my Works, I shall endeavour at a Stile and Air suitable to their Understanding. When I say this, I must be understood to mean, that I shall not lower but exalt[3] the Subjects I treat upon. Discourse for their Entertainment, is not to be debased but refined. A Man may appear learned, without talking Sentences; as in his ordinary Gesture he discovers he can dance, tho' he does not cut Capers. In a Word, I shall take it for the greatest Glory of my Work, if among reasonable Women this Paper may furnish *Tea-Table Talk*.[4] In order to it, I shall treat on Matters which

[1] The first declaration of what is to become one of the major intentions of the *Spectator*—a concern with the dress, education, talents, proper duties, &c., of 'the most beautiful Part of the Creation' (No. 57).

[2] Foreign observers frequently comment on this characteristic of the English. 'In short, such is the *Complaisance* for the Sex in general, that it is not to be paralelled, and has given birth to the Proverb, That *England is the Paradise of Women*' (Miège, p. 220).

[3] 'To dignify, ennoble' (the earliest example in *OED* in this sense).

[4] One of Steele's later periodicals (Dec. 1715—Mar. 1716) was called *The Tea Table*.

relate to Females as they are concern'd to approach or fly from the other Sex, or as they are tyed to them by Blood, Interest, or Affection. Upon this Occasion I think it but reasonable to declare, that whatever Skill I may have in Speculation, I shall never betray what the Eyes of Lovers say to each other in my Presence. At the same Time I shall not think my self obliged by this Promise to conceal any false Protestations which I observe made by Glances in publick Assemblies; but endeavour to make both Sexes appear in their Conduct what they are in their Hearts. By this Means Love, during the Time of my Speculations, shall be carried on with the same Sincerity as any other Affair of less Consideration. As this is the greatest Concern, Men shall be from henceforth liable to the greatest Reproach for Misbehaviour in it. Falshood in Love shall hereafter bear a blacker Aspect, than Infidelity in Friendship or Villany in Business. For this great and good End, all Breaches against that noble Passion, the Cement of Society, shall be severely examined. But this and all other Matters loosely hinted at now and in my former Papers, shall have their proper Place in my following Discourses: The present writing is only to admonish the World, that they shall not find me an idle but a very busy Spectator.   R

No. 5
[ADDISON]

Tuesday, March 6, 1711[1]

Spectatum admissi risum teneatis? . . .
                                        Hor.

AN Opera may be allowed to be extravagantly lavish in its Decorations, as its only Design is to gratify the Senses, and keep up

---

[1] *Motto.* Horace, *Ars Poetica*, 5:
          Admitted to the sight, would you not laugh?

In pointing out the aesthetic absurdities of the Italian opera Addison carries on the views of the *Tatler*, which as early as No. 4 had ridiculed this form of art which affords 'the shallow Satisfaction of the Eyes and Ears only'. According to Isaac Bickerstaff (*Tatler* 4) it was Dennis who had been most affected by the operas: 'a Great Critick fell into Fits in the Gallery, at seeing, not only Time and Place, but Languages and Nations confus'd in the most incorrigible Manner.' Dennis's *Essay on the Opera's after the Italian Manner* (1706), subtitled 'with some reflections on the damage which they may bring to the public' (*Critical Works*, ed. Hooker, i. 382–93), is one of the earliest in a long line of attacks in the first half of the eighteenth century (see Hooker's note, i. 522–3, and, for satire on opera, Nicoll, pp. 230–3). Unlike

an indolent Attention in the Audience. Common Sense however requires, that there should be nothing in the Scenes and Machines which may appear Childish and Absurd. How would the Wits of King *Charles*'s Time have laughed to have seen *Nicolini*[1] exposed to a Tempest in Robes of Ermin, and sailing in an open Boat upon a Sea of Paste-Board? What a Field of Raillery would they have been let into, had they been entertain'd with painted Dragons spitting Wild-fire, enchanted Chariots drawn by *Flanders* Mares, and real Cascades in artificial Land-skips? A little Skill in Criticism would inform us that Shadows and Realities ought not to be mix'd together in the same Piece; and that Scenes, which are designed as the Representations of Nature, should be filled with Resemblances, and not with the Things themselves. If one would represent a wide Champian Country filled with Herds and Flocks, it would be ridiculous to draw the Country only upon the Scenes, and to crowd several Parts of the Stage with Sheep and Oxen. This is joining together Inconsistencies, and making the Decoration partly Real and partly Imaginary. I would recommend what I have here said, to the Directors, as well as to the Admirers, of our Modern Opera.

As I was walking in[a] the Streets about a Fortnight ago, I saw an

---

[a] in] *om. Fol.*

Addison, Dennis is concerned chiefly with the decline in manners, the failure of opera to teach public virtue and public spirit, and the danger to morality which comes from the 'effeminate Airs' of the opera. Towards the end of his essay, Dennis considers briefly its aesthetic shortcomings, and says of Italy, 'where an Opera is most advanc'd, there is no one who can write either Verse or Prose, nor any one who can judge of them' (i. 391). Addison on the whole takes the opera less seriously, and bases his attack from the point of view not of morals but of taste. During the twenty-two months of the original series of the *Spectator* its advertisements record the presentation of eleven different operas and a total of ninety performances: *Rinaldo* (20 performances), *Antiochus* (17), *Hydaspes* (16), *Almahide* (11), *Amleto* (7), *Hercules* and *Calypso and Telemachus* (5 each), *The Faithful Shepherd* (4), *Clotilda* and *The Triumph of Love* (2 each), and *Pyrrhus and Demetrius* (1).

[1] Nicola Grimaldi, known as Nicolini (1673–1732), was a Neapolitan singer, a male contralto, who had come to England in 1708. His first London appearance seems to have been on 14 Dec. 1708, in Haym's arrangement of Alessandro Scarlatti's *Pirro e Demetrio*, translated into English by Owen Swiney, the manager of the Haymarket. Nicolini sang in Italian, the rest of the cast in English. He soon became extremely popular, singing such roles as Prenesto in *Camilla*, Tigranes in *Thomyris*, *Queen of Scythia*, and the title-part in *Hydaspes* (cf. No. 13). He seems to have been a friend of both Addison and Steele. Hughes, in a letter to him, dated 4 Feb. 1709–10, says he had told Steele of the obliging manner in which Nicolini had spoken of Mr. Bicker-staff, 'en disant que vous aviez beaucoup d'inclination à étudier l'Anglois pour avoir seulement le plaisir de lire le *Tatler*' (Hughes, *Correspondence*, Dublin, 1773, i. 33–34). In *Tatler* 115 Steele pays a very high compliment to his acting ability as well as his singing. At the time of the present essay he was singing in *Rinaldo*, the new opera by Handel (see below).

ordinary Fellow carrying a Cage full of little Birds upon his Shoulder; and, as I was wondering with my self what Use he would put them to, he was met very luckily by an Acquaintance, who had the same Curiosity. Upon his asking him what he had upon his Shoulder, he told him, that he had been buying Sparrows for the Opera. Sparrows for the Opera, says his Friend, licking his Lips, what are they to be roasted? No, no, says the other, they are to enter towards the end of the first Act, and to fly about the Stage.

This strange Dialogue awakened my Curiosity so far that I immediately bought the Opera, by which means I perceived that the Sparrows were to act the part of Singing Birds in a delightful Grove: though upon a nearer Enquiry I found the Sparrows put the same Trick upon the Audience, that Sir *Martin Mar-all*[1] practised upon his Mistress; for, though they flew in Sight, the Musick proceeded from a Consort of Flagellets and Bird-calls which was planted behind the Scenes. At the same time I made this Discovery, I found by the Discourse of the Actors, that there were great Designs on foot for the Improvement of the Opera; that it had been proposed to break down a part of the Wall, and to surprize the Audience with a Party of an hundred Horse, and that there was actually a Project of bringing the *New-River*[2] into the House, to be employed in Jetteaus and Water-works. This Project, as I have since heard, is post-poned 'till the Summer-Season; when it is thought the Coolness that proceeds from Fountains and Cascades will be more acceptable and refreshing to People of Quality. In the mean time, to find out a more agreeable Entertainment for the Winter-Season, the Opera of *Rinaldo*[3] is filled with Thunder and Lightning, Illumina-

---

[1] *Sir Martin Mar-all, or the Feigned Innocence*, adapted by Dryden from the Duke of Newcastle's translation of Molière's *L'Étourdi* (and from Quinault's *L'Amant indiscret*), was first acted at Lincoln's Inn Fields Theatre on 15 Aug. 1667 (Pepys). In Act V, scene i, Sir Martin is advised by his man Warner: 'Get up into your window, and set two candles by you; take my landlord's lute in your hand, and fumble on it, and make grimaces with your mouth, as if you sung; in the meantime I'll play in the next room in the dark, and consequently your mistress, who will come to her balcony over against you, will think it to be you.' But Sir Martin 'continues fumbling, and gazing on his Mistress' after the song is concluded, and the trick is discovered. Although by no means a popular play at this time, it had had three performances in 1710, the last of which was on 4 Dec. at Drury Lane, with Bullock in the part of Sir Martin and Powell as Warner.

[2] An artificial stream of water, brought from Amwell and Chadwell through Islington to the New River Head or reservoir, whence it ran underground through wooden mains and other pipes to parts of London. The 'Jetteaus and Water-works' were a popular feature of opera presentation. *Pyrrhus and Demetrius* is advertised for performance on 3 Jan. 1710-11 'with the Addition of a New Cascade Scene after the Italian manner' (*Daily Courant*).

[3] The opera by Handel (who had just come to England, in November or December

tions, and Fireworks; which the Audience may look upon without catching Cold, and indeed without much Danger of being burnt; for there are several Engines filled with Water, and ready to play at a Minute's Warning, in case any such Accident should happen. However, as I have a very great Friendship for the Owner of this Theater,[1] I hope that he has been wise enough to *insure* his House before he would let this Opera be acted in it.

It is no wonder, that those Scenes should be very surprizing, which were contrived by two Poets of different Nations, and raised by two Magicians of different Sexes. *Armida*[2] (as we are told in the Argument) was an *Amazonian* Enchantress, and poor Seignior *Cassani* (as we learn from the *Persons represented*) a Christian Conjurer (*Mago Christiano*). I must confess I am very much puzzled to find how an *Amazon* should be versed in the Black Art, or how a good Christian, for such is the Part of the Magician, should[a] deal with the Devil.

To consider the Poets after the Conjurers, I shall give you a Taste of the *Italian*, from the first Lines of his Preface. *Eccoti, benigno Lettore,*[3] *un Parto di poche Sere, che se ben nato di Notte, non è però aborto di Tenebre, mà si farà conoscere Figlio d'Apollo con qualche Raggio di*

---

[a] how a good Christian . . . should] how a Christian should *Fol.*

1710) opened at the Haymarket on 24 Feb. The fourth performance was advertised for 6 Mar., the day this number of the *Spectator* appeared. It had nine performances during February and March, and after the pre-Easter recess was given six times, in April, May, and June—a total of fifteen performances. The libretto, based on the episode of Rinaldo and Armida in Tasso, was written in Italian by Giacomo Rossi, with an English version by Aaron Hill. (The text, Italian and English, is to be found in Hill's *Dramatic Works*, 1760, i. 71–143.) The part of Rinaldo was sung by Nicolini, that of Armida by Signora Elisabetta Piloti Schiavonetti, and that of the heroine Almirena by Isabella Girardeau. Act I, scene v, represents 'Armida in the Air, in a Chariot drawn by two huge Dragons, out of whose Mouths issue Fire and Smoke', and the following scene is 'A delightful Grove in which the Birds are heard to sing, and seen flying up and down among the Trees'. The episode of Nicolini 'in an open boat' on 'a calm and sun-shiny Sea' occurs at the beginning of Act II. Act III opens with 'A dreadful prospect of a mountain horribly steep . . .', with 'rocks, and caves, and waterfalls'. In Act I, scene iii, Argantes is 'drawn through the gate in a triumphal chariot, the horses white and led in by armed Blackamoors'.

1 The reference seems to be to Owen Swiney, who, together with Wilks, Cibber, and Doggett, had managed the Haymarket through the greater part of 1709 and 1710. In Nov. 1710 an agreement had been made whereby operas alone were to be given at the Haymarket.

2 Armida, 'Incantatrice, Regina di Damasco', was sung by Signora Elisabetta Piloti Schiavonetti, described as 'Virtuosa di S. A. E. d'Hanover'. The alto part of the Magician, 'Mago Christiano', was taken by Giuseppe Cassani, who had come to London from Italy in 1708.

3 The opening words of the preface, 'Il Poeta al Lettore', and signed Giacomo Rossi. He speaks of 'il signor Hendel, Orfeo del nostro secolo', who, to Rossi's amazement, had composed the music in two weeks' time.

*Parnasso. Behold, gentle Reader, the Birth of a few Evenings, which tho'
it be the Offspring of the Night, is not the Abortive of Darkness, but will
make it self known to be the Son of* Apollo, *with a certain Ray of* Parnassus.
He afterwards proceeds to call Minheer[a] *Hendel* the *Orpheus* of our
Age, and to acquaint us, in the same Sublimity of Stile, that he
Composed this Opera in a Fortnight. Such are the Wits, to whose
Tastes we so ambitiously conform our selves. The Truth of it is, the
finest Writers among the Modern *Italians*, express themselves in
such a florid form of Words, and such tedious Circumlocutions, as
are used by none but Pedants in our own Country; and at the same
time, fill their Writings with such poor Imaginations and Conceits,
as our Youths are ashamed of, before they have been Two Years at
the University. Some may be apt to think, that it is the difference
of Genius which produces this difference in the Works of the two
Nations; but to show there is nothing in this, if we look into the
Writings of the old *Italians*, such as *Cicero* and *Virgil*, we shall find
that the *English* Writers, in their way of thinking and expressing
themselves, resemble those Authors much more than the Modern
Italians pretend to do. And as for the Poet himself, from whom the
Dreams of this Opera are taken, I must entirely agree with Monsieur
Boileau, that one Verse in *Virgil*, is worth all the *Clincant* or Tinsel
of *Tasso*.[1]

But to return to the Sparrows; there have been so many Flights
of them let loose in this Opera, that it is feared the House will never
get rid of them; and that in other Plays, they may make their
Entrance in very wrong and improper Scenes, so as to be seen

[a] Minheer] Seignior *Fol. Corrected in Errata (No. 6)*

---

[1] Boileau, *Satires* 9. 176. According to A. F. B. Clark (*Boileau and the French Classical
Critics in England*, Paris, 1925, p. 338) none of Boileau's judgements 'had such a success
as that terse one in which he contrasted "Tasso's tinsel" with "Virgil's gold"'. Bk.
IV, chap. iv of Clark's work deals with Tasso's reputation at this time and discusses
the influence of this passage in the *Spectator*. It was not until the publication of Hurd's
Letters on Chivalry and Romance in 1762 that Tasso's prestige began to recover from
this double blow. In No. ix of the *Letters* Hurd writes: 'A lucky word in a verse,
which sounds well and every body gets by heart, goes further than a volume of just
criticism. In short, the exact, but cold Boileau happened to say something of the
clinquant of Tasso; and the magic of this word, like the report of Astolfo's horn in
Ariosto, overturned at once the solid and well-built reputation of the *Italian* poetry.
It is not perhaps strange that this potent word should do its business in *France*. What
was less to be expected, it put us into a fright on this side the water. Mr. Addison,
who gave the law in taste here, took it up, and sent it about the kingdom in his
polite and popular essays. It became a sort of watchword among the critics; and,
on the sudden, nothing was heard, on all sides, but the *clinquant* of Tasso' (*Works*,
1811, iv. 314).

flying in a Lady's Bed-Chamber, or pearching upon a King's Throne; besides the Inconveniencies which the Heads of the Audience may sometimes suffer from them. I am credibly informed, that there was once a Design of casting into an Opera, the Story of *Whittington*[1] and his Cat, and that in order to it, there had been got together a great Quantity of Mice; but Mr. *Rich*,[2] the Proprietor of the Play-House, very prudently considered that it would be impossible for the Cat to kill them all, and that consequently the Princes of his Stage might be as much infested with Mice, as the Prince of the Island was before the Cat's arrival upon it; for which Reason, he would not permit it to be Acted in his House. And indeed I cannot blame him; for, as he said very well upon that Occasion, I do not hear that any of the Performers in our Opera, pretend to equal the famous Pied Piper, who made all the Mice of a great Town in *Germany* follow his Musick, and by that means cleared the Place of those little Noxious Animals.

Before I dismiss this Paper, I must inform my Reader, that I hear there is a Treaty on Foot with *London* and *Wise*[3] (who will be appointed Gardiners of the Play-House)[a] to furnish the Opera of *Rinaldo* and *Armida* with an Orange-Grove; and that the next time it is Acted, the Singing Birds will be Personated by Tom-Tits: The Undertakers being resolved to spare neither Pains nor Mony, for the Gratification of the Audience.   C

---

[a] *Wise* (who ... Play-House)] *Wise*, who ... Play-House, *Fol. Corrected to parentheses in Errata (No. 6)*

---

[1] For this puppet 'opera' see No. 14.

[2] Christoper Rich for many years controlled Drury Lane Theatre, where he had revived such English operas as *The Tempest* and *King Arthur*, with elaborate stage effects, and later successfully introduced Italian opera. Addison is here doubtless thinking of these earlier productions of opera at Drury Lane; by this time Rich had been restrained by an order of silence from exercising his patent, and could in no sense be regarded as the proprietor of either house. He died on 4 Nov. 1714.

[3] The famous firm of gardeners, whose nursery at Brompton Park, near Kensington, helped to popularize the fashion of formal Dutch gardens. George London founded the nursery in 1681 and took into partnership Henry Wise, who after London's death in 1714 was appointed 'Master Gardner of all his Majesty's Royal Gardens and Plantations in *England*' (*Pol. State*, Jan. 1715, p. 57). Their abridgement of J. de La Quintinie's *Compleat Gard'ner* was published in 1699 (reprinted 1704 and 1710), and in 1706 Tonson published a compilation under the title *The Retir'd Gard'ner* in two volumes. Volume I was translated from *Le Jardinier solitaire* by F. Gentil, and Volume II from *Le Jardinier fleuriste et historiographe* by L. Liger. The whole work is announced as 'Revis'd, with several Alterations and Additions, which render it proper for our English Culture', by George London and Henry Wise. This is one of Tonson's publications most frequently advertised in the *Spectator*. For the contribution of Wise to the art of the formal garden see David Green, *Gardener to Queen Anne* (1956).

No. 6   *Wednesday, March 7, 1711*[1]
[STEELE]

> *Credebant hoc grande Nefas, & Morte piandum,*
> *Si Juvenis Vetulo non assurrexerat . . .*
>
> Juv.

I KNOW no Evil under the Sun so great as the Abuse of the Understanding, and yet there is no one Vice more common. It has diffus'd it self through both Sexes and all Qualities of Mankind; and there is hardly that Person to be found, who is not more concern'd for the Reputation of Wit and Sense, than Honesty and Virtue. But this unhappy Affectation of being Wise rather than Honest, Witty than Good-natur'd, is the Source of most of the ill Habits of Life. Such false Impressions are owing to the abandon'd Writings of Men of Wit, and the awkard Imitation of the rest of Mankind.

For this Reason, Sir ROGER was saying last Night, That he was of Opinion none but Men of fine Parts deserve to be hanged. The Reflections of such Men are so delicate upon all Occurrences which they are concern'd in, that they should be expos'd to more than ordinary Infamy and Punishment, for offending against such quick Admonitions as their own Souls give them, and blunting the fine Edge of their Minds in such a Manner, that they are no more shocked at Vice and Folly, than Men of slower Capacities. There is no greater Monster in Being, than a very ill Man of great Parts: He lives like a Man in a Palsy, with one Side of him dead. While perhaps he enjoys the Satisfaction of Luxury, of Wealth, of Ambition, he has lost the Taste of Good-will, of Friendship, of Innocence. *Scarecrow*, the Beggar in *Lincoln's-Inn-Fields*, who disabled himself in his Right-Leg, and asks Alms all Day to get himself a warm Supper and a Trull at Night, is not half so despicable a Wretch as such a Man of Sense. The Beggar has no Relish above Sensations; he finds Rest more agreeable than Motion; and while he has a warm Fire and his Doxy, never reflects that he deserves to be whipped. Every Man who terminates his Satisfactions and Enjoyments within the Supply of his own Necessities and Passions, is, says Sir ROGER, in my Eye

---

[1] *Motto.* Juvenal, *Satires*, 13. 54–55:
It was looked upon as a great sin, worthy of death, if a young man did not rise before an elder.

as poor a Rogue as *Scarecrow*. But, continued he, for the Loss of publick and private Virtue, we are beholden to your Men of Parts forsooth; it is with them no matter what is done, so it is done with an Air. But to me who am so whimsical in a corrupt Age as to act according to Nature and Reason, a selfish Man in the most shining Circumstance and Equipage, appears in the same Condition with the Fellow abovementioned, but more contemptible, in Proportion to what more he robs the Publick of and enjoys above him. I lay it down therefore for a Rule, That the whole Man is to move together; that every Action of any Importance, is to have a Prospect of publick Good; and that the general Tendency of our indifferent Actions, ought to be agreeable to the Dictates of Reason, of Religion, of good Breeding; without this, a Man, as I before have hinted, is hopping instead of walking, he is not in his entire and proper Motion.

While the honest Knight was thus bewildering himself in good Starts, I look'd intentively[1] upon him, which made him I thought collect his Mind a little. What I aim at, says he, is, to represent, That I am of Opinion, to polish our Understandings and neglect our Manners is of all things the most inexcusable. Reason should govern Passion, but instead of that, you see, it is often subservient to it; and as unaccountable as one would think it, a wise Man is not always a good Man. This Degeneracy is not only the Guilt of particular Persons, but also at some times of a whole People; and perhaps it may appear upon Examination, that the most polite Ages are the least virtuous. This may be attributed to the Folly of admitting Wit and Learning as Merit in themselves, without considering the Application of them. By this Means it becomes a Rule, not so much to regard what we do, as how we do it. But this false Beauty will not pass upon Men of honest Minds and true Taste: Sir *Richard Blackmore*[2] says, with as much good Sense as Virtue, *It is a mighty Dishonour and Shame to employ excellent Faculties and abundance of Wit, to humour and please Men in their Vices and Follies. The great Enemy of Mankind, notwithstanding his Wit and Angelick Faculties, is the most odious Being in the whole Creation.* He goes on soon after to say very generously, That he undertook the writing of his Poem *to*

---

[1] Intentively, i.e. intently. This quotation is the last in *OED* for this word, which is marked *Obs.* or *arch.*

[2] Preface to *Prince Arthur*, 1695 (Spingarn, iii. 233–4). Steele omits the second sentence from the passage: 'Such a one is more hateful as an *ill Man* than valuable as a *good Poet*.'

rescue the Muses out of the Hands of Ravishers, to restore them to their sweet and chaste Mansions, and to engage them in an Employment suitable to their Dignity. This certainly ought to be the Purpose of every Man who appears in Publick; and whoever does not proceed upon that Foundation, injures his Country as fast as he succeeds in his Studies. When Modesty[1] ceases to be the chief Ornament of one Sex, and Integrity of the other, Society is upon a wrong Basis, and we shall be ever after without Rules to guide our Judgment in what is really becoming and ornamental. Nature and Reason direct one thing, Passion and Humour another: To follow the Dictates of the two latter, is going into a Road that is both endless and intricate; when we pursue the other, our Passage is delightful, and what we aim at easily attainable.

I do not doubt but *England* is at present as polite a Nation as any in the World; but any Man who thinks can easily see, that the Affectation of being gay and in fashion has very near eaten up our good Sense and our Religion. Is there any thing so just, as that Mode and Gallantry should be built upon exerting our selves in what is proper and agreeable to the Institutions of Justice and Piety among us? And yet is there any thing more common, than that we run in perfect Contradiction to them? All which is supported by no other Pretension, than that it is done with what we call a good Grace.

Nothing ought to be held laudable or becoming, but what Nature it self should prompt us to think so. Respect to all kind of Superiours is founded methinks upon Instinct; and yet what is so ridiculous as Age? I make this abrupt Transition to the Mention of this Vice more than any other, in order to introduce a little Story,[2] which I think a pretty Instance that the most polite Age is in danger of being the most vicious.

'It happen'd at *Athens*, during a publick Representation of some Play exhibited in honour of the Common-wealth, that an old Gentleman came too late for a Place suitable to his Age and Quality. Many of the young Gentlemen who observed the Difficulty and Confusion he was in, made Signs to him that they would accommodate him if he came where they sate: The good Man bustled through the Crowd

---

[1] Cf. *Tatler* 84: 'There is nothing in Woman so graceful and becoming as Modesty. . . . Without it, Simplicity and Innocence appear rude, Reading and good Sense masculine, Wit and Humour lascivious.'

[2] Plutarch, 'Sayings of Spartans', *Moralia* 235C–235E; Cicero, *De Senectute*, 18. 63. Budgell later uses it in *A Letter to Cleomenes* (1731), pp. 158–9.

accordingly; but when he came to the Seats to which he was invited, the Jest was to sit close, and expose him, as he stood out of Countenance, to the whole Audience. The Frolick went round all the *Athenian* Benches. But on those Occasions there were also particular Places assigned for Foreigners: When the good Man skulked towards the Boxes appointed for the *Lacedemonians*, that honest People, more virtuous than polite, rose up all to a Man, and with the greatest Respect received him among them. The *Athenians* being suddenly touch'd with a Sense of the *Spartan* Virtue and their own Degeneracy, gave a Thunder of Applause; and the old Man cry'd out, *The* Athenians *understand what is good, but the* Lacedemonians *practice it.*'

R

No. 7   *Thursday, March 8*, 1711[1]
[ADDISON]

Somnia, terrores magicos, miracula, Sagas,
Nocturnos lemures, portentaque Thessala rides?
                                                            Hor.

GOING Yesterday to Dine with an old Acquaintance, I had the Misfortune to find his whole Family very much dejected. Upon asking him the Occasion of it, he told me that his Wife had dreamt a very strange Dream the Night before, which they were afraid portended some Misfortune to themselves or to their Children. At her coming into the Room I observed a settled Melancholy in her Countenance, which I should have been troubled for, had I not heard from whence it proceeded. We were no sooner sat down, but, after having looked upon me a little while, *My Dear*, says she, turning to her Husband, *you may now see the Stranger*[2] *that was in the Candle last Night.* Soon after this, as they began to talk of Family Affairs, a little Boy at the lower end of the Table told her, that he

---

[1] *Motto.* Horace, *Epistles*, 2. 2. 208–9:
  Dreams, terrors of magic, marvels, witches, nocturnal ghosts, and portents of Thessaly . . . do you laugh at these?
[2] 'Any of the things which are popularly imagined to forebode the coming of an unexpected visitor, e.g. a floating tea-leaf in the cup; an excrescence on the wick of a candle, causing guttering; a piece of soot flapping on the bar of the grate; a moth flying towards one' (*OED*). The earliest example in *OED* is dated 1838.

was to go into Join-hand[1] on *Thursday*: Thursday? says she, *no Child, if it please God, you shall not begin upon* Childermas-day;[2] *tell your Writing-Master that* Friday *will be soon enough*. I was Reflecting with my self on the Odness of her Fancy, and wondering that any Body would establish it as a Rule to lose a Day in every Week. In the midst of these my Musings she desired me to reach her a little Salt upon the Point of my Knife, which I did in such a Trepidation and hurry of Obedience, that I let it drop by the way; at which she immediately startled, and said it fell towards her. Upon this I looked very blank; and, observing the Concern of the whole Table, began to consider my self, with some Confusion, as a Person that had brought a Disaster upon the Family. The Lady however recovering her self, after a little space, said to her Husband with a Sigh, *My Dear, Misfortunes never come Single*. My Friend, I found, acted but an under Part at his Table, and being a Man of more Good-nature than Understanding, thinks himself obliged to fall in with all the Passions and Humours of his Yoke-fellow: *Do not you remember, Child*, says she, *that the Pidgeon-House fell the very Afternoon that our careless Wench spilt the Salt upon the Table? Yes*, says he, *My Dear, and the next Post brought us an Account of the Battel of* Almanza.[3] The Reader may guess at the Figure I made, after having done all this Mischief. I dispatched my Dinner as soon as I could, with my usual Taciturnity; when, to my utter Confusion, the Lady seeing me quitting[a] my Knife and Fork, and laying them across one another upon my Plate, desired me that I would humour her so far as to take them out of that Figure, and place them side by side. What the Absurdity was which I had committed I did not know, but I suppose

---

[a] quitting] cleaning *Fol.*

[1] Cursive handwriting. *The Paul's Scholar's Copy Book*, by John Rayner, 'containing the Round and Round-Text Hands, with Alphabets at large of the Greek and Hebrew, and Joyning Pieces of each', is advertised in *Tatler* 144.

[2] Childermas-day, or Innocents' Day (28 Dec.) 'used to be reckoned about the most unlucky throughout the year, and in former times, no one who could possibly avoid it, began any work, or entered on any undertaking, on this anniversary' (Chambers's *Book of Days*). See also Lean, *Collectanea*, ii. 235. The reference to losing 'a day in every week' is not clear; possibly in the first draft of the essay an allusion had been made to Friday as an unlucky day for beginning work.

[3] Lord Galway was defeated here on 25 Apr. (N.S.) 1707, in a decisive battle of the war in Spain. The unhappy news reached England on 31 May, O.S. (Postscript to *Post Boy*, 2 June 1707). Almanza had recently been called to public attention, when the House of Lords in Jan. 1711 made an extended inquiry into the affairs of Spain. The Earl of Galway was summoned to appear before the Lords on 6 Jan., and a long and acrimonious debate followed, reported in the *Political State of Great Britain*, Feb. 1711, pp. 74-183.

there was some traditionary Superstition in it; and therefore, in obedience to the Lady of the House, I disposed of my Knife and Fork in two parallel Lines, which is the figure I shall always lay them in for the future, tho' I do not know any Reason for it.

It is not difficult for a Man to see that a Person has conceived an Aversion to him. For my own part, I quickly found, by the Lady's Looks, that she regarded me as a very odd kind of Fellow, with an unfortunate Aspect: For which Reason I took my leave immediately after Dinner, and withdrew to my own Lodgings. Upon my Return home, I fell into a profound Contemplation on the Evils that attend these superstitious Follies[1] of Mankind; how they subject us to imaginary Afflictions, and additional Sorrows that do not properly come within our Lot. As if the natural Calamities of Life were not sufficient for it, we turn the most indifferent Circumstances into Misfortunes, and suffer as much from trifling Accidents, as from real Evils. I have known the shooting of a Star spoil a Night's Rest, and have seen a Man in Love grow pale and lose his Appetite, upon the plucking of a Merry-thought.[2] A Screech-Owl at Midnight has alarm'd a Family, more than a Band of Robbers; nay, the Voice of a Cricket hath struck more Terrour, than the Roaring of a Lion. There is nothing so inconsiderable, which[a] may not appear dreadful to an Imagination that is filled with Omens and Prognosticks. A Rusty Nail, or a crooked Pin, shoot up into Prodigies.

I remember I was once in a mixt Assembly, that was full of Noise and Mirth, when on a sudden an old Woman unluckily observed there were thirteen of us in Company. This Remark struck a pannick Terror into several who[b] were present, insomuch that one or two of the Ladies were going to leave the Room; but a Friend of mine taking notice that one of our female Companions was

---

[a] which] that Fol.   [b] who] that Fol.

---

[1] Many of these are discussed in John Trenchard's *Natural History of Superstition*, published by Mrs. Baldwin on 15 Apr. 1709 (*Daily Courant*) and frequently advertised by her. It is largely devoted to exposing visionaries and fanatics, melancholy and hypochondriacal persons. 'Nor are there wanting People otherwise of good understanding, who are affected with the falling of a Salt-Seller, crossing of a Hare, croaking of a Raven, howling of Dogs, screaching of Owls, the motion of Worms in a Bed-steed, mistaken for Death-Watches, and other as sensles and trifling Accidents' (p. 11).
[2] The custom of pulling apart the wish-bone of an owl. The term 'merry-thought' is derived, according to the *British Apollo* (1 Dec. 1708), 'from the Pleasant Fancies, that commonly arise upon the Breaking of that Bone'.

big with Child, affirm'd there were fourteen in the Room, and that instead of portending one of the Company should die, it plainly foretold one of them should be born. Had not my Friend found this Expedient to break the Omen, I question not but half the Women in the Company would have fallen sick that very Night.

An old Maid, that is troubled with the Vapours, produces infinite Disturbances of this kind among her Friends and Neighbours. I know a Maiden Aunt, of a great Family, who is one of these Anti-quated *Sybils*, that forebodes and prophesies from one end of the Year to the other. She is always seeing Apparitions, and hearing Death-Watches; and was the other Day almost frighted out of her Wits by the great House-Dog, that howled in the Stable at a time when she lay ill of the Tooth-ach. Such an extravagant Cast of Mind engages Multitudes of People, not only in impertinent Terrors, but in supernumerary Duties of Life, and arises from that Fear and Ignorance which are natural to the Soul of Man. The Horrour with which we entertain the Thoughts of Death (or indeed of any future Evil) and the Uncertainty of its Approach, fill a melancholy Mind with innumerable Apprehensions and Suspicions, and consequently dispose it to the Observation of such groundless Prodigies and Predictions. For as it is the chief Concern of Wise-Men, to retrench the Evils of Life by the Reasonings of Philosophy; it is the Employ-ment of Fools, to multiply them by the Sentiments of Superstition.

For my own part, I should be very much troubled were I en-dowed with this Divining Quality, though it should inform me truly of every thing that can befall me. I would not anticipate the Relish of any Happiness, nor feel the Weight of any Misery, before it actually arrives.

I know but one way of fortifying my Soul against these gloomy Presages and Terrours of Mind, and that is, by securing to my self the Friendship and Protection of that Being, who disposes of Events, and governs Futurity. He sees, at one View, the whole Thread of my Existence, not only that Part of it which I have already pass'd through, but that which runs forward into all the Depths of Eternity. When I lay me down to Sleep, I recommend my self to his Care; when I awake, I give my self up to his Direction. Amidst all the Evils that threaten me, I will look up to him for Help, and question not but he will either avert them, or turn them to my Advantage. Though I know neither the Time nor the Manner of the Death I am to die, I am not at all sollicitous about it, because I am sure that he knows them both, and that he will not fail to comfort and support me under them.[a]   C

No. 8   *Friday, March 9, 1711*[1]

[ADDISON]

> *At* Venus *obscuro gradientes aere sepsit,*
> *Et multo Nebulæ circum Dea fudit amictu,*
> *Cernere ne quis eos . . .*
>   Virg.

I SHALL here communicate to the World a couple of Letters, which I believe will give the Reader as good an Entertainment as any that I am able to furnish him[b] with, and therefore shall make no Apology for them.

To the SPECTATOR, &c.

SIR,

'I AM one of the Directors of the Society for the Reformation of Manners,[2] and therefore think my self a proper Person for your Correspondence. I have thoroughly examined the present State of Religion in *Great-Britain*, and am able to acquaint you with the predominant Vice of every Market-Town in the whole Island. I can tell you the Progress that Virtue has made in all our Cities, Boroughs, and Corporations; and know as well the evil Practices that are committed in *Berwick* or *Exeter*, as what is done in my own Family. In a Word, Sir, I have my Correspondents in the remotest

---

[a] *Letters are Directed for the* Spectator, *to be left with Mr.* Buckley *at the* Dolphin *in* Little-Britain. *Fol.*   [b] him] them *Fol.*

---

[1] *Motto.* Virgil, *Aeneid*, 1. 411–13:
> They march obscure, for *Venus* kindly shrowds,
> With Mists, their Persons, and involves in Clouds:
> That, thus unseen, their Passage none might stay,
> Or force to tell the Causes of their Way. DRYDEN.

[2] Several societies began to be formed for this purpose early in the reign of William and Mary and published annual reports of their progress 'in suppressing profaneness and debauchery'. They are described in Tutchin's *Observator* (24 Mar. 1702/3), which gives a specimen of the Agreement to which members subscribe. Josiah Woodward's *Account of the Societies for Reformation of Manners in England and Ireland* (1698) reached an 11th edition by 1702.

Parts of the Nation, who send me up punctual Accounts from time to time of all the little Irregularities that fall under their Notice in their several Districts and Divisions.

'I am no less acquainted with the particular Quarters and Regions of this great Town, than with the different Parts and Distributions of the whole Nation. I can describe every Parish by its Impieties, and can tell you in which of our Streets Lewdness prevails, which Gaming has taken the Possession of, and where Drunkenness has got the better of them both. When I am disposed to raise a Fine for the Poor, I know the Lanes and Allies that are inhabited by common Swearers.[1] When I would encourage the Hospital of *Bridewell*[2] and improve the Hempen Manufacture, I am very well acquainted with all the Haunts and Resorts of Female Nightwalkers.

'After this short Account of my self, I must let you know, that the Design of this Paper is to give you Information of a certain irregular Assembly which I think falls very properly under your Observation, especially since the Persons it is composed of are Criminals too considerable for the Animadversions of our Society. I mean, Sir, the Midnight Masque,[3] which has of late been very frequently held in one of the most conspicuous Parts of the Town, and which I hear will be continued with Additions and Improvements. As all the Persons who compose this lawless Assembly are masqued, we dare not attack any of them in *our Way*, lest we should send a Woman of Quality to *Bridewell* or a Peer of *Great-Britain* to the *Counter*:[4]

[1] The curing of a common swearer is described in *Tatler* 13.
[2] Founded in 1553, this was a hospital or asylum for decayed tradesmen and also 'a House of Correction for idle Vagrants, loose and disorderly Servants, Nightwalkers, Strumpets, &c.' (Hatton, p. 734). It was situated near St. Bride's Church, near the east end of Fleet Street. Ned Ward's *London Spy*, part vi, contains a description of the occupants of both sexes beating hemp.
[3] Masquerades, held at Lambeth-Wells, Spring Garden, and elsewhere, were the cause of much scandal. Belinda, in Pope's *Rape of the Lock*, is warned against the dangers of 'Courtly Balls, and Midnight Masquerades' (i. 72). The following advertisement appears in No. 53:

At the Request of several Foreigners lately arrived, The Masquerade in Old Spring Garden, Charing Cross, will be this present Tuesday, being the First Day of May. Note, That upon this Occasion a Gentleman is pleased to give for the Diversion of the Masquers, an Entertainment of Musick, both Vocal and Instrumental, by some of the best Masters in London. This Entertainment will begin exactly at Ten a Clock. Tickets may be had at Mr. Thurmonds's in King's Court, Russel-street, Covent-Garden, and at the House in Spring Garden; price Half a Guinea. No person whatsoever to be admitted Unmask'd or Arm'd.

Another, to be held on 5 Dec. 1711, is advertised in No. 239 (vol. ii).
[4] The Counter was a prison attached to a city court, where debtors and night revellers were sent to await trial. There was one in the Poultry.

Besides, that their Numbers are so very great, that I am afraid they would be able to rout our whole Fraternity, tho' we were accompanied with all our Guard of Constables. Both these Reasons which secure them from our Authority, make them obnoxious to yours; As both their Disguise and their Numbers will give no particular Person Reason to think himself affronted by you.

'If we are rightly inform'd, the Rules that are observed by this new Society are wonderfully contriv'd for the Advancement of Cuckoldom. The Women either come by themselves or are introduced by Friends, who are obliged to quit them upon their first Entrance, to the Conversation of any Body that addresses himself to them. There are several Rooms where the Parties may retire, and, if they please, show their Faces by Consent. Whispers, Squeezes, Nods, and Embraces, are the innocent Freedoms of the Place. In short, the whole Design of this libidinous Assembly seems to terminate in Assignations and Intrigues; and I hope you will take effectual Methods by your publick Advice and Admonitions, to prevent such a promiscuous Multitude of both Sexes from meeting together in so clandestine a Manner.

I am,
Your humble Servant,
And Fellow-Labourer,
T. B.'

Not long after the Perusal of this Letter I received another upon the same Subject; which by the Date and Stile of it, I take to be written by some young Templer.

SIR,   *Middle-Temple,* 1710–11.

'WHEN a Man has been guilty of any Vice or Folly, I think the best Attonement he can make for it is to warn others not to fall into the like. In order to this I must acquaint you, that some Time in *February* last I went to the *Tuesday's* Masquerade. Upon my first going in I was attacked by half a Dozen female Quakers, who seem'd willing to adopt me for a Brother; but upon a nearer Examination I found they were a Sisterhood of Coquets disguised in that precise Habit. I was soon after taken out to dance, and as I fancied, by a Woman of the first Quality, for she was very tall, and moved gracefully. As soon as the Minuet was over, we ogled one another through our Masques; and as I am very well read in *Waller,*

37

I repeated to her the four following Verses out of his Poem to
Vandike.

> *The heedless Lover does not know*
> *Whose Eyes they are that wound him so;*
> *But confounded with thy Art,*
> *Enquires her Name that has his Heart.*[1]

I pronounced these Words with such a languishing Air, that I had
some Reason to conclude I had made a Conquest. She told me that
she hoped my Face was not akin to my Tongue; and looking upon
her Watch, I accidentally discovered the Figure of a Coronet on the
back Part of it. I was so transported with the Thought of such an
Amour, that I plied her from one Room to another with all the
Gallantries I could invent; and at length brought things to so happy
an Issue, that she gave me a private Meeting the next Day, without
Page or Footman, Coach or Equipage. My Heart danced in Raptures;
but I had not lived in this golden Dream above three Days, before
I found good Reason to wish that I had continued true to my
Landress. I have since heard by a very great Accident, that this fine
Lady does not live far from *Covent-Garden,* and that I am not the
first Cully whom she has pass'd her self upon for a Countess.

'Thus, Sir, you see how I have mistaken a *Cloud* for a *Juno;*[2] and
if you can make any use of this Adventure, for the Benefit of those
who may possibly be as vain young Coxcombs as my self, I do most
heartily give you Leave.

I am,

SIR,

Your most humble Admirer,

B. L.'

I design to visit the next Masquerade my self, in the same Habit
I wore at *Grand Cairo*; and till then shall suspend my Judgment of
this Midnight Entertainment.[3]   C

---

[1] Waller, *To Vandyck*, 5–8.

[2] When Jupiter discovered that his guest Ixion had fallen in love with Juno, he
ordered that 'one of the Queens Maids of Honour called *Nephele*, or *Cloud*, should be
dressed with the Queens Apparel, and brought to *Ixion*, who enjoy'd her, thinking
it was the Queen her self' (Danet, 'Ixion').

[3] In *Tatler* 215 Mr. Bickerstaff makes a similar reply to the Petition of Linendrapers
complaining of naked bosoms: 'Before I answer this Petition, I am inclined to examine
the Offenders my self.'

> *. . . Tigris agit rabidâ cum tigride pacem*
> *Perpetuam, sævis inter se convenit ursis.*
>
> Juv.

MAN is said to be a Sociable Animal,[2] and, as an Instance of it, we may observe, that we take all Occasions and Pretences of forming our selves into those little Nocturnal Assemblies, which are commonly known by the Name of *Clubs*.[3] When a Sett of Men find themselves agree in any Particular, tho' never so trivial, they establish themselves into a kind of Fraternity, and meet once or twice a Week, upon the Account of such a Fantastick Resemblance. I know a considerable Market-town, in which there was a Club of Fat-Men,[4] that did not come together (as you may well suppose) to entertain one another with Sprightliness and Wit, but to keep one another in Countenance: The Room, where the Club met, was something of the largest, and had two Entrances, the one by a Door of a moderate Size, and the other by a Pair of Folding-Doors. If a Candidate for this Corpulent Club could make his Entrance through the first, he was looked upon as unqualifyed; but if he stuck in the Passage, and could not force his Way through it, the Folding-Doors were immediately thrown open for his Reception, and he was saluted as a Brother. I have heard that this Club, tho' it consisted but of fifteen Persons, weighed above three Tun.

In Opposition to this Society, there sprung up another composed of Scare-Crows and Skeletons, who being very meagre and envious,

---

[1] *Motto*. Juvenal, *Satires*, 15. 163–4:
       Tiger with tiger, bear with bear, you'll find
       In leagues offensive and defensive join'd. TATE.

[2] Aristotle, *Politics*, 1252B.

[3] Addison's description of these (some actual and others clearly fictitious) is one of the important contemporary accounts of an institution which was to play so large a part in eighteenth-century social life; many other clubs are described in later papers. Ned Ward's *Secret History of the Clubs* (1709), later expanded into the *Satyrical Reflections on Clubs*, gives an equally vivid if less decorous account. In 1711 was published the curious little book by James Puckle entitled *The Club: or a Dialogue between Father and Son*, the history of which is described in Austin Dobson's *Eighteenth Century Vignettes* (3rd ser.). John Timbs's *Clubs and Club Life in London* (1872) gives much curious information on the subject; the best recent account is *The Clubs of Augustan London*, by Robert J. Allen (Cambridge, Mass., 1933).

[4] Like the 'Scare-Crows and Skeletons' this belongs to the class of imaginary clubs so popular in Queen Anne literature as the vehicle for personal and political satire (see Allen, chap. iii, 'The Fictitious Club').

did all they could to thwart the Designs of their Bulky Brethren, whom they represented as Men of Dangerous Principles; till at length they worked them out of the Favour of the People, and consequently out of the Magistracy. These Factions tore the Corporation in Pieces for several Years, till at length they came to this Accommodation; that the two Bailiffs of the Town should be annually chosen out of the two Clubs; by which Means the principal Magistrates are at this Day coupled like Rabbets,[1] one fat and one lean.

Every one has heard of the Club, or rather the Confederacy, of the *Kings*.[2] This grand Alliance was formed a little after the Return of King *Charles* the Second, and admitted into it Men of all Qualities and Professions, provided they agreed in this Sir-name of *King*, which, as they imagined, sufficiently declared the Owners of it to be altogether untainted with Republican and Anti-Monarchical Principles.

A Christian Name[3] has likewise been often used as a Badge of Distinction, and made the Occasion of a Club. That of the *George*'s,

---

[1] By coupling them the game-dealer was able to get rid of the lean ones. Cf. Swift's *Complete Collection of Genteel and Ingenious Conversation* (1738), where (Dialogue 3) Lady Smart says: 'You must know, the Man and his Wife are coupled like Rabbets, a fat and a lean . . .' (p. 194).

[2] Club of the Kings. The following announcement appears in the *Daily Courant* of 28 May 1703:

A General Meeting of the Surname of *KING*, being appointed to be held at Mr. *John King*'s at the Rummer Tavern in *White-Chappel*, *London*, on Saturday the 29th of this instant *May* 1703. And whereas there may be many Persons of that Surname, whose Habitations the Stewards do not know, they are desir'd to take Tickets (for 2s. 6d.) at the Rummer above mention'd, or from Mr. *King* at the King's-Arms Tavern in *Wild-street* near *Lincolns-Inn-Fields*, or from Mr. *King* at the Feathers in *Warwick-Lane*.

[3] The Club of Georges, 'still fresh in every one's Memory', Allen considers (p. 176) as fictitious. There is evidence, however, that surnames at least provided an excuse for establishing such 'a kind of Fraternity'. The *Post-Man* for 26 Oct. 1703 announces that 'In respect to the antient Name of WESTON, several Gentlemen of the same Name, are, for better Society, desirous to meet at the House of Tho. Weston, being the Red Lyon and Ball in the Old Baily, on the 5th of Nov. next, at 2 of the Clock Afternoon'. Two years later, 'All Gentlemen and others whose Sirnames are Abraham' are likewise desired to meet others of the like name, 'to constitute a Friendly meeting' (*Post-Man*, 27 and 30 Oct. 1705). 'A Mutual Society of the Name of Clark' meets 'at J. Clark's at the Thatcht House in Ave-mary Lane near Pater-Noster-Row', we read in the *Daily Courant* of 25 Feb. 1706: 'All Gentlemen and Tradesmen are desir'd to meet their Name-sakes at the Place aforesaid every Monday Evening, between the Hours of Six and Eight.' Clubs were formed also on geographical bases. 'For the Encouragement of Trade and Mutual Society, several Persons Natives of the County of WILTS, do intend to meet every Wednesday at 3 a Clock, at the Ship and Castle Tavern in Cornhil' (*Post-Man*, 16 Feb. 1702/3). 'A Club or Society of Men born in the City and County of Gloucester' met on Wednesdays 'at the Sign of the City of Bristol in Friday-street, Cheapside' (*Post-Man*, 16 Jan. 1705 and 20 Aug. 1706).

which used to meet at the Sign of the *George*, on St. *George's* Day, and swear *Before George*, is still fresh in every one's Memory.

There are at present in several Parts of this City, what they call *Street-Clubs*, in which the chief Inhabitants of the Street converse together every Night. I remember, upon my enquiring after Lodgings in *Ormond-Street*,[1] the Landlord, to recommend that Quarter of the Town, told me, there was at that time a very good Club in it; he also told me, upon further Discourse with him, that two or three noisy Country Squires, who were settled there the Year before, had considerably sunk the Price of House-Rent; and that the Club (to prevent the like Inconveniencies for the future) had thoughts of taking every House that became vacant into their own Hands, till they had found a Tenant for it, of a Sociable Nature and good Conversation.

The *Hum-Drum* Club,[2] of which I was formerly an unworthy Member, was made up of very honest Gentlemen, of peaceable Dispositions, that used to sit together, smoak their Pipes, and say nothing 'till Mid-night. The *Mum* Club[3] (as I am informed) is an Institution of the same Nature, and as great an Enemy to Noise.

After these two innocent Societies, I cannot forbear mentioning a very mischievous one, that was erected in the Reign of King *Charles* the Second: I mean, *the Club of Duellists*,[4] in which none was to be admitted that had not fought his Man. The President of it was said to have killed half a dozen in single Combat; and as for the other Members, they took their Seats according to the Number of their Slain. There was likewise a Side-Table, for such as had only drawn Blood, and shown a laudable Ambition of taking the first Opportunity to qualify themselves for the first Table. This Club, consisting only of Men of Honour, did not continue long, most of the Members of it being put to the Sword, or hanged, a little after its Institution.

---

[1] Between Red Lion Street and Devonshire Street, north of Red Lion Square.

[2] Thomas Burnet seems to refer to this club in a letter to George Duckett of 15 Mar. 1712: 'I have worn off all the Spleen the Club had at me and am become once more a very acceptable member. Nay, having lost you the Supporter of my mirth and gaiety, I begin to be *humdrum* enough even for them' (*Letters of Thomas Burnet to George Duckett, 1712–1722*, ed. by David Nichol Smith, Oxford, Roxburghe Club, 1914, p. 2). Since this follows a description of the Mohocks one may suspect that Addison's account of the Hum-Drum Club covers a jest readily recognizable to readers of his own circle.

[3] It is possible that this title had a punning significance, since mum was also the name of a beer.

[4] The first attack upon a subject later to become one of the serious preoccupations of the *Spectator*.

Our Modern celebrated Clubs are founded upon Eating and Drinking, which are Points wherein most Men agree, and in which the Learned and Illiterate, the Dull and the Airy, the Philosopher and the Buffoon, can all of them bear a Part. The *Kit-Cat*[1] it self is said to have taken its Original from a Mutton-Pye. The *Beef-Steak*,[2] and *October* Clubs[3] are neither of them averse to Eating and Drinking, if we may form a Judgment of them from their respective Titles.

When Men are thus knit together, by a Love of Society, not a Spirit of Faction, and don't meet to censure or annoy those that are absent, but to enjoy one another: When they are thus combined for their own Improvement, or for the Good of others, or at least to relax themselves from the Business of the Day, by an innocent and chearful Conversation, there may be something very useful in these little Institutions and Establishments.

I cannot forbear concluding this Paper with a Scheme of Laws that I met with upon a Wall in a little Ale-house: How I came thither I may inform my Reader at a more convenient time. These Laws were enacted by a Knot of Artizans and Mechanicks, who used to meet every Night; and as there is something in them which gives

[1] This famous club of prominent Whigs was founded about 1700 and seems to have met first at the house of Christopher Cat; Hearne, 6 Dec. 1705, calls him Christopher Catling (*Remarks and Collections*, i. 116). The elder Jacob Tonson acted as secretary, and in 1703 the headquarters were moved to his villa at Barn-Elms in Surrey. Here the famous series of portraits by Godfrey Kneller were hung, now in the National Portrait Gallery. Besides such prominent leaders as Halifax, Somers, Sunderland, Marlborough, Godolphin, and Walpole, the club included the best-known literary men among the Whigs: Addison, Steele, Garth, Vanbrugh, Congreve, and Walsh.

[2] This social club flourished early in Queen Anne's reign. William King's *Miscellanies in Prose and Verse* (1705) is dedicated 'To the Right Honourable Lords and Gentlemen, Members of the Immortal Beef-Steak Clubb', where, says the preface, 'every valuable Quality reigns differently, but are all cemented by the Ties of Good Nature and Good Humour'. His *Art of Cookery* (1709) also pays tribute to the club and connects the name of Richard Estcourt, the actor, with it. According to Chetwood (*General History of the Stage*, Dublin, 1749, p. 143), Estcourt 'was made Providore of the Beef-Stake-Club, and for a Mark of Distinction, wore their Badge, which was a small Gridiron of Gold, hung about his Neck with a green Silk Ribbon'. In No. 260 (28 Dec. 1711)(vol. ii) an advertisement announces that Estcourt will on the first of January open the Bumper Tavern in James Street, Covent Garden; and it seems likely that the meetings of the club were henceforth held here (cf. the letter in No. 264 (vol. ii) from Sir Roger de Coverley to Estcourt, beginning 'Old Comical Ones').

[3] Swift writes to Stella on 18 Feb. 1711: 'We are plagued here with an October Club, that is, a set of above a hundred parliament-men of the country, who drink October beer at home, and meet every evening at a tavern near the parliament, to consult affairs, and drive things on to extreams against the Whigs, to call the old ministry to account, and get off five or six heads.' It was made up of Jacobites and extreme Tories. For a satirical description see Defoe's *Review*, 13 Mar. 1710/11. Part I of Defoe's *Secret History of the October Club* was published on 21 Apr. 1711 (advertisement in No. 45), and early in 1712 Swift brought out anonymously *Some Advice humbly offer'd to the members of the October Club, in an effort to restrain their activities.*

us a pretty Picture of low Life, I shall transcribe them Word for Word.

RULES *to be observed in the* Two-penny Club, *erected in this Place, for the Preservation of Friendship and good Neighbourhood.*

I. Every Member at his first coming in shall lay down his Two Pence.

II. Every Member shall fill his Pipe out of his own Box.

III. If any Member absents himself he shall forfeit a Penny for the Use of the Club, unless in case of Sickness or Imprisonment.[1]

IV. If any Member swears or curses, his Neighbour may give him a Kick upon the Shins.

V. If any Member tells Stories in the Club that are not true, he shall forfeit for every third Lie an Half-Penny.

VI. If any Member strikes another wrongfully, he shall pay his Club for him.[2]

VII. If any Member brings his Wife into the Club, he shall pay for whatever she drinks or smoaks.

VIII. If any Member's Wife comes to fetch him Home from the Club, she shall speak to him without the Door.

IX. If any Member calls another Cuckold, he shall be turned out of the Club.

X. None shall be admitted into the Club that is of the same Trade with any Member of it.

XI. None of the Club shall have his Cloaths or Shoes made or mended, but by a Brother Member.

XII. No Non-juror shall be capable of being a Member.

The Morality of this little Club is guarded by such wholesome Laws and Penalties, that I question not but my Reader will be as well pleased with them, as he would have been with the *Leges Convivales*[3] of *Ben. Johnson*, the Regulations of an old *Roman* Club cited by *Lipsius*,[4] or the Rules of a *Symposium*[5] in an ancient *Greek* Author.   C

¹ Cf. Miège, p. 138: 'The Use of *Clubs*, so frequent in *London*, especially among Traders, is a good way to improve a diverting and useful Correspondence. The way of 'em is, for a select Company of Men to meet at a certain Hour in the Evening at a publick House, where they talk of Trade, News, *&c.* each paying his Club (or Quota) as limited before hand. The Absent are also to pay, and that is laid up till there be enough for a Treat.'

² In the obsolete meaning 'share of joint expense due from an individual' (*OED*),

³ See Ben Jonson's *Works*, ed. Herford and Simpson, viii. 656.

⁴ For his 'De ritu conviviorum apud Romanos' see his *Opera* (1675), iii. 1476.

⁵ 'A convivial meeting for drinking, conversation, and intellectual entertainment' (the earliest quotation in this sense in *OED*).

No. 10   *Monday, March 12, 1711*[1]
[ADDISON]

Non aliter quam qui adverso vix flumine lembum
Remigiis subigit: si brachia forte remisit,
Atque illum in præceps prono rapit alveus amni.
                                 Virg.

IT is with much Satisfaction that I hear this great City inquiring Day by Day after these my Papers, and receiving my Morning Lectures with a becoming Seriousness and Attention. My Publisher tells me, that there are already Three Thousand[2] of them distributed every Day: So that if I allow Twenty Readers to every Paper, which I look upon as a modest Computation, I may reckon about Threescore thousand Disciples in *London* and *Westminster*, who I hope will take care to distinguish themselves from the thoughtless Herd of their ignorant and unattentive Brethren. Since I have raised to my self so great an Audience, I shall spare no Pains to make their Instruction agreeable, and their Diversion useful. For which Reasons I shall endeavour to enliven Morality with Wit, and to temper Wit with Morality, that my Readers may, if possible, both Ways find their Account in the Speculation of the Day. And to the End that their Virtue and Discretion may not be short transient intermitting Starts of Thought, I have resolved to refresh their Memories from Day to Day, till I have recovered them out of that desperate State of Vice and Folly into which the Age is fallen. The Mind that lies fallow but a single Day, sprouts up in Follies that are only to be killed by a constant and assiduous Culture. It was said of *Socrates*,[3] that he brought Philosophy down from Heaven, to inhabit among Men; and I shall be ambitious to have it said of me, that I have brought Philosophy out of Closets and Libraries, Schools and Colleges, to dwell in Clubs and Assemblies, at Tea-Tables, and in Coffee-Houses.

I would therefore in a very particular Manner recommend these my Speculations to all well regulated Families, that set apart an

---

[1] *Motto.* Virgil, *Georgics*, I. 201–3:

As if one, whose oars can scarce force his skiff against the stream, should by chance slacken his arms, and lo! headlong down the current the channel sweeps it away.

[2] The first statement as to the success of the *Spectator*, after less than two weeks of publication.

[3] Cicero, *Tusculan Disputations*, 5. 4. 10.

Hour in every Morning for Tea and Bread and Butter; and would earnestly advise them for their Good to order this Paper to be punctually served up, and to be looked upon as a Part of the Tea Equipage.[1]

Sir *Francis Bacon*[2] observes, that a well-written Book compared with its Rivals and Antagonists, is like *Moses's* Serpent, that immediately swallow'd up and devoured those of the *Ægyptians*. I shall not be so vain as to think, that where the SPECTATOR appears, the other publick Prints will vanish; but shall leave it to my Readers Consideration, whether, Is it not much better to be let into the Knowledge of ones-self, than to hear what passes in *Muscovy* or *Poland*;[3] and to amuse our selves with such Writings as tend to the wearing out of Ignorance, Passion, and Prejudice, than such as naturally conduce to inflame Hatreds and make Enmities irreconcileable?

In the next Place, I would recommend this Paper to the daily Perusal of those Gentlemen whom I cannot but consider as my good Brothers and Allies, I mean the Fraternity of Spectators who live in the World without having any thing to do in it; and either by the Affluence of their Fortunes, or Laziness of their Dispositions, have no other Business with the rest of Mankind but to look upon them. Under this Class of Men are comprehended all contemplative Tradesmen, titular Physitians, Fellows of the Royal Society,[4] Templers that are not given to be contentious, and Statesmen that are out of Business. In short, every one that considers the World as a Theatre,

---

[1] Cf. *Tatler* 86.

[2] *Advancement of Learning*, book ii, int. 14: 'The great quantity of books maketh a show rather of superfluity than lack; which surcharge nevertheless is not to be remedied by making no more books, but by making more good books, which, as the serpent of Moses, mought devour the serpents of the enchanters' (World's Classics ed., p. 74). For the Biblical passage (the reference is to Aaron's serpent) see Exod. vii. 10–12.

[3] Cf. Shadwell's *Epsom Wells*, I. i, where Clodpate, who is described as loving the Gazettes, says: 'I do so love to hear of *Wisnowisky*, *Potosky*, General *Wrangle*, and Count *Tot*, and all those brave Fellows.' In the *Tatler* the Political Upholsterer 'was much more inquisitive to know what passed in *Poland* than in his own Family' and was concerned 'by some News he had lately read from *Muscovy*' (*Tatler* 155). See also *Tatlers* 160 and 178.

[4] This mild censure of the amateurs of natural science continues Addison's earlier attacks on the members of the Royal Society in *Tatlers* 119, 216, 221, and 236. Addison concludes *Tatler* 236 by saying that 'they seem to be in a Confederacy against Men of polite Genius, noble Thought, and diffusive Learning; and chuse into their Assemblies such as have no Pretence to Wisdom, but Want of Wit; or to natural Knowledge, but Ignorance of every Thing else.... When I meet with a young Fellow that is an humble Admirer of the Sciences, but more dull than the rest of the Company, I conclude him to be a Fellow of the Royal Society.'

and desires to form a right Judgment of those who are the Actors on it.

There is another Set of Men that I must likewise lay a Claim to, whom I have lately called the Blanks of Society,[1] as being altogether unfurnish'd with Ideas, till the Business and Conversation of the Day has supplied them. I have often considered these poor Souls with an Eye of great Commiseration, when I have heard them asking the first Man they have met with, whether there was any News stirring? and by that Means gathering together Materials for thinking. These needy Persons do not know what to talk of, till about twelve a Clock in the Morning; for by that Time they are pretty good Judges of the Weather, know which Way the Wind sits, and whether the *Dutch* Mail be come in. As they lie at the Mercy of the first Man they meet, and are grave or impertinent all the Day long, according to the Notions which they have imbibed in the Morning, I would earnestly entreat them not to stir out of their Chambers till they have read this Paper, and do promise them that I will daily instil into them such sound and wholesome Sentiments, as shall have a good Effect on their Conversation for the ensuing twelve Hours.

But there are none to whom this Paper will be more useful, than to the female World. I have often thought there has not been sufficient Pains taken in finding out proper Employments and Diversions for the Fair ones. Their Amusements seem contrived for them rather as they are Women, than as they are reasonable Creatures; and are more adapted to the Sex, than to the Species. The Toilet is their great Scene of Business, and the right adjusting of their Hair the principal Employment of their Lives. The sorting of a Suit of Ribbons, is reckon'd a very good Morning's Work; and if they make an Excursion to a Mercer's or a Toy-shop,[2] so great a Fatigue makes them unfit for any thing else all the Day after. Their more serious Occupations are Sowing and Embroidery, and their greatest Drudgery the Preparation of Jellies and Sweetmeats. This, I say, is the State of ordinary Women; tho' I know there are Multitudes of those of a more elevated Life and Conversation, that move in an exalted Sphere of Knowledge and Virtue, that join all the Beauties of the Mind to the Ornaments of Dress, and inspire a kind

[1] See No. 4.
[2] 'A shop for the sale of trinkets, knick-knacks, or small ornamental articles; a fancy shop. *arch.*' (*OED*).

of Awe and Respect, as well as Love, into their Male-Beholders. I hope to encrease the Number of these by publishing this daily Paper, which I shall always endeavour to make an innocent if not an improving Entertainment, and by that Means at least divert the Minds of my female Readers from greater Trifles. At the same Time, as I would fain give some finishing Touches to those which are already the most beautiful Pieces in humane Nature, I shall endeavour to point out all those Imperfections that are the Blemishes, as well as those Virtues which are the Embellishments, of the Sex. In the mean while I hope these my gentle Readers, who have so much Time on their Hands, will not grudge throwing away a Quarter of an Hour in a Day on this Paper, since they may do it without any Hindrance to Business.

I know several of my Friends and Well-wishers are in great Pain for me, lest I should not be able to keep up the Spirit of a Paper which I oblige my self to furnish every Day: But to make them easy in this Particular, I will promise them faithfully to give it over as soon as I grow dull. This I know will be Matter of great Raillery to the small Wits;[1] who will frequently put me in mind of my Promise, desire me to keep my Word, assure me that it is high Time to give over, with many other little Pleasantries of the like Nature, which Men of a little smart Genius cannot forbear throwing out against their best Friends, when they have such a Handle given them of being witty. But let them remember, that I do hereby enter my Caveat against this Piece of Raillery.   C

No. 11   *Tuesday, March* 13, 1711[2]
[STEELE]

Dat veniam corvis, vexat censura columbas.

Juv.

*A*RIETTA is visited by all Persons of both Sexes, who have any Pretence to Wit and Gallantry. She is in that time of Life which is neither affected with the Follies of Youth, or Infirmities of Age; and her Conversation is so mixed with Gaiety and Prudence, that she is

---

[1] This prediction of the small wits' raillery is fulfilled in *The Review* of 18 Aug. 1711, which contains an anecdote of a man complaining of the *Spectator*'s dullness.
[2] *Motto.* Juvenal, *Satires,* 2. 63:
He shows indulgence toward the crows and censures the doves.

agreeable both to the Young and the Old. Her Behaviour is very frank, without being in the least blameable; and as she is out of the Tract of any amorous or ambitious Pursuits of her own, her Visitants entertain her with Accounts of themselves very freely, whether they concern their Passions or their Interests. I made her a Visit this Afternoon, having been formerly introduced to the Honour of her Acquaintance, by my Friend *Will. Honeycomb,* who has prevailed upon her to admit me sometimes into her Assembly, as a civil, inoffensive Man. I found her accompanied with one Person only, a Common-Place Talker, who, upon my Entrance, rose, and after a very slight Civility sat down again; then turning to *Arietta,* pursued his Discourse, which I found was upon the old Topick, of Constancy in Love. He went on with great Facility in repeating what he talks every Day of his Life; and, with the Ornaments of insignificant Laughs and Gestures, enforced his Arguments by Quotations out of Plays and Songs, which allude to the Perjuries of the Fair, and the general Levity of Women. Methought he strove to shine more than ordinarily in his Talkative Way, that he might insult my Silence, and distinguish himself before a Woman of *Arietta*'s Taste and Understanding. She had often an Inclination to interrupt him, but could find no Opportunity, 'till the Larum ceased of its self; which it did not 'till he had repeated and murdered the celebrated Story of the *Ephesian* Matron.[1]

Arietta seemed to regard this Piece of Raillery as an Outrage done to her Sex, as indeed I have always observed that Women, whether out of a nicer Regard to their Honour, or what other Reason I cannot tell, are more sensibly touched with those general Aspersions, which are cast upon their Sex, than Men are by what is said of theirs.

When she had a little recovered her self from the serious Anger she was in, she replied in the following manner.

Sir, When I consider, how perfectly new all you have said on this Subject is, and that the Story you have given us is not quite two thousand Years Old, I cannot but think it a Piece of Presumption to dispute with you: But your Quotations put me in Mind of the Fable of the Lion and the Man.[2] The Man walking with that noble

[1] The story is told in Part II of the *Satyricon* (*Satyrical Works of Titus Petronius Arbiter in Prose and Verse,* 1708, pp. 171–5).
[2] Aesop, Fable 219. It appears in La Fontaine (book iii, Fable 10) as 'Le Lion abattu par l'homme'. It is related as a Persian fable in Chardin's *Voyages* (Amsterdam, 1711), v. 193. See L'Estrange, *Fables of Æsop* (1692), Fable 240.

Animal, showed him, in the Ostentation of Human Superiority, a Sign of a Man killing a Lion. Upon which the Lion said very justly, *We Lions are none of us Painters, else we could show a hundred Men killed by Lions, for one Lion killed by a Man.* You Men are Writers, and can represent us Women as Unbecoming as you please in your Works, while we are unable to return the Injury. You have twice or thrice observed in your Discourse, that Hipocrisy is the very Foundation of our Education; and that an Ability to dissemble our Affections, is a professed Part of our Breeding. These, and such other Reflections, are sprinkled up and down the Writings of all Ages, by Authors, who leave behind them Memorials of their Resentment against the Scorn of particular Women, in Invectives against the whole Sex. Such a Writer, I doubt not, was the celebrated *Petronius*, who invented the pleasant Aggravations of the Frailty of the *Ephesian* Lady; but when we consider this Question between the Sexes, which has been either a Point of Dispute or Raillery ever since there were Men and Women, let us take Facts from plain People, and from such as have not either Ambition or Capacity to embellish their Narrations with any Beauties of Imagination. I was the other Day amusing my self with *Ligon's* Account of *Barbadoes*; and, in Answer to your well-wrought Tale, I will give you (as it dwells upon my Memory) out of that honest Traveller, in his fifty fifth Page, the History of *Inkle* and *Yarico*.[1]

Mr. *Thomas Inkle* of *London*, aged 20 Years, embarked in the *Downs* on the good Ship called the *Achilles*, bound for the *West-Indies*, on

---

[1] Richard Ligon's *True and Exact History of the Island of Barbados* (1657), p. 55. Ligon, who had himself sailed in the *Achilles* to the West Indies, describes Yarico as an Indian slave who had borne a child to one of the Christian servants in the colony. Later, when the men on an English ship which had put in there are surprised and attacked, 'a young man amongst them straggling from the rest, was met by this Indian maid, who upon first sight fell in love with him, and hid him close from her countrymen (the Indians) in a cave, and there fed him, till they could safely go down to the shoar where the ship lay at anchor, expecting the return of their friends. But at last, seeing them upon the shoar, sent the long'Boat for them, took them aboard, and brought them away. But the youth, when he came a shoar in the Barbadoes, forgot the kindness of the poor maid, that had ventured her life for his safety, and sold her for a slave, who was as free born as he: And so poor Yarico for her love, lost her liberty.' The name Inkle ('a kind of linen tape, or the thread or yarn from which it is made'), the characterization of the young merchant, and his seduction of Yarico —these are all Steele's additions to Ligon's anecdote. It was this version in the *Spectator* which caught the fancy of eighteenth-century readers, and the theme became enormously popular not only in England but also on the Continent. For a full list of the poems, novelettes, and plays, in English, French, German, Swedish, &c., and a discussion of the various developments of the theme see Lawrence M. Price, *Inkle and Yarico Album* (Berkeley, California, 1937). Chamfort's one-act play, *La Jeune Indienne* (1764), based on this story, has been edited by Gilbert Chinard (Princeton, 1945).

the 16th of *June* 1647, in order to improve his Fortune by Trade and Merchandize. Our Adventurer was the third Son of an eminent Citizen, who had taken particular Care to instill into his Mind an early Love of Gain, by making him a perfect Master of Numbers, and consequently giving him a quick View of Loss and Advantage, and preventing the natural Impulses of his Passions, by Prepossession towards his Interests. With a Mind thus turned, young *Inkle* had a Person every way agreeable, a ruddy Vigour in his Countenance, Strength in his Limbs, with Ringlets of fair Hair loosely flowing on his Shoulders. It happened, in the Course of the Voyage, that the *Achilles*, in some Distress, put into a Creek on the Main of *America*, in Search of Provisions: The Youth, who is the Hero of my Story, among others, went ashore on this Occasion. From their first Landing they were observed by a Party of *Indians*, who hid themselves in the Woods for that Purpose. The *English* unadvisedly marched a great distance from the Shore into the Country, and were intercepted by the Natives, who slew the greatest Number of them. Our Adventurer escaped among others, by flying into a Forest. Upon his coming into a remote and pathless Part of the Wood, he threw himself, tired and breathless,[a] on a little Hillock, when an *Indian* Maid rushed from a Thicket behind him: After the first Surprize, they appeared mutually agreeable to each other. If the *European* was highly Charmed with the Limbs, Features, and wild Graces of the Naked *American*; the *American* was no less taken with the Dress, Complexion and Shape of an *European*, covered from Head to Foot. The *Indian* grew immediately enamoured of him, and consequently sollicitous for his Preservation: She therefore conveyed him to a Cave, where she gave him a Delicious Repast of Fruits, and led him to a Stream to slake his Thirst. In the midst of these good Offices, she would sometimes play with his Hair, and delight in the Opposition of its Colour, to that of her Fingers: Then open his Bosome, then laugh at him for covering it. She was, it seems, a Person of Distinction, for she every day came to him in a different Dress, of the most beautiful Shells, Bugles and Bredes.[1] She likewise brought him a great many Spoils, which her other Lovers had presented to her; so that his Cave was richly adorned with all the spotted Skins of Beasts, and most Party-coloured Feathers of Fowls,

[a] himself, tired and breathless,] himself breathless *Fol.*

---

[1] Tube-shaped glass beads and braiding.

which that World afforded. To make his Confinement more tolerable, she would carry him in the Dusk of the Evening, or by the
favour of Moon-light, to unfrequented Groves and Solitudes, and
show him where to lye down in Safety, and sleep amidst the Falls
of Waters, and Melody of Nightingales. Her Part was to watch and
hold him in her Arms, for fear of her Country-men, and wake him[a]
on Occasions to consult his Safety. In this manner did the Lovers
pass away their Time, till they had learn'd a Language of their own,
in which the Voyager communicated to his Mistress, how happy
he should be to have her in his Country, where she should be
Cloathed in such Silks as his Wastecoat was made of, and be carried
in Houses drawn by Horses, without being exposed to Wind or
Weather. All this he promised her the Enjoyment of, without such
Fears and Alarms as they were there Tormented with. In this tender
Correspondence these Lovers lived for several Months, when *Yarico*,
instructed by her Lover, discovered a Vessel on the Coast, to which
she made Signals, and in the Night, with the utmost Joy and
Satisfaction accompanied him to a Ships-Crew of his Country-Men,
bound for *Barbadoes*. When a Vessel from the Main arrives in that
Island, it seems the Planters come down to the Shoar, where there is
an immediate Market of the *Indians* and other Slaves, as with us of
Horses and Oxen.

To be short, Mr. *Thomas Inkle*, now coming into *English* Territories,
began seriously to reflect upon his loss of Time, and to weigh with
himself how many Days Interest of his Mony he had lost during his
Stay with *Yarico*. This Thought made the Young Man very pensive,
and careful what Account he should be able to give his Friends of
his Voyage. Upon which Considerations, the prudent and frugal
young Man sold *Yarico* to a *Barbadian* Merchant; notwithstanding
that the poor Girl, to incline him to commiserate her Condition,
told him that she was with Child by him: But he only made use of
that Information, to rise in his Demands upon the Purchaser.

I was so touch'd with this Story, (which I think should be always
a Counterpart to the *Ephesian* Matron) that I left the Room with
Tears in my Eyes; which a Woman of *Arietta*'s good Sense, did, I
am sure, take for greater Applause, than any Compliments I could
make her.   R

[a] wake him] wake *Fol.*

No. 12   *Wednesday, March 14, 1711*[1]
[ADDISON]

> . . . *Veteres avias tibi de pulmone revello.*
>   Per.

AT my coming to *London*, it was some time before I could settle my self in a House to my likeing. I was forced to quit my first Lodgings, by reason of an officious Land-lady, that would be asking me every Morning how I had slept. I then fell into an honest Family, and lived very happily for above a Week; when my Land-lord, who was a jolly good-natur'd Man, took it into his Head that I wanted Company, and therefore would frequently come into my Chamber to keep me from being alone. This I bore for Two or Three Days; but telling me one Day that he was afraid I was melancholy, I thought it was high time for me to be gone, and accordingly took new Lodgings that very Night. About a Week after, I found my jolly Land-lord, who, as I said before was an honest hearty Man, had put me into an Advertisement of the *Daily Courant*,[2] in the following Words. *Whereas a melancholy Man left his Lodgings on* Thursday *last in the Afternoon, and was afterwards seen going towards* Islington;[3] *If any one can give Notice of him to R. B. Fishmonger in the* Strand, *he shall be very well rewarded for his Pains.* As I am the best Man in the World to keep my own Counsel, and my Land-lord the Fishmonger not knowing my Name, this Accident of my Life was never discovered to this very Day.

I am now settled with a Widow-woman, who has a great many Children, and complies with my Humour in every thing. I do not remember that we have exchang'd a Word together these Five Years; my Coffee comes into my Chamber every Morning without asking for it; if I want Fire I point to my Chimney, if Water to my Bason: Upon which my Land-lady nodds, as much as to say she takes my Meaning, and immediately obeys my Signals. She has likewise model'd her Family so well, that when her little Boy

---

[1] *Motto.* Persius, *Satires,* 5. 92:

> I pluck the old wives' notions from your breast.

[2] The *Daily Courant* was printed by Samuel Buckley, one of the printers of the *Spectator* (cf. No. 1), from 1702 until 1714. Beginning with the issue of 25 Sept. 1714 the imprint reads: 'Printed by S. Gray, and Sold by Ferd. Burleigh in Amen-Corner.'

[3] This may be the origin of the supposition, advanced by Nichols and other early editors, that Addison's papers signed 'I' were written from Islington. There is no evidence that either Addison or Steele ever lived there.

offers to pull me by the Coat or prattle in my Face, his eldest Sister immediately calls him off and bids him not disturb the Gentleman. At my first entering into the Family, I was troubled with the Civility of their rising up to me every time I came into the Room; but my Land-lady observing that upon these Occasions I always cried pish and went out again, has forbidden any such Ceremony to be used in the House; so that at present I walk into the Kitchin or Parlour without being taken notice of, or giving any Interruption to the Business or Discourse of the Family. The Maid will ask her Mistress (tho' I am by) whether the Gentleman is ready to go to Dinner, as the Mistress (who is indeed an excellent House-wife) scolds at the Servants as heartily before my Face as behind my Back. In short, I move up and down the House and enter into all Companies, with the same Liberty as a Cat or any other domestick Animal, and am as little suspected of telling any thing that I hear or see.

I remember last Winter there were several young Girls of the Neighbourhood sitting about the Fire with my Land-lady's Daughters, and telling Stories of Spirits and Apparitions.[1] Upon my opening the Door the young Women broke off their Discourse, but my Land-lady's Daughters telling them that it was no Body but the Gentleman (for that is the Name which I go by in the Neighbour-hood as well as in the Family) they went on without minding me. I seated my self by the Candle that stood on a Table at one End of the Room; and pretending to read a Book that I took out of my Pocket, heard several dreadful Stories of Ghosts as pale as Ashes that had stood at the Feet of a Bed,[2] or walked over a Church-yard by Moon-light: And of others that had been conjured into the *Red-Sea*,[3] for disturbing People's Rest, and drawing their Curtains at Midnight; with many other old Womens Fables of the like Nature. As one Spirit raised another, I observed that at the End of every Story the whole Company closed their Ranks and crouded about the Fire: I took Notice in particular of a little Boy, who was so attentive to every Story, that I am mistaken if he ventures to go to bed by himself this Twelvemonth. Indeed they talked so long, that

---

[1] *The Possibility of Apparitions, being an Answer to this Question, Whether can Departed Souls . . . so appear as to be visibly seen and conversed with here on Earth*, 'by a Divine of the Church of England', is advertised in the *Post-Man* for 8 Oct. 1705.

[2] The last example of this plural usage in *OED* is dated *c.* 1710.

[3] The Butler, in Addison's *Drummer* (II. i), advises paying the conjurer, so that he will 'take pains upon the Ghost, and lay him, look ye, in the Red-Sea—and then he's laid for ever'.

the Imaginations of the whole Assembly were manifestly crazed, and I am sure will be the worse for it as long as they live. I heard one of the Girls, that had looked upon me over her Shoulder, asking the Company how long I had been in the Room, and whether I did not look paler than I used to do. This put me under some Apprehensions that I should be forced to explain my self if I did not retire; for which Reason I took the Candle in my Hand, and went up into my Chamber, not without wondering at this unaccountable Weakness in reasonable Creatures, that they should love[a] to astonish and terrify one another. Were I a Father, I should take a particular Care to preserve my Children from these little Horrours of Imagination, which they are apt to contract when they are young, and are not able to shake off when they are in Years. I have known a Soldier that has enter'd a Breach, affrighted at his own Shadow; and look pale upon a little scratching at his Door, who the Day before had march'd up against a Battery of Cannon. There are Instances of Persons, who have been terrify'd, even to Distraction, at the Figure of a Tree or the shaking of a Bull-rush. The Truth of it is, I look upon a sound Imagination as the greatest Blessing of Life, next to a clear Judgment and a good Conscience. In the mean Time, since there are very few whose Minds are not more or less subject to these dreadful Thoughts and Apprehensions, we ought to arm our selves against them by the Dictates of Reason and Religion, *to pull the old Woman out of our Hearts* (as *Persius* expresses it in the Motto of my Paper,) and extinguish those impertinent Notions which we imbibed at a Time that we were not able to judge of their Absurdity. Or if we believe, as many wise and good Men have done, that there are such Phantoms and Apparitions as those I have been speaking of, let us endeavour to establish to our selves an Interest in him who holds the Reins of the whole Creation in his Hand, and moderates them after such a Manner, that it is impossible for one Being to break loose upon another without his Knowledge and Permission.

For my own Part, I am apt to join in Opinion with those who believe that all the Regions of Nature swarm with Spirits; and that we have Multitudes of Spectators on all our Actions, when we think our selves most alone: But instead of terrifying my self with such a Notion, I am wonderfully pleased to think that I am always engaged with such an innumerable Society in searching out the Wonders of the Creation, and joining in the same Consort of Praise and Adoration.

---

[a] Creatures, that they should love] Creatures, who love *Fol.*

Milton[1] has finely described this mixed Communion of Men and Spirits in Paradise; and had doubtless his Eye upon a Verse in old *Hesiod*,[2] which is almost Word for Word the same with his third Line in the following Passage.

> . . . *Nor think, though Men were none,*
> *That Heav'n would want Spectators, God want Praise:*
> *Millions of spiritual Creatures walk the Earth*
> *Unseen, both when we wake and when we sleep;*
> *All these with ceaseless Praise his Works behold*
> *Both Day and Night. How often from the Steep*
> *Of ecchoing Hill or Thicket, have we heard*
> *Celestial Voices to the midnight Air,*
> *Sole, or responsive each to others Note,*
> *Singing their great Creator: Oft in Bands,*
> *While they keep Watch, or nightly Rounding walk,*
> *With heav'nly Touch of instrumental Sounds,*
> *In full harmonick Number join'd, their Songs*
> *Divide the Night, and lift our Thoughts to Heaven.*   C

No. 13   *Thursday, March* 15, 1711[3]

ADDISON]

Dic mihi si fueras tu Leo qualis eris?

Mart.

THERE is nothing that of late Years has afforded Matter of greater Amusement to the Town than Signior *Nicolini*'s Combat with a Lion in the *Hay-Market*, which has been very[a] often exhibited to the general Satisfaction of most of the Nobility and Gentry in the Kingdom of *Great Britain*. Upon the first Rumour of this intended Combat, it was confidently affirmed, and is still

---

[a] very] so *Fol.*

---

[1] *Paradise Lost*, iv. 675–88.
[2] *Works and Days*, 1. 250–1. Hesiod's poems occupy pp. 2–115 of Ralph Winterton's *Poetae minores graeci* (Cambridge, 1635), a book which Addison frequently uses (ed. 1677, p. 15, contains the verse cited here).
[3] *Motto.* Martial, *Epigrams*, 12. 92. 4:
       Tell me, if you were a lion what kind would you be?

believed by many in both Galleries, that there would be a tame Lion[1] sent from the *Tower* every Opera Night, in order to be killed by *Hydaspes*;[2] this Report, tho' altogether groundless, so universally prevailed in the upper Regions of the Play-House, that some of the most refined Politicians in those Parts of the Audience gave it out in Whisper, that the Lion was a Cousin-German of the Tyger who made his Appearance in King *William*'s Days,[3] and that the Stage would be supplied with Lions at the publick Expence, during the whole Session. Many likewise were the Conjectures of the Treatment which this Lion was to meet with from the hands of Signior *Nicolini*; some suppos'd that he was to Subdue him in *Recitatevo*,[4] as

[1] The lions and other animals kept in the Tower were among the sights always shown to visitors. Thomas Brockbank in 1695 was shown not only the lions but also 'a Linx, a Leopard, a Cat a Mountain' and several other animals (*Diary and Letter Book*, ed. by R. Trappes-Lomax, p. 94), and Isaac Bickerstaff writes in *Tatler* 30: 'I took Three Lads who are under my Guardianship a rambling in an Hackney-Coach, to show 'em the Town, as the Lions, the Tombs, *Bedlam*, and the other Places which are Entertainments to raw Minds. . . .'

[2] *L'Idaspe fedele* by Francesco Mancini, with libretto probably by Giovanni Candi, was one of the most popular of the Italian operas in 1711 and 1712 (16 performances are advertised in the *Spectator*). *Idaspe* and *Almahide* were the first operas to be sung wholly in Italian in London (Grove). *Hydaspes* was first given on 23 Mar. 1709/10, with Nicolini in the title role. The struggle with the lion was much talked of at the time. Lady Mary Wortley Montagu, in an undated letter to Mrs. Hewet, describes a performance in which she 'saw Nicolini strangle a lion with great gallantry. But he represented nakedness so naturally, I was surprised to see those ladies stare at him without any confusion, that pretend to be so violently shocked at a poor *double entendre* or two in a comedy . . .' (*Letters*, ed. W. Moy Thomas, i. 31). The German traveller, Zacharias Conrad von Uffenbach, gives a more detailed account of a performance at the Haymarket on 10 June 1710. 'The best of the females is Margarite de l'Epine. . . . The conductor is Pepusch from Brandenburg, who is known everywhere for his amazingly elegant compositions. The scenery and properties had all been made expressly for the opera and were very fine, though not as costly as those in Italy; but the costumes were of the finest and the performances were in all things most natural and uncommonly elegant. In especial the representation of the lion with which Hidaspes has to fight was incomparably fine. The fellow who played him was not only wrapped in a lion-skin, but, moreover, nothing could be seen of his feet, which usually betray the fact that a man is hidden within. We were filled with surprise at the way in which the fellow could spring about so nimbly on the ground on all fours as well as on his hind legs. The singers expressed so well the emotions they must represent that I have never seen the like, above all Nicolini, who excels all actors in the world in this respect' (*London in 1710, from the Travels of Zacharias Conrad von Uffenbach*, translated and edited by W. H. Quarrell and Margaret Mare (London, Faber, 1934), pp. 17–18). See also *Autobiography and Correspondence of Mary Granville, Mrs. Delany*, ed. Lady Llanover (1861), i. 16.

[3] *The Post-Man*, 2 Mar. 1698/9, announces an encounter to take place at the Cock Pit Royal on 9 Mar. 'betwixt the East India Tyger, that was lately shown in the Stocks Market . . ., and three large Bear Dogs'. On 11 Mar. the same newspaper reported: 'On *Thursday* last the Tyger which was shewn about Town, was baited at the Cockpit by 4 Dogs, one after another. The first Dog was almost killed, but the other three fought so well, that one may say it was a Drawn Battel, and some believe they would have been too hard for him, had not a large Collar saved his Throat.'

[4] In *A Second Tale of a Tub*, by Thomas Burnet and George Duckett (1715), Dionysius 'mounts his Horse *Coirocephalus*, and like a Champion on a Coronation

Orpheus used to serve the wild Beasts in his time, and afterwards to knock him on the head; some fancied that the Lion would not pretend to lay his Paws upon the Hero, by Reason of the received Opinion, that a Lion will not hurt a Virgin. Several, who pretended to have seen the Opera in *Italy*, had inform'd their Friends, that the Lion was to act a Part in *High-Dutch*, and roar twice or thrice to a thorough Base, before he fell at the Feet of *Hydaspes*. To clear up a Matter that was so variously reported, I have made it my Business to examine whether this pretended Lion is really the Savage he appears to be, or only a Counterfeit.

But before I communicate my Discoveries, I must acquaint the Reader, that upon my walking behind the Scenes last Winter, as I was thinking on something else, I accidentally justled against a monstrous Animal that extreamly startled me, and upon my nearer Survey of it, appeared to be a Lion-Rampant. The Lion, seeing me very much surprized, told me, in a gentle Voice, that I might come by him if I pleased: *For* (says he) *I do not intend to hurt any body.* I thanked him very kindly, and passed by him. And in a little time after saw him leap upon the Stage, and act his Part with very great Applause. It has been observ'd by several, that the Lion has changed his manner of Acting twice or thrice since his first Appearance; which will not seem strange, when I acquaint my Reader that the Lion has been changed upon the Audience three several times. The first Lion was a Candle-snuffer, who being a Fellow of a testy, cholerick Temper over-did his Part, and would not suffer himself to be killed so easily as he ought to have done; besides, it was observ'd of him, that he grew more surly every time he came out of the Lion; and having dropt some Words in ordinary Conversation, as if he had not fought his best, and that he suffered himself to be thrown upon his Back in the Scuffle, and that he would wrestle with Mr. *Nicolini* for what he pleased, out of his Lion's Skin, it was thought proper to discard him: And it is verily believed to this Day, that had he been brought upon the Stage another time, he would certainly have done Mischief. Besides, it was objected against the first Lion, that he reared himself so high upon his hinder Paws, and walked in so erect a Posture, that he looked more like an old Man than a Lion.

The second Lion was a Taylor by Trade, who belonged to the

Day, . . . or like NICHOLINI, when he kills a Lion in *Recitativo* . . ., rides out into the Streets, and pulls the *Plug* out of his Horses Posteriors' (p. 211).

Play-House, and had the Character of a mild and peaceable Man in his Profession. If the former was too furious, this was too sheepish, for his Part; insomuch that after a short modest Walk upon the Stage, he would fall at the first Touch of *Hydaspes*, without grappling with him, and giving him an Opportunity of showing his Variety of *Italian* Tripps: It is said indeed, that he once gave him a Ripp in his flesh-colour Doublet, but this was only to make work for himself, in his private Character of a Taylor. I must not omit, that it was this second Lion who[a] treated me with so much Humanity behind the Scenes.

The Acting Lion at present is, as I am informed, a Country Gentleman, who does it for his Diversion, but desires his Name may be concealed. He says very handsomely in his own Excuse, that he does not Act for Gain, that he indulges an innocent Pleasure in it, and that it is better to pass away an Evening in this manner, than in Gaming and Drinking: But at the same time says, with a very agreeable Raillery upon himself, that if his Name should be known, the ill-natured World might call him, *The Ass in the Lion's Skin.*[1] This Gentleman's Temper is made out of such a happy Mixture of the Mild and the Cholerick, that he out-does both his Predecessors, and has drawn together greater Audiences than have been known in the Memory of Man.

I must not conclude my Narrative, without taking Notice of a groundless Report that has been raised, to a Gentleman's Disadvantage, of whom I must declare my self an Admirer; namely, that Signior *Nicolini* and the Lion have been seen sitting peaceably by one another, and smoking a Pipe together, behind the Scenes; by which their common Enemies would insinuate, that it is but a sham Combat which they represent upon the Stage: But upon Enquiry I find, that if any such Correspondence has passed between them, it was not till the Combat was over, when the Lion was to be looked upon as dead, according to the received Rules of the *Drama*. Besides, this is what is practised every day in *Westminster-Hall*, where nothing is more usual than to see a Couple of Lawyers, who have been tearing each other to pieces in the Court, embracing one another as soon as they are out of it.

I would not be thought, in any part of this Relation, to reflect

[a] who] that *Fol.*

---

[1] L'Estrange, *Fables of Æsop* (1692), Fable 224.

upon Signior *Nicolini*, who in Acting this Part only complies with the wretched Taste of his Audience; he knows very well, that the Lion has many more Admirers than himself; as they say of the famous *Equestrian* Statue[1] on the *Pont-Neuf* at *Paris*, that more People go to see the Horse, than the King who sits upon it. On the contrary, it gives me a just Indignation, to see a Person whose Action gives new Majesty to Kings, Resolution to Heroes, and Softness to Lovers, thus sinking from the Greatness of his Behaviour, and degraded into the Character of *the* London *Prentice*.[2] I have often wished that our Tragœdians would copy after this great Master in Action. Could they make the same use of their Arms and Legs, and inform their Faces with as significant Looks and Passions, how glorious would an *English* Tragedy appear with that Action which is capable of giving a Dignity to the forced Thoughts, cold Conceits, and unnatural Expressions of an *Italian* Opera. In the mean time, I have related this Combat of the Lion, to show what are at present the reigning Entertainments of the Politer Part of *Great Britain*.

Audiences have often been reproached by Writers for the Coarseness of their Taste, but our present Grievance does not seem to be the Want of a good Taste, but of Common Sense.[a]   C

[a] *Letters are Directed for the* Spectator, *to be left with* Mr. Buckley *at the* Dolphin *in* Little-Britain. *Fol.*

---

[1] This was the statue of Henri IV, formerly on the Pont-Neuf, mainly the work of Giovanni Bologna; it was erected in 1614 and melted into cannon in 1792. John Evelyn (24 Dec. 1643) describes this 'famous statue of Henry le grand on horse-back exceeding the natural proportion by much . . .' (*Diary*, ed. E. S. de Beer, ii. 92).

[2] A popular street ballad. In Vol. i of the Bagford Ballads in the British Museum it is entitled:

> The Honour of a LONDON PRENTICE. Being an Account of his Matchless Manhood and brave Adventures done in Turkey, and by what means he married the King's Daughter, &c. To the Tune of, *All you that love Goodfellows*, &c. London: Printed by and for W.O. and sold by the Booksellers of Pye-corner and London-bridge.

There are many references to it in the literature of the day. In Arbuthnot's *John Bull Still in his Senses* (1712), chap. vii, Mrs. Bull is blamed 'that she would not allow her Maids and Apprentices the Benefit of *John Bunyan*, the *London-Apprentice*, or the *Seven Champions*, in the Black Letter' (*History of John Bull*, ed. Herman Teerink, p. 192). See also the Earl of Dorset's 'Epilogue on the Revival of Every Man in his Humour', line 48; and Tom Brown's *Letters to Gentlemen and Ladies* (*Works*, 1715, iii. 236). John Ashton, *Chap-Books of the Eighteenth Century* (1882), pp. 227-9, gives further examples.

No. 14   *Friday, March 16, 1711*[1]

[STEELE]

> . . . *Teque his, Infælix, exue monstris.*
>
>   Ovid

I WAS reflecting this Morning upon the Spirit and Humour of the publick Diversions Five and twenty Years ago, and those of the present Time; and lamented to my self, that tho' in those Days they neglected their Morality, they kept up their Good Sense; but that the *beau Monde* at present, is only grown more childish, not more innocent, than the former. While I was in this Train of Thought, an odd Fellow whose Face I have often seen at the Play-house, gave me the following Letter with these Words, Sir, *The Lyon presents his humble Service to you, and desired me to give this into your own Hands.*

> *From my Den in the* Hay-Market, March 15.

SIR,

'I HAVE read all your Papers, and have stifled my Resentment against your Reflections upon Operas, till that of this Day, wherein you plainly insinuate that Signior *Grimaldi* and my self have a Correspondence more friendly than is consistent with the Valour of his Character, or the Fierceness of mine. I desire you would for your own Sake forbear such Intimations for the future; and must say it is a great Piece of Ill-nature in you, to shew so great an Esteem for a Foreigner, and to discourage a *Lyon* that is your own Country-man.

'I take notice of your Fable of the Lyon and Man,[2] but am so equally concerned in that Matter, that I shall not be offended to which soever of the Animals the Superiority is given. You have mis-represented me in saying that I am a Country-Gentleman who act only for my Diversion; whereas, had I still the same Woods to range in which I once had when I was a Fox-hunter, I should not resign my Manhood for a Maintenance; and assure you, as low as my Circum-stances are at present, I am so much a Man of Honour, that I would scorn to be any Beast for Bread but a Lyon.

> Yours, *&c.*'

I had no sooner ended this, than one of my Land-lady's Children

---

[1] *Motto.* Ovid, *Metamorphoses,* 4. 591:
        Unhappy man, put off this monstrous shape.
[2] See No. 11.

brought me in several others, with some of which I shall make up my present Paper, they all having a Tendency to the same Subject, *viz.* the Elegance of our present Diversions.

SIR,   *Covent-Garden, March* 13.

'I HAVE been for twenty Years Under-Sexton of this Parish of St. *Paul's Covent-Garden,*[1] and have not missed tolling in to Prayers six times in all those Years; which Office I have performed to my great Satisfaction, till this Fortnight last past, during which Time I find my Congregation take the Warning of my Bell, Morning and Evening, to go to a Puppet-show[2] set forth by one *Powell* under the *Piazzas.*[3] By this Means I have not only lost my two Customers, whom I used to place for six Pence a Piece over-against Mrs *Rachel Eyebright,* but Mrs *Rachel* her self is gone thither also. There now

---

[1] Ward's *London Spy,* part ix, describes 'a *Sanctified* Troop of *Females* flocking to their *Devotions*' at this Church. 'These, says my Friend, are a *Pious* sort of *Creatures,* that are much given to go to *Church,* and may be seen there every Day at *Prayers,* as constantly as the *Bell* Rings; and if you were to Walk the other way, you might meet as many *Young Gentlemen* from the *Temple* and *Grays-Inn,* going to Joyn with them in their *Devotions . . .*' (Casanova Society, 1924, p. 217).

[2] The puppet-shows so popular at this time were under the conduct of Martin Powell (not to be confused with the actor George Powell). Nichols (note to *Tatler* 16) describes him as 'a deformed cripple' who 'made Punch utter many things, that would not have been endured in any other way of communication'. Powell had exhibited his marionettes in Bath and other provincial towns (see *Tatlers* 37, 44, 50, 77, and 115), but early in 1710 removed to London, where at 'Punch's Theatre', at the upper end of St. Martin's Lane, joining Litchfield-street, he presented burlesques of operas and various comical entertainments. On 1 May 1710 the Four Indian Kings visited his theatre to witness 'an incomparable Entertainment, call'd, The Last Years Campaigne' (playbill reproduced in R. P. Bond, *Queen Anne's American Kings,* Oxford, 1952, facing p. 4). In Jan. 1711 Punch's Theatre was removed 'to the 7 Stars in the Little-Piazza Covent-Garden, (being a Place both warmer and fitter to receive Persons of Quality, &c.)' (*Daily Courant,* 27 Jan.). Here in the new site adjoining what was later Tavistock Row were presented 'The History of King Bladud, Founder of the Bath', 'The City-Rake, or Punch turn'd Quaker', 'The History of Whittington, thrice Lord Mayor of London: with variety of new scenes in imitation of the Italian Opera's', 'Orpheus's Journey to Hell', 'The Vertuous Wife, or Innocence in Danger', and (throughout the week in which this number of the *Spectator* appeared) 'Heroick Love, with variety of Scenes, Pageantry and Machinary, in imitation of the Italian Opera's'. It was at this theatre, on the other side of Covent Garden from St. Paul's Church, that Punch continued to entice the Under-Sexton's 'customers' from their prayers. According to Thomas Seccombe in the *DNB* Powell was largely responsible for the form taken by the drama of Punch and Judy. He died in 1729. Tickell's poem, 'Kensington Garden', 79-82, refers to the puppet-show:

> Whoe'er on *Powell's* dazling Stage display'd,
> Hath fam'd King *Pepin* and his Court survey'd,
> May guess, if old by modern Things we trace,
> The Pomp and Splendor of the Fairy-race.

[3] 'On the North and East Sides [of the Square] are Rows of very good and large Houses, called the Piazzo's, sustained by Stone Pillars to support the Buildings, under which are Walks, broad and convenient, paved with Freestone' (Strype's edition of Stow's *Survey of London,* 1720, vi. 89).

appear among us none but a few ordinary People, who come to Church only to say their Prayers, so that I have no Work worth speaking of but on *Sundays*. I have placed my Son at the *Piazzas* to acquaint the Ladies that the Bell rings for Church, and that it stands on the other Side of the *Garden*; but they only laugh at the Child.

'I desire you would lay this before all the World, that I may not be made such a Tool for the Future, and that Punchinello may chuse Hours less canonical. As things are now, Mr. *Powell* has a full Congregation, while we have a very thin House; which if you can Remedy, you will very much oblige,

Sir,

Your, &c.'

The following Epistle I find is from the Undertaker of the Masquerade.[1]

SIR,

'I HAVE observed the Rules of my Masque so carefully, (in not enquiring into Persons) that I cannot tell whether you were one of the Company or not last *Tuesday*; but if you were not, and still design to come, I desire you would, for your own Entertainment, please to admonish the Town, that all Persons indifferently are not fit for this Sort of Diversion. I could wish, Sir, you could make them understand, that it is a kind of acting to go in Masquerade, and a Man should be able to say or do things proper for the Dress in which he appears. We have now and then Rakes in the Habit of *Roman* Senators, and grave Politicians in the Dress of Rakes. The Mis-

---

[1] See No. 8. A masquerade 'with several Comical Dances' at Lambeth Wells is announced in the *Daily Courant* of 2 Sept. 1713 for the following evening: 'The Room will be darken'd and Candles lighted during the time of Dancing, which will continue till 9 a Clock.' An anonymous poem, *The Masquerade* (by Mrs. Centlivre?), inscribed to the Duke d'Aumont and published by Lintott in 1713, describes a masquerade held at Somerset House on 17 Aug. 1713.

> Here Witches, Devils, Conjurers, Hags are found,
> And there the midnight Watchman takes his Round:
> Swans, Eagles, Owls, and ominous Birds appear,
> That seem to threaten falling Virtue near;
> There wanton Nuns at Liberty you spy,
> Their Relicks, Beads and Orisons thrown by:
> The Rural Nymphs and Satyrs trip along,
> And pretty Milkmaids mingle in the Throng:
> The sprightly Templer leaves the noisie Bar,
> And comes to make a Motion to the Fair. (26–35)

The letter in this number suggests the possibilities for indecorous conversation and loose conduct which become a frequent theme in the novels and plays of the century. For 'the Undertaker of the Masquerade', J. J. Heidegger, see No. 31.

fortune of the thing is, that People dress themselves in what they have a Mind to be, and not what they are fit for. There is not a Girl in the Town, but let her have her Will in going to a Masque, and she shall dress as a Shepherdess. But let me beg of them to read the *Arcadia*,[1] or some other good Romance, before they appear in any such Character at my House. The last Day we presented, every Body was so rashly habited, that when they came to speak to each other, a Nymph with a Crook had not a Word to say but in the pert Stile of the Pit Bawdry; and a Man in the Habit of a Philosopher was speechless, till an Occasion offered of expressing himself in the Refuse of the Tyring-Rooms. We had a Judge that danced a Minuet, with a Quaker for his Partner, while half a dozen Harlequins stood by as Spectators: A *Turk* drank me off two Bottles of Wine, and a *Jew* eat me up half a Ham of Bacon. If I can bring my Design to bear, and make the Maskers preserve their Characters in my Assemblies, I hope you will allow there is a Foundation laid for more elegant and improving Gallantries than any the Town at present affords; and consequently, that you will give your Approbation to the Endeavours of,

Sir,
Your most obedient humble Servant.'

I am very glad the following Epistle obliges me to mention Mr. *Powell* a second Time in the same Paper; for indeed there cannot be too great Encouragement given to his Skill in Motions,[2] provided he is under proper Restrictions.

SIR,

'THE Opera at the *Hay-Market*, and that under the little *Piazza* in *Covent-Garden*, being at present the Two leading Diversions of the Town; and Mr. *Powell* professing in his Advertisements to set up *Whittington*[3] *and his Cat* against *Rinaldo and Armida*, my

---

[1] Sidney's *Arcadia* is one of the books in Leonora's Library (No. 37).

[2] 'Motions' has the obsolete sense of 'a puppet-show'. The last example given in *OED* is dated 1678.

[3] The story of Dick Whittington and his cat had long been a popular theme in chap-books, ballads, and puppet-shows. Pepys at Southwark Fair 'saw the puppet show of Whittington, which was pretty to see' on 21 Sept. 1668, and the booths at Bartholomew Fair frequently presented 'the famous Story of Whittington Lord Mayor of London, being set off with variety of Pageantry and Decorations suitable to the Subject', as the advertisement reads (*Daily Courant*, 19 Aug. 1706). It had been presented at Punch's Theatre on 23 Feb. 1711 'with Variety of New Scenes in Imitation of the Italian Opera's' (*Daily Courant*) and nine times thereafter in Feb., Mar., and Apr.

Curiosity led me the Beginning of last Week to view both these Performances, and make my Observations upon them.

'First therefore, I cannot but observe that Mr. *Powell* wisely forbearing to give his Company a Bill of Fare before-hand, every Scene is new and unexpected; whereas it is certain, that the Undertakers of the *Hay-Market*, having raised too great an Expectation in their printed Opera, very much disappoint their Audience on the Stage.

'The King of *Jerusalem* is obliged to come from the City on foot, instead of being drawn in a triumphant Chariot by white Horses, as my Opera-Book had promised me; and thus while I expected *Armida*'s Dragons should rush forward towards *Argantes*,[1] I found the Hero was obliged to go to *Armida*, and hand her out of her Coach. We had also but a very short Allowance of Thunder and Lightning; tho' I cannot in this Place omit doing Justice to the Boy who had the Direction of the Two painted Dragons, and made them spit Fire and Smoke: He flash'd out his Rosin in such just Proportions and in such due Time, that I could not forbear conceiving Hopes of his being one Day a most excellent Player. I saw indeed but Two things wanting to render his whole Action compleat, I mean the keeping his Head a little lower, and hiding his Candle.

'I observe that Mr. *Powell* and the Undertakers had both the same Thought, and I think, much about the same time, of introducing Animals on their several Stages, tho' indeed with very different Success. The Sparrows and Chaffinches[2] at the *Hay-Market* fly as yet very irregularly over the Stage; and instead of perching on the Trees and performing their Parts, these young Actors either get into the Galleries or put out the Candles; whereas Mr. *Powell* has so well disciplin'd his Pig,[3] that in the first Scene he and Punch dance a Minuet together. I am informed however, that Mr. *Powell* resolves to excell his Adversaries in their own Way; and introduce Larks in

---

[1] For these features of *Rinaldo* see No. 5.

[2] See No. 5.

[3] In *A Second Tale of a Tub: or, the History of Robert Powel the Puppet-Show-Man* (by Thomas Burnet and George Duckett), published in 1715, a list of Punch's 'incomparable Dramas' is given, concluding with 'the Pleasant and Comical Humours of *Valentini*, *Nicolini*, and the tuneful warbling Pig of *Italian Race*' (pp. 218–19). Among the papers of M. L. S. Clements at Ashfield Lodge, Cootehill, co. Cavan, is an undated letter (11 May 1711, since it mentions the Dering–Thornhill duel 'two days ago') from 'P. L. to Mr. Molesworth' and describing the puppet-show of 'Mr. Porrel'. 'He has turned his ordinary show into an opera in ridicule of *Hydaspes*, in which Punch most heroically kills a pig and sings an *Io Pean* in Italian music, this has affronted Nicolino and he threatens to tread the stage no more' (*Hist. MSS. Comm., Various Collections*, viii (1913), 251).

his next Opera of *Susanna* or *Innocence betrayed*, which will be exhibited next Week with a Pair of new Elders.[1]

'The Moral of Mr. *Powell*'s Drama is violated I confess by Punch's national Reflections on the *French*, and King *Harry*'s laying his Leg upon thea Queen's Lap in too ludicrous a manner before so great an Assembly.

'As to the Mechanism and Scenary, every thing indeed was uniform and of a Piece, and the Scenes were managed very dexterously; which calls on me to take Notice, that at the *Hay-Market* the Undertakers forgetting to change their Side-Scenes,[2] we were presented with a Prospect of the Ocean in the midst of a delightful Grove; and tho' the Gentlemen on the Stage had very much contributed to the Beauty of the Grove by walking up and down between the Trees, I must own I was not a little astonish'd to see a well-dress'd young Fellow in a full-bottom'd Wigg, appear in the Midst of the Sea, and without any visible Concern taking Snuff.

'I shall only observe one thing further, in which both Dramas agree; which is, that by the Squeak of their Voices the Heroes of each are Eunuchs; and as the Wit in both Pieces are equal, I must prefer the Performance of Mr. *Powell*, because it is in our own Language.

I am, &c.'b

R

a the] his *Fol.*   b *ADVERTISEMENT. On the first of April will be performed at the Play-house in the* Hay-market *an Opera call'd* The Cruelty of Atreus. *N.B. The Scene wherein* Thyestes *eats his own Children, is to be performed by the famous Mr* Psalmanazar,[3] *lately arrived from* Formosa: *The whole Supper being set to Kettle-drums. Fol.*

---

1 'The History of Chast Susannah, and the 2 wicked Elders' is advertised for performance at Punch's Opera at Litchfield Street End for 16 Nov. 1710. 'The Figures being drest in Hebrew and Babilonian Habits; with that diverting Figure of the Jesuit, where you'll see a Woman Quaker Holding Forth from his Head, and is delivered with an Antick from his Body with the Scaramouch and Tumbler, &c. all the Figures performed by Powell, with Scenes and Machines, with a Prologue coherent to the Play' (*Post-Man*, 16 Nov. 1710).

2 For the use of lateral side scenes at this time alongside of back-cloth and wings see Nicoll, p. 29.

3 George Psalmanazar (1679?–1763) had already published his *History of Formosa* some years before (1704). A second edition appeared in 1705, and on 18 July 1707 was published *An Enquiry into the Objections against George Psalmanaazaar of Formosa* (*Daily Courant*).

'The humour of the strictures on the Opera in these Papers is pointed: it is said, the *Pope*, on reading them, laughed till his sides shook. There are very many Numbers besides this, that well merit the attention of such as pretend to distinguish with wonderful facility between Addison's and Steele's Papers' (Nichols).

No. 15
[ADDISON]

Saturday, March 17, 1711[1]

Parva leves capiunt animos . . .
Ovid

WHEN I was in *France*, I used to gaze with great Astonishment at the Splendid Equipages, and Party-coloured Habits, of that Fantastick Nation.[2] I was one Day in particular contemplating a Lady, that sate in a Coach adorned with gilded *Cupids*, and finely painted with the Loves of *Venus* and *Adonis*. The Coach was drawn by six milk-white Horses, and loaden[3] behind with the same Number of powder'd Foot-men. Just before the Lady were a Couple of beautiful Pages, that were stuck among the Harness, and by their gay Dresses, and smiling Features, looked like the elder Brothers of the little Boys that were carved and painted in every Corner of the Coach.

The Lady was the unfortunate *Cleanthe*, who afterwards gave an Occasion to a pretty melancholy Novel. She had, for several Years, received the Addresses of a Gentleman, whom, after a long and intimate Acquaintance she forsook, upon the Account of this shining Equipage, which had been offered to her by one of Great Riches, but a Crazy Constitution. The Circumstances in which I saw her, were, it seems, the Disguises only of a broken Heart, and a kind of Pageantry to cover Distress; for in two Months after she was carried to her Grave with the same Pomp and Magnificence: being sent thither partly by the Loss of one Lover, and partly by the Possession of another.

I have often reflected with my self on this unaccountable Humour in Woman-kind, of being smitten with every thing that is showy and superficial; and on the numberless Evils that befall the Sex,

---

[1] *Motto.* Ovid, *Ars Amatoria*, 1. 159:
Light minds are taken with little things.

[2] Mr. Spectator here and elsewhere views the French as a 'ludicrous Nation' (No. 45, a vain and lively people, light and talkative, politically enslaved, and in battle 'already cowed and accustomed to flight' (No. 167). The *Spectator*'s views cannot be attributed entirely to political animus; Swift in *Examiner* 32 (published just two days earlier) describes them as 'a People, whose Genius seems wholly turned to singing, and dancing, and prating; to Vanity and Impertinence; who lay so much Weight upon Modes and Gestures; whose Essentialities are generally so very superficial; who are usually so serious upon Trifles, and so trifling upon what is serious . . .' (*Prose Works*, ed. H. Davis, iii. 107).

[3] This obsolete form of the past participle continues through the century (the last quotation in *OED* is dated 1792) and occurs frequently in the *Spectator*.

from this light, fantastical Disposition. I my self remember a young Lady, that was very warmly sollicited by a Couple of importunate Rivals, who for several Months together did all they could to recommend themselves, by Complacency of Behaviour, and Agreeableness of Conversation. At length, when the Competition was doubtful, and the Lady undetermined in her Choice, one of the young Lovers very luckily bethought himself of adding a supernumerary Lace to his Liveries, which had so good an Effect that he married her the very Week after.

The usual Conversation of ordinary Women very much cherishes this Natural Weakness of being taken with Outside and Appearance. Talk of a new-married Couple, and you immediately hear whether they keep their Coach and six, or eat in Plate: Mention the Name of an absent Lady, and it is ten to one but you learn something of her Gown and Petticoat. A Ball is a great Help to Discourse, and a Birth-Day furnishes Conversation for a Twelve-month after. A Furbelow of precious Stones, an Hat buttoned with a Diamond, a Brocade Waistcoat or Petticoat, are standing Topicks. In short, they consider only the Drapery of the Species, and never cast away a Thought on those Ornaments of the Mind, that make Persons Illustrious in themselves, and Useful to others. When Women are thus perpetually dazling one anothers Imaginations, and filling their Heads with nothing but Colours, it is no Wonder that they are more attentive to the superficial Parts of Life, than the solid and substantial Blessings of it. A Girl, who has been trained up in this kind of Conversation, is in danger of every Embroidered Coat that comes in her Way. A Pair of fringed Gloves[1] may be her Ruin. In a word, Lace and Ribbons, Silver and Gold Galloons,[2] with the like glittering Gew-Gaws, are so many Lures to Women of weak Minds or low Educations, and, when artificially[3] displayed, are able to fetch down the most airy Coquet from the wildest of her Flights and Rambles.

True Happiness is of a retired Nature, and an Enemy to Pomp and Noise; it arises, in the first place, from the Enjoyment of ones self; and, in the next, from the Friendship and Conversation of a few

[1] Isaac Bickerstaff considered it impossible 'to reckon up all the Virgins that have fallen a Sacrifice to a Pair of fringed Gloves' (*Tatler* 151).

[2] A galloon was 'a kind of narrow, close-woven ribbon or braid, of gold, silver, or silk thread, used for trimming articles of apparel' (*OED*). In *Tatler* 270 Ralph Nab, haberdasher of hats, presents a petition to Mr. Bickerstaff complaining of the 'almost universal' use of gold and silver galloons upon hats.

[3] Here, as commonly in the *Spectator*, in the obsolete sense of 'artistically, designed with skill'.

select Companions. It loves Shade and Solitude, and naturally haunts Groves and Fountains, Fields and Meadows: In short, it feels every thing it wants within it self, and receives no Addition from Multitudes of Witnesses and Spectators. On the contrary, false Happiness loves to be in a Crowd, and to draw the Eyes of the World upon her. She does not receive any Satisfaction from the Applauses which she gives her self, but from the Admiration which she raises in others. She flourishes in Courts and Palaces, Theatres and Assemblies, and has no Existence but when she is looked upon.

Aurelia, tho' a Woman of Great Quality, delights in the Privacy of a Country Life, and passes away a great part of her Time in her own Walks and Gardens. Her Husband, who is her Bosom Friend, and Companion in her Solitudes, has been in Love with her ever since he knew her. They both abound with good Sense, consummate Virtue, and a mutual Esteem; and are a perpetual Entertainment to one another. Their Family is under so regular an Oeconomy, in its Hours of Devotion and Repast, Employment and Diversion, that it looks like a little Common-Wealth within it self. They often go into Company, that they may return with the greater Delight to one another; and sometimes live in Town not to enjoy it so properly as to grow weary of it, that they may renew in themselves the Relish of a Country Life. By this means they are Happy in each other, beloved by their Children, adored by their Servants, and are become the Envy, or rather the Delight, of all that know them.

How different to this is the Life of *Fulvia*![1] she considers her Husband as her Steward, and looks upon Discretion, and good House-Wifery, as little domestick Virtues, unbecoming a Woman of Quality. She thinks Life lost in her own Family, and fancies her self out of the World when she is not in the Ring,[2] the Play-House, or the Drawing-Room: She lives in a perpetual Motion of Body, and Restlesness of Thought, and is never easie in any one Place when she thinks there is more Company in another. The missing of an

[1] Too much significance should not, of course, be attached to these names, but Fulvia, the wife of Marc Antony, is described by Plutarch as 'a woman not born for spinning or housewifery' (*Antony*, x. 3).
[2] The circular road in Hyde Park, forming a popular ride and promenade in fine weather. In his account of Hyde Park Misson writes: 'Here the People of Fashion take the Diversion of the Ring: In a pretty high Place, which lies very open, they have surrounded a Circumference of two or three hundred Paces Diameter with a sorry Kind of Ballustrade, or rather with Poles plac'd upon Stakes, but three Foot from the Ground; and the Coaches drive round and round this. When they have turn'd for some Time round one Way, they face about and turn t'other: So rowls the World' (p. 126).

Opera the first Night, would be more afflicting to her than the Death of a Child. She pities all the valuable Part of her own Sex, and calls every Woman of a prudent modest retired Life, a poor-spirited, unpolished Creature. What a Mortification would it be to *Fulvia*, if she knew that her setting her-self to View is but exposing her self, and that she grows Contemptible by being Conspicuous.

I cannot conclude my Paper, without observing that *Virgil* has very finely touched upon this Female Passion for Dress and Show, in the Character of *Camilla*; who, tho' she seems to have shaken off all the other Weaknesses of her Sex, is still described as a Woman in this Particular. The Poet tells us, that after having made a great Slaughter of the Enemy, she unfortunately cast her Eye on a *Trojan* who[a] wore an embroidered Tunick, a beautiful Coat of Mail, with a Mantle of the finest Purple. *A Golden Bow*, says he, *hung upon his Shoulder; his Garment was buckled with a Golden Clasp, and his Head covered with an Helmet of the same shining Mettle.* The *Amazon* immediately singled out this well-dressed Warrior, being seized with a Woman's Longing for the pretty Trappings that he was adorned with:

> . . . *Totumque incauta per agmen*
> *Fœmineo prædæ & spoliorum ardebat amore.*[1]

This heedless Pursuit after these glittering Trifles, the Poet (by a nice concealed Moral) represents to have been the Destruction of his Female Hero.   C

---

[a] who] that *Fol.*

---

[1] Virgil, *Aeneid* ,11. 781–2:
> Him, the fierce Maid beheld with ardent Eyes;
> Fond and Ambitious of so Rich a Prize:
> Or that the Temple might his Trophees hold,
> Or else to shine her self in *Trojan* Gold:
> Blind in her haste, she chases him alone,
> And seeks his Life, regardless of her own. DRYDEN.

Le Bossu (book iv, chap. ii) uses this example to point the same moral: 'the Motives the Poet gives her are looked upon as a Woman's greedy Desire. This Levity of the Sex makes *Camilla* forget her Dignity, and the taking Care of her Safety, and 'tis followed with very mischievous Effects' (ii. 104).

No. 16   *Monday, March* 19, 1711[1]

[ADDISON]

Quod verum atque decens curo & rogo, & omnis in hoc sum.
                                               Hor.

I HAVE receiv'd a Letter, desiring me to be very satyrical upon the little Muff[2] that is now in Fashion; another informs me of a Pair of silver Garters buckled below the Knee, that have been lately seen at the *Rainbow* Coffee-house[3] in *Fleet-street*; a third sends me an heavy Complaint against fringed Gloves.[4] To be brief, there is scarce an Ornament of either Sex which one or other of my Correspondents has not inveighed against with some Bitterness, and recommended to my Observation. I must therefore, once for all inform my Readers, that it is not my Intention to sink the Dignity of this my Paper with Reflections upon Red-heels or Top-knots,[5] but rather to enter into the Passions of Mankind, and to correct those depraved Sentiments that give Birth to all those little Extravagancies which appear in their outward Dress and Behaviour. Foppish and fantastick Ornaments are only Indications of Vice, not criminal in themselves. Extinguish Vanity in the Mind, and you naturally retrench the little Superfluities of Garniture and Equipage. The Blossoms will fall of themselves, when the Root that nourishes them is destroyed.

I shall therefore, as I have said, apply my Remedies to the first Seeds and Principles of an affected Dress, without descending to the Dress it self; though at the same time I must own, that I have Thoughts of creating an Officer under me to be entituled *The Censor of small Wares*,[6] and of allotting him one Day in a Week for the Execu-

---

[1] *Motto.* Horace, *Epistles*, I.I.II:
         I now design to seek what's good and true,
         And that alone. CREECH.

[2] Men carried muffs at this period; Addison's Upholsterer had 'a loose great Coat and a Muff' (*Tatler* 155). Among the lost articles advertised for in the *Daily Courant* of 5 Mar. 1704/5 is 'a Man's Muff with a brass Ring to it'.

[3] There were at least six coffee-houses of this name; the one in Fleet Street was near Lintot's book-shop. According to Ashton (ii. 228) it was still in existence in 1882.

[4] Cf. No. 15.

[5] Red-heeled shoes are described as 'essential Parts of the Habit belonging to the Order of *smart Fellows*' in *Tatler* 26. The top-knot was a bow of ribbon worn on the head by ladies.

[6] Mr. Spectator asks his correspondents to let him know whether they approve this project. From the fact that 'a petty Censorship' does not become one of the features of the *Spectator* it is possible to infer that letters were received vetoing the proposal; at any rate, beyond a reference in No. 619 (vol. iv) nothing more is heard of the project. The *Original Letters* printed by Lillie in 1725 contains one from 'J. C.' on

tion of such his Office. An Operator of this Nature might act under me with the same Regard as a Surgeon to a Physitian; the one might be employ'd in healing those Blotches and Tumours which break out in the Body, while the other is sweetning the Blood and rectifying the Constitution. To speak truly, the young People of both Sexes are so wonderfully apt to shoot out into long Swords or sweeping Trains,[1] bushy Head-dresses or full-bottom'd Perriwigs, with several other Incumbrances of Dress, that they stand in Need of being pruned very frequently, lest they should be oppressed[a] with Ornaments, and over-run with the Luxuriency of their Habits. I am much in doubt, whether I should give the Preference to a Quaker that is trimmed close and almost cut to the Quick, or to a Beau that is loaden with such a Redundance of Excrescencies. I must therefore desire my Correspondents to let me know how they approve my Project, and whether they think the erecting of such a petty Censorship may not turn to the Emolument of the Publick; for I would not do any thing of this Nature rashly and without Advice.

There is another Set of Correspondents to whom I must address my self in the second Place; I mean such as fill their Letters with private Scandal, and black Accounts of particular Persons and Families. The World is so full of Ill-nature, that I have Lampoons sent me by People who[b] cannot spell, and Satyrs compos'd by those who scarce know how to write. By the last Post in particular I receiv'd a Packet of Scandal which[c] is not legible; and have a whole Bundle of Letters in Womens Hands that are full of Blots and Calumnies, insomuch that when I see the Name *Cælia*, *Phillis*, *Pastora*, or the like, at the Bottom of a Scrawl, I conclude on course[2] that it

---

 a frequently . . . oppressed] frequently that they may not be oppressed *Fol.*
b who] that *Fol.*   c which] that *Fol.*

---

the subject: 'Since you have so generously given leave to your correspondents to give you their sentiments freely on the point of a petty-censorship, for my part I freely declare against it, especially to through away so much time and paper on such frivolous impertinences. When I come to bind up my spectators in a volume (for I take them daily, and constantly drink a dish of tea over them) how poor a figure will fifty two leaves make in my book, filled with top-knots, muffs, scarfs, and riding-hoods? besides, that day my tea will lose its relish, for I cannot bear those trifling pieces of low life. No, Sir, rather advance human nature, by reaching home to the corrupt affections of both sexes, and thereby make your paper equally serviceable as delightful to men of sense and virtue as to small wits and triflers . . .' (i. 191).
[1] Cf. *Rape of the Lock*, i. 84: 'Peers and Dukes, and all their sweeping Train.'
[2] The last quotation in *OED* for this obsolete phrase.

brings me some Account of a fallen Virgin, a faithless Wife, or an amorous Widow.[1] I must therefore inform these my Correspondents, that it is not my Design to be a Publisher of Intreagues and Cuckoldoms, or to bring little infamous Stories out of their present lurking Holes into broad Day light. If I attack the Vicious, I shall only set upon them in a Body; and will not be provoked by the worst Usage I can[a] receive from others, to make an Example of any particular Criminal. In short, I have so much of a *Drawcansir* in me, that I shall pass over a single Foe to charge whole Armies.[2] It is not *Lais* or *Silenus*, but the Harlot and the Drunkard, whom I shall endeavour to expose; and shall consider the Crime as it appears in a Species, not as it is circumstanced in an Individual. I think it was *Caligula* who wished the whole City of *Rome* had but one Neck, that he might behead them at a Blow.[3] I shall do out of Humanity what that Emperour would have done in the Cruelty of his Temper, and aim every Stroak at a collective Body of Offenders. At the same Time I am very sensible, that nothing spreads a Paper like private Calumny and Defamation; but as my Speculations are not under this Necessity, they are not exposed to this Temptation.

In the next Place I must apply my self to my Party-Correspondents, who are continually teazing me to take Notice of one anothers Proceedings. How often am I asked by both Sides, if it is possible for me to be an unconcerned Spectator of the Rogueries that are committed by the Party which is opposite to him that writes the Letter. About two Days since I was reproached with an old *Grecian* Law, that forbids any Man to stand as a Neuter or a Looker-on in the Divisions of his Country.[4] However, as I am very sensible my[b]

[a] Usage I can] Usage that I can *Fol.*   [b] sensible my] sensible that my *Fol.*

---

[1] Betterton's play, *The Amorous Widow, or the Wanton Wife* had been given recently at Drury Lane Theatre (on 9 January), with Mrs. Oldfield in the chief role.

[2] In the *Rehearsal*, V. i. 354, Drawcansir, after engaging in the battle between foot- and great-hobby-horses, says:

> Others may boast a single man to kill,
> But I the blood of thousands daily spill.

[3] Suetonius, *Caligula* 30, and quoted by Seneca (*De Ira*, 3. 19. 2). See also Nos. 246 (vol. ii) and 435 (vol. iv).

[4] According to Plutarch, Solon made a 'peculiar and surprising' law, which ordained that a man who in time of faction takes neither side shall be disfranchised (*Solon*, 20. 1). Aristotle (*Constitution of Athens*, 8. 5) also mentions the law, which was directed against those citizens who waited to see what the outcome of a given political struggle might be. Addison praises this 'remarkable law of Solon' in *Free-holder* 13.

Paper would lose its whole Effect, should it run into the Outrages of a Party, I shall take Care to keep clear of every thing which[a] looks that Way. If I can any way asswage private Inflamations, or allay publick Ferments, I shall apply my self to it with my utmost Endeavours; but will never let my Heart reproach me with having done any thing towards encreasing[b] those Feuds and Animosities that extinguish Religion, deface Government, and make a Nation miserable.

What I have said under the three foregoing Heads, will, I am afraid, very much retrench the Number of my Correspondents: I shall therefore acquaint my Reader, that if he has started any Hint which he is not able to pursue, if he has met with any surprizing Story which he does not know how to tell, if he has discovered any epidemical Vice which has escaped my Observation, or has heard of any uncommon Vertue which he would desire to publish; in short, if he has any Materials that can furnish out an innocent Diversion, I shall promise him my best Assistance in the working of them up for a publick Entertainment.

This Paper my Reader will find was intended for an Answer to a Multitude of Correspondents; but I hope he will pardon me if I single out one of them in particular, who has made me so very humble a Request, that I cannot forbear complying with it.

To the SPECTATOR.

SIR,   *March* 15, 1710–11.

'I AM at present so unfortunate, as to have nothing to do but to mind my own Business; and therefore beg of you that you will be pleased to put me into some small Post under you. I observe that you have appointed your Printer and Publisher to receive Letters and Advertisements for the City of *London*, and shall think my self very much honoured by you, if you will appoint me to take in Letters and Advertisements for the City of *Westminster* and the Dutchy of *Lancaster*.[1] Tho' I cannot promise to fill such an Employ-

---

[a] which] that *Fol.*   [b] towards encreasing] towards the encreasing *Fol.*

---

[1] A district or liberty outside the freedom of London, extending roughly from Cecil Street west of Beaufort Buildings to Temple Bar. The Savoy Palace, Somerset House, and Essex House, in this district, had formerly belonged to the Duke of Lancaster.

ment with sufficient Abilities, I will endeavour to make up with Industry and Fidelity what I want in Parts and Genius. I am,

Sir,

Your most obedient Servant,

Charles Lillie.'[1]

C

No. 17

[STEELE]

. . . *Tetrum ante Omnia vultum.*

Juv.

SINCE our Persons are not of our own Making, when they are such as appear Defective or Uncomely, it is, methinks, an honest and laudable Fortitude to dare to be Ugly; at least to keep our selves from being abashed with a Consciousness of Imperfections which we cannot help, and in which there is no Guilt. I would not defend an haggard Beau, for passing away much time at a Glass, and giving Softnesses and Languishing Graces to Deformity. All I intend

---

[1] Lillie was a perfumer, with a shop at 'the corner of Beaufort Buildings in the Strand', who had also acted as agent in the distribution of the *Tatler*. A letter from him is printed in *Tatler* 92, 'to beg the Favour of being advantagiously exposed in your Paper, chiefly for the Reputation of Snuff'. In *Tatler* 94 Steele praises his orange-flower water, his snuff, and his other 'Helps to Discourse', and in *Tatler* 96 denies a rumour that Lillie and Isaac Bickerstaff are partners. 'However, since the said *Charles* has promised that all his Customers shall be mine, I must desire all mine to be his; and dare answer for him, that if you ask in my Name for Snuff, Hungary or Orange-Water, you shall have the best the Town affords at the cheapest Rate.' There are many other references to Lillie in the *Tatler*, and when the collected volumes appeared in 1710–11 the imprint read 'London, Printed: And to be deliver'd to Subscribers, by *Charles Lillie*, Perfumer, at the Corner of *Beauford-Buildings* in the *Strand*; and *John Morphew* near *Stationers-Hall*.' With No. 16 of the *Spectator* Lillie's name is added to that of Mrs. Anne Baldwin as a shop 'where Advertisements are taken in', and throughout the run of the periodical Lillie seems to have been active in assisting its circulation. In 1725 he brought out by subscription in two volumes *Original and Genuine Letters sent to the Tatler and Spectator, during the Time those Works were publishing: None of which have been before Printed*, with a dedication to Steele and a commendatory letter from him. Lillie, whose career seems to have closed about 1740, brought together a large collection of recipes which was later edited by Colin Mackenzie and published in 1822 under the title of *The British Perfumer, Snuff-Manufacturer, and Colourman's Guide; being a Collection of Choice Receipts and Observations, proved in an extensive Practice of Thirty Years, in the above Branches of Trade.*

[2] *Motto.* Juvenal, *Satires*, 10. 191:

Above all a repulsive face.

is, that we ought to be contented with our Countenance and Shape, so far, as never to give our selves an uneasie Reflection on that Subject. It is to the ordinary People, who are not accustomed to make very proper Remarks on any Occasion, matter of great Jest, if a Man enters with a prominent Pair of Shoulders into an Assembly, or is distinguished by an Expansion of Mouth, or Obliquity of Aspect. It is happy for a Man, that has any of these Odnesses about him, if he can be as merry upon himself, as others are apt to be upon that Occasion: When he can possess himself with such a Chearfulness, Women and Children, who were at first frighted at him, will afterwards be as much pleased with him. As it is barbarous in others to railly him for natural Defects, it is extreamly agreeable when he can Jest upon himself for them.

Madam *Maintenon*'s first Husband[1] was an Hero in this Kind, and has drawn many Pleasantries from the Irregularity of his Shape, which he describes as very much resembling the Letter Z. He diverts himself likewise by representing to his Reader the Make of an Engine and Pully, with which he used to take off his Hat. When there happens to be any thing ridiculous in a Visage, and the Owner of it thinks it an Aspect of Dignity, he must be of very great Quality to be exempt from Raillery: The best Expedient therefore is to be pleasant upon himself. Prince *Harry* and *Falstaffe*, in *Shakespear*, have carry'd the Ridicule upon Fat and Lean as far as it will go. *Falstaffe* is Humourously called *Woolsack*, *Bed-presser*, and *Hill of Flesh*; *Harry*, a *Starveling*, an *Elves-Skin*, a *Sheath*, a *Bow-case*, and a *Tuck*.[2] There is, in several incidents of the Conversation between them, the Jest still kept up upon the Person. Great Tenderness and Sensibility in this Point is one of the greatest Weaknesses of Self-love; for my own part, I am a little unhappy in the Mold of my Face,[3] which is not quite so long as it is broad: Whether this might not partly arise from my opening my Mouth much seldomer than other People, and by Consequence not so much lengthning the Fibres of my Visage,

---

[1] Paul Scarron (1610–60), who married in 1652 Françoise d'Aubigné, afterwards Madame de Maintenon and wife to Louis XIV. Although a helpless cripple, he drew 'many Pleasantries' from his deformity, in the Preface to his *Roman Comique* (1651): 'My Legs and Thighs in the first place compose an obtuse Angle, then an equal one, and lastly an acute. My Thighs and Body make another, and my Head leaning perpetually over my Belly, I fancy makes me not very unlike the Letter Z' (*Whole Comical Works*, 2nd ed., 1703, sig. A4).

[2] *1 Henry IV*, II. iv. 149, 268–74. Betterton's *King Henry IV with the Humours of Sir John Falstaff* had been given at Drury Lane on 2 Dec. 1710, with Estcourt as Falstaff and Wilks as the Prince.

[3] The portraits of Steele by Kneller and Thornhill show the 'shortness' of his face.

I am not at leisure to determine. However it be, I have been often put out of Countenance by the Shortness of my Face, and was formerly at great Pains in concealing it by wearing a Periwigg with an high Foretop, and letting my Beard grow. But now I have thoroughly got over this Delicacy, and could be contented it were much shorter, provided it might qualify me for a Member of the Merry Club, which the following Letter gives me an Account of. I have recieved it from *Oxford*, and as it abounds with the Spirit of Mirth and good Humour, which is natural to that Place, I shall set it down Word for Word as it came to me.

Most Profound Sir,

'HAVING been very well entertained, in the last of your Speculations that I have yet seen, by your Specimen upon Clubs, which I therefore hope you will continue, I shall take the Liberty to furnish you with a brief Account of such a one as perhaps you have not seen in all your Travels, unless it was your Fortune to touch upon some of the woody Parts of the *African* Continent, in your Voyage to or from *Grand Cairo*. There have arose in this University, (long since you left us without saying any thing) several of these inferior Hebdomadal Societies, as *the Punning Club*, *the Witty Club*, and amongst the rest *the Handsom Club*; as a Burlesque upon which, a certain merry Species, that seem to have come into the World in Masquerade, for some Years last past have associated themselves together, and assum'd the Name of *the Ugly Club*:[1] This ill-favoured Fraternity consists of a President and twelve Fellows; the Choice of which is not confin'd by Patent to any particular Foundation, (as St. *John*'s Men would have the World believe, and have therefore erected a separate Society within themselves) but Liberty is left to elect from any School in *Great Britain*, provided the Candidates be within the Rules of the Club, as set forth in a Table entitled *The Act of Deformity*. A Clause or two of which I shall transmit to you.

'I. That no Person whatsoever shall be admitted without a visible Quearity[2] in his Aspect, or peculiar Cast of Countenance; of which the President and Officers for the time being are to determine, and the President to have the casting Voice.

---

[1] Among Lillie's *Original Letters* is one from Frances Frightful, desiring admission into the society and offering to produce 'certificates of my unparalelled distortions' (i. 193). *The Ugly Club*, a dramatic caricature 'founded on the Seventeenth Number of the Spectator' and written by 'Edmund Spenser, the Younger', was performed at Drury Lane on 6 June 1798.
[2] The first example of the word in *OED*.

'II. That a singular Regard be had, upon Examination, to the Gibbosity of the Gentlemen that offer themselves, as Founders Kinsmen, or to the Obliquity of their Figure, in what sort soever.

'III. That if the Quantity of any Man's Nose be eminently mis-calculated, whether as to Length or Breadth, he shall have a just Pretence to be elected.

'*Lastly*, That if there shall be two or more Competitors for the same Vacancy, *cæteris paribus*, he that has the thickest Skin to have the Preference.

'Every fresh Member, upon his first Night, is to entertain the Company with a Dish of Cod-fish, and a Speech in praise of *Æsop*;[1] whose Portraiture they have in full Proportion, or rather Disproportion, over the Chimney; and their Design is, as soon as their Funds are sufficient, to purchase the Heads of *Thersites*, *Duns Scotus*, *Scarron*, *Hudibras*, and the old Gentleman in *Oldham*, with all the celebrated ill Faces of Antiquity, as Furniture for the Club Room.[2]

'As they have always been profess'd Admirers of the other Sex, so they unanimously declare that they will give all possible Encouragement to such as will take the Benefit of the Statute, tho' none yet have appeared to do it.

'The worthy President, who is their most devoted Champion, has lately shown me two Copies of Verses composed by a Gentleman of his Society; the first, a Congratulatory Ode inscrib'd to Mrs. *Touchwood*,[3] upon the loss of her two Fore-teeth; the other, a Panegyrick upon Mrs. *Andiron*'s left Shoulder. Mrs. *Vizard* (he says) since the Small Pox, is grown tolerably ugly, and a top Tost in the Club; but I never hear him so lavish of his fine things, as upon old *Nell*

[1] Æsop's ugliness is described in the *Life* by Maximus Planudes: 'in his person deformed, to the highest degree: Flat-nos'd, Hunch-Back'd, Blobber-Lipp'd; a Long Miss-shapen Head; his Body Crooked all over, Big-Belly'd, Baker-legg'd, and his Complexion so swarthy, that he took his very Name from't; for *Æsop* is the same with *Æthiop*' (L'Estrange, *Fables of Æsop*, 1692, p. 1). The full-page plate opposite p. 1 in L'Estrange depicts Æsop as a hunchback. In *Guardian* 92 (by Pope) Dick Distick thinks 'Æsop was not a jot properer or handsomer than he is represented by the common pictures'. Vanbrugh's comedy *Æsop* (1697) had been revived at Drury Lane on 5 Dec. 1710, with Cibber in the ugly deformed title-part.
[2] Thersites, bandy-legged and lame in one foot, is introduced in the *Iliad* (2. 216–19). 'The deformities of Dun Scotus were probably the exaggeration of his opponents the Thomists, and through them became a tradition' (G. Gregory Smith). For the deformity of Hudibras see especially I. i. 285–302. The 'old Gentleman in Oldham' is Loyola, in Satire 3 ('Loyola's Will') of Oldham's *Satyrs upon the Jesuits* (1681):

His bristling Hairs stick up, his Eye-Balls glow,
And from his Mouth long flakes of Drivel flow (26–27).
[3] This may recall the violent aunt, Lady Touchwood, in Congreve's *Double Dealer* (1693).

Trot, who constantly officiates at their Table; her he even adores, and extolls as the very Counterpart of Mother *Shipton*;[1] in short, *Nell* (says he) is one of the Extraordinary Works of Nature; but as for Complexion, Shape, and Features, so valued by others, they are all meer Outside and Symmetry, which is his Aversion. Give me leave to add, that the President is a facetious, pleasant Gentleman, and never more so, than when he has got (as he calls 'em) his dear Mummers about him; and he often protests it does him good to meet a Fellow with a right genuine Grimmace in his Air, (which is so agreeable in the generality of the *French* Nation;) and as an Instance of his Sincerity in this particular, he gave me a sight of a List in his Pocket-book of all of this Class, who for these five Years have fallen under his Observation, with himself at the Head of 'em, and in the Rear (as one of a promising and improving Aspect)

SIR,

Your Obliged and

Oxford,

March 12, 1710.

Humble Servant,

Alexander Carbuncle.'

R

No. 18   *Wednesday, March 21, 1711*[2]
[ADDISON]

  . . . Equitis quoque jam migravit ab aure voluptas
Omnis ad incertos oculos & gaudia vana.

Hor.

IT is my Design in this Paper to deliver down to Posterity a faithful Account of the *Italian* Opera, and of the gradual Progress

---

[1] In *The Life and Death of Mother Shipton* (1684) by Richard Head her ill looks are described in chap. iv: 'Her Neck so strangely distorted, that her right shoulder was forced to be a supporter to her head, it being propt up by the help of her Chin, in such sort, that the right side of her Body stood much lower than the left; like the reeling of a Ship that sails with a side wind' (p. 10). In *Tatler* 89 a stone-cutter who 'improved' statues is recalled: 'I remember a *Venus*, that by the Nose he had given her, look'd like Mother *Shipton*.' One of the new operas 'now fitting' at Punch's Theatre (*Daily Courant*, 11 Apr. 1712) is 'The Life of Mother Shipton and Downfal of Cardinal Woolsey'.

[2] *Motto.* Horace, *Epistles*, 2. 1. 187–8:

      But now our *Nobles* too are Fops and Vain,
      Neglect the Sense, but love the Painted Scene. CREECH.

which it has made upon the *English* Stage: For there is no Question but our great Grand-children will be very curious to know the Reason why their Forefathers used to sit together like an Audience of Foreigners in their own Country, and to hear whole Plays acted before them in a Tongue which they did not understand.

Arsinoe[1] was the first Opera that gave us a Taste of *Italian* Musick. The great Success this[a] Opera met with, produced some Attempts of forming Pieces upon *Italian* Plans, which[b] should give a more natural and reasonable Entertainment than what can be met with in the elaborate Trifles of that Nation. This alarm'd the Poetasters and Fidlers of the Town, who were used to deal in a more ordinary Kind of Ware; and therefore laid down an establish'd Rule, which is receiv'd as such to this Day,[c] *That nothing is capable of being well set to Musick, that is not Nonsense.*

This Maxim was no sooner receiv'd, but we immediately fell to translating the *Italian* Operas; and as there was no great Danger of hurting the Sense of those extraordinary Pieces, our Authors would often make Words of their own which[d] were entirely foreign to the Meaning of the Passages they[e] pretended to translate; their chief Care being to make the Numbers of the *English* Verse answer to those of the *Italian*, that both of them might go to the same Tune. Thus the famous Song in *Camilla*,[2]

[a] Success this] Success which this *Fol.* this very Day, *Fol.*   [b] which] that *Fol.*   [c] this Day,] this very Day, *Fol.*   [d] which] that *Fol.*   [e] Passages they] Passages which they *Fol.*

---

[1] *Arsinoe, Queen of Cyprus*, was first produced at Drury Lane on 16 Jan. 1705, with Mrs. Tofts in the title-role. The libretto by Peter Motteux was based on an Italian piece by Tomaso Stanzani, and the music was composed or adapted by Thomas Clayton, probably with the assistance of Charles Dieupart and Nicolo Haym (cf. No. 258 (vol. ii)). Clayton was also responsible for the music of Addison's opera *Rosamond*. The statement made here regarding the primacy of *Arsinoe* is supported by a modern authority: 'Although it was, strictly speaking, an English opera, the history of Italian opera in England begins with *Arsinoe*, as there is a steady development, from the mere translation of an Italian libretto to the actual insertion of Italian airs in *Camilla* (1706) to *Almahide* (1710) and *L'Idaspe fedele* (1710)' (Alfred Loewenberg, *Annals of Opera*, 1943, p. 57).

[2] This opera, based on the episode in the *Æneid*, was the most successful work of Antonio Maria Bononcini (his brother Giovanni is thought to have been the composer of *Almahide*). It was originally given at Naples in 1696, as *Il Trionfo di Camilla, Regina de' Volsci*, with libretto by Silvio Stampiglia. The music was adapted by Nicolo Haym and the English libretto prepared by Owen Swiney for its performance at Drury Lane in March 1706. Mrs. Tofts sang the title-role, and the part of Latinus was taken by Turner. It seems to have been first sung in English, but later it was done partly in English and partly in Italian. It was the most successful Italian opera in England at this time; Nicoll lists sixty-four performances in the years 1706–9.

Barbara si t'intendo, &c.

Barbarous Woman, yes, I know your Meaning,

which expresses the Resentments of an angry Lover, was translated into that *English* Lamentation

Frail are a Lover's Hopes, &c.[1]

And it was pleasant enough to see the most refined Persons of the *British* Nation dying away and languishing to Notes that were filled with a Spirit of Rage and Indignation. It happen'd also very frequently, where the Sense was rightly translated, the necessary Transposition of Words which[a] were drawn out of the Phrase of one Tongue into that of another, made the Musick appear very absurd in one Tongue that was very natural in the other. I remember an *Italian* Verse that ran thus Word for Word,

And turn'd my Rage into Pity;

which the *English* for Rhime sake translated,

And into Pity turn'd my Rage.

By this Means the soft Notes that were adapted to *Pity* in the *Italian*, fell upon the Word *Rage* in the *English*; and the angry Sounds that were tuned[b] to *Rage* in the Original, were made to express *Pity* in the Translation. It oftentimes happen'd likewise, that the finest Notes in the Air fell upon the most insignificant Words in the Sentence. I have known the Word *And* pursu'd through the whole Gamut, have been entertain'd with many a melodious *The*, and have heard the most beautiful Graces, Quavers and Divisions bestow'd upon *Then, For,* and *From*; to the eternal Honour of our *English* Particles.

The next Step to our Refinement, was the introducing of *Italian* Actors into our Opera; who sung their Parts in their own Language, at the same Time that our Countrymen perform'd theirs in our native Tongue. The King or Hero of the Play generally spoke in *Italian*, and his Slaves answer'd him in *English*: The Lover frequently made his Court, and gain'd the Heart of his Princess in a Language which she did not understand. One would have thought it very difficult to have carry'd on Dialogues after this Manner, without an

---

a which] that *Fol.*   b tuned] turn'd *Fol. Corrected in Errata (No. 19).*

---

[1] The song in Act I, scene v, by Turnus, played by 'Mr. Hughs'.

Interpreter between the Persons that convers'd together; but this was the State of the *English* Stage for about three Years.

At length the Audience grew tir'd of understanding Half the Opera, and therefore to ease themselves intirely of the Fatigue of Thinking, have so order'd it at Present that the whole Opera is perform'd in an unknown Tongue. We no longer understand the Language of our own Stage; insomuch that I have often been afraid, when I have seen our *Italian* Performers chattering in the Vehemence of Action, that they have been calling us Names, and abusing us among themselves; but I hope, since we do put such an entire Confidence in them, they will not talk against us before our Faces, though they may do it with the same Safety as if it were[a] behind our Backs. In the mean Time I cannot forbear thinking how naturally an Historian, who writes Two or Three hundred Years hence, and does not know the Taste of his wise Fore-fathers, will make the following Reflection, *In the Beginning of the Eighteenth Century the* Italian *Tongue was so well understood in* England, *that Opera's were acted on the publick Stage in that Language.*

One scarce knows how to be serious in the Confutation of an Absurdity that shews itself at the first Sight. It does not want any great Measure of Sense to see the Ridicule of this monstrous Practice; but what makes it the more astonishing, it is not the Taste of the Rabble, but of Persons of the greatest Politeness, which has establish'd it.

If the *Italians* have a Genius for Musick above the *English*, the *English* have a Genius for other Performances of a much higher Nature, and capable of giving the Mind a much nobler Entertainment. Would one think it was possible (at a Time when an Author lived that was able to write the *Phaedra* and *Hippolitus*)[1] for a People to be so stupidly fond of the *Italian* Opera, as scarce to give a Third Days Hearing to that admirable Tragedy? Musick is certainly a very agreeable Entertainment, but if it would take the entire Possession of our Ears, if it would make us incapable of hearing Sense, if it would exclude Arts that have a much greater Tendency to the

[a] were] was *Fol.*

---

[1] *Phaedra and Hippolitus*, by Addison's friend Edmund Smith, was produced at the Haymarket on 21 Apr. 1707, with further performances on 22, 25, and 26 Apr., Mrs. Barry and Betterton taking the two chief parts. It was published on 19 June 1707 (*Daily Courant*). The Prologue, written by Addison, ridicules the taste for Italian opera, and concludes with the hope that 'you will your Foreign Taste command, | To bear, for once, with what you understand'.

Refinement of humane Nature: I must confess I would allow it no better Quarter than *Plato*[1] has done, who banishes it out of his Commonwealth.

At present, our Notions of Musick are so very uncertain, that we do not know what it is we like; only, in general, we[a] are transported with any thing that is not *English*: So it be of a foreign Growth, let it be *Italian*, *French*, or *High-Dutch*, it is the same thing. In short, our *English* Musick is quite rooted out, and nothing yet planted in its stead.

When a Royal Palace is burnt to the Ground, every Man is at Liberty to present his Plan for a new one; and tho' it be but indifferently put together, it may furnish several Hints that may be of Use to a good Architect. I shall take the same Liberty in a following Paper, of giving my Opinion upon the Subject of Musick,[2] which I shall lay down only in a problematical Manner to be considered by those who are Masters in the Art. 　　　　　　C

No. 19 　　　　　　　　*Thursday, March 22, 1711*[3]
[STEELE]

Di bene fecerunt, inopis me quodque pusilli
Finxerunt animi, rarò & perpauca loquentis.

Hor.

OBSERVING one Person behold another, who was an utter Stranger to him, with a Cast of his Eye, which, methought, expressed an Emotion of Heart very different from what could be

---

[a] like; only, in general, we] like, only, in general, that we *Fol.*

---

[1] *Republic* 398C–399E.

[2] A letter from R. T. (Lillie, i. 233) deplores the lack of encouragement given to English music: 'The opera-house is wholly in the hands of foreigners; and the house in drury-lane is not suffered to have any musical entertainments: so that our English masters are totally excluded from all opportunities of shewing themselves; and we are compelled to have Italian musick or none: or if at any time we have an English opera, it must be composed or put together by foreigners; and what strange work they make with our words is obvious enough, and which you have pleasantly exposed in one of your papers.'

[3] *Motto.* Horace, *Satires*, I. 4. 17–18:

Thank Heaven that made me slow, and gave a Pen
That writes but little, and but now and then. CREECH.

raised by an Object so agreeable as the Gentleman he looked at, I began to consider, not without some secret Sorrow, the Condition of an Envious Man. Some have fancied that Envy has a certain Magical Force in it, and that the Eyes of the Envious have by their Fascination blasted the Enjoyments of the Happy. Sir *Francis Bacon* says,[1] Some have been so curious as to remark the Times and Seasons when the Stroke of an Envious Eye is most effectually pernicious, and have observed that it has been when the Person envied has been in any Circumstance of Glory and Triumph. At such a time the Mind of the Prosperous Man goes, as it were, abroad, among things without him, and is more exposed to the Malignity. But I shall not dwell upon Speculations so abstracted as this, or repeat the many excellent Things which one might collect out of Authors upon this miserable Affection; but keeping in the road of common Life, consider the Envious Man with relation to these three Heads, His Pains, His Reliefs, and His Happiness.

The Envious Man is in Pain upon all Occasions which ought to give him Pleasure. The Relish of his Life is inverted, and the Objects which administer the highest Satisfaction to those who are exempt from this Passion, give the quickest Pangs to Persons who are subject to it. All the Perfections of their Fellow-Creatures are odious: Youth, Beauty, Valour and Wisdom are Provocations of their Displeasure. What a Wretched and Apostate State is this! To be offended with Excellence, and to hate a Man because we Approve him! The Condition of the Envious Man is the most Emphatically miserable; he is not only incapable of rejoicing in another's Merit or Success, but lives in a World wherein all Mankind are in a Plot against his Quiet, by studying their own Happiness and Advantage. *Will. Prosper* is an honest Tale-bearer, he makes it his business to join in Conversation with Envious Men. He points to such an handsom Young Fellow, and whispers that he is secretly married to a Great Fortune: When they doubt, he adds Circumstances to prove it; and never fails to aggravate their Distress, by assuring 'em that to his knowledge he has an Uncle will leave him some Thousands. *Will.* has many Arts of this kind to torture this sort of Temper, and delights in it. When

---

[1] Essay 9: 'Nay some have beene so curious, as to note, that the Times, when the Stroke, or Percussion of an *Envious Eye* doth most hurt, are, when the *Partie envied* is beheld in Glory, or Triumph; For that sets an Edge upon *Envy*; And besides, at such times, the Spirits of the *person Envied*, doe come forth, most into the outward Parts, and so meet the Blow' (paragraph 1). The subject of envy and emulation is also the theme of *Medley* 23, published earlier in this month (5 Mar.).

he finds them change colour, and say faintly They wish such a Piece of News is true, he has the Malice to speak some good or other of every Man of their Acquaintance.

The Reliefs of the Envious Man are those little Blemishes and Imperfections, that discover themselves in an Illustrious Character. It is matter of great Consolation to an Envious Person, when a Man of Known Honour does a thing Unworthy himself: Or when any Action which was well executed, upon better Information appears so alter'd in its Circumstances that the Fame of it is divided among many, instead of being attributed to One. This is a secret Satisfaction to these Malignants; for the Person whom they before could not but admire, they fancy is nearer their own Condition as soon as his Merit is shared among others. I remember some Years ago there came out an Excellent Poem, without the Name of the Author. The little Wits, who were incapable of Writing it, began to pull in Pieces the supposed Writer. When that would not do, they took great Pains to suppress the Opinion that it was his. That again failed. The next Refuge was to say it was overlook'd by one Man, and many Pages wholly written by another. An honest Fellow, who sate among a Cluster of them in debate on this Subject, cryed out, *Gentlemen, if you are sure none of you your selves had an hand in it, you are but where you were, whoever writ it.* But the most usual Succour to the Envious, in cases of nameless Merit in this kind, is to keep the Property, if possible, unfixed, and by that means to hinder the Reputation of it from falling upon any particular Person. You see an Envious Man clear up his Countenance, if in the Relation of any Man's Great Happiness in one Point, you mention his Uneasiness in another. When he hears such a one is very rich he turns Pale, but recovers when you add that he has many Children. In a Word, the only sure Way to an Envious Man's Favour, is not to deserve it.

But if we consider the Envious Man in Delight, it is like reading the Seat of a Giant in a Romance; the Magnificence of his House consists in the many Limbs of Men whom he has slain. If any who promised themselves Success in any Uncommon Undertaking miscarry in the Attempt, or he that aimed at what would have been Useful and Laudable, meets with Contempt and Derision, the Envious Man, under the Colour of hating Vainglory, can smile with an inward Wantonness of Heart at the ill Effect it may have upon an honest Ambition for the future.

Having throughly considered the Nature of this Passion, I have made it my Study how to avoid the Envy that may acrue to me from these my Speculations; and if I am not mistaken in my self, I think I have a Genius to escape it. Upon hearing in a Coffee-House one of my Papers commended, I immediately apprehended the Envy that would spring from that Applause; and therefore gave a Description of my Face the next Day; being resolved as I grow in Reputation for Wit, to resign my Pretensions to Beauty. This, I hope, may give some Ease to those unhappy Gentlemen, who do me the Honour to torment themselves upon the Account of this my Paper. As their Case is very deplorable, and deserves Compassion, I shall sometimes be dull, in Pity to them, and will from time to time administer Consolations to them by further Discoveries of my Person. In the mean while, if any one says the *Spectator* has Wit, it may be some Relief to them, to think that he does not show it in Company. And if any one praises his Morality, they may comfort themselves by considering that his Face is none of the longest.   R

No. 20   *Friday, March* 23, 1711¹

[STEELE]

        . . . κυνὸς ὄμματ᾽ ἔχων . . .
                        Hom.

AMONG the other hardy Undertakings which I have propos'd to my self, that of the Correction of Impudence is what I have very much at Heart. This in a particular Manner is my Province as SPECTATOR; for it is generally an Offence committed by the Eyes, and that against such as the Offenders would perhaps never have an Opportunity of injuring any other Way. The following Letter is a Complaint of a young Lady, who sets forth a Trespass of this Kind, with that Command of her self as befits Beauty and Innocence, and yet with so much Spirit as sufficiently expresses her Indignation. The whole Transaction is performed with the Eyes; and the Crime is no less than employing them in such a Manner, as to divert the Eyes of others from the best Use they can make of them, even looking up to Heaven.

¹ *Motto.* Homer, *Iliad*, 1. 225: Having dog's eyes.

SIR,

'THERE never was (I believe) an acceptable Man, but had some awkard Imitators. Ever since the SPECTATOR appear'd, have I remarked a kind of Men, whom I choose to call *Starers*; that without any regard to Time, Place, or Modesty, disturb a large Company with their impertinent Eyes. Spectators make up a proper Assembly for a Puppet-Show or a Bear-Garden; but devout Supplicants and attentive Hearers, are the Audience one ought to expect in Churches. I am, Sir, Member of a small pious Congregation near one of the North Gates of this City; much the greater Part of us indeed are Females, and used to behave our selves in a regular attentive Manner, till very lately one whole Isle has been disturbed with one of these monstrous Starers: He's the Head taller than any one in the Church; but for the greater Advantage of exposing himself, stands upon a Hassock, and commands the whole Congregation, to the great Annoyance of the devoutest Part of the Auditory; for what with Blushing, Confusion, and Vexation, we can neither mind the Prayers nor Sermon. Your Animadversion upon this Insolence, would be a great Favour to

Sir,
Your most humble Servant,
S. C.'

I have frequently seen of this Sort of Fellows; and do not think there can be a greater Aggravation of an Offence, than that it is committed where the Criminal is protected by the Sacredness of the Place which he violates. Many Reflexions of this Sort might be very justly made upon this Kind of Behaviour, but a *Starer* is not usually a Person to be convinced by the Reason of the thing; and a Fellow that is capable of shewing an impudent Front before a whole Congregation, and can bear being a publick Spectacle, is not so easily rebuked as to amend by Admonitions. If therefore my Correspondent does not inform me, that within Seven Days after this Date the Barbarian does not at least stand upon his own Legs only, without an Eminence, my Friend WILL. PROSPER[1] has promised to take an Hassock opposite to him, and stare against him in Defence of the Ladies. I have given him Directions, according to the most exact Rules of Opticks, to place himself in such a manner that he shall meet his Eyes wherever he throws them: I have Hopes that when .

---

[1] See No. 19.

WILL. confronts him, and all the Ladies, in whose Behalf he engages him, cast kind Looks and Wishes of Success at their Champion, he will have some Shame, and feel a little of the Pain he has so often put others to, of being out of Countenance.

It has indeed been Time out of Mind generally remarked, and as often lamented, that this Family of Starers have infested publick Assemblies: And I know no other Way to obviate so great an Evil, except in the Case of fixing their Eyes upon Women, some Male Friend will take the Part of such as are under the Oppression of Impudence, and encounter the Eyes of the Starers wherever they meet them. While we suffer our Women to be thus impudently attacked, they have no Defence, but in the End to cast yielding Glances at the Starers: And in this Case, a Man who has no Sense of Shame has the same Advantage over his Mistress, as he who has no Regard for his own Life has over his Adversary. While the Generality of the World are fetter'd by Rules, and move by proper and just Methods; he who has no Respect to any of them, carries away the Reward due to that Propriety of Behaviour, with no other Merit, but that of having neglected it.

I take an impudent Fellow to be a sort of Outlaw in Good-Breeding, and therefore what is said of him no Nation or Person can be concerned for. For this Reason, one may be free upon him. I have put my self to great Pains in considering this prevailing Quality which we call Impudence, and have taken notice that it exerts itself in a different Manner, according to the different Soils wherein such Subjects of these Dominions, as are Masters of it, were born. Impudence in an *Englishman*, is sullen and insolent; in a *Scotchman* it is untractable and rapacious; in an *Irishman* absurd and fawning: As the Course of the World now runs, the impudent *Englishman* behaves like a surly Land-lord, the *Scot* like an ill-received Guest, and the *Irishman* like a Stranger who knows he is not welcome. There is seldom any thing entertaining either in the Impudence of a *South* or *North Briton*; but that of an *Irishman* is always Comick: A true and genuine Impudence is ever the Effect of Ignorance, without the least Sense of it: The best and most successful Starers now in this Town, are of that Nation; they have usually the Advantage of the Stature mentioned in the above Letter of my Correspondent, and generally take their Stands in the Eye of Women of Fortune: Insomuch that I have known one of them, three Months after he came from Plough, with a tolerable good Air lead out a Woman from a Play, which one of our

THE SPECTATOR

own Breed, after four Years at *Oxford* and two at the *Temple*, would have been afraid to look at.

I cannot tell how to account for it, but these People have usually the Preference to our own Fools in the Opinion of the sillier Part of Womankind. Perhaps it is that an *English* Coxcomb is seldom so obsequious as an *Irish* one; and when the Design of pleasing is visible, an Absurdity in the Way toward it is easily forgiven.

But those who are downright impudent, and go on without Reflection that they are such; are more to be tolerated, than a Set of Fellows among us who profess Impudence with an Air of Humour, and think to carry off the most inexcusable of all Faults in the World, with no other Apology than saying in a gay Tone, *I put an impudent Face upon the Matter.* No, no Man shall be allowed the Advantages of Impudence, who is conscious that he is such: If he knows he is impudent, he may as well be otherwise; and it shall be expected that he blush, when he sees he makes another do it. For nothing can attone for the Want of Modesty; without which Beauty is ungraceful, and Wit detestable.   R

No. 21   *Saturday, March 24, 1711*[1]
[ADDISON]

. . . *Locus est & pluribus Umbris.*
Hor.

I AM sometimes very much troubled, when I reflect upon the three great Professions of Divinity, Law and Physick; how they are each of them over-burdened with Practitioners, and filled with Multitudes of Ingenious Gentlemen that starve one another.

We may divide the Clergy into Generals, Field-Officers, and Subalterns.[2] Among the first we may reckon Bishops, Deans and Arch-Deacons. Among the second are Doctors of Divinity, Pre-

[1] *Motto.* Horace, *Epistles* I. 5. 28:
There's room too for several uninvited guests.

[2] Dr. Norman Sykes, after quoting this paragraph, writes: 'The traditional comparison of the church to an army, accepted generally as a compliment, was especially congenial to the genius of the eighteenth century, which interpreted it as lending an august authority to the contemporary practice whereby circumstances of birth and seniority determined the prospects of promotion in both national institutions' (*Church and State in England in the XVIIIth Century*, Cambridge, 1934, p. 147). See his excellent chap. iv, 'The Ladder of Preferment'.

NO. 21, SATURDAY, MARCH 24, 1711

bendaries, and all that wear Scarfs.[1] The rest are comprehended under the Subalterns. As for the first Class, our Constitution preserves it from any Redundancy of Incumbents, notwithstanding Competitors are numberless. Upon a strict Calculation, it is found that there has been a great Exceeding of late Years in the second Division, several Brevets having been granted for the converting of Subalterns into Scarf-Officers; insomuch that within my Memory the price of Lutestring[2] is raised above two Pence in a Yard. As for the Subalterns, they are not to be numbred. Should our Clergy once enter into the corrupt Practice of the Laity, by the splitting of their Freeholds,[3] they would be able to carry most of the Elections in *England*.

The Body of the Law is no less encumbered with superfluous Members, that are like *Virgil's* Army,[4] which he tells us was so crouded many[a] of them had not Room to use their Weapons. This prodigious Society of Men may be divided into the Litigious and Peaceable. Under the first are comprehended all those who are carried down in Coach-fulls to *Westminster-Hall*, every Morning in Term-time. *Martial's* Description of this Species of Lawyers is full of Humour:

Iras & Verba locant.[5]

Men that hire out their Words and Anger; that are more or less passionate according as they are paid for it, and allow their Client a quantity of Wrath proportionable to the Fee which they receive from him. I must however observe to the Reader, that above three Parts of those whom I reckon among the Litigious, are such as are only quarrelsome in their Hearts, and have no Opportunity of showing their Passion at the Bar. Nevertheless, as they do not know what Strifes may arise, they appear at the Hall every Day, that they may show themselves in a Readiness to enter the Lists, whenever there shall be Occasion for them.

a crouded many] crouded that many *Fol.*

---

[1] In ecclesiastical usage 'a band of silk or other material worn round the neck, with the two ends pendent from the shoulders in front, as a part of clerical costume' (*OED*). At this time it denoted specifically the scarf worn by a nobleman's chaplain. On 11 Dec. 1710 Swift 'dined with Mrs. Vanhomrigh, to desire them to buy me a scarf' (*Journal to Stella*).
[2] 'A kind of glossy silk fabric' (*OED*).
[3] The meaning is, that if the clergy followed the example of landholders and cut up their glebes and tithes into forty-shilling freeholds (the requirement for voting) they could control most of the elections.
[4] *Aeneid*, 10. 432-3.
[5] The line is not from Martial, but from Seneca (*Hercules Furens*, 173-4).

The Peaceable Lawyers are, in the first place, many of the Benchers of the several Inns of Court, who seem to be the Dignitaries of the Law, and are endowed with those Qualifications of Mind that accomplish a Man rather for a Ruler, than a Pleader. These Men live peaceably in their Habitations, Eating once a Day, and Dancing once a Year,[1] for the Honour of their respective Societies.

Another numberless Branch of Peaceable Lawyers, are those young Men who being placed at the Inns of Court in order to study the Laws of their Country, frequent the Play-House more than *Westminster-Hall*, and are seen in all publick Assemblies, except in a Court of Justice. I shall say nothing of those Silent and Busie Multitudes that are employed within Doors, in the drawing up of Writings and Conveyances; nor of those greater Numbers that palliate their want of Business with a Pretence to such Chamber-practice.

If, in the third place, we look into the Profession of Physick, we shall find a most formidable Body of Men: The Sight of them is enough to make a Man serious, for we may lay it down as a Maxim, that When a Nation abounds in Physicians it grows thin of People. Sir *William Temple*[2] is very much puzzled to find out a Reason why the Northern Hive, as he calls it, does not send out such prodigious Swarms, and over-run the World with *Goths* and *Vandals*, as it did formerly; but had that Excellent Author observed that there were no Students in Physick among the Subjects of *Thor* and *Woden*, and that this Science very much flourishes in the North at present, he might have found a better Solution for this Difficulty, than any of those he has made use of. This Body of Men, in our own Country, may be described like the *British* Army[3] in *Caesar*'s time: Some of them slay in Chariots, and some on Foot. If the Infantry do less Execution than the Charioteers, it is because they cannot be carried so soon into all Quarters of the Town, and dispatch so much Business in so short a Time. Besides this Body of Regular Troops, there are Stragglers, who without being duly listed and enrolled, do infinite Mischief to those who are so unlucky as to fall into their Hands.

[1] Cf. Ward's *London Spy*, part xiii: 'like the Great *Old Dons* of the *Law*, when they Dance the *Measures* in an *Inns-of-Court-Hall* upon the first Day of *Christmas*' (Casanova Society, 1924, p. 305). Cf. also Dugdale's *Origines Juridiciales*, chap. lvii (3rd ed. 1680), p. 161.   [2] Miscellanea, part ii (*Works*, 1720, i. 212).

[3] Caesar, *Commentaries*, 4. 33: The Britons 'would forsake their Chariots, and fight on foot, to a vast Advantage, tho' our Cavalry on both sides were equally match'd . . .' (*Commentaries made English*, by Capt. Martin Bladen, 2nd ed., 1712, p. 86).

There are, besides the abovementioned, innumerable Retainers to Physick, who, for want of other Patients, amuse themselves with the stifling of Cats in an Air Pump, cutting up Dogs alive, or impaling of Insects upon the point of a Needle for Microscopical Observations;[1] besides those that are employed in the gathering of Weeds, and the Chase of Butterflies: Not to mention the Cockleshell-Merchants and Spider-catchers.

When I consider how each of these Professions are crouded with Multitudes that seek their Livelihood in them, and how many Men of Merit there are in each of them, who may be rather said to be of the Science, than the Profession; I very much wonder at the Humour of Parents, who will not rather chuse to place their Sons in a way of Life where an honest Industry cannot but thrive, than in Stations where the greatest Probity, Learning and Good Sense may miscarry. How many Men are Country-Curates,[2] that might have made themselves Aldermen of *London*, by a right Improvement of a smaller Sum of Mony than what is usually laid out upon a learned Education? A sober, frugal Person, of slender Parts and a slow Apprehension, might have thrived in Trade, tho' he starves upon Physick; as a Man would be well enough pleased to buy Silks of one, whom he would not venture to feel his Pulse. *Vagellius* is careful, studious and obliging, but withal a little thick-skull'd; he has not a single Client, but might have had abundance of Customers. The Misfortune is, that Parents take a Liking to a particular Profession, and therefore desire their Sons may be of it. Whereas, in so great an Affair of Life, they should consider the Genius and Abilities of their Children, more than their own Inclinations.

It is the great Advantage of a trading Nation, that there are very few in it so dull and heavy, who may not be placed in Stations of Life which may give them an Opportunity of making their Fortunes. A well-regulated Commerce is not, like Law, Physick or Divinity, to be overstocked with Hands; but, on the contrary, flourishes by Multitudes, and gives Employment to all its Professors. Fleets of

---

[1] The labours of the virtuosi are also ridiculed in *Tatler* 216: 'It is indeed wonderful to consider, that there should be a Sort of learned Men, who are wholly employed in gathering together the Refuse of Nature, if I may call it so, and hoarding up in their Chests and Cabinets such Creatures as others industriously avoid the Sight of.' The same number reproduces the will of Nicholas Gimcrack, the Virtuoso of Shadwell's comedy. See also *Tatlers* 119 and 216 for references to the dissection of a dog, the gathering of weeds, and the collection of butterflies.

[2] On this point see chap. v, 'The Clerical Subalterns', in Norman Sykes, *Church and State in England in the XVIIIth Century*.

Merchantmen are so many Squadrons of floating Shops, that vend our Wares and Manufactures in all the Markets of the World, and find out Chapmen[1] under both the Tropicks.   C

No. 22   *Monday, March 26, 1711*[2]
[STEELE]

> *Quodcunque ostendis mihi sic, incredulus odi.*
> Hor.

THE Word *Spectator* being most usually understood as one of the Audience at publick Representations in our Theatres, I seldom fail of many Letters relating to Plays and Operas. But indeed there are such monstrous things done in both, that if one had not been an Eye-witness of them, one could not believe that such Matters had really been exhibited. There is very little which concerns human Life, or is a Picture of Nature, that is regarded by the greater Part of the Company. The Understanding is dismissed from our Entertainments. Our Mirth is the Laughter of Fools, and our Admiration the Wonder of Idiots; else such improbable, monstrous, and incoherent Dreams could not go off as they do, not only without the utmost Scorn and Contempt, but even with the loudest Applause and Approbation. But the Letters of my Correspondents will represent this Affair in a more lively Manner, than any Discourse of my own; I shall therefore[a] give them to my Reader with only this Preparation, that they all come from Players, and that the business of Playing is now so managed, that you are not to be surprised when I say one or two of them are rational, others sensitive and vegetative Actors, and others wholly inanimate.[b] I shall not place these as I have named them, but as they have Precedence in the Opinion of their Audiences.

---

[a] shall therefore] therefore shall *Fol.*   [b] Players . . . inanimate.] Players, one or two of whom are rational . . . inanimate. *Fol.*

---

[1] Purchaser; customer. Now *Obs.* or *dial.* (*OED*).
[2] *Motto.* Horace, *Ars poetica*, 188:
     And whatsoever contradicts my Sense,
     I hate to see, and never can believe. ROSCOMMON.

Mr. SPECTATOR,

'**Y**OUR having been so humble as to take Notice of the Epistles of other Animals,[1] emboldens me, who am the wild Boar[2] that was killed by Mrs. *Tofts*, to represent to you, That I think I was hardly used in not having the Part of the Lyon in *Hydaspes*[3] given to me. It would have been but a natural Step for me to have personated that noble Creature, after having behaved my self to Satisfaction in the Part above-mention'd: But that of a Lyon, is too great a Character for one that never trod the Stage before but upon two Legs. As for the little Resistance which I made, I hope it may be excused, when it is considered that the Dart was thrown at me by so fair an Hand. I must confess I had but just put on my Brutality; and *Camilla*'s Charms were such, that beholding her erect Mien, hearing her charming Voice, and astonish'd with her graceful Motion, I could not keep up to my assumed Fierceness, but died like a Man.

I am,
Sir,
Your most humble Servant,
Thomas Prone.'

Mr. SPECTATOR,

'**T**HIS is to let you understand, that the Play-house is a Representation of the World in nothing so much as in this Particular, That no one rises in it according to his Merit. I have acted several Parts of Houshold-stuff with great Applause for many Years: I am one of the Men in the Hangings in the *Emperour of the Moon*;[4] I have twice performed the third Chair in an *English* Opera; and have rehearsed the Pump in the *Fortune Hunters*.[5] I am now

---

[1] No. 14.
[2] In the opera *Camilla* (Act I, scene ii) Prenesto, the young son of Latinus, is saved by Camilla:

Enter PRENESTO: *The Boar pursuing him.*

PRENESTO. O Heav'ns! who defends me?
CAMILLA. My Arm. [*She throws a Dart, and kills the Boar.*

'A wild-boar, killed by Mrs. Tofts' is in the Inventory of stage effects listed in *Tatler* 42. *Camilla* had not been given since 13 Dec. 1709. For Mrs. Tofts, who had now retired from the stage and was living in Italy, see No. 443 (vol. iv).
[3] See No. 13.
[4] Mrs. Behn's farce, adapted from the French *Harlequin l'Empereur dans le Monde de la Lune*, was first produced in 1687 and had been revived at Drury Lane on 10 and 26 Apr. 1710. At Penkethman's New Theatre in Greenwich it was given on 22 July 1710, 'With a New Invention first Contriv'd by Monsieur St. Everimont, which Represents a Suit of Hangings, which in an Instant is Transform'd to Men and Women' (*Daily Courant*).
[5] *The Fortune-Hunters: or, Two Fools Well Met*, a comedy by James Carlisle (Carlile),

grown old, and hope you will recommend me so effectually, as that I may say something before I go off the Stage: In which you will do a great Act of Charity to

Your most humble Servant,

William Screne.'

Mr. SPECTATOR,

'UNDERSTANDING that Mr. *Screne* has writ to you, and desired to be raised from dumb and still Parts; I desire, if you give him Motion or Speech, that you would advance me in my Way, and let me keep on in what I humbly presume I am a Master, to wit, in representing human and still Life together. I have several times acted one of the finest Flower-pots in the same Opera wherein Mr. *Screne* is a Chair; therefore upon his Promotion, request that I may succeed him in the Hangings[1] with my Hand in the Orange-Trees.

Your humble Servant,

Ralph Simple.'

Drury-Lane, March 24. 1710-11.

SIR,

'I SAW your Friend the Templar this Evening in the Pit, and thought he looked very little pleased with the Representation of the mad Scene of the *Pilgrim*.[2] I wish, Sir, you would do us the Favour to animadvert frequently upon the false Taste the Town is in, with Relation to Plays as well as Operas. It certainly requires a Degree of Understanding to play justly; but such is our Condition, that we are to suspend our Reason to perform our Parts. As to

was first given at Drury Lane in 1689. Its most recent performance was at the Haymarket, on 25 Oct. 1709 (it was soon after this revived at Drury Lane on 15 May 1711). At the end of Act II the inebriated Mr. Spruce (one of Norris's roles) encounters his wife's gallant, Young Wealthy (played by Mountfort) by the pump in a garden; he 'gropes up and down, and takes hold of Mr. Wealthy's hand instead of the pump'.

[1] In *The Emperour of the Moon* 'the Front of the Scene is only a Curtain or Hangings to be drawn up at Pleasure' (p. 25). In Act II, scene iii, Scaramouch places a company of masqueraders 'all in the Hanging, in which they make the Figures, where they stand without Motion in Postures' and here Harlequin is 'plac'd on a Tree in the Hangings' (p. 27).

[2] *The Pilgrim.* Fletcher's play, altered by Vanbrugh (1700), was revived at Drury Lane on 30 April 1707, with Cibber as the mad Englishman, and thereafter played frequently. The most recent performance had been at the Haymarket on 10 Nov. 1710. Act III, scene v, shows 'the interior of a madhouse', and the English madman calls from his cell, 'Give me some Drink'. When the First Keeper interposes, 'O ho, here's the English Man', the madman says, 'Fill me a thousand Pots, and froth 'em, froth 'em; down o' your knees, you Rogues, and pledge me roundly; one, two, three —and four.'

Scenes of Madness, you know, Sir, there are noble Instances of this Kind in *Shakespear*; but then it is the Disturbance of a noble Mind, from generous and humane Resentments: It is like that Grief which we have for the Decease of our Friends: It is no Diminution, but a Recommendation of humane Nature, that in such Incidents Passion gets the better of Reason; and all we can think to comfort ourselves, is impotent against half what we feel. I will not mention that we had an Idiot[1] in the Scene, and all the Sense it is represented to have, is that of Lust. As for my self, who have long taken Pains in personating the Passions, I have to Night acted only an Appetite: The Part I play'd is Thirst, but it is represented as written rather by a Drayman than a Poet. I come in with a Tub about me, that Tub hung with Quart-potts; with a full Gallon at my Mouth. I am ashamed to tell you that I pleased very much, and this was introduced as a Madness; but sure it was not humane Madness, for a Mule or an Ass[a] may have been as dry as ever I was in my Life.

> *I am,*
> *Sir,*
> *Your most obedient*
> *and humble Servant.*'

> *From the* Savoy *in the* Strand.[2]

Mr. SPECTATOR,

'IF you can read it with dry Eyes, I give you this Trouble to acquaint you, that I am the unfortunate King *Latinus*,[3] and believe I am the first Prince that dated from this Palace since *John*

---

[a] Ass] Horse *Fol*.

---

[1] In Act III there is a 'She-Fool', for whom the licentious part is written. The conversation between her and the two keepers immediately follows the above scene of the English madman.

[2] The Savoy, in the Strand, just west of Somerset House, had once been a palace belonging to John of Gaunt. By this time most of the buildings had been rented to private individuals or replaced by tenements. Two parts which had not yet fallen into private hands were the building used as a church and that reserved as a ward or barracks for soldiers. See Strype's edition of Stow's *Survey* (1720), iv. 112.

[3] In *Camilla* (II. x) King Latinus speaks a number of lines in recitative, including those given on p. 96. (The part was taken by Turner.) The sudden entry of 'King Latinus' into the army is referred to in a mock-advertisement which appeared a few weeks earlier (6 Feb.) in *The Grouler: or, Diogenes Robb'd of his Tub*: 'All Emperors, Kings, Princes, and other inferior Potentates, who have vulgarly made their Appearances at the *Opera*, *Theatre-Royal*, *Greenwich*, or *Windmill-hill*, are desir'd to keep close to their Garrets, for the Preservation of their Persons, the rude pressing Gang paying no Regard to their Characters, have insolently made the famous King *Latinus* Prisoner.'

of *Gaunt*. Such is the Uncertainty of all human Greatness, that I who lately never moved without a Guard, am now pressed as a common Soldier, and am to sail with the first fair Wind against my Brother *Lewis* of *France*. It is a very hard thing to put off a Character which one has appeared in with Applause: This I experienced since the Loss of my Diadem; for upon quarrelling with another Recruit, I spoke my Indignation out of my Part *in recitativo*;

> *... Most audacious Slave*
> *Darest thou an angry Monarch's Fury brave?*

The Words were no sooner out of my Mouth, when a Sergeant knock'd me down, and ask'd me if I had a Mind to Mutiny, in talking things no Body understood. You see, Sir, my unhappy Circumstances; and if by your Mediation you can procure a Subsidy for a Prince (who never failed to make all that beheld him merry at his Appearance,) you will merit the Thanks of

> *Your Friend*,
> The King of *Latium*.'

ADVERTISEMENT.
For the Good of the Publick.

Within two Doors of the Masquerade,[1] *lives an eminent* Italian *Chirurgeon arriv'd from the Carnaval at* Venice, *of great Experience in private Cures. Accommodations are provided and Persons admitted in their masquing Habits.*

He has cur'd since his coming thither, in less than a Fortnight, Four Scaramouches, a Mountebank Doctor, Two Turkish *Bassas, Three Nuns, and a Morris Dancer.*

Venienti occurrite Morbo.[2]

N. B. *Any Person may agree by the Great*,[3] *and be kept in Repair by the Year. The Doctor draws Teeth without pulling off your Mask.*

R

---

[1] See No. 14.
[2] Meet the coming disease. Persius, *Satires*, 3. 64.
[3] 'Of work done: at a fixed price for the whole amount. Now *dial*.' (*OED*).

*Sævit atrox Volscens, nec teli conspicit usquam
Auctorem, nec quo se ardens immittere possit.*
Vir.

THERE is nothing that more betrays a base, ungenerous Spirit, than the giving of secret Stabs to a Man's Reputation. Lampoons and Satyrs, that are written with Wit and Spirit, are like poison'd Darts, which not only inflict a Wound, but make it incurable. For this Reason I am very much troubled when I see the Talents of Humour and Ridicule in the Possession of an ill-natured Man. There cannot be a greater Gratification to a barbarous and inhuman Wit, than to stir up Sorrow in the Heart of a private Person, to raise Uneasiness among near Relations, and to expose whole Families to Derision, at the same time that he remains unseen and undiscovered. If, besides the Accomplishments of being Witty and Ill-natured, a Man is vicious into the bargain, he is one of the most mischievous Creatures that can enter into a Civil Society. His Satyr will then chiefly fall upon those who ought to be the most exempt from it. Virtue, Merit, and every thing that is Praise-worthy, will be made the Subject of Ridicule and Buffoonry. It is impossible to enumerate the Evils which arise from these Arrows that fly in the dark, and I know no other Excuse that is or can be made for them, than that the Wounds they give are only Imaginary, and produce nothing more than a secret Shame or Sorrow in the Mind of the suffering Person. It must indeed be confess'd, that a Lampoon or a Satyr do not carry in them Robbery or Murder; but at the same time, how many are there that would not rather lose a considerable Sum of Mony, or even Life it self, than be set up as a Mark of Infamy and Derision? And in this Case a Man should consider, that an Injury is not to be measured by the Notions of him that gives, but of him that receives it.

Those who can put the best Countenance upon the Outrages of

---

[1] *Motto.* Virgil, *Aeneid*, 9. 420–1:

Fierce Volcens storms with rage, yet descries not him who sent the dart, nor where to vent his rage.

According to Nichols ,a copy of the first 12mo edition of the *Spectator* 'with MS. notes by a Spanish merchant (Mr. Blundel), who lived at the time of the original publication' bore the following endorsement at the top of this paper: 'The character of Dr. Swift.'

this nature which are offered them, are not without their secret Anguish. I have often observed a Passage in *Socrates's* Behaviour at his Death,[1] in a Light wherein none of the Criticks have considered it. That excellent Man, entertaining his Friends a little before he drank the Bowl of Poison with a Discourse on the Immortality of the Soul, at his entering upon it says, that he does not believe any the most Comick Genius can censure him for talking upon such a Subject at such a Time. This Passage, I think, evidently glances upon *Aristophanes*,[2] who writ a Comedy on purpose to ridicule the Discourses of that Divine Philosopher: It has been observed by many Writers, that *Socrates* was so little moved at this piece of Buffoonry, that he was several times present at its being acted upon the Stage, and never expressed the least Resentment of it. But with Submission, I think the Remark I have here made shows us that this unworthy Treatment made an Impression upon his Mind, though he had been too wise to discover it.

When *Julius Cæsar*[3] was Lampoon'd by *Catullus*, he invited him to a Supper, and treated him with such a generous Civility, that he made the Poet his Friend ever after. Cardinal *Mazarine*[4] gave the same kind of Treatment to the Learned *Quillet*, who had reflected upon his Eminence in a famous *Latin* Poem. The Cardinal sent for him, and after some kind Expostulations upon what he had written, assured him of his Esteem, and dismissed him with a Promise of the next good Abby that should fall, which he accordingly conferr'd upon him in a few Months after. This had so good an Effect upon the Author, that he dedicated the second Edition of his Book to the Cardinal, after having expunged the Passages which had given him Offence.

[1] Plato, *Phaedo* 40.

[2] In *The Clouds* Socrates is introduced as an example of the sophistical system of education.

[3] Suetonius, *Julius Caesar* 73. Addison's source, however, is probably Bayle, art. 'Catullus': 'He compos'd some Satyrical Verses against *Caesar*, that serv'd only to set forth the Moderation of the offended Person; he was not silent indeed about the heinous Injury that he had receiv'd from him; but he was contented to oblige the Poet to make him Satisfaction, and the same Day he invited him to Supper.'

[4] Addison's account is a paraphrase of Bayle, art. 'Quillet', Remark C. The *Callipaedia* of Claude Quillet was first published at Leyden in 1655, with some derogatory references to Cardinal Mazarin and his family. These were omitted in the second edition, published at Paris in 1656. The book is advertised in No. 57:

Callipædiæ; or, an Art how to have Handsome Children. Written in Latin by the Abbot Quillet. To which is added Pædotrophiæ; or the Art of Nursing and Breeding up Children. Written in Latin by Monsieur St. Marthe, Physician to Henry the Third of France. Now done into English Verse. Printed for John Morphew near Stationers-Hall.

Sextus Quintus[1] was not of so generous and forgiving a Temper. Upon his being made Pope, the Statue of *Pasquin* was one Night dressed in a very dirty Shirt, with an Excuse written under it, that he was forced to wear foul Linnen because his Laundress was made a Princess. This was a Reflection upon the Pope's Sister, who, before the Promotion of her Brother, was in those mean Circumstances that *Pasquin* represented her. As this Pasquinade made a great noise in *Rome*, the Pope offered a Considerable Sum of Mony to any Person that should discover the Author of it. The Author relying upon his Holiness's Generosity, as also on some private Overtures which he had received from him, made the Discovery himself; upon which the Pope gave him the Reward he had promised, but at the same time, to disable the Satyrist for the future, ordered his Tongue to be cut out, and both his Hands to be chopped off. *Aretine*[2] is too trite an Instance. Every one knows that all the Kings of *Europe* were his Tributaries. Nay, there is a Letter of his extant, in which he makes his Boasts that he had laid the Sophy of *Persia* under Contribution.

Though in the various Examples which I have here drawn together, these several great Men behaved themselves very differently towards the Wits of the Age who had reproached them, they all of them plainly showed that they were very sensible of their Reproaches, and consequently that they received them as very great Injuries. For my own part, I would never trust a Man that I thought was capable of giving these secret Wounds, and cannot but think that he would hurt the Person, whose Reputation he thus assaults, in his Body or in his Fortune, could he do it with the same Security. There is indeed something very barbarous and inhuman in the ordinary Scriblers of Lampoons. An Innocent young Lady shall be exposed, for an unhappy Feature. A Father of a Family turn'd to Ridicule, for some domestick Calamity. A Wife be made uneasy all her Life, for a misinterpreted Word or Action. Nay, a good, a temperate and a just Man, shall be put out of Countenance, by the Representation of those Qualities that should do him Honour. So pernicious a thing is Wit, when it is not tempered with Virtue and Humanity.

---

[1] Sixtus V. The story is told by Gregorio Leti in Book VII of his life of Sixtus V. See *L'Histoire de la vie du pape Sixte cinquieme*, nouvelle edition, revuë, augmentée (Paris: chez André Pralard, 1698), ii. 70–72.

[2] See Bayle, art. 'Aretin' and Remark A, which quotes the passage regarding 'the Sophy of Persia'.

I have indeed heard of heedless, inconsiderate Writers, that without any Malice have sacrificed the Reputation of their Friends and
Acquaintance to a certain Levity of Temper, and a silly Ambition of
distinguishing themselves by a Spirit of Raillery and Satyr: As if it
were not infinitely more honourable to be a Good-natured Man,
than a Wit. Where there is this little petulant Humour in an Author,
he is often very mischievous without designing to be so. For which
Reason I always lay it down as a Rule, that an indiscreet Man is
more hurtful than an ill-natured one; for as the one[a] will only attack
his Enemies, and those he wishes ill to, the other injures indifferently
both Friends and Foes. I cannot forbear, on this occasion, transcribing a Fable out of Sir *Roger L'Estrange*,[1] which accidentally lies before
me. 'A Company of Waggish Boys were watching of Frogs at the
side of a Pond, and still as any of 'em put up their Heads, they'd be
pelting them down again with Stones. *Children* (says one of the Frogs)
you never consider that though this may be Play to you, 'tis Death to us.'

As this Week[2] is in a manner set apart and dedicated to Serious
Thoughts, I shall indulge my self in such Speculations as may not
be altogether unsuitable to the Season; and in the mean time, as the
settling in our selves a Charitable Frame of Mind is a Work very
proper for the Time, I have in this Paper endeavour'd to expose that
particular Breach of Charity which has been generally over-look'd
by Divines, because they are but few who can be guilty of it.   C

No. 24   *Wednesday, March* 28, 1711[3]
[STEELE]

Accurrit quidam, notus mihi nomine tantum;
Arreptaque manu, Quid agis, dulcissime rerum?
                                                            Hor.

THERE are in this Town a great Number of insignificant People
who are by no Means fit for the better sort of Conversation,

[a] one] *1721*; former *Fol, 8vo, 12mo*

[1] *Fables of Æsop and other eminent Mythologists* (1692), Fable 398. Steele uses this
fable in the *Theatre* No. 2 (5 Jan. 1720), ed. Nichols (1790), i. 14.
[2] Good Friday fell on 30 Mar. in 1711. A general fast was appointed for Wednesday,
28 Mar.
[3] *Motto.* Horace, *Satires*, 1. 9. 3–4:
       A Fop came up, by name scarce known to me,
       He seiz'd my hand, and cry'd, *Dear Sir how d'ye.* CREECH.

and yet have an impertinent Ambition of appearing with those to whom they are not welcome. If you walk in the *Park*, one of them will certainly joyn with you, tho' you are in Company with Ladies; if you drink a Bottle, they will find your Haunts. What makes such Fellows[a] the more burdensome, is, that they neither offend or please so far as to be taken Notice of for either. It is I presume for this Reason that my Correspondents are willing by my Means to be rid of them. The two following Letters are writ by Persons who suffer by such impertinence. A worthy old Batchelour, who sets in[1] for his Dose of Claret every Night at such an Hour, is teized by a Swarm of them; who because they are sure of Room and good Fire, have taken it in their Heads to keep a sort of Club in his Company; tho' the sober Gentleman himself is an utter Enemy to such Meetings.

Mr. SPECTATOR,

'THE Aversion I for some Years have had to Clubs in general, gave me a perfect Relish for your Speculation on that Subject; but I have since been extremely mortified, by the malicious World's ranking me amongst the Supporters of such impertinent Assemblies. I beg Leave to state my Case fairly; and that done, I shall expect Redress from your judicious Pen.

'I am, Sir, a Batchelour of some standing, and a Traveller; my Business, to consult my own Humour, which I gratify without controuling other People's; I have a Room and a whole Bed to my self; and I have a Dog, a Fiddle, and a Gun; they please me, and injure no Creature alive. My chief Meal is a Supper, which I always make at a Tavern. I am constant to an Hour, and not ill-humour'd; for which Reasons, tho' I invite no Body, I have no sooner supp'd, than I have a Crowd about me of that sort of good Company that know not whither else to go. It is true every Man pays his Share, yet as they are Intruders, I have an undoubted Right to be the only Speaker, or at least the loudest; which I maintain, and that to the great Emolument of my Audience. I sometimes tell them their own in pretty free Language; and sometimes divert them with merry Tales, according as I am in Humour. I am one of those who live in Taverns to a great Age, by a sort of regular Intemperance; I never go to Bed drunk, but always fluster'd; I wear away very gently; am

___

[a] such Fellows] these People *Fol.*

___

[1] To set in for, i.e. to set to work, begin (upon something). *Obs.* except *dial.* (*OED*).

apt to be peevish, but never angry. Mr. SPECTATOR, If you have
kept various Company, you know there is in every Tavern in Town
some old Humourist or other, who is Master of the House as much
as he that keeps it. The Drawers are all in Awe of him; and all the
Customers who frequent his Company, yield him a sort of comical
Obedience. I do not know but I may be such a Fellow as this my
self. But I appeal to you, whether this is to be called a Club, because
so many Impertinents will break in upon me, and come without
Appointment? *Clinch*[1] of *Barnet* has a nightly Meeting, and shows to
every one that will come in and pay; but then he is the only Actor.
Why should People miscall things? If his is allow'd to be a Consort,
why mayn't mine be a Lecture? However, Sir, I submit to you, and
am,

Sir,

Your most obedient, &c.

Tho. Kimbow.'

Good Sir,

'YOU and I were press'd against each other last Winter in a
Crowd, in which uneasy Posture we suffer'd together for
almost Half an Hour. I thank you for all your Civilities ever since,
in being of my Acquaintance wherever you meet me. But the other
Day you pull'd off your Hat to me in the *Park,* when I was walking

---

[1] Clinch, or Clench, of Barnet was a popular entertainer of the day, described in
Tatler 51 as 'an artful Person' who did 'Feats of Activity with his Throat and Wind-
pipe'. The nature of his performance can best be described by quoting one of his
frequent advertisements (from No. 533):

> AN Entertainment by Mr. CLINCH of BARNET, who imitates the Flute, Double
> Curtel, the Organ with 3 Voices, the Horn, Huntsman and Pack of Hounds, the
> Sham-Doctor, the Old Woman, the Drunken-Man, the Bells: All Instruments are
> performed by his natural Voice. To which is added an Essex Song by Mr. Clinch
> himself. To be seen this present Evening at 7 a Clock, at the Queen's-Arms Tavern
> on Ludgate-Hill. Price 1s.

He seems to have begun at Bartholomew Fair before the close of the seventeenth
century; in one of Tom Brown's letters upon the breaking up of the fair (dated
12 Sept. 1699) there is a reference to 'the famous Mr. *Clinch* of *Barnet* with his Kit [i.e.
fiddle] and Organ' (*Works of Monsieur Voiture*, 1705, p. 107). From 1704 his advertisements appear frequently in the *Daily Courant,* announcing appearances in London
taverns and ale-houses, generally from October to May, and at such places as Tunbridge Wells and Epsom Old Wells during the summer months. In 1708 and 1709
the advertisements contain the additional item of 'a Tune by his 6 Children, himself
playing upon the Violin and his Voice the same Time'. At the time of this essay he
was appearing at the Fountain Tavern 'at Chairing-Cross'. He was still giving his
performances as late as 1722. His death is announced in the *London Daily Post and
General Advertiser,* 24 Dec. 1734: 'A few Days since died, aged about 70, the famous
Mr. Clench of Barnet, who diverted the Town many Years, with imitating a Drunken
Man, old Woman, Pack of Hounds, &c.' The *Gentleman's Magazine* (xiv. 703) places
his death on 18 Dec.

with my Mistress: She did not like your Air, and said she wonder'd what strange Fellows I was acquainted with. Dear Sir, consider it is as much as my Life is Worth, if she should think we were intimate; therefore I earnestly intreat you for the Future to take no Manner of Notice of,

Sir,

Your obliged humble Servant,

Will. Fashion.'

A like[a] Impertinence is also very troublesome to the superior and more intelligent Part of the fair Sex. It is, it seems, a great Inconvenience, that those of the meanest Capacities will pretend to make Visits, tho' indeed they are qualify'd rather to add to the Furniture of the House (by filling an empty Chair) than to the Conversation they come into when they visit. A Friend of mine hopes for Redress in this Case, by the Publication of her Letter in my Paper; which she thinks those she would be rid of will take to themselves. It seems to be written with an Eye to one of those pert giddy unthinking Girls, who upon the Recommendation only of an agreeable Person and a fashionable Air, take themselves to be upon a Level with Women of the greatest Merit.

Madam,

'I TAKE this Way to acquaint you with what common Rules and Forms would never permit me to tell you otherwise; to wit, that you and I, tho' Equals in Quality and Fortune, are by no Means suitable Companions. You are, 'tis true, very pretty, can dance, and make a very good Figure in a publick Assembly; but alass, Madam, you must go no further; Distance and Silence are your best Recommendations; therefore let me beg of you never to make me any more Visits. You come in a literal Sense to see one, for you have nothing to say. I do not say this that I would by any Means lose your Acquaintance; but I would keep it up with the Strictest Forms of good Breeding. Let us pay Visits, but never see one another: If you will be so good as to deny your self always to me, I shall return the Obligation by giving the same Orders to my Servants. When Accident makes us meet at a third Place, we may mutually lament the Misfortune of never finding one another at home, go in the same Party to a Benefit-Play, and smile at each other and put down

---

[a] A like] This *Fol.*

Glasses as we pass in our Coaches. Thus we may enjoy as much of each others Friendship as we are capable: For there are some People who are to be known only by Sight, with which sort of Friendship I hope you will always honour,

Madam,
Your most obedient humble Servant,
Mary Tuesday.

'*P.S.* I subscribe my self by the Name of the Day I keep,[1] that my supernumerary Friends may know who I am.'

ADVERTISEMENT.

To prevent all Mistakes that may happen among Gentlemen of the other End of the Town, who come but once a Week to St. James's *Coffee-house, either by miscalling the Servants, or requiring such things from them as are not properly within their respective Provinces; this is to give Notice, that* Kidney,[2] *Keeper of the Book-Debts of the outlying Customers, and Observer of those who go off without paying, having resign'd that Employment, is succeeded by* John Sowton; *to whose Place of Enterer of Messages and first Coffee-Grinder* William Bird *is promoted; and* Samuel Burdock *comes as Shooe-Cleaner in the Room of the said* Bird.

R

[1] The new fashion of keeping certain days for visits is satirized in William Burnaby's *The Ladies Visiting-Day*, published in 1701. In the opening scene Courtine says, 'I thought the Design of these Visiting-Days had been for the Womens innocent Pleasure, to settle the Fashions, detract the Absent, and compare Intreagues'. To this Polidore replies, 'Yes, and to secure 'em against Discoveries, the Gallant might be surpris'd, if they had not Set days for other Visiters!' (*Dramatic Works*, ed. F. E. Budd, p. 202). The method of keeping accounts of visiting days is noted in *Tatler* 109.

[2] The waiter at the St. James's Coffee-house, frequently referred to by Isaac Bickerstaff: he 'has the Ear of the greatest Politicians who come hither' (*Tatler* 1), he 'has long convers'd with, and fill'd Tea for the most consummate Politicians' (*Tatler* 69), &c. His name is given as Humphrey Kidney in a letter from him in *Tatler* 56. For an earlier use of the name cf. Ben Jonson, *Staple of News*, II. iii.

Thursday, March 29, 1711[1]

. . . Ægrescitque medendo.
Vir.

The following Letter will explain it self, and needs no Apology.

SIR,

'I AM one of that sickly Tribe who are commonly known by the
Name of *Valetudinarians*,[2] and do confess to you, that I first con-
tracted this ill Habit of Body, or rather of Mind, by the Study of
Physick. I no sooner began to peruse Books of this Nature, but I
found my Pulse was irregular,[3] and scarce ever read the Account of
any Disease that I did not fancy my self afflicted with. Doctor
Sydenham's learned Treatise[4] of Feavers threw me into a lingring
Hectick, which hung upon me all the while I was reading that
excellent Piece. I then applied my self to the Study of several
Authors, who have written upon Phthisical Distempers, and by
that means fell into a Consumption, 'till at length, growing very
fat, I was in a manner shamed out of that Imagination. Not long
after this I found in my self all the Symptoms of the Gout, except
Pain, but was cured of it by a Treatise upon the Gravel, written by
a very Ingenious Author, who (as it is usual for Physicians to convert
one Distemper into another) eased me of the Gout by giving me the
Stone. I at length studied my self into a Complication of Distempers;
but, accidentally taking into my Hand that Ingenious Discourse
written by *Sanctorius*,[5] I was resolved to direct my self by a Scheme

---

¹ *Motto.* Virgil, *Aeneid*, 12. 46: Growing worse with the healing.
² Still a new word in English; the earliest example in *OED* is dated 1703. Cf.
No. 395 (vol. iii), where Budgell uses it in a figurative sense.
³ Tickell, in the Preface to the collected edition of Addison's *Works* in 1721, notes
as 'one circumstance very remarkable, that, from his cradle, he never had a regular
pulse' (I. xvi). Steele questions this fact, in his angry letter to Congreve prefixed to
the second edition of the *Drummer* in 1722 (*Correspondence*, ed. Blanchard, p. 512).
⁴ An English version of Sydenham's Latin treatise was published in 1694 under
the title, *The Compleat Method of Curing almost all Diseases: to which is added, An Exact
Description of their several Symptoms.* The *Whole Works*, translated by John Pechy, M.D.,
of the College of Physicians in London, appeared in 1696 and reached a fourth edition
by 1705.
⁵ *Medicina Statica: or, Rules of Health, in eight Sections of Aphorisms,* 'originally written
by Sanctorius Chief Professor of Physick at Padua, English'd by J[ohn] D[avies]',
was published in 1676. The frontispiece portrays the mathematical chair mentioned
here: 'From which Chair we gain two advantages; the former, by finding out the
daily insensible perspiration of our bodies; which perspiration not well consider'd,
Medicine proves for the most part vain and ineffectual: for all indispositions almost
are the productions of a lesser, or larger, perspiration than is requisite. The latter in

of Rules, which I had collected from his Observations. The Learned World are very well acquainted with that Gentleman's Invention; who, for the better carrying on of his Experiments, contrived a certain Mathematical Chair, which was so Artificially hung upon Springs, that it would weigh any thing as well as a Pair of Scales. By this means he discovered how many Ounces of his Food pass'd by Perspiration, what quantity of it was turned into Nourishment, and how much went away by the other Channels and Distributions of Nature.

'Having provided my self with this Chair, I used to Study, Eat, Drink, and Sleep in it; insomuch that I may be said, for these three last Years, to have lived in a Pair of Scales. I compute my self, when I am in full Health, to be precisely Two Hundred Weight, falling short of it about a Pound after a Day's Fast, and exceeding it as much after a very full Meal; so that it is my continual Employment, to trim the Ballance between these two Volatile Pounds in my Constitution. In my ordinary Meals I fetch my self up to two Hundred Weight and a half Pound;[a] and if after having dined I find my self fall short of it, I drink just so much Small Beer, or eat such a quantity of Bread, as is sufficient to make me weight. In my greatest Excesses I do not transgress more than the other half Pound; which, for my Healths sake, I do the first *Monday* in every Month. As soon as I find my self duly poised after Dinner, I walk till I have perspired five Ounces and four Scruples;[1] and when I discover, by my Chair, that I am so far reduced, I fall to my Books, and Study away three Ounces more. As for the remaining Parts of the Pound, I keep no account of them. I do not dine and sup by the Clock, but by my Chair, for when that informs me my Pound of Food is exhausted I conclude my self to be hungry, and lay in another with all Diligence. In my Days of Abstinence I lose a Pound and an half, and on solemn Fasts am two Pound lighter than on other Days in the Year.

'I allow my self, one Night with another, a Quarter of a Pound of Sleep within a few Grains more or less; and if upon my rising I find that I have not consumed my whole quantity, I take out the rest in

---

[a] a half Pound;] *8vo*; an half; *Fol.*; half a Pound; *12mo*.

that, having seated our selves in this Chair, we perceive, during our refection, when we are come to that just proportion of meat, and drink, beyond which, or short of which, we are prejudic'd' (sig. A5). Another translation, by John Quincy, was published in 1712. In Shadwell's *True Widow* (published 1679) young Maggot has 'an Engine to weigh my self, when I sit down to write, or think'.
[1] In apothecaries' weight a scruple is one-twenty-fourth of an ounce.

my Chair. Upon an exact Calculation of what I expended and received the last Year, which I always register in a Book, I find the Medium to be two hundred weight, so that I cannot discover that I am impaired one Ounce in my Health during a whole Twelvemonth. And yet, Sir, notwithstanding this my great Care to ballast my self equally every Day, and to keep my Body in its proper Poise, so it is that I find my self in a sick and languishing Condition. My Complexion is grown very sallow, my Pulse low, and my Body Hydropical.[1] Let me therefore beg you, Sir, to consider me as your Patient, and to give me more certain Rules to walk by than those I have already observed, and you will very much oblige

Your most Humble Servant.'

This Letter puts me in mind of an *Italian* Epitaph[2] written on the Monument of a *Valetudinarian*; *Stavo ben, ma per star Meglio, sto qui*: Which it is impossible to translate. The Fear of Death often proves mortal, and sets People on Methods to save their Lives, which infallibly destroy them. This is a Reflection made by some Historians, upon observing that there are many more thousands killed in a Flight than in a Battel, and may be applied to those Multitudes of Imaginary Sick Persons that break their Constitutions by Physick, and throw the mselves into the Arms of Death, by endeavouring to escape it. This Method is not only dangerous, but below the Practice of a Reasonable Creature. To consult the Preservation of Life, as the only End of it, To make our Health our Business, To engage in no Action that is not part of a Regimen, or course of Physick, are Purposes so abject, so mean, so unworthy human Nature, that a generous Soul would rather die than submit to them. Besides that a continual Anxiety for Life vitiates all the Relishes of it, and casts a Gloom over the whole Face of Nature; as it is impossible we should take Delight in any thing that we are every Moment afraid of losing.

I do not mean, by what I have here said, that I think any one to blame for taking due Care of their Health. On the contrary, as Cheerfulness of Mind, and Capacity for Business, are in a great measure the Effects of a well-tempered Constitution, a Man cannot be at too much Pains to cultivate and preserve it. But this Care, which we are prompted to, not only by common Sense, but by Duty

---

[1] Dropsical. Very common in 17th c. and now *rare* (*OED*).
[2] Dryden quotes this in the Dedication to the *Aeneis* (*Essays*, ed. Ker, ii. 169). Nichols translates: 'I was well, but by trying to be better, I am here.'

and Instinct, should never engage us in groundless Fears, melancholly Apprehensions and imaginary Distempers, which are natural to every Man who is more anxious to live than how to live. In short, the Preservation of Life should be only a secondary Concern, and the Direction of it our Principal. If we have this Frame of Mind, we shall take the best Means to preserve Life, without being oversollicitous about the Event; and shall arrive at that Point of Felicity which *Martial*[1] has mentioned as the Perfection of Happiness, of neither fearing nor wishing for Death.

In answer to the Gentleman, who tempers his Health by Ounces and by Scruples, and instead of complying with those natural Sollicitations of Hunger and Thirst, Drowsiness or Love of Exercise, governs himself by the Prescriptions of his Chair, I shall tell him a short Fable.[2] *Jupiter*, says the Mythologist, to reward the Piety of a certain Country-man, promised to give him what ever he would ask. The Country-man desired that he might have the Management of the Weather in his own Estate: He obtained his Request, and immediately distributed Rain, Snow and Sunshine among his several Fields, as he thought the Nature of the Soil required. At the end of the Year, when he expected to see a more than ordinary Crop, his Harvest fell infinitely short of that of his Neighbours: Upon which (says the Fable) he desired *Jupiter* to take the Weather again into his own Hands, or that otherwise he should utterly ruin himself.

C

No. 26   *Friday, March 30, 1711*[3]
[ADDISON]

Pallida mors æquo pulsat pede pauperum tabernas
   Regumque turres. O beate Sesti,
Vitæ summa brevis spem nos vetat incohare longam.
   Jam te premet nox, fabulæque manes,
Et domus exilis Plutonia . . .

                                   Hor.

WHEN I am in a serious Humour, I very often walk by my self in *Westminster* Abbey;[4] where the Gloominess of the Place,

[1] *Epigrams*, 10. 47. 13.
[2] L'Estrange, *Fables of Æsop* (1692), No. 435 (one of the 'Fables by several Authors').
[For footnotes 3 and 4 see opposite page.

and the Use to which it is applied, with the Solemnity of the Building, and the Condition of the People who lye in it, are apt to fill the Mind with a kind of Melancholy, or rather Thoughtfulness, that is not disagreeable. I Yesterday pass'd a whole Afternoon in the Church-yard, the Cloysters, and the Church, amusing my self with the Tomb-stones and Inscriptions that I met with in those several Regions of the Dead. Most of them recorded nothing else of the buried Person, but that he was born upon one Day and died upon another: The whole History of his Life, being comprehended in those two Circumstances that are common to all Mankind. I could not but look upon these Registers of Existence, whether of Brass or Marble, as a kind of Satyr upon the departed Persons; who had left no other Memorial of them, but that they were born and that they died. They put me in mind of several Persons mentioned in the Battles of Heroic Poems, who have sounding Names given them, for no other Reason but that they may be killed, and are celebrated for nothing but being knocked on the Head.

Γλαῦκόν τε Μέδοντά τε Θερσίλοχόν τε. Hom.
Glaucumque, Medontaque, Thersilochumque. Virg.[1]

The Life of these Men is finely described in Holy Writ,[2] by *the Path of an Arrow* which is immediately closed up and lost.

Upon my going into the Church, I entertain'd my self with the digging of a Grave; and saw in every Shovel-full of it that was thrown up, the Fragment of a Bone or Skull intermixt with a kind of fresh mouldering Earth that some time or other had a Place in the Composition of an humane Body. Upon this, I began to consider with my self what innumerable Multitudes of People lay confus'd together under the Pavement of that ancient Cathedral; how Men and Women, Friends and Enemies, Priests and Soldiers, Monks and

---

[1] Homer, *Iliad*, 17. 216. Virgil, *Aeneid*, 6. 483.
[2] *Wisdom of Solomon*, 5. 12.

---

[3] *Motto.* Horace, *Odes*, 1. 4. 13–17:
With equal foot, Rich friend, impartial Fate
Knocks at the Cottage, and the Palace Gate:
Life's span forbids Thee to extend thy Cares,
And stretch thy Hopes beyond thy Years:
Night soon will seize, and, You must quickly go
To story'd Ghosts, and *Pluto's* house below. CREECH.

[4] On 1 Feb. 1711 (*Post Man*) Curll had published *The Antiquities of St. Peters, or the Abbey Church of Westminster from its original to this time*. The subtitle reads: 'containing all the inscriptions, epitaph's, &c. upon the tombs and gravestones, with the lives, marriages and issue, of the most eminent personages therein reposited.'

Prebendaries, were crumbled amongst one another, and blended together in the same common Mass; how Beauty, Strength, and Youth, with Old-age, Weakness, and Deformity, lay undistinguish'd in the same promiscuous Heap of Matter.

After having thus surveyed this great Magazine of Mortality, as it were in the Lump, I examined it more particularly by the Accounts which I found on several of the Monuments which[a] are raised in every Quarter of that ancient Fabrick. Some of them were covered with such extravagant Epitaphs, that, if it were possible for the dead Person to be acquainted with them, he would blush at the Praises which his Friends have[b] bestow'd upon him. There are others so excessively modest, that they deliver the Character of the Person departed in *Greek* or *Hebrew*, and by that Means are not understood once in a Twelve-month. In the poetical Quarter, I found there were Poets who[c] had no Monuments, and Monuments which[d] had no Poets. I observed indeed that the present War had filled the Church with many of these uninhabited Monuments, which had been erected to the Memory of Persons whose Bodies were perhaps buried in the Plains of *Blenheim*[1] or in the Bosom of the Ocean.

I could not but be very much delighted with several modern Epitaphs, which are written with great Elegance of Expression and Justness of Thought, and therefore do Honour to the Living as well as to the Dead. As a Foreigner is very apt to conceive an Idea of the Ignorance or Politeness of a Nation from the Turn of their publick Monuments and Inscriptions, they should be submitted to the Perusal of Men of Learning and Genius before they are put in Execution. Sir *Cloudesly Shovel*'s Monument[2] has very often given me great Offence: Instead of the brave rough *English* Admiral, which was the distinguishing Character of that plain gallant Man, he is represented on his Tomb by the Figure of a Beau, dress'd in a long Perriwig, and reposing himself upon Velvet Cushions under a

[a] which] that *Fol.*   [b] have] had *Fol.*   [c] who] that *Fol.*   [d] which] that *Fol.*

---

[1] The number of British soldiers killed at the battle of Blenheim (13 Aug., N.S., 1704) is estimated by Trevelyan (i. 433) at 672.

[2] Sir Cloudesley Shovell was shipwrecked on the rocks of Scilly, in his voyage from Toulon, 22 Oct. 1707. The monument described here is still to be seen in the south aisle of the Abbey; for the inscription see Le Neve, *Monumenta Anglicana*, i. 126–7. Trevelyan (ii. 311) quotes Addison's description of the monument and adds: 'One could almost wish these words might be inscribed in stone and placed beside the monument in the Abbey.'

Canopy of State. The Inscription is answerable to the Monument; for instead of celebrating the many remarkable Actions he had performed in the Service of his Country, it acquaints us only with the Manner of his Death, in which it was impossible for him to reap any Honour. The *Dutch*, whom we are apt to despise for want of Genius, shew an infinitely greater Taste of Antiquity and Politeness in their Buildings and Works of this Nature, than what we meet with in those of our own Country. The Monuments of their Admirals, which have been erected at the publick Expence, represent 'em like themselves; and are adorn'd with rostral Crowns and naval Ornaments, with beautiful Festoons of Sea-weed, Shells, and Coral.[a]

But to return to our Subject. I have left the Repository of our *English* Kings for the Contemplation of another Day, when I shall find my Mind disposed for so serious an Amusement. I know that Entertainments of this Nature, are apt to raise dark and dismal Thoughts in timorous Minds and gloomy Imaginations; but for my own Part, though I am always serious, I do not know what it is to be melancholy; and can therefore take a View of Nature in her deep and solemn Scenes, with the same Pleasure as in her most gay and delightful ones. By this Means I can improve my self with those Objects, which others consider with Terrour. When I look upon the Tombs of the Great, every Emotion of Envy dies in me; when I read the Epitaphs of the Beautiful, every inordinate Desire goes out; when I meet with the Grief of Parents upon a Tomb-stone, my Heart melts with Compassion; when I see the Tomb of the Parents themselves, I consider the Vanity of grieving for those whom we must quickly follow: When I see Kings lying by those who deposed them, when I consider rival Wits plac'd Side by Side, or the holy Men that divided the World with their Contests and Disputes, I reflect with Sorrow and Astonishment on the little Competitions, Factions, and Debates of Mankind. When I read the several Dates of the Tombs, of some that dy'd Yesterday, and some six hundred Years ago, I consider that great Day when we shall all of us be Contemporaries, and make our Appearance together.[1]

C

---

[a] Festoons . . . Coral.] Festoons of Shells and Coral. *Fol.*

---

[1] This paper appropriately appeared on Good Friday.

No. 27   *Saturday, March 31, 1711*[1]
[STEELE]

> *Ut nox longa quibus Mentitur amica, diesque*
> *Longa videtur opus debentibus, ut piger Annus*
> *Pupillis, quos dura premit Custodia matrum,*
> *Sic mihi Tarda fluunt ingrataque Tempora, quæ spem*
> *Consiliumque morantur agendi Gnaviter, id quod*
> *Æquè pauperibus prodest, Locupletibus æquè,*
> *Æquè neglectum pueris senibusque nocebit.*
>
> Hor.

THERE is scarce a thinking Man in the World, who is involved in the Business of it, but lives under a secret Impatience of the Hurry and Fatigue he suffers, and has formed a Resolution to fix himself, one time or other, in such a State as is suitable to the End of his Being. You hear Men every Day in Conversation profess, that all the Honour, Power and Riches which they propose to themselves, cannot give Satisfaction enough to reward them for half the Anxiety they undergo in the Pursuit, or Possession of them. While Men are in this Temper, (which happens very frequently) how inconsistent are they with themselves? They are wearied with the Toil they bear, but cannot find in their Hearts to relinquish it; Retirement is what they want, but they cannot betake themselves to it: While they pant after Shade and Covert, they still affect to appear in the most glittering Scenes of Life: But sure this is but just as reasonable as if a Man should call for more Lights, when he has a mind to go to Sleep.

Since then it is certain that our own Hearts deceive us in the Love of the World, and that we cannot command our selves enough to resign it, tho' we every Day wish our selves disengaged from its Allurements; let us not stand upon a Formal taking of Leave, but wean our selves from them, while we are in the midst of them.

---

[1] *Motto.* Horace, *Epistles*, 1. 1. 20–26:

> As Night to those their Mistress fails appears,
> As Days to Labourers, and as long the Years,
> When Jealous Mothers curb, to eager Heirs:
> So dull, and so ingrate my Time doth flow,
> Which hinders what I hope and wish to do:
> What done will profit Rich and Poor, what long
> Forborn, prove equal harm to Old and Young. CREECH.

It is certainly the general Intention of the greater Part of Mankind to accomplish this Work, and live according to their own Approbation, as soon as they possibly can: But since the Duration of Life is so incertain, and that has been a common Topick of Discourse ever since there was such a thing as Life it self, how is it possible that we should defer a Moment the beginning to Live according to the Rules of Reason?

The Man of Business has ever some one Point to carry, and then he tells himself he'll bid adieu to all the Vanity of Ambition: The Man of Pleasure resolves to take his leave at least, and part civilly with his Mistress: But the Ambitious Man is entangled every Moment in a fresh Pursuit, and the Lover sees new Charms in the Object he fancy'd he could abandon. It is therefore a fantastical way of thinking, when we promise our selves an Alteration in our Conduct from change of Place, and difference of Circumstances; the same Passions will attend us where-ever we are, till they are Conquer'd, and we can never live to our Satisfaction in the deepest Retirement, unless we are capable of living so in some measure amidst the Noise and Business of the World.

I have ever thought Men were better known, by what could be observed of them from a Perusal of their private Letters, than any other way. My Friend, the Clergyman, the other Day, upon serious Discourse with him concerning the Danger of Procrastination, gave me the following Letters from Persons with whom he lives in great Friendship and Intimacy, according to the good Breeding and good Sense of his Character. The first is from a Man of Business, who is his Convert; The second from one of whom he conceives good Hopes; The third from one who is in no State at all, but carryed one way and another by starts.

SIR,

'I KNOW not with what Words to express to you the Sense I have of the high Obligation you have laid upon me, in the Penance you enjoined me of doing some Good or other, to a Person of Worth, every Day I live. The Station I am in furnishes me with daily Opportunities of this kind: And the Noble Principle with which you have inspired me, of Benevolence to all I have to deal with, quickens my Application in every thing I undertake. When I relieve Merit from Discountenance,[1] when I assist a Friendless

---

[1] The fact or state of being put out of countenance. *Obs.* The last quotation in *OED* is dated 1656.

Person, when I produce conceal'd Worth, I am displeas'd with my self, for having design'd to leave the World in order to be Virtuous. I am sorry you decline the Occasions which the Condition I am in might afford me of enlarging your Fortunes; but know I contribute more to your Satisfaction, when I acknowledge I am the better Man, from the Influence and Authority you have over,

SIR,

Your most Oblig'd, and

Most Humble Servant,

R. O.'

SIR,

'I AM intirely convinced of the Truth of what you were pleas'd to say to me, when I was last with you alone. You told me then of the silly way I was in; but you told me so, as I saw you loved me, otherwise I could not obey your Commands in letting you know my Thoughts so sincerely as I do at present. I know *the Creature for whom I resign so much of my Character*, is all that you said of her; but then the Trifler has something in her so undesigning and harmless, that her Guilt in one kind disappears by the Comparison of her Innocence in another. Will you, Virtuous Men, allow no alteration of Offences? Must Dear *Chloe* be called[a] by the hard Name you pious People give to common Women? I keep the solemn Promise I made you, in writing to you the State of my Mind, after your kind Admonition; and will endeavour to get the better of this Fondness, which makes me so much her humble Servant, that I am almost asham'd to Subscribe my self Yours,

T. D.'

SIR,

'THERE is no State of Life so Anxious as that of a Man who does not live according to the Dictates of his own Reason. It will seem odd to you, when I assure you that my Love of Retirement first of all brought me to Court; but this will be no Riddle, when I acquaint you that I placed my self here with a Design of getting so much Mony as might enable me to Purchase a handsome Retreat in the Country. At present my Circumstances enable me, and my Duty prompts me, to pass away the remaining Part of My Life in such a Retirement as I at first proposed to my self; but to my great Misfortune I have intirely lost the Relish of it, and shou'd now

---

[a] Must Dear *Chloe* be called] Must Dear   be called *Fol.*

return to the Country with greater Reluctance than I at first came to Court. I am so unhappy, as to know that what I am fond of are Trifles, and that what I neglect is of the greatest Importance: In short, I find a Contest in my own Mind between Reason and Fashion. I remember you once told me, that I might live in the World, and out of it, at the same time. Let me beg of you to explain this Paradox more at large to me, that I may conform my Life, if possible, both to my Duty and my Inclination.

> *I am*
> *Your most Humble Servant,*
> R. B.'ª

R

No. 28
[ADDISON]

Monday, April 2, 1711[1]

> . . . *Neque semper arcum*
> *Tendit Apollo.*

Hor.

I SHALL here present my Reader with a Letter from a Projector, concerning a new Office which he thinks may very much contribute to the Embellishment of the City, and to the driving Barbarity out of our Streets. I consider it as a Satyr upon Projectors[2] in general, and a lively Picture of the whole Art of Modern Criticism.ᵇ

SIR,

'OBSERVING that you have Thoughts of creating certain Officers under you, for the Inspection of several petty Enormities which you your self cannot attend to; and finding daily

---

ª *Letters are Directed*
   For The Spectator,
      To be left at Mr. *Buckley's*
         in *Little-Britain.*
   Post paid.   *Fol.*
ᵇ I consider . . . Criticism.] It is as follows. *Fol.*

---

[1] *Motto.* Horace, *Odes*, 2. 10. 19–20: Nor does Apollo always bend his bow.
[2] Projector. Literally, one who forms a project or designs some enterprise, but at this period usually with invidious connotation: a schemer, one who lives by his wits, a speculator, a cheat (*OED*).

Absurdities hung out upon the Sign-Posts[1] of this City, to the great Scandal of Foreigners, as well as those of our own Country, who are curious Spectators of the same: I do humbly propose, that you would be pleased to make me your Superintendant of all such Figures and Devices as are or shall be made use of on this Occasion; with full Powers to rectify or expunge whatever I shall find irregular or defective. For want of such an Officer, there is nothing like sound Literature and good Sense to be met with in those Objects, that are every where thrusting themselves out to the Eye, and endeavouring to become visible. Our Streets are filled with blue Boars, black Swans, and red Lions; not to mention flying Pigs, and Hogs in Armour, with many other Creatures more extraordinary than any in the Desarts of *Africk*. Strange! that one who has all the Birds and Beasts in Nature to chuse out of, should live at the Sign of an *Ens Rationis*![2]

'My first Task therefore should be, like that of *Hercules*, to clear the City from Monsters. In the second Place I would forbid, that Creatures of jarring and incongruous Natures should be joined together in the same Sign; such as the Bell and the Neats-Tongue, the Dog and Gridiron. The Fox and Goose may be supposed to have met, but what has the Fox and the Seven Stars to do together? and when did the Lamb[a] and Dolphin ever meet, except upon a Sign-Post? As for the Cat and Fiddle, there is a Conceit in it, and therefore I do not intend that any thing I have here said should affect it.

---

[a] Lamb] Sheep *Fol.*

---

[1] *Tatler* 18 had deplored their inaccuracy: 'Many a Man has lost his Way and his Dinner by this general Want of Skill in Orthography: For, considering that the Painters are usually so very bad, that you cannot know the Animal under whose Sign you are to live that Day, How must the Stranger be misled, if it be wrong spell'd, as well as ill painted?' At this period sign-boards were the chief means of distinguishing houses. The modern system of numbering was almost unknown: Hatton (p. 65) notes Prescot street, Goodmans Fields, as unusual: 'Instead of Signs, the Houses here are distinguished by Numbers, as the Stair Cases in the *Inns of Court* and *Chancery*.' According to Misson, the signs 'are commonly very large, and jutt out so far, that in some narrow Streets they touch one another; nay, and run cross almost quite to the other Side' (p. 302). Tom Brown's *Amusements Serious and Comical* (Amusement VIII) describes a walk through the streets of London, where the variety and 'contradictory Language' of the signs puzzle the visitor. 'Here we saw *Joseph's* Dream, the *Bull* and *Mouth*, the *Hen* and *Razor*, the *Ax* and *Bottle*, the *Whale* and *Crow*, the *Shovel* and *Boot*, the *Leg* and *Star*, the *Bible* and *Swan*, the *Frying-Pan* and *Drum*, the *Lute* and *Tun*, the *Hog* in *Armour*, and a thousand others, that the wise Men that put them there can give no Reason for' (*Works*, 3rd ed., 1715, iii. 67–68).
[2] The scholastic term applied to a fantastic or mythical animal ('a being formed by the mind'). Cf. Cowley, note to *Davideis*, ii. 452: 'These are called by the *Schoolmen*, *Entia Rationis*, but are rather *Entia Imaginationis*, or *Phantastique Creatures*' (*Poems*, ed. Waller, p. 313).

I must however observe to you upon this Subject, that it is usual for a young Tradesman, at his first setting up, to add to his own Sign that of the Master whom he serv'd; as the Husband after Marriage, gives a Place to his Mistress's Arms in his own Coat. This I take to have given Rise to many of those Absurdities which are committed over our Heads, and, as I am inform'd, first occasion'd the three Nuns and a Hare, which we see so frequently joined together. I would therefore establish certain Rules, for the determining how far one Tradesman may *give* the Sign of another, and in what Cases he may be allowed to quarter it with his own.

'In the third Place, I would enjoin every Shop to make use of a Sign which bears some Affinity to the Wares in which it deals. What can be more inconsistent, than to see a Bawd at the Sign of the Angel, or a Taylor at the Lion? A Cook should not live at the Boot, nor a Shooemaker at the roasted Pig; and yet for want of this Regulation, I have seen a Goat set up before the Door of a Perfumer, and the *French* King's Head at a Sword-Cutler's.

'An ingenious Foreigner observes, that several of those Gentlemen who value themselves upon their Families, and overlook such as are bred to Trade, bear the Tools of their Forefathers in their Coats of Arms.[1] I will not examine how true this is in Fact: But though it may not be necessary for Posterity thus to set up the Sign of their Fore-fathers; I think it highly proper for those who actually profess the Trade, to show some such Marks of it before their Doors.

'When the Name gives an Occasion for an ingenious Sign-post, I would likewise advise the Owner to take that Opportunity of letting the World know who he is. It would have been ridiculous for the ingenious Mrs. *Salmon*[2] to have lived at the Sign of the Trout; for which Reason she has erected before her House, the Figure of the Fish that is her Name-sake. Mr. *Bell*[3] has likewise distinguish'd

---

[1] 'Les Armoiries des nouvelles Maisons, sont pour la plus grande partie, les Enseignes de leurs anciennes boutiques' (*Menagiana*, 3rd ed., 1715, iii. 350).

[2] Mrs. Salmon's waxworks, in Fleet Street near Temple Bar, were one of the popular attractions of the time. One of the handbills, listing her curiosities, is printed in Ashton, i. 282-3. One of the burlesque 'Notes upon Notes' printed in the Lintott *Odes of Horace* in 1712 (part iv, p. 7) refers to 'the Famous Mrs. *Salmon* at the *Salmon* near *Chancery-Lane* in *Fleet-street*, who gives out that she has now the greatest Beauties, not only of the *British* Court, but of all *Europe*, to be seen in Wax-work at her House'. The death of 'Mr. Salmon, the famous Waxwork Man . . . at his House in Fleet-street' is announced in Applebee's *Original Weekly Journal*, 3 Jan. 1718/19. For an illustration of the exterior of the waxworks see Claud Golding, *London: the City* (Hale, 1951), facing p. 116.

[3] There was a Bell Ale-house at the corner of Silver-street in Woodstreet (*Post Boy*, 29 June 1710).

himself by a Device of the same Nature: And here, Sir, I must beg Leave to observe to you, that this particular Figure of a Bell, has given Occasion to several Pieces of Wit in this Kind. A Man of your Reading, must know that *Abel Drugger*[1] gain'd great Applause by it in the Time of *Ben. Johnson.* Our Apocryphal Heathen God,[2] is also represented by this Figure; which in Conjunction with the Dragon, make a very handsome Picture in several of our Streets. As for the Bell-Savage, which is the Sign of a savage Man standing by a Bell, I was formerly very much puzzled upon the Conceit of it, till I accidentally fell into the reading of an old Romance translated out of the *French*; which gives an Account of a very beautiful Woman who was found in a Wilderness, and is called in the *French la belle Sauvage*;[3] and is every where translated by our Countrymen the Bell-Savage. This Piece of Philology will, I hope, convince you that I have made Sign-posts my Study, and consequently qualified my self for the Employment which I sollicit at your Hands. But before I conclude my Letter, I must communicate to you another Remark which I have made upon the Subject with which I am now entertaining you, namely, that I can give a shrewd Guess at the Humour of the Inhabitant by the Sign that hangs before his Door. A surly cholerick Fellow, generally makes Choice of a Bear; as Men of milder Dispositions, frequently live at the Lamb. Seeing a Punch-Bowl painted upon a Sign near *Charing-Cross*, and very curiously garnished, with a couple of Angels hovering over it and squeezing a Lemmon into it, I had the Curiosity to ask after the Master of the House, and found upon Enquiry, as I had ghessed by the little *Agréemens* upon his Sign, that he was a *Frenchman.* I know, Sir, it is not requisite for me to enlarge upon these Hints to a Gentleman of your great Abilities; so humbly recommending my self to your Favour and Patronage,

I remain. *&c.*'

I shall add to the foregoing Letter, another which came to me by the same Penny-Post.

[1] Jonson's *Alchemist*, II. i.
[2] *The History of Bel and of the Dragon* (cf. No. 73). The Monthly Society of Assurance upon Lives had offices at the Bell and Dragon at Lincoln's Inn Back Gate (*Post Man*, 31 Mar. 1711).
[3] Many derivations have been offered for the name of this inn on Ludgate Hill. The 'philology' advanced by this correspondent represents one current theory of the origin of the phrase. Cf. Jacob Larwood and John Camden Hotten, *English Inn Signs* (Chatto & Windus, 1951), p. 290.

From my own Apartment near Charing-Cross.

Honoured Sir,

'HAVING heard that this Nation is a great Encourager of Ingenuity, I have brought with me a Rope-dancer[1] that was caught in one of the Woods belonging to the Great *Mogul*.[2] He is by Birth a Monkey; but swings upon a Rope, takes a Pipe of Tobacco, and drinks a Glass of Ale, like any reasonable Creature. He gives great Satisfaction to the Quality; and if they will make a Subscription for him, I will send for a Brother of his out of *Holland* that is a very good Tumbler, and also for another of the same Family whom I design for my *Merry-Andrew*,[3] as being an excellent Mimick, and the greatest Drole in the Country where he now is. I hope to have this Entertainment in a Readiness for the next Winter; and doubt not but it will please more than the Opera or Puppet-Show. I will not say that a Monkey is a better Man than some of the Opera Heroes; but certainly he is a better Representative of a Man, than the most artificial Composition of Wood and Wire. If you will be pleased to give me a good Word in your Paper, you shall be every Night a Spectator at my Show for nothing.

I am, *&c.*'

C

No. 29   *Tuesday, April 3, 1711*[4]

[ADDISON]

. . . Sermo linguâ concinnus utrâque
Suavior: ut Chio nota si commista Falerni est.

Hor.

THERE is nothing that has more[a] startled our *English* Audience, than the *Italian Recitativo* at its first Entrance upon the Stage.

[a] that has more] that more *Fol.*

---

1 Rope-dancers and tumblers 'from Europe' were among the popular features of the booths at Bartholomew Fair and elsewhere. The following advertisement (*Daily Courant*, 1 May 1706) illustrates the marvels here satirized:
At the Widow Barnes, Mr. Evans's, and Mr. Finley's Booth, over-against Mr. Penkethman's, during the usual time of May-Fair are to be seen the most famous Rope-Dancers of Europe, who perform such strange and surprizing things as were never before seen, and which are almost incredible to relate.
2 The Emperors of Delhi were usually given this name.
3 The traditional name for a mountebank's assistant.
4 *Motto.* Horace, *Satires*, I. 10. 23–24:
A style, where both tongues make a happy blend, has more charm, as when the Falernian wine is mixed with Chian.

People were wonderfully surprized to hear Generals singing the Word of Command, and Ladies delivering Messages in Musick. Our Country-men could not forbear laughing when they heard a Lover chanting out a Billet-doux, and even the Superscription of a Letter set to a Tune. The Famous Blunder in an old Play of *Enter a King and two Fidlers Solus*,[1] was now no longer an Absurdity, when it was impossible for a Hero in a Desart, or a Princess in her Closet, to speak any thing unaccompanied with Musical Instruments.

But however this *Italian* Method of acting in *Recitativo* might appear at first hearing, I cannot but think it much more just than that which prevailed in our *English* Opera before this Innovation: The Transition from an Air to Recitative Musick being more natural than the passing from a Song to plain and ordinary Speaking, which was the common Method in *Purcell's* Opera's.[2]

The only Fault I find in our present Practice is the making use of *Italian Recitativo* with *English* Words.

To go to the Bottom of this Matter, I must observe, that the Tone, or (as the *French* call it) the Accent of every Nation in their ordinary Speech is altogether different from that of every other People, as we may see even in the *Welsh* and *Scotch*, who[a] border so near upon us. By the Tone or Accent, I do not mean the Pronunciation of each particular Word, but the Sound of the whole Sentence. Thus it is very common for an *English* Gentleman, when he hears a *French* Tragedy, to complain that the Actors all of them speak in a Tone; and therefore he very wisely prefers his own Country-men, not considering that a Foreigner complains of the same Tone in an *English* Actor.

_a who] that *Fol.*

. [1] This 'famous blunder' remains unidentified.

[2] The 'operas' during the Restoration period were for the most part dramatic spectacles with songs interspersed. (Cf. Peter Motteux, *Gentleman's Journal*, Jan. 1691/2, p. 5.) Henry Purcell (1659–95) composed incidental music for several plays, such as *The Tempest* and *The Indian Queen*, but except for *Dido and Aeneas* these are more properly described as 'operas with dialogue'. A concert of Purcell's music was given shortly after the publication of this essay. It is advertised in No. 58:

At the Desire of several Persons of Quality. For the Benefit of Mr. Cuthbert, Lovelace and White. At Stationer's-Hall near Ludgate, on Wednesday the 9th of May, will be a Consort of Vocal and Instrumental Musick by the best Performers; particularly, several select Entertainments of the following (English) Operas, viz. The Indian Queen, King Arthur, the Fairy Queen, and Dioclesian; the Masque in Timon of Athens, the Pastoral in the Libertine; with several Songs out of the St. Cæcelia's Musick: All compos'd by that great Master the late Mr. Henry Purcell. Tickets are deliver'd at Garraway's and Robin's in Exchange-Ally, Will's and Batson's in Cornhill, Sam's in Ludgate-street, St. James's and Smyrna Coffee-houses at St. James's, and at the Hall, at 5 s. per Ticket. Beginning at 6 a Clock.

For this Reason, the Recitative Musick in every Language should be as different as the Tone or Accent of each Language, for otherwise what may properly express a Passion in one Language, will not do it in another. Every one who has been long in *Italy* knows very well, that the Cadences in the *Recitativo* bear a remote Affinity to the Tone of their Voices in ordinary Conversation, or to speak more properly, are only the Accents of their Language made more Musical and Tuneful.

Thus the Notes of Interrogation, or Admiration, in the *Italian* Musick (if one may so call them) which resemble their Accents in Discourse on such Occasions, are not unlike the ordinary Tones of an *English* Voice when we are angry; insomuch that I have often seen our Audiences extreamly mistaken as to what has been doing upon the Stage, and expecting to see the Hero knock down his Messenger, when he has been asking[a] him a Question; or fancying that he quarrels with his Friend, when he only bids him Good-morrow.

For this Reason the *Italian* Artists cannot agree with our *English* Musicians, in admiring *Purcell's* Compositions, and thinking his Tunes so wonderfully adapted to his Words, because both Nations do not always express the same Passions by the same Sounds.

I am therefore humbly of Opinion, that an *English* Composer should not follow the *Italian* Recitative too servilely, but make use of many gentle Deviations from it, in Compliance with his own Native Language. He may Copy out of it all the lulling Softness and *Dying Falls*[1] (as *Shakespear* calls them,) but should still remember that he ought to accommodate himself to an *English* Audience, and by humouring the Tone of our Voices in ordinary Conversation, have the same Regard to the Accent of his own Language, as those Persons had to theirs whom he professes to imitate. It is observed, that several of the singing Birds of our own Country learn to sweeten their Voices, and mellow the Harshness of their natural Notes, by practising under those that come from warmer Climates. In the same manner I would allow the *Italian* Opera to lend our *English* Musick as much as may grace and soften it, but never entirely to annihilate and destroy it. Let the Infusion be as strong as you please, but still let the Subject Matter of it be *English*.

[a] been asking] been only asking *Fol.*

---

[1] *Twelfth Night*, I. i. 4.

A Composer should fit his Musick to the Genius of the People, and consider that the Delicacy of Hearing, and Taste of Harmony, has been formed upon those Sounds which every Country abounds with: In short, that Musick is of a Relative Nature, and what is Harmony to one Ear, may be Dissonance to another.

The same Observations which I have made upon the Recitative part of Musick, may be applied to all our Songs and Airs in general.

Signior *Baptist Lully*[1] acted like a Man of Sense in this Particular. He found the *French* Musick extreamly defective, and very often barbarous: However, knowing the Genius of the People, the Humour of their Language, and the prejudiced Ears he[a] had to deal with, he did not pretend to extirpate the *French* Musick, and plant the *Italian* in its stead; but only to Cultivate and Civilize it with innumerable Graces and Modulations which he borrow'd from the *Italian*. By this means the *French* Musick is now perfect in its kind; and when you say it is not so good as the *Italian*, you only mean that it does not please you so well, for there is scarce[b] a *Frenchman* who would not wonder to hear you give the *Italian* such a Preference. The Musick of the *French* is indeed very properly adapted to their Pronunciation and Accent, as their whole Opera wonderfully favours the Genius of such a gay airy People. The Chorus in which that Opera abounds, gives the Parterre[2] frequent Opportunities of joining in Consort with the Stage. This Inclination of the Audience to Sing along with the Actors,[3] so prevails with them, that I have sometimes known the Performer on the Stage do no more in a Celebrated Song, than the Clerk of a Parish Church, who serves

[a] Ears he] Ears that he *Fol.*   [b] scarce] not *Fol.*

[1] Jean Baptiste Lully (1632–87) became director of the opera at the French court and composed some fourteen operas, one of which, *Proserpine* (produced at St-Germain 3 Feb. 1680 and at Paris on 19 Nov.), is referred to in the next paragraph. For the *recitativo secco* of the Italians he substituted accompanied recitative (Grove).

[2] The part of the ground-floor of the auditorium of a theatre behind the orchestra. (This is the earliest example of the word in this sense in *OED*.)

[3] Gay's *Epistle to Pulteney* (1720) contains an account of a visit to the French opera, in which 'The Hero strutts, and the whole audience sings' (192):

Hard chance had plac'd me near a noisie throat,
That in rough quavers bellow'd ev'ry note.
Pray Sir, says I, suspend a-while your song,
The Opera's drown'd; your lungs are wondrous strong;
I wish to hear your *Roland*'s ranting strain,
While he with rooted forests strows the plain.
Sudden he shrugs surprize, and answers quick,
Monsieur apparemment n'aime pas la musique.
Then turning round, he join'd th' ungrateful noise;
And the loud Chorus thunder'd with his voice. (195–204)

only to raise the Psalm, and is afterwards drown'd in the Musick of the Congregation. Every Actor that comes on the Stage is a Beau.[1] The Queens and Heroines are so Painted, that they appear as Ruddy and Cherry-cheek'd as Milk-maids. The Shepherds are all Embroider'd, and acquit themselves in a Ball better than our *English* Dancing-Masters. I have seen a couple of Rivers appear in red Stockings; and *Alpheus*,[2] instead of having his Head cover'd with Sedge and Bull-Rushes, making Love in a fair full-bottom'd Perriwig, and a Plume of Feathers, but with a Voice so full of Shakes and Quavers that I should have thought the Murmurs of a Country Brook the much more agreeable Musick.

I remember the last Opera I saw in that merry Nation, was the Rape of *Proserpine*, where *Pluto*, to make the more tempting Figure, puts himself in a *French* Equipage, and brings *Ascalaphus* along with him as his *Valet de Chambre*. This is what we call Folly and Impertinence; but what the *French* look upon as Gay and Polite.

I shall add no more to what I have here offer'd than that Musick, Architecture and Painting, as well as Poetry and Oratory, are to deduce their Laws and Rules from the general Sense and Taste of Mankind, and not from the Principles of those Arts themselves; or in other Words, the Taste is not to conform to the Art, but the Art to the Taste. Musick is not design'd to please only Chromatick Ears,[3] but all that are capable of distinguishing harsh from disagreeable Notes. A Man of an ordinary Ear is a Judge whether a Passion is express'd in proper Sounds, and whether the Melody of those Sounds be more or less pleasing.   C

---

[1] Addison had written from Paris an account of the opera in a letter to Congreve, dated August 1699, which is recalled in the present essay: 'I cou'd have wisht for your company last night at ye Opera where you would have seen paint enough on ye actors Faces to have Dawbed a whole street of sign-posts. Every man that comes upon the Stage is a Beau: the Shepherds are all Embroiderd, Pluto has his Valet de chambre, and a couple of Riders appears in Red Stockins. Alpheus throws aside his Sedge and makes Love in a Fair periwig and a plume of Feathers but with such a horrid voice that [one] woud think the murmurs of a Country-Brook much better music' (Letters, ed. Graham, p. 4).

[2] For the legend of Alpheus and Arethusa see Ovid, *Metamorphoses*, 5. 572–641.

[3] This is the earliest example in *OED* of 'chromatic' in a figurative sense.

No. 30
[STEELE]

Wednesday, April 4, 1711[1]

Si, Mimnermus uti censet, sine amore Jocisque
Nil est Jucundum; vivas in amore Jocisque.

Hor.

ONE common Calamity makes Men extremely affect each other, tho' they differ in every other Particular. The Passion of Love is the most general Concern among Men; and I am glad to hear by my last Advices from *Oxford*, that there are a Set of Sighers in that University, who have erected themselves into a Society in honour of that tender Passion. These Gentlemen are of that Sort of Inamoratos, who are not so very much lost to common Sense, but that they understand the Folly they are guilty of; and for that Reason separate themselves from all other Company, because they will enjoy the Pleasure of talking incoherently, without being ridiculous to any but each other. When a Man comes into the Club, he is not obliged to make any Introduction to his Discourse, but at once, as he is seating himself in his Chair, speaks in the Thread of his own Thoughts, 'She gave me a very obliging Glance, She never look'd so well in her Life as this Evening,' or the like Reflection, without Regard to any other Members of the Society; for in this Assembly they do not meet to talk to each other, but every Man claims the full Liberty of talking to himself. Instead of Snuff-boxes and Canes, which are usual Helps to Discourse with other young Fellows, these have each some Piece of Ribband, a broken Fan, or an old Girdle, which they play with while they talk of the fair Person remember'd by each respective Token. According to the Representation of the Matter from my Letters, the Company appear like so many Players rehearsing behind the Scenes; one is sighing and lamenting his Destiny in beseeching Terms, another declaring he will break his Chain, and another in dumb-Show, striving to express his Passion by his Gesture. It is very ordinary in the Assembly for one of a sudden to rise and make a Discourse concerning his Passion in general, and describe the Temper of his Mind in such a Manner, as that the whole Company shall join in the Description, and feel

---

[1] *Motto*. Horace, *Epistles*, 1. 6. 65–66:

If, as Mimnermus thinks, nothing can be pleasant without love and mirth, then live in love and mirth.

the Force of it. In this Case, if any Man has declared the Violence of his Flame in more pathetick Terms, he is made President for that Night, out of respect to his superiour Passion.

We had some Years ago in this Town a Set of People who met and dressed like Lovers, and were distinguished by the Name of the *Fringe-Glove Club*;[1] but they were Persons of such moderate Intellects even before they were impaired by their Passion, that their Irregularities could not furnish sufficient Variety of Folly to afford daily new Impertinencies; by which Means that Institution dropp'd. These Fellows could express their Passion in nothing but their Dress; but the *Oxonians* are phantastical now they are Lovers, in proportion to their Learning and Understanding before they became such. The Thoughts of the ancient Poets on this agreeable Phrenzy, are translated in honour of some modern Beauty; and *Chloris* is won to Day, by the same Compliment that was made to *Lesbia*[2] a thousand Years ago. But as far as I can learn, the Patron of the Club is the renowned Don *Quixote*.[3] The Adventures of that gentle Knight are frequently mention'd in the Society, under the Colour of laughing at the Passion and themselves: But at the same Time, tho' they are sensible of the Extravagancies of that unhappy Warriour, they do not observe, that to turn all the Reading of the best and wisest Writings into Rapsodies of Love, is a Phrenzy no less diverting than that of the aforesaid accomplish'd *Spaniard*. A Gentleman who, I hope, will continue his Correspondence, is lately admitted into the Fraternity, and sent me the following Letter.

SIR,

'SINCE I find you take Notice of Clubs, I beg Leave to give you an Account of one in *Oxford*, which you have no where mention'd, and perhaps never heard of. We distinguish our selves by

---

[1] For fringed gloves see No. 16.

[2] *The Adventures of Catullus, and History of his Amours with Lesbia, intermixt with translations of his choicest poems,* translated from the French 'by several hands', was published in 1707.

[3] The 'Genius and discerning Spirit' of Cervantes are praised in *Tatler* 178. D'Urfey's stage version of *Don Quixote*, in three parts, was produced in 1695–6. The *Daily Courant* of 17 Dec. 1702 advertises as published 'this day':

The History of the Renowned Don Quixote de la Mancha: Written in Spanish by Miguel de Cervantes Saavedra; Translated from the Original by several Hands, and publish'd by Peter Motteux. In 4 Volumes in 12º, with Sculptures. Printed for Sam. Buckley at the Dolphin in Little Britain, and Sold by the Booksellers of London and Westminster. Those that have the Two First Volumes already, may have the Two Last apart.

Ned Ward's version, in 'Hudibrastic Verse', appeared in 1711.

the Title of the *Amorous Club*,[1] are all Votaries of *Cupid*, and Admirers of the Fair-Sex. The Reason that we are so little known in the World, is the Secresy which we are obliged to live under in the University. Our Constitution runs counter to that of the Place wherein we live: For in Love there are no Doctors, and we all profess so high Passion, that we admit of no Graduates in it. Our Presidentship is bestow'd according to the Dignity of Passion; our Number is unlimited; and our Statutes are like those of the Druids, recorded in our own Breasts only, and explained by the Majority of the Company. A Mistress, and a Poem in her Praise, will introduce any Candidate: Without the latter no one can be admitted; for he that is not in love enough to rhime, is unqualified for our Society. To speak disrespectfully of any Woman, is Expulsion from our gentle Society. As we are at present all of us Gown-men, instead of duelling when we are Rivals, we drink together the Health of our Mistress. The Manner of doing this sometimes indeed creates Debates; on such Occasions we have Recourse to the Rules of Love among the Antients.

Naevia[2] *sex Cyathis, septem Justina bibatur.*

This Method of a Glass to every Letter of her Name, occasioned the other Night a Dispute of some Warmth. A young Student, who is in Love with Mrs. *Elizabeth Dimple*, was so unreasonable as to begin her Health under the Name of *Elizabetha*; which so exasperated the Club, that by common Consent we retrenched it to *Betty*. We look upon a Man as no Company, that does not sigh five times in a Quarter of an Hour; and look upon a Member as very absurd, that is so much himself as to make a direct Answer to a Question. In fine, the whole Assembly is made up of absent Men,[3] that is, of such Persons as have lost their Locality, and whose Minds and Bodies never keep Company with one another. As I am an unfortunate

---

[1] This may be compared with the Sweet-meat Club of *The Female Tatler*, No. 5 (R. J. Allen, *The Clubs of Augustan London*, pp. 167–8).

[2] Martial, *Epigrams*, I. 71. 1. Cf. Camden, *Remains concerning Britain* (ed. 1674), p. 71:

> Or how the amorous Romans kissed the Cup with a health so often at their meetings, as there were letters in their Mistresses names, according to that of merry *Martial* of his two wenches, *Naevia* which had six letters, and *Justina* that had seven in her name.
>
> *Nævia sex cyathis, septem Justina bibatur.*

(In Martial the line reads *Lævia* . . . .)

[3] Absent men, i.e. absent-minded. This is the earliest example in *OED* of this use. See also No. 77.

Member of this distracted Society, you cannot expect a very regular Account of it; for which Reason, I hope you will pardon me that I so abruptly subscribe my self,

Sir,

Your most obedient

humble Servant,

T. B.

'I forgot to tell you, that *Albina*, who has six Votaries in this Club, is one of your Readers.'

R

No. 31

[ADDISON]

Sit mihi fas audita loqui! . . .

Vir.

LAST Night, upon my going into a Coffee-House not far from the *Hay-Market* Theatre, I diverted my self for above half an Hour with overhearing the Discourse of one, who, by the Shabbiness of his Dress, the Extravagance of his Conceptions, and the Hurry of his Speech, I discovered to be of that Species who are generally distinguished by the Title of Projectors. This Gentleman, for I found he was treated as such by his Audience, was entertaining a whole Table of Listners with the Project of an Opera, which he told us had not cost him above two or three Mornings in the Contrivance, and which he was ready to put in Execution, provided he might find his Account in it. He said, that he had observed the great Trouble and Inconvenience which Ladies were at, in travelling up and down to the several Shows that are exhibited in different Quarters of the Town. The dancing Monkies[2] are in one Place; the Puppet Show in another; the Opera in a third; not to mention the Lions, that are almost a whole Day's Journey from the Politer Part of the Town. By this means People of Figure are forced to lose half

---

[1] *Motto.* Virgil, *Aeneid*, 6. 266: May I be allowed to tell what I have heard!
[2] The dancing monkeys (cf. No. 28), the puppet show, the opera, and the lions in the Tower—these sum up the attractions of London for the ladies and 'people of figure'. The puppet show and opera are frequently linked in later essays.

the Winter after their coming to Town, before they have seen all the strange Sights about it. In order to remedy this great Inconvenience, our Projector drew out of his Pocket the Scheme of an Opera, Entitled, *The Expedition of* Alexander[1] *the Great*; in which he had disposed all[a] the remarkable Shows about Town, among the Scenes and Decorations of his Piece. The Thought, he confest, was not originally his own, but that he had taken the Hint of it from several Performances which he had seen upon our Stage: In one of which there was a Rary-Show;[2] in another, a Ladder-dance;[3] and in others a Posture-Man,[4] a moving Picture,[5] with many Curiosities of the like nature.

 [a] disposed all] disposed of all *Fol.*

---

[1] Lee's *The Rival Queens, or the Death of Alexander the Great*, first produced in 1677, was still a standard piece in the repertory at Drury Lane Theatre. It had had three performances in 1710. On 29 June 1710 it had been burlesqued at the Haymarket as 'A Comical Tragedy, call'd The Rival Queans; with the Humours of Alexander the Great', in which Cibber had appeared as Alexander, Estcourt as Clytus, Bullock as Roxana, and Bullock Junior as Statira.

[2] A Rary-Show, or raree-show, was a peep-show carried about on a man's back in a long box. See the letter signed S. T. in No. 271 (vol. ii).

[3] In *Tatler* 12 Steele had complained that Christopher Rich 'brought in upon us, to get in his Money, Ladder-dancers, Rope-dancers, Juglers, and Mountebanks, to strut in the Place of *Shakespear*'s Heroes, and *Johnson*'s Humourists'. One Robinson had long been advertised as the 'Master Ladder-Dancer of England'; performing at the Great Booth at Stepney, 'he stands on the uppermost Step of the Ladder and turns himself quite round, which no Man ever did, or can do besides himself; playing on the Violin, with several other things' (*Daily Courant*, 7 Apr. 1705).

[4] Nos. 41 and 42 in Marcellus Laroon's *Cryes of the City of London* depict posture-men; in No. 42 Clark, 'the English Posture Master' is shown standing on his right leg and holding his left leg up over his head, while a monkey at his side imitates him. 'The Surprizing Mr. Higgins, Posture-Master, that lately perform'd in the Queen's Theatre in the Hay-Market' is advertised to appear at the Ship Tavern in Greenwich on 14 Mar. 1710 (*Daily Courant*). In No. 246 is advertised:

At the Duke of Marlborough's Head in Fleet-street, in the great Room, is to be seen the famous Posture-Master of Europe, who far exceeds the deceased Posture Masters Clarke and Higgins: He extends his Body into all deformed Shapes; makes his Hip and Shoulder Bones meet together; lays his Head upon the Ground, and turns his Body round twice or thrice, without stirring his Face from the Place; stands upon one Leg, and extends the other in a perpendicular Line half a Yard above his Head; and extends his Body from a Table, with his Head a Foot below his Heels, having nothing to balance his Body but his Feet: With several other Postures too tedious to mention. Likewise a Child of about 9 Years of Age, that shews such Postures as never was seen perform'd by one of his Age. Also the famous English Artist, who turns his Balls into living Birds; and takes an empty Bag, which after being turn'd, trod, and stampt on, produces some Hundreds of Eggs, and at last a living Hen. Side-Boxes 2s. Pit 1s. To be perform'd at 6 a Clock every Evening.

This advertisement is repeated in Nos. 269, 298, &c. In Nos. 386 and 394 the performance is advertised to be given 'at the New Tunbridge Wells by the New River Head, in the Dancing Room'.

[5] 'The most Famous and Curious Original Moving Picture which came from

This *Expedition of Alexander* opens with his consulting the Oracle at *Delphos*, in which the dumb Conjurer,[1] who has been visited by so many Persons of Quality of late Years, is to be introduced as telling him his Fortune: At the same time *Clench* of *Barnet*[2] is represented in another Corner of the Temple, as ringing the Bells of *Delphos*, for joy of his Arrival. The Tent of *Darius* is to be Peopled by the Ingenious Mrs. *Salmon*,[3] where *Alexander* is to fall in Love with a Piece of Wax-Work, that represents the beautiful *Statira*. When *Alexander* comes into that Country, in which *Quintus Curtius*[4] tells us the Dogs were so exceeding fierce that they would not loose their Hold, tho' they were cut to pieces Limb by Limb, and that they would hang upon their Prey by their Teeth when they had nothing but a Mouth left, there is to be a Scene of *Hockley in the Hole*,[5] in which is to be represented all the Diversions of that Place, the Bull-baiting only excepted, which cannot possibly be exhibited in the Theatre, by Reason of the Lowness of the Roof. The several Woods in *Asia*, which *Alexander* must be supposed to pass through, will give the Audience a Sight of Monkies dancing upon Ropes, with the many other Pleasantries of that ludicrous Species. At the same time, if there chance to be any Strange Animals in Town, whether Birds or Beasts, they may be either let loose among the Woods, or driven across the Stage by some of the Country People of *Asia*. In the last great Battel, *Pinkethman*[6] is to personate King *Porus*

Germany, that was designed for the Elector of Bavaria', was being displayed at the Duke of Marlborough's Head in Fleet-street early in 1709 (*Post Boy*, 12 Mar.). A rival was displayed for the first time on 29 Dec. 1709, 'next Door to the Grecian's Head Coffee-House, over against Cecil-street in the Strand', described as 'a PICTURE finely drawn, by an extraordinary Master, which has many curious and wonderfully pleasing and surprising Motions in it, all natural' (*Tatler* 113). Another is advertised at 'Mr David Randall's in Channel-Row, Westminster' (*Post-Man*, 14 Jan. 1709/10 and 20 Jan. 1710/11), and still another 'at the Green-Man, the Upper-end of King-street, near Bloomsbury-Square, going into the Long Fields' (*Daily Courant*, 8 Apr. 1710). The moving picture at the Duke of Marlborough's Head is again being shown in 1710 and 1711 (see notes to No. 414 (vol. iii)).

[1] Duncan Campbell, the 'dumb fortune-teller' of *Tatler* 14, was a popular oracle of the day. Shortly before, he had published an advertisement in the *Post Boy* (27 Mar.) defending himself against a charge of treasonable activities and announcing that he 'still lives at his own House in *Drury-lane*, where all Persons may apply themselves, as usual, for his Advice, *&c*.' Defoe published in 1720 a *History of the Life and Adventures of Mr. Duncan Campbell, a Gentleman, who, though deaf and dumb, writes down any strange Name at first Sight, with their future Contingencies of Fortune.*

[2] See No. 24.

[3] See No. 28.

[4] *Life and Death of Alexander the Great*, 9. 1. 31–33.

[5] The Bear Garden at Hockley in the Hole, near Clerkenwell Green, was a popular resort for bear-baiting and prize-fights. No. 436 (vol. iv) contains an account of a 'trial of skill' there.

[6] William Penkethman (or Pinkethman) was one of the most popular actors

upon an Elephant, and is to be encounter'd by *Powell*, representing *Alexander* the Great upon a Dromedary, which nevertheless Mr. *Powell*[1] is desired to call by the Name of *Bucephalus*. Upon the Close of this great decisive Battel, when the two Kings are thoroughly reconciled, to shew the mutual Friendship and good Correspondence that reigns between them, they both of them go together to a Puppet Show, in which the ingenious Mr. *Powell, Junior,*[2] may have an Opportunity of displaying his whole Art of Machinery, for the Diversion of the two Monarchs. Some at the Table urged that a Puppet Show was not a suitable Entertainment for *Alexander* the Great; and that it might be introduced more properly, if we suppose the Conqueror touched upon that Part of *India* which is said to be inhabited by the Pigmies. But this Objection was looked upon as frivolous, and the Proposal immediately over-ruled. Our Projector further added, that after the Reconciliation of these two Kings they might invite one another to Dinner, and either of them entertain his Guest with the *German* Artist,[3] Mr. *Pinkethman's* Heathen

and showmen of the day. For years he had conducted a booth at May Fair, Bartholomew Fair, and elsewhere; he appeared regularly in the plays at Drury Lane; and in the summer of 1710 he opened a theatre of his own in Greenwich. (See Sybil Rosenfeld, *Strolling Players and Drama in the Provinces 1660–1765*, Cambridge, 1939, chap. xiii.) Among his recent roles at Drury Lane were those of Frible in *Epsom Wells*, Trim in *The Funeral*, Old Bell-air in *The Man of Mode*, and Humphry Gubbin in *The Tender Husband* (a role which he created). At a production of *The Silent Woman*, followed by *The Stage Coach*, at Drury Lane on 31 May 1709 Penkethman, it is advertised, 'will speak an Epilogue riding on an Ass' (*Daily Courant*). 'Like that merry Fellow PINKETHMAN on an Elephant' is one of the similes in Burnet and Duckett', *Second Tale of a Tub* (p. 211). He died at Richmond on 20 Sept. 1725 (*Weekly Journal*, 25 Sept.).

[1] George Powell appears in *Tatler* 3 as 'that Famous and Heroick Actor . . . who formerly play'd *Alexander the Great* in all Places, tho' he is lately grown so reserv'd, as to act it only on the Stage'. Powell in fact was given to intemperance (see Cibber's *Apology*, chap. vii), and at this time was near the end of his career. He created the role of Orestes in *The Distrest Mother* at Drury Lane on 17 Mar. 1712, and his last role of importance was that of Portius in *Cato*. He died on 14 Dec. 1714. In *The Rival Queens* at Penkethman's theatre in Greenwich (5 and 6 July 1710) he had played the part of Alexander.

[2] Martin Powell, the master of the puppet show (see No. 14). At this date Punch's Theatre was presenting

The History of King Bladud, Founder of the Bath. The Figures being drest after the manner of the Ancient Britains. With the Walks, Groves, and Representation of the King's-Bath and new Pump-house. The Figures of Ladies and Gentlemen all moving in real Water.

[3] This may refer to the operator of the 'moving picture' mentioned in the preceding paragraph, but more likely to the posture-master advertised in the *Flying Post* of 8 Dec. 1698:

The greatest Wonder in Nature that ever was seen. There is arrived from *Germany* the most famous Artist in the World, the like never seen before, born without Arms, he has had the Honour to be shown before the Emperor of *Germany*, the great Czar of *Moscovy*, the Kings of *Denmark* and *Sweedland*. He performs wonderful

Gods,[1] or any of the like Diversions, which shall then chance to be in vogue.

This Project was receiv'd with very great Applause by the whole Table. Upon which the Undertaker told us, that he had not yet communicated to us above half his Design; for that *Alexander* being a *Greek*, it was his Intention that the whole Opera should be acted in that Language, which was a Tongue he was sure would wonderfully please the Ladies, especially when it was a little raised and rounded by the *Ionick* Dialect; and could not but be acceptable[a] to the whole Audience, because there are fewer of them who understand *Greek* than *Italian*. The only Difficulty that remained, was, how to get Performers, unless we could persuade some Gentlemen of the Universities to learn to Sing, in order to qualify themselves for the Stage; but this Objection soon vanished, when the Projector informed us that the *Greeks* were at present the only Musicians in the *Turkish* Empire, and that it would be very easy for our Factory at *Smyrna* to furnish us every Year with a Colony of Musicians, by the Opportunity of the *Turkey* Fleet; besides, says he, if we want any

---

[a] be acceptable] be wonderfully acceptable *Fol.*

Actions of Body, to the great Admiration of all Spectators; he Fences with his Foot as well as some with their Hand, he flings a Dart or Sword thro a Board, he walks upon his Toes and stands upon one, he lays one Foot behind his Neck and hops on the other . . .; he writes with his right Foot, left Foot and Mouth five several sorts of Languages. . . . He is to be seen from Ten in the Morning till Six at Night, at Mr. *Francis Strut*'s at the *Civet-Cat*, Perfumer, over-against *Exeter-Change* in the *Strand*.

Ward's *London Spy* (Part I) mentions a trickster with false dice and cards, 'which he handles with more gainful *Dexterity* than the *German Artist*' (Casanova Society, 1924, p. 10); and in *Medley* 4 (23 Oct. 1710) the author of *Faults on Both Sides* is described as 'as great a Master of the Mystery of our State of Clock-work, as the *German* of his own Moving-Picture'.

[1] 'Mr. Penkethman's Wonderful Invention, call'd the Pantheon: Or, the Temple of the Heathen-gods,' is advertised in No. 43, to be seen 'in the Little Piazza's Covent-Garden, in the same House where Punch's Opera is'. It is described more fully in Nos. 181, 184, and 192:

At the Duke of Marlborough's Head in Fleetstreet, is now to be seen a new Invented Machine, composed of five curious Pictures, with moving Figures, representing the History of the Heathen Gods, which move as Artificially as if Living: the like not seen before in Europe. The whole contains near an hundred Figures, besides Ships, Beasts, Fish, Fowl and other Embellishments, some near a Foot in height; all which have their respective and peculiar Motions, their very Heads, Legs and Arms, Hands and Fingers, Artificially moving to what they perform, and setting one Foot before another like Living Creatures, in such a manner that nothing but Nature it self can excel it. It will continue to be seen every Day from 10 in the Morning 'till 10 at Night. The Prices 1s. 6d. 1s. and the lowest 6d.

single Voice for any lower part in the Opera, *Lawrence*[1] can learn to speak *Greek*, as well as he does *Italian*, in a Fortnight's time.

The Projector having thus settled Matters, to the good liking of all that heard him, he left his Seat at the Table, and planted himself before the Fire, where I had unluckily taken my Stand for the Convenience of over-hearing what he said. Whether he had observed me to be more attentive than ordinary, I cannot tell, but he had not stood by me above a quarter of a Minute, but he turned short upon me on a sudden, and catching me by a Button of my Coat, attack'd me very abruptly after the following manner. Besides, Sir, I have heard of a very extraordinary Genius for Musick[2] that lives in *Switzerland*, who has so strong a Spring in his Fingers, that he can make the Board of an Organ sound like a Drum, and if I could but procure a Subscription of about Ten Thousand Pound every Winter, I would undertake to fetch him over, and oblige him by Articles to set every thing that should be sung upon the *English* Stage. After this he looked full in my Face, expecting I wou'd make an Answer, when, by good Luck, a Gentleman that had entered the Coffee-House since the Projector applied himself to me, hearing him talk of his *Swiss* Compositions, cry'd out with a kind of Laugh, Is our Musick then to receive further Improvements from *Switzerland*? This alarm'd the Projector, who immediately let go my Button, and turned about to answer him. I took the Opportunity of the Diversion, which seemed to be made in favour of me, and laying down my Penny upon the Bar, retired with some Precipitation.   C

[1] A tenor singer in the Italian opera. He sang in *Thomyris, Queen of Scythia* at Drury-Lane on 18 Dec. 1707, appeared as the Messenger in Addison and Clayton's *Rosamond*, and took the part of the Herald in the first performance of *Rinaldo* on 24 Feb. 1711. His name also occurs in concerts (at York-buildings on 17 Apr. 1710, and in the Great Room at Richmond-Wells on 21 July 1711).

[2] John Jacob Heidegger, a native of Switzerland, had become assistant manager of the opera at the Haymarket, and seems to have been famous chiefly for his ugliness. Pope, in a note to the original *Dunciad* (i. 244), refers to him as 'a strange Bird from Switzerland'. Nichols speaks of his 'uncommonly disagreeable' person and his 'ugly face, scarcely human' (note to *Tatler* 18). He died 'aged near 90' on 4 Sept. 1749 (*Gentleman's Magazine*, xix. 429). Cf. 'Memoirs of John James Heidegger', *London Magazine*, Oct. 1779, pp. 452-3.

Nil illi larva aut tragicis opus esse Cothurnis.
Hor.

THE late Discourse concerning the Statutes of the *Ugly-Club*[2]
having been so well received at *Oxford*, that, contrary to the
strict Rules of the Society, they have been so partial as to take my
own Testimonial, and admit me into that select Body; I could not
restrain the Vanity of publishing to the World the Honour which
is done me. It is no small Satisfaction, that I have given Occasion
for the President's shewing both his Invention and Reading to such
Advantage as my Correspondent reports he did: But it is not to be
doubted there were many very proper Hums and Pauses in his
Harangue, which lose their Ugliness in the Narration, and which
my Correspondent (begging his Pardon) has no very good Talent
at representing. I very much approve of the Contempt the Society
has of Beauty: Nothing ought to be laudable in a Man, in which his
Will is not concerned; therefore our Society can follow Nature, and
where she has thought fit, as it were, to mock herself, we can do so
too, and be merry upon the Occasion.

Mr. SPECTATOR,

'YOUR making publick the late Trouble I gave you, you will
find to have been the Occasion of this: Who should I meet at
the Coffee-house Door t'other Night, but my old Friend Mr. President? I saw somewhat had pleas'd him; and assoon as he had cast
his Eye upon me, "Oho, Doctor, rare News from *London* (says he);
the SPECTATOR has made honourable Mention o' th' Club (Man)
and publish'd to the World his sincere Desire to be a Member, with
a recommendatory Description of his Phiz: And tho' our Constitution has made no particular Provision for short Faces, yet, his being
an extraordinary Case, I believe we shall find an Hole for him to
creep in at; for I assure you he is not against the Canon; and if his
Sides are as compact as his Joles,[3] he need not disguise himself to
make one of us." I presently call'd for the Paper to see how you

[1] *Motto.* Horace, *Satires*, I. 5. 64:
    He would need neither mask nor tragic buskin [to increase his nátural de-
formity of face].
[2] See No. 17.
[3] Joles (i.e. jowls), here in the sense of cheeks.

look'd in Print; and after we had regal'd our selves awhile upon the pleasant Image of our Proselite, Mr. President told me I should be his Stranger at the next Night's Club: Where we were no sooner come, and Pipes brought, but Mr. President began an Harangue upon your Introduction to my Epistle; setting forth with no less Volubility of Speech than Strength of Reason, "That a Speculation of this Nature was what had been long and much wanted; and that he doubted not but it would be of inestimable Value to the Publick, in reconciling even of Bodies and Souls; in composing and quieting the Minds of Men under all corporal Redundancies, Deficiencies, and Irregularities whatsoever; and making every one sit down content in his own Carcass, tho' it were not perhaps so mathematically put together as he could wish." And again, "How that for want of a due Consideration of what you first advance, *viz.* that our Faces are not of our own chusing, People had been transported beyond all good Breeding, and hurry'd themselves into unaccountable and fatal Extravagancies: As, how many impartial Looking-glasses had been censur'd and calumniated, nay and sometimes shiver'd into ten thousand Splinters, only for a fair Representation of the Truth? How many Headstrings and Garters had been made accessary, and actually forfeited, only because Folks must needs quarrel with their own Shadows? And who (continues he) but is deeply sensible, that one great Source of the Uneasiness and Misery of human Life, especially amongst those of Distinction, arises from nothing in the World else, but too severe a Contemplation of an indefeasible Contexture of our external Parts, or certain natural and invincible Dispositions to be fat or lean? When a little more of Mr. SPECTATOR's Philosophy would take off all this; and in the mean Time let them observe, that there's not one of their Grievances of this Sort, but perhaps in some Ages of the World has been highly in vogue; and may be so again, nay, in some Country or other ten to one is so at this Day. My Lady *Ample* is the most miserable Woman in the World, purely of her own making: She even grudges her self Meat and Drink, for fear she should thrive by 'em; and is constantly crying out, In a Quarter of an Year more I shall be quite out of all manner of Shape! Now this Lady's Misfortune seems to be only this, that she is planted in a wrong Soil; for, go but t'other Side of the Water, its a Jest at *Harlem* to talk of a Shape under eighteen Stone. There[a] wise Traders regulate their Beauties as they do their Butter,

---

[a] There] These *Fol.*, *8vo*, *12mo*

by the Pound; and Miss *Cross*, when she first arriv'd in the *Low-Countries*, was not computed to be so handsom as Madam *Van Brisket* by near half a Tun. On the other Hand, there's 'Squire *Lath*, a proper Gentleman of Fifteen hundred Pound *per Annum*, as well as of an unblameable Life and Conversation; yet would not I be the Esquire for half his Estate; for if it was as much more, he'd freely part with 't all for a Pair of Legs to his Mind: Whereas in the Reign of our first King *Edward* of glorious Memory, nothing more modish than a Brace of your fine taper Supporters; and his Majesty without an Inch of Calf, manag'd Affairs in Peace and War as laudably as the bravest and most politick of his Ancestors; and was as terrible to his Neighbours under the royal Name of *Long-shanks*,[1] as *Cœur de Lion* to the *Saracens* before him. If we look farther back into History we shall find, that *Alexander* the Great[2] wore his Head a little o'er the left Shoulder; and then not a Soul stirr'd out till he had adjusted his Neck Bone; the whole Nobility address'd the Prince and each other obliquely, and all Matters of Importance were concerted and carried on in the *Macedonian* Court with their Polls on one Side. For about the first Century nothing made more Noise in the World than *Roman* Noses, and then not a Word of 'em till they reviv'd again in Eighty eight.[3] Nor is it so very long since *Richard* the Third set up half the Backs of the Nation; and high Shoulders, as well as high Noses, were the Top of the Fashion. But to come to our selves, Gentlemen, tho' I find by my quinquennial Observations that we shall never get Ladies enough to make a Party in our own Country, yet might we meet with better Success among some of our Allies. And what think you if our Board sate for a *Dutch* Piece? Truly I am of Opinion, that as odd as we appear in Flesh and Blood, we should be no such strange things in Metzo-Tinto. But this Project may rest till our Number is compleat; and this being our Election Night, give me Leave to propose Mr. SPECTATOR: You see his Inclinations, and perhaps we may not have his Fellow."

'I found most of 'em (as it is usual in all such Cases) were prepar'd;

---

[1] According to Sir Richard Baker, Edward I 'was tall of Stature, higher than ordinary men by head and shoulders, and thereof called *Longshank*' (*Chronicle of the Kings of England*, ed. 1684, p. 102).

[2] Plutarch, *Alexander*, 4. 1. Cf. *Tatler* 77: '*Alexander the Great* had a wry Neck, which made it the Fashion in his Court to carry their Heads on one Side when they came into the Presence.'

[3] William III was remembered for his Roman nose. In compliment to him 'Dryden in the plates to his translation of Virgil, had Æneas always represented with a Roman Nose' (Nichols).

but one of the Seniors (whom by the by Mr. President had taken all this Pains to bring over) sate still, and cocking his Chin, which seemed only to be levell'd at his Nose, very gravely declar'd, "That in case he had had sufficient Knowledge of you, no Man should have been more willing to have served you; but that he, for his Part, had always had regard to his own Conscience, as well as other Peoples Merit; and he did not know but that you might be a handsome Fellow; for as for your own Certificate, it was every Body's Business to speak for themselves." Mr. President immediately retorted, "A handsome Fellow! why he's a Wit (Sir) and you know the Proverb"; and to ease the old Gentleman of his Scruples, cry'd, "That for Matter of Merit it was all one, you might wear a Mask." This threw him into a Pause, and he looked desirous of three Days to consider on 't; but Mr. President improved the Thought, and follow'd him up with an old Story, "That Wits were privileg'd to wear what Masks they pleased in all Ages; and that a Vizard had been the constant Crown of their Labours, which was generally presented them by the Hand of some Satyr, and sometimes of *Apollo* himself:" For the Truth of which he appeal'd to the Frontispiece of several Books, and particularly to the *English Juvenal*,[1] to which he referred him; and only added, "That such Authors were the *Larvati*,[2] or *Larvâ donati* of the Ancients." This clear'd up all, and in the Conclusion you were chose probationer; and Mr. President put round your Health as such, protesting "That tho' indeed he talk'd of a Vizard, he did not believe all the while you had any more Occasion for it than the Cat-a-mountain;" so that all you have to do now is to pay your Fees, which here are very reasonable if you are not imposed upon; and you may stile your self *Informis Societatis Socius*: Which I am desired to acquaint you with; and upon the same I beg you to accept of the Congratulation of,

Sir,

Oxford,   *Your oblig'd humble Servant,*

March 21.   A. C.'

R

[1] The frontispiece of the 2nd edition of Dryden's *Juvenal and Persius* (published by Tonson in 1697) represents Apollo presenting the mask of satire to Juvenal. This is repeated in the 3rd and 4th editions (1702 and 1711), both printed for Tonson. The same engraving is used before Creech's translation of the satires of Horace (1684).

[2] *Larva*, the Latin word for mask, seems also to have had the meaning of disembodied spirit. Danet explains Larvae as 'Ghosts of wicked Men wandering up and down after their death; Phantoms who fight good Men, and torment the wicked. The word *Larva*, in the singular number is taken for a Vizard, that frights Children, like *Larvae* or bad Genius's.' Addison discusses 'the *Larva* or *Persona*' of the Roman actors in the *Remarks on Italy* (1705), p. 324.

> *Fervidus tecum Puer, & solutis*
> *Gratiæ zonis, properentque Nymphæ,*
> *Et parum comis sine te Juventas,*
> *Mercuriusque.*
>
> Hor. ad Venerem.

A FRIEND of mine has two Daughters, whom I will call *Lætitia* and *Daphne*; The Former is one of the Greatest Beauties of the Age in which she lives, the Latter no way remarkable for any Charms in her Person. Upon this one Circumstance of their Outward Form, the Good and Ill of their Life seems to turn. *Lætitia* has not, from her very Childhood, heard any thing else but Commendations of her Features and Complexion, by which means she is no other than Nature made her, a very beautiful Outside. The Consciousness of her Charms has render'd her insupportably Vain and Insolent, towards all who have to do with her. *Daphne*, who was almost Twenty before one civil thing had ever been said to her, found her self obliged to acquire some Accomplishments to make up for the want of those Attractions which she saw in her Sister. Poor *Daphne* was seldom submitted to in a Debate wherein she was concerned; her Discourse had nothing to recommend it but the good Sense of it, and she was always under a necessity to have very well considered what she was to say before she uttered it; while *Lætitia* was listen'd to with Partiality, and Approbation sate in the Countenances of those she conversed with, before she communicated what she had to say. These Causes have produced suitable Effects, and *Lætitia* is as insipid a Companion, as *Daphne* is an agreeable one. *Lætitia*, confident of Favour, has studied no Arts to please; *Daphne*, despairing of any Inclination towards her Person, has depended only on her Merit. *Lætitia* has always something in her Air that is sullen, grave and disconsolate. *Daphne* has a Countenance that appears chearful, open and unconcerned. A Young Gentleman saw *Lætitia* this Winter at a Play, and became her Captive. His Fortune was such, that he wanted very little Introduction to speak his Sentiments

[1] *Motto.* Horace, *Odes*, 1. 30. 5–8:
  With thee let hasten thy ardent child; the Graces, too, with girdles all unloosed, the Nymphs, and Youth, unlovely without thee, and Mercury!

to her Father. The Lover was admitted with the utmost Freedom into the Family, where a constrain'd Behaviour, severe Looks, and distant Civilities, were the highest Favours he could obtain of *Lætitia*; while *Daphne* used him with the good Humour, Familiarity and Innocence of a Sister: Insomuch that he would often say to her, *Dear* Daphne, *wert thou but as Handsome as* Lætitia!—She received such Language with that ingenuous and pleasing Mirth, which is natural to a Woman without Design. He still Sighed in vain for *Lætitia*, but found certain Relief in the agreeable Conversation of *Daphne*. At length, heartily tired with the haughty Impertinence of *Lætitia*, and charmed with repeated Instances of good Humour he had observ'd in *Daphne*, he one Day told the latter, that he had something to say to her he hoped she would be pleased with.— *Faith* Daphne, continued he, *I am in Love with thee, and despise thy Sister sincerely.* The manner of his declaring himself gave his Mistress occasion for a very hearty Laughter.—*Nay*, says he, *I knew you would Laugh at me, but I'll ask your Father.* He did so; the Father received his Intelligence with no less Joy than Surprize, and was very glad he had now no Care left but for his *Beauty*, which he thought he could carry to Market at his Leisure. I do not know any thing that has pleased me so much a great while, as this Conquest of my Friend *Daphne*'s. All her Acquaintance congratulate her upon her Chance-Medley,[1] and laugh at that premeditating Murderer her Sister. As it is an Argument of a light Mind, to think the worse of our selves for the Imperfections of our Persons, it is equally below us to value our selves upon the Advantages of them. The Female World seem to be almost incorrigibly gone astray in this Particular; for which Reason, I shall recommend the following Extract out of a Friend's Letter to the Profess'd Beauties, who are a People almost as unsufferable as the Profess'd Wits.

'Monsieur *St. Evremont*[2] has concluded one of his Essays, with affirming, that the last Sighs of a Handsome Woman are not so much for the Loss of her Life, as of her Beauty. Perhaps this Raillery is pursu'd too far, yet it is turn'd upon a very obvious Remark, that

[1] Chance-medley 'signifies the casual killing of a Man, not altogether without the Killer's fault, tho' without an evil intent. . . . It is also call'd *Manslaughter by Misadventure*' (Cowell's *Law Dictionary*, 1708).

[2] Saint-Evremond, 'Of the Complacency that Women take in their Beauty': 'Let a fair Person retire to what Place she pleases, let her Condition be what it will, yet her Charms and Features are still dear to her, even in the time of Sickness; and if her Sickness goes as far as Death, the last Sigh that goes from her, is more for the Loss of her Beauty, than that of her Life' (*Works*, 1714, i. 160).

Woman's strongest Passion is for her own Beauty, and that she values it as her Favourite Distinction. From hence it is that all Arts, which pretend to improve or preserve it, meet with so general a Reception among the Sex. To say nothing of many False Helps, and Contraband Wares of Beauty, which are daily vended in this great Mart, there is not a Maiden-Gentlewoman, of a good Family in any County of *South-Britain*, who has not heard of the Virtues of *May-Dew*,[1] or is unfurnish'd with some Receipt or other in Favour of her Complexion; and I have known a Physician of Learning and Sense, after Eight Years Study in the University, and a Course of Travels into most Countries of *Europe*, owe the first raising of his Fortunes to a Cosmetick Wash.[2]

'This has given me Occasion to consider how so Universal a Disposition in Womankind, which springs from a laudable Motive, the Desire of Pleasing, and proceeds upon an Opinion, not altogether groundless, that Nature may be help'd by Art, may be turn'd to their Advantage. And, methinks, it wou'd be an acceptable Service to take them out of the Hands of Quacks and Pretenders, and to prevent their imposing upon themselves, by discovering to them the true Secret and Art of improving Beauty.

'In order to this, before I touch upon it directly, it will be necessary to lay down a few Preliminary Maxims, *viz.*

'That no Woman can be Handsome by the Force of Features alone, any more than she can be Witty only by the Help of Speech.

'That Pride destroys all Symmetry and Grace, and Affectation is a more terrible Enemy to fine Faces than the Small-Pox.

---

[1] Dew gathered in the month of May was thought to have medicinal and cosmetic properties. In Shadwell's *Virtuoso* (III. i) Sir Samuel Harty has among the best pomatums of Europe 'one rare, one made of a Lamb's Caul and *May* Dew'. In *Guardian* 158, by Addison, a young woman whose chief aim has been to make herself lovely explains that she passed her time 'in bottling up *May*-dew, inventing White-washes, mixing Colours . . .'.

[2] An advertisement appearing in Nos. 25, 31, and frequently thereafter reads:

This Chrystal Cosmetick approv'd of by the worthy Dr. Paul Chamberline, (viz.) By washing Morning or Evening, cures all red Faces proceeding from what cause soever, it takes off all Morphews, Pimples and Freckles; it's of a soft Nature, cleansing and adorning the Face and Hands of both Sexes in a very Beautiful Manner, and may be used with as much safety as Milk, having in it no Mercury (so frequently made use of) or any other thing that may be prejudicial to the Body, being the best of this Nature now extant. Price of the larger Bottle six Shillings, the lesser three Shillings. Sold at Mr. Allcrofts over against the Royal Exchange, Cornhill, Mr. Jackson's the Corner of Wood-Street, Cheapside; formerly sold at the Comb, but now removed to the Seven Stars under St. Dunstans Church, Fleet-Street, Mrs. Bracknocks at the upper end of St. Jame's (*sic*) Street, Piccadillie. Note, to prevent counterfeits, each single Bottle with Directions is tied and sealed with this Coat of Arms, being a Frett with a Lion Rampant on a Canon.

'That no Woman is capable of being Beautiful, who is not incapable of being False.

'And that what wou'd be Odious in a Friend, is Deformity in a Mistress.

'From these few Principles, thus laid down, it will be easie to prove, that the true Art of assisting Beauty consists in Embellishing the whole Person by the proper Ornaments of virtuous and commendable Qualities. By this Help alone it is, that those who are the Favourite Work of Nature, or, as Mr. *Dryden*[1] expresses it, the Porcelain Clay of human Kind, become animated, and are in a Capacity of exerting their Charms: And those who seem to have been neglected by her, like Models wrought in haste, are capable, in a great measure, of finishing what She has left imperfect.

'It is, methinks, a low and degrading Idea of that Sex, which was created to refine the Joys, and soften the Cares of Humanity, by the most agreeable Participation, to consider them meerly as Objects of Sight. This is abridging them of their natural Extent of Power, to put them upon a Level with their Pictures at *Kneller*'s.[2] How much nobler is the Contemplation of Beauty heighten'd by Virtue, and commanding our Esteem and Love, while it draws our Observation? How faint and spiritless are the Charms of a Coquet, when compar'd with the real Loveliness of *Sophronia*'s Innocence, Piety, good Humour and Truth; Virtues which add a new Softness to her Sex, and even beautify her Beauty! That Agreeableness, which must otherwise have appeared no longer in the modest Virgin, is now preserv'd in the tender Mother, the prudent Friend, and the faithful Wife. Colours, artfully spread upon Canvas, may entertain the Eye, but not affect the Heart; and she, who takes no Care to add to the natural Graces of her Person any excelling Qualities, may be allow'd still to amuse, as a Picture, but not to triumph as a Beauty.

'When *Adam* is introduc'd by *Milton*[3] describing *Eve* in Paradise, and relating to the Angel the Impressions he felt upon seeing her at her first Creation, he does not represent her like a *Grecian Venus*

---

[1] *Don Sebastian*, I. i:

> Ay; These look like the Workmanship of Heav'n:
> This is the porcelain clay of human kind,
> And therefore cast into these noble moulds.

[2] Sir Godfrey Kneller, a German who had come to England in 1675, was at this time the most successful painter in London. He had a studio in his magnificent house in Great Queen Street, Lincoln's Inn Fields, and here the great and the fashionable of the day came to have their portraits done. In the autumn of 1711 he became Governor of the first Academy of Art in London (see No. 555 (vol. iv)).

[3] *Paradise Lost*, viii. 488–9.

by her Shape or Features, but by the Lustre of her Mind which shone in them, and gave them their Power of charming.

> *Grace was in all her Steps, Heav'n in her Eye,*
> *In all her Gestures Dignity and Love.*

'Without this irradiating Power the proudest Fair One ought to know, whatever her Glass may tell her to the contrary, that her most perfect Features are Uninform'd[1] and Dead.

'I cannot better close this Moral, than by a short Epitaph written by *Ben. Johnson,* with a Spirit which nothing cou'd inspire but such an Object as I have been describing.

> *Underneath this Stone doth lye*
> *As much Virtue as cou'd die;*
> *Which when alive did Vigour give*
> *To as much Beauty as cou'd live.*[2]

> *I am, SIR,*
> *Your most humble Servant,*
> R. B.'[3]

R

No. 34

[ADDISON]

Monday, April 9, 1711[4]

> *. . . parcit*
> *Cognatis maculis similis fera . . .*
> Juv.

THE Club of which I am a Member, is very luckily compos'd of such Persons as are engag'd in different Ways of Life, and

[1] Not animated. The *OED* gives one quotation earlier than this, from Swift's *Vindication of Bickerstaff* (1709).

[2] The passage quoted is lines 3–6 of Jonson's 'Epitaph on Elizabeth, L. H.' (Epigrammes, cxxiiii):

> Vnder-neath this stone doth lye
> As much beautie, as could dye:
> Which in life did harbour giue
> To more vertue, then doth liue.
> (*Works,* ed. Herford and Simpson, viii. 79.)

[3] This letter is in the list of Hughes's contributions to the *Spectator* (Preface to John Hughes's *Poems and Essays,* 1735, vol. i, p. xxiv) drawn up by William Duncombe, his brother-in-law. This attribution has been generally accepted by editors, although Gregory Smith suggested that R. B. might stand for 'the moral vein of Richard Blackmore'.

[4] *Motto.* Juvenal, *Satires,* 15. 159–60:
> Wild animals spare animals with spotted skins like their own.

deputed as it were out of the most conspicuous Classes of Mankind: By this Means I am furnish'd with the greatest Variety of Hints and Materials, and know every thing that passes in the different Quarters and Divisions, not only of this great City, but of the whole Kingdom. My Readers too have the Satisfaction to find, that there is no Rank or Degree among them who have not their Representative in this Club, and that there is always some Body present who will take Care of their respective Interests, that nothing may be written or publish'd to the Prejudice or Infringement of their just Rights and Privileges.

I last Night sat very late in company with this select Body of Friends, who entertain'd me with several Remarks which they and others had made upon these my Speculations, as also with the various Success which they had met with among their several Ranks and Degrees of Readers. WILL. HONEYCOMB told me, in the softest Manner he could, That there were some Ladies (but for your Comfort, says WILL. they are not those of the most Wit) that were offended at the Liberties I had taken with the Opera and the Puppet-Show: That some of them were likewise very much surpriz'd, that I should think such serious Points as the Dress and Equipage of Persons of Quality, proper Subjects for Raillery.

He was going on, when Sir ANDREW FREEPORT took him up short, and told him, That the Papers he hinted at, had done great Good in the City, and that all their Wives and Daughters were the better for them: And further added, That the whole City thought themselves very much obliged to me for declaring my generous Intentions to scourge Vice and Folly as they appear in a Multitude, without condescending to be a Publisher of particular Intrigues and Cuckoldoms. In short, says Sir ANDREW, if you avoid that foolish beaten Road of falling upon Aldermen and Citizens, and employ your Pen upon the Vanity and Luxury of Courts, your Paper must needs be of general Use.

Upon this my Friend the TEMPLAR told Sir ANDREW, That he wonder'd to hear a Man of his Sense talk after that Manner; that the City had always been the Province for Satyr; and that the Wits of King *Charles*'s Time jested upon nothing else during his whole Reign. He then shew'd by the Examples of *Horace*, *Juvenal*, *Boileau*,[1] and the best Writers of every Age, that the Follies of the Stage and Court had never been accounted too sacred for Ridicule, how great

[1] His death (on 13 Mar. N.S.) is announced in the *Daily Courant* of 17 Mar. 1711.

soever the Persons might be that patroniz'd them. But after all, says he, I think your Raillery has made too great an Excursion, in attacking several Persons of the Inns of Court; and I do not believe you can shew me any Precedent for your Behaviour in that Particular. My good Friend Sir ROGER DE COVERLY, who had said nothing all this while, began his Speech with a Pish! and told us, That he wonder'd to see so many Men of Sense so very serious upon Fooleries. Let our good Friend, says he, attack every one that deserves it: I would only advise you, Mr. SPECTATOR, applying himself to me, to take Care how you meddle with Country Squires: They are the Ornaments of the *English* Nation; Men of good Heads and sound Bodies! and let me tell you, some of them take it ill of you that you mention Fox-hunters with so little Respect.

Captain SENTRY spoke very sparingly on this Occasion. What he said was only to commend my Prudence in not touching upon the Army, and advised me to continue to act discreetly in that Point.

By this Time I found every Subject of my Speculations was taken away from me by one or other of the Club; and began to think my self in the Condition of the good Man[1] that had one Wife who took a Dislike to his grey Hairs, and another to his black, till by their picking out what each of them had an Aversion to, they left his Head altogether bald and naked.

While I was thus musing with my self, my worthy Friend the Clergy-man, who, very luckily for me, was at the Club that Night, undertook my Cause. He told us, That he wonder'd any Order of Persons should think themselves too considerable to be advis'd: That it was not Quality, but Innocence which exempted Men from Reproof: That Vice and Folly ought to be attacked wherever they could be met with, and especially when they were placed in high and conspicuous Stations of Life. He further added, That my Paper

[1] Æsop, *Fable* 162. In *Æsop Naturaliz'd* (3rd ed., 1711, p. 101) it appears as Fable CXXV: The Old Man and his Two Wives:

An Old sort o' Beaux, an unmortified Dunce,
Wou'd hardily marry Two Women at once.
The one was a Beauty, and dazzl'd his Eyes;
The other was Old enough, but very wise.
The Beauty dispatcht all his Hairs that were gray,
Lest they should his Weakness or Dotage betray.
Old Madam pull'd up the black Hairs by the Root,
Which did not his Age, nor his Gravity suit.
Thus worse than old Time did the poor Bully fare,
Before and behind he was left without Hair.

Cf. also La Fontaine (Book I, Fable XVII), 'L'Homme entre deux âges, & ses deux Maîtresses'.

would only serve to aggravate the Pains of Poverty, if it chiefly expos'd those who are already depress'd, and in some Measure turn'd into Ridicule, by the Meanness of their Conditions and Circumstances. He afterwards proceeded to take Notice of the great Use this Paper might be of to the Publick, by reprehending those Vices which are too trivial for the Chastisement of the Law, and too fantastical for the Cognizance of the Pulpit. He then advis'd me to prosecute my Undertaking with Chearfulness; and assur'd me, that whoever might be displeas'd with me, I should be approv'd by all those whose Praises do Honour to the Persons on whom they are bestow'd.

The whole Club pays a particular Deference to the Discourse of this Gentleman, and are drawn into what he says as much by the candid and ingenuous Manner with which he delivers himself, as by the Strength of Argument and Force of Reason which he makes use of. WILL. HONEYCOMBE immediately agreed, that what he had said was right; and that for his Part, he would not insist upon the Quarter which he had demanded for the Ladies. Sir ANDREW gave up the City with the same Frankness. The TEMPLAR would not stand out; and was followed by Sir ROGER and the CAPTAIN: Who all agreed that I should be at Liberty to carry the War into what Quarter I pleased; provided I continued to combat with Criminals in a Body, and to assault the Vice without hurting the Person.[1]

This Debate, which was held for the Good of Mankind, put me in Mind of that which the *Roman* Triumvirate[2] were formerly engaged in, for their Destruction. Every Man at first stood hard for his Friend, till they found that by this Means they should spoil their Proscription: And at length, making a Sacrifice of all their Acquaintance and Relations, furnished out a very decent Execution.

Having thus taken my Resolutions to march on boldly in the Cause of Virtue and good Sense, and to annoy their Adversaries in whatever Degree or Rank of Men they may be found: I shall be deaf for the future to all the Remonstrances that shall be made to me on this Account. If *Punch*[3] grows[a] extravagant, I shall reprimand him very freely: If the Stage becomes a Nursery of Folly and Impertin-

---

[a] grows] grow *Fol.*

---

[1] Martial, *Satires*, 10. 33. 10: *Parcere personis, dicere de vitiis.*
[2] The Second Triumvirate, of Octavius, Antony, and Lepidus (Plutarch, *Life of Antony*, 19. 2; *Life of Cicero*, 46. 4). Cf. also Shakespeare's *Julius Caesar*, IV. i.
[3] See No. 14.

ence, I shall not be afraid to animadvert upon it. In short, If I meet with any thing in City, Court, or Country, that shocks Modesty or good Manners, I shall use my utmost Endeavours to make an Example of it. I must however intreat every particular Person, who does me the Honour to be a Reader of this Paper, never to think himself, or any one of his Friends or Enemies, aimed at in what is said: For I promise him, never to draw a faulty Character which does not fit at least a Thousand People; or to publish a single Paper, that is not written in the Spirit of Benevolence and with a Love to Mankind.

C

No. 35   *Tuesday, April 10, 1711*[1]
[ADDISON]

> *Risu inepto res ineptior nulla est.*
> Mart.

AMONG all kinds of Writing, there is none in which Authors are more apt to miscarry than in Works of Humour, as there is none in which they are more ambitious to excell. It is not an Imagination that teems with Monsters, an Head that is filled with extravagant Conceptions, which is capable of furnishing the World with Diversions of this nature; and yet if we look into the Productions of several Writers, who set up for Men of Humour, what wild irregular Fancies, what unnatural Distortions of Thought, do we meet with? If they speak Nonsense, they believe they are talking Humour; and when they have drawn together a Scheme of absurd, inconsistent Idea's, they are not able to read it over to themselves without laughing. These poor Gentlemen endeavour to gain themselves the Reputation of Wits and Humourists, by such monstrous

---

[1] *Motto.* Catullus, *Carmina*, 39. 16:
Nothing is more silly than an ill-tim'd laugh.

This paper, the first of the critical essays in the *Spectator*, is preliminary to the series on true and false wit (Nos. 58–63). Here, however, as in No. 23, the emphasis is on the needless cruelty inflicted by writers of lampoon and satire. The genealogy of true and false wit introduces a device very popular in Addison's day, with relationships humorously depicted by means of a family tree. Swift had drawn up a similar genealogy, of true and false merit, in *Examiner* 30, just a few weeks earlier (1 Mar. 1711).

Conceits as almost qualify them for *Bedlam*;[1] not considering that Humour should always lye under the Check of Reason, and that it requires the Direction of the nicest Judgment, by so much the more as it indulges it self in the most boundless Freedoms. There is a kind of Nature that is to be observed in this sort of Compositions, as well as in all other, and a certain Regularity of Thought which[a] must discover the Writer to be a Man of Sense, at the same time that he appears altogether given up to Caprice: For my part, when I read the delirious Mirth of an unskilful Author, I cannot be so barbarous as to divert my self with it, but am rather apt to pity the Man, than to laugh at any thing he writes.

The Deceas'd Mr. *Shadwell*,[2] who had himself a great deal of the Talent, which I am treating of, represents an empty Rake, in one of his Plays, as very much surprized to hear one say that breaking of Windows was not Humour; and I question not but several *English* Readers will be as much startled to hear me affirm, that many of those raving incoherent Pieces, which are often spread among us, under odd Chymerical Titles, are rather the Offsprings of a Distempered Brain, than Works of Humour.

It is indeed much easier to describe what is not Humour, than what is; and very difficult to define it otherwise than as *Cowley*[3] has done Wit, by Negatives. Were I to give my own Notions of it, I would deliver them after *Plato*'s manner, in a kind of Allegory, and by supposing Humour to be a Person, deduce to him all his Qualifications, according to the following Genealogy. TRUTH was the Founder of the Family, and the Father of GOOD SENSE. GOOD SENSE was the Father of WIT, who married a Lady of a Collateral Line called MIRTH, by whom he had Issue HUMOUR. HUMOUR therefore being the youngest of this Illustrious Family, and descended from Parents of such different Dispositions, is very various and unequal in his Temper; sometimes you see him putting on grave Looks and a solemn Habit, sometimes airy in his Behaviour and fantastick in his Dress: Insomuch that at different times he

---

[a] which] that *Fol.*

[1] Hatton (pp. 731–3) gives an account of the new structure on the south side of Moor-fields, completed in 1676, with apartments 'for 150 Lunatick Persons'. Ward's *London Spy* (Part III) describes a visit to Bedlam.

[2] (Shadwell had died in 1692.) The breaking of windows is a frequent theme of satire in Shadwell's description of the rakes of his day: *The Woman-Captain, The Squire of Alsatia, The Scowrers, Epsom Wells,* &c.

[3] 'Of Wit', especially stanzas 3–7 (*Poems,* ed. Waller, pp. 16–18).

appears as serious as a Judge, and as jocular as a *Merry-Andrew*.[1] But as he has a great deal of the Mother in his Constitution, whatever Mood he is in, he never fails to make his Company laugh.

But since there is an Impostor abroad, who takes upon him[a] the Name of this young Gentleman, and would willingly pass for him in the World; to the end that well-meaning Persons may not be imposed upon by Cheats,[b] I would desire my Readers, when they meet with this Pretender,[c] to look into his Parentage, and to examine him strictly, whether or no he be remotely allied to TRUTH, and lineally descended from GOOD SENSE? if not, they may conclude him a Counterfeit. They may likewise distinguish him by a loud and excessive Laughter, in which he seldom gets his Company to join with him. For as TRUE HUMOUR generally looks serious, whilst every Body laughs about him;[d] FALSE HUMOUR is always laughing, whilst every Body about him looks serious. I shall only add, if he has not in him a Mixture of both Parents, that is, if he wou'd pass for the Offspring of WIT without MIRTH, or MIRTH without WIT, you may conclude him to be altogether Spurious, and a Cheat.

The Impostor of whom I am speaking, descends Originally from FALSEHOOD, who was the Mother of NONSENSE, who was brought to Bed of a Son called FRENZY, who Married one of the Daughters of FOLLY, commonly known by the Name of LAUGHTER, on whom he begot that Monstrous Infant of which I have been here speaking. I shall set down at length the Genealogical Table of FALSE HUMOUR, and, at the same time, place under it the Genealogy of TRUE HUMOUR, that the Reader may at one View behold their different Pedigrees and Relations.

FALSEHOOD.

NONSENSE.

FRENZY. — LAUGHTER.

FALSE HUMOUR.

TRUTH.

GOOD SENSE.

WIT. — MIRTH.

HUMOUR.

[a] there is . . . upon him] there are several Impostors abroad, who take upon them *Fol.*   [b] Cheats,] Counterfeits, *Fol.*   [c] this Pretender,] any of these Pretenders, *Fol.*   [d] laughs about him;] laughs that is about him; *Fol.*

[1] See No. 28.

I might extend the Allegory, by mentioning several of the Children of FALSE HUMOUR, who are more in Number than the Sands of the Sea, and might in particular enumerate the many Sons and Daughters which he has begot in this Island. But as this would be a very invidious Task, I shall only observe in general, that FALSE HUMOUR differs from the TRUE, as a Monkey does from a Man.

First of all, He is exceedingly given to little Apish Tricks and Buffooneries.

Secondly, He so much delights in Mimickry, that it is all one to him whether he exposes by it Vice and Folly, Luxury and Avarice; or, on the contrary, Virtue and Wisdom, Pain and Poverty.

Thirdly, He is wonderfully unlucky, insomuch that he will bite the Hand that feeds him,[1] and endeavour to ridicule both Friends and Foes indifferently. For having but small Talents, he must be merry where he *can*, not where he *should*.

Fourthly, Being intirely void of Reason, he pursues no Point either of Morality or Instruction, but is Ludicrous only for the sake of being so.

Fifthly, Being incapable of any thing but Mock-Representations, his Ridicule is always Personal, and aimed at the Vicious Man, or the Writer; not at the Vice, or at the Writing.

I have here only pointed at the whole Species of False Humourists, but as one of my principal Designs in this Paper is to beat down that malignant Spirit, which discovers it self in the Writings of the present Age, I shall not scruple, for the future, to single out any of the small Wits, that infest the World with such Compositions as are ill-natured, immoral and absurd. This is the only Exception which I shall make to the General Rule I have prescribed my self, of *attacking Multitudes*. Since every honest Man ought to look upon himself as in a Natural State of War with the Libeller and Lampooner, and to annoy them where-ever they fall in his way, this is but retaliating upon them and treating them as they treat others.　　　　　　C

---

[1] An early example of this phrase (not in *OED*, Apperson, or Tilley).

> . . . *Immania monstra*
> *Perferimus* . . .
>> Virg.

I SHALL not put my self to any further Pains for this Day's
Entertainment, than barely to publish the Letters and Titles of
Petitions from the Play-house, with the Minutes I have made upon
the Latter for my Conduct in Relation to them.

Drury-Lane, April[a] *the 9th.*[2]

'Upon reading the Project which is set forth in one of your late
Papers,[3] of making an Alliance between all the Bulls, Bears, Elephants,
and Lions, which are separately expos'd to publick View in the
Cities of *London* and *Westminster;* together with the other Wonders,
Shows and Monsters, whereof you made respective Mention in the
said Speculation; We, the chief Actors of this Play-house, met and
sat upon the said Design. It is with great Delight that We expect
the Execution of this Work; and in order to contribute to it, We
have given Warning to all our Ghosts to get their Livelihoods where
they can, and not to appear among us after Day-break of the 16th
Instant. We are resolved to take this Opportunity to part with every
thing which does not contribute to the Representation of humane
Life; and shall make a free Gift of all animated Utensils to your
Projector. The Hangings you formerly mention'd, are run away;
as are likewise a Sett of Chairs,[4] each of which was met upon two
Legs going through the *Rose* Tavern at two this Morning. We hope,
Sir, you will give proper Notice to the Town that We are endeavour-
ing at these Regulations; and that We intend for the future to shew
no Monsters, but Men who are converted into such by their own
Industry and Affectation. If you will please to be at the House to

---

^a *April*] *1729; March* Fol., *8vo, 12mo*

---

[1] *Motto.* Virgil, *Aeneid*, 3. 583–4: We endure frightful monsters.
[2] Since the letter refers to Nos. 31 and 22, the date is obviously an error.
April 9th was probably intended. Gregory Smith suggests that the initials at the
end of this letter may stand for Thomas Doggett, the actor.
[3] No. 31.
[4] No. 22.

Night, you will see me do my Endeavour to shew some unnatural Appearances which are in vogue among the Polite and Well-bred. I am to represent, in the Character of a fine Lady dancing, all the Distortions which are frequently taken for Graces in Mein and Gesture. This, Sir, is a Specimen of the Method we shall take to expose the Monsters which come within the Notice of a regular Theatre; and we desire nothing more gross may be admitted by you Spectators for the future. We have cashier'd three Companies of Theatrical Guards, and design our Kings shall for the future make love and sit in Council without an Army; and wait only your Direction, whether you will have them reinforce King *Porus* or join the Troops of *Macedon.* Mr. *Penkethman*[1] resolves to consult his *Pantheon* of Heathen Gods in Opposition to the Oracle of *Delphos,* and doubts not but he shall turn the Fortunes of *Porus* when he personates him. I am desir'd by the Company to inform you, that they submit to your Censures; and shall have you in greater Veneration than *Hercules*[2] was in of old, if you can drive Monsters from the Theatre; and think your Merit will be as much greater than his, as to convince is more than to conquer.

> *I am,*
> *Sir,*
> *Your most obedient Servant,*
> T. D.'

SIR,

'WHEN I acquaint you with the great and unexpected Vicissitudes of my Fortune, I doubt not but I shall obtain your Pity and Favour. I have for many Years last past been Thunderer[3] to the Play-house; and have not only made as much Noise out of the Clouds as any Predecessor of mine in the Theatre that ever bore that Character, but also have descended and spoke on the Stage as the bold Thunder in the *Rehearsal.*[4] When they got me down thus low, they thought fit to degrade me further, and make me a Ghost. I was contented with this for these two last Winters; but they carry their Tyranny still further, and not satisfy'd that I am banish'd from above Ground, they have given me to understand that I am wholly

---

[1] King Porus . . . Penkethman. No. 31.

[2] In No. 28 Mr. Spectator had compared his labours in another field to those of Hercules.

[3] The first example in *OED* of the word in this sense.

[4] *The Rehearsal* (I. i. 414–19). It had been recently given at Drury Lane (29 Jan.) with Johnson in the role of Thunder.

to depart their Dominions, and taken from me even my subterraneous Employment. Now, Sir, what I desire of you is, that if your Undertaker thinks fit to use Fire-Arms (as other Authors have done) in the Time of *Alexander*, I may be a Cannon against *Porus*, or else provide for me in the Burning of *Persepolis*, or what other Method you shall think fit.

Salmoneus[1] of *Covent-Garden*.'

The Petition of all the Devils of the Play-house in behalf of themselves and Families, setting forth their Expulsion from thence, with Certificates of their good Life and Conversation, and praying Relief.

The Merit of this Petition referr'd to Mr. Chr. Rich,[2] *who made them Devils.*

The Petition of the Grave-digger in *Hamlet*,[3] to command the Pioneers in the Expedition of *Alexander*.

Granted.

The Petition of *William Bullock*[4] to be *Hephestion* to *Penkethman the Great.*

Granted.

ADVERTISEMENT.

A Widow Gentlewoman, well born both by Father and Mother's Side, being the Daughter of Thomas Prater, *once an eminent Practitioner in the Law, and of* Letitia Tattle, *a Family well known in all Parts of this Kingdom, having been reduc'd by Misfortunes to wait on several great Persons, and for some Time to be Teacher at a Boarding-School of young Ladies; giveth Notice to the Publick, That she hath lately taken a House near* Bloomsbury-Square, *commodiously situated next the Fields in a good Air; where she teaches all Sorts of Birds of the loquacious Kind, as Parrots, Starlings, Magpies, and others, to imitate humane Voices in greater Perfection than ever yet was practis'd. They are not only instructed to pronounce Words distinctly, and in a proper Tone and Accent, but to speak the Language with*

---

[1] Salmoneus, son of Aeolus, paid a cruel penalty while imitating the fires of Jove and the thunders of Olympus (*Aeneid*, 6. 585–6). Cf. No. 592 (vol. iv).

[2] Christopher Rich. See No. 5.

[3] Johnson had played this part in a performance at Drury Lane on 24 Mar.

[4] He had taken the part of Bonniface in *The Beaux' Stratagem* on 2 Apr. at Drury Lane, and on 5 Apr. (with Doggett and Penkethman) played one of the witches in *Macbeth*—in general, minor low comedy parts. During the week in which this essay appeared he was playing Sir Bookish Outside in *Injured Love, or the Lady's Satisfaction* (Genest, ii. 478). In the preceding summer at Penkethman's Theatre (5 and 6 July) 'Mr. Bullock, Jun.' had played Hephestion in *The Rival Queens*, with Powell as Alexander. Bullock had three sons, all of them actors—Christopher, Hildebrand, and William—and the reference here may therefore be to William Bullock, Jun.

great Purity and Volubility of Tongue, together with all the fashionable Phrases and Compliments now in use either at Tea Tables or visiting Days.[1] Those that have good Voices may be taught to sing the newest Opera-Airs, and if requir'd, to speak either Italian or French, paying something extraordinary above the common Rates. They whose Friends are not able to pay the full Prices, may be taken as Half-boarders. She teaches such as are design'd for the Diversion of the Publick, and to act in enchanted Woods on the Theatres, by the Great. As she has often observ'd with much Concern how indecent an Education is usually given these innocent Creatures, which in some Measure is owing to their being plac'd in Rooms next the Street, where, to the great Offence of chaste and tender Ears, they learn Ribaldry, obscene Songs, and immodest Expressions from Passengers and idle People, as also to cry Fish and Card-matches,[2] with other useless Parts of Learning to Birds who have rich Friends, She has fitted up proper and neat Apartments for them in the back Part of her said House; where she suffers none to approach them but her self, and a Servant Maid who is deaf and dumb, and whom she provided on purpose to prepare their Food and cleanse their Cages, having found by long Experience how hard a thing it is for those to keep Silence who have the Use of Speech, and the Dangers her Scholars are expos'd to by the strong Impressions that are made by harsh Sounds and vulgar Dialects. In short, if they are Birds of any Parts or Capacity, she will undertake to render them so accomplish'd in the Compass of a Twelve-month, that they shall be fit Conversation for such Ladies as love to chuse their Friends and Companions out of this Species.   R

No. 37

[ADDISON]

Thursday, April 12, 1711[3]

> *. . . Non illa colo calathisve Minervæ*
> *Fœmineas assueta manus . . .*
>
> Virg.

SOME Months ago, my Friend Sir ROGER being in the Country, enclosed a Letter to me, directed to a certain Lady whom I shall

---

[1] See No. 24.

[2] Vendors of eels, mackerel, flounders, &c., are depicted in Marcellus Laroon's *Cryes of the City of London.* No. 2 shows a young woman crying 'Any Card matches or Save alls'. A card-match was a piece of card dipped in melted sulphur.

[3] *Motto.* Virgil, *Aeneid*, 7. 805–6:
     Unbred to spinning, in the loom unskill'd. DRYDEN.

here call by the Name of *Leonora*,[1] and as it contained Matters of Consequence, desired me to deliver it to her with my own Hand. Accordingly I waited upon her Ladyship pretty early in the Morning, and was desired by her Woman to walk into her Lady's Library, till such time as she was in a Readiness to receive me. The very sound of a *Lady's Library* gave me a great Curiosity to see it; and, as it was some time before the Lady came to me, I had an Opportunity of turning over a great many of her Books, which were ranged together in a very beautiful Order. At the End of the *Folio's* (which were finely bound and gilt) were great Jars of *China* placed one above another in a very noble piece of Architecture. The *Quarto's* were separated from the *Octavo's* by a pile of smaller Vessels, which rose in a delightful[a] Pyramid. The *Octavo's* were bounded by Tea Dishes of all Shapes, Colours and Sizes, which were so disposed on a wooden Frame, that they looked like one continued Pillar indented with the finest Strokes of Sculpture, and stained with the greatest Variety of Dyes. That Part of the Library which was designed for the Reception of Plays and Pamphlets, and other loose Papers, was enclosed in a kind of Square, consisting of one of the prettiest Grotesque Works[2] that ever I saw, and made up of Scaramouches,[3] Lions, Monkies, Mandarines, Trees, Shells, and a thousand other odd Figures in *China* Ware. In the midst of the Room was a little Japan Table, with a Quire of gilt Paper upon it, and on the Paper a Silver Snuff-box[4] made in the shape of a little Book. I found there were[b] several other Counterfeit Books upon the upper Shelves, which were carved in Wood, and served only to fill up the Number, like Faggots[5] in the Muster of a Regiment. I was wonderfully pleased with such a mixt

---

[a] a delightful] a very delightful *Fol.*   [b] found there were] found that there were *Fol.*

---

[1] For conjectures as to the original of Leonora see No. 140 (vol. ii).

[2] Grotesque is 'a kind of decorative painting or sculpture, representing portions of human and animal forms, fantastically combined and interwoven with foliage and flowers'. *OED* quotes Shaftesbury's *Characteristics*: "Tis the perfection of certain grotesque-painters, to keep as far from nature as possible' (iii. 6).

[3] See No. 283 (vol. iii).

[4] For the various kinds see Hugh McCausland, *Snuff and Snuff-Boxes* (1951).

[5] A faggot was 'a person temporarily hired to supply a deficiency at the muster, or on the roll of a company or regiment; a dummy' (*OED*). A notice in the *Daily Courant* for 21 Feb. 1711 reads: 'All Persons who have been Defrauded by Faggots and others who are Listed in the Foot-Guards, are desir'd to leave their Particular Cases in Writing at Margaret's Coffee-house next the Feathers Tavern in Cheapside, and Care shall be taken to lay the same before the Committee of the Honourable the House of Commons appointed to Inquire into those Abuses.'

kind of Furniture, as seemed very suitable both to the Lady and the Scholar, and did not know at first whether I should fancy my self in a Grotto, or in a Library.

Upon my looking into the Books, I found there were some few which the Lady had bought for her own use, but that most of them had been got together, either because she had heard them praised, or because she had seen the Authors of them. Among several that I examin'd, I very well remember these that follow.

Ogleby's Virgil.[1]
Dryden's Juvenal.[2]
Cassandra.[3]
Cleopatra.[4]
Astræa.[5]
Sir *Isaac Newton's* Works.[6]
The *Grand Cyrus:*[7] With a Pin stuck in one of the middle Leaves.

---

[1] John Ogilby translated the *Works* of Virgil in 1649, 1650, and 1654. A reprint of this translation 'adorned with Cutts', printed for T. Varnam and J. Osborne, is advertised in the *Term Catalogues* for Easter 1711 (Arber, iii. 677).

[2] The *Satires* of Juvenal and Persius, translated by Dryden 'and Several other Eminent Hands', appeared in 1693.

[3] *Cassandra*, the romance by La Calprenède, appeared originally in 1642–5 in ten volumes. Partial translations were published before the Restoration, and the whole work was done into English by Sir Charles Cotterell in 1676 (*Term Catalogues*, Michaelmas 1675, Arber, i. 224). A translation 'by several hands' was published in 1705 as *The Famous History of Cassandra: Containing many Admirable Adventures of the most Illustrious Persons of either Sex.*

[4] *Cleopatra*, also by La Calprenède, was first published in 1647, in twelve volumes. There were several English translations, of which the best known is Robert Loveday's *Hymen's Prœludia, or Love's Masterpiece, being the first part of that much admired Romance, intituled Cleopatra* (1652). The following eleven parts were published in the next decade, and there were later editions after the Restoration.

[5] This is the very influential pastoral romance of Honoré d'Urfé, *L'Astrée, où par plusieurs histoires et sous personnes de bergers et d'autres sont déduits les divers effets de l'honnête amitié*, published in five parts 1607–27 and as a whole in 1633. A partial translation was made by John Pyper as early as 1620, and the whole was translated into English in three volumes in 1657–8.

[6] Newton's chief works published by this date were the *Principia mathematica* (1687), the *Opticks* (1704), and *Arithmetica universalis* (1707).

[7] *Artamène ou le grand Cyrus* was a romance by Madeleine de Scudéry (1649–53, 10 vols.). An English translation by F. G. in five folio volumes was published 1653–5. The four French romances, together with *Clelia* mentioned below, which Sir Roger found in Leonora's library are representative of the tales of love and gallantry which had such a great vogue in the late seventeenth century. 'In England', wrote Sir Walter Scott, 'they continued to be read by our grandmothers during the Augustan age of English, and while Addison was amusing the world with his wit, and Pope by his poetry, the ladies were reading Clelia, Cleopatra, and the Grand Cyrus. The fashion did not decay till about the reign of George I . . .' (*Essay on Romance, Miscellaneous Prose Works*, Edinburgh, 1827, vi. 256). In the opening scene of Steele's *Tender Husband* (1705) Biddy Tipkin is described as a young woman who 'has spent all her solitude in reading romances, her head is full of shepherds, knights, flowery meads, groves, and streams, so that if you talk like a man of this world to

Pembroke's Arcadia.[1]
Lock of Human Understanding.[2] With a Paper of Patches in it.
A Spelling Book.[3]
A Dictionary[4] for the Explanation of hard Words.
Sherlock upon Death.[5]
The fifteen Comforts of Matrimony.[6]
Sir *William Temple's* Essays.[7]
Father *Malbranche's* Search after Truth, translated into *English*.[8]
A Book of Novels.
The Academy of Compliments.[9]
Culpepper's Midwifery.[10]
The Ladies Calling.[11]

her, you do nothing'; whereupon Clerimont says, 'Oh, let me alone—I have been a great traveller in fairy-land myself, I know Oroondates; Cassandra, Astraea and Clelia are my intimate acquaintance'. On the vogue of the romances in England see Thomas P. Haviland, *The Roman de longue haleine on English Soil* (Philadelphia, 1931).

[1] *The Countesse of Pembrokes Arcadia*, by Sir Philip Sidney, was published in 1590 and frequently reprinted during the seventeenth century (13th edition, 1674). It is this romance which Lettice studies, 'by a small candle', in Steele's *Lying Lover* (IV. ii).

[2] The 6th edition, 'with large Additions', of Locke's *Essay concerning Human Understanding* (1690), in two volumes, printed for A. and J. Churchill at the Black Swan in Paternoster-row, is advertised in No. 16 (19 Mar. 1711).

[3] There were, of course, many of these. Joseph Hazard, at the Golden-Bible in Stationers-Court, within Ludgate, advertises, among other books, 'a new British Spelling-Book; Hawkin's and Young's Spelling-Book, and others' (*Post Boy*, 24 Mar. 1711).

[4] *Glossographia Anglicana Nova*, a dictionary of 'hard words' in English (1707), has been suggested for this, but it seems more likely that the popular *Cocker's English Dictionary* (first published in 1704) is meant. For this book see DeWitt T. Starnes and Gertrude E. Noyes, *The English Dictionary from Cawdrey to Johnson, 1604–1755* (Chapel Hill, N.C., 1946), chap. x.

[5] *A Practical Discourse concerning Death*, by William Sherlock, Dean of St. Paul's and Master of the Temple, was published in 1689 and had reached a 13th edition by 1705. In No. 289 (vol. iii) Addison speaks of its great popularity and calls it 'one of the strongest Persuasives to a religious Life that ever was written in any Language'. A passage from it is quoted in No. 513 (vol. iv).

[6] The English version (1682) of the popular *Quinze joies de mariage*. The 1705 edition has the subtitle, 'A looking-glass for all those who have enter'd in that holy and comfortable state'.

[7] *Miscellanea* appeared in three parts, 1680, 1690, and 1701.

[8] Malebranche's *Recherche de la vérité* (1674–5, 2 vols.) was translated by Thomas Taylor in 1694 and by R. Sault in the same year. Taylor's translation, *Father Malebranche his Treatise concerning, The Search after Truth*, had a second edition in 1700.

[9] There were many editions of this compilation. One dated 1705 bears the title, *The Compleat Academy of Complements: containing first, Choice sentences, with variety of similitudes, and comparisons; also the best complemental letters. Second, The art of courtship and genteel breeding, with discourses proper for this ingenious age, so far surpassing any thing of this nature. Together with a collection of the newest songs that are sung at court and play-house*. Printed for E. Tracy, and T. Ballard.

[10] *A Directory for Midwives*, by Nicolas Culpeper, was published in 1651. Another edition is advertised in the *Term Catalogues*, Hilary 1701 (Arber, iii. 234).

[11] *The Ladies Calling: by the Author of the Whole Duty of Man*, i.e. by Richard Allestree (Oxford, 1673), was frequently reprinted.

Tales in Verse by Mr. *Durfey*:[1] Bound in Red Leather, gilt on the Back, and doubled down in several places.

All the Classick Authors in Wood.

A Set of *Elzivers*[2] by the same Hand.

Clelia.[3] Which opened of it self in the Place that describes two Lovers in a Bower.

Baker's Chronicle.[4]

Advice to a Daughter.[5]

The New *Atalantis*,[6] with a Key to it.

Mr. *Steel's* Christian Heroe.

A Prayer Book: With a Bottle of *Hungary* Water[7] by the side of it.

[1] Thomas D'Urfey's *Tales Tragical and Comical* appeared in 1704.

[2] Elzevier (spelt variously in the eighteenth century) was the name of a family of printers in Holland, famous chiefly for their elegant editions of the classics.

[3] Madeleine de Scudéry's *Clélie, histoire romaine*, was published in 1654–60, in ten volumes, and translated (1655–61) by John Davies and G. Havers.

[4] *A Chronicle of the Kings of England from the Time of the Romans Government unto the Raigne of King Charles* (1643) was a favourite book of Sir Roger's (No. 269 (vol. ii)). It was reprinted, with continuations, throughout the seventeenth century. *Tatler* 264 satirizes coffee-house speakers who 'draw Parallels out of *Baker's Chronicle* to almost every Part of Her Majesty's Reign'.

[5] *The Lady's New-Years Gift; or, Advice to a Daughter* (by George Savile, Marquis of Halifax) was published in 1688, went through many editions, and was included in his *Miscellanies* of 1700. In No. 26 is advertised:

Miscellanies by the late Lord Marquis of Hallifax, viz. Advice to a Daughter. The Character of a Trimmer. The Anatomy of an Equivalent. A Letter to a Dissenter, cautions for Choice of Parliament Men. A rough Draught of a new Model at Sea. Maxims of State, &c. Printed for D. Midwinter at the three Crowns in St. Paul's Church-yard.

[6] Mrs. Manley's *Secret Memoirs and Manners of several Persons of Quality of both Sexes, from the new Atalantis, an Island in the Mediterranean; written originally in Italian* appeared in 1709 in two volumes (26 May and 20 Oct.). A third volume, with an ironic dedication to Steele, had been published in the spring of 1710 (*Correspondence* of Steele, ed. Blanchard, pp. 30–31).

[7] A popular compound of wine, rosemary, and lavender flowers, used as both a cosmetic and a medicine. The recipe for making it is given in chap. xxii of Charles Lillie's *British Perfumer* (ed. Colin Mackenzie, 1822), p. 142. In No. 209 is advertised:

Hungary Water, right and fine, large half Pint (Flint) Bottles, Sold for 15d. per Bottle at Mr. Strahan's, Bookseller over against the Royal Exchange in Cornhil, Young Man's Coffee-house at Charing-cross, Mitchel's Coffee-house in Crutchet Fryars, and no where else in Town. Those that want quantities to send in the Country, or beyond Sea, may be supplied at Mr. Strahan's aforesaid, and have great Encouragement. Note, It is the same sort by which Isabella Queen of Hungary so long preserved her Life and Health, she always poured a small quantity in the Water she washed her Hands and Face withal, which wonderfully refreshed the Spirits, comforted the Nerves, and preserved Beauty; she used it with great Success in odd Pains and the Rheumatism, by rubbing the Part by the Fire, and before all things commends it for Pains in the Head, and for the Vapours being smelled to, for a cold Stomach, and to help Digestion, nothing better than a little in a Draught of Ale in the Morning. It ought to be used by all Barbers to wash Gentlemens Heads and Faces after Shaving, I mean to pour a little in the Water; and by Bagnio-keepers, who should pour some of these Bottles over the Gentlemen and Ladies when they come out of the Bath.

Dr. *Sacheverell's* Speech.[1]
Fielding's Tryal.[2]
Seneca's Morals.[3]
Taylor's holy living and dying.[4]
La Ferte's Instructions for Country Dances.[5]

I was taking a Catalogue in my Pocket-Book of these, and several other Authors, when *Leonora* entred, and upon my presenting her with the Letter from the Knight, told me, with an unspeakable Grace, that she hoped Sir ROGER was in good Health: I answered *Yes*, for I hate long Speeches, and after a Bow or two retired.

Leonora was formerly a celebrated Beauty, and is still a very lovely Woman. She has been a Widow for two or three Years, and being unfortunate in her first Marriage, has taken a Resolution never to

---

[1] *The Speech of Henry Sacheverell D.D. upon his Impeachment at the Bar of the House of Lords, March 7, 1709/10* had at least six editions during 1710. See Abbie T. Scudi, *The Sacheverell Affair* (New York, 1939), p. 141.

[2] *The Arraignment, Tryal and Conviction of Robert Feilding, Esq; for Felony, in Marrying her Grace the Dutchess of Cleveland, his first Wife, Mrs. Mary Wadsworth, being then alive* is advertised as 'Just Publish'd' in the *Daily Courant* of 20 Feb. 1707/8. The trial, one of the sensations of the decade, had been held at the Old Bailey in December 1706. This book, 'with copies of the several Letters between him and his first Wife; the learned Arguments of the Council; and the whole Proceedings against Mr. Feilding in Doctors Commons: Perused by one of the Judges present at the Tryal', was still being advertised in 1710 (*Examiner*, 16 Nov.). It was published by J. Morphew.

[3] *Seneca's Morals, by way of Abstract* (by Sir Roger L'Estrange) was first published in 1678 and ran through many editions.

[4] *The Rule and Exercises of Holy Living* (1650) and *The Rule and Exercises of Holy Dying* (1651) were frequently reprinted together.

[5] *A Discourse or Explications of the Grounds of Dancing*, 'by Mr. Fert, Dancing Master, which may be had at his Lodgings, at the Sign of the Lamb and Still in Compton-street, over against the Back door of St. Ann's Church', is advertised in the *Post-Man* of 13 Feb. 1711. In *Spectator* 52 and 54 is advertised:

Mr. Fert Dancing-Master, who keeps his School in Compton street Soho, over-against St. Ann's Church Back-door, where he teaches on Mondays, Wednesdays and Fridays; gives Notice to the Publick, That at the Desire of several Gentlemen in the City, he teaches on Tuesdays and Thursdays at the George in Finch-lane Threadneedle-street, near the Royal-Exchange: He likewise teaches abroad; and plays very well on the Violin.

In Nos. 265, 267, and 269 he announces that he 'has lately taken the great Dancing Room at the corner of Thrift-street Soho' for lessons and that if 'any Ladies or Gentlemen desire to be Taught at their own Houses, send to him he will Wait upon them'. His 'Explanation of the Grounds of Dancing, and a Sett of new Courants, Minuet[s], Rigadoons, &c. All Compos'd by Mr. Fert' are advertised in No. 543; at this time he is 'at his Dancing Room in Peter's-Yard at the upper end of Castle street near Leicester Fields'. Two years later, in Nos. 613 and 631, his advertisement reads:

Anth. Fert, Dancing-Master, who has the most easie Manner of teaching Ladies and Gentlemen, and has lately composed a new Dance, is willing to teach at private Houses at one Guinea per Month, or in any Boarding School at reasonable Rates. Enquire for him at the following Places, viz. Mr. Fraigneau's, a Confectioner, at the Orange Tree in the Pell-mell, or at Mr. Loquet's Master of Languages in Lamb-Alley Abchurch-lane over-against Pontac's.

venture upon a second. She has no Children to take care of, and leaves the Management of her Estate to my good Friend Sir ROGER. But as the Mind naturally sinks into a kind of Lethargy, and falls asleep, that is not agitated by some Favourite Pleasures and Pursuits, *Leonora* has turned all the Passions of her Sex, into a Love of Books and Retirement. She converses chiefly with Men, (as she has often said her self) but it is only in their Writings; and admits of very few Male-Visitants, except my Friend Sir ROGER, whom she hears with great Pleasure, and without Scandal. As her Reading has lain very much among Romances, it has given her a very particular Turn of Thinking, and discovers it self even in her House, her Gardens and her Furniture. Sir ROGER has entertained me an Hour together with a Description of her Country-Seat, which is Situated in a kind of Wilderness, about an Hundred Miles distant from *London*, and looks like a little Enchanted Palace. The Rocks about her are shaped into Artificial Grottoes covered with Wood-Bines and Jessamines. The Woods are cut into shady Walks, twisted into Bowers, and filled with Cages of Turtles. The Springs are made to run among Pebbles, and by that means taught to Murmur very agreeably. They are likewise collected into a Beautiful Lake, that is Inhabited by a Couple of Swans, and empties it self by a little Rivulet which runs through a Green Meadow, and is known in the Family by the Name of *The Purling Stream*. The Knight likewise tells me, that this Lady preserves her Game better than any of the Gentlemen in the Country, not (says Sir ROGER,) that she sets so great a Value upon her Partridges and Pheasants, as upon her Larks and Nightingales. For she says that every Bird which is killed in her Ground, will spoil a Consort, and that she shall certainly miss him the next Year.

When I think how odly this Lady is impoved by Learning, I look upon her with a mixture of Admiration and Pity. Amidst these Innocent Entertainments which she has formed to her self, how much more Valuable does she appear than those of her Sex, who[a] employ themselves in Diversions that are less Reasonable, tho' more in Fashion? What Improvements would a Woman have made, who is so Susceptible of Impressions from what she reads, had she been guided to such Books as have a tendency to enlighten the Understanding and rectify the Passions, as well as to those which are of little more use than to divert the Imagination?

[a] who] that *Fol.*

But the manner of a Lady's Employing her self usefully in Reading shall be the Subject of another Paper,[1] in which I design to recommend such particular Books as may be proper for the Improvement of the Sex. And as this is a Subject of a very nice Nature, I shall desire my Correspondents to give me their Thoughts upon it.   C

No. 38   *Friday, April* 13, 1711[2]
[STEELE]

. . . Cupias non placuisse nimis.
Mart.

A LATE Conversation which I fell into, gave me an Opportunity of observing a great deal of Beauty in a very handsome Woman, and as much Wit in an ingenious Man, turned into Deformity in the one, and Absurdity in the other, by the meer Force of Affectation.[3] The Fair One had something in her Person upon which her Thoughts were fixed, that she attempted to shew to Advantage in every Look, Word, and Gesture. The Gentleman was as diligent to do Justice to his fine Parts, as the Lady to her beauteous Form: You might see his Imagination on the Stretch to find out something uncommon, and what they call bright,[4] to entertain her; while she writhed herself into as many different Postures to engage him. When she

[1] See No. 92. The suggestion of 'a *Female Library*' had been made in *Tatler* 248, 'for the better Improvement of the Fair Sex', and the subject is revived from time to time in the *Spectator*. In 1714 Tonson published, in three volumes, *The Ladies Library*, announced on the title-page as 'Written by a Lady' and 'Published by Mr. Steele', actually a compilation by Steele of material from Tillotson, Fénelon, Bishop Fleetwood, Scott's *Christian Life*, and three of the titles listed in Leonora's library—Taylor's *Holy Living*, Halifax's *Advice to a Daughter*, and *The Ladies Calling*. 'The Reader is to understand', says the Preface to vol. i, 'that the Papers which compose the following Volumes came into my Hands upon the frequent mention in the *Spectator* of a *Ladies Library*. They are suppos'd to be collected out of the several Writings of our greatest Divines, and are dispos'd under proper Heads, in order to fix in the Mind general Rules for Conduct in all the Circumstances of the Life of Woman.'
[2] *Motto.* Martial, *Epigrams*, 6. 29. 8: Affect not to please too much.
[3] A favourite theme of Steele's. Cf. *Tatler* 77, where varieties of affectation are analysed, and the motive traced to 'that noble Thirst of Fame and Reputation which is planted in the Hearts of all Men'.
[4] A relatively new word in the sense of lively, clever, brilliant, applied to conversation, writings, &c. (*OED*). In *Tatler* 31 Steele gives an example of current 'bright Conversation'.

laugh'd, her Lips were to sever at a greater Distance than ordinary to shew her Teeth: Her Fan was to point to somewhat at a Distance, that in the Reach she may discover the Roundness of her Arm; then she is utterly mistaken in what she saw, falls back, smiles at her own Folly, and is so wholly discompos'd, that her Tucker[1] is to be adjusted, her Bosom expos'd, and the whole Woman put into new Airs and Graces. While she was doing all this, the Gallant had Time to think of something very pleasant to say next to her, or make some unkind Observation on some other Lady to feed her Vanity. These unhappy Effects of Affectation, naturally led me to look into that strange State of Mind which so generally discolours the Behaviour of most People we meet with.

The learned Dr. *Burnet*,[2] in his Theory of the Earth, takes Occasion to observe, That every Thought is attended with Consciousness and Representativeness; the Mind has nothing presented to it, but what is immediately followed by a Reflection or Conscience,[3] which tells you whether that which was so presented is graceful or unbecoming. This Act of the Mind discovers it self in the Gesture, by a proper Behaviour in those whose Consciousness goes no further than to direct them in the just Progress of their present Thought or Action; but betrays an Interruption in every second Thought, when the Consciousness is employ'd in too fondly approving a Man's own Conceptions; which sort of Consciousness is what we call Affectation.

As the Love of Praise is implanted in our Bosoms as a strong Incentive to worthy Actions, it is a very difficult Task to get above a Desire of it for things that should be wholly indifferent. Women, whose Hearts are fixed upon the Pleasure they have in the Consciousness that they are the Objects of Love and Admiration, are ever

[1] Addison defines the tucker in *Guardian* 100: 'a certain Female Ornament by some called a Tucker, and by others the Neck-piece, being a slip of fine Linnen or Muslin that used to run into a small kind of ruffle round the uppermost Verge of the Womens Stays, and by that means covered a great part of the Shoulders and Bosom.' This and several later numbers of the *Guardian* deal with the dangers resulting from the discontinuance of the tucker.

[2] Thomas Burnet's *Telluris theoria sacra*, published in 1681 and 1689 in two volumes, was translated into English in 1684 and 1690. In book ii, chap. x, he writes: 'In a *Thought* there are two things, *Consciousness*, and a *Representation*; Consciousness is in all Thoughts indifferently, whether distinct or confus'd, for no man thinks but he is conscious that he thinks, nor perceives any thing but he is conscious that he perceives it; there is also in a Thought, especially if it be distinct, a representation; 'tis the image of that we think upon, and makes its Object present to the Mind' (ed. 1684, i. 302).

[3] In the now obsolete sense of 'consciousness, internal conviction'. Cf. 'the Conscience of a good Fame' in No. 153 (vol. ii).

changing the Air of their Countenances, and altering the Attitude of their Bodies, to strike the Hearts of their Beholders with new Sense of their Beauty. The dressing Part of our Sex, whose Minds are the same with the sillyer Part of the other, are exactly in the like uneasy Condition to be regarded for a well-tied Cravat, an Hat cocked[1] with an unusual Briskness, a very well-chosen Coat, or other Instances of Merit, which they are impatient to see unobserved.

But this apparent Affectation, arising from an ill govern'd Consciousness, is not so much to be wonder'd at in such loose and trivial Minds as these: But when you see it reign in Characters of Worth and Distinction, it is what you cannot but lament, not without some Indignation. It creeps into the Heart of the wise Man, as well as that of the Coxcomb. When you see a Man of Sense look about for Applause, and discover an itching Inclination to be commended; lay Traps for a little Incense, even from those whose Opinion he values in nothing but his own Favour; Who is safe against this Weakness? or who knows whether he is guilty of it or not? The best Way to get clear of such a light Fondness for Applause, is, to take all possible Care to throw off the Love of it upon Occasions that are not in themselves[a] laudable; but, as it appears, we hope for no Praise from them. Of this Nature are all Graces in Mens Persons, Dress, and bodily Deportment; which will naturally be winning and attractive if we think not of them, but lose their Force in proportion to our Endeavour to make them such.

When our Consciousness turns upon the main Design of Life, and our Thoughts are employ'd upon the chief Purpose either in Business or Pleasure, we shall never betray an Affectation, for we cannot be guilty of it: But when we give the Passion for Praise an unbridled Liberty, our Pleasure in little Perfections, robs us of what is due to us for great Virtues and worthy Qualities. How many excellent Speeches and honest Actions are lost, for want of being indifferent where we ought? Men are oppress'd with regard to their Way of speaking and acting; instead of having their Thought bent upon what they shou'd do or say, and by that Means bury a Capacity for great things, by their fear of failing in indifferent things. This, perhaps, cannot be call'd Affectation; but it has some Tincture of it, at

---

[a] are not in themselves] are in themselves *Fol. Corrected in Errata (No. 40)*

---

[1] Cocking the hat is defined by Johnson as 'to set up the hat with an air of petulance and pertness'. The phrase occurs frequently in the *Spectator*.

least so far, as that their Fear of erring in a thing of no Consequence, argues they wou'd be too much pleas'd in performing it.

It is only from a thorough Disregard to himself in such Particulars, that a Man can act with a laudable Sufficiency: His Heart is fix'd upon one Point in view; and he commits no Errours, because he thinks nothing an Errour but what deviates from that Intention.

The wild Havock Affectation makes in that Part of the World which shou'd be most polite, is visible wherever we turn our Eyes: It pushes Men not only into Impertinencies in Conversation, but also in their premeditated Speeches. At the Bar it torments the Bench, whose Business it is to cut off all Superfluities in what is spoken before it by the Practitioner; as well as several little Pieces of Injustice which arise from the Law it self. I have seen it make a Man run from the Purpose before a Judge,[1] who was, when at the Bar himself, so close and logical a Pleader, that with all the Pomp of Eloquence in his Power, he never spoke a Word too much.

It might be born even here, but it often ascends the Pulpit[2] it self; and the Declaimer, in that sacred Place, is frequently so impertinently witty, speaks of the last Day it self with so many quaint Phrases, that there is no Man who understands Raillery, but must resolve to sin no more: Nay, you may behold him sometimes in Prayer for a proper Delivery of the great Truths he is to utter, humble himself with so very well turn'd Phrase, and mention his own Unworthiness in a Way so very becoming, that the Air of the pretty Gentleman is preserv'd, under the Lowliness of the Preacher.

I shall end this with a short Letter I writ the other Day to a very witty Man, over-run with the Fault I am speaking of.

---

[1] 'This seems to be intended as a compliment to Chancellor Cowper' (Nichols). William Cowper, at this time William Lord Cowper, Baron of Wingham, had served as Lord Chancellor from May 1707 until September 1710, when the Tories came into office. Steele had dedicated vol. iii of the *Tatler* to him, and Hughes praises him as 'Manilius' in No. 467 (vol. iv) of the *Spectator*.

[2] Cf. Thomas Pope Blount's *De re poetica*, Part I (1694), p. 90:

Dr. *Burnet*, the present Bishop of *Salisbury*, remarks [in the Preface to his translation of More's *Utopia* in 1684], That the *English Language* has wrought it self out, both of the fulsome Pedantry, under which it labour'd long ago, and the trifling way of dark and unintelligible Wit, that came after *that*, and out of the course Extravagance of *Canting* that succeeded *this*: But as one Extream commonly produces another, so we were beginning to fly into a Sublime pitch, of a strong but false Rhetorick, which had much corrupted, not only the *Stage*, but even the *Pulpit*; two places, that though they ought not to be named together, much less to resemble one another; yet (says *Burnet*) it cannot be denied, but the Rule and Measure of Speech is generally taken from them: but that florid Strain is almost quite worn out, and is become *now* as ridiculous as it was once admired . . . .

Dear Sir,

'I SPENT some Time with you the other Day, and must take the Liberty of a Friend to tell you of the unsufferable Affectation you are guilty of in all you say and do. When I gave you an Hint of it, you ask'd me whether a Man is to be cold to what his Friends think of him? No; but Praise is not to be the Entertainment of every Moment: He that hopes for it[1] must be able to suspend the Possession of it till proper Periods of Life, or Death it self. If you would not rather be commended than be Praise-worthy, contemn little Merits; and allow no Man to be so free with you, as to praise you to your Face. Your Vanity by this Means will want its Food. At the same time your Passion for Esteem will be more fully gratify'd; Men will praise you in their Actions: Where you now receive one Compliment, you will then receive twenty Civilities. Till then you will never have of either, further than

Sir,

Your humble Servant.'

R[2]

No. 39   *Saturday, April* 14, 1711[3]

[ADDISON]

Multa fero, ut placem genus irritabile vatum,
Cum scribo . . . .

Hor.

AS a perfect Tragedy[4] is the Noblest Production of Human Nature, so it is capable of giving the Mind one of the most delightful and most improving Entertainments. A Virtuous Man (says *Seneca*)[5]

[1] W. Papenheim (*Die Charakterschilderungen im Tatler, Spectator und Guardian,* Leipzig, 1930) cites this passage and others in this essay as examples of borrowing from La Bruyère. The resemblances are not close.

[2] On 20 Oct. 1715 young Dudley Ryder wrote in his diary: 'Read the 38th *Spectator,* was extremely pleased because I felt everything I read [in] it was designed against the fault that I find myself extremely guilty of, and that is a too great desire and love of applause in things which are in themselves the least commendable. I have continually a desire of pleasing in my eye and this gives birth and life to every pursuit or engagement, whatever I do carries an air of affectation along with it' (*Diary,* ed. W. Matthews, p. 121).

[3] *Motto.* Horace, *Epistles,* 2. 2. 102–3:
> A Thousand things I suffer to asswage
> The waspish Poets, and to cool their rage;
> Because I write my self. CREECH.

[4] Addison here follows Aristotle (*Poetics* 26); seventeenth-century critics, especially in France, had generally placed the epic above tragedy.

[5] *De Providentia,* 2. 8–9.

163

strugling with Misfortunes, is such a Spectacle as Gods might look upon with Pleasure: And such a Pleasure it is which one meets with in the Representation of a well-written Tragedy. Diversions of this kind wear out of our Thoughts every thing that is mean and little. They cherish and cultivate that Humanity which is the Ornament of our Nature. They soften Insolence, sooth Affliction, and subdue the Mind to the Dispensations of Providence.

It is no Wonder therefore that in all the Polite Nations of the World, this part of the *Drama* has met with Publick Encouragement.

The Modern Tragedy excells that of *Greece* and *Rome*, in the Intricacy and Disposition of the Fable; but, what a Christian Writer would be ashamed to own, falls infinitely short of it in the Moral Part of the Performance.

This I may[a] show more at large hereafter; and in the mean time, that I may contribute something towards the Improvement of the *English* Tragedy, I shall take notice, in this and in other following Papers, of some particular Parts in it that seem liable to Exception.

Aristotle observes,[1] that the *Iambick* Verse in the *Greek* Tongue was the most proper for Tragedy: Because at the same time that it lifted up the Discourse from Prose, it was that which approached nearer to it than any other kind of Verse. For, says he, we may observe that Men in Ordinary Discourse very often speak *Iambicks*, without taking Notice of it. We may make the same Observation of our *English* Blank Verse,[2] which often enters into our Common Discourse, though we do not attend to it, and is such a due Medium between Rhyme and Prose, that it seems wonderfully adapted to Tragedy. I am therefore very much offended when I see a Play in Rhyme, which is as absurd in *English*, as a Tragedy of *Hexameters* would have been in *Greek* or *Latin*. The Solæcism is, I think, still

---

[a] may] shall *Fol.*

---

[1] *Poetics,* 4. 14. 'Iambicks are of all sorts of Verse, the most proper for Conversation; this is a certain Sign of it, that we often make Iambicks, in talking to one another' (*Aristotle's Art of Poetry: translated from the original Greek, according to Mr. Theodore Goulston's Edition, together with Mr. D'Acier's notes translated from the French,* 1705, p. 34). Citations from the *Poetics*, unless otherwise noted, are from this edition. Dacier's French version is listed in the Sale Catalogue of Addison's library in 1799 (two copies), as well as this English translation of 1705.

[2] The question of blank verse, or rhyme, in tragedy had been discussed frequently in the seventeenth century. Dryden argues the advantages of rhyme in the Epistle Dedicatory of *The Rival Ladies* (1664) and discusses the relative merits of rhyme and blank verse in the *Essay of Dramatic Poesy* (1668). Sir Robert Howard (Preface to *Four New Plays*, 1665) and Dryden (*Defence of an Essay of Dramatic Poesy*, 1668) consider the question further.

greater, in those Plays that have some Scenes in Rhyme and some in Blank Verse, which are to be looked upon as two several Languages; or where we see some particular Similies dignifyed with Rhyme, at the same time that every thing about them lyes in Blank Verse. I would not however debar the Poet from concluding his Tragedy, or, if he pleases, every Act of it, with two or three Couplets, which may have the same Effect as an Air in the *Italian* Opera after a long *Recitativo*, and give the Actor a graceful *Exit*. Besides that we see a Diversity of Numbers in some Parts of the Old Tragedy, in order to hinder the Ear from being tired with the same continued Modulation of Voice. For the same Reason I do not dislike the Speeches in our *English* Tragedy that close with an *Hemistick*, or half Verse, notwithstanding the Person who speaks after it begins a new Verse, without filling up the preceding one; Nor with abrupt Pauses and Breakings-off in the middle of a Verse, when they humour any Passion that is expressed by it.

Since I am upon this Subject, I must observe that our *English* Poets have succeeded much better in the Stile, than in the Sentiments of their Tragedies. Their Language is very often Noble and Sonorous, but the Sense either very trifling or very common. On the contrary, in the Ancient Tragedies, and indeed in those of *Corneille* and *Racine*,[1] tho' the Expressions are very great, it is the Thought that bears them up and swells them. For my own part, I prefer a noble Sentiment that is depressed with homely Language, infinitely before a Vulgar one that is blown up with all the Sound and Energy of Expression. Whether this Defect in our Tragedies may arise from Want of Genius, Knowledge, or Experience in the Writers, or from their Compliance with the vicious Taste of their Readers, who are better Judges of the Language than of the Sentiments, and consequently relish the one more than the other, I cannot determine. But I believe it might rectify the Conduct both of the one and of the other, if the Writer laid down the whole Contexture of his Dialogue in plain *English*, before he turned it into Blank Verse; and if the Reader, after the Perusal of a Scene, would consider the naked Thought of every Speech in it, when divested of all its Tragick Ornaments; By this means, without being imposed upon by Words, we may judge impartially of the Thought, and consider whether it

---

[1] Cf. Saint-Evremond ('A Dissertation on Racine's Tragedy, call'd The Grand Alexander'): 'Some of his Thoughts are strong and bold; his Expressions equal the Force of his Thoughts' (*Works*, 1714, i. 272).

be natural or great enough for the Person that utters it, whether it deserves to shine in such a Blaze of Eloquence, or show it self in such a variety of Lights as are generally made use of by the Writers of our *English* Tragedy.

I must in the next place observe, that when our Thoughts are great and just, they are often obscured by the sounding Phrases, hard Metaphors,[1] and forced Expressions in which they are cloathed. *Shakespear* is often very Faulty in this Particular. There is a fine Observation in *Aristotle*[2] to this purpose, which I have never seen quoted. The Expression, says he, ought to be very much laboured in the unactive Parts of the Fable, as in Descriptions, Similitudes, Narrations, and the like; in which the Opinions, Manners and Passions of Men are not represented; for these, (namely the Opinions, Manners and Passions,) are apt to be obscured by Pompous Phrases, and Elaborate Expressions. *Horace*,[3] who Copy'd most of his Criticisms after *Aristotle*, seems to have had his Eye on the foregoing Rule, in the following Verses:

> *Et Tragicus plerumque dolet Sermone pedestri,*
> *Telephus & Peleus, cum pauper & exul uterque,*
> *Projicit Ampullas & sesquipedalia verba,*
> *Si curat cor Spectantis tetigisse querelâ.*

> *Tragœdians too lay by their State, to Grieve.*
> Peleus *and* Telephus,[4] *Exil'd and Poor,*
> *Forget their Swelling and Gigantick Words.*
>
> Ld. ROSCOMMON.

Among our Modern *English* Poets, there is none who was better turned for Tragedy than *Lee*;[5] if instead of favouring the Impetuosity of his Genius, he had restrained it, and kept it within its proper

---

[1] Cf. Dryden, Preface to *The State of Innocence* (1677): 'Virgil and Horace, the severest writers of the severest age, have made frequent use of the hardest metaphors, and of the strongest hyperboles . . .' (*Essays*, ed. W. P. Ker, i. 183).

[2] *Poetics*, 24. 11: 'Thus ought we to reserve all the Ornaments of the Diction, for these weak parts: Those that have either good Sentiments, or Manners, have no occasion for them. A Brillant, or Glorious Expression, damages them rather, and serves only to hide their Beauty' (pp. 408-9). Dacier's note on this passage: 'Those Places which have Beautiful Sentiments, have no occasion for the Ornaments of the Diction, because these Ornaments would only obscure them' (p. 432).

[3] *Ars poetica*, 95-98.

[4] Subjects of tragedies by Sophocles and Euripides. 'These two Princes having been driven out of their Dominions, came to beg Assistance in *Greece*, and went up and down dress'd like Beggars' (Roscommon's note).

[5] Nathaniel Lee (1649?-92), one of the most influential writers of tragedy in the late seventeenth century, and at this time commonly ranked with Dryden.

Bounds. His Thoughts are wonderfully suited to Tragedy, but frequently lost in such a Cloud of Words, that it is hard to see the Beauty of them: There is an infinite Fire in his Works, but so involved in Smoak, that it does not appear in half its Lustre. He frequently succeeds in the Passionate Parts of the Tragedy, but more particularly where he slackens his Efforts, and eases the Stile of those Epithets and Metaphors, in which he so much abounds. What can be more Natural, more Soft, or more Passionate, than that Line in *Statira*'s Speech,[1] where she describes the Charms of *Alexander*'s Conversation?

Then he would talk, good Gods! How he would talk!

That unexpected Break in the Line, and turning the Description of his manner of Talking into an Admiration of it, is inexpressibly Beautiful, and wonderfully suited to the fond Character of the Person that speaks it. There is a Simplicity in the Words, that outshines the utmost Pride of Expression.

Otway[2] has followed Nature in the Language of his Tragedy, and therefore shines in the Passionate Parts, more than any of our *English* Poets. As there is something Familiar and Domestick in the Fable of his Tragedy, more than in those of any other Poet, he has little Pomp, but great Force in his Expressions. For which Reason, tho' he has admirably succeeded in the tender and melting Part of his Tragedies, he sometimes falls into too great a Familiarity of Phrase in those Parts, which, by *Aristotle*'s Rule, ought to have been raised and supported by the Dignity of Expression.

It has been observed by others, that this Poet has founded his Tragedy of *Venice Preserved*[3] on so wrong a Plot, that the greatest Characters in it are those of Rebels and Traitors. Had the Hero of

[1] *The Rival Queens* (cf. No. 31), I. i: Then he will talk, good Gods how he will talk!

[2] Thomas Otway (1652–85). For his reputation in the eighteenth century see Aline Mackenzie Taylor, *Next to Shakespeare: Otway's Venice Preserved and The Orphan and their History on the London Stage* (Durham, N.C., 1950). As to Otway's 'following Nature', Dryden, in the preface to Du Fresnoy's *Art of Painting* (1695), thought that the passions were truly touched in *Venice Preserved*, 'though perhaps there is somewhat to be desired, both in the grounds of them, and in the height and elegance of expression; but nature is there, which is the greatest beauty' (*Essays*, ed. Ker, ii. 145). Mrs. Taylor, who quotes this passage, adds: 'During the eighteenth century, however, Addison's criticism, not Dryden's, was quoted in handbooks and prefaces for the readers of Otway's plays' (p. 250).

[3] *Venice Preserved, or a Plot Discovered* was first acted in 1682, just after the excitement of the 'Popish Plot', which it, of course, satirizes. The play had in consequence long been a great favourite with the Tories, and Addison's comment here states the Whig view of the play admirably. 'By the middle of the century', writes Mrs. Taylor, 'Addison's charge had become one of the clichés of criticism' (p. 40 n.).

his Play discovered the same good Qualities in the Defence of his Country, that he showed for its Ruin and Subversion, the Audience could not enough pity and admire him: But as he is now represented we can only say of him, what the *Roman* Historian[1] says of *Catiline*, that his Fall would have been Glorious (*si pro Patriâ sic concidisset*) had he so fallen in the Service of his Country.   C

No. 40   *Monday, April* 16, 1711[2]
[ADDISON]

> *Ac ne forte putes me, quæ facere ipse recusem,*
> *Cum recte tractent alii, laudare maligne;*
> *Ille per extentum funem mihi posse videtur*
> *Ire Poeta, meum qui pectus inaniter angit,*
> *Irritat, mulcet, falsis terroribus implet,*
> *Ut magus; & modo me Thebis, modo ponit Athenis.*
>
> Hor.

THE *English* Writers of Tragedy are possessed with a Notion, that when they represent a virtuous or innocent Person in Distress, they ought not to leave him till they have delivered him out of his Troubles, or made him triumph over his Enemies. This Errour they have been led into by a ridiculous Doctrine in modern Criticism, that they are obliged to an equal Distribution of Rewards and Punishments, and an impartial Execution of poetical Justice.[3]

---

[1] Lucius Annaeus Florus, *Epitome*, 2. 12.

[2] *Motto.* Horace, *Epistles*, 2. 1. 208–13:

And lest, perchance, you may think that I begrudge praise when others are handling well what I decline to try myself, methinks that poet is able to walk a tight rope, who with airy nothings wrings my heart, inflames, soothes, fills it with vain alarms like a magician, and sets me down now at Thebes, now at Athens.

[3] This paper, according to Pope's *Narrative of Dr. Robert Norris* (1713), was the occasion of the 'strange and deplorable frenzy' of John Dennis on the morning of 17 May 1712, when he entered Lintott's shop 'and opening one of the Volumes of the *Spectator*, in the large Paper, did suddenly, without the least Provocation, tear out that of N° [40] where the Author treats of Poetical Justice, and cast it into the Street' (*Prose Works*, ed. Ault, i. 166). Dennis replied in a letter 'To the Spectator, upon his Paper on the 16th of April', printed with Dennis's *Essay on the Genius and Writings of Shakespear*, 1712 (published on 15 Nov. 1711), and reprinted in Dennis's *Original Letters* in 1721 (ii. 407–16). E. N. Hooker (*Critical Works* of Dennis, ii. 435–6) points out that it was personal resentment against Steele which caused Dennis to compose this letter since 'he believed that Steele was conducting a campaign to undermine his reputation'. Hooker, in a long note on this passage in Dennis, shows that Dennis's

Who were the first that established this Rule I know not; but I am sure it has no Foundation in Nature, in Reason, or in the Practice of the Ancients. We find that Good and Evil happen alike to all Men on this Side the Grave; and as the principal Design of Tragedy is to raise Commiseration and Terrour in the Minds of the Audience, we shall defeat this great End, if we always make Virtue and Innocence happy and successful. Whatever Crosses and Disappointments a good Man suffers in the Body of the Tragedy, they will make but small Impression on our Minds, when we know that in the last Act he is to arrive at the End of his Wishes and Desires. When we see him engaged in the Depth of his Afflictions, we are apt to comfort ourselves, because we are sure he will find his Way out of them; and that his Grief, how great soever it may be at present, will soon terminate in Gladness. For this Reason the ancient Writers of Tragedy treated Men in their Plays, as they are dealt with in the World, by making Virtue sometimes happy and sometimes miserable, as they found it in the Fable which they made choice of, or as it might affect their Audience in the most agreeable Manner. *Aristotle*[1] considers the Tragedies that were written in either of these Kinds, and observes, That those which ended unhappily, had always pleased the People, and carried away the Prize in the publick Disputes of the Stage, from those that ended happily. Terrour and Commiseration leave a pleasing Anguish in the Mind; and fix the Audience in such a serious Composure of Thought, as is much more lasting and delightful than any little transient Starts of Joy and Satisfaction. Accordingly we find, that more of our *English* Tragedies have succeeded, in which the Favourites of the Audience sink under their Calamities, than those in which they recover themselves out of them. The best Plays[2] of this Kind are the *Orphan*, *Venice preserv'd*,

application of the doctrine was not quite so extreme as his theory. Addison's position in the present essay endorses that of Steele in *Tatler* 82:

> The wise *Athenians*, in their Theatrical Performances, laid before the Eyes of the People the greatest Afflictions which could befal human Life, and insensibly polish'd their Tempers by such Representations. Among the Modern, indeed there has arose a Chimerical Method of disposing the Fortune of the Persons represented, according to what they call Poetical Justice; and letting none be unhappy, but those who deserve it. In such Cases, an intelligent Spectator, if he is concern'd, knows he ought not to be so; and can learn nothing from such a Tenderness, but that he is a weak Creature, whose Passions cannot follow the Dictates of his Understanding.

[1] *Poetics* 13. 4–6.
[2] With the exception of *Theodosius*, all the plays in this list were a part of the current repertory at Drury Lane. *The Orphan, or the Unhappy Marriage*, by Otway, had been given on 27 Feb., with Mrs. Bradshaw in the role of Monimia. *Venice Preserved*

Alexander the Great, *Theodosius*, *All for Love*, *Oedipus*, *Oroonoko*, *Othello*, &c. *King Lear*[1] is an admirable Tragedy of the same Kind, as *Shakespear* wrote it; but as it is reformed according to the chymerical Notion of poetical Justice, in my humble Opinion it has lost half its Beauty. At the same time I must allow, that there are very noble Tragedies which have been framed upon the other Plan, and have ended happily; as indeed most of the good Tragedies, which have been written since the starting of the abovementioned Criticism, have taken this Turn: As the *Mourning Bride*,[2] *Tamerlane*, *Ulysses*, *Phaedra* and *Hyppolitus*, with most of Mr. *Dryden*'s. I must also allow, that many of *Shakespear*'s, and several of the celebrated Tragedies of Antiquity, are cast in the same Form. I do not therefore dispute against this Way of writing Tragedies, but against the Criticism that would establish this as the only Method; and by that Means would very much cramp the *English* Tragedy, and perhaps give a wrong Bent to the Genius of our Writers.

The Tragi-Comedy,[3] which is the Product of the *English* Theatre, is one of the most monstrous Inventions that ever enter'd into a Poet's Thoughts. An Author might as well think of weaving the Adventures of *Æneas* and *Hudibras* into one Poem, as of writing such a motly Piece of Mirth and Sorrow. But the Absurdity of these Performances is so very visible, that I shall not insist upon it.

The same Objections which are made to Tragi-Comedy, may in some Measure be apply'd to all Tragedies that have a double Plot[4]

(cf. No. 39) was produced on 16 Jan. For *The Rival Queens*, by Lee, see No. 31; *Theodosius, or the Force of Love* is also by Lee. *All for Love, or the World Well Lost*, by Dryden, had been last given on 2 May 1709. *Oedipus*, by Dryden and Lee, had performances at Penkethman's Theatre on 3 and 31 Aug. 1710. *Oroonoko*, by Thomas Southerne, had been given on 9 and 19 Dec. 1710, and *Othello* on 18 Jan. 1711, with Booth in the title-role. Dennis's comment on this list is that 'there are not two of those which he commends, whose principal Characters can be said to be innocent, and consequently there are not two of them where there is not a due Observance of poetical Justice' (Hooker, ii. 21). As Hooker notes, the one exception would be *Oedipus*.
[1] Tate's adaptation had been given at Drury Lane on 30 Nov. 1710, with Powell as Lear.
[2] *The Mourning Bride*, by Congreve, had been given at Drury Lane on 18 Jan. 1710. For its reputation at this time see Emmett Avery, *Congreve's Plays on the Eighteenth-Century Stage* (New York, 1951). *Tamerlane* and *Ulysses* are both by Rowe; the former was given at Drury Lane on 7 Mar. 1710 and at Penkethman's Theatre in Greenwich on 30 Sept. 1710; the latter had not been performed since 1705. For *Phaedra and Hippolitus*, by Edmund Smith, see No. 18.
[3] Addison may be recalling the attack on this 'drama of our own invention' by Lisideius in Dryden's *Essay of Dramatic Poesy* (*Essays*, ed. Ker, i. 57).
[4] In Dryden's *Essay of Dramatic Poesy* Neander offers a similar justification: 'Our plays, besides the main design, have under-plots or by-concernments, of less considerable persons and intrigues, which are carried on with the motion of the main plot . . .' (*Essays*, ed. Ker, i. 70).

in them; which are likewise more frequent upon the *English* Stage, than upon any other: For tho' the Grief of the Audience, in such Performances, be not chang'd into another Passion, as in Tragi-Comedies; it is diverted upon another Object, which weakens their Concern for the principal Action, and breaks the Tide of Sorrow, by throwing it into different Channels. This Inconvenience, how-ever, may in a great Measure be cur'd, if not wholly remov'd, by the skilful Choice of an Under-Plot, which may bear such a near Relation to the principal Design, as to contribute towards the Com-pletion of it, and be concluded by the same Catastrophe.

There is also another Particular, which may be reckon'd among the Blemishes, or rather the false Beauties, of our *English* Tragedy: I mean those particular Speeches, which are commonly known by the Name of *Rants*.[1] The warm and passionate Parts of a Tragedy, are always the most taking with the Audience; for which Reason we often see the Players pronouncing, in all the Violence of Action, several Parts of the Tragedy which the Author writ with great Temper, and design'd that they should have been so acted. I have seen *Powell* very often raise himself a loud Clap by this Artifice. The Poets that were acquainted with this Secret, have given frequent Occasion for such Emotions in the Actor, by adding Vehemence to Words where there was no Passion, or inflaming a real Passion into Fustian. This hath filled the Mouths of our Heroes with Bombast; and given them such Sentiments, as proceed rather from a Swelling than a Greatness of Mind. Unnatural Exclamations, Curses, Vows, Blasphemies, a Defiance of Mankind, and an Outraging of the Gods, frequently pass upon the Audience for tow'ring Thoughts, and have accordingly met with infinite Applause.

I shall here add a Remark, which I am afraid our Tragick Writers may make an ill use of. As our Heroes are generally Lovers, their Swelling and Blustring upon the Stage very much recommends

---

[1] Granville's Preface to *Heroick Love* (1698) concludes: 'It often indeed happens, that the Audience is best pleas'd where the Author is most out of countenance, and that part of the Performance which the Writer Suspects, the Spectator chiefly approves. When we observe how little notice is taken of the noble and sublime [Thoughts] and Expressions of Mr. *Dryden* in *Oedipus*, and what Applause is given to the Rants and the Fustian of Mr. *Lee*, what can we say, but that Madmen are only fit to write, when nothing is esteem'd Great and Heroick but what is un-intelligible' (p. 5). Colley Cibber devotes a long passage in the *Apology* (chap. iv) to 'the furious fustian and turgid rants' in *The Rival Queens*. 'The unskilful actor, who imagin'd all the merit of delivering those blazing rants lay only in the strength and strain'd exertion of the voice, began to tear his lungs, upon every false or slight occasion, to arrive at the same applause' (Everyman edition, p. 61).

them to the fair Part of their Audience. The Ladies are wonderfully pleas'd to see a Man insulting Kings, or affronting the Gods, in one Scene, and throwing himself at the Feet of his Mistress in another. Let him behave himself insolently towards the Men, and abjectly towards the fair one, and it is ten to one but he proves a Favourite of the Boxes. *Dryden* and *Lee*, in several of their Tragedies, have practis'd this Secret with good Success.

But to shew how a *Rant* pleases beyond the most just and natural Thought that is not pronounced with Vehemence, I would desire the Reader, when he sees the Tragedy of *Oedipus*,[1] to observe how quietly the Hero is dismiss'd at the End of the third Act, after having pronounc'd the following Lines, in which the Thought is very natural, and apt to move Compassion.

> *To you, good Gods, I make my last Appeal,*
> *Or clear my Virtues, or my Crimes reveal.*
> *If in the Maze of Fate I blindly run,*
> *And backward trod those Paths I sought to shun;*
> *Impute my Errours to your own Decree,*
> *My Hands are guilty, but my Heart is free.*

Let us then observe with what Thunder-claps of Applause he leaves the Stage, after the Impieties and Execrations at the End of the fourth Act; and you will wonder to see an Audience so cursed and so pleased at the same Time.

> *O that as oft I have at* Athens *seen,*
> [Where, by the Way, there was no Stage till many
>   Years after *Oedipus.*]
> *The Stage arise, and the big Clouds descend;*
> *So now, in very Deed, I might behold,*
> *This pond'rous Globe, and all yon marble Roof,*
> *Meet, like the Hands of* Jove, *and crush Mankind.*
> *For all the Elements, &c.*

ADVERTISEMENT.

Having spoken of Mr. Powell,[2] as sometimes raising himself Applause from the ill Taste of an Audience; I must do him the Justice to own, that he

---

[1] The two passages from *Oedipus* are quoted with several verbal changes. In *The Drummer* Addison closes Act I with a tag facetiously chosen from the second act of *Oedipus*:

> Clasp'd in the Folds of Love, I'd meet my Doom,
> And act my Joys, tho' Thunder shook the Room.

[2] This performance of *The Indian Emperor*, with Powell as Cortez, is advertised in No. 41.

is excellently form'd for a Tragœdian, and, when he pleases, deserves the Admiration of the best Judges; as I doubt not but he will in the Conquest of Mexico, *which is acted for his own Benefit To-morrow Night.*   C

No. 41   *Tuesday, April* 17, 1711[1]
[STEELE]

> . . . *Tu non inventa reperta es.*
> Ovid.

COMPASSION for the Gentleman who writes the following Letter, should not prevail upon me to fall upon the Fair Sex, if it were not that I find they are frequently Fairer than they ought to be. Such Impostures are not to be tolerated in Civil Society; and I think his Misfortune ought to be made publick, as a Warning for other Men always to Examine into what they Admire.

SIR,
'SUPPOSING you to be a Person of General Knowledge, I make my Application to you on a very particular Occasion. I have a great Mind to be rid of my Wife, and hope, when you consider my Case, you will be of Opinion I have very just Pretentions to a Divorce. I am a mere Man of the Town, and have very little Improvement, but what I have got from Plays. I remember in *The Silent Woman*[2] the Learned Dr. *Cutberd,* or Dr. *Otter* (I forget which) makes one of the Causes of Separation to be *Error Personæ,* when a Man marries a Woman, and finds her not to be the same Woman whom he intended to marry, but another. If that be Law, it is, I presume, exactly my Case. For you are to know, Mr. *Spectator,* that there are Women who do not let their Husbands see their Faces 'till they are married.

---

[1] *Motto.* Adapted from Ovid, *Metamorphoses,* 1. 654–5:
Undiscovered thou art discovered.

[2] Ben Jonson, *Epicoene, or the Silent Woman,* v. i:
CUTBEARD. The first is *impedimentum erroris.*
OTTER. Of which there are several species.
CUTBEARD. Ay, as *error personae.*
OTTER. If you contract yourself to one person, thinking her another.
The Silent Woman had been given recently (5 Mar.) at Drury Lane, with Estcourt as Otter, and Norris as Cutbeard.

'Not to keep you in suspense, I mean plainly, that part of the Sex who paint. They are some of them so Exquisitely skilful this Way, that give them but a Tolerable Pair of Eyes to set up with, and they will make Bosom, Lips, Cheeks, and Eyebrows, by their own Industry. As for my Dear, never Man was so inamour'd as I was of her fair Forehead, Neck and Arms, as well as the bright Jett of her Hair; but to my great Astonishment, I find they were all the Effect of Art: Her Skin is so Tarnished with this Practice, that when she first wakes in a Morning, she scarce seems young enough to be the Mother of her whom I carried to Bed the Night before. I shall take the Liberty to part with her by the first Opportunity, unless her Father will make her Portion suitable to her real, not her assumed, Countenance. This I thought fit to let him and her know by your means.

I am, SIR,

Your most Obedient,

Humble Servant.'

I cannot tell what the Law, or the Parents of the Lady, will do for this Injured Gentleman, but must allow he has very much Justice on his side. I have indeed very long observed this Evil, and distinguished those of our Women who wear their own, from those in borrowed Complexions, by the *Picts*[1] and the *British*. There does not need any great Discernment to judge which are which. The *British* have a lively, animated Aspect; The *Picts*, tho' never so Beautiful, have dead, uninformed[2] Countenances. The Muscles of a real Face sometimes swell with soft Passion, sudden Surprize, and are flushed with agreeable Confusions, according as the Objects before them, or the Ideas presented to them, affect their Imagination. But the *Picts* behold all things with the same Air, whether they are Joyful or Sad; The same fix'd Insensibility appears upon all Occasions. A *Pict*, tho' she takes all that Pains to invite the Approach of Lovers, is obliged to keep them at a certain Distance; a Sigh in a Languishing Lover, if fetched too near her, would dissolve a Feature; and a Kiss snatched by a Forward one, might transfer the Complexion

---

[1] Cf. Robert Plot, *Natural History of Stafford-shire* (Oxford, 1686), p. 34: 'The ancient *Britans* painted their bodies with *woad* and were exceeding long lived; and some have thought the *Picts* had their name from hence. . . .' Caesar (*Commentaries*, 5. 14) had described the British as men who 'paint themselves blue with Woad, that they may look the more dreadful to their Enemies in Battel' (trans. Martin Bladen, 1712, p. 85). Steele's use of the word in the now obsolete sense of 'one who paints the face' is the earliest example in *OED*.

[2] See No. 33.

of the Mistress to the Admirer. It is hard to speak of these false Fair Ones,[1] without saying something uncomplaisant, but I would only recommend to them to consider how they like coming into a Room new Painted; they may assure themselves, the near Approach of a Lady who uses this Practice is much more offensive.

WILL. HONEYCOMB told us, one Day, an Adventure he once had with a *Pict*. This Lady had Wit, as well as Beauty, at Will, and made it her Business to gain Hearts, for no other Reason, but to rally the Torments of her Lovers. She would make great Advances to insnare Men, but without any manner of Scruple break off when there was no Provocation. Her Ill-Nature and Vanity made my Friend very easily Proof against the Charms of her Wit and Conversation; but her beauteous Form, instead of being blemished by her Falshood and Inconstancy, every Day increased upon him, and she had new Attractions every time he saw her. When she observed WILL. irrevocably her Slave, she began to use him as such, and after many steps toward such a Cruelty, she at last utterly banished him. The unhappy Lover strove in vain, by servile Epistles, to revoke his Doom, till at length he was forced to the last Refuge, a round Sum of Mony to her Maid. This corrupt Attendant placed him early in the Morning behind the Hangings in her Mistress's Dressing-Room. He stood very conveniently to observe, without being seen. The *Pict* begins the Face she designed to wear that Day, and I have heard him protest she had worked a full half Hour before he knew her to be the same Woman. As soon as he saw the Dawn of that Complexion, for which he had so long languished, he thought fit to break[2] from his Concealment, repeating that of *Cowley*:[3]

> *Th' adorning Thee, with so much Art,*
> *Is but a barbarous Skill;*
> *'Tis like the Pois'ning of a Dart,*
> *Too apt before to kill.*

The *Pict* stood before him in the utmost Confusion, with the prettiest Smirk imaginable on the finish'd side of her Face, pale as Ashes on the other. HONEYCOMB seized all her Gally-Pots and Washes, and carried off his Handkerchief full of Brushes, Scraps of

[1] Swift writes to Stella on 21 Dec. 1711: 'I was to see lady ——, who is just up after lying-in; and the ugliest sight I have seen, pale, dead, old and yellow, for want of her paint. She has turned my stomach. But she will soon be painted, and a beauty again.'
[2] The earliest example of this use of the verb in *OED*.
[3] 'The Waiting-Maid', in *The Mistress*, stanza iv (*Poems*, ed. Waller, p. 138).

Spanish Wool,[1] and Phials of Unguents. The Lady went into the Country, the Lover was cured.

It is certain no Faith ought to be kept with Cheats, and an Oath made to a *Pict* is of it self void. I would therefore exhort all the *British* Ladies to single them out, nor do I know any but *Lindamira*, who should be Exempt from Discovery; for her own Complexion is so delicate, that she ought to be allowed the Covering it with Paint, as a Punishment for chusing to be the worst Piece of Art extant, instead of the Masterpiece of Nature. As for my part, who have no Expectations from Women, and Consider them only as they are part of the Species, I do not half so much fear offending a Beauty, as a Woman of Sense; I shall therefore produce several Faces which have been in Publick this many Years, and never appeared; it will be a very pretty Entertainment in the Play-House (when I have abolished this Custom) to see so many Ladies, when they first lay it down, *incog.* in their own Faces.

In the mean time, as a Pattern for improving their Charms, let the Sex study the agreeable *Statira*. Her Features are enlivened with the Chearfulness of her Mind, and good Humour gives an Alacrity to her Eyes. She is Graceful without Affecting an Air, and Unconcerned without appearing Careless. Her having no manner of Art in her Mind, makes her want none in her Person.

How like is this Lady, and how unlike is a *Pict*, to that Description Dr. *Donne*[2] gives of his Mistress?

> *. . . Her Pure and Eloquent Blood*
> *Spoke in her Cheeks, and so distinctly Wrought,*
> *That one would almost say her Body Thought.*

ADVERTISEMENT.

A young Gentlewoman of about Nineteen Years of Age (bred in the Family of a Person of Quality lately deceased,) who Paints the Finest Flesh-colour, wants a Place, and is to be heard of at the House of Minheer Grotesque, *a* Dutch *Painter in* Barbican.[3]

[1] Wool treated with dye and used as a cosmetic. The 'true use of Spanish-wool and beautifying-creams' is mentioned in a letter in Lillie (ii. 180).
[2] 'Of the Progress of the Soul (the Second Anniversary)', 244–6 ('That one might almost say . . .'). Although these lines had, of course, been quoted before (e.g. in the Epistle Dedicatory to Lee's *Theodosius*), Steele's use of them in this essay (the only reference to Donne in the *Spectator*) very likely gave them a certain currency in the eighteenth century. They are quoted in *Tom Jones* (IV. ii)—the only quotation from Donne in the novel.
[3] A continuation of Long Lane. Hatton calls it 'a considerable Street, between Aldersgate Westerly and Red Cross street Easterly' (pp. 4–5).

N.B. She is also well skilled in the Drapery-part, and puts on Hoods and mixes Ribbands so as to suit the Colours of the Face with great Art and Success. R¹

No. 42   *Wednesday, April 18, 1711*²
ADDISON]

Garganum mugire putes nemus aut mare Thuscum,
Tanto cum strepitu ludi spectantur, & artes,
Divitiæque peregrinæ; quibus oblitus actor
Cum stetit in Scena, concurrit dextera lævæ.
Dixit adhuc aliquid? Nil sane. Quid placet ergo?
Lana Tarentino violas imitata veneno.

Hor.

ARISTOTLE³ has observ'd, that ordinary Writers in Tragedy endeavour to raise Terrour and Pity in their Audience, not by proper Sentiments and Expressions, but by the Dresses and Decorations⁴ of the Stage. There is something of this Kind very ridiculous

---

¹ A letter (Lillie, i. 330–5) signed Aurelia and dated from Covent-garden, 23 May, defends feminine methods of making themselves agreeable:

There is nothing you impute to us, but what with equal justice may be retorted on your own sex: your nice distinction between Picts and Britons may find a proper place among the men. Mr. Lillie can testify the truth of this matter, and that their Valets can paint flesh-colour as well as the young gentlewomen that you put in your advertisement. If their artificial noses, cheeks, and complections, were taken from them, they would appear as despicable as Will. Honeycomb's mistress; if their rhetorick oaths and dammes were taken out, what vacancies and interruptions would be in their discourse; but if you strip them of their borrowed wit out of plays and poems, they would become speechless and unfit for society (i. 334).

² *Motto.* Horace, *Epistles*, 2. 1. 202–7:

As when the Winds dash Waves against the Shore,
Or lash the Woods, and all the Monsters Roar;
So great the shout when rich and strangely drest,
The Player comes, they clap his gawdy Vest.
Well hath the Actor spoken? *Not a Line:*
Why then d'ye clap? Oh, Sir, *his Cloaths are fine.* CREECH.

³ *Poetics*, 14. 1–3.
⁴ In *Tatler* 42 Addison had in a similar vein of raillery described the costumes and stage equipment at Drury Lane. The 'Inventory' of the movables of Christopher Rich, 'who is breaking up House-keeping', included such items as 'An Imperial Mantle, made for *Cyrus the Great*, and worn by *Julius Caesar*, *Bajazet*, King *Harry* the Eighth, and Signior *Valentini*', and 'A Plume of Feathers, never used but by *Oedipus* and the Earl of *Essex*'.

in the *English* Theatre. When the Author has a Mind to terrify us, it thunders; when he would make us melancholy, the Stage is darken'd. But among all our tragick Artifices, I am the most offended at those which are made use of to inspire us with magnificent Ideas of the Persons that speak. The ordinary Method of making an Heroe, is to clap a huge Plume of Feathers upon his Head, which rises so very high, that there is often a greater Length from his Chin to the Top of his Head, than to the Sole of his Foot. One would believe, that we thought a great Man and a tall Man the same thing. This very much embarrasses the Actor, who is forced to hold his Neck extremely stiff and steady all the while he speaks; and notwithstanding any Anxieties which he pretends for his Mistress, his Country, or his Friends, one may see by his Action, that his greatest Care and Concern is to keep the Plume of Feathers from falling off his Head. For my own Part, when I see a Man uttering his Complaints under such a Mountain of Feathers, I am apt to look upon him rather as an unfortunate Lunatick, than a distress'd Heroe. As these superfluous Ornaments upon the Head make a great Man, a Princess generally receives her Grandeur from those additional Incumbrances that fall into her Tail: I mean the broad sweeping Train that follows her in all her Motions, and finds constant Employment for a Boy who stands behind her to open and spread it to Advantage. I do not know how others are affected at this Sight, but, I must confess, my Eyes are wholly taken up with the Page's Part; and as for the Queen, I am not so attentive to any thing she speaks, as to the right adjusting of her Train, lest it should chance to trip up her Heels, or incommode her, as she walks to and fro upon the Stage. It is, in my Opinion, a very odd Spectacle, to see a Queen venting her Passion in a disordered Motion, and a little Boy taking Care all the while that they do not ruffle the Tail of her Gown. The Parts that the two Persons act on the Stage at the same Time, are very different: The Princess is afraid lest she should incur the Displeasure of the King her Father, or lose the Heroe her Lover, whilst her Attendant is only concern'd lest she should entangle her Feet in her Petticoat.

We are told, that an ancient tragick Poet,[1] to move the Pity of his Audience for his exiled Kings and distressed Heroes, used to make the Actors represent them in Dresses and Cloaths that were threadbare and decay'd. This Artifice for moving Pity, seems as ill con-

---

[1] Roscommon, in a note to Horace's *Ars poetica* 96, cites Aristophanes' *Frogs* (IV. ii), where Aeschylus says to Euripides: 'You dress Kings in Rags to move Pity.'

triv'd, as that we have been speaking of to inspire us with a great Idea of the Persons introduc'd upon the Stage. In short, I would have our Conceptions rais'd by the Dignity of Thought and Sublimity of Expression, rather than by a Train of Robes or a Plume of Feathers.

Another mechanical Method of making great Men, and adding Dignity to Kings and Queens, is to accompany them with Halberts and Battle-axes.[1] Two or three Shifters of Scenes,[2] with the two Candle-Snuffers, make up a compleat Body of Guards upon the *English* Stage; and by the Addition of a few Porters dress'd in red Coats, can represent above a dozen Legions. I have sometimes seen a Couple of Armies drawn up together upon the Stage, when the Poet has been dispos'd to do Honour to his Generals. It is impossible for the Reader's Imagination to multiply twenty Men into such prodigious Multitudes, or to fancy that two or three hundred thousand Soldiers are fighting in a Room of forty or fifty Yards in Compass. Incidents of such Nature should be told, not represented.

> *. . . Non tamen intus*
> *Digna geri promes in scenam: multaque tolles*
> *Ex oculis, quæ mox narret facundia præsens.* Hor.[3]

> *Yet there are things improper for a Scene,*
> *Which Men of Judgment only will relate.* L. Roscom.

I should therefore, in this Particular, recommend to my Countrymen the Example of the *French* Stage, where the Kings and Queens always appear unattended, and leave their Guards behind the Scenes. I should likewise be glad if we imitated the *French* in banishing from our Stage the Noise of Drums, Trumpets, and Huzzas; which is sometimes so very great, that when there is a Battle in the *Hay-Market* Theatre,[4] one may hear it as far as *Charing-Cross*.

I have here only touched upon those Particulars which are made use of to raise and aggrandize the Persons of a Tragedy; and shall

---

[1] The Inventory of the movables of Christopher Rich cited above concludes: 'There are also Swords, Halberts, Sheep-Hooks, Cardinals Hats, Turbants, Drums, Gally-Pots. . . .'

[2] In *The Rehearsal*, V. i, Bayes says, 'I sum up my whole battle in the representation of two persons only—no more—and yet so lively that, I vow to gad, you would swear ten thousand men were at it, really engaged'.

[3] Horace, *Ars poetica*, 182–4.

[4] Since 20 Nov. 1710 the Haymarket Theatre had been used exclusively for opera, and Addison's examples refer to the tragedies at Drury Lane. Unless this is an oversight it suggests that the essay may have been written some time earlier.

shew in another Paper the several Expedients which are practiced by Authors of a vulgar Genius to move Terrour, Pity, or Admiration, in their Hearers.

The Taylor and the Painter often contribute to the Success of a Tragedy more than the Poet. Scenes affect ordinary Minds as much as Speeches; and our Actors are very sensible, that a well-dress'd Play has sometimes brought them as full Audiences, as a well-written one. The *Italians* have a very good Phrase to express this Art of imposing upon the Spectators by Appearances: They call it the *Fourberia della Scena, The Knavery or trickish Part of the Drama*. But however the Show and Outside of the Tragedy may work upon the Vulgar, the more understanding Part of the Audience immediately see through it and despise it.

A good Poet will give the Reader a more lively Idea of an Army or a Battle in a Description, than if he actually saw them drawn up in Squadrons and Batallions, or engaged in the Confusion of a Fight. Our Minds should be open'd to great Conceptions and inflamed with glorious Sentiments by what the Actor speaks, more than by what he appears. Can all the Trappings or Equipage of a King or Hero, give *Brutus* half that Pomp and Majesty which he receives from a few Lines in *Shakespear?*　　　　　　　　　　　　　　C

No. 43　　　　　　　　　　　　　　*Thursday, April* 19, 1711[1]
[STEELE]

> *Hæ tibi erunt artes; pacisque imponere morem,*
> *Parcere Subjectis, & debellare Superbos.*
>
> 　　　　　　　　　　　　　　　　　　　Virg.

THERE are Crowds of Men, whose great Misfortune it is that they were not bound to Mechanick Arts or Trades; it being absolutely necessary for them to be led by some continual Task or Employment. These are such as we commonly call Dull Fellows; Persons, who for want of something to do, out of a certain Vacancy

---

[1] *Motto.* Virgil, *Aeneid*, 6. 852–3:

> Disposing Peace, and War, thy own Majestick Way.
> To tame the Proud, the fetter'd Slave to free;
> These are Imperial Arts, and worthy thee. DRYDEN.

of Thought, rather than Curiosity, are ever meddling with things for which they are unfit. I cannot give you a Notion of them better than by presenting you with a Letter from a Gentleman, who belongs to a Society of this Order of Men, residing at *Oxford*.

Oxford, April 13. 1711.

SIR, *Four a Clock in the Morning.*

'IN some of your late Speculations,[1] I find some Sketches towards an History of Clubs: But you seem to me to shew them in somewhat too ludicrous a Light. I have well weigh'd that Matter, and think, that the most important Negotiations may best be carry'd on in such Assemblies. I shall therefore, for the good of Mankind, (which, I trust, you and I are equally concern'd for) propose an Institution of that Nature for Example sake.

'I must confess, the Design and Transactions of too many Clubs are trifling, and manifestly of no Consequence to the Nation or Publick Weal: Those I'll give you up. But you must do me then the Justice to own, that nothing can be more useful or laudable, than the Scheme we go upon. To avoid Nicknames and Witticisms, we call our selves *The Hebdomadal Meeting*: Our President continues for a Year at least, and sometimes four or five: We are all Grave, Serious, Designing[2] Men, in our Way:[3] We think it our Duty, as far as in us lies, to take care the Constitution receives no Harm,—*Ne quid detrimenti Res capiat publica*[4]—To Censure Doctrines, or Facts, Persons, or Things, which we don't like; To settle the Nation at home, and to carry on the War abroad, where and in what manner we see fit: If other People are not of our Opinion, we can't help that. 'Twere better they were. Moreover, we now and then condescend to direct, in some measure, the little Affairs of our own University.

'Verily, Mr. *Spectator*, we are much offended at the Act[5] for Importing *French* Wines: A Bottle or two of good Solid Edifying Port,[6] at

---

[1] Nos. 9, 17, 24, 30, 32.

[2] Not in the usual modern sense, but as 'characterized by constructive forethought'. *OED* gives one example earlier than this.

[3] See *OED*, 'way', 14 f. This is the earliest example of the phrase used in this limiting sense.

[4] Roman consuls were granted unlimited authority and instructed to look after the preservation of the city. Cf. Sallust, *Bell. Catil.* 29. 2: 'Dent operam consules ne quid respublica detrimenti capiat.'

[5] An act had been recently passed allowing the importation of French wines. The bill was read a third time on 10 Mar. and carried, 193 to 68 (*Journals of House of Commons*, xvi. 543); it was accepted by the House of Lords on 16 Mar. (*Political State*, Apr. 1711, p. 349).

[6] The Methuen Treaty of 1703 had provided that England should import Portuguese wines at one-third less duty than those of France.

Honest *George*'s, made a Night Cheerful, and threw off Reserve. But this plaguy *French* Claret, will not only cost us more Mony, but do us less good: Had we been aware of it, before it had gone too far, I must tell you, we would have petitioned to be heard upon that Subject. But let that pass.

'I must let you know likewise, good Sir, that we look upon a certain Northern Prince's March,[1] in Conjunction with Infidels, to be palpably against our good Will and Liking; and, for all Monsieur *Palmquist*,[2] a most dangerous Innovation; and we are by no means yet sure, that some People are not at the bottom on't. At least, my own private Letters leave Room for a Politician, well vers'd in matters of this Nature, to suspect as much, as a Penetrating Friend of mine tells me.

'We think we have at last done the Business with the Male-contents in *Hungary*,[3] and shall clap up a Peace there.

'What the Neutrality Army[4] is to do, or what the Army in *Flanders*, and what two or three other Princes, is not yet fully determin'd among us; and we wait impatiently for the coming in of the next *Dyer*'s,[5] who, you must know, is our Authentick Intelligence,

[1] Charles XII of Sweden, after his defeat by the Russians under Peter I at Poltava in July 1709 had fled south to Bender (modern Tighina, in Bessarabia), where he took refuge with the Grand Signior (the 'conjunction with infidels'), and the newspapers of this time were filled with speculations as to the outcome.

[2] Monsieur Palmquist was the Envoy-Extraordinary of Charles XII to the United Provinces of the Netherlands. The *London Gazette* of 15 Feb. 1711 prints the following dispatch from The Hague: 'The Ministers of the Allies have deliver'd Monsieur Palmquist, the Swedish Envoy, a new Project for the Preservation of the Neutrality in the North, whereupon an Express has been sent to his Swedish Majesty at Bender, and another to the Senate in Sweden, on that Subject.'

[3] According to a dispatch from Vienna of 9 May, 'Our City is filled with Joy for the Peace with the Malecontents, the whole Kingdom of Hungary and Principality of Transylvania being restored to Quiet, and brought under Obedience again to the House of Austria; which will increase its Strength and Treasure, and be a great Relief to the Inhabitants of this City and Country' (*Daily Courant*, 17 May 1711).

[4] In 1710 Great Britain, the States-General, and the Emperor of Germany had concluded a treaty guaranteeing the neutrality of the States of the Empire during the troubled state of affairs in Sweden. At this time no one was quite sure what Charles XII would do, and the newspapers repeat many rumours of marches and counter-marches. The *Post Boy* of 6 Mar. repeats a dispatch from The Hague (6 Mar., N.S.): 'The Declaration of the Envoy of Sweden, That his Master cannot consent to the Act of Neutrality agreed upon here, for the Tranquillity of the Empire, makes us long to know how the Guaranty-Army will be form'd and employ'd.'

[5] Dyer's *News-Letter*, published by John Dyer in a type resembling handwriting, was a favourite among country Tory readers, including Sir Roger de Coverley (No. 127 (vol. ii)). In Addison's *Drummer* (II. i) Vellum believes his master is alive, 'because the news of his death was first published in Dyer's Letter'. 'Mr. *Dyer*, who is justly look'd upon by all the Foxhunters in the Nation as the greatest Statesman our Country has produc'd' (*Tatler* 18), died on 6 Sept. 1713, and his news-letter was then discontinued.

our *Aristotle* in Politicks. And 'tis indeed but fit there should be some Dernier Resort, the absolute Decider of all Controversies.

'We were lately inform'd, that the Gallant Train'd-Bands had patroll'd all Night long about the Streets of *London*: We indeed could not imagine any Occasion for it, we guess'd not a Tittle on't aforehand, we were in nothing of the Secret; and that City Trades-men, or their Apprentices, should do Duty, or Work, during the Holidays, we thought absolutely Impossible: But *Dyer* being Positive in it, and some Letters from other People, who had talk'd with some who had it from those who should know, giving some Countenance to it, the Chairman reported from the Committee, appointed to examine into that Affair, That 'twas Possible, there might be some-thing in't. I have much more to say to you, but my Two good Friends and Neighbours, *Dominic* and *Slyboots*, are just come in, and the Coffee's ready.

I am, in the mean time,
Mr. SPECTATOR,
Your Admirer, and
Humble Servant,
Abraham Froth.'[1]

You may observe the Turn of their Minds tends only to Novelty,

[1] Thomas Hearne comments on this paper on 22 Apr.: 'Memorandum that there is a Daily paper comes out call'd *The Spectator*, written, as is suppos'd, by the same Hand that writ the *Tattler*, viz. Captain *Steel*. In one of these papers is a Letter written from *Oxon.* at four Clock in the Morning & subscrib'd *Abraham Froth*. It ridicules our Hebdomadal Meetings. The said *Abraham Froth* is design'd for Dr *Arthur Charlett* an empty, frothy Man, & indeed the Letter personates him incomparably well, being written, as he uses to do, upon great variety of Things, & yet about Nothing of Moment. It brings in his Cronys George Clarke of All Souls, Dr Wm Lancaster provost of Queens & Dr Gardiner warden of All-Souls. Dr Lancaster is call'd in it *Sly-Boots* & Dr Gardiner is call'd in it *Dominick*. Queen's people are angry at it, & the Common room say there 'tis silly, dull stuff, & they are seconded by some that have been of the same College. But Men that are indifferent commend it highly, as it deserves' (*Remarks and Collections*, ed. C. E. Doble, iii. 153–4). Later, on 2 May, Hearne mentions 'Dr Charlet, or *Abraham Froth*' (iii. 157).

Dr. Arthur Charlett (1655–1722) had been Master of University College since 1692. He was a learned man, but 'was ever meddling in matters that did not con-cern him' (*DNB*).

Dr. Bernard Gardiner (1668–1726), the 'Dominic' of this letter, had been elected Warden of All Souls College in 1702. He is described in *DNB* as 'a conscientious, indomitable, stern, uncompromising man' who was particularly disliked by Hearne. Later (1712–15) as Vice-Chancellor he was with Wake 'the chief means of saving his university from the consequences of its pronounced and prevalent Jacobitism'.

Dr. William Lancaster (1650–1717), Provost of Queen's, and Vice-Chancellor from 1706 to 1710, is often referred to by Hearne in derogatory language: he is 'a second *Smooth-boots*' (21 Mar. 1706/7), 'the present smooth-booted Provost' (24 Apr. 1707), 'old Smoothboots the Vice-Chancellor' (11 Mar. 1708–9), &c.

and not Satisfaction in any thing. It would be Disappointment to them, to come to Certainty in any thing, for that would Gravel them, and put an end to their Enquiries, which dull Fellows do not make for Information, but for Exercise. I do not know but this may be a very good way of accounting for what we frequently see, to wit, that dull Fellows prove very good Men of Business. Business relieves them from their own Natural Heaviness, by furnishing them with what to do; whereas Business to Mercurial Men, is an Interruption from their real Existence and Happiness. Tho' the dull part of Mankind are harmless in their Amusements, it were to be wished they had no vacant Time, because they usually undertake something that makes their Wants conspicuous, by their manner of supplying them. You shall seldom find a dull Fellow of good Education, but (if he happens to have any Leisure upon his Hands,) will turn his Head to one of those two Amusements, for all Fools of Eminence, Politicks or Poetry. The former of these Arts, is the Study of all dull People in general; but when Dulness is lodged in a Person of a quick Animal Life, it generally exerts it self in Poetry. One might here mention a few Military Writers, who give great Entertainment to the Age, by reason that the Stupidity of their Heads is quickned by the Alacrity of their Hearts. This Constitution in a dull Fellow, gives Vigour to Nonsense, and makes the Puddle boil, which would otherwise Stagnate. The *British Prince,*[1] that Celebrated Poem, which was written in the Reign of King *CHARLES* the Second, and deservedly called by the Wits of that Age *Incomparable,* was the Effect of such an Happy Genius as we are speaking of. From among many other Disticks no less to be quoted on this Account, I cannot but recite the two following Lines.

---

[1] *The Brittish Princes: an Heroick Poem*, written by the Honourable Edward Howard Esq., was published in 1669. The lines which Steele inaccurately quotes occur in Book II, canto i (p. 96):

> A Robe of *Arthurs*, *Albianus* wears
> Which his great Lineage, and Atchievments bears;
> Kept sacred to adorn his mighty line,
> When Temples with their offer'd Trophies shine.
> A Vest as Admir'd *Vortiger* had on,
> Which from this Islands foes his Grandsire won;
> Whose artful colour pass'd the *Tyrian* Dye,
> Oblig'd to triumph in this Legacy.

Howard became the butt of much contemporary ridicule for this poem. Lord Buckhurst and Thomas Sprat both addressed lines to Howard 'on his incomparable, incomprehensible poem' (*Works of Celebrated Authors*, 1750, i. 189–90; ii. 374). For other attacks see A. J. Bull, 'Thomas Shadwell's Satire on Edward Howard', *Review of English Studies*, vi (1930), 312–15.

A Painted Vest Prince Voltager *had on,*
Which from a Naked Pict *his Grandsire won.*

Here if the Poet had not been Vivacious, as well as Stupid, he could not in the Warmth and Hurry of Nonsense, have been[a] capable of forgetting that neither Prince *Voltager*, nor his Grandfather, could strip a Naked Man of his Doublet; but a Fool of a colder Constitution, would have stay'd to have Flea'd the *Pict*, and made Buff[1] of his Skin, for the Wearing of the Conqueror.

To bring these Observations to some useful Purpose of Life, what I would propose should be, that we imitated those Wise Nations, wherein every Man learns some Handycraft Work. Would it not employ a Beau prettily enough, if instead of eternally playing with a Snuff-Box, he spent some part of his Time in making one. Such a Method as this, would very much conduce to the Publick Emolument, by making every Man Living good for something; for there would then be no one Member of Human Society, but would have some little Pretension for some Degree in it; like him who came to *Will*'s Coffee-House, upon the Merit of having writ a Posie of a Ring.[2]   R

No. 44   *Friday, April* 20, 1711[3]
[ADDISON]

Tu quid ego & populus mecum desideret audi.

Hor.

AMONG the several Artifices which are put in Practice by the Poets to fill the Minds of an[b] Audience with Terrour, the first Place is due to Thunder and Lightning,[4] which are often made use

---

[a] could not in the Warmth and Hurry of Nonsense, have been] could in the Warmth and Hurry of Nonsense, been *Fol.*   [b] an] the *Fol.*

---

[1] Leather made of buffalo- or ox-hide. Now obsolete.
[2] Examples of verses in rings are given in W. W[instanley], *The New Help to Discourse* (4th ed., 1695), pp. 184–5. For the custom of writing verses and emblems in rings see Joan Evans, *English Posies and Posy Rings* (1931).
[3] *Motto.* Horace, *Ars poetica*, 153:
    Now hear what I and with me the public expect.
[4] See No. 36.

of at the Descending of a God or the Rising of a Ghost, at the Vanishing of a Devil, or at the Death of a Tyrant. I have known a Bell[1] introduced into several Tragedies with good Effect; and have seen the whole Assembly in a very great Alarm all the while it has been ringing. But there is nothing which delights and terrifies our *English* Theatre so much as a Ghost, especially when he appears in a bloody Shirt. A Spectre has very often saved a Play, though he has done nothing but stalked across the Stage, or rose through a Cleft of it, and sunk again without speaking one Word. There may be a proper Season for these several Terrours; and when they only come in as Aids and Assistances to the Poet, they are not only to be excused, but to be applauded. Thus the sounding of the Clock in *Venice preserv'd*,[2] makes the Hearts of the whole Audience quake; and conveys a stronger Terrour to the Mind, than it is possible for Words to do. The Appearance of the Ghost in *Hamlet* is a Master-piece in its kind, and wrought up with all the Circumstances that can create either Attention or Horrour. The Mind of the Reader is wonderfully prepared for his Reception by the Discourses that pre-cede it: His dumb Behaviour at his first Entrance, strikes the Imagination very strongly; but every Time he enters, he is still more terrifying. Who can read the Speech with which young *Hamlet* accosts him, without trembling?

> Hor. *Look, my Lord, it comes.*
> Ham. *Angels and Ministers of Grace defend us.*
> *Be thou a Spirit of Health, or Goblin damn'd;*
> *Bring with thee Airs from Heav'n, or Blasts from Hell;*
> *Be thy Events wicked or charitable;*
> *Thou com'st in such a questionable Shape*
> *That I will speak to thee. I'll call thee* Hamlet,
> *King, Father, Royal* Dane: *Oh! Oh! Answer me,*
> *Let me not burst in Ignorance; but tell*
> *Why thy canoniz'd Bones, hearsed in Death,*
> *Have burst their Cearments? Why the Sepulchre*
> *Wherein we saw thee quietly inurn'd,*
> *Hath op'd his ponderous and marble Jaws*
> *To cast thee up again? What may this mean?*

---

[1] Pope has a note on 'Tolling Bell' in *Dunciad* (1729), ii. 220: 'A mechanical help to the Pathetic, not unuseful to the modern writers of Tragedy.'

[2] In the scene of parting between Jaffeir and Belvidera (Act V) the passing-bell tolls for Pierre.

That thou dead Coarse again in compleat Steel,
Revisit'st thus the Glimpses of the Moon,
Making Night hideous?[1]

I do not therefore find Fault with the Artifices abovementioned when they are introduced with Skill, and accompanied by proportionable Sentiments and Expressions in the Writing.

For the moving of Pity, our principal Machine is the Handkerchief; and indeed in our common Tragedies, we should not know very often that the Persons are in Distress by any thing they say, if they did not from time to time apply their Handkerchiefs to their Eyes. Far be it from me to think of banishing this Instrument of Sorrow from the Stage; I know a Tragedy could not subsist without it: All that I would contend for, is, to keep it from being misapplied. In a Word, I would have the Actor's Tongue sympathize with his Eyes.

A disconsolate Mother[2] with a Child in her Hand, has frequently drawn Compassion from the Audience, and has therefore gained a Place in several Tragedies. A Modern Writer that observed how this had took in other Plays, being resolved to double the Distress, and melt his Audience twice as much as those before him had done, brought a Princess upon the Stage with a little Boy in one Hand and a Girl in the other. This too had a very good Effect. A third Poet, being resolved to outwrite all his Predecessors, a few Years ago introduced three Children, with great Success: And as I am inform'd, a young Gentleman who is fully determin'd to break the most obdurate Hearts, has a Tragedy by him, where the first Person that appears upon the Stage, is an afflicted Widow in her Mourning-Weeds, with half a Dozen fatherless Children attending her, like those that usually hang about the Figure of Charity. Thus several Incidents that are beautiful in a good Writer, become ridiculous by falling into the Hands of a bad one.

But among all our Methods of moving Pity or Terrour, there is none so absurd and barbarous, and what more exposes us to the Contempt and Ridicule of our Neighbours, than that dreadful butchering of one another which is so very frequent upon the *English* Stage. To delight in seeing Men stabb'd, poyson'd, rack'd, or impaled, is certainly the Sign of a cruel Temper: And as this is often

---

[1] *Hamlet*, I. iv. 38–54.
[2] Possibly an allusion to Dryden's *All for Love*, Act III, where Octavia enters, 'leading Antony's two little daughters'.

practis'd before the *British* Audience, several *French* Criticks,[1] who think these are grateful Spectacles to us, take Occasion from them to represent us as a People that delight in Blood. It is indeed very odd, to see our Stage strow'd with Carcasses in the last Scene of a Tragedy; and to observe in the Ward-robe of the Play-house[2] several Daggers, Poniards, Wheels, Bowls for Poison, and many other Instruments of Death. Murders and Executions are always transacted behind the Scenes in the *French* Theatre; which in general is very agreeable to the Manners of a polite and civiliz'd People: But as there are no Exceptions to this Rule on the *French* Stage, it leads them into Absurdities almost as ridiculous as that which falls under our present Censure. I remember in the famous Play of *Corneille*,[3] written upon the Subject of the *Horatii* and *Curiatii*; the fierce young Heroe who had overcome the *Curiatii* one after another, (instead of being congratulated by his Sister for his Victory, being upbraided by her for having slain her Lover,) in the Height of his Passion and Resentment kills her. If any thing could extenuate so brutal an Action, it would be the doing of it on a sudden, before the Sentiments of Nature, Reason, or Manhood could take Place in him. However, to avoid *publick Blood-shed*, as soon as his Passion is wrought to its Height, he follows his Sister the whole Length of the Stage, and forbears killing her till they are both withdrawn behind the Scenes. I must confess, had he murder'd her before the Audience,

[1] Rapin (*Reflections on Aristotle's Treatise of Poesie*, 1694, part ii, chaps. xx, xxiii) notes that the English 'love Blood in their Sports, by the Quality of their Temperament' and that 'The *English* have more of *Genius* for *Tragedy* than other People, as well by the Spirit of their Nation which delights in Cruelty, as also by the Character of their Language which is proper for great Expressions' (*Whole Critical Works*, 1706, ii. 210, 219–20). Steele, who quotes this in *Tatler* 134, add: 'I must own, there is something very horrid in the publick Executions of an *English* Tragedy. Stabbing and Poisoning, which are performed behind the Scenes in other Nations, must be done openly among us to gratify the Audience.' The point is frequently made by foreign observers, particularly French. 'There is a violent Conflict', says Misson, 'between the *French* and *English* about the Composition of Plays; for here they laugh at the Unity of Time, Place, and Action, and at all the Laws of *Aristotle's* Stage and ours. They make no Scruple also to stab you four or five Persons in the same Play, before the Eyes of all the Spectators' (p. 220). See further Ascoli (1930), i. 434–5.
[2] This recalls the 'Inventory' described in *Tatler* 42 (see above, No. 42).
[3] Corneille's *Horace* (1640). The incident occurs in Act IV, scene v. In his *Examen* of this play, published in 1660, Corneille states that most critics felt the death of Camille had spoiled the end of his tragedy—curiously enough because the violent scene was sometimes presented before the eyes of the audience. 'On l'attribue communément à ce qu'on voit cette mort sur la scène; ce qui seroit plutôt la faute de l'actrice que la mienne, parce que quand elle voit son frère mettre l'épée à la main, la frayeur, si naturelle au sexe, lui doit faire prendre la fuite, et recevoir le coup derrière le théâtre, comme je le marque dans cette impression' (*Œuvres*, ed. C. Marty-Laveaux, iii. 273). In the text of the play the directions indicate clearly that the action takes place off stage.

the Indecency might have been greater; but as it is, it appears very unnatural, and looks like killing in cold Blood. To give my Opinion upon this Case; the Fact ought not to have been represented, but to have been told if there was any Occasion for it.

It may not be unacceptable to the Reader, to see how *Sophocles*[1] has conducted a Tragedy under the like delicate Circumstances. *Orestes* was in the same Condition with *Hamlet* in *Shakespear*, his Mother having murder'd his Father, and taken Possession of his Kingdom in Conspiracy with her Adulterer. That young Prince therefore, being determin'd to revenge his Father's Death upon those who filled his Throne, conveys himself by a beautiful Stratagem into his Mother's Apartment with a Resolution to kill her. But because such a Spectacle would have been too shocking to the Audience, this dreadful Resolution is executed behind the Scenes: The Mother is heard calling out to her Son for Mercy; and the Son answering her, that she shew'd no Mercy to his Father: After which she shrieks out that she is wounded, and by what follows we find that she is slain. I don't remember that in any of our Plays there are Speeches made behind the Scenes, tho' there are other Instances of this Nature to be met with in those of the Ancients: And I believe my Reader will agree with me, that there is something infinitely more affecting in this dreadful Dialogue between the Mother and her Son behind the Scenes, than cou'd have been in any thing transacted before the Audience. *Orestes* immediately after meets the Usurper at the Entrance of his Palace; and by a very happy Thought of the Poet avoids killing him before the Audience, by telling him that he should live some Time in his present Bitterness of Soul before he would dispatch him, and by ordering[a] him to retire into that Part of the Palace where he had slain his Father, whose Murther he would revenge in the very same Place where it was committed. By this Means the Poet observes that Decency, which *Horace* afterwards establish'd by a Rule, of forbearing to commit Parricides or unnatural Murthers before the Audience.

[a] and by ordering] and ordering *Fol.*

---

[1] Rowe, in his 'Account of the Life of Shakespeare' prefixed to the *Works* (1709), makes a similar comparison between the behaviour of Hamlet and Orestes. The death of Clytemnestra off stage is frequently cited in illustration of the classical 'rule', e.g. by Corneille in his *Discours de la tragédie*, 1660 (*Œuvres*, ed. C. Marty-Laveaux, i. 78). Actually, in Sophocles' *Electra*, it is not Orestes but Electra who says that Clytemnestra 'shew'd no Mercy to his Father'.

Nec coram populo natos Medea *trucidet.*[1]

Let not Medea *draw her murth'ring Knife,*
And spill her Childrens Blood upon the Stage;

The *French* have therefore refin'd too much upon *Horace*'s Rule, who never design'd to banish all Kinds of Death from the Stage, but only such as had too much Horrour in them, and which would have a better Effect upon the Audience when transacted behind the Scenes. I would therefore recommend to my Countrymen the Practice of the ancient Poets, who were very sparing of their publick Executions, and rather chose to perform them behind the Scenes, if it could be done with as great an Effect upon the Audience. At the same Time I must observe, that though the devoted Persons of the Tragedy were seldom slain before the Audience, which has generally something ridiculous in it, their Bodies were often produced after their Death, which has always in it something melancholy or terrifying; so that the killing on the Stage does not seem to have been avoided only as an Indecency, but also as an Improbability.[2]

Nec pueros coram populo Medea *trucidet;*
Aut humana palam coquat exta nefarius Atreus;
Aut in Avem Progne *vertatur,* Cadmus *in anguem,*
Quodcunque ostendis mihi sic, incredulus odi. Hor.

Medea[3] *must not draw her murth'ring Knife,*
Nor Atreus[4] *there his horrid Feast prepare.*
Cadmus *and* Progne's[5] *Metamorphosis,*
(*She to a Swallow turn'd, he to a Snake*)
And whatsoever contradicts my Sense,
I hate to see, and never can believe. L. Roscom.

I have now gone through the several dramatick Inventions which

[1] Horace, *Ars poetica,* 185.
[2] Cf. Dacier's comment (p. 276):
There are things which the Audience ought to see, and there are others which they ought only to hear related. If this order is inverted, and that is related which ought to be seen, and that is exposed to the sight, which ought to be only related, 'tis such a fault as will certainly spoil the Poem. A Poet has need of a great deal of Judgment, and Ingenuity, not to leave any of those Incidents behind the Scene, which will affect the Audience by being seen: And to hide those which might offend by reason of their Cruelty, or be found fault with for the want of probability.
[3] In the play of Euripides.
[4] Atreus, in Greek legend, murdered the children of his brother Thyestes and served them as a feast to their father.
[5] See Ovid, *Metamorphoses,* 4. 576; 6. 668.

are made use of by the ignorant[a] Poets to supply the Place of Tragedy, and by the skilful[b] to improve it; some of which I could wish entirely rejected, and the rest to be used with Caution. It would be an endless Task to consider Comedy in the same Light, and to mention the innumerable Shifts that small Wits put in practice to raise a Laugh. *Bullock* in a short Coat, and *Norris*[1] in a long one, seldom fail of this Effect. In ordinary Comedies, a broad and a narrow brim'd Hat are different Characters. Sometimes the Wit of the Scene lies in a Shoulder-Belt, and sometimes in a Pair of Whiskers. A Lover running about the Stage,[2] with his Head peeping out of a Barrel, was thought a very good Jest in King *Charles* the Second's Time; and invented by one of the first Wits of that Age. But because Ridicule is not so delicate as Compassion, and because the Objects[c] that make us laugh are infinitely more numerous than those that make us weep, there is a much greater Latitude for comick than tragick Artifices, and by consequence a much greater Indulgence to be allow'd them.   C

No. 45   *Saturday, April 21, 1711*[3]
[ADDISON]

Natio Comœda est . . .

Juv.

THERE is nothing which I more desire than a safe and honourable Peace,[4] tho' at the same time I am very apprehensive of

---

 [a] by the ignorant] by ignorant *Fol.*   [b] by the skilful] by skilful ones *Fol.*
[c] and because the Objects] and as the Objects *Fol.*

---

[1] William Bullock (1657?–1740?) is described in *Tatler* 7 as well qualified for the part of Biskett in *Epsom Wells* because he 'has a peculiar Talent of looking like a Fool'. His height is mentioned in *Tatler* 188. Henry Norris (1665–1730?), the comic actor, became famous as Dicky in Farquhar's *Constant Couple, or a Trip to the Jubilee* and was thereafter known as 'Jubilee Dicky'. Bullock and Norris are paired in one of Penketh-man's drolls at Southwark Fair in 1714: 'The Constant Lovers; or, Sir Paul Slouch, alias, Sir Timothy Little-Wit. With the comical Humours of his Man Trip. The Parts of Sir Timothy and his Man to be acted by Bullock and Jubilee-Dicky, and the part of Old Buzzard by Penkethman himself' (*Daily Courant*, 2 Sept. 1714).

[2] Dufoy, 'a saucy impertinent French-man', in Etherege's *Comical Revenge, or Love in a Tub* (IV. vi, vii; V. i).

[3] *Motto.* Juvenal, *Satires*, 3. 100: They are a nation of play-actors.

[4] Although the Preliminaries of Peace were not made known until the following autumn (they were printed in the *Daily Courant* on 13 Oct.), the Tory ministers were

many ill Consequences that may attend it. I do not mean in regard to our Politicks, but to our Manners. What an Inundation of Ribbons and Brocades will break in upon us? What Peals of Laughter and Impertinence shall we be exposed to? For the Prevention of these great Evils, I could heartily wish that there was an Act of Parliament for Prohibiting the Importation of *French* Fopperies.[1]

The Female Inhabitants of our Island have already received very strong Impressions from this ludicrous Nation, tho' by the Length of the War (as there is no Evil which has not some Good attending it) they are pretty well worn out and forgotten. I remember the time when some of our well-bred Country Women kept their *Valet de Chambre*, because forsooth, a Man was much more handy about them than one of their own Sex. I my self have seen one of these Male *Abigails* tripping about the Room with a Looking-Glass in his hand, and combing his Lady's Hair a whole Morning together. Whether or no there was any Truth in the Story of a Lady's being got with Child by one of these her Hand-maids I cannot tell, but I think at present the whole Race of them is extinct in our own Country.

About the Time that several of our Sex were taken into this kind of Service, the Ladies likewise brought up the Fashion of receiving Visits in their Beds.[2] It was then looked upon as a piece of Ill Breeding, for a Woman to refuse to see a Man, because she was not stirring; and a Porter would have been thought unfit for his Place, that could have made so awkward an Excuse. As I love to see every thing that is new, I once prevail'd upon my Friend WILL. HONEY-COMB to carry me along with him to one of these Travell'd Ladies, desiring him, at the same time, to present me as a Foreigner who could not speak *English*, that so I might not be obliged to bear a Part in the Discourse. The Lady, tho' willing to appear undrest, had put on her best Looks, and painted her self for our Reception. Her Hair appeared in a very nice Disorder, as the Night-Gown which was thrown upon her Shoulders was ruffled with great Care. For

already conducting secret negotiations with the enemy, and rumours of peace were now circulating, particularly after the death of the young Emperor Joseph I on 17 Apr., N.S. (reported in the *Post Boy* of 19 Apr., two days before the publication of this number).

[1] For the popularity of things French in the social life of the time see L. Charlanne, *L'Influence française en Angleterre au XVIIᵉ siècle* (Paris, 1906), part i, chaps. i and ii.
[2] The custom of the *ruelle*, or the morning visit in the bedroom or boudoir, was one of the affectations of the modish. Will Honeycomb, in No. 530 (vol. iv), calls himself an *homme de ruelle*.

my part, I am so shocked with every thing which looks immodest in the Fair Sex, that I could not forbear taking off my Eye from her when she moved in her Bed, and was in the greatest Confusion imaginable every time she stirred a Leg or an Arm. As the Coquets, who introduced this Custom, grew old, they left it off by degrees, well knowing that a Woman of Threescore may kick and tumble her Heart out, without making any Impressions.

Sempronia[1] is at present the most profest Admirer of the *French* Nation, but is so modest as to admit her Visitants no farther than her Toilet. It is a very odd Sight that beautiful Creature makes, when she is talking Politicks with her Tresses flowing about her Shoulders, and examining that Face in the Glass, which does such Execution upon all the Male Standers-by. How prettily does she divide her Discourse between her Woman and her Visitants? What sprightly Transitions does she make from an Opera or a Sermon, to an Ivory Comb or a Pin-Cushion? How have I been pleased to see her interrupted in an Account of her Travels, by a Message to her Foot man? and holding her Tongue, in the midst of a Moral Reflection, by applying the tip of it to a Patch.[2]

There is nothing which exposes a Woman to greater Dangers, than that Gaiety and Airiness of Temper, which are Natural to most of the Sex. It should be therefore the Concern of every Wise and Virtuous Woman, to keep this Sprightliness from degenerating into Levity. On the contrary, the whole Discourse and Behaviour of the *French* is to make the Sex more Fantastical, or (as they are pleased to term it,) *more awaken'd*,[3] than is consistent either with Virtue or Discretion. To speak Loud in Publick Assemblies, to let every one hear you Talk of Things that should only be mentioned in Private, or in Whisper, are looked upon as Parts of a refined Education. At the same time, a Blush is unfashionable, and Silence more ill-bred than any thing that can be spoken. In short, Discretion and Modesty,

---

[1] Sempronia was the woman who, according to Sallust (*Bellum Catilinae*, 25. 2), was able to dance more skilfully than an honest woman need (the motto of No. 67) and who had often committed many crimes of masculine daring. Cf. *Tatler* 33.

[2] Misson contrasts the use of patches among the French and English. 'The Use of Patches is not unknown to the *French* Ladies; but she that wears them must be young and handsome. In *England*, young, old, handsome, ugly, all are *bepatch'd* 'till they are Bed-rid. I have often counted fifteen Patches, or more, upon the swarthy wrinkled Phiz of an old Hag threescore and ten, and upwards. Thus the *English* Women refine upon our Fashions' (p. 214).

[3] The equivalent of the French *éveillé*. In Etherege's *Man of Mode* (IV. i) Sir Fopling describes a pretty young woman as 'more *éveillée* than our English women commonly are'.

which in all other Ages and Countries have been regarded as the greatest Ornaments of the Fair Sex, are considered as the Ingredients of narrow Conversation, and Family Behaviour.

Some Years ago, I was at the Tragedy of *Macbeth*,[1] and unfortunately placed my self under a Woman of Quality that is since Dead; who, as I found by the Noise she made, was newly returned from *France*. A little before the rising of the Curtain, she broke out into a loud Soliloquy, *When will the dear Witches*[2] *enter*; and immediately upon their first Appearance, asked a Lady that sat three Boxes from her, on her Right Hand, if those Witches were not charming Creatures. A little after, as *Betterton* was in one of the finest Speeches of the Play, she shook her Fan at another Lady, who sat as far on the left Hand, and told her with a Whisper, that might be heard all over the Pit, We must not expect to see *Balloon*[3] to Night. Not long after, calling out to a young Baronet by his Name, who sat three Seats before me, she asked him whether *Macbeth*'s Wife was still alive; and (before he could give an Answer) fell a talking of the Ghost of *Banquo*. She had by this time formed a little Audience to her self, and fixed the Attention of all about her. But as I had a mind to hear the Play, I got out of the Sphere of her Impertinence, and planted my self in one of the remotest Corners of the Pit.

This pretty Childishness of Behaviour is one of the most refined Parts of Coquetry, and is not to be attained in Perfection, by Ladies that do not Travel for their Improvement. A natural and unconstrained Behaviour has something in it so agreeable, that it is no wonder to see People endeavouring after it. But at the same time, it is so very hard to hit, when it is not Born with us, that People often make themselves Ridiculous in attempting it.

---

[1] One of Betterton's principal roles during his last years. He played this part at the Haymarket on 27 and 29 Dec. 1707, 10 Jan. 1708, and 17 Dec. 1709; and at Drury Lane on 24 Apr. 1708, 16 Oct. 1708, 6 Jan. 1709, and 20 May 1709. He died on 28 Apr. 1710; Steele devotes *Tatler* 167 (4 May 1710) to praise of his acting, particularly in Shakespearian roles.

[2] Norris, Bullock, and Bowen customarily took these parts in the performances at Drury Lane.

[3] Balon was a French dancer, who had performed for some time in London. 'On Easter Monday, at the New Theatre in Little Lincoln's Inn Fields, will be an entertainment of Dancing, performed by Monsieur Balon newly arrived from Paris' (*Post-Man*, 6 Apr. 1699). See also the *Flying Post* of the same date, and the *Post Boy*, 15 Apr. 1699. Cibber (*Apology*, chap. ix) mentions him as one of 'the, then, most famous dancers of the French opera' who were 'at several times, brought over at extraordinary rates, to revive that sickly appetite which plain sense and nature had satiated' (Everyman edition, p. 161).

NO. 45, SATURDAY, APRIL 21, 1711

A very Ingenious *French* Author[1] tells us, that the Ladies of the Court of *France*, in his Time, thought it ill Breeding, and a kind of Female Pedantry, to pronounce an hard Word right; for which Reason they took frequent occasion to use hard Words, that they might shew a Politeness in murdering them. He further adds, that a Lady of some Quality at Court, having accidentally made use of an hard Word in a proper Place, and Pronounced it right, the whole Assembly was out of Countenance for her.

I must however be so just to own, that there are many Ladies who have Travell'd several thousands of Miles without being the worse for it, and have brought Home with them all the Modesty, Discretion and good Sense, that they went abroad with. As on the contrary, there are great Numbers of *Travell'd* Ladies, who[a] have lived all their Days within the Smoak of *London*. I have known a Woman that never was out of the Parish of St. *James's*, betray[b] as many Foreign Fopperies in her Carriage, as she could have Gleaned up in half the Countries of *Europe*.
C

No. 46   *Monday, April 23, 1711*[2]
[ADDISON]

Non bene junctarum discordia semina rerum.
Ovid.

WHEN I want Materials for this Paper, it is my Custom to go abroad in quest of Game; and when I meet any proper Subject, I take the first Opportunity of setting down an Hint of it upon

[a] who] that *Fol.*   [b] betray] with *Fol.*

---

[1] Cf. La Bruyère, *Les Caractères*, v, 'De la Société et de la Conversation':

Quelques femmes de la ville ont la délicatesse de ne pas savoir ou de n'oser dire le nom des rues, des places et de quelques endroits publics qu'elles ne croient pas assez nobles pour être connus. ... Si l'on feint quelquefois de ne pas se souvenir de certains noms que l'on croit obscurs, et si l'on affecte de les corrompre en les prononçant, c'est par la bonne opinion qu'on a du sien (ed. Servois et Rébelliau, p. 145).

In *The Ladies Library* Steele, in a passage which comes from Fénelon's *Education of a Daughter*, speaks of women's fashionable deficiencies in spelling and pronunciation. 'Is it not shameful to see how Women of *Wit* and *Politeness* neglect the common Rudiments of Education? Tis enough for them to understand what they *read*, if they do not know how to *pronounce* it, and *read* with a Grace' (i. 16).

[2] *Motto.* Ovid, *Metamorphoses*, I. 9: The jarring seeds of ill-consorted things.

195

Paper. At the same Time I look into the Letters of my Correspondents, and if I find any thing suggested in them that may afford
Matter of Speculation, I likewise enter a Minute of it in my Collection of Materials. By this Means I frequently carry about me a whole
Sheet full of Hints, that would look like a Rhapsody of Nonsense to
any Body but my self: There is nothing in them but Obscurity and
Confusion, Raving and Inconsistency. In short, they are my Speculations in the first Principles, that (like the World in its Chaos) are
void of all Light, Distinction, and Order.

About a Week since there happened to me a very odd Accident,
by Reason of one of these my Papers of Minutes which I had accidentally dropped at *Lloyd*'s Coffee-house,[1] where the Auctions are usually
kept. Before I missed it, there were a Cluster of People who had
found it, and were diverting themselves with it at one End of the
Coffee-house: It had raised so much Laughter among them before
I had observed what they were about, that I had not the Courage
to own it. The Boy of the Coffee-house, when they had done with it,
carried it about in his Hand, asking every Body if they had dropped
a written Paper; but no Body challenging it, he was ordered by those
merry Gentlemen who had before perused it, to get up into the
Auction Pulpit[2] and read it to the whole Room, that if any one would
own it they might. The Boy accordingly mounted the Pulpit, and
with a very audible Voice read as follows.

MINUTES.

Sir *Roger de Coverly*'s Country-Seat——Yes, for I hate long Speeches
——Query, if a good Christian may be a Conjuror——*Childermas-
day*, Saltseller, House-Dog, Screech-Owl, Cricket,——Mr. *Thomas
Inkle* of *London*, in the good Ship called the *Achilles. Yarico*——

1 Lloyd's Coffee-house was first established about 1687 in Tower Street, from
which it was removed in 1691 to Lombard Street. Ships and merchandise auctions
were frequently held there, 'by inch of candle', as well as book auctions. See Warren
R. Dawson, 'The London Coffee-houses and the beginnings of Lloyd's', *Essays by
Divers Hands: Transactions of the Royal Society of Literature*, N.S., xi (1932), 69–111. A
letter from Lloyd's to Isaac Bickerstaff (*Tatler* 268) represents 'That this Coffee-house
being provided with a Pulpit for the Benefit of such Auctions that are frequently
made in this Place, it is our Custom, upon the first coming in of the News, to order
a Youth, who officiates as the Kidney of the Coffee-house, to get into the Pulpit, and
read every Paper with a loud and distinct Voice, while the whole Audience are sipping
their respective Liquors'. Sales of wines at Lloyd's are frequently advertised in the
Spectator, beginning in No. 59.
2 See the above quotation from the *Tatler*. The earliest example of 'pulpit' in this
sense in *OED* is from 1738.

Egrescitque medendo——Ghosts——The Lady's Library——*Lion* by Trade a Taylor——Dromedary called *Bucephalus*——Equipage the Lady's *summum bonum*——*Charles Lillie* to be taken Notice of—— Short Face a Relief to Envy——Redundancies in the three Professions——King *Latinus* a Recruit——Jew devouring an Ham of Bacon——*Westminster-Abby*——*Grand Cairo*——Procrastination—— *April* Fools——Blue Boars, Red Lyons, Hogs in Armour——Enter a King and two Fidlers *solus*——Admission into the Ugly Club—— Beauty, how improveable——Families of true and false Humour ——The Parrot's School-Mistress——Face half *Pict* half *British*—— No Man to be an Hero of a Tragedy under six Foot——Club of Sighers——Letters from Flower-Pots, Elbow-Chairs, Tapestry-Figures, Lion, Thunder——The Bell rings to the Puppet-Show—— Old Woman with a Beard married to a smock-faced[1] Boy——My next Coat to be turn'd up with Blue——Fable of Tongs and Grid-iron——Flower Dyers——The Soldier's Prayer——Thank ye for nothing says the Gally-Pot——*Pactolus* in Stockings, with golden Clocks to them——Bamboos, Cudgels, Drum-sticks——Slip of my Land-lady's eldest Daughter——The black Mare with a Star in her Forehead——The Barber's Pole——*Will. Honeycomb's* Coat-pocket ——*Cæsar's* Behaviour and my own in Parallel Circumstances—— Poem in Patch-work——*Nulli gravis est percussus Achilles*[2]——The Female Conventicler——The Ogle-Master.

The reading of this Paper made the whole Coffee-house very merry; some of them concluded it was written by a Madman, and others by some Body that had been taking Notes out of the Spectator. One who had the Appearance of a very substantial Citizen, told us with several politick Winks and Nods, that he wished there was no more in the Paper than what was expressed in it: That for his Part, he looked upon the Dromedary, the Gridiron, and the Barber's Pole, to signify something more than what is usually meant by those Words; and that he thought the Coffee-man could not do better, than to carry the Paper to one of the Secretaries of State. He further added, that he did not like the Name of the outlandish Man with the Golden Clock in his Stockings. A young *Oxford* Scholar,[a] who chanced to be with his Uncle at the Coffee-house, discovered to us

[a] A young *Oxford* Scholar,] A young *Oxonian*, Fol.

---

[1] Smock-fac'd, i.e. having a pale smooth face. Now rare (*OED*).
[2] Nobody resents the slaughter of Achilles (Juvenal, *Satires*, 1. 163).

THE SPECTATOR

who this *Pactolus*[1] was; and by that Means turn'd the whole Scheme of this worthy Citizen into Ridicule. While they were making their several Conjectures upon this innocent Paper, I reached out my Arm to the Boy, as he was coming out of the Pulpit, to give it me; which he did accordingly. This drew the Eyes of the whole Company upon me; but after having cast a cursory Glance over it, and shook my Head twice or thrice at the reading of it, I twisted it into a kind of Match, and litt my Pipe with it. My profound Silence, together with the Steadiness of my Countenance, and the Gravity of my Behaviour during this whole Transaction, raised a very loud Laugh on all Sides of me; but as I had escaped all Suspicion of being the Author, I was very well satisfied, and applying my self to my Pipe and the *Postman*, took no further Notice[a] of any thing that passed about me.

My Reader will find, that I have already made use of above half the Contents of the foregoing Paper; and will easily suppose, that those Subjects which are yet untouched, were such Provisions as I had made for his future Entertainment. But as I have been unluckily prevented by this Accident, I shall only give him the Letters which relate to the two last Hints. The first of them I should not have published, were I not informed that there is many an Husband who suffers very much in his private Affairs by the indiscreet Zeal of such a Partner as is hereafter mentioned; to whom I may apply the barbarous Inscription quoted by the Bishop of *Salisbury*[2] in his Travels; *Dum nimia pia est, facta est impia.*

SIR,

'I AM one of those unhappy Men that are plagued with a Gospel-Gossip,[3] so common among Dissenters (especially Friends).

[a] no further Notice] no Notice *Fol.*

---

[1] Probably a jest on the name of the river in Lydia, in which Midas had bathed, and famed for its golden sands (Ovid, *Metamorphoses*, 11. 87).

[2] For this inscription, at Lyons, see Gilbert Burnet, *Some Letters containing an Account of what seemed most remarkable in travelling through Switzerland, Italy, some Parts of Germany, &c. in the Years 1685 and 1686* (Amsterdam, 1686), p. 5: 'Quae dum Nimia pia fuit, facta est impia.' Chalmers adds a translation: 'Through too much piety she became impious.'

[3] The *Spectator*'s first allusion to the Quakers, the object of so much derision at this time. One of the spectacles at Punch's theatre in the preceding autumn had been that of 'a Woman Quaker Holding Forth' (*Post-Man*, 16 Nov. 1710). On 26 Nov. 1711 and following days his performance was that of 'The Town Rake, or Punch turn'd Quaker' (*Daily Courant*). Misson describes a woman-preacher among the Quakers:

To set her a preaching, you have nothing to do, but to carry two or three Ladies into the Meeting; the Moment Mrs. Doctor spies a Ribbon, the Spirit moves her, and she falls into one of her Fits; up she gets upon the Bottom of some Tub, with

Lectures in the Morning, Church-Meetings at Noon, and Prepara-tion-Sermons[1] at Night, take up so much of her Time, 'tis very rare she knows what we have for Dinner, unless when the Preacher is to be at it. With him come a Tribe, all Brothers and Sisters it seems; while others really such, are deemed no Relations. If at any Time I have her Company alone, she is a meer Sermon Popgun, repeating and discharging Texts, Proofs, and Applications so perpetually, that however weary I may go to Bed, the Noise in my Head will not let me sleep till towards Morning. The Misery of my Case, and great Numbers of such Sufferers, plead your Pity and speedy Relief; otherwise must expect, in a little Time, to be lectured, preached, and prayed into Want, unless the Happiness of being sooner talked to Death prevent it.

> *I am,* &c.
> R. G.'

The second Letter, relating to the Ogleing Master, runs thus.

Mr. SPECTATOR,

'I AM an *Irish* Gentleman, that have travelled many Years for my Improvement; during which Time I have accomplished my self in the whole Art of Ogling, as it is at present practised in all the polite Nations of *Europe*. Being thus qualified, I intend, by the Advice of my Friends, to set up for an Ogling-Master.[2] I teach the Church Ogle in the Morning, and the Play-house Ogle by Candle-light. I have also brought over with me a new flying Ogle fit for the Ring; which I teach in the Dusk of the Evening, or in any Hour of the Day by darkning one of my Windows. I have a Manuscript by me called *The compleat Ogler*, which I shall be ready to shew you upon any Occasion: In the mean Time, I beg you will publish the Substance of this Letter in an Advertisement, and you will very much oblige,

> *Your,* &c.'
> C

her pinch'd up Cap, and her screw'd up Countenance; she Sighs, she Groans, she Snorts through the Nose, and then out she bursts into such a Jargon as no mortal Man can make Head or Tail of (pp. 228-9).

[1] The earliest example of this word in *OED* (Supplement) is dated 1843.

[2] Cf. No. 20 (on Starers). The *British Apollo* of 5 Feb. 1711 contains a request from Tranquilla for a definition 'of the Ogling-Art, or Speaking by the Eyes'. The answer given is: 'As for an *Ogling-Grammar*, we know of none such, or that the Art is Grammatically taught, but we judge the Theatre the most proper School to learn it in.' See *OED*, 'ogle', for examples of this fairly new word. Cynthio in *Tatler* 22 declares 'there is nothing but Ogling with Skill carries a Woman. . . . This requires an exquisite Judgment, to take the Language of her Eyes to yours exactly, and not let yours talk too fast for hers.'

No. 47
[ADDISON]

Tuesday, April 24, 1711[1]

Ride si sapis. . . .
Mart.

MR. HOBBS,[2] in his Discourse of Human Nature, which, in my humble Opinion, is much the best of all his Works, after some very curious Observations upon Laughter, concludes thus: 'The Passion of Laughter is nothing else but sudden Glory arising from some sudden Conception of some Eminency in our selves, by Comparison with the Infirmity of others, or with our own formerly: For Men laugh at the Follies of themselves past, when they come suddenly to Remembrance, except they bring with them any present Dishonour.'

According to this Author therefore, when we hear a Man laugh excessively, instead of saying he is very Merry, we ought to tell him he is very Proud. And indeed, if we look into the bottom of this Matter, we shall meet with many Observations to confirm us in his Opinion. Every one laughs at some Body that is in an inferior State of Folly to himself. It was formerly the Custom for every great House in *England* to keep a tame Fool[3] dress'd in Petticoats, that the Heir of the Family might have an opportunity of joking upon him, and divert himself with his Absurdities. For the same Reason Ideots are still in request in most of the Courts of *Germany*, where there is not a Prince of any great Magnificence who has not two or three dress'd, distinguish'd, undisputed Fools in his Retinue, whom the rest of the Courtiers are always breaking their Jests upon.

The *Dutch*, who are more famous for their Industry and Application, than for Wit and Humour, hang up in several of their Streets what they call the Sign of the *Gaper*, that is, the Head of an Ideot dress'd in a Cap and Bells, and gaping in a most immoderate manner: This is a standing Jest at *Amsterdam*.

Thus every one diverts himself with some Person or other that is

---

[1] *Motto.* Martial, *Epigrams*, 2. 41. 1: Laugh if you are wise.
[2] Hobbes, *Human Nature* (1650), ix. 13 (*Elements of Law*, I. ix. 13). For other statements by Hobbes on the subject see Clarence D. Thorpe, *The Aesthetic Theory of Thomas Hobbes* (1940), pp. 145–8.
[3] In the Middle Ages and later, professional fools were a recognized class at court and in the families of the wealthy. The Earl of Suffolk's jester, Dicky Pearce, is the subject of an epitaph by Swift. Many examples are given in John Doran's *History of Court Fools* (1858).

below him in Point of Understanding, and triumphs in the Superiority of his Genius, whilst he has such Objects of Derision before his
Eyes. Mr. *Dennis*[1] has very well expressed this in a Couple of
humorous Lines, which are part of a Translation of a Satire in
Monsieur *Boileau.*

> *Thus one Fool lolls his Tongue out at another,*
> *And shakes his empty Noddle at his Brother.*

Mr. *Hobbs's* Reflection gives us the Reason why the insignificant
People above-mention'd are Stirrers up of Laughter among Men of
a gross Taste: But as the more Understanding Part of Mankind do
not find their Risibility affected by such ordinary Objects, it may
be worth the while to examine into the several Provocatives of
Laughter in Men of superior Sense and Knowledge.

In the first Place I must observe, that there is a Set of merry
Drolls, whom the common People of all Countries admire, and seem
to love so well, *that they could eat them,* according to the old Proverb:[2]
I mean those circumforaneous[3] Wits whom every Nation calls by
the Name of that Dish of Meat which it loves best. In *Holland*
they are termed *Pickled Herrings;*[4] in *France, Jean Pottages;* in *Italy,*

[1] Boileau, *Satire* iv (to the Abbé Le Vayer). In his reply, 'To the Spectator upon
his Paper on the 24th of April', published with his *Essay on Shakespear* (see above,
No. 40), Dennis admits the authorship of the ridiculous couplet, but states that
he had written it thirty years before, when he was 'a very Boy', and regrets that
Steele (who was generally believed to be Mr. Spectator at this time) did not quote
some of his more mature work, such as his 'Battle of Ramillia'. Steele, he says,
'discover'd more than a common Satisfaction when you were present with your
Friend Mr. *A.* at the reading those Verses in Manuscript' (*Critical Works,* ed. Hooker,
ii. 24). In the *Critical Specimen* (by Pope?) of 1711 one of the jibes at Dennis is: 'How
he writ upon occasion (*vide Spect.* 47.) two good Lines, being the most wonderful and
surprizing Adventure in the whole Book' (Pope, *Prose Works,* ed. Ault, i. 15). The
couplet from Boileau and the reference in *Tatler* 4 to the critic driven frantic by an
Italian opera (see above, No. 5) are the only overt allusions to Dennis in the *Tatler*
and the *Spectator,* according to Hooker (Dennis, *Critical Works,* ii, p. lvii), at him,
remarks on poetic justice in Nos. 40 (vol. i) and 548 (vol. iv) are directed but the
and there is generally an air of contemptuous silence toward Dennis in the critical
papers. 'The fact that Addison wrote at large of Milton and the sublime without
mentioning Dennis would seem to indicate that he had no great affection for the
critic and no extraordinary respect for his writings, and also that the critic's views on
Milton and the sublime were not generally familiar to the large body of readers for
whom the *Spectator* was designed' (ibid.).

[2] Apperson (s.v. 'love', verb) quotes this from the *Spectator* and cites two earlier
examples: 'I love thee like pudding, if thou wert pie I'd eat thee' (Ray's *English
Proverbs,* 1678) and 'I love you so that I could eat ye' (S. Wesley, *Maggots,* 1685).

[3] Strolling from market to market; vagrant. Cf. Burton, *Anatomy of Melancholy:*
'circumforanean Rogues and Gipsies' (I. ii. 1. v).

[4] A clown, buffoon, merry-andrew. According to the *OED* the term originated in
German and appears in Dutch in 1648; this quotation is the earliest example in English. Pickle Herring, however, occurs earlier in the advertisements of the drolls. An
advertisement of rope-dancing at the Widow Barnes's Booth at Bartholomew Fair

Maccaronies;[1] and in *Great Britain*, *Jack Puddings*.[2] These merry Wags, from whatsoever Food they receive their Titles, that they may make their Audiences laugh, always appear in a Fool's Coat, and commit such Blunders and Mistakes in every Step they take, and every Word they utter, as those who listen to them would be ashamed of. But this little Triumph of the Understanding, under the Disguise of Laughter, is no where more visible than in that Custom which prevails every where among us on the First Day of the present Month, when every Body takes it in his Head to make as many Fools as he can. In proportion as there are more Follies discover'd, so there is more Laughter raised on this Day than on any other in the whole Year. A Neighbour of mine, who is a Haberdasher by Trade, and a very shallow conceited Fellow, makes his Boasts that for these Ten Years successively he has not made less than an Hundred *April* Fools.[3] My Landlady had a falling out with him about a Fortnight ago, for sending every one of her Children upon some *Sleeveless Errand*, as she terms it. Her eldest Son went to buy an Halfpenny worth of Inkle[4] at a Shoemakers; the eldest Daughter

concludes: 'Together with the diverting Entertainment of your Old Friend Picle Herring, the chief of all his imitating Brethren' (*Daily Courant*, 23 Aug. 1705). Tom Brown also refers to 'the merry Conceits of the little Pickle-herring' at Bartholomew Fair in 1699 (*Works of Voiture . . .*, 1705, p. 100). 'The diverting Humours of your Old Friend Pickle-Herring' continue to be advertised in the entertainments of rope-dancing in the Widow Barnes's Company in 1714 (*Daily Courant*, 9 Nov.).

[1] Italian *maccherone*, stupid fellow.

[2] 'A buffoon, clown, or merry-andrew, especially one attending on a mountebank' (*OED*). Cf. Shadwell, preface to *The Humorists* (1671): 'The rabble of little people are more pleas'd with *Jack Puddings* being soundly kick'd, or having a Custard handsomely thrown in his face, than with all the wit in Plays . . .' (Spingarn, ii. 155). In Shadwell's *Sullen Lovers* (II. i) Emilia says to Lady Vaine, 'I had as leave stand among the Rabble, to see a Jack-pudding eat a Custard, as trouble my self to see a Play'. See also Robert Wolseley, preface to *Valentinian* (1685) in Spingarn, iii. 14. The 'Fool's Coat' of many colours is alluded to in *Tatler* 19.

[3] Tom Brown, 'To Mons. de la —— his Correspondent in Paris, writ in the Person of a Frenchman, of what he observ'd in London', writes: 'Among other Customs, I observ'd one very *singular*, and *antient*, and *still* kept on foot, which is, to make *Fools* of People on the first Day of *April*. I cou'd never inform my self what gave the first Rise to so *odd* a Custom; but methinks they might let it alone; for since three Parts in four of the People are Fools *every* Day in the Year, what *occasion* is there to set a Day *apart* for it' (*Works*, 4th ed., 1715, i. 241). On this custom see A. R. Wright, *British Calendar Customs: England*, vol. ii, ed. T. E. Lones (1938), pp. 171–6, where the earliest reference given is from *Dawks's News Letter*, 2 Apr. 1698: 'yesterday being the 1st of April, several persons were sent to the Tower Ditch to see the lions washed'. When or how the custom originated, writes Mr. Lones, may never be known. The earliest quotation in *OED* is dated 1687. Swift writes to Stella on 1 Apr. 1711: 'The Duke of Buckingham's house fell down last night with an earth-quake, and is half swallowed up;—Won't you go and see it?—An April fool, an April fool, oh ho, young women.' The 'sleeveless errand' on which April fools are sent is a much older expression and occurs, for example, in Shakespeare, *Troilus and Cressida*, v. iv. 9.

[4] See No. 11.

was dispatch'd half a Mile to see a Monster; and, in short, the whole Family of innocent Children made *April* Fools. Nay, my Landlady her self did not escape him. This empty Fellow has laughed upon these Conceits ever since.

This Art of Wit is well enough, when confined to one Day in a Twelve-month; But there is an ingenious Tribe of Men sprung up of late Years, who are for making *April* Fools every Day in the Year. These Gentlemen are commonly distinguished by the name of *Biters*;[1] a Race of Men that are perpetually employ'd in laughing at those Mistakes which are of their own Production.

Thus we see, in proportion as one Man is more refined than another, he chuses his Fool out of a lower or higher Class of Mankind; or, to speak in a more Philosophical Language, that secret Elation and Pride of Heart which is generally call'd Laughter, arises in him from his comparing himself with an Object below him, whether it so happens that it be a Natural or an Artificial Fool. It is indeed very possible that the Persons we laugh at may in the main of their Characters be much wiser Men than our selves, but if they would have us laugh at them, they must fall short of us in those Respects which stir up this Passion.

I am afraid I shall appear too Abstracted[2] in my Speculations, if I show that when a Man of Wit makes us laugh, it is by betraying some Oddness or Infirmity in his own Character, or in the Representation which he makes of others; and that when we laugh at a Brute or even at an[a] Inanimate thing, it is at some Action or Incident that bears a remote Analogy to any Blunder or Absurdity in reasonable Creatures.

But to come into common Life, I shall pass by the Consideration of those Stage Coxcombs that are able to shake a whole Audience, and take Notice of a particular sort of Men who are such Provokers of Mirth in Conversation, that it is impossible for a Club or Merry-meeting to subsist without them; I mean, those honest Gentlemen

---

[a] even at an] even an *Fol.*

[1] For *bite* see No. 156 (vol. ii). A biter is described in *Tatler* 12 as 'a dull Fellow, that tells you a Lye with a grave Face, and laughs at you for knowing him no better than to believe him'. Cf. Swift, letter to the Rev. William Tisdall (16 Dec. 1703): 'I will teach you a way to outwit Mrs. Johnson: it is a new-fashioned way of being witty, and they call it a *bite*. You must ask a bantering question, or tell some damned lie in a serious manner, and then she will answer or speak as if you were in earnest; and then cry you, "Madam, there's a *bite*"' (*Correspondence*, ed. F. Elrington Ball, i. 40). Rowe's comedy, *The Biter*, was produced on 4 Dec. 1704.

[2] Used in the now obsolete sense of 'abstruse, difficult'.

that are always exposed to the Wit and Raillery of their Well-wishers and Companions; that are pelted by Men, Women and Children, Friends and Foes, and, in a word, stand as *Butts* in Conversation, for every one to shoot at that pleases. I know several of these *Butts*,¹ who are Men of Wit and Sense, though by some odd turn of Humour, some unlucky Cast in their Person or Behaviour, they have always the Misfortune to make the Company merry. The Truth of it is, a Man is not qualified for a *Butt*, who has not a good deal of Wit and Vivacity, even in the ridiculous side of his Character. A stupid *Butt* is only fit for the Conversation of ordinary People: Men of Wit require one that will give them Play, and bestir himself in the absurd part of his Behaviour. A *Butt* with these Accomplishments, frequently gets the Laugh of his side, and turns the Ridicule upon him that attacks him. Sir *John Falstaff*² was an Hero of this Species, and gives a good Description of himself in his Capacity of a *Butt*, after the following manner; *Men of all Sorts* (says that merry Knight) *take a pride to gird at me. The Brain of Man is not able to invent any thing that tends to Laughter more than I invent, or is invented on me. I am not only Witty in my self, but the Cause that Wit is in other Men.*

C

No. 48   *Wednesday, April 25, 1711*³
[STEELE]

> *. . . Per multas aditum sibi sæpe figuras*
> *Repperit . . .*
>   Ovid.

MY Correspondents take it ill if I do not from Time to Time let them know I have received their Letters. The most effectual Way will be to publish some of them that are upon important Subjects; which I shall introduce with a Letter of my own that I writ a Fortnight ago to a Fraternity who thought fit to make me an honourary Member.

---

¹ 'Addison may have had Dennis in mind' (H. G. Paul, *John Dennis, his Life and Criticism*, N.Y., 1911, p. 65).
² *2 Henry IV*, I. ii. 7–12.
³ *Motto.* Ovid, *Metamorphoses*, 14. 652–3:
   Through various disguises he often found access.

To the President and Fellows of the Ugly Club.[1]

May it please your Deformities,
    'I have received the Notification of the Honour you have done
me, in admitting me into your Society. I acknowledge my Want of
Merit, and for that Reason shall endeavour at all Times to make up
my own Failures, by introducing and recommending to the Club
Persons of more undoubted Qualifications than I can pretend to.
I shall next Week come down in the Stage Coach, in order to take
my Seat at the Board; and shall bring with me a Candidate of each
Sex. The Persons I shall present to you, are an old Beau and a
modern *Pict*.[2] If they are not so eminently gifted by Nature as our
Assembly expects, give me Leave to say their acquired Ugliness is
greater than any that has ever appear'd before you. The Beau has
varied his Dress every Day of his Life for these thirty Years last past,
and still added to the Deformity he was born with. The *Pict* has
still greater Merit towards us; and has, ever since she came to Years
of Discretion, deserted the handsom Party, and taken all possible
Pains to acquire the Face in which I shall present her to your Consideration and Favour.

I *am,*
Gentlemen,
Your most obliged
Humble Servant,
The SPECTATOR.'

'P.S.[a] I desire to know whether you admit People of Quality.'

Mr. SPECTATOR,   *April* 17.
'TO shew you there are among us of the vain weak Sex, some
    that have Honesty and Fortitude enough to dare to be ugly,
and willing to be thought so; I apply my self to you, to beg your
Interest and Recommendation to the Ugly Club. If my own Word
will not be taken, (tho' in this Case a Woman's may) I can bring
credible Witness of my Qualifications for their Company, whether
they insist upon Hair, Forehead, Eyes, Cheeks, or Chin; to which
I must add, that I find it easier to lean to my left Side than my right.
I hope I am in all Respects agreeable: And for Humour and Mirth,
I'll keep up to the President himself. All the Favour I'll pretend to

[a] P.S.] *om. Fol.*

---

[1] Nos. 17, 32.   [2] No. 41.

is, that as I am the first Woman has appear'd desirous of good Company and agreeable Conversation, I may take and keep the upper End of the Table. And indeed I think they want a Carver, which I can be after as ugly a Manner as they can wish. I desire your Thoughts of my Claim as soon as you can. Add to my Features the Length of my Face, which is full half Yard; tho' I never knew the Reason of it till you gave one for the Shortness of yours. If I knew a Name ugly enough to belong to the above-described Face, I would feign one; but, to my unspeakable Misfortune, my Name is the only disagreeable Prettiness about me; so prithee make one for me that signifies all the Deformity in the World: You understand *Latin*, but be sure bring it in with my being, in the Sincerity of my Heart,

Your most frightful Admirer
And Servant.
Hecatissa.'

Mr. SPECTATOR,

'I READ your Discourse upon Affectation,[1] and from the Remarks made in it examined my own Heart so strictly, that I thought I had found out its most secret Avenues, with a Resolution to be aware of them for the Future. But alass! to my Sorrow I now understand, that I have several Follies which I do not know the Root of. I am an old Fellow, and extremely troubled with the Gout; but having always a strong Vanity towards being pleasing in the Eyes of Women, I never have a Moment's Ease, but I am mounted in high-heel'd Shoes with a glased Wax-leather Instep. Two Days after a severe Fit I was invited to a Friend's House in the City, where I believ'd I should see Ladies; and with my usual Complaisance crippled my self to wait upon them: A very sumptuous Table, agreeable Company, and kind Reception, were but so many importunate[2] Additions to the Torment I was in. A Gentleman of the Family observed my Condition; and soon after the Queen's Health, he, in the Presence of the whole Company, with his own Hands degraded me into an old Pair of his own Shooes. This Operation, before fine Ladies, to me (who am by Nature a Coxcomb,) was suffered with the same Reluctance as they admit the Help of Men in their greatest Extremity. The Return of Ease made me forgive the rough Obligation laid upon me, which at that time reliev'd my Body from a Dis-

---

[1] No. 38.
[2] In the obsolete sense of burdensome, grievous.

temper, and will my Mind for ever from a Folly. For the Charity received I return my Thanks this Way.

Your most humble Servant.'

Epping, April 18.

SIR,

'WE have your Papers here the Morning they come out, and we have been very well entertained with your last,[1] upon the false Ornaments of Persons who represent Heroes in a Tragedy. What made your Speculation come very seasonably among us is, that we have now at this Place a Company of Strolers, who are very far from offending in the impertinent Splendour of the Drama. They are so far from falling into these false Gallantries, that the Stage is here in its original Situation of a Cart. *Alexander* the Great[2] was acted by a Fellow in a Paper Cravat. The next Day, the Earl of *Essex*[3] seemed to have no Distress but his Poverty: And my Lord *Foppington*[4] the same Morning wanted any better Means to shew himself a Fop, than by wearing Stockings of different Colours. In a Word, tho' they have had a full Barn for many Days together, our Itinerants are still so wretchedly poor, that without[5] you can prevail to send us the Furniture you forbid at the Play-house, the Heroes appear only like sturdy Beggars, and the Heroines Gipsies. We have had but one Part which was performed and dressed with Propriety, and that was Justice *Clodpate*:[6] This was so well done, that it offended Mr. Justice *Overdo*,[7] who, in the Midst of our whole Audience, was (like *Quixote* in the Puppet-Show)[8] so highly provoked that he told

[1] No. 42.

[2] See No. 31. It is mentioned in *Tatler* 16 (17 May 1709) as acted by a company of strolers at Bath.

[3] *The Unhappy Favourite, or the Earl of Essex*, by John Banks (1681) had been given at Drury Lane on 20 Nov. and 28 Dec. 1710 with Wilks and Mrs. Knight in the principal roles. Five performances at Drury Lane are advertised during the run of the *Spectator* in 1711–12.

[4] Lord Foppington was Cibber's role in his own play, *The Careless Husband*, first produced on 7 Dec. 1704. He acted this part in a performance at Drury Lane on 19 Feb. 1711.

[5] Without, with the meaning 'unless', is marked by Johnson as 'not in use, except in conversation'. Formerly common in literary use, later colloquial or archaic, and now chiefly illiterate (*OED*).

[6] Justice Clodpate, 'an immoderate hater of London', is a character in Shadwell's *Epsom-Wells*, given at the Haymarket on 12 Apr. 1710 and at Drury Lane on 1 Dec. 1710, each time with Johnson in this role. It was also given at Penkethman's Theatre on 20 July 1710, with Leigh as Clodpate.

[7] Justice Overdo is in Jonson's *Bartholomew Fair*, produced recently at Drury Lane (8 Mar. 1711).

[8] *Don Quixote*, part ii, chap. xxvi.

them, If they would move Compassion, it should be in their own Persons, and not in the Characters of distressed Princes and Potentates: He told them, If they were so good at finding the Way to Peoples Hearts, they should do it at the End of Bridges or Church-Porches, in their proper Vocation of Beggars. This, the Justice says, they must expect, since they could not be contented to act Heathen Warriours and such Fellows as *Alexander*, but must presume to make a Mockery of one of the Quorum.

Your Servant.'

R

No. 49
[STEELE]

Thursday, April 26, 1711[1]

. . . *Hominem pagina nostra sapit.*
Mart.

IT is very natural for a Man who is not turned[2] for Mirthful Meetings of Men, or Assemblies of the fair Sex, to delight in that sort of Conversation which we find in Coffee-houses. Here a Man, of my Temper, is in his Element; for, if he cannot talk, he can still be more agreeable to his Company, as well as pleased in himself, in being only an Hearer. It is a Secret known but to few, yet of no small use in the Conduct of Life, that when you fall into a Man's Conversation, the first thing you should consider is, whether he has a greater Inclination to hear you, or that you should hear him. The latter is the more general Desire, and I know very able Flatterers that never speak a word in Praise of the Persons from whom they obtain daily Favours, but still practise a skilful Attention to whatever is uttered by those with whom they converse. We are very Curious to observe the Behaviour of Great Men and their Clients; but the same Passions and Interests move Men in lower Spheres; and I (that have nothing else to do, but make Observations) see in every Parish, Street, Lane, and Alley of this Populous City, a little Potentate that has his Court, and his Flatterers who lay Snares for his Affection and Favour, by the same Arts that are practised upon Men in higher Stations.

---

[1] *Motto.* Martial, *Epigrams*, 10. 4. 10: Our book savours of the man.
[2] Naturally adapted, fitted, or 'cut out' for some pursuit. *Obs.* (*OED*).

In the Place I most usually frequent, Men differ rather in the time of Day in which they make a Figure, than in any real Greatness above one another. I, who am at the Coffee-house at Six in a Morning, know that my Friend *Beaver*[1] the Haberdasher has a Levy of more undissembled Friends and Admirers, than most of the Courtiers or Generals of *Great Britain*. Every Man about him has, perhaps, a News Paper in his Hand, but none can pretend to guess what Step will be taken in any one Court of *Europe*, 'till Mr. *Beaver* has thrown down his Pipe, and declares what Measures the Allies must enter into upon this new Posture of Affairs. Our Coffee-house is near one of the Inns of Court, and *Beaver* has the Audience and Admiration of his Neighbours from Six 'till within a Quarter of Eight, at which time he is interrupted by the Students of the House; some of whom are ready Dress'd for *Westminster*, at Eight in a Morning, with Faces as busie as if they were retain'd in every Cause there; and others come in their Night-Gowns to Saunter[2] away their Time, as if they never designed to go thither. I do not know that I meet, in any of my Walks, Objects which move both my Spleen and Laughter so effectually, as those Young Fellows at the *Grecian*,[3] *Squire's*, *Searle's*, and all other Coffee-houses adjacent to the Law, who rise early for no other purpose but to publish their Laziness. One would think these young *Virtuoso's* take a gay Cap and Slippers, with a Scarf and Party-colour'd Gown, to be Ensigns of Dignity; for the vain Things approach each other with an Air, which shows they regard one another for their Vestments. I have observed, that the Superiority among these proceeds from an Opinion of Gallantry and Fashion: The Gentleman in the Strawberry Sash, who presides so much over the rest, has, it seems, subscribed to every Opera this last Winter, and is supposed to receive Favours from one of the Actresses.

When the Day grows too busie for these Gentlemen to enjoy any longer the Pleasures of their *Deshabilé*, with any manner of Confidence, they give Place to Men who have Business or good Sense

---

[1] James Heywood, a wholesale linen-draper of Fish Street Hill, has been suggested as the original of this character. See Austin Dobson, *Selections from Steele*, pp. 467, 473. For Heywood see No. 268 (vol. ii).

[2] To loiter over one's work, to dawdle. *Obs*. (*OED*).

[3] See No. 1. Squire's Coffee-house was situated in Fuller's-Rents in Holborn, a street extending north from High Holborn to Field Court in Gray's Inn. It is here that Sir Roger invites Mr. Spectator 'to smoke a Pipe with him over a Dish of Coffee' (No. 269 (vol. ii)). Searle's Coffee-house stood on the corner of Searle and Portugal Streets, south of Lincoln's Inn Fields. All three coffee-houses were near the Inns of Court—the Grecian by the Temple, Squire's by Gray's Inn, and Searle's by Lincoln's Inn.

in their Faces, and come to the Coffee-house either to transact Affairs or enjoy Conversation. The Persons to whose Behaviour and Discourse I have most regard, are such as are between these two sorts of Men: Such as have not Spirits too Active to be happy and well pleased in a private Condition, nor Complexions too warm to make them neglect the Duties and Relations of Life. Of these sort of Men consist the worthier Part of Mankind; of these are all good Fathers, generous Brothers, sincere Friends, and faithful Subjects. Their Entertainments are derived rather from Reason than Imagination: Which is the Cause that there is no Impatience or Instability in their Speech or Action. You see in their Countenances they are at home, and in quiet Possession of the present Instant, as it passes, without desiring to Quicken it by gratifying any Passion, or prosecuting any new Design. These are the Men formed for Society, and those little Communities which we express by the Word *Neighbourhoods*.

The Coffee-house is the Place of Rendezvous to all that live near it, who are thus turned to relish calm and ordinary Life. *Eubulus* presides over the middle Hours of the Day, when this Assembly of Men meet together. He enjoys a great Fortune handsomely, without launching into Expence, and exerts many noble and useful Qualities, without appearing in any publick Employment. His Wisdom and Knowledge are serviceable to all that think fit to make use of them; and he does the Office of a Council, a Judge, an Executor, and a Friend to all his Acquaintance, not only without the Profits which attend such Offices, but also without the Deference and Homage which are usually paid to them. The giving of Thanks is displeasing to him. The greatest Gratitude you can show him, is to let him see you are the better Man for his Services; and that you are as ready to oblige others, as he is to oblige you.

In the private Exigencies of his Friends he lends, at legal Value, considerable Sums, which he might highly increase by rolling[1] in the Publick Stocks. He does not consider in whose Hands his Mony will improve most, but where it will do most Good.

Eubulus has so great an Authority in his little Diurnal Audience, that when he shakes his Head at any Piece of publick News, they all of them appear dejected; and, on the contrary, go home to their

---

[1] The sense here is identified in *OED* ('roll', 19b) as 'to dabble, speculate in (stocks)' and marked obsolete. This quotation provides the only actual instance of the word known in this sense.

Dinners with a good Stomach and chearful Aspect, when *Eubulus* seems to intimate that Things go well. Nay, their Veneration towards him is so great, that when they are in other Company they speak and act after him; are Wise in his Sentences, and are no sooner sat down at their own Tables, but they hope or fear, rejoice or despond as they saw him do at the Coffee-house. In a word, every Man is *Eubulus* as soon as his Back is turn'd.

Having here given an Account of the several Reigns that succeed each other from Day-break 'till Dinner-time,[1] I shall mention the Monarchs of the Afternoon on another occasion, and shut up the whole Series of them with the History of *Tom* the Tyrant;[2] who, as first Minister of the Coffee-house, takes the Government upon him between the Hours of Eleven and Twelve at Night, and gives his Orders in the most Arbitrary manner to the Servants below him, as to the Disposition of Liquors, Coal and Cinders.   R

No. 50   *Friday, April 27, 1711*[3]
[ADDISON]

Nunquam aliud Natura, aliud Sapientia dicit.
                                                                    Juv.

W HEN the four *Indian* Kings[4] were in this Country about a Twelve-month ago, I often mix'd with the Rabble and followed them a whole Day together, being wonderfully struck with the Sight of every thing that is new or uncommon. I have, since their Departure, employed a Friend to make many Enquiries of their

---

[1] Steele had written in *Tatler* 263: 'In my own Memory, the Dinner has crept by degrees from Twelve a Clock to Three, and where it will fix no body knows.' In the *Journal to Stella* Swift speaks of dining on 10 July 1711 with the Lord Treasurer: 'we did not sit down till four'; and again on the 28th with him at Windsor at five o'clock. See also Ashton, i. 186.

[2] Apparently the waiter at White's chocolate-house, the 'Sir Thomas' mentioned in *Tatlers* 16 and 26.

[3] *Motto*. Juvenal, *Satires*, 14. 321:
        Never does nature say one thing and wisdom another.

[4] In April 1710 four Iroquois sachems, or 'Kings', had visited London, accompanied by Col. Peter Schuyler and other colonial leaders, in order to solicit aid from the home government for military operations against the French in Canada. They had an audience of Queen Anne on 19 April, and were taken to see the principal sights of London. For an account of the visit and its echoes in contemporary journalism see Richmond P. Bond, *Queen Anne's American Kings* (Oxford, 1952).

Landlord[1] the Upholsterer relating to their Manners and Conversa-
tion, as also concerning the Remarks which they made in this
Country: For next to the forming a right Notion of such Strangers,
I should be desirous of learning what Ideas they have conceived of us.

The Upholsterer finding my Friend very inquisitive about these
his Lodgers, brought him some time since a little Bundle of Papers,
which he assured him were written by King *Sa Ga Yean Qua Rash
Tow*, and, as he supposes, left behind by some Mistake. These
Papers are now translated, and contain abundance of very odd
Observations, which I find this little Fraternity of Kings made
during their Stay in the Isle of *Great Britain*. I shall present my
Reader with a short Specimen of them in this Paper, and may perhaps communicate more to him hereafter. In the Article of *London*
are the following Words, which without Doubt are meant of the
Church of St. *Paul*.[2]

'On the most rising Part of the Town there stands a huge House,
big enough to contain the whole Nation of which I am King. Our
good Brother *E Tow O Koam* King of the *Rivers*, is of Opinion it was
made by the Hands of that great God to whom it is consecrated.
The Kings of *Granajah* and of the *Six Nations*[3] believe that it was
created with the Earth, and produced on the same Day with the
Sun and Moon. But for my own Part, by the best Information that
I could get of this Matter, I am apt to think that this prodigious Pile
was fashioned into the Shape it now bears by several Tools and
Instruments, of which they have a wonderful Variety in this
Country. It was probably at first an huge mis-shapen Rock[4] that
grew upon the Top of the Hill, which the Natives of the Country
(after having cut it into a kind of regular Figure) bored and hollowed
with incredible Pains and Industry, till they had wrought in it all

---

[1] While in London the chiefs were lodged at the Two Crowns and Cushions in
King Street, Covent Garden, the shop of Thomas Arne the upholsterer (father of
Thomas Arne the musician and Mrs. Cibber the actress). *Tatler* 171 describes how
the kings 'did Honour to the Person where they lodged' by bestowing upon him the
name Cadaroque, 'the Name of the strongest Fort in their Part of the World'.

[2] St. Paul's Cathedral, designed by Sir Christopher Wren to replace the old building burnt in the Great Fire of 1666, had just been completed. Although services
were held in the choir as early as 1697, the last stone was not laid into position until
1710, by the surveyor's son Christopher Wren.

[3] Addison is here alluding, not very clearly, to the third and fourth kings, 'Oh
Nee Yeath Ton No Prow', called in England King of Ganajahhore, and 'Te Yee Neen
Ho Ga Prow', known as Emperor, and 'the ranking sachem of the quartet, at least
in ability and influence' (Bond, p. 39).

[4] Possibly a reminiscence of an anecdote in Martin Martin's *Description of the
Western Islands of Scotland* (1703), pp. 297–8. See Boswell's *Life of Johnson*, ed. Hill–
Powell, i. 450.

those beautiful Vaults and Caverns into which it is divided at this Day. As soon as this Rock was thus curiously scooped to their Liking, a prodigious Number of Hands must have been employed in chipping the Outside of it, which is now as smooth as the Surface of a Pebble;[a] and is in several Places hewn out into Pillars that stand like the Trunks of so many Trees bound about the Top with Garlands of Leaves. It is probable that when this great Work was begun, which must have been many Hundred Years ago, there was some Religion among this People; for they give it the Name of a Temple, and have a Tradition that it was designed for Men to pay their Devotions in. And indeed, there are several Reasons which make us think, that the Natives of this Country had formerly among them some sort of Worship; for they set apart every seventh Day as sacred: But upon my going into one of these[b] holy Houses on that Day, I could not observe any Circumstance of Devotion in their Behaviour: There was indeed a Man in Black who was mounted above the rest, and seemed to utter something with a great deal of Vehemence; but as for those underneath him, instead of paying their Worship to the Deity of the Place, they were most of them bowing and curtisying to one another, and a considerable Number of them fast asleep.

'The Queen of the Country appointed two Men to attend us, that had enough of our Language to make themselves understood in some few Particulars. But we soon perceived these two were great Enemies to one another, and did not always agree in the same Story. We could make a Shift to gather out of one of them, that this Island was very much infested with a monstrous Kind of Animals, in the Shape of Men, called *Whigs*; and he often told us, that he hoped we should meet with none of them in our Way, for that if we did, they would be apt to knock us down for being Kings.

'Our other Interpreter used to talk very much of a kind of Animal called a *Tory*, that was as great a Monster as the *Whig*, and would treat us as ill for being Foreigners. These two Creatures, it seems, are born with a secret Antipathy to one another, and engage when they meet as naturally as the Elephant and the Rhinoceros. But as we saw none of either of these Species, we are apt to think that our Guides deceived us with Misrepresentations and Fictions, and amused us with an Account of such Monsters as are not really in their Country.

[a] the Surface of a Pebble;] polished Marble; *Fol.*   [b] these] those *Fol.*

'These Particulars we made a Shift to pick out from the Discourse of our Interpreters; which we put together as well as we could, being able to understand but here and there a Word of what they said, and afterwards making up the Meaning of it among our selves. The Men of the Country are very cunning and ingenious in handicraft Works; but withal so very idle, that we often saw young lusty raw-boned Fellows carried up and down the Streets in little covered Rooms[1] by a Couple of Porters who are hired for that Service. Their Dress is likewise very barbarous, for they almost strangle themselves about the Neck, and bind their Bodies with many Ligatures, that we are apt to think are the Occasion of several Distempers among them which our Country is entirely free from. Instead of those beautiful Feathers with which we adorn our Heads, they often buy up a monstrous Bush of Hair, which covers their Heads, and falls down in a large Fleece below the Middle of their Backs; with which they walk up and down the Streets, and are as proud of it as if it was of their own Growth.

'We were invited to one of their publick Diversions, where we hoped to have seen the great Men of their Country running down a Stag or pitching a Bar, that we might have discover'd who were the Persons of the greatest Abilities among them;[a] but instead of that, they conveyed us into an huge Room lighted up with abundance of Candles, where this lazy People sat still above three Hours to see several Feats of Ingenuity performed by others, who it seems were paid for it.

'As for the Women of the Country, not being able to talk with them, we could only make our Remarks upon them at a Distance. They let the Hair of their Heads grow to a great Length; but as the Men make a great Show with Heads of Hair that are none of their own, the Women, who they say have very fine Heads of Hair, tie it up in a Knot and cover it from being seen. The Women look like Angels, and would be more beautiful than the Sun, were it not for little black Spots[2] that are apt to break out in their Faces, and sometimes rise in very odd Figures. I have observed that those little

---

[a] the Persons . . . among them;] the Men of the greatest Perfections in their Country; *Fol.*

---

[1] Cf. Koenig (p. 219): 'The Gentlemen are carryed . . . in Chairs, (or Sedans) which are here very cheap, a Guinea a Week, or a Shilling per Hour, and your Chairmen serve you for Porters, to run on Errands, as your Gondaliers do at *Venice.*'

[2] Patches are discussed later in No. 81.

Blemishes wear off very soon; but when they disappear in one Part of the Face, they are very apt to break out in another, insomuch that I have seen a Spot upon the Forehead in the Afternoon, which was upon the Chin in the Morning.'

The Author then proceeds to shew the Absurdity of Breeches and Petticoats, with many other curious Observations, which I shall reserve for another Occasion. I cannot however conclude this Paper without taking Notice, That amidst these wild Remarks there now and then appears something very reasonable. I cannot[a] likewise forbear observing, That we are all guilty in some Measure of the same narrow Way of Thinking which we meet with in this Abstract of the *Indian* Journal; when we fancy the Customs, Dresses, and Manners of other Countries are ridiculous and extravagant, if they do not resemble those of our own.   C[1]

No. 51   *Saturday, April 28, 1711*[2]
[STEELE]

Torquet ab Obscenis jam nunc Sermonibus Aurem!
                                                            Hor.

Mr. SPECTATOR,

'MY Fortune, Quality and Person, are such as render me as Conspicuous as any Young Woman in Town. It is in my Power to enjoy it in all its Vanities, but I have, from a very careful Education, contracted a great Aversion to the forward Air and Fashion which is practised in all Publick Places and Assemblies. I attribute this very much to the Stile and Manners of our Plays: I

---

[a] cannot] can't *Fol.*

[1] On the day following the publication of this paper Swift wrote in the *Journal to Stella*: 'The *Spectator* is written by Steele, with Addison's help: 'tis often very pretty. Yesterday it was made of a noble hint I gave him long ago for his *Tatlers*, about an Indian supposed to write his travels into England. I repent he ever had it. I intended to have written a book on that subject. I believe he has spent it all in one paper, and all the under-hints there are mine too; but I never see him or Addison.' On 29 April one J. H. writes to the *Spectator* complaining of improbabilities in the account: 'the memoirs you are pleased to father on the four Indian kings, are no more genuine than those that go under the name of the Turkish spy' (Lillie, i. 259).

[2] *Motto.* Horace, *Epistles*, 2. 1. 127:

Even then he turns the ear from obscene words.

was last Night at the *Funeral*,[1] where a Confident Lover in the Play, speaking of his Mistress, Cries out—*Oh that* Harriot! *to fold these Arms about the Waste of that Beauteous strugling, and at last yielding Fair!* Such an Image as this ought, by no means, to be presented to a Chaste and Regular Audience. I expect your Opinion of this Sentence, and recommend to your Consideration, as a SPECTATOR, the Conduct of the Stage at present, with Relation to Chastity and Modesty.

> *I am, SIR,*
> *Your Constant Reader,*
> *and Well-Wisher.'*

The Complaint of this Young Lady is so just, that the Offence is gross enough to have displeased Persons who cannot pretend to that Delicacy and Modesty, of which she is Mistress. But there is a great deal to be said in Behalf of an Author; if the Audience would but consider the Difficulty of keeping up a sprightly Dialogue for five Acts together, they would allow a Writer, when he wants Wit, and can't please any otherwise, to help it out with a little Smuttiness. I will answer for the Poets, that no one ever writ Bawdry[a] for any other Reason but Dearth of Invention. When the Author cannot strike out of himself any more of that which he has superior to those who make up the Bulk of his Audience, his natural Recourse is to that which he has in common with them; and a Description which gratifies a sensual Appetite will please, when the Author has nothing about him to delight[b] a refined Imagination. It is to such a Poverty we must impute this and all other Sentences in Plays, which are of this kind, and which are commonly term'd Luscious Expressions.

This Expedient, to supply the Deficiences of Wit, has been used, more or less, by most of the Authors who have succeeded on the Stage; tho' I know but one who has professedly writ a Play upon

---

[a] Bawdry] Bawdy *Fol.*   [b] about him to delight] else to gratifie *Fol.*

---

[1] *The Funeral.* Steele's first comedy, published in December 1701. The passage quoted is from the first edition (II. i); the revised text reads:

> CAMPLEY. O that Harriot! to Embrace that Beauteous—
> LORD HARDY. Ay Tom . . .

The Funeral had been performed, with Wilks as Campley, at Drury Lane on 26 Apr., i.e. the Thursday evening before the publication of this paper. The letter, purporting to be written on Friday the 27th, may be genuine; if so, very little time was allowed Steele for the writing of the essay, delivery to the printer, setting up in type, and delivery to readers by Saturday morning. One suspects the correspondent to be Steele himself.

the Basis of the Desire of Multiplying our Species, and that is the Polite Sir *George Etherege*; if I understand what the Lady would be at, in the Play called *She would if she could*.[1] Other Poets have, here and there, given an Intimation that there is this Design, under all the Disguises and Affectations which a Lady may put on; but no Author, except this, has made sure Work of it, and put the Imaginations of the Audience upon this one Purpose, from the Beginning to the End of the Comedy. It has always fared accordingly; for whether it be, that all who go to this Piece would if they could, or that the Innocents go to it, to guess only what *She would if she could*, the Play has always been well received.

It lifts an heavy empty Sentence, when there is added to it a lascivious Gesture of Body; and when it is too low to be raised even by that, a flat Meaning is enlivened by making it a double one. Writers, who want *Genius*, never fail of keeping this Secret in reserve, to create a Laugh, or raise a Clap. I, who know nothing of Women but from seeing Plays, can give great Guesses at the whole Structure of the fair Sex, by being innocently placed in the Pitt, and Insulted by the Petticoats of their Dancers; the Advantages of whose pretty Persons are a great help to a dull Play. When a Poet flags in writing Lusciously, a pretty Girl can move Lasciviously, and have the same good Consequence for the Author. Dull Poets in this Case use their Audiences, as dull Parasites do their Patrons; when they cannot longer divert them with their Wit or Humour, they bait their Ears with something which is agreeable to their Temper, though below their Understanding.[a] *Apicius*[2] cannot resist being pleased, if you give him an Account of a delicious Meal; or *Clodius*,[3] if you describe a Wanton Beauty: Tho' at the same time, if you do not awake those Inclinations in them, no Men are better Judges of what is just and delicate in Conversation. But, as I have before observed, it is easier to talk to the Man, than to the Man of Sense.

It is remarkable, that the Writers of least Learning are best skill'd

[a] when they cannot longer . . . Understanding.] when they cannot longer divert him with their Wit or Humour, they bait his Ears with something which is agreeable to his Temper, though below his Understanding. *Fol.*

[1] Etherege's comedy had been produced at Drury Lane on 19 Mar., with Mrs. Knight as Lady Cockwood.
[2] M. Gabius Apicius was a famous gourmet of the time of Tiberius (see Martial, *Epigrams*, 3. 22).
[3] P. Clodius Pulcher, the noted profligate who profaned the mysteries of the Bona Dea (cf. No. 217 (vol. ii)).

in the luscious Way. The Poetesses of the Age have done Wonders in this kind; and we are obliged to the Lady who writ *Ibrahim*,[1] for introducing a preparatory Scene to the very Action, when the Emperor throws his Handkerchief as a Signal for his Mistress to follow him into the most retired part of the Seraglio. It must be confessed his *Turkish* Majesty went off with a good Air, but, me-thought, we made but a sad Figure who waited without. This ingenious Gentlewoman, in this piece of Bawdry, refined upon an Author of the same Sex, who, in the *Rover*,[2] makes a Country Squire strip to his Holland Drawers. For *Blunt* is disappointed, and the Emperor is understood to go on to the utmost. The Pleasantry of Stripping almost Naked has been since practised (where indeed it should have been begun) very successfully at *Bartholomew* Fair.[3]

It is not here to be omitted, that in one of the above-mentioned Female Compositions, the *Rover* is very frequently sent on the same Errand; as I take it, above once every Act. This is not wholly un-natural, for, they say, the Men-Authors draw themselves in their

---

[1] *Ibrahim, the thirteenth Emperour of the Turks*, a tragedy by Mrs. Mary Pix, first given in 1696. It was not in the current repertory; Genest (ii. 74–75) records a per-formance on 20 Oct. 1702. It was revived on 14 Mar. 1715. For Madeleine de Scudéry's novel, *Ibrahim ou l'illustre Bassa* (1641) and later treatments of the theme, see Clarence D. Rouillard, *The Turk in French History, Thought and Literature (1520–1660)* (Paris, 1940), pp. 546–71. The scene mentioned by Steele occurs in Act I; the stage directions (p. 4) read: 'The Scene draws and discovers the Ladies set in Order for the Sultans Choice, who takes out his Handkerchief, and walks round them; whilst *Sheker Para* talks to *Achmet*. . . . The Sultan drops his Handkerchief, which the Lady falling prostrate, kisses, and takes up, and is led off by two Eunuchs; the Sultan following, the Scene shuts upon the rest.' The dropping of a handkerchief seems to have been recognized as a symbol even before Mrs. Pix's play. In the opening scene of Shadwell's *Scowrers* (1691) Sir William Rant's valet announces to his master that he has lodged two wenches 'in two several Apartments of your Seraglio, not knowing which of them you would vouchsafe your Handkerchief to'.

[2] *The Rover, or the Banish't Cavaliers* (1677), by Mrs. Aphra Behn. The disappoint-ment of Blunt refers to a trick played upon him by Lucetta in Act III, scene ii. As Blunt 'goes toward the Bed in his shirt, Drawers, &c.' he 'lights on a Trap, and is let down'. *The Rover* had been given recently at Drury Lane (on 22 Mar.), with Estcourt in the role of Ned Blunt.

[3] Bartholomew Fair began each year on St. Bartholomew's Day (24 Aug.) in the three-acre plot known as West Smithfield, north of Newgate. The first part, lasting three days, featured a cattle fair; 'but that for Toys, and the Diversions of Drolls, Rope-dancing, and strange Creatures, lasts a Fortnight' (Hatton, p. 87). Henry Morley's *Memoirs of Bartholomew Fair* (1857) gives many anecdotes. 'A Letter from an Actress of the Play House, to a Stroler in the Country, concerning Reformation of Manners, and the Suppression of Drolls in Bartholomew Fair', published in *A Pacquet from Will's: or, a Collection of Diverting Letters* (2nd ed., 1705), explains Steele's allusion. Although the drolls and music houses are to be suppressed, 'they have suffer'd the Dancers of the Ropes, to stir up Concupiscence in Youth, by showing at once, both their Ar—s and their Activity' (p. 221). According to Nichols it was the appearance of Lady Mary, a rope-dancer at Bartholomew Fair, which gave occasion to Steele's 'very proper animadversion'.

chief Characters, and the Women-Writers may be allow'd the same Liberty. Thus, as the Male Wit gives his Hero a great Fortune, the Female gives her Heroin a good Gallant at the end of the Play. But, indeed, there is hardly a Play one can go to, but the Hero or fine Gentleman of it struts off upon the same account, and leaves us to consider what good Office he has put us to, or to employ our selves as we please. To be plain, a Man who frequents Plays, would have a very respectful Notion of himself, were he to recollect how often he has been used as a Pimp to ravishing Tyrants, or successful Rakes. When the Actors make their *Exit* on this good Occasion, the Ladies are sure to have an examining Glance from the Pit, to see how they relish what passes, and a few lewd Fools are very ready to employ their Talents upon the Composure or Freedom of their Looks. Such Incidents as these make some Ladies wholly absent themselves from the Play-House; and others never miss the first Day of a Play,[1] lest it should prove too luscious to admit their going with any Countenance to it on the second.

If Men of Wit, who think fit to write for the Stage, instead of this pitiful way of giving Delight, would turn their Thoughts upon raising it from good natural Impulses as are in the Audience, but are Choaked up by Vice and Luxury, they would not only please, but befriend us at the same time. If a Man had a mind to be new in his way of Writing, might not he, who is now represented as a fine Gentleman, tho' he betrays the Honour and Bed of his Neighbour and Friend, and lyes with half the Women in the Play, and is at last rewarded with her of the best Character in it, I say, upon giving the Comedy another Cast, might not such a one divert the Audience quite as well, if at the Catastrophe he were found out for a Traytor, and met with Contempt accordingly. There is seldom a Person devoted to above one Darling Vice at a time, so that there is room enough to catch at Mens Hearts to their Good and Advantage, if the Poets will attempt it with the Honesty which becomes their Characters.

There is no Man who loves his Bottle or his Mistress, in a manner so very abandon'd, as not to be capable of relishing an agreeable Character, that is, no way a Slave to either of those Pursuits. A Man that is Temperate, Generous, Valiant, Chaste, Faithful and Honest,

---

[1] 'On the first night of the exhibition of a new play, virtuous women about this time came to see it in masks, then worn by women of the town, as the characteristic mark of their being prostitutes' (Nichols).

may, at the same time, have Wit, Humour,[a] Mirth, good Breeding, and Gallantry. While he exerts these latter Qualities, twenty Occasions might be invented to shew he is Master of the other noble Virtues. Such Characters wou'd smite and reprove the Heart of a Man of Sense, when he is given up to his Pleasures. He would see he has been mistaken all this while, and be convinced that a sound Constitution and an innocent Mind are the true Ingredients for becoming and enjoying Life. All Men of true Taste would call a Man of Wit, who should turn his Ambition this way, a Friend and Bene-factor to his Country; but I am at a loss what Name they would give him, who makes use of his Capacity for contrary Purposes.   R

No. 52   *Monday, April* 30, 1711[1]
[STEELE]

> *Omnes ut Tecum meritis pro Talibus annos*
> *Exigat, & pulchra faciat Te prole parentem.*
>   Virg.

AN ingenious Correspondent, like a sprightly Wife, will always have the last Word. I did not think my last Letter[2] to the deformed Fraternity would have occasioned any Answer, especially since I had promised them so sudden a Visit: But as they think they cannot shew too great a Veneration for my Person, they have already sent me up an Answer. As to the Proposal of a Marriage between my self and the matchless *Hecatissa*, I have but one Objection to it; which is, That all the Society will expect to be acquainted with her; and who can be sure of keeping a Woman's Heart long, where she may have so much Choice? I am the more alarmed at this, because the Lady seems particularly smitten with Men of their Make.

I believe I shall set my Heart upon her; and think never the worse of my Mistress for an Epigram[3] a smart Fellow writ, as he thought,

---

[a] Humour,] Honour, *Fol. Corrected in Errata* (*No. 53*)

[1] *Motto.* Virgil, *Aeneid*, i. 74–75:
> For these thy great Deserts she shall be thine,
> And make thee Father of a happy Line.

[2] No. 48.

[3] This is one of the epigrams ascribed to Martial (iv. *De Vetula*).

against her; it does but the more recommend her to me. At the same Time I cannot but discover that his Malice is stolen from *Martial*.

> *Tacta places, Audita places, si non videare*
> *Tota places, neutro, si videare, places.*

> *Whilst in the Dark on thy soft Hand I hung,*
> *And heard the tempting* Syren *in thy Tongue,*
> *What Flames, what Darts, what Anguish I endur'd?*
> *But when the Candle enter'd I was cur'd.*

'Your Letter to us we have receiv'd, as a signal Mark of your Favour and brotherly Affection. We shall be heartily glad to see your short Face in *Oxford*: And since the Wisdom of our Legislature has been immortaliz'd in your Speculations, and our personal Deformities in some sort by you recorded to all Posterity; we hold our selves in Gratitude bound to receive with the highest Respect, all such Persons as for their extraordinary Merit you shall think fit from Time to Time to recommend unto the Board. As for the Pictish Damsel, we have an easy Chair prepar'd at the upper End of the Table; which we doubt not but she will grace with a very hideous Aspect, and much better become the Seat in the native and unaffected Uncomeliness of her Person, than with all the superficial Airs of the Pencil, which (as you have very ingeniously observ'd)[1] vanish with a Breath, and the most innocent Adorer may deface the Shrine with a Salutation, and in the literal Sense of our Poets, snatch and imprint his balmy Kisses, and devour her melting Lips: In short, the only Faces of the Pictish Kind that will endure the Weather, must be of Dr. *Carbuncle's*[2] Die, tho' his, in truth, has cost him a World the Painting; but then he boasts with *Zeuxis*, *In eternitatem pingo*;[3] and oft jocously tells the Fair ones, Would they acquire Colours that would stand kissing, they must no longer Paint but Drink for a Complexion: A Maxim that in this our Age has been pursu'd with no ill Success; and has been as admirable in its Effects, as the famous Cosmetick[4] mention'd in the *Post-man*, and invented

[1] No. 41.
[2] For Carbuncle's letters see Nos. 17 and 32.
[3] Plutarch, *Life of Pericles*, 159 D; 'On having many Friends', *Moralia*, 94 F; see Bayle, art. 'Zeuxis', Remark H. Among the ancients Zeuxis 'was most famous for his colouring' (Dryden, 'Parallel of Poetry and Painting', *Essays*, ed. Ker, ii. 148).
[4] There are many cosmetics advertised in the *Post-Man*—'The Royal Beautifier', sold only at Lemery's Head at Charing Cross; the 'Incomparable Beautifying Cream', sold only at Mr. Lawrence's Toyshop, &c.—as well as in the *Spectator*. One of the most frequently advertised is the 'Christal Cosmetick approv'd of by the worthy

by the renowned *British Hippocrates* of the Pestle and Mortar; making the Party, after a due Course, rosy, hale and airy; and the best and most approv'd Receipt now extant for the Feaver o' th' Spirits. But to return to our female Candidate, who, I understand, is return'd to her self, and will no longer hang out false Colours; as she is the first of her Sex that has done us so great an Honour, she will certainly, in a very short Time, both in Prose and Verse, be a Lady of the most celebrated Deformity now living; and meet with Admirers here as frightful as her self. But being a long-headed Gentlewoman, I am apt to imagine she has some further Design than you have yet penetrated; and perhaps has more Mind to the SPECTATOR than any of his Fraternity, as the Person of all the World she could like for a Paramour: And if so, really I cannot but applaud her Choice; and should be glad, if it might lie in my Power, to effect an amicable Accommodation betwixt two Faces of such different Extremes, as the only possible Expedient to mend the Breed, and rectify the Phiziognomy of the Family on both Sides. And again, as she is a Lady of a very fluent Elocution, you need not fear that your first Child will be born dumb, which otherwise you might have some Reason to be apprehensive of. To be plain with you, I can see nothing shocking in it; for tho' she has not a Face like a *John-Apple*,[1] yet, as a late Friend of mine, who at Sixty five ventur'd on a Lass of Fifteen, very frequently, in the remaining five Years of his Life, gave me to understand, That, as old as he then seem'd, when they were first married he and his Spouse could both make but Fourscore; so may Madam *Hecatissa* very justly alledge hereafter, That, as long visag'd as she may then be thought, upon their Wedding-day Mr. SPECTATOR and she had but Half an Ell of Face betwixt them: And this my very worthy Predecessor Mr. Sergeant *Chin* always maintain'd to be no more than the true oval Proportion between Man and Wife.

Dr. Paul Chamberlaine' (quoted above in notes to No. 33). Another advertised in *Spectator* 124 and frequently thereafter is:

The famous Bavarian Red Liquor:

Which gives such a delightful blushing Colour to the Cheeks of those that are White or Pale, that it is not [to] be distinguished from a natural fine Complexion, nor perceived to be artificial by the nearest Friend. Is nothing of Paint, or in the least hurtful, but good in many Cases to be taken inwardly. It renders the Face delightfully handsome and beautiful; is not subject to be rubb'd off like Paint, therefore cannot be discovered by the nearest Friend. It is certainly the best Beautifier in the World. Is sold only at Mr. Payn's Toyshop, at the Angel and Crown in St. Paul's Church-yard near Cheapside, at 3s. 6d. a Bottle, with Directions.

[1] 'An apple said to keep two years, and to be ripe when much withered' (*OED*).

But as this may be a new thing to you, who have hitherto had no Expectations from Women, I shall allow you what Time you think fit to consider on't; not without some Hope of seeing at last your Thoughts hereupon subjoyn'd to mine, and which is an Honour much desired by

Sir,
Your assured Friend,
And most humble Servant,
Hugh Goblin Præses.'

The following Letter has not much in it, but as it is written in my own Praise I cannot for my Heart suppress it.

SIR,

'YOU propos'd in your SPECTATOR of last *Tuesday*[1] Mr. *Hobbs's* Hypothesis, for solving that very odd Phænomenon of Laughter. You have made the Hypothesis valuable by espousing it your self; for had it continued Mr. *Hobbs's*, no Body would have minded it. Now here this perplex'd Case arises, A certain Company laugh'd very heartily upon the Reading of that very Paper of yours: And the Truth on't is, he must be a Man of more than ordinary Constancy that could stand it out against so much Comedy, and not do as we did. Now there are few Men in the World so far lost to all good Sense, as to look upon you to be a Man in a State of Folly *inferior to himself.* Pray then, how do you justify your Hypothesis of Laughter?

'Thursday, *the 26th of*   *Your most humble,*
  the Month of Fools.'   Q. R.'

SIR,

'IN answer to your Letter, I must desire you to recollect your self; and you will find, that when you did me the Honour to be so merry over my Paper, you laugh'd at the Ideot, the *German* Courtier, the Gaper, the Merry-Andrew, the Haberdasher, the Biter, the Butt, and not at

Your humble Servant,
The SPECTATOR.'

R

[1] See No. 47.

No. 53   *Tuesday, May 1, 1711*[1]
[STEELE]

. . . Aliquando bonus dormitat Homerus.
Hor.

MY Correspondents grow so numerous, that I cannot avoid frequently inserting their Applications to me.

Mr. SPECTATOR,

'I AM glad I can inform you, that your Endeavours to adorn that Sex, which is the fairest Part of the visible Creation, are well receiv'd, and like to prove not unsuccessful. The Triumph of *Daphne*[2] over her Sister *Letitia* has been the Subject of Conversation at several Tea-Tables where I have been present; and I have observ'd the fair Circle not a little pleas'd to find you considering them as reasonable Creatures, and endeavouring to banish that *Mahometan* Custom[3] which had too much prevail'd even in this Island, of treating Women as if they had no Souls. I must do them the Justice to say, that there seems to be nothing wanting to the finishing of these lovely Pieces of Human Nature, besides the turning and applying their Ambition properly, and the keeping them up to a Sense of what is their true Merit. *Epictetus*,[4] that plain honest Philosopher, as little as he had of Gallantry, appears to have understood them, as well as the Polite *St. Evremont*,[5] and has hit this Point very luckily. *When Young Women,* says he, *arrive at a certain Age, they hear themselves call'd* Mistresses, *and are made to believe that their only Business is to please the Men; They immediately begin to dress, and place all their Hopes in the adorning of their Persons; it is therefore,* continues he, *worth the while to endeavour by all Means to make them sensible that the Honour pay'd to them is only upon Account of their conducting themselves with Virtue, Modesty, and Discretion.*

---

¹ *Motto.* Horace, *Ars poetica*, 359 (altered):
    Homer himself hath been observ'd to nod. ROSCOMMON.

² No. 33.
³ Writers on Turkey were fond of pointing out that women in Islam occupied a degraded position and were even barred from Paradise. According to Jean de Thévenot, *Travels into the Levant* (1687), part i, p. 56, 'The Turks do not believe that women go to Heaven, and hardly account them Rational Creatures'. For earlier examples see Clarence D. Rouillard, *The Turk in French History, Thought and Literature* (*1520–1660*) (Paris, 1940), pp. 267–8, 324–6.
⁴ *Epictetus his Morals, with Simplicius his Comment*, translated by George Stanhope (1694), p. 486.
⁵ Cf. No. 33.

'Now to pursue the Matter yet further, and to render your Cares for the Improvement of the Fair Ones more effectual, I wou'd propose a new Method, like those Applications which are said to convey their Virtue by Sympathy;[1] and that is, that in order to embellish the Mistress, you shou'd give a new Education to the Lover, and teach the Men not to be any longer dazl'd by false Charms and unreal Beauty. I cannot but think that if our Sex knew always how to place their Esteem justly, the other wou'd not be so often wanting to themselves in deserving it. For as the being enamour'd with a Woman of Sense and Virtue is an Improvement to a Man's Understanding and Morals, and the Passion is ennobled by the Object which inspires it; so on the other Side, the appearing amiable to a Man of a wise and elegant Mind, carries in it self no small Degree of Merit and Accomplishment. I conclude therefore, that one way to make the Women yet more agreeable is, to make the Men more Virtuous.

> I am, SIR,
> Your most humble Servant,
> R. B.'[2]

SIR, *April 26.*

'YOURS of *Saturday* last[3] I read, not without some Resentment; but I will suppose when you say you expect an Inundation of Ribbons and Brocades, and to see many new Vanities which the Women will fall into upon a Peace with *France*, that you intend only the unthinking part of our Sex: And what Methods can reduce them to Reason is hard to imagine.

'But, Sir, there are others yet that your Instructions might be of great use to, who, after their best Endeavours, are sometimes at a loss to acquit themselves to a Censorious World: I am far from thinking you can altogether disapprove of Conversation between Ladies and Gentlemen, regulated by the Rules of Honour and Prudence, and have thought it an Observation not ill made, that where that was wholly denied the Women lost their Wit, and the Men their good Manners. 'Tis sure, from those improper Liberties you

---

[1] The 'sympathetic powder' was thought to heal wounds by 'sympathy' or affinity on being applied to a cloth stained with blood from the wound (or to the weapon with which the wound was inflicted). See Sir Kenelm Digby, *A Late Discourse touching the Cure of Wounds by the Powder of Sympathy* (1658).

[2] This letter is listed as by John Hughes in Duncombe's preface to Hughes's *Poems* (1735). Like the letter in No. 33 this is signed R. B. and also cites St. Evremond.

[3] No. 45.

mentioned, that a sort of undistinguishing People shall banish from their Drawing-Rooms the best bred Men in the World, and condemn those that do not. Your stating this Point might, I think, be of good use, as well as much oblige,

SIR,

Your Admirer, and

most Humble Servant,

ANNA BELLA.'

No Answer to this, 'till Anna Bella *sends a Description of those she calls the Best bred Men in the World.*

Mr. SPECTATOR,

'I AM a Gentleman who for many Years last past have been well know to be truly Splenatick, and that my Spleen[1] arises from having contracted so great a Delicacy, by reading the best Authors, and keeping the most refined Company, that I cannot bear the least Impropriety of Language, or Rusticity of Behaviour. Now, Sir, I have ever look'd upon this as a wise Distemper, but by late Observations find that every heavy Wretch, who has nothing to say, excuses his Dulness by complaining of the Spleen. Nay, I saw, the other Day, two Fellows in a Tavern Kitchen set up for it, call for a Pint and Pipes, and only by Guzling Liquor to each other's Health, and wafting Smoak in each other's Face, pretend to throw off the Spleen. I appeal to you, whether these Dishonours are to be done to the Distemper of the Great and the Polite. I beseech you, Sir, to inform these Fellows that they have not the Spleen, because they cannot talk without the help of a Glass at their Mouths, or convey their Meaning to each other without the Interposition of Clouds. If you

---

[1] The spleen—in women the vapours—was the fashionable distemper so often referred to in the literature of the day. Of contemporary accounts the best known is perhaps Pope's description of the Cave of the Spleen in book iv of *The Rape of the Lock.* For other references see Lawrence Babb, *The Elizabethan Malady* (East Lansing, Mich., 1951). The symptoms of the spleen, or the vapours, would seem to indicate maladies now called 'nervous disorders'. The following advertisement appears first in No. 124 and several times thereafter:

The Vapours in Women infallibly Cured in an Instant, so as never to return again, by an admirable Chymical Secret, a few drops of which takes off a Fit in a Moment, dispels Sadness, clears the Head, takes away all Swimming, Giddiness, Dimness of Sight, Flushings in the Face, &c. to a Miracle, and most certainly prevents the Vapours returning again; for by Rooting out the very Cause it perfectly Cures as Hundreds have experienc'd: It also strengthens the Stomach and Bowels, and causes Liveliness and settled Health. Is sold only at Mrs. Osborn's, Toy-shop, at the Rose and Crown under St. Dunstan's Church in Fleet-street, at 2s. 6d. the Bottle, with directions.

will not do this with all speed, I assure you, for my part, I will wholly quit the Disease, and for the future be merry with the Vulgar.

I am, SIR,
Your Humble Servant.'

SIR,

'THIS is to let you understand, that I am a reformed Starer,[1] and conceived a Detestation for that Practice from what you have writ upon the Subject. But as you have been very severe upon the Behaviour of us Men at Divine Service, I hope you will not be so apparently partial to the Women, as to let them go wholly unobserved. If they do every thing that is possible to attract our Eyes, are we more culpable than they for looking at them? I happen'd last *Sunday* to be shut into a Pew, which was full of young Ladies in the Bloom of Youth and Beauty. When the Service began, I had not room to kneel at the Confession, but as I stood kept my Eyes from wandring as well as I was able, 'till one of the young Ladies, who is a Peeper, resolved to bring down my Looks, and fix my Devotion on her self. You are to know, Sir, that a Peeper works with her Hands, Eyes, and Fan; one of which is continually in motion, while she thinks she is not actually the Admiration of some Ogler or Starer in the Congregation. As I stood utterly at a loss how to behave my self, surrounded as I was, this Peeper so placed her self as to be kneeling just before me. She display'd the most beautiful Bosom imaginable, which heav'd and fell with some fervour, while a delicate well-shaped Arm held a Fan over her Face. It was not in Nature to command ones Eyes from this Object; I could not avoid taking notice also of her Fan, which had on it various Figures, very improper to behold on that occasion. There lay in the Body of the Piece a *Venus*, under a Purple Canopy furled with curious Wreaths of Drapery, half naked, attended with a Train of *Cupids*, who were busied in Fanning her as she slept. Behind her was drawn a Satyr peeping over the silken Fence, and threatning to break through it. I frequently offer'd to turn my Sight another way, but was still detained by the Fascination of the Peeper's Eyes, who had long practised a skill in them, to recal the parting Glances of her Beholders. You see my Complaint, and hope you will take these mischievous People, the Peepers, into your Consideration: I doubt

---

[1] See No. 20.

not but you will think a Peeper as much more pernicious than a Starer, as an Ambuscade is more to be feared than an open Assault.

I am, SIR,

Your most Obedient Servant.'

This Peeper using both Fan and Eyes to be consider'd as a Pict, *and proceed accordingly.*

King Latinus[1] *to the* Spectator, *Greeting.*

'THO' some may think we descend from our Imperial Dignity, in holding Corespondence with a private *Litterati*; yet as we have great Respect to all Good Intentions for our Service, we do not esteem it beneath us to return you our Royal Thanks for what you published in our Behalf, while under Confinement in the Inchanted Castle of the *Savoy*, and for your Mention of a Subsidy for a Prince in Misfortune. This your timely Zeal has inclined the Hearts of divers to be aiding unto us, if we could propose the Means. We have taken their Good-will into Consideration, and have contrived a Method which will be easy to those who shall give the Aid, and not unacceptable to us who receive it. A Consort of Musick shall be prepared at *Haberdashers-hall*[2] for *Wednesday* the Second of *May*, and we will honour the said Entertainment with our own Presence, where each Person shall be assessed but at two Shillings and Six Pence. What we expect from you is, that you publish these our Royal Intentions, with Injunction that they be read at all Tea-Tables within the Cities of *London* and *Westminster*, and so we bid you heartily Farewell.

Latinus, *King of the* Volscians.'

Given at our Court in Vinegar
Yard,[3] *Story the* 3d *from the*
Earth. April 28, 1711.

R

---

[1] See No. 22.

[2] Haberdashers-hall was on the north side of Maiden Lane near Woodstreet, not far from Aldersgate. It was a plain brick building with a large hall paved with marble, and here musical concerts were frequently held. Two days before the date of this letter the following advertisement appeared in No. 49:

At Stationers-Hall, this present Thursday the 26th of this Instant, will be perform'd a Consort of Vocal and Instrumental Musick, by the best Masters, for the Benefit of Mr. Dean; beginning at Seven a Clock. Tickets at Half a Crown each.

[3] Vinegar Yard was a small street running west from Drury Lane just south of Drury Lane Theatre. Latinus was a character in the opera *Camilla* (see Nos. 18 and 22).

. . . Strenua nos exercet inertia.

Hor.

THE following Letter[2] being the first that I have received from the learned University of *Cambridge*, I could not but do my self the Honour of publishing it. It gives an Account of a new Sect of Philosophers which has arose in that famous Residence of Learning; and is, perhaps, the only Sect this Age is likely to produce.

Mr. SPECTATOR,   *Cambridge, April 26.*

'BELIEVING you to be an universal Encourager of liberal Arts and Sciences, and glad of any Information from the learned World, I thought an Account of a Sect of Philosophers very frequent among us, but not taken Notice of, as far as I can remember, by any Writers either ancient or modern, would not be unacceptable to you. The Philosophers of this Sect are in the Language of our University call'd *Lowngers*. I am of Opinion, that, as in many other things, so likewise in this, the Ancients have been defective; *viz.* in mentioning no Philosophers of this Sort. Some indeed will affirm that they are a kind of Peripateticks, because we see them continually walking about. But I would have these Gentlemen consider, that though the ancient Peripateticks walk'd much, yet they wrote much also; (witness, to the Sorrow of this Sect, *Aristotle* and others): Whereas it is notorious that most of our Professors never lay out a Farthing either in Pen, Ink, or Paper. Others are for deriving them from *Diogenes*, because several of the leading Men of the Sect have a great deal of the cynical Humour in them, and delight much in Sun-shine. But then again, *Diogenes*[3] was content to have his constant Habitation in a narrow Tub; whilst our Philosophers are so far from being of his Opinion, that it's Death to them to be confin'd within the Limits of a good handsome convenient Chamber but for Half an Hour. Others there are, who from the Clearness of their Heads deduce the Pedigree of *Lowngers* from that great Man (I think it was either *Plato*[4] or

---

[1] *Motto.* Horace, *Epistles*, I. II. 28: A busy idleness destroys our care. Steele later used this as the motto for the folio version of No. 284 (vol. iii).

[2] This letter has been attributed by early editors to Lawrence Eusden.

[3] See Diogenes Laertius, 6. 23.

[4] *Apology* 21D.

Socrates) who after all his Study and Learning profess'd, That all he then knew was, that he knew nothing. You easily see this is but a shallow Argument, and may be soon confuted.

'I have with great Pains and Industry made my Observations from Time to Time upon these Sages; and having now all Materials ready, am compiling a Treatise, wherein I shall set forth the Rise and Progress of this famous Sect, together with their Maxims, Austerities, Manner of living, *&c.* Having prevail'd with a Friend who designs shortly to publish a new Edition of *Diogenes Laertius*, to add this Treatise of mine by way of Supplement; I shall now, to let the World see what may be expected from me (first begging Mr. SPECTATOR's Leave that the World may see it) briefly touch upon some of my chief Observations, and then subscribe my self your humble Servant. In the first Place I shall give you two or three of their Maxims: The fundamental one, upon which their whole System is built, is this, *viz.* That Time being an implacable Enemy to and Destroyer of all things, ought to be paid in his own Coin, and be destroy'd and murder'd without Mercy by all the Ways that can be invented. Another favourite Saying of theirs is, That Business was design'd only for Knaves, and Study for Blockheads. A Third seems to be a ludicrous one, but has a great Effect upon their Lives; and is this, That the Devil is at Home.[1] Now for their Manner of Living: And here I have a large Field to expatiate in; but I shall reserve Particulars for my intended Discourse, and now only mention one or two of their principal Exercises. The elder Proficients employ themselves in inspecting *mores hominum multorum*,[2] in getting acquainted with all the Signs and Windows in the Town. Some are arriv'd to so great Knowledge, that they can tell every time any Butcher kills a Calf, every time any old Woman's Cat is in the Straw; and a thousand other Matters as important. One antient Philosopher contemplates two or three Hours every Day over a Sun-Dial; and is true to the Dial

> . . . *As the Dial to the Sun*
> *Although it be not shone upon.*[3]

Our younger Students are content to carry their Speculations as yet

[1] For earlier examples of this proverb see Apperson, 'Devil' (56).
[2] 'The various customs of mankind'. Horace, *Ars Poetica*, 142.
[3] *Hudibras*, III. ii. 175–6 ('shin'd upon').

no farther than Bowling-Greens,[1] Billiard-Tables,[2] and such like Places: This may serve for a Sketch of my Design; in which I hope I shall have your Encouragement.

I am,
Sir,
Yours.'

I must be so just as to observe I have formerly seen of this Sect at our other University; tho' not distinguished by the Appellation which the learned Historian, my Correspondent, reports they bear at *Cambridge.* They were ever looked upon as a People that impaired themselves more by their strict Application to the Rules of their Order, than any other Students whatever. Others seldom hurt themselves, any further than to gain weak Eyes and sometimes Head-Aches; but these Philosophers are seized all over with a general Inability, Indolence, and Weariness, and a certain Impatience of the Place they are in, with an Heaviness in removing to another.

The *Lowngers* are satisfied with being merely Part of the Number of Mankind, without distinguishing themselves from amongst them. They may be said rather to suffer their Time to pass, than to spend it, without Regard to the past, or Prospect of the future. All they know of Life is only the present Instant, and do not taste even that. When one of this Order happens to be a Man of Fortune, the Expence of his Time is transferred to his Coach and Horses, and his Life is to be measured by their Motion, not his own Enjoyments or Sufferings. The chief Entertainment one of these Philosophers can possibly propose to himself, is to get a Relish of Dress: This, methinks, might diversify the Person he is weary of (his own dear self) to himself. I have known these two Amusements make one of these Philosophers make a tollerable Figure in the World; with Variety of Dresses in publick Assemblies in Town, and quick Motion of his Horses out of it, now to *Bath,* now to *Tunbridge,* then to *New-Market,* and then to *London,* he has in Process of Time brought it to pass, that his Coach and his Horses have been mentioned in all those Places. When the *Lowngers* leave

---

[1] Bowling was popular at this time, and the number of bowling-greens increased greatly during the reign of Queen Anne (see Ashton, i. 324). The *Daily Courant* of 14 Apr. 1711 announces the opening of three bowling-greens for the following week —'at Marribone', at the Three Crowns 'at Stock-Newington', and at the Cockpit 'the back-side of Gray's-Inn'.

[2] Billiards were played at this time not only in private houses but also in coffee-houses. See Ashton, i. 322.

an Academick Life, and instead of this more elegant Way of appearing in the polite World, retire to the Seats of their Ancestors, they usually join a Pack of Dogs, and employ their Days in defending their Poultry from Foxes: I do not know any other Method that any of this Order has ever taken to make a Noise in the World; but I shall enquire into such about this Town as have arriv'd at the Dignity of being *Lowngers* by the Force of natural Parts, without having ever seen an University; and send my Correspondent, for the Embellishment of his Book, the Names and History of those who pass their Lives without any Incidents at all; and how they shift Coffee-houses and Chocolate-houses[1] from Hour to Hour, to get over the insupportable Labour of doing nothing.   R

No. 55
[ADDISON]

Thursday, May 3, 1711[2]

> . . . *Intus, & in jecore ægro*
> *Nascuntur Domini* . . .
>   Pers.

MOST of the Trades, Professions, and Ways of Living among Mankind, take their Original either from the Love of Pleasure or the Fear of Want. The former, when it becomes too violent, degenerates into *Luxury*, and the latter into *Avarice*. As these two Principles of Action draw different Ways, *Persius* has given us a very humorous Account of a young Fellow who was rouzed out of his Bed, in order to be sent upon a long Voyage by *Avarice*, and afterwards over-persuaded and kept at Home by *Luxury*. I shall set down at length the Pleadings of these two imaginary Persons, as they are in the Original,[3] with Mr. *Dryden's* Translation of them.

> *Mane, piger, stertis: surge inquit Avaritia; eja*
> *Surge. Negas, Instat, surge inquit. Non queo. Surge.*

[1] There was no real distinction between these, since coffee, chocolate (and tea) were served at both.
[2] *Motto.* Persius, *Satires*, 5. 129–30:
> But if thy passions lord it in thy breast,
> Art thou not still a slave, and still oppress'd? DRYDEN.
[3] Persius, *Satires*, 5. 132–55. Dryden's translation, 189–227 (line 193: The tyrant Lucre; lines 208–9: Nothing retards thy voyage, now, unless | Thy other lord forbids, Voluptuousness).

Et quid agam? Rogitas? Saperdas advehe Ponto,
Castoreum, stuppas, hebenum, thus, lubrica Coa.
Tolle recens primus piper è sitiente camelo.
Verte aliquid; jura. Sed Jupiter Audiet. Eheu!
Baro, regustatum digito terebrare salinum
Contentus perages, si vivere cum Jove tendis.
Jam pueris pellem succinctus & œnophorum aptas;
Ocyus ad Navem. Nil obstat quin trabe vastâ
Ægæum rapias, nisi solers Luxuria ante
Seductum moneat; quo deinde, insane ruis? Quo?
Quid tibi vis? Calido sub pectore mascula bilis
Intumuit, quam non extinxerit urna cicutæ?
Tun' mare transilias? Tibi tortâ cannabe fulto
Cœna sit in transtro? Veientanumque rubellum
Exhalet vapida læsum pice sessilis obba?
Quid petis? Ut nummi, quos hic quincunce modesto
Nutrieras, pergant avidos sudare deunces?
Indulge genio: carpamus dulcia; nostrum est
Quod vivis; cinis, & manes, & fabula fies.
Vive memor lethi: fugit hora. Hoc quod loquor, inde est.
En quid agis? Duplici in diversum scinderis hamo.
Hunccine, an hunc sequeris? . . .

    Whether alone, or in thy Harlot's Lap,
When thou would'st take a lazy Morning's Nap;
Up, Up, says *AVARICE*; thou snor'st again,
Stretchest thy Limbs, and yawn'st, but all in vain.
The rugged Tyrant no Denial takes;
At his Command th'unwilling Sluggard wakes.
What must I do? he cries; What? says his Lord:
Why rise, make ready, and go streight Aboard:
With Fish, from *Euxine* Seas, thy Vessel freight;
Flax, Castor, *Coan* Wines, the precious Weight
Of Pepper, and *Sabean* Incense, take   ⎫
With thy own Hands, from the tir'd Camel's Back, ⎬
And with Post-haste thy running Markets make. ⎭
Be sure to turn the Penny; Lye and Swear,
'Tis wholesome Sin: But *Jove*, thou say'st, will hear.
Swear, Fool, or Starve; for the *Dilemma's* even:
A Tradesman thou! and hope to go to Heav'n?

Resolv'd for Sea, the Slaves thy Baggage Pack,
Each saddled with his Burden on his Back:
Nothing retards thy Voyage, now; but He,
That soft voluptuous Prince, call'd *LUXURY*;
And he may ask this civil Question; Friend,
What dost thou make a Shipboard? To what end?
Art thou of *Bethlem*'s noble College free?
Stark, staring mad, that thou wou'dst tempt the Sea?
Cubb'd[1] in a Cabbin, on a Mattress laid,
On a brown *George*,[2] with lowsie Swobbers fed,
Dead Wine that stinks of the *Borachio*,[3] sup
From a foul Jack,[4] or greasie Maple Cup?
Say, wou'dst thou bear all this, to raise thy Store,
From Six i'th'Hundred, to Six Hundred more?
Indulge, and to thy Genius freely give:
For, not to live at Ease, is not to live:
Death stalks behind thee, and each flying Hour
Does some loose Remnant of thy Life devour.
Live, while thou liv'st; for Death will make us all,
A Name, a nothing but an Old Wife's Tale.

Speak; wilt thou *Avarice*, or *Pleasure* chuse
To be thy Lord? Take one, and one refuse.

When a Government flourishes in Conquests, and is secure from foreign Attacks, it naturally falls into all the Pleasures of Luxury; and as these Pleasures are very expensive, they put those who are addicted to them upon raising fresh Supplies of Mony, by all the Methods of Rapaciousness and Corruption; so that Avarice and Luxury very often become one complicated Principle of Action, in those whose Hearts are wholly set upon Ease, Magnificence, and Pleasure. The most Elegant and Correct of all the *Latin* Historians[5] observes, that in his time, when the most formidable States of the World were subdued by the *Romans*, the Republick sunk into those two Vices of a quite different Nature, Luxury and Avarice: And

---

[1] Cooped, confined. *Obs.* exc. *dial.* (*OED*).
[2] A loaf of a coarse kind of brown bread.
[3] A leather bottle or bag used in Spain for wine.
[4] A leathern jug or tankard.
[5] Sallust, *Bellum Catilinae*, 5. 4: 'alieni appetens, sui profusus.' For the *elegantia orationis* of Sallust cf. Aulus Gellius, *Noctes Atticae*, 4. 15. 1.

accordingly describes *Catiline* as one who coveted the Wealth of other Men, at the same time that he squandred away his own. This Observation on the Commonwealth, when it was in its height of Power and Riches, holds good of all Governments that are settled in a State of Ease and Prosperity. At such times Men naturally endeavour to outshine one another in Pomp and Splendor, and having no Fears to alarm them from abroad, indulge themselves in the Enjoyment of all the Pleasures they can get into their Possession; which naturally produces Avarice, and an immoderate Pursuit after Wealth and Riches.

As I was humouring my self in the Speculation of these two great Principles of Action, I could not forbear throwing my Thoughts into a little kind of Allegory or Fable, with which I shall here present my Reader.

There were two very powerful Tyrants engaged in a perpetual War against each other: The Name of the first was LUXURY, and of the second AVARICE. The Aim of each of them was no less than Universal Monarchy over the Hearts of Mankind. *Luxury* had many Generals under him, who did him great Service, as *Pleasure*, *Mirth*, *Pomp*, and *Fashion*. *Avarice* was likewise very strong in his Officers, being faithfully served by *Hunger*, *Industry*, *Care* and *Watchfulness*: He had likewise a Privy-Counsellor who was always at his Elbow, and whispering something or other in his Ear: the Name of this Privy-Counsellor was *Poverty*. As *Avarice* conducted himself by the Counsels of *Poverty*, his Antagonist was entirely guided by the Dictates and Advice of *Plenty*, who was his first Counsellor and Minister of State, that concerted all his Measures for him, and never departed out of his sight. While these two great Rivals were thus contending for Empire, their Conquests were very various. *Luxury* got Possession of one Heart, and *Avarice* of another. The Father of a Family would often range himself under the Banners of *Avarice*, and the Son under those of *Luxury*. The Wife and Husband would often declare themselves on the two different Parties; nay, the same Person would very often side with one in his Youth, and revolt to the other in his old Age. Indeed the Wise Men of the World stood *Neuter*; but alas! their Numbers were not considerable. At length, when these two Potentates had wearied themselves with waging War upon one another, they agreed upon an Interview, at which neither of their Counsellors were to be present. It is said that *Luxury* began the Parly, and after having represented the endless State of War in which they were engaged, told his Enemy, with a Frankness of Heart which is natural to him, that he believed they two should be very good Friends, were it not for the Instigations of *Poverty*, that pernicious Counsellor, who made an ill use of his Ear, and filled him with groundless Apprehensions and Prejudices. To this *Avarice* replied, that he looked upon *Plenty*, (the first Minister of his Antagonist) to be a much more destructive Counsellor than *Poverty*, for that he was perpetually suggesting Pleasures, banishing all the necessary Cautions against Want, and consequently undermining those Principles on which the Government of *Avarice* was founded. At last, in order to an Accommodation, they agreed upon this Preliminary; That each of them should immediately dismiss his Privy-Counsellor. When things were thus far adjusted towards a Peace, all other Differences were soon accommodated, insomuch that for the future they resolved to live as good Friends and Confederates, and to share between them whatever Conquests were made on either side. For this Reason, we now find *Luxury* and *Avarice* taking Possession of the same Heart, and dividing the same Person between them. To which I shall only add, that since the discarding of the Counsellors above mentioned, *Avarice* supplies *Luxury* in the room of *Plenty*, as *Luxury* Prompts *Avarice* in the place of *Poverty*.

C

No. 56
[ADDISON]

Friday, May 4, 1711[1]

Felices errore suo . . .
Lucan.

THE *Americans*[2] believe that all Creatures have Souls, not only Men and Women, but Brutes, Vegetables, nay even the most inanimate things, as Stocks and Stones. They believe the same of all the Works of Art, as of Knives, Boats, Looking-glasses: And that as any of these things perish, their Souls go into another World, which is inhabited by the Ghosts of Men and Women. For this Reason

[1] *Motto*. Lucan, *Pharsalia*, i. 459: Happy in their error.
[2] This number may have been suggested by the visit of the four Indian Kings (No. 50).

they always place by the Corpse of their dead Friend a Bow and Arrows, that he may make use of the Souls of them in the other World, as he did of their wooden Bodies in this. How absurd soever such an Opinion as this may appear, our *European* Philosophers have maintain'd several Notions altogether as improbable. Some of *Plato's* Followers in particular, when they talk of the World of Ideas, entertain us with Substances and Beings no less extravagant and chymerical. Many *Aristotelians* have likewise spoken as unintelligibly of their substantial Forms. I shall only instance *Albertus Magnus,*[1] who in his Dissertation upon the Load-stone observing that Fire will destroy its magnetick Vertues, tells us that he took particular Notice of one as it lay glowing amidst an Heap of burning Coals, and that he perceiv'd a certain blue Vapour to arise from it, which he believed might be the *substantial Form,* that is, in our *West-Indian* Phrase, the *Soul* of the Load-stone.

There is a Tradition among the *Americans,* that one of their Countrymen descended in a Vision to the great Repository of Souls, or, as we call it here, to the other World; and that upon his Return he gave his Friends a distinct Account of every thing he saw among those Regions of the Dead. A Friend of mine, whom I have formerly mentioned, prevailed upon one of the Interpreters of the *Indian* Kings, to enquire of them, if possible, what Tradition they have among them of this Matter: Which, as well as he could learn by those many Questions which he asked them at several Times, was in Substance as follows.

The Visionary, whose Name was *Marraton,*[2] after having travelled for a long Space under an hollow Mountain, arrived at length on the Confines of this World of Spirits; but could not enter it by reason of a thick Forest made up of Bushes, Brambles, and pointed Thorns, so perplexed and interwoven with one another, that it was impossible to find a Passage through it. Whilst he was looking about for some Track[a] or Path-way that might be worn in any Part of it, he saw an huge Lion couched under the Side of it, who kept his Eye upon him in the same Posture as when he watches for his Prey. The *Indian*

[a] Track] Tract *Fol. Corrected in Errata (No. 58)*

[1] St. Albert, Bishop of Ratisbon (1193–1280). His works were published at Leyden in 1651, in 21 volumes.
[2] It is perhaps worth noting that two of the four Indian Kings had names including 'Ton'.

immediately started back, whilst the Lion rose with a Spring, and leaped towards him. Being wholly destitute of all other Weapons, he stooped down to take up an huge Stone in his Hand; but to his infinite Surprize grasped nothing, and found the supposed Stone to be only the Apparition of one. If he was disappointed on this Side, he was as much pleased on the other, when he found the Lion, which had seized on his left Shoulder, had no Power to hurt him, and was only the Ghost of that ravenous Creature which it appeared to be. He no sooner got rid of his impotent Enemy, but he marched up to the Wood, and after having surveyed it for some Time, endeavoured to press into one Part of it that was a little thinner than the rest; when again, to his great Surprize, he found the Bushes made no Resistance, but that he walked through Briars and Brambles with the same Ease as through the open Air; and, in short, that the whole Wood was nothing else but a Wood of Shades. He immediately concluded, that this huge Thicket of Thorns and Brakes was designed as a kind of Fence or quick-set Hedge to the Ghosts it inclosed; and that probably their soft Substances might be torn by these subtle Points and Prickles, which were too weak to make any Impressions in Flesh and Blood. With this Thought he resolved to travel through this intricate Wood; when by Degrees he felt a Gale of Perfumes breathing upon him, that grew stronger and sweeter in proportion as he advanced. He had not proceeded much further when he observed the Thorns and Briars to end, and give Place to a thousand beautiful green Trees covered with Blossoms of the finest Scents and Colours, that formed a Wilderness of Sweets, and were a kind of Lining to those ragged Scenes which he had before passed through. As he was coming out of this delightful Part of the Wood, and entering upon the Plains it inclosed, he saw several Horsemen rushing by him, and a little while after heard the Cry of a Pack of Dogs. He had not listned long before he saw the Apparition of a milke-white Steed, with a young Man on the Back of it, advancing upon full Stretch after the Souls of about an hundred Beagles that were hunting down the Ghost of an Hare, which ran away before them with an unspeakable Swiftness. As the Man on the milke-white Steed came by him, he looked upon him very attentively, and found him to be the young Prince *Nicharagua*, who died about Half a Year before, and by reason of his great Vertues, was at that Time lamented over all the Western Parts of *America*.

He had no sooner got out of the Wood, but he was entertained with such a Landskip of flowry Plains, green Meadows, running Streams, sunny Hills, and shady Vales, as were not to be represented[a] by his own Expressions, nor, as he said, by the Conceptions of others. This happy Region was peopled with innumerable Swarms of Spirits, who applied themselves to Exercises and Diversions according as their Fancies led them. Some of them were tossing the Figure of a Coit;[1] others were pitching the Shadow of a Bar; others were breaking the Apparition of an Horse; and Multitudes employing themselves upon ingenious Handicrafts with the Souls of *departed Utensils*; for that is the Name which in the *Indian* Language they give their Tools when they are burnt or broken. As he travelled through this delightful Scene, he was very often tempted to pluck the Flowers that rose every where about him in the greatest Variety and Profusion, having never seen several of them in his own Country: But he quickly found that though they were Objects of his Sight, they were not liable to his Touch. He at length came to the Side of a great River, and being a good Fisherman himself stood upon the Banks of it some time to look upon an Angler that had taken a great many Shapes of Fishes, which lay flouncing up and down by him.

I should have told my Reader, that this *Indian* had been formerly married to one of the greatest Beauties of his Country, by whom he had several Children. This Couple were so famous for their Love and Constancy to one another, that the *Indians* to this Day, when they give a married Man Joy of his Wife, wish that they may live together like *Marraton* and *Yaratilda*. *Marraton* had not stood long by the Fisherman when he saw the Shadow of his beloved *Yaratilda*, who had for some time fixed her Eye upon him, before he discovered her. Her Arms were stretched out towards him, Floods of Tears ran down her Eyes; her Looks, her Hands, her Voice called him over to her; and at the same Time seemed to tell him that the River was unpassable. Who can describe the Passion made up of Joy, Sorrow, Love, Desire, Astonishment, that rose in the *Indian* upon the Sight of his dear *Yaratilda*? He could express it by nothing but his Tears, which ran like a River down his Cheeks as he looked upon her. He had not stood in this Posture long, before he plunged into the Stream that lay before him; and finding it to be nothing but the Phantom of a River, walked on the Bottom of it till he arose on the other Side.

[a] represented] described *Fol.*

---

[1] An obsolete spelling of quoit.

At his Approach *Taratilda* flew into his Arms, whilst *Marraton* wished himself disencumbered of that Body which kept her from his Embraces. After many Questions and Endearments on both Sides, she conducted him to a Bower which she had dressed with her own Hands, with all the Ornaments that could be met with in those blooming Regions. She had made it gay beyond Imagination, and was every Day adding something new to it. As *Marraton* stood astonished at the unspeakable Beauty of her Habitation, and ravished with the Fragrancy that came from every Part of it, *Taratilda* told him that she was preparing this Bower for his Reception, as well knowing that his Piety to his God and his faithful Dealing towards Men would certainly bring him to that happy Place whenever his Life should be at an End. She then brought two of her Children to him, who died some Years before, and resided with her in the same delightful Bower, advising him to breed up those others which were still with him in such a Manner, that they might hereafter all of them meet together in this happy Place.

The Tradition tells us further, that he had afterwards a Sight of those dismal Habitations which are the Portion of ill Men[1] after Death; and mentions several Molten Seas of Gold, in which were plunged the Souls of barbarous *Europeans*, who[a] put to the Sword so many Thousands of poor *Indians* for the Sake of that precious Metal: But having already touched upon the chief Points of this Tradition, and exceeded the Measure of my Paper, I shall not give any further Account of it.   C[2]

[a] *Europeans*, who] *Europeans* that *Fol.*

---

[1] Ill, in the sense of morally evil, is marked as *obs.*, except *dial.*, in *OED*.
[2] 'This little fanciful paper is written, throughout, in the very spirit of its author. All the graces of imagination, are here joined with all the light and lustre of expression: but it was not for nothing (as the concluding moral shews) that so much wit and elegance was employed on this subject. See his introduction to No. 152, in the *Tatler*' (Hurd).

Quem præstare potest mulier galeata pudorem,
Quæ fugit à Sexu? . . .

Juv.

WHEN the Wife of *Hector*, in *Homer*'s *Iliads*,[2] discourses with
her Husband about the Battel in which he was going to
engage, the Hero, desiring her to leave that Matter to his Care,
bids her go to her Maids and mind her Spinning: By which the Poet
intimates, that Men and Women ought to busie themselves in their
proper Spheres, and on such Matters only as are suitable to their
respective Sex.

I am at this time acquainted with a Young Gentleman, who has
passed a great Part of his Life in the Nursery, and, upon Occasion,
can make a Caudle or a Sack Posset[3] better than any Man in *England*.
He is likewise a wonderful Critick in Cambrick and Muslins, and
will talk an Hour together upon a Sweet-meat. He entertains his
Mother every Night with Observations that he makes both in Town
and Court: As what Lady shows the nicest Fancy in her Dress;
what Man of Quality wears the fairest Wig; who has the finest
Linnen, who the prettiest Snuff-box, with many other the like
curious Remarks that may be made in good Company.

On the other hand I have very frequently the Opportunity of
seeing a Rural *Andromache*,[4] who came up to Town last Winter, and
is one of the greatest Fox Hunters in the Country. She talks of
Hounds and Horses, and makes nothing of leaping over a Six bar
Gate. If a Man tells her a waggish Story, she gives him a Push with
her Hand in jest, and calls him an impudent Dog; and if her Servant
neglects his Business, threatens to kick him out of the House. I have

---

[1] *Motto*. Juvenal, *Satires*, 6. 252–3:
        What Sense of Shame in such a Breast can lye?
        Innur'd to Arms, and her own Sex to fly? DRYDEN.

[2] *Iliad*, 6. 490–3.

[3] A Cawdle or Posset-Drink is mentioned in No. 143 (vol. ii). Cf. John Houghton,
Collection, 20 May 1698: 'When women are delivered of children, or, as we say, lie in,
the nurses feed them much with caudle, which is made with pounded oat-meal boil'd
in water, and with seeds or spice, to which they add ale, and sometimes white-wine,
and sweeten it with sugar; and this is generally a treat to any that make a visit'
(ed. 1727, ii. 294).

[4] *Tatler* 37 had described 'Mrs. *Alse Copswood*, the *Yorkshire* Huntress, who is come
to Town lately, and moves as if she were on her Nag, and going to take a Five-Bar
Gate; and is as loud as if she were following her Dogs.'

heard her, in her Wrath, call a Substantial Trades-man a Lousy-Cur; and remember one Day, when she could not think of the Name of a Person, she described him, in a large Company of Men and Ladies, by the Fellow with the Broad Shoulders.

If those Speeches and Actions, which in their own Nature are indifferent, appear ridiculous when they proceed from a wrong Sex, the Faults and Imperfections of one Sex transplanted into another, appear black and monstrous. As for the Men, I shall not in this Paper any further concern my self about them, but as I would fain contribute to make Woman-kind, which is the most beautiful Part of the Creation, entirely amiable, and wear out all those little Spots and Blemishes that are apt to rise among the Charms which Nature has poured out upon them, I shall dedicate this Paper to their Service. The Spot which I would here endeavour to clear them of, is that Party Rage which of late Years is very much crept into their Conversation. This is, in its nature, a Male Vice, and made up of many angry and cruel Passions that are altogether repugnant to the Softness, the Modesty, and those other endearing Qualities which are natural to the Fair Sex. Women were formed to temper Mankind, and sooth them into Tenderness and Compassion, not to set an Edge upon their Minds, and blow up in them those Passions which are too apt to rise of their own Accord. When I have seen a pretty Mouth uttering Calumnies and Invectives, what would not I have given to have stopt it? How have I been troubled to see some of the finest Features in the World grow pale, and tremble with Party Rage? *Camilla*[1] is one of the greatest Beauties in the *British* Nation, and yet values her self more upon being the *Virago*[2] of one Party, than upon being the Toast[3] of both. The Dear Creature, about a Week ago, encountred the fierce and beautiful *Penthesilea* across a Tea-Table, but in the height of her Anger, as her Hand chanced to shake with the Earnestness of the Dispute, she scalded her Fingers, and spilt a Dish of Tea upon her Petticoat. Had not this Accident broke off the Debate, no Body knows where it would have ended.

There is one Consideration which I would earnestly recommend

[1] Camilla, the warrior maiden, and Penthesilea, Queen of the Amazons (*Aeneid*, 7. 803; 11. 648–63).   [2] Lat. *virago*, a man-like or heroic woman.

[3] A lady who is named as the person to whom a company is requested to drink; often one who is the reigning belle of the season (*OED*). For various interpretations of the origin of this new word see *Tatlers* 24 and 31. The language of this passage ('the Virago of one Party ... the Toast of both') is reminiscent of Addison's advice to Pope, 'not to be content with the praise of half the nation' (Sherburn, *Early Career of Pope*, p. 68).

to all my Female Readers, and which, I hope, will have some weight with them. In short it is this, that there is nothing so bad for the Face as Party Zeal. It gives an ill-natured Cast to the Eye, and a disagreeable Sourness to the Look; Besides, that it makes the Lines too strong, and flushes them worse than Brandy. I have seen a Woman's Face break out in Heats, as she has been talking against a great Lord, whom she had never seen in her Life; and indeed never knew a Party Woman that kept her Beauty for a Twelve-month. I would therefore advise all my Female Readers, as they value their Complexions, to let alone all Disputes of this Nature; though, at the same time, I would give free Liberty to all superannuated motherly Partizans to be as violent as they please, since there will be no danger either of their spoiling their Faces, or of their gaining Converts.

[a]For my own part, I think a Man makes an odious and despicable Figure, that is violent in a Party; but a Woman is too sincere to mitigate the Fury of her Principles with Temper and Discretion, and to act with that Caution and Reservedness which are requisite in our Sex. When this unnatural Zeal gets into them, it throws them into ten thousand Heats and Extravagancies; their generous Souls set[b] no Bounds to their Love or to their Hatred; and whether a Whig or Tory, a Lap-Dog or a Gallant, an Opera or a Puppet-Show, be the Object of it, the Passion, while it reigns, engrosses the whole Woman.

I remember when Dr. *Titus Oates*[1] was in all his Glory, I accompanied my Friend WILL. HONEYCOMB in a Visit to a Lady of his Acquaintance: We were no sooner sat down, but upon casting my Eyes about the Room, I found in almost every Corner of it a Print[2] that represented the Doctor in all Magnitudes and Dimensions. A little after, as the Lady was discoursing my Friend,[3] and held her

---

[a] *No new paragraph in Fol.*   [b] Souls set] Souls (I mean those of ordinary Women) set *Fol. Corrected in Errata (No. 58)*

---

[1] Titus Oates was 'in his Glory' at the time of the Popish Plot in 1679–80, but the present 'doctor' is Henry Sacheverell, whose trial in 1710 had aroused the passions of the mob and helped in the fall of the Whig ministry. *Tatler* 142 describes the enthusiasm of the Tory ladies for 'the doctor' during his trial (27 Feb. to 23 Mar. 1710).

[2] The *Post Boy* of 11 Feb. 1709/10 advertises 'The true Effigies of Dr. Henry Sacheverel, curiously perform'd in Metzotinto, from off a Copper-Plate, done after the Original Painting of Mr. Gibson'.

[3] This transitive use of the verb is noted by *OED* as very common down to 1750 and now *obs.* or *arch.*

Snuff-Box in her Hand, who should I see in the Lid of it but the Doctor. It was not long after this, when she had occasion for her Handkerchief, which upon the first opening discover'd among the Plaites of it the Figure of the Doctor. Upon this my Friend WILL. who loves Raillery, told her, That if he was in Mr. *Truelove's* Place (for that was the Name of her Husband) he should be made as uneasie by a Handkerchief as ever *Othello* was. *I am afraid*, said she, *Mr.* HONEYCOMB, *you are a Tory; tell me truly, are you a Friend to the Doctor or not?* WILL. instead of making her a Reply, smiled in her Face (for indeed she was very pretty) and told her that one of her Patches was dropping off. She immediately adjusted it, and looking a little seriously, *Well*, says she, *I'll be hang'd if you and your silent Friend there are not against the Doctor in your Hearts, I suspected as much by his saying nothing.* Upon this she took her Fan[1] into her Hand, and upon the opening[a] of it again display'd to us the Figure of the Doctor, who was placed with great Gravity among the Sticks of it. In a word, I found that the Doctor had taken Possession of her Thoughts, her Discourse, and most of her Furniture; but finding my self pressed too close by her Question, I wink'd upon my Friend to take his Leave, which he did accordingly.   C

No. 58
[ADDISON]

Monday, May 7, 1711[2]

Ut pictura poesis erit . . .
Hor.

NOTHING is so much admired and so little understood as Wit. No Author that I know of has written professedly upon it;

---

[a] upon the opening] upon opening *Fol.*

[1] Part of the Tory campaign of propaganda in the summer of 1710 was the sale of ans showing the doctor's picture. 'Emblematical FANS, with the true Effigies of the Reverend Dr. *Henry Sacheverell* done to the Life, and several curious Hieroglyphicks in Honour of the Church of England, finely painted and mounted on extraordinary genteel Sticks, are to be sold only at Mrs. Beardwell's, next the Red-Cross-Tavern, in Blackfriars' (*Supplement*, 21 Aug. 1710; *Post Boy*, 24 Aug. 1710). Mrs. Beardwell was printer of the Tory *Post Boy*. Her advertisement in the *Supplement* of 11 Sept. 1710 warns of counterfeits, 'for such are abroad; the Figure whereof, that is put to represent Dr. *Sacheverell*, might as well be call'd *Ben Hoadly*; whereas these *Emblematical Fans* have the said Doctor's Effigies curiously done to the Life, as any one who knows the Doctor, and will give himself the Trouble to see them, may be satisfy'd'. A letter in Lillie (i. 353–6) comments on this number (cf. No. 217 (vol. ii)).

[2] *Motto.* Horace, *Ars poetica*, 361: A poem will be like a picture . . .

and as for those who make any Mention of it, they only treat on the Subject as it has accidentally fallen in their Way, and that too in little short Reflections, or in general declamatory Flourishes, without entering into the Bottom of the Matter. I hope therefore I shall perform an acceptable Work to my Countrymen if I treat at large upon this Subject; which I shall endeavour to do in a Manner suitable to it, that I may not incur the Censure which a famous Critick[1] bestows upon one who had written a Treatise upon *the Sublime* in a low groveling Stile. I intend to lay aside a whole Week for this Undertaking, that the Scheme of my Thoughts may not be broken and interrupted; and I dare promise my self, if my Readers will give me a Week's Attention, that this great City will be very much changed for the better by next *Saturday* Night. I shall endeavour to make what I say intelligible to ordinary Capacities; but if my Readers meet with any Paper that in some Parts of it may be a little out of their Reach, I would not have them discouraged, for they may assure themselves the next shall be much clearer.

As the great and only End of these my Speculations is to banish Vice and Ignorance out of the Territories of *Great Britain*, I shall endeavour as much as possible to establish among us a Taste of polite Writing. It is with this View that I have endeavoured to set my Readers right in several Points relating to Operas and Tragedies; and shall from Time to Time impart my Notions of Comedy, as I think they may tend to its Refinement and Perfection. I find by my Bookseller that these Papers of Criticism, with that upon Humour, have met with a more kind Reception than indeed I could have hoped for from such Subjects; for which Reason I shall enter upon my present Undertaking with greater Chearfulness.

In this and one or two following Papers I shall trace out the History of false Wit, and distinguish the several Kinds of it as they have prevailed in different Ages of the World. This I think the more necessary at present, because I observed there were Attempts on foot last Winter to revive some of those antiquated Modes of Wit that have been long exploded out of the Common-wealth of Letters. There were several Satyrs and Panegyricks handed about in Acrostick, by which Means some of the most arrant undisputed Blockheads about the Town began to entertain ambitious Thoughts, and to set up for polite Authors. I shall therefore describe at length those

[1] Longinus thus criticizes Caecilius, the Sicilian rhetorician, as writing in a humbler style than the argument demands.

many Arts of false Wit, in which a Writer does not shew himself a Man of a beautiful Genius, but of great Industry.

The first Species of false Wit which I have met with is very venerable for its Antiquity, and has produced several Pieces which have lived very near as long as the *Iliad* it self: I mean those short Poems printed among the minor *Greek* Poets, which resemble the Figure of an Egg,[1] a Pair of Wings, an Ax, a Shepherd's Pipe, and an Altar.

[a]As for the first, it is a little oval Poem, and may not improperly be called a Scholar's Egg. I would endeavour to hatch it, or, in more intelligible Language, to translate it into *English*, did not I find the Interpretation of it very difficult; for the Author seems to have been more intent upon the Figure of his Poem, than upon the Sense of it.

The Pair of Wings consist of twelve Verses, or rather Feathers, every Verse decreasing gradually in its Measure according to its Situation in the Wing. The Subject of it (as in the rest of the Poems which follow) bears some remote Affinity with the Figure, for it describes a God of Love, who is always painted with Wings.

The Ax methinks would have been a good Figure for a Lampoon, had the Edge of it consisted of the most satyrical Parts of the Work; but as it is in the Original, I take it to have been nothing else but the Posy of an Ax which was consecrated to *Minerva*, and was thought to have been the same that *Epeus*[2] made use of in the building of the *Trojan* Horse; which is a Hint I shall leave to the Consideration of the Criticks. I am apt to think that the Posy was written originally upon the Ax, like those which our modern Cutlers inscribe upon their Knives; and that therefore the Posy still remains in its ancient Shape, though the Ax it self is lost.

The Shepherd's Pipe may be said to be full of Musick, for it is composed of nine different Kinds of Verses, which[b] by their several Lengths resemble the nine Stops of the old musical Instrument, that[c] is likewise the Subject of the Poem.

The Altar is inscribed with the Epitaph of *Troilus* the Son of *Hecuba*; which, by the Way, makes me believe, that these false

[a] *No new paragraph in Fol.*   [b] which] that *Fol.*   [c] of the old musical Instrument, that] of that old musical Instrument, which *Fol.*

[1] Poems in typographical shapes are found in English in the sixteenth century and are discussed in Puttenham's *Art of English Poesie* (1589). See Margaret Church, 'The First English Pattern Poems', *PMLA*, lxi (1946), 636–50. Addison's source, however, is the *Poetae Minores Graeci* of Ralph Winterton (see note to No. 12). The order of examples (egg, wings, axe, shepherd's pipe, and altar) and the details of each follow Winterton's anthology (ed. Cambridge, 1677, pp. 314–29).

[2] *Aeneid*, 2. 264.

Pieces of Wit are much more ancient than the Authors to whom they are generally ascribed; at least I will never be perswaded, that so fine a Writer as *Theocritus*[1] could have been the Author of any such simple Works.

It was impossible for a Man to succeed in these Performances who[a] was not a kind of Painter, or at least a Designer: He was first of all to draw the Out-line of the Subject which he intended to write upon, and afterwards conform the Description to the Figure of his Subject. The Poetry was to contract or dilate itself according to the Mould in which it was cast. In a Word, the Verses were to be cramped or extended to the Dimensions of the Frame that was prepared for them; and to undergo the Fate of those Persons whom the Tyrant *Procrustes* used to lodge in his Iron Bed; if they were too short he stretched them on a Rack, and if they were too long chopped off a Part of their Legs, till they fitted the Couch which he had prepared for them.

Mr. *Dryden*[2] hints at this obsolete kind of Wit in one of the following Verses, in his *Mac Fleckno*;[b] which an *English* Reader cannot understand, who does not know that there are those little Poems abovementioned in the Shape of Wings and Altars.

> *. . . Chuse for thy Command*
> *Some peaceful Province in Acrostick Land;*
> *There may'st thou* Wings *display and* Altars *raise,*
> *And torture one poor* Word *a thousand Ways.*

This Fashion of false Wit was revived by several Poets of the last Age, and in particular may be met with among Mr. *Herbert*'s Poems;[3] and if I am not mistaken, in the Translation of *Du Bartas*.[4] I do not remember any other Kind of Work among the Moderns which more resembles the Performances I have mentioned, than that famous Picture[5] of King *Charles* the First, which has the whole Book of *Psalms*

---

a who] that *Fol.*   b in his *Mac Fleckno*;] *om. Fol.*

---

[1] Winterton (pp. 328–9) describes the altar as by Simias of Rhodes 'or, according to others', by Theocritus.

[2] *Mac Flecknoe*, 205–8 ('There thou may'st Wings display, and Altars raise, | And torture one poor Word ten thousand Ways').

[3] *The Temple*, 13th edition, is advertised in *Term Catalogues*, Easter 1711 (Arber, iii. 677).

[4] Joshua Sylvester, in his translation of the *Divine Weeks and Works* (1608) includes in the Dedication several 'Anagrammata regia': 'IACOBVS STVART: Justa Scrutabo', 'IAMES STVART: A iust Master', etc. Among the other preliminary pieces is 'An Acrostick Sonnet, to his friend M. Iosva Silvester, by R. N.'

[5] When Samuel Sorbière came to St. John's College at Oxford he entered 'a large

written in the Lines of the Face and the Hair of the Head. When I was last at *Oxford* I perused one of the Whiskers; and was reading the other, but could not go so far in it as I would have done, by reason of the Impatience of my Friends and Fellow-Travellers, who all of them pressed to see such a Piece of Curiosity. I have since heard, that there is now an eminent Writing-Master in Town, who has transcribed all the *Old Testament* in a full-bottom'd Perriwig; and if the Fashion should introduce the thick Kind of Wigs which were in Vogue some few Years ago, he promises to add two or three supernumerary Locks that shall contain all the *Apocrypha*. He designed this Wig originally for King *William*, having disposed of the two Books of *Kings* in the two Forks of the Foretop; but that glorious Monarch dying before the Wig was finished, there is a Space left in it for the Face of any one that has a mind to purchase it.

But to return to our ancient Poems in Picture, I would humbly propose, for the Benefit of our modern Smatterers in Poetry, that they would imitate their Brethren among the Ancients in those ingenious Devices. I have communicated this Thought to a young Poetical Lover of my Acquaintance, who intends to present his Mistress with a Copy of Verses made in the Shape of her Fan; and if he tells me true, has already finished the three first Sticks of it. He has likewise promised me to get the Measure of his Mistress's Marriage-Finger, with a Design to make a Posie in the Fashion of a Ring which shall exactly fit it. It is so very easy to enlarge upon a good Hint, that I do not question but my ingenious Readers will apply what I have said to many other Particulars; and that we shall see the Town filled in a very little Time with Poetical Tippets, Handkerchiefs, Snuff-Boxes, and the like Female Ornaments. I shall therefore conclude with a Word of Advice to those admirable *English* Authors who call themselves Pindarick Writers,[1] that they would apply themselves to this Kind of Wit without Loss of Time, as being provided better than any other Poets with Verses of all Sizes and Dimensions.   C

Wainscotted Gallery, wherein I found no other Ornament than the Picture of King *Charles* I. which they took out of a Cover, and shewed here for a Rarity, because the Hair of his Head was made up of Scripture Lines, wrought wonderfully small, and more particularly of the Psalms of *David* in *Latin*' (*A Voyage to England*, 1709, pp. 42–43). R. Plot, *Natural History of Oxfordshire* (Oxford, 1677), pp. 276–7, also mentions this and a similar picture of King James as 'pretty *curiosities*'. For other examples of portraits made with writing characters see *Menagiana*, 3rd ed., 1715, i. 141–2.

[1] See also Nos. 147 and 160 (vol. ii).

Operose Nihil agunt.

Sen.

THERE is nothing more certain than that every Man would be a Wit if he could, and notwithstanding Pedants of pretended Depth and Solidity are apt to decry the Writings of a polite Author, as *Flash* and *Froth*, they all of them show upon Occasion that they would spare no Pains to arrive at the Character of those whom they seem to despise. For this Reason we often find them endeavouring at Works of Fancy, which cost them infinite Pangs in the Production. The Truth of it is, a Man had better be a Gally-Slave than a Wit, were one to gain that Title by those Elaborate Trifles which have been the Inventions of such Authors as were often Masters of Great Learning but no Genius.

In my last Paper I mentioned some of these false Wits among the Ancients, and in this shall give the Reader two or three other Species of 'em that flourished in the same early Ages of the World. The first I shall produce are the *Lipogrammatists*[2] or *Letter-droppers* of Antiquity, that would take an Exception, without any Reason, against some particular Letter in the Alphabet, so as not to admit it once into a whole Poem. One *Tryphiodorus*[3] was a great Master in this kind of Writing. He composed an *Odissey* or Epic Poem on the Adventures of *Ulysses*, consisting of four and twenty Books, having entirely banished the Letter *A* from his first Book, which was called *Alpha* (as *Lucus a non lucendo*)[4] because there was not an *Alpha* in it. His Second Book was inscribed *Beta*, for the same Reason. In short, the Poet excluded the whole four and twenty Letters in their turns, and

---

[1] *Motto.* Seneca, *De brevitate vitae*, 13. 1: They laboriously do nothing.
[2] The earliest example of this word in English (*OED*). 'Les Grecs ont fait des Ouvrages Lipogrammatiques, c'est-à-dire, dans lesquels une lettre de l'alphabet manque. C'est de cette maniere que Tryphiodore a fait son Odyssée; il n'y avoit point d'α dans le premier livre, point de β dans le second, & ainsi des autres' (*Menagiana*, 1715, iii. 329). Examples are given in James Appleton Morgan, *Macaronic Poetry* (N.Y., 1872), pp. 12–15.
[3] A Greek grammarian and epic poet of the middle half of the fifth century B.C. According to Suidas he wrote a lipogrammatic *Odyssey* in 24 books, from each of which a letter of the alphabet was successively excluded.
[4] Proverbial for far-fetched etymologies. According to Quintilian (1. 6. 34) *Lucus*, a grove, is so called because, from the dense shade, there is very little light there (*Lucus, quia, umbra opacus, parum luceat*).

showed them, one after another, that he could do his Business without them.

It must have been very pleasant to have seen this Poet avoiding the reprobate Letter, as much as another would a false Quantity, and making his Escape from it through the Several *Greek* Dialects, when he was pressed with it in any particular Syllable. For the most apt and elegant Word in the whole Language was rejected, like a Diamond with a Flaw in it, if it appeared blemish'd with a wrong Letter. I shall only observe upon this Head, that if the Work I have here mentioned had been now extant, the *Odissey* of *Tryphiodorus*, in all probability, would have been oftner quoted by our learned Pedants, than the *Odissey* of *Homer*. What a perpetual Fund would it have been of obsolete Words and Phrases, unusual Barbarisms and Rusticities,[1] absurd Spellings and complicated Dialects? I make no Question but it would have been looked upon as one of the most valuable Treasuries of the *Greek* Tongue.

I find likewise among the Ancients that ingenious kind of Conceit, which the Moderns distinguish by the Name of a *Rebus*,[2] that does not sink a Letter but a whole Word, by substituting a Picture in its place. When *Cæsar* was one of the Masters of the *Roman* Mint, he placed the Figure of an Elephant upon the Reverse of the publick Mony; the Word *Cæsar* signifying an Elephant in the *Punick* Language. This was artificially contrived by *Cæsar*, because it was not lawful for a private Man to stamp his own Figure upon the Coin of the Commonwealth. *Cicero*, who was so call'd from the Founder of his Family, that was marked on the Nose with a little Wenn like a Vetch (which is *Cicer* in *Latin*) instead of *Marcus Tullius Cicero*, ordered the Words *Marcus Tullius* with the Figure of a Vetch at the end of 'em to be inscribed on a publick Monument. This was done probably to shew that he was neither ashamed of his Name or Family, notwithstanding the Envy of his Competitors had often reproach'd him with both. In the same manner we read of a famous

---

[1] Rusticity. A rustic expression (the earliest example of the word in this sense in *OED*).

[2] The section on 'Rebus, or Name-devises' in Camden's *Remains concerning Britain* (1605) provides most of the illustrations here (ed. 1674, pp. 210–15). 'Our great Master *Cicero* in a Dedication of his to his gods, inscribed *Marcus Tullius* and that little pulse less than a pease, which we call (I think) a chich-pease, and the *Latines Cicer*, instead of *Cicero*. As in the Coins of *Julius Caesar* we have seen an Elephant, for so *Caesar* signifieth in the *Mauritanian* Tongue . . .' (pp. 214–15). In the first of the *Dialogues upon Ancient Medals* Addison names the statue of Marcus Aurelius on horseback, along with the Hercules Farnese, the Venus de' Medici, and the Apollo Belvedere, as 'perhaps the four most beautiful Statues extant' (Guthkelch, ii. 292).

Building that was marked in several Parts of it with the Figures of a Frog and a Lizard: Those Words in *Greek* having been the Names of the Architects, who by the Laws of their Country were never permitted to inscribe their own Names upon their Works. For the same Reason it is thought, that the Forelock of the Horse in the Antique Equestrian Statue of *Marcus Aurelius*, represents at a distance the shape of an Owl, to intimate the Country of the Statuary, who, in all probability, was an *Athenian*. This kind of Wit was very much in Vogue among our own Country-men about an Age or two ago, who did not practise it for any oblique Reason, as the Ancients above-mentioned, but purely for the sake of being Witty. Among innumerable Instances that may be given of this Nature, I shall produce the Device of one Mr. *Newberry*, as I find it mention'd by our learned *Camden*[1] in his Remains. Mr. *Newberry*, to represent his Name by a Picture, hung up at his Door the Sign of a Yew-tree, that had several Berries upon it, and in the midst of them a great golden *N* hung upon a Bough of the Tree, which by the help of a little false Spelling made up the Word *N-ew-berry*.

I shall conclude this Topick with a *Rebus*, which has been lately hewn out in Free stone, and erected over two of the Portals of *Blenheim* House,[2] being the Figure of a monstrous Lion tearing to pieces a little Cock. For the better understanding of which Device, I must acquaint my *English* Reader that a Cock has the Misfortune to be called in *Latin* by the same Word that signifies a *French*-Man, as a Lion is the Emblem of the *English* Nation. Such a Device in so noble a Pile of Building looks like a Pun in an Heroic Poem; and I am very sorry the truly ingenious Architect would suffer the Statuary to blemish his excellent Plan with so poor a Conceit: But I hope what I have said will gain Quarter for the Cock, and deliver him out of the Lion's Paw.

[1] *Remains* (ed. 1674), p. 556:

Those devices that express Names by bodies are termed *Rebus*, in old times esteemed ingenious devices, but in ours ridiculous.

Master *Newbury* the Stationer, devised for himself an Ewtree with the Berries, and a great N. hanging upon a Snag in the midst of the Tree, which could not chuse but make *Newbery*.

[2] Blenheim House, at this time still uncompleted. The figure of the lion and cock is still to be seen over the entrance. The 'truly ingenious Architect' was Sir John Vanbrugh, and the 'Statuary' Grinling Gibbons. In No. 75 is advertised:

With Her Majesty's Royal Privilege and Licence, there is now Printing an Exact Description of the Palace of Blenheim in Oxfordshire, in a large Folio. Illustrated with the Plans, Sections and Perspectives. Engraven by the best Hands on Copper Plates. Several of which being already finished, are this Day published by Jacob Tonson, at Shakespear's Head over-against Catherine-street in the Strand.

I find likewise in ancient Times the Conceit of making an Eccho talk sensibly, and give rational Answers. If this could be excusable in any Writer it would be in *Ovid*,[1] where he introduces the Eccho as a Nymph, before she was worn away into nothing but a Voice. The learned *Erasmus*,[2] tho' a Man of Wit and Genius, has composed a Dialogue upon this silly kind of Device, and made use of an Eccho who seems to have been a very extraordinary Linguist, for she answers the Person she talks with in *Latin*, *Greek* and *Hebrew*, according as she found the Syllables which she was to repeat in any of those learned Languages. *Hudibras*,[3] in Ridicule of this false kind of Wit, has described *Bruin* bewailing the Loss of his Bear to a solitary Eccho, who is of great use to the Poet in several Disticks, as she does not only repeat after him, but helps out his Verse, and furnishes him with *Rhymes*.

> *He rag'd, and kept as heavy a Coil as*
> *Stout* Hercules *for loss of* Hylas;
> *Forcing the Vallies to repeat*
> *The Accents of his sad Regret:*
> *He beat his Breast, and tore his Hair,*
> *For Loss of his dear Crony Bear,*
> *That Eccho from the hollow Ground*
> *His doleful Wailings did resound*
> *More wistfully, by many times,*
> *Than in small Poets Splay-foot Rhymes,*
> *That make her, in their rueful Stories,*
> *To answer to Int'rogatories,*
> *And most unconscionably depose*
> *Things of which She nothing knows:*
> *And when she has said all she can say,*
> *'Tis wrested to the Lover's Fancy.*
> *Quoth he, O whither, wicked* Bruin,
> *Art thou fled to my—Eccho, Ruin?*
> *I thought th'hadst scorn'd to budge a Step*
> *For Fear.* (*Quoth Eccho*) Marry guep.
> *Am not I here to take thy Part!*
> *Then what has quell'd thy stubborn Heart?*

[1] *Metamorphoses*, 3. 356 ff.
[2] *Colloquia Familiaria* (Lyon, 1533), pp. 490–2. The Echo poem consists of a dialogue between Iuvenis and Echo, on the subject of studies. Echo answers in Latin and Greek, though not in Hebrew.
[3] *Hudibras*, I. iii. 183–220. (It is Orsin who is bewailing the loss of the bear.)

Have these Bones rattled, and this Head
So often in thy Quarrel bled?
Nor did I ever winch or grudge it,
For thy dear Sake. (Quoth she) Mum budget.
Think'st thou 'twill not be laid i'th'Dish
Thou turn'dst thy Back? Quoth Eccho, Pish.
To run from those th'hadst overcome
Thus cowardly? Quoth Eccho, Mum.
But what a-vengeance makes thee fly
From me too, as thine Enemy?
Or if thou hadst no Thought of me,
Nor what I have endur'd for Thee,
Yet Shame and Honour might prevail
To keep thee thus from turning Tail:
For who wou'd grudge to spend his Blood in
His Honour's Cause? Quoth she, a Pudding.

C

No. 60 *Wednesday, May 9, 1711*[1]

[ADDISON]

Hoc est quod palles? Cur quis non prandeat, Hoc est?

Per. Sat. 3.

SEVERAL Kinds of false Wit that vanished[a] in the refined Ages of the World, discovered themselves again in the Times of Monkish Ignorance.

As the Monks were the Masters of all that little Learning which was then extant, and had their whole Lives entirely disengaged from Business, it is no Wonder that several of them who wanted Genius for higher Performances, employed many Hours in the Composition of such Tricks in Writing as required much Time and little

---

[a] Several Kinds . . . vanished] The several Kinds of false Wit that vanished and disappeared *Fol.*

---

[1] *Motto.* Persius, *Satires*, 3. 85:
   Is it for this that you grow pale and go without your dinner?

Capacity. I have seen half the *Æneid* turn'd into *Latin* Rhymes[1] by one of the *Beaux Esprits* of that dark Age; who says in his Preface to it, that the *Æneid* wanted nothing but the Sweets of Rhyme to make it the most perfect Work in its Kind. I have likewise seen an Hymn in Hexameters to the Virgin *Mary*,[2] which filled a whole Book, tho' it consisted but of the eight following Words;

Tot, tibi, sunt, Virgo, dotes, quot, sidera, Cœlo.
Thou hast as many Virtues, O Virgin, as there are Stars in Heaven.

The Poet rung the Changes[a] upon these eight several Words, and by that Means made his Verses almost as numerous as the Virtues and the Stars which they celebrated. It is no Wonder that Men who had so much Time upon their Hands, did not only restore all the antiquated Pieces of false Wit, but enriched the World with Inventions of their own. It was to this Age that we owe the Production of Anagrams,[3] which is nothing else but a Transmutation of one Word into another, or the turning of the same Set of Letters into different Words; which may change Night into Day, or Black into White, if Chance, who is the Goddess that presides over these Sorts of Composition, shall so direct. I remember a witty Author, in Allusion to this Kind of Writing, calls his Rival, who (it seems) was distorted, and had his Limbs set in Places that did not properly belong to them, *The Anagram of a Man.*[4]

[a] Changes] Chymes *Fol.*

---

[1] I have not discovered the name of the medieval writer who made this experiment.
[2] The *Epigrammatum selectorum libri v* (Antwerp, 1616) of the Jesuit poet Bernard van Bauhuysen (or Bauhusius) contains (p. 74) an inscription to the Virgin Mary concluding with this line, which, according to its author could be arranged in 1,022 ways without impairing the sense or metre. In the following year Henri Dupuy (or Van de Putte) is said to have accomplished this feat, in his *Pietatis Thaumata in Proteum parthenicum unius libri versum, et unius versus librum, stellarum numeris sive formis 1022 variatum* (Antwerp, 1617). Tom Brown's 'Dialogue II: The Late Converts Exposed' mentions '*Scribonius* himself, or another of the Society that rung two and twenty thousand Changes upon the Eight Bells of the Virgin *Mary*'s good Qualities' (*A Collection of All the Dialogues*, 1704, p. 192). See *Biographie universelle*, art. 'Bauhuys'; *N & Q*, 1st ser., xii (1855), 222; 10th ser., ix (1908), 134–5.
[3] 'The Anagrame, or poesie transposed' is discussed in Puttenham (1589), and there is a section on anagrams in Camden's *Remains* (ed. 1674, pp. 216–27). For contemporary examples of anagrams and acrostics see W. Winstanley, *New Help to Discourse* (4th ed., 1695), pp. 185–9.
[4] I have not found the 'witty author' who coined this phrase. *Hudibras*, III. i. 771–2, has been cited by earlier editors, but the phrasing is only generally similar. Butler's couplet reads:

> His Body, that stupendous Frame,
> Of all the World the Anagram.

When the Anagrammatist takes a Name to work upon, he considers it at first as a Mine not broken up, which will not shew the Treasure it contains till he shall have spent many Hours in the Search of it: For it is his Business to find out one Word that conceals itself in another, and to examine the Letters in all the Variety of Stations in which they can possibly be ranged. I have heard of a Gentleman who, when this Kind of Wit was in fashion, endeavoured to gain his Mistress's Heart by it. She was one of the finest Women of her Age, and known by the Name of the Lady *Mary Boon*.[a] The Lover not being able to make any thing of *Mary*, by certain Liberties indulged to this Kind of writing converted it into *Moll*; and after having shut himself up for half a Year, with indefatigable Industry produced an Anagram. Upon the presenting it to his Mistress, who was a little vexed in her Heart to see her self degraded into *Moll Boon*, she told him, to his infinite Surprize, that he had mistaken her Sirname, for that it was not *Boon* but *Bohun*.

> . . . *Ibi omnis*
> *Effusus labor* . . . .[1]

The Lover was thunder-struck with his Misfortune, insomuch that in a little Time after he lost his Senses, which indeed had been very much impaired by that continual Application he had given to his Anagram.

The Acrostick[2] was probably invented about the same Time with the Anagram, tho' it is impossible to decide whether the Inventor of the one or the other were[b] the greater Blockhead. The *Simple* Acrostick is nothing but the Name or Title of a Person or Thing made out of the initial Letters of several Verses, and by that Means written, after the Manner of the *Chinese*,[3] in a perpendicular Line. But besides these there are *Compound* Acrosticks, where the principal Letters stand two or three deep. I have seen some of them where the

---

[a] known by . . . *Mary Boon*,] was called by the Name of *Mary Boon*. Fol. *Corrected in Errata (No. 61)*   [b] were] was *Fol.*

---

[1] Virgil, *Georgics*, 4. 491–2:
Straight all his Hopes exhal'd in empty Smoke;
And his long Toils were forfeit for a Look. DRYDEN.

[2] This, like the anagram, is found before the Middle Ages. Cicero gives examples in *De Divinatione*, 2. 54. 111–12. See the long article 'Akrostichis' in Pauly-Wissowa.

[3] Sir William Temple, 'Of Heroick Virtue', says of the Chinese: 'Their Writing is neither from the Left Hand to the Right like the *European*, nor from Right to Left like the *Asiatick* Languages, but from Top to Bottom of the Paper in one strait Line, and then beginning again at the Top till the Side be full' (*Works*, 1720, i. 201).

Verses have not only been edged by a Name at each Extremity, but have had the same Name running down like a Seam through the Middle of the Poem.

There is another near Relation of the Anagrams and Acrosticks, which is commonly called[a] a Chronogram.[1] This Kind of Wit appears very often on many modern Medals, especially those of *Germany*, when they represent in the Inscription the Year in which they were coined. Thus we see on a Medal of *Gustavus Adolphus*[2] the following Words, CHRIstVs DuX ergo trIVMphVs. If you take the Pains to pick the Figures out of the several Words, and range them in their proper Order, you will find they amount to MDCXVVVII, or 1627, the Year in which the Medal was stamped: For as some of the Letters distinguish themselves from the rest, and overtop their Fellows, they are to be considered in a double Capacity, both as Letters and as Figures. Your laborious *German* Wits will turn over a whole Dictionary for one of these ingenious Devices. A Man would think they were searching after an apt classical Term, but instead of that they are looking out a Word that has an L, an M, or a D in it. When therefore we meet with any of these Inscriptions, we are not so much to look in 'em for the Thought, as for the Year of the Lord.

The *Bouts Rimez*[3] were the Favourites of the *French* Nation for a whole Age together, and that at a Time when it abounded in Wit and Learning. They were a List of Words that rhyme to one another, drawn up by another Hand, and given to a Poet, who was to make a Poem to the Rhymes in the same Order that they were placed upon the List: The more uncommon the Rhymes were, the more extraordinary was the Genius of the Poet that could accommodate his Verses to them. I don't know any greater Instance of the Decay of Wit and Learning among the *French* (which generally follows the

---

[a] called] known by the Name of *Fol*.

[1] The Chronogram seems to have arisen in the seventeenth century. See James Hilton's *Chronograms, 5,000 and more in number* (1882) and *Chronograms continued and concluded* (1885).

[2] Gustavus II (1594–1632), King of Sweden, killed at Lützen 16 Nov. 1632. In the third of the *Dialogues on Medals*, apparently written shortly after his continental tour but not published until 1721, Addison uses this example and comments on the work of 'your laborious German wits' in the same language as in this paragraph, adding: 'There are foreign Universities where this kind of wit is so much in vogue, that as you praise a man in *England* for being an excellent Philosopher or Poet, it is an ordinary character among them to be a great Chronogrammatist. These are probably, says *Cynthio*, some of those mild provinces of Acrostic land, that Mr. *Dryden* has assigned to his Anagrams, Wings and Altars' (Guthkelch, ii. 388–9). It seems likely that Addison drew on already written notes for parts of these essays on wit.

[3] Bouts-rimés. This is the first example of the word in English (*OED*).

Declension of Empire), than the endeavouring to restore this foolish Kind of Wit. If the Reader will be at the Trouble to see Examples of it, let him look into the new *Mercure Galant;*[1] where the Author every Month gives a List of Rhymes to be filled up by the Ingenious, in order to be communicated to the Publick in the *Mercure* for the succeeding Month. That for the Month of *November* last, which[a] now lies before me, is as follows.

– – – – – – – – – – – – – – *Lauriers*
– – – – – – – – – – – – – – *Guerriers*
– – – – – – – – – – – – – – – *Musette*
– – – – – – – – – – – – – – – *Lisette*

– – – – – – – – – – – – – – *Cesars*
– – – – – – – – – – – – – – – *Etendars*
– – – – – – – – – – – – – – – *Houlette*
– – – – – – – – – – – – – – *Folette*

One would be amazed to see so learned a Man as *Menage*[2] talking seriously on this Kind of Trifle in the following Passage.

Monsieur de la Chambre *has told me, that he never knew what he was going to write when he took his Pen into his Hand; but that one Sentence always produced another. For my own Part, I never knew what I should write next when I was making Verses. In the first Place I got all my Rhymes together, and was afterwards perhaps three or four Months in filling them up. I one Day shewed Monsieur* Gombaud *a Composition of this Nature, in which among others I had made use of the four following Rhymes,* Amaryllis, Phillis, Marne, Arne, *desiring him to give me his Opinion of it. He told me immediately, That my Verses were good for nothing. And upon my asking his Reason, he said, Because the Rhymes are too common; and for that Reason easy to be put into Verse. Marry, says I, if it be so, I am very well rewarded for all the Pains I have been at. But by Monsieur* Gombaud's *Leave, notwithstanding the Severity of the Criticism, the Verses were good.* Vid. MENAGIANA.[3] Thus far the learned *Menage,* whom I have translated Word for Word.

[a] *November* last, which] *November,* which *Fol.*

---

[1] The *Mercure Galant,* founded in 1672, was a monthly periodical, with literary and theatrical news, fugitive pieces in verse and prose, &c. The editor from 1710 to 1714 was Charles Rivière Dufresny.

[2] An account of Giles Ménage (1613–92) will be found in Bayle, who calls him 'one of the most learn'd Men of his Time, and the *Varro* of the XVIIth Century'.

[3] *Menagiana* was first published in 1693. This passage will be found in the 3rd

The first Occasion of these *Bouts Rimez* made them in some Manner excusable, as they were Tasks which the *French* Ladies used to impose on their Lovers. But when a grave Author, like him abovementioned, tasked himself, could there be any thing more ridiculous? Or would not one be apt to believe that the Author played booty,[a] and did not make his List of Rhymes till he had finished his Poem?

I shall only add, that this Piece of false Wit has been finely ridiculed by Monsieur *Sarasin*[1] in a Poem entituled, *La Defaite des Bouts-Rimez, The Rout of the Bouts-Rimez.*

I must subjoyn to this last Kind of Wit the double Rhymes,[2] which are used in Doggerel Poetry, and generally applauded by ignorant Readers. If the Thought of the Couplet in such Compositions is good, the Rhyme adds little[b] to it; and if bad, it will not be in the Power of the Rhyme to recommend it. I am afraid that great Numbers of those who admire the incomparable *Hudibras*, do it more on Account of these Doggerel Rhymes than of the Parts that really deserve Admiration. I am sure I have heard the

> *Pulpit, Drum Ecclesiastick,*
> *Was beat with Fist instead of a Stick.*[3]

and

> *There was an antient sage Philosopher*
> *Who had read* Alexander Ross[4] *over.*

more frequently quoted, than the finest Pieces of Wit in the whole Poem.   C[5]

---

[a] booty,] double, *Fol.*   [b] little] nothing *Fol.*

---

edition (1715), ii. 355–6. Marin Cureau de la Chambre (1594–1669), Physician to the King, was author of the *Art de connaître les hommes.* Jean-Ogier de Gombauld (d. 1666) was admitted to the Académie Française in 1635, the year of its founding, with a discourse on the *je ne sais quoi.*

[1] The works of Jean-François Sarrasin (1603–54) were printed by Ménage in 1656 (see *Menagiana*, i. 30, 447). 'Dulot vaincu, ou la défaite des bouts-rimez' is a mock-heroic poem in four cantos, in which Sarrasin ridicules Dulot, the supposed inventor of *bouts-rimés.*

[2] Bysshe's *Art of English Poetry* (chap. ii, sect. iii) cites Dryden's opinion that they should seldom be used in heroic verse. Bysshe adds: 'but they are very graceful in the Lyrick, to which, as well as to the Burlesque, those Rhymes more properly belong' (8th ed., 1737, i. 22). (Bysshe uses these two couplets from *Hudibras* by way of illustration.)

[3] *Hudibras*, I. i. 11–12; I. ii. 1–2. Cf. *Tatler* 132.

[4] Alexander Ross (1590–1654), a Scottish clergyman and chaplain to Charles I, was author of *Pansebia, or a View of all Religions* (1653).

[5] A letter from T. Plainway at the Rainbow Coffee-house (Lillie, i. 262–3) praises 'your falling foul upon those vices in wit, as, altars, axes, acrosticks, chronograms, epigrams, anagrams, &c.', and suggests that Mr. Spectator now employ his forces 'in reducing and bringing in those out-laws in sense, the minters of words, who break

Non equidem hoc studeo, bullatis ut mihi nugis
Pagina turgescat, dare pondus idonea fumo.

Pers.

THERE is no kind of false Wit which has been so recommended by the Practice of all Ages, as that which consists in a Jingle of Words, and is comprehended under the general Name of *Punning*.[2] It is indeed impossible to kill a Weed, which the Soil has a natural Disposition to produce. The Seeds of Punning are in the Minds of all Men, and tho' they may be subdued by Reason, Reflection and good Sense, they will be very apt to shoot up in the greatest Genius, that is not broken and cultivated by the Rules of Art. Imitation is natural to us, and when it does not raise the Mind to Poetry, Painting, Musick, or other more noble Arts, it often breaks out in Punns and Quibbles.

Aristotle,[3] in the Eleventh Chapter of his Book of Rhetorick, describes two or three kinds of Punns, which he calls Paragrams, among the Beauties of good Writing, and produces Instances of them out of some of the greatest Authors in the *Greek* Tongue. *Cicero*[4] has

in upon our tongue, and may be as prejudicial to the speaking good English, as the Goths and Vandals were to the arts and sciences . . .'. This may have suggested Nos. 135 and 165 (vol. ii).

[1] *Motto.* Persius, *Satires*, 5. 19–20:

Indeed, it is no aim of mine that my page should swell with pretentious trifles, fit only to give solidity to smoke.

[2] *Tatler* 32 calls punning 'an Enormity which has been reviv'd (after being long oppress'd)', and the *Spectator* generally considers the pun only an example of false wit (cf. the censure of Milton's puns in No. 297 (vol. iii)), though Addison himself occasionally puns, as in the play on the words *pie* and *piety* in No. 85, and many of his friends were addicted to the practice, particularly Swift. *Guardian* 36 is given over to an 'Apology for Punning'. For the origin of the word *pun* see *OED*, which considers it as probably one of the clipped words like *mob* which came into fashionable slang at or after the Restoration. The *OED* also quotes from John Norris's *Reflections upon the Conduct of Humane Life* (1690): 'This great Mystery of Disputation is nothing else but a meer Tossing of Words backward and forward, sometimes without any meaning, which is Canting; and sometimes with more Meanings than one, which is Punning' (ed. 1691, p. 58). Peter Motteux, in the preface to his translation of Rabelais (1708), defends the puns, clenches, conundrums, and quibbles in his author. They were used, he maintains, by Aristophanes, Plautus, and Tully. 'They were doubtless better lik'd in those times, than they are now; and we find them in as great a Number in almost all the Writers of the last Age, that pretended to Wit; nor have Rhetoricians refus'd to teach or use the Figure *Antanaclasis*' (p. civ).

[3] *Rhetoric*, 3. 11. 7. Paragram is defined in *OED* as 'a kind of play upon words, consisting in the alteration of one letter or group of letters of a word'.

[4] *De Oratore*, 2. 61–63.

sprinkled several of his Works with Punns, and in his Book where he lays down the Rules of Oratory, quotes abundance of Sayings as Pieces of Wit, which also upon Examination prove arrant Punns. But the Age in which *the Punn* chiefly flourished, was the Reign of King *James* the First.[1] That learned Monarch was himself a tolerable Punnster, and made very few Bishops or Privy-Counsellors that had not some time or other signalized themselves by a Clinch, or a *Conundrum*.[2] It was therefore in this Age that the Punn appeared with Pomp and Dignity. It had before been admitted into merry Speeches and ludicrous Compositions, but was now delivered with great Gravity from the Pulpit, or pronounced in the most solemn manner at the Council-Table. The greatest Authors, in their most serious Works, made frequent use of Punns. The Sermons of Bishop *Andrews*,[3] and the Tragedies of *Shakespear*,[4] are full of them. The Sinner was punned into Repentance by the former, as in the Latter nothing is more usual than to see a Hero weeping and quibbling for a dozen Lines together.

I must add to these great Authorities, which seem to have given a kind of Sanction to this Piece of false Wit, that all the Writers of Rhetorick have treated of Punning with very great Respect, and divided the several kinds of it into hard Names, that are reckoned among the Figures of Speech, and recommended as Ornaments in Discourse. I remember a Country School-master of my Acquaintance told me once, that he had been in Company with a Gentleman whom he looked upon to be the greatest *Paragrammatist*[5] among the Moderns. Upon Enquiry, I found my learned Friend had dined that

[1] The pedantry of the 'learned monarch' is referred to in the *Dunciad* (iv. 175 80). His prose works (*Daemonologie, Basilikon Doron*, the *Counterblaste to Tobacco*, &c.) were collected and edited by James Montagu, the Bishop of Winchester, in 1616.

[2] The meaning here is the obsolete one of pun or word-play. The modern sense of 'riddle in form of question' does not come into use until the latter half of the century (*OED*).

[3] Lancelot Andrewes (1555–1626), Bishop of Winchester. His sermons had long been criticized for their metaphysical and 'witty' adornments. Andrewes was held to be representative of the old style, as Tillotson was of the new; hence 'praise of the latter is frequently combined with depreciation of the former' (*DNB*). For criticism of Andrewes by Thomas Tenison, Robert South, and others, see George Williamson, *The Senecan Amble* (1951), pp. 248–74.

[4] Rowe, in his 'Account of Shakespeare' (1709), makes a similar comment: 'As for his Jingling sometimes, and playing upon Words, it was the common Vice of the Age he liv'd in: And if we find it in the Pulpit, made use of as an Ornament to the Sermons of some of the Gravest Divines of those Times; perhaps it may not be thought too light for the Stage' (p. xxiii).

[5] The earliest example of this word in English (*OED*). For paragram see above, p. 259, n. 3.

Day with Mr. *Swan*,[1] the famous Punnster; and desiring him to give me some Account of Mr. *Swan*'s Conversation, he told me that he generally talked in the *Paranomasia*,[2] that he sometimes gave into the *Plocè*,[3] but that in his humble Opinion he shined most in the *Antanaclasis*.[4]

I must not here omit, that a famous University[5] of this Land was formerly very much Infested with Punns; but whether or no this might not arise from the Fens and Marshes in which it was situated, and which are now drain'd, I must leave to the Determination of more skilful Naturalists.

After this short History of Punning, one would wonder how it should be so entirely banish'd out of the Learned World, as it is at present, especially since it had found a Place in the Writings of the most ancient Polite Authors. To account for this, we must consider, that the first Race of Authors, who were the great Heroes in Writing, were destitute of all Rules and Arts of Criticism; and for that Reason, though they excel later Writers in Greatness of Genius, they fall short of them in Accuracy and Correctness. The Moderns cannot reach their Beauties, but can avoid their Imperfections. When the World was furnish'd with these Authors of the first Eminence, there grew up another Set of Writers, who gained themselves a Reputation by the Remarks which they made on the Works of those who preceded them. It was one of the Employments of these Secondary Authors, to distinguish the several kinds of Wit by Terms of Art, and to consider them as more or less perfect, according as they were founded in Truth. It is no wonder therefore, that even such Authors as *Isocrates*, *Plato* and *Cicero*, should have such little

---

[1] 'Honest Mr. Swan', as a maker of puns and clenches, is mentioned by Dryden in the *Discourse concerning Satire* (1693) (*Essays*, ed. Ker, ii. 95; see also other references to Swan in Ker's note, ii. 285). Wycherley addressed a poem to him: 'A Panegyric, on Quibling; to the, that way, Ingenious Mr. Swan' (*Works*, ed. M. Summers, iii. 163–5).

[2] An obsolete and incorrect spelling of *paronomasia*. Cf. *OED*.

[3] Lit. *plaiting*. 'The repetition of a word in an altered or more expressive sense, or for the sake of emphasis' (*OED*).

[4] The repetition of a word in a different or even contrary sense. Johnson defines it as a figure of speech, 'when the same word is repeated in a different, if not in a contrary signification; as *In thy youth learn some craft, that in thy old age thou mayest get thy living without craft*'.

[5] Cambridge. Cf. John Henley, 'An Oration on Grave Conundrums, and Serious Buffoons': 'All Schools, especially *Westminster*, train up Scholars to declaim in an ironical Manner, and make Sharp and Burlesque Epigrams and Poems. Colleges are famous for the like; Puns are a main Education in *Cambridge*; and practis'd and profess'd in all Exercises and Conversation' (*Oratory Transactions*, no. vi (1729), p. 12.

Blemishes as are not to be met with in Authors of a much inferior Character, who have written since those several Blemishes were discover'd. I do not find that there was a proper Separation made between Punns and true[a] Wit by any of the ancient Authors, except *Quintilian* and *Longinus*. But when this Distinction was once settled, it was very natural for all Men of Sense to agree in it. As for the Revival of this false Wit, it happen'd about the time of the Revival of Letters,[1] but as soon as it was once detected, it immediately vanish'd and disappear'd. At the same time there is no Question, but as it has sunk in one Age and rose in another, it will again recover it self in some distant Period of Time, as Pedantry and Ignorance shall prevail upon Wit and Sense. And, to speak the Truth, I do very much apprehend, by some of the last Winter's Productions, which had their Sets of Admirers, that our Posterity will in a few Years degenerate into a Race of Punnsters: At least, a Man may be very excusable for any Apprehensions of this kind, that has seen *Acrosticks* handed about the Town with great Secresie and Applause; to which I must also add a little *Epigram* called the *Witches Prayer*,[2] that fell into Verse when it was read either backward or forward, excepting only, that it Cursed one way and Blessed the other. When one sees there are actually such Pains-takers[3] among our *British* Wits, who can tell what it may end in? If we must Lash one another, let it be with the manly Strokes of Wit and Satyr; for I am of the old Philosopher's Opinion, That if I must suffer from one or the other, I would rather it should be from the Paw of a Lion,[4] than the Hoof of an Ass. I do not speak this out of any Spirit of Party. There is a most crying Dulness on both sides. I have seen Tory *Acrosticks* and Whig *Anagrams*, and do not quarrel with either of them, because they are *Whigs* or *Tories*, but because they are *Anagrams* and *Acrosticks*.

But to return to Punning. Having pursued the History of a Punn, from its Original to its Downfal, I shall here define it to be a Conceit arising from the use of two Words that agree in the Sound, but

---

[a] true] fine *Fol.*

---

[1] The earliest example in *OED* of this phrase for 'the Renaissance in its literary aspect' is dated 1785.

[2] See *Hudibras*, I. iii. 343–4; Congreve, *Love for Love*, IV. xxi; Blackmore, *Satyr against Wit*, 348–9; &c.

[3] This is the last quotation in *OED* for this obsolete word.

[4] Cf. L'Estrange, *Fables of Æsop*, no. 14.

differ in the Sense. The only way therefore to try a Piece of Wit[1] is to translate it into a different Language, if it bears the Test you may pronounce it true; but if it vanishes in the Experiment, you may conclude it to have been[a] a Punn. In short, one may say of a Punn as the Country-man described his Nightingale, that it is *vox & prætereà nihil*,[2] a Sound, and nothing but a Sound. On the contrary, one may represent true Wit by the Description which *Aristinetus*[3] makes of a fine Woman, When she is *dress'd* she is Beautiful, when she is *undress'd* she is Beautiful: Or, as *Mercerus* has translated it more Emphatically,[b] *Induitur, formosa est: Exuitur, ipsa forma est.*   C

No. 62

[ADDISON]

Friday, May 11, 1711[4]

Scribendi recte Sapere est & principium & fons.

Hor.

MR. *LOCK*[5] has an admirable Reflection upon the Difference of Wit and Judgment, whereby he endeavours to shew the Reason why they are not always the Talents of the same Person. His Words are as follow: *And hence, perhaps, may be given some Reason of that common Observation, That Men who have a great deal of Wit and prompt Memories, have not always the clearest Judgment, or deepest Reason. For Wit lying most in the Assemblage of Ideas, and putting those together*

---

   [a] have been] be *Fol.*   [b] more Emphatically,] *om. Fol.*

[1] Cf. Addison's *Dialogues upon Ancient Medals*, ii: 'A pun can be no more engraven than it can be translated. When the word is construed into its idea the double meaning vanishes' (Guthkelch, ii. 362–3).
[2] Plutarch, 'Sayings of Spartans', *Moralia* 233A, and frequently quoted, e.g. Burton, *Anatomy*, 'Democritus Junior to the Reader'; Bayle, 'Cornelio Musso', Remark C.
[3] Aristenetus (book i, letter 1). See *Menagiana*, 1715, ii. 176–7: 'J'ai rendu quelques pensées d'Aristenet en vers Grecs. Par exemple, celle, où en parlant d'une beauté, il dit qu'elle étoit belle étant vétuë, mais qu'elle étoit la beauté même étant nuë. . . . Mercier beau-pere de M. Saumaise a merveilleusement bien exprimé la premiére par ces mots: *Induitur, formosa est: exuitur, ipsa forma est.*'
[4] *Motto*. Horace, *Ars poetica*, 309: Of writing well the source and fount is wisdom.
[5] Locke, *Essay concerning Humane Understanding*, II. xi. 2. This definition had also been quoted approvingly by Addison in his Notes on Ovid (1704), where many of the arguments and illustrations in these essays on true, mixed, and false wit are to be found. See Guthkelch, i. 133–47, particularly pp. 143–4. The same distinction between wit and judgement is also made by Robert Boyle, *Occasional Reflections upon Several Subiects* (1665), sect. iii, chap. v (p. 46).

with Quickness and Variety, wherein can be found any Resemblance or Congruity thereby to make up pleasant Pictures and agreeable Visions in the Fancy; Judgment, on the contrary, lies quite on the other Side, In separating carefully one from another, Ideas wherein can be found the least Difference, thereby to avoid being misled by Similitude and by Affinity to take one thing for another. This is a Way of proceeding quite contrary to Metaphor and Allusion; wherein, for the most Part, lies that Entertainment and Pleasantry of Wit which strikes so lively on the Fancy, and is therefore so acceptable to all People.

This is, I think, the best and most philosophical Account that I have ever met with of Wit, which generally, tho' not always, consists in such a Resemblance and Congruity of Ideas as this Author mentions. I shall only add to it, by way of Explanation, That every Resemblance of Ideas is not that which we call Wit, unless it be such an one that gives *Delight* and *Surprize* to the Reader: These two Properties seem essential to Wit, more particularly the last of them. In order therefore that the Resemblance in the Ideas be Wit, it is necessary that the Ideas should not lie too near one another in the Nature of things; for where the Likeness is obvious, it gives no Surprize. To compare one Man's Singing to that of another, or to represent the Whiteness of any Object by that of Milk and Snow, or the Variety of its Colours by those of the Rainbow, cannot be called Wit, unless, besides this obvious Resemblance, there be some further Congruity discovered in the two Ideas that is capable of giving the Reader some Surprize. Thus when a Poet tells us, the Bosom of his Mistress is as white as Snow, there is no Wit in the Comparison;[1] but when he adds, with a Sigh, that it is as cold too, it then grows into Wit. Every Reader's Memory may supply him with innumerable Instances of the same Nature. For this Reason, the Similitudes in Heroick Poets, who endeavour rather to fill the Mind with great Conceptions, than to divert it with such as are new and surprizing, have seldom any thing in them that can be called Wit. Mr. *Lock*'s Account of Wit, with this short Explanation, comprehends most of the Species of Wit, as Metaphors, Similitudes,

---

[1] 'Upon the Constellation of Beauties that were lately seen in Greenwitch-Park', by Captain Ayloffe (in 'A Collection of Poems by Persons of Honour and Quality, Corrected and revis'd, by Mr. Tho. Brown') contains the couplet:

> Her Breast is like a Heap of sollid Snow,
> Boasting its Colour, and its coldness too.

(*Second Volume of Miscellaneous Works, written by George, late Duke of Buckingham, Collected . . . by the late ingenious Mr. Tho. Brown* (1705), p. 78.)

Allegories, Ænigmas, Mottos, Parables, Fables, Dreams, Visions, dramatick Writings, Burlesque, and all the Methods of Allusion: As there are many other Pieces of Wit (how remote soever they may appear at first Sight from the foregoing Description) which upon Examination will be found to agree with it.

As *true Wit* generally consists in this Resemblance and Congruity of Ideas, *false Wit* chiefly consists in the Resemblance and Congruity sometimes of single Letters, as in Anagrams, Chronograms, Lipograms, and Acrosticks: Sometimes of Syllables, as in Ecchos and Doggerel Rhymes: Sometimes of Words, as in Punns and Quibbles; and sometimes of whole Sentences or Poems, cast into the Figures of *Eggs*, *Axes*, or *Altars*: Nay some carry the Notion of Wit so far, as to ascribe it even to external Mimickry;[1] and to look upon a Man as an ingenious Person, that can resemble the Tone, Posture, or Face of another.

As *true Wit* consists in the Resemblance of Ideas, and *false Wit* in the Resemblance of Words, according to the foregoing Instances; there is another kind of Wit which consists partly in the Resemblance of Ideas, and partly in the Resemblance of Words; which for Distinction Sake I shall call *mixt Wit*. This Kind of Wit is that which abounds in *Cowley*,[2] more than in any Author that ever wrote. Mr. *Waller* has likewise a great deal of it. Mr. *Dryden* is very sparing in it. *Milton* had a Genius much above it. *Spencer* is in the same Class with *Milton*. The *Italians*, even in their Epic Poetry, are full of it. Monsieur *Boileau*, who formed himself upon the ancient Poets, has every where rejected it with Scorn. If we look after mixt Wit among the *Greek* Writers, we shall find it no where but in the Epigrammatists. There are indeed some Strokes of it in the little Poem ascribed to *Musæus*,[3] which by that, as well as many other Marks, betrays it self to be a modern Composition. If we look into the *Latin* Writers, we find none of this mixt Wit in *Virgil*, *Lucretius*, or

---

[1] One of the types of 'creeping and cringing Wit' described in Henry Barker's *The Polite Gentleman* (1700) is the man who merely seeks to amuse and provoke laughter (p. 16).

[2] Cowley, Waller, Dryden, Milton, and Spenser are all treated in Addison's early poem, 'An Account of the Greatest English Poets' (1694), where Cowley's fault is described as 'only wit in its excess'.

[3] The 'Hero and Leander' is printed in Winterton, *Poetae Minores Graeci*, pp. 330–47. Cf. *Menagiana* (1715, ii. 6–7): 'Jule Scaligèr a cru que Musée auteur du petit Poëme de Leandre & Héro, étoit l'ancien Musée; mais il s'est trompé, & Scaligèr son fils l'a avoué lui-même. Ce dernier Musée étoit un Grammairien. Il a fait ce Poëme où il a réussi.' See also Theobald's 'Essay on the Hero and Leander of Musaeus', prefixed to his translation in *The Grove* (1721).

Catullus; very little in *Horace*, but a great deal of it in *Ovid*, and scarce any thing else in *Martial*.

Out of the innumerable Branches of mixt Wit, I shall chuse one Instance which may be met with in all the Writers of this Class. The Passion of Love in its Nature has been thought to resemble Fire; for which Reason the Words Fire and Flame are made use of to signify Love. The witty Poets therefore have taken an Advantage from the doubtful Meaning of the Word Fire, to make an infinite Number of Witticisms. *Cowley*[1] observing the cold Regard of his Mistress's Eyes, and at the same Time their Power of producing Love in him, considers them as Burning-Glasses made of Ice; and finding himself able to live in the greatest Extremities of Love, concludes the Torrid Zone to be habitable. When his Mistress has read his Letter written in Juice of Lemmon by holding it to the Fire, he desires her to read it over a second time by Love's Flames. When she weeps, he wishes it were inward Heat that distilled those Drops from the Limbeck.[2] When she is absent he is beyond eighty, that is, thirty Degrees nearer the Pole than when she is with him. His ambitious Love is a Fire that naturally mounts upwards, his happy Love is the Beams of Heaven, and his unhappy Love Flames of Hell. When it does not let him sleep, it is a Flame that sends up no Smoak; when it is opposed by Counsel and Advice, it is a Fire that rages the more by the Wind's blowing upon it. Upon the dying of a Tree in which he had cut his Loves, he observes that his written Flames had burnt up and withered the Tree. When he resolves to give over his Passion, he tells us that one burnt like him for ever dreads the Fire. His Heart is an *Ætna*, that instead of *Vulcan*'s Shop encloses *Cupid*'s Forge in it. His endeavouring to drown his Love in Wine, is throwing Oil upon the Fire. He would insinuate to his Mistress, that the Fire of Love, like that of the Sun (which produces so many living Creatures)[a] should not only warm but beget. Love in another Place

---

[a] many living Creatures)] many Creatures) *Fol.*

[1] The examples of mixt wit are taken from his collection, *The Mistress*. Burning-glasses: 'The Vain Love', lines 1–4. The Torrid Zone: 'The Request', stanza 4. His Letter: 'Written in Juice of Lemmon', stanza 4. When she weeps: 'Weeping', stanza 4. When she is absent: 'The Parting', stanza 3. His ambitious Love: 'My Fate', stanzas 1, 3. When it does not let him sleep: 'Sleep', stanza 1. When it is opposed: 'Counsel' (ii), stanza 2. Upon the Dying of a Tree: 'The Tree', stanza 1. When he resolves: 'Love given over', stanza 4. An Aetna: 'The Monopoly', stanza 1. Throwing Oil: 'The Incurable', stanza 4. The Fire of Love: 'The Parting', stanza 6. Love . . . cooks Pleasure: 'Answer to the Platonicks', 11–12. The Poet's Heart: 'The Heart Fled Again', stanza 4. A Ship set on Fire: 'Love Given Over', stanza 2.

[2] i.e. alembic.

cooks Pleasure at his[a] Fire. Sometimes the Poet's[b] Heart is frozen in every Breast, and sometimes scorched in every Eye. Sometimes he is drowned in Tears, and burnt in Love, like a Ship set on fire in the Middle of the Sea.

The Reader may observe in every one of these Instances, that the Poet mixes the Qualities of Fire with those of Love; and in the same Sentence speaking of it both as a Passion and as real Fire, surprizes the Reader with those seeming Resemblances or Contradictions that make up all the Wit in this kind of Writing. Mixt Wit[1] therefore is a Composition of Punn and true Wit, and is more or less perfect as the Resemblance lies in the Ideas or in the Words: Its Foundations are laid partly in Falsehood and partly in Truth: Reason puts in her Claim for one Half of it, and Extravagance for the other. The only Province therefore for this kind of Wit, is Epigram,[2] or those little occasional Poems that in their own Nature are nothing else but a Tissue of Epigrams. I cannot conclude this Head of *mixt Wit*, without owning that the admirable Poet out of whom I have taken the Examples of it, had as much true Wit as any Author that ever writ; and indeed all other Talents of an extraordinary Genius.

It may be expected, since I am upon this Subject, that I should take Notice of Mr. *Dryden*'s Definition[3] of Wit; which, with all the Deference that is due to the Judgment of so great a Man, is not so properly a Definition of Wit, as of good Writing in general. Wit, as he defines it, is 'a Propriety of Words and Thoughts adapted to the Subject.' If this be a true Definition of Wit, I am apt to think that *Euclid* was[c] the greatest Wit that ever set Pen to Paper: It is certain there never was a greater Propriety of Words and Thoughts adapted to the Subject, than what that Author has made use of in his Elements. I shall only appeal to my Reader, if this Definition agrees with any Notion he has of Wit: If it be a true one, I am sure Mr. *Dryden* was not only a better Poet, but a greater Wit than

---

[a] his] its *Fol.*   [b] the Poet's] his *Fol.*   [c] was] is *Fol.*

---

[1] See Robert L. Morris, 'Addison's *Mixt Wit*', *Modern Language Notes*, lvii (1942), 666–8.

[2] Here used in the sense of 'a pointed or antithetical saying'.

[3] 'A propriety of thoughts and words; or, in other terms, thoughts and words elegantly adapted to the subject' (*Apology* prefixed to *The State of Innocence*, 1677; Ker, i. 190). For censure of Addison in omitting the word 'elegantly' from this definition see George Williamson, *The Senecan Amble* (1951), p. 355 n. In *Tatler* 62 'The Evening was spent at our Table in Discourse of Propriety of Words and Thoughts, which is Mr. *Dryden*'s Definition of Wit'.

Mr. *Cowley*, and *Virgil* a much more facetious Man than either *Ovid* or *Martial*.

Bouhours,[1] whom I look upon to be the most penetrating of all the *French* Criticks, has taken Pains to shew, That it is impossible for any Thought to be beautiful which is not just, and has not its Foundation in the Nature of things: That the Basis of all Wit is Truth; and that no Thought can be valuable, of which good Sense is not the Ground-work. *Boileau*[2] has endeavoured to inculcate the same Notion in several Parts of his Writings, both in Prose and Verse. This is that natural Way of writing, that beautiful Simplicity, which we so much admire in the Compositions of the Ancients; and which no Body deviates from, but those who want Strength of Genius to make a Thought shine in its own natural Beauties. Poets who want this Strength of Genius to give that majestick Simplicity to Nature, which we so much admire in the Works of the Ancients, are forced to hunt after foreign Ornaments, and not to let any Piece of Wit of what Kind soever escape them. I look upon these Writers as *Goths* in Poetry, who, like those in Architecture, not being able to come up to the beautiful Simplicity of the old *Greeks* and *Romans*, have endeavoured to supply its Place with all the Extravagancies of an irregular Fancy. Mr. *Dryden*[3] makes a very handsome Observation on *Ovid*'s writing a Letter from *Dido* to *Æneas* in the following Words: '*Ovid* (says he, speaking of *Virgil*'s Fiction of *Dido* and *Æneas*) takes it up after him, even in the same Age, and makes an ancient Heroine of *Virgil*'s new-created *Dido*; dictates a Letter for her just before her Death to the ungrateful Fugitive; and, very unluckily for himself, is for measuring a Sword with a Man so much superiour in Force to him, on the same Subject. I think I may be

---

[1] The Jesuit grammarian and critic, Dominique Bouhours (1628–1702). His influential *Manière de bien penser dans les ouvrages d'esprit* was published in 1687 (2nd edition, revised and corrected, at Amsterdam, 1692). It consists of four dialogues between Eudoxe, the exponent of good taste and admirer of the Ancients, and Philanthe, who prefers the more showy literature of the Spanish and Italians. Addison is referring to the discussion of 'ingenious thoughts' in the first dialogue, where Eudoxe explains: 'La verité est la premiére qualité, & comme le fondement des pensées: les plus belles sont vitieuses; ou plûtost celles qui passent pour belles, & qui semblent l'estre, ne le sont pas en effet; si ce fond leur manque' (p. 9).

[2] In the preface to the 1701 edition of his *Works* Boileau writes: 'What is a New, Brilliant, Extraordinary Thought? It is not, as the Ignorant persuade themselves, a Thought which no Body ever had, nor ought to have. But on the contrary, a Thought which every Body ought to have had, and which some one bethinks himself of expressing the First. *Wit* is not *Wit*, but as it says something every Body thought of, and that in a lively, delicate, and New Manner' (*Works*, 1711–12, i, pp. ii–iii).

[3] 'Dedication of the Aeneis', 1697 (*Essays*, ed. Ker, ii. 193–4).

Judge of this, because I have translated both. The famous Author of the Art of Love has nothing of his own; he borrows all from a greater Master in his own Profession, and, which is worse, improves nothing which he finds: Nature fails him, and being forced to his old Shift, he has Recourse to Witticism. This passes indeed with his soft Admirers, and gives him the Preference to *Virgil* in their Esteem.'

Were not I supported by so great an Authority as that of Mr. *Dryden*, I should not venture to observe, That the Taste of most of our *English* Poets, as well as Readers, is extremely *Gothick*. He quotes Monsieur *Segrais* for a threefold Distinction of the Readers of Poetry: In the first of which he comprehends the Rabble of Readers, whom he does not treat as such with regard to their Quality, but to their Numbers and the Coarseness of their Taste. His Words are as follow: '*Segrais*[1] has distinguished the Readers of Poetry, according to their Capacity of judging, into three Classes. [He might have said the same of Writers too if he had pleased.] In the lowest Form he places those whom he calls *Les Petits Esprits*, such things as are our upper-Gallery Audience in a Play-house; who like nothing but the Husk and Rind of Wit, prefer a Quibble, a Conceit, an Epigram, before solid Sense and elegant Expression: These are Mob-Readers. If *Virgil* and *Martial* stood for Parliament-Men, we know already who would carry it. But though they make the greatest Appearance in the Field, and cry the loudest, the best on't is they are but a Sort of *French* Huguenots, or *Dutch* Boors, brought over in Herds, but not naturalized; who have not Lands of two Pounds *per Annum* in *Parnassus*, and therefore are not privileg'd to poll. Their Authors are of the same Level, fit to represent them on a Mountebank's Stage, or to be Masters of the Ceremonies in a Bear-Garden: Yet these are they who have the most Admirers. But it often happens, to their Mortification, that as their Readers improve their Stock of Sense, (as they may by reading better Books, and by Conversation with Men of Judgment) they soon forsake them.'

I must not dismiss this Subject without observing,[a] that as Mr. *Lock* in the Passage above-mentioned has discovered the most fruitful Source of Wit, so there is another of a quite contrary Nature to

---

[a] I must not . . . observing,] I would not break the Thread of this Discourse without observing, *Fol. Corrected in Errata (No. 63): for* without *read* with

---

[1] Ker, ii. 223 ff. Jean Regnauld de Segrais (d. 1701) was a member of the circle of the Hôtel de Rambouillet. His dissertation on Virgil, prefixed to his translation of the *Aeneid* and the *Georgics*, is quoted by Dryden.

it, which does likewise branch it self out into several Kinds. For not only the *Resemblance* but the *Opposition* of Ideas does very often pro-duce Wit; as I cou'd shew in several little Points, Turns, and Anti-theses, that I may possibly enlarge upon in some future Speculation.

C

No. 63   *Saturday, May* 12, 1711[1]
[ADDISON]

> *Humano Capiti cervicem pictor Equinam*
> *Jungere si velit & varias inducere plumas*
> *Undique collatis membris, ut turpiter atrum*
> *Desinat in piscem mulier formosa supernè;*
> *Spectatum admissi risum teneatis, amici?*
> *Credite, Pisones, isti tabulæ fore librum*
> *Persimilem, cujus, velut ægri somnia, vanæ*
> *Finguntur species . . .*
>
> Hor.

IT is very hard for the Mind to disengage it self from a Subject in which it has been long employed. The Thoughts will be rising of themselves from time to time, tho' we give them no Encourage-ment; as the Tossings and Fluctuations of the Sea continue several hours after the Winds are laid.

It is to this that I impute my last Night's Dream or Vision, which[a] formed into one Continued Allegory the several Schemes of Wit, whether False, Mixed, or True, that have been the Subject of my late Papers.

---

a which] that *Fol.*

---

[1] *Motto.* Horace, *Ars poetica*, 1-8:
> If in a Picture (*Piso*) you should see
> A handsom Woman with a Fishes Tail,
> Or a Man's Head upon a Horse's Neck,
> Or Limbs of Beasts of the most diff'rent kinds,
> Cover'd with Feathers of all sorts of Birds,
> Would you not laugh, and think the Painter mad?
> Trust me, that Book is as ridiculous,
> Whose incoherent Stile (like sick Mens Dreams)
> Varies all Shapes, and mixes all Extremes. ROSCOMMON.

Methoughts I was transported into a Country that was filled with Prodigies and Enchantments, Governed by the Goddess of FALSE-HOOD, and entitled the *Region of false Wit*. There was nothing in the Fields, the Woods, and the Rivers, that appeared natural. Several of the Trees blossom'd in Leaf-Gold, some of them produced Bone-Lace, and some of them precious Stones. The Fountains bubbled in an Opera Tune, and were filled with Stags, Wild-Boars, and Mermaids, that lived among the Waters, at the same time that Dolphins and several kinds of Fish played upon the Banks, or took their Pastime in the Meadows. The Birds had many of them Golden Beaks, and human Voices. The Flowers perfumed the Air with Smells of Incense, Amber-Greese and Pulvillios,[1] and were so inter-woven with one another, that they grew up in Pieces of Embroidery. The Winds were fill'd with Sighs and Messages of distant Lovers. As I was walking to and fro in this enchanted Wilderness, I could not forbear breaking out into Soliloquies upon the several Wonders which lay before me, when to my great Surprise I found there were artificial Ecchoes in every Walk, that by Repetitions of certain Words which I spoke, agreed with me, or contradicted me, in every thing I said. In the midst of my Conversation with these invisible Companions, I discover'd in the Center of a very dark Grove a Monstrous Fabrick built after the *Gothick* manner, and covered with innumerable Devices in that barbarous kind of Sculpture. I immediately went up to it, and found it to be a kind of Heathen Temple consecrated to the God of *Dullness*.[2] Upon my Entrance I saw the Deity of the Place dressed in the Habit of a Monk, with a Book in one Hand and a Rattle in the other. Upon his right Hand was *Industry*, with a Lamp burning before Her; and on his left *Caprice*, with a Monky sitting on her Shoulder. Before his Feet there stood an *Altar* of a very odd Make, which, as I afterwards found, was shaped in that manner, to comply with the Inscription that surrounded it. Upon the Altar there lay several Offerings of *Axes*, *Wings*, and *Eggs*, cut in Paper, and inscribed with Verses. The Temple was filled with Votaries, who applied themselves to different Diversions, as their Fancies directed them. In one Part of it I saw a Regiment of *Anagrams*, who were continually in motion, turning to the Right or to the Left, facing about, doubling their Ranks,

[1] Pulvillio (Ital. *polviglio*), cosmetic or perfumed powder for powdering the wig or perfuming the person.
[2] A general term for slowness, obtuseness, and bad writing generally—the eighteenth-century equivalent of bad art. Cf. Dryden's *Mac Flecknoe*, Pope's *Dunciad*, &c.

shifting their Stations, and throwing themselves into all the Figures and Counter-marches of the most changeable and perplexed Exercise.

Not far from these was a Body of *Acrosticks*, made up of very disproportioned Persons. It was disposed into three Columns, the Officers planting themselves in a Line on the left Hand of each Column. The Officers were all of them at least Six Foot high, and made three Rows of very proper Men; but the Common Soldiers, who[a] filled up the Spaces between the Officers, were such Dwarfs, Cripples, and Scare-Crows, that one could hardly look upon them without laughing. There were behind the *Acrosticks* two or three files of *Chronograms*, which differed only from the former, as their Officers were equipped (like the Figure of Time) with an Hourglass in one Hand, and a Scythe in the other, and took their Posts promiscuously among the Private Men whom they commanded.

In the Body of the Temple, and before the very Face of the Deity, methoughts I saw the Phantom of *Tryphiodorus*[1] the *Lipo-grammatist*, engaged in a Ball with four and twenty Persons, who pursued him by turns through all the Intricacies and Labyrinths of a Country Dance, without being able to overtake him.

Observing several to be very busie at the Western End of the *Temple*, I enquired into what they were doing, and found there was in that Quarter the great Magazine of *Rebus*'s. These were several things of the most different Natures tied up in Bundles, and thrown upon one another in heaps like Faggots. You might behold[b] an Anchor, a Night-rail,[2] and an Hobby-horse bound up together. One of the Workmen seeing me very much surprized, told me, there was an infinite deal of Wit in several of those Bundles, and that he would explain them to me if I pleased: I thanked him for his Civility, but told him I was in very great haste at that time. As I was going out of the Temple, I observed in one Corner of it a Cluster of Men and Women laughing very heartily, and diverting themselves at a Game of *Crambo*.[3] I heard several *double Rhymes* as I passed by them, which raised a great deal of Mirth.

Not far from these was another Set of Merry People engaged at a Diversion, in which the whole Jest was to mistake one Person for another. To give occasion for these ludicrous Mistakes, they were

---

[a] who] which *Fol.*   [b] behold] see *Fol.*

[1] See No. 59.   [2] A dressing-gown or negligee.
[3] A game in which one player gives a word or line of verse to which each of the others has to find a rime (*OED*).

divided into Pairs, every Pair being covered from Head to Foot with the same kind of Dress, though, perhaps, there was not the least Resemblance in their Faces. By this means an old Man was sometimes mistaken for a Boy, a Woman for a Man, and a Black-a-moor for an *European*, which very often produced great Peals of Laughter. These I guess'd to be a Party of *Punns*. But being very desirous to get out of this World of Magick, which[a] had almost turned my Brain, I left the Temple, and crossed over the Fields that lay about it with all the speed I could make. I was not gone far before I heard the Sound of Trumpets and Alarms, which[b] seemed to proclaim the March of an Enemy; and, as I afterwards found, was in reality what I apprehended it. There appear'd at a great distance a very shining Light, and in the midst of it a Person of a most beautiful Aspect; her Name was TRUTH. On her Right Hand there marched a Male Deity, who[c] bore several Quivers on his Shoulders, and grasped several Arrows in his Hand. His Name was *Wit*. The Approach of these two Enemies filled all the Territories of *False Wit* with an unspeakable Consternation, insomuch that the Goddess of those Regions appear'd in Person upon her Frontiers with the several inferior Deities, and the different Bodies of Forces which I had before seen in the Temple, who were now drawn up in Array, and prepared to give their Foes a warm Reception. As the March of the Enemy was very slow, it gave time to the several Inhabitants who border'd upon the *Regions of* FALSEHOOD to draw their Forces into a Body, with a Design to stand upon their Guard as Neuters, and attend the Issue of the Combat.

I must here inform my Reader, that the Frontiers of the Enchanted Region, which I have before described, were inhabited by the Species of MIXED WIT, who made a very odd Appearance when they were Mustered together in an Army. There were Men whose Bodies were stuck full of Darts, and Women whose Eyes were burning Glasses: Men that had Hearts of Fire, and Women that had Breasts of Snow. It would be endless to describe several Monsters of the like Nature, that composed this great Army; which immediately fell asunder, and divided it self into two Parts; the one half throwing themselves behind the Banners of TRUTH, and the others behind those of FALSEHOOD.

The Goddess of FALSEHOOD was of a Gigantick Stature, and advanced some Paces before the Front of her Army; but as the

a which] that *Fol.*　　b which] that *Fol.*　　c who] that *Fol.*

THE SPECTATOR

dazling Light, which flowed from TRUTH, began to shine upon her, she faded insensibly; insomuch that in a little space she looked rather like an huge Phantom, than a real Substance. At length, as the Goddess of TRUTH approached still nearer to her, she fell away entirely, and vanish'd amidst the Brightness of her Presence; so that there did not remain the least Trace or Impression of her Figure in the Place where she had been seen.

As at the rising of the Sun the Constellations grow thin, and the Stars go out one after another, 'till the whole Hemisphere is extinguish'd; such was the vanishing of the Goddess; and not only of the Goddess her self, but of the whole Army that attended her, which sympathized with their Leader, and shrunk into Nothing, in Proportion as the Goddess disappeared. At the same time the whole Temple sunk, the Fish betook themselves to the Streams, and the wild Beasts to the Woods: The Fountains recovered their Murmurs, the Birds their Voices, the Trees their Leaves, the Flowers their Scents, and the whole Face of Nature its true and genuine Appearance. Tho' I still continued asleep, I fancy'd my self as it were awaken'd out of a Dream, when I saw this Region of Prodigies restor'd to Woods and Rivers, Fields and Meadows.

Upon the Removal of that wild Scene of Wonders, which had very much disturbed my Imagination, I took a full Survey of the Persons of WIT and TRUTH, for indeed it was impossible to look upon the first, without seeing the other at the same time. There was behind them a strong and compact Body of Figures. The Genius of *Heroic Poetry* appeared with a Sword in her Hand, and a Lawrel on her Head. *Tragedy* was crowned with Cypress, and covered with Robes dipped in Blood. *Satyr* had Smiles in her Look, and a Dagger under her Garment. *Rhetorick* was known by her Thunderbolt; and *Comedy* by her Mask. After several other Figures, *Epigram* marched up in the Rear, who had been posted there at the beginning of the Expedition, that he might not revolt to the Enemy, whom he was suspected to favour in his Heart. I was very much awed and delighted with the Appearance of the God of *Wit*; there was something so amiable and yet so piercing in his Looks, as inspired me at once with Love and Terrour. As I was gazing on him to my unspeakable Joy, he took a Quiver of Arrows from his Shoulder, in order to make me a Present of it, but as I was reaching out my Hand to receive it of him, I knocked it against a Chair, and by that means awaked.

C

> . . . *Hic vivimus Ambitiosa*
> *Paupertate omnes* . . .
>   Juv.

THE most improper things we commit in the Conduct of our
Lives, we are led into by the Force of Fashion. Instances might
be given, in which a prevailing Custom makes us act against the
Rules of Nature, Law, and common Sense: But at present I shall
confine my Consideration of the Effect it has upon Men's Minds,
by looking into our Behaviour when it is the Fashion to go into
Mourning. The Custom of representing the Grief we have for the
Loss of the Dead by our Habits, certainly had its Rise from the real
Sorrow of such as were too much distressed to take the proper Care
they ought of their Dress. By Degrees it prevailed, that such as had
this inward Oppression upon their Minds, made an Apology for not
joining with the rest of the World in their ordinary Diversions, by
a Dress suited to their Condition. This therefore was at first assumed
by such only as were under real Distress, to whom it was a Relief
that they had nothing about them so light and gay, as to be irksome
to the Gloom and Melancholy of their inward Reflections, or that
might misrepresent them to others. In Process of Time this laudable
Distinction of the Sorrowful was lost, and Mourning is now worn
by Heirs and Widows. You see nothing but Magnificence and
Solemnity in the Equipage of the Relict, and an Air of Release[a] from
Servitude in the Pomp of a Son who has lost a wealthy Father. This
Fashion of Sorrow is now become a generous Part of the Ceremonial
between Princes and Soveraigns, who in the Language of all Nations
are stiled Brothers to each other, and put on the Purple upon the
Death of any Potentate with whom they live in Amity. Courtiers,
and all who wish themselves such, are immediately seized with Grief
from Head to Foot upon this Disaster to their Prince; so that one
may know by the very Buckles of a Gentleman-Usher, what Degree
of Friendship any deceased Monarch maintained with the Court
to which he belongs. A good Courtier's Habit and Behaviour is

---

[a] of Release] a Release *Fol.*

---

[1] *Motto.* Juvenal, *Satires*, 3. 182–3: We all live in a state of pretentious poverty.

hieroglyphical on these Occasions: He deals much in Whispers, and you may see he dresses according to the best Intelligence.

The general Affectation among Men, of appearing greater than they are, makes the whole World run into the Habit of the Court. You see the Lady, who the Day before was as various as a Rainbow, upon the Time appointed for beginning to mourn, as dark as a Cloud. This Humour does not prevail only on those whose Fortunes can support any Change in their Equipage, not on those only whose Incomes demand the Wantonness of new Appearances; but on such also who have just enough to cloath them. An old Acquaintance of mine of Ninety Pounds a Year, who has naturally the Vanity of being a Man of Fashion deep at his Heart, is very much put to it to bear the Mortality of Princes. He made a new black Suit upon the Death of the King of *Spain*, he turned it for the King of *Portugal*,[1] and he now keeps his Chamber while it is scowring for the Emperour. He is a good Oeconomist in his Extravagance, and makes only a fresh black Button upon his iron-grey Suit for any Potentate of small Territories; he indeed adds his Crape Hatband for a Prince whose Exploits he has admired in the *Gazette*.[2] But whatever Complements may be made on these Occasions, the true Mourners are the Mercers, Silkmen, Lacemen and Milliners. A Prince of a merciful and royal Disposition would reflect with great Anxiety upon the Prospect of his Death, if he considered what Numbers would be reduced to Misery by that Accident only: He would think it of Moment enough to direct, that in the Notification of his Departure, the Honour done to him might be restrained to those of the Houshold of the Prince to whom 'it should be signified. He would think a general Mourning to be in a less Degree the same Ceremony which is practised in barbarous Nations, of killing their Slaves to attend the Obsequies of their Kings.

I had been wonderfully at a Loss for many Months together, to guess at the Character of a Man who came now and then to our Coffee-house:[3] He ever ended a News-paper with this Reflexion, *Well, I see all the foreign Princes are in good Health.* If you asked, Pray

---

[1] Charles II of Spain had died in November 1700; Don Pedro (Peter II) of Portugal in December 1706. The Emperor Joseph I died on 17 Apr., N.S., 1711; the news was announced in the *Post Boy* of 19 Apr., shortly before the publication of this essay.

[2] Steele served as writer for the *Gazette*, the official government publication, from 1707 to October 1710.

[3] This character recalls the Political Upholsterer of the *Tatler* 'who was in greater Pain and Anxiety of Mind for King *Augustus*'s Welfare, than that of his nearest Relations' (*Tatler* 155)

NO. 64, MONDAY, MAY 14, 1711

Sir, What says the *Postman* from *Vienna*, he answered, *Make us thank-ful, the* German *Princes are all well*; what does he say from *Barcelona, He does not speak but that the Country agrees very well with the new Queen.* After very much Enquiry, I found this Man of universal Loyalty was a wholesale Dealer in Silks and Ribbands: His Way is, it seems, if he hires a Weaver or Workman, to have it inserted in his Articles, 'That all this shall be well and truly performed, provided no foreign Potentate shall depart this Life within the Time abovementioned.' It happens in all publick Mournings, that the many Trades which depend upon our Habits, are during that Folly either pinched with present Want, or terrified with the apparent Approach of it. All the Atonement which Men can make for wanton Expences, (which is a Sort of insulting the Scarcity under which others labour) is, that the Superfluities of the Wealthy give Supplies to the Necessities of the Poor; but instead of any other Good arising from the Affectation of being in courtly Habits of Mourning, all Order seems to be des-troyed by it; and the true Honour which one Court does to another on that Occasion, loses its Force and Efficacy. When a foreign Minister beholds the Court of a Nation (which flourishes in Riches and Plenty) lay aside upon the Loss of his Master all Marks of Splen-dour and Magnificence, tho' the Head of such a joyful People, he will conceive a greater Idea of the Honour done his Master, than when he sees the Generality of the People in the same Habit. When one is afraid to ask the Wife of a Tradesman whom she has lost of her Family; and after some Preparation endeavours to know whom she mourns for; how ridiculous is it to hear her explain her self, That we have lost one of the House of *Austria*? Princes are elevated so highly above the rest of Mankind, that it is a presumptuous Dis-tinction to take a Part in Honours done to their Memories, except we have Authority for it, by being related in a particular Manner to the Court which pays that Veneration to their Friendship, and seems to express on such an Occasion the Sense of the Uncertainty of humane Life in general, by assuming the Habit of Sorrow[1] tho' in the full Possession of Triumph and Royalty.   R[2]

[1] The Earl Marshal's Order for Mourning is printed in the *Gazette* for 28 Apr.: 'This is to signifie the Queen's Command, That, upon the Death of the Emperor, Her Majesty intends to go into Mourning on *Sunday* next [29 Apr.], and doth expect, That the Peers, and all other Persons, should wear Black Cloth, with plain Linnen, Black Swords and White Gloves. And that the Peeresses, and other Ladies, wear Black Silk, Laune Linnen, and White Gloves.'
[2] Defoe's Review of 19 May comments on this number and discusses the motives for mourning the death of the Emperor.

No. 65   *Tuesday, May* 15, 1711[1]
[STEELE]

> *. . . Demetri, teque, Tigelli,*
> *Discipularum inter Jubeo plorare cathedras.*
>   Hor.

AFTER having at large explained what Wit is, and described the false Appearances of it, all that Labour seems but an useless Enquiry, without some Time be spent in considering the Application of it. The Seat of Wit, when one speaks as a Man of the Town and the World, is the Play-house; I shall therefore fill this Paper with Reflections upon the Use of it in that Place. The Application of Wit in the Theatre has as strong an Effect upon the Manners of our Gentlemen, as the Taste of it has upon the Writings of our Authors. It may, perhaps, look like a very Presumptuous Work, tho' not Foreign from the Duty of a SPECTATOR, to tax the Writings of such as have long had the general Applause of a Nation: But I shall always make Reason, Truth, and Nature the Measures of Praise and Dispraise; if those are for me, the Generality of Opinion is of no Consequence against me; if they are against me, the General Opinion cannot long support me.

Without further Preface, I am going to look into some of our most Applauded Plays, and see whether they deserve the Figure they at present bear in the Imaginations of Men, or not.

In reflecting upon these Works, I shall chiefly dwell upon that for which each respective Play is most celebrated. The present Paper shall be employed upon Sir *Foplin Flutter*.[2] The Received Character of this Play is, That it is the Pattern of Gentile Comedy. *Dorimant* and *Harriot* are the Characters of Greatest Consequence, and if these are Low and Mean, the Reputation of the Play is very Unjust.

I will take for granted, that a fine Gentleman should be honest in his Actions, and refined in his Language. Instead of this, our Hero, in this Piece, is a direct Knave in his Designs, and a Clown in his

---

[1] *Motto.* Horace, *Satires*, I. 10. 90–91:
> Demetrius and Tigellius, know your place;
> Go hence, and whine among the school-boy race.

[2] Etherege's comedy, *The Man of Mode, or Sir Fopling Flutter* (1676), had been given at Drury Lane on 20 Apr., with the following cast: Sir Fopling, Cibber; Dorimant, Wilks; Medley, Mills; Old Bell-Air, Penkethman; Young Bell-Air, Bullock Junior; Shoe-maker, Bowen; Loveit, Mrs. Oldfield; Belinda, Mrs. Rogers; Harriet, Mrs. Santlow; Emilia, Mrs. Porter.

Language. *Bellair* is his Admirer and Friend, in return for which, because he is forsooth a greater Wit than his said Friend, he thinks it reasonable to perswade him to Marry a young Lady, whose Virtue, he thinks, will last no longer than 'till she is a Wife, and then she cannot but fall to his Share, as he is an irresistible fine Gentleman. The Falshood to Mrs. *Loveit*, and the Barbarity of Triumphing over her Anguish for losing him, is another Instance of his Honesty, as well as his good Nature. As to his fine Language; he calls the Orange Woman, who, it seems, is inclined to grow Fat, *An Over-grown Jade, with a Flasket of Guts before her*; and salutes her with a pretty Phrase of, *How now, Double Tripe?*[1] Upon the Mention of a Country Gentle-woman, whom he knows nothing of, (no one can imagine why) he *will lay his Life she is some awkard, ill-fashioned Country Toad, who not having above four Dozen of Hairs on her Head, has adorned her Baldness with a large white Fruz, that she may look Sparkishly in the Fore-front of the King's Box at an old Play.* Unnatural Mixture of senseless Common Place!

As to the Generosity of his Temper, he tells his poor Footman, *If he did not wait better*—he would turn him away, in the insolent Phrase of, *I'll Uncase you.*

Now for Mrs. *Harriot*: She laughs at Obedience to an absent Mother, whose Tenderness *Busie* describes to be very exquisite, for *that*[a] *she is so pleased with finding* Harriot *again, that she cannot chide her for being out of the Way.*[2] This Witty Daughter, and Fine Lady, has so little Respect for this good Woman, that she Ridicules her Air in taking Leave, and cries, *In what Struggle is my poor Mother yonder? See, See, her Head tottering, her Eyes staring, and her under Lip trembling.*[3] But all this is atoned for, because *she has more Wit than is usual in her Sex, and as much Malice, tho' she is as Wild as you would wish her, and has a Demureness in her Looks that makes it so surprising!*[4] Then to recommend her as a fit Spouse for his Hero, the Poet makes her speak her Sense of Marriage very ingeniously. *I Think*, says she, *I might be brought to endure him, and that is all a reasonable Woman should expect in an Husband.*[5] It is, methinks, unnatural that we are not made to understand how she that was bred under a silly pious old Mother, that would never trust her out of her Sight, came to be so Polite.

[a] very exquisite, for *that*] so exquisite, *that Fol.*

---

[1] The quotations in this paragraph and the next are all from the opening scene.
[2] Act III, scene iii. [3] Act IV, scene i.
[4] Act I, scene i. [5] Act III, scene i.

It cannot be denied, but that the Negligence of every thing, which engages the Attention of the sober and valuable Part of Mankind, appears very well drawn in this Piece: But it is denied, that it is necessary to the Character of a Fine Gentleman, that he should in that manner Trample upon all Order and Decency. As for the Character of *Dorimant*, it is[a] more of a Coxcomb than that of *Foplin*. He says of one of his Companions,[1] that a good Correspondence between them is their mutual Interest. Speaking of that Friend, he declares, their being much together *makes the Women think the better of his Understanding, and judge more favourably of my Reputation. It makes him pass upon some for a Man of very good Sense, and me upon others for a very civil Person.*

This whole celebrated Piece is a perfect Contradiction to good Manners, good Sense, and common Honesty; and as there is nothing in it but what is built upon the Ruin of Virtue and Innocence, according to the Notion of Merit in this Comedy, I take the Shoo-maker to be, in reality, the fine Gentleman of the Play: For it seems he is an Atheist, if we may depend upon his Character as given by the Orange-Woman, who is her self far from being the lowest in the Play. She says of a Fine Man, who is *Dorimant's* Companion, There *is not such another Heathen in the Town, except the Shoe-maker.* His Pre-tention to be the Hero of the *Drama* appears still more in his own Description of his way of Living with his Lady. *There is,* says he, *never a Man in Town lives more like a Gentleman with his Wife than I do; I never mind her Motions; she never enquires into mine. We speak to one another civilly, hate one another heartily; and because it is Vulgar to Lye and Soak together, we have each of us our several Settle-Bed.* That of *Soaking together* is as good as if *Dorimant* had spoken it himself; and, I think, since he puts Humane Nature in as ugly a Form as the Circumstance will bear, and is a staunch Unbeliever, he is very much Wronged in having no part of the good Fortune bestowed in the last Act.

To speak plainly of this whole Work, I think nothing but being lost to a Sense of Innocence and Virtue can make any one see this Comedy, without observing more frequent Occasion to move Sorrow and Indignation, than Mirth and Laughter. At the same time I allow it to be Nature, but it is Nature in its utmost Corruption and Degeneracy.   R[2]

---

[a] it is] is it *Fol.*

[1] Bellair. The remaining quotations are again from the opening scene.
[2] Dennis replied to this paper in his *Defence of Sir Fopling Flutter* in 1722 (*Critical*

> *Motus Doceri gaudet Jonicos*
> *Matura Virgo, & fingitur Artibus*
> *Jam nunc, & incestos amores*
> *De Tenero meditatur Ungui.*
>
> Hor.

THE two following Letters[2] are upon a Subject of very great Importance, tho' expressed without any Air of Gravity.

To the SPECTATOR.

SIR,

'I TAKE the Freedom of asking your Advice in Behalf of a young Country Kinswoman of mine who is lately come to Town, and under my Care for her Education. She is very pretty, but you can't imagine how unform'd a Creature it is. She comes to my Hands just as Nature left her, half finish'd, and without any acquir'd Improvements. When I look on her I often think of the *Belle Sauvage*[3] mention'd in one of your Papers. Dear Mr. SPECTATOR, help me to make her comprehend the visible Graces of Speech, and the dumb Eloquence of Motion; for she is at present a perfect Stranger to both. She knows no Way to express her self but by her Tongue, and that always to signify her Meaning. Her Eyes serve her yet only to see with, and she is utterly a Forreigner to the Language of Looks and Glances. In this I fancy you could help her better than any Body. I have bestow'd two Months in teaching her to sigh when she is not concern'd, and to smile when she is not pleas'd; and am asham'd to own she makes little or no Improvement. Then she is no more able now to walk, than she was to go at a Year old. By Walking you will easily know I mean that regular but easy Motion, which gives our Persons so irresistible a Grace as if we mov'd to Musick, and is

Works, ed. Hooker, ii. 241–50), arguing that while Dorimant might not be 'the Pattern of Gentile Comedy' by present-day standards, Etherege was writing according to Restoration standards of conduct and hence 'was oblig'd to accommodate himself to that Notion of a fine Gentleman, which the Court and the Town both had at the Time of the writing of this Comedy' (ii. 244).

[1] *Motto.* Horace, *Odes*, 3. 6. 21–24.

The maiden early takes delight in learning Grecian dances, and trains herself in coquetry e'en now, and plans unholy amours, from childhood.

[2] These are by John Hughes (Duncombe, vol. i, p. xxxiv).

[3] No. 28.

a Kind of disengag'd Figure, or, if I may so speak, recitative Dancing. But the Want of this I cannot blame in her, for I find she has no Ear, and means nothing by Walking but to change her Place. I cou'd pardon too her Blushing if she knew how to carry her self in it, and if it did not manifestly injure her Complexion.

'They tell me you are a Person who have seen the World, and are a Judge of fine Breeding; which makes me ambitious of some Instructions from you for her Improvement: Which when you have favour'd me with, I shall further advise with you about the Disposal of this fair Forrester in Marriage; for I will make it no Secret to you, that her Person and Education are to be her Fortune.

I am,

Sir,

Your very humble Servant,

Celimene.'

SIR,

'BEING employed by *Celimene* to make up and send to you her Letter, I make bold to recommend the Case therein mentioned to your Consideration, because she and I happen to differ a little in our Notions. I, who am a rough Man, am afraid the young Girl is in a fair Way to be spoiled: Therefore pray Mr. SPECTATOR let us have your Opinion of this fine thing called *Fine Breeding*; for I am afraid it differs too much from that plain thing called *Good Breeding*.

Your most humble Servant.'

The general Mistake among us in the educating our Children, is, That in our Daughters we take Care of their Persons and neglect their Minds; in our Sons, we are so intent upon adorning their Minds, that we wholly neglect their Bodies. It is from this that you shall see a young Lady celebrated and admired in all the Assemblies about Town; when her elder Brother is afraid to come into a Room. From this ill Management it arises, That we frequently observe a Man's Life is half spent before he is taken Notice of; and a Woman in the Prime of her Years is out of Fashion and neglected. The Boy I shall consider upon some other Occasion, and at present stick to the Girl: And I am the more inclined to this, because I have several Letters which complain to me that my female Readers have not understood me for some Days last past, and take themselves to be unconcerned in the present Turn of my Writings. When a Girl is safely brought from her Nurse, before she is capable of forming one simple Notion of any thing in Life, she is delivered to the Hands of her Dancing-Master; and with a Collar round her Neck,[1] the pretty wild thing is taught a fantastical Gravity of Behaviour, and forced to a particular Way of holding her Head, heaving her Breast, and moving with her whole Body; and all this under Pain of never having an Husband, if she steps, looks, or moves awry. This gives the young Lady wonderful Workings of Imagination, what is to pass between her and this Husband that she is every Moment told of, and for whom she seems to be educated. Thus her Fancy is engaged to turn all her Endeavours to the Ornament of her Person, as what must determine her Good and Ill in this Life; and she naturally thinks, if she is tall enough she is wise enough for any thing for which her Education makes her think she is designed. To make her an agreable Person is the main Purpose of Her Parents; to that is all their Cost, to that all their Care directed; and from this general Folly of Parents we owe our present numerous Race of Coquets. These Reflections puzzle me, when I think of giving my Advice on the Subject of managing the wild thing mentioned in the Letter of my Correspondent. But sure there is a middle Way to be followed; the Management of a young Lady's Person is not to be overlooked, but the Erudition[2] of her Mind is much more to be regarded. According as this is managed, you will see the Mind follow the Appetites of the Body, or the Body express the Virtues of the Mind.

Cleomira[3] dances with all the Elegance of Motion imaginable; but her Eyes are so chastised with the Simplicity and Innocence of her Thoughts, that she raises in her Beholders Admiration and good Will, but no loose Hope or wild Imagination. The true Art in this Case is, To make the Mind and Body improve together; and if possible, to make Gesture follow Thought, and not let Thought be employed upon Gesture.   R

[1] A correspondent in *N & Q,* 5 ser., vii (1877), 415, identifies this as the steel 'backboard and collar' which she had worn in her teens.

It consisted of a steel backboard about seven or eight inches wide and nine or ten inches long, which was fastened on by a strap round the waist and one round each shoulder, which drew them back and expanded the chest. From the centre of this backboard rose a slight strong steel bar, so arranged that it could be moved up or down according to the length of the neck of the wearer, and at the top of this bar was a round steel collar (covered with black ribbon so that it should not hurt the skin), which opened with a snap and hinge, and when adjusted the wearer's head was thus drawn back on a line with the spine. This was by no means painful, but, of course, irksome.

[2] Used here in the now obsolete meaning of cultivation, instruction, education. The last example in *OED* in this sense is dated 1749.

[3] Cf. *Tatler* 61.

No. 67
[BUDGELL]

Thursday, May 17, 1711[1]

Saltare elegantiùs quam necesse est probæ.
Sal.

*L*UCIAN,[2] in one of his Dialogues, introduces a Philosopher chiding his Friend for his being a Lover of Dancing, and a Frequenter of Balls. The other undertakes the Defence of his Favourite Diversion, which, he says, was at first invented by the Goddess *Rhea*, and preserved the Life of *Jupiter* himself, from the Cruelty of his Father *Saturn*. He proceeds to shew, that it had been Approved by the greatest Men in all Ages; that *Homer* calls *Merion* a *Fine Dancer*;[3] and says, That the graceful Mein and great Agility which he had acquired by that Exercise, distinguished him above the rest in the Armies, both of *Greeks* and *Trojans*.

He adds, that *Pyrrhus* gained more Reputation by Inventing the Dance which is called after his Name, than by all his other Actions: That the *Lacedemonians*, who were the bravest People in *Greece*, gave great Encouragement to this Diversion, and made their *Hormus*[4] (a Dance much resembling the *French Brawl*) famous over all *Asia*: That there were still extant some *Thessalian* Statues erected to the Honour of their best Dancers: And that he wondred how his Brother Philosopher could declare himself against the Opinions of those two Persons, whom he professed so much to Admire, *Homer* and *Hesiod*;[5] the latter of which compares Valour and Dancing together; and says, That *the Gods have bestowed Fortitude on some Men, and on others a Disposition for Dancing*.

Lastly, He puts him in mind that *Socrates*[6] (who, in the Judgment of *Apollo*, was the Wisest of Men) was not only a professed Admirer of this Exercise in others, but learned it himself when he was an Old Man.

[1] *Motto.* Sallust, *Bellum Catilinae*, 25. 2:
        She danced with an elegance unbecoming modesty.

[2] *The Dance*, 8–25. In the *Works of Lucian translated . . . by several eminent hands* (1711), iii. 402–32.
[3] *Iliad*, 13. 249; 16. 617–18.
[4] Hormus (Gk. ὅρμος), a dance performed in a ring by youths and maidens alternately. Brawl: a kind of French dance resembling a cotillion.
[5] Budgell has confused the references here. Lucian mentions both Homer and Hesiod as praising the art of the dance, but it is Homer, not Hesiod, whom he quotes as to the two gifts of the gods (*Iliad*, 13. 730–1).
[6] Xenophon, *Symposium*, 2. 17–20.

The Morose Philosopher is so much affected by these, and some other Authorities, that he becomes a Convert to his Friend, and desires he would take him with him when he went to his next Ball.

I love to shelter my self under the Examples of Great Men; and, I think, I have sufficiently shewed that it is not below the Dignity of these my Speculations, to take Notice of the following Letter, which, I suppose, is sent me by some substantial Tradesman about *Change.*

SIR,

'I AM a Man in Years, and by an honest Industry in the World have acquired enough to give my Children a liberal Education, though I was an utter Stranger to it my self. My eldest Daughter, a Girl of Sixteen, has for some time been under the Tuition of Monsieur *Rigadoon,*[1] a Dancing-Master in the City; and I was prevailed upon by her and her Mother to go last Night to one of his Balls. I must own to you, Sir, that having never been at any such Place before, I was very much pleased and surprized with that part of his Entertainment which he called *French Dancing.*[2] There were several Young Men and Women, whose Limbs seemed to have no other Motion, but purely what the Musick gave them. After this Part was over, they began a Diversion which they call *Country Dancing,*[3] and wherein there were also some things not disagreeable, and divers *Emblematical Figures,* Composed, as I guess, by Wise Men, for the Instruction of Youth.

'Among the rest I observed one, which, I think, they call *Hunt the Squirrel,*[4] in which while the Woman flies the Man pursues her; but as soon as she turns, he runs away, and she is obliged to follow.

[1] This was 'a lively and somewhat complicated dance for two persons' (*OED*), of Italian or Provençal origin. See Violet Alford, 'The Rigaudon', *J. Eng. Folk Dance and Song Society,* Dec. 1941, pp. 70–74. An 'English Rigaudon' is advertised in 1706: *The Art of Dancing, . . . done from the French of Monsieur Feuillet, with many Alterations in the Characters, and an Addition of the English Rigaudon and French Bretagne:* By P. Siris, Dancing-Master' (*Gazette,* 28 Mar., 'this day published'). In 1711 John Walsh brought out *The Rigadoon Royal, Mr. Isaac's New Dance made for Her Majesty's Birth Day 1711* (William C. Smith, *Bibliography of the Musical Works published by John Walsh* [1948], no. 383).

[2] Cf. *Tatler* 88.

[3] A generic name for all English dances of rural or native origin (already in the seventeenth century contrasted with French dances); specifically, applied to dances in which an indefinite number of couples stand up face to face in two long lines. On its introduction into France the name was changed to *Contre-danse,* which has been erroneously assumed to be the original form (*OED*).

[4] 'An outdoor game in which one player is chased by another who must follow all his windings in and out of a ring formed by the remaining players; also called *Cat and Mouse*' (*OED*).

'The Moral of this Dance does, I think, very aptly recommend Modesty and Discretion to the Female Sex.

'But as the best Institutions are liable to Corruptions, so, Sir, I must acquaint you that very great Abuses are crept into this Entertainment. I was amazed to see my Girl handed by, and handing young Fellows with so much Familiarity; and I could not have thought it had been in the Child. They very often made use of a most impudent and lascivious Step called *Setting*,[1] which I know not how to describe to you, but by telling you that 'tis the very reverse of *Back to Back*. At last an impudent young Dog bid the Fidlers play a Dance called *Mol. Pately*,[2] and after having made two or three Capers, ran to his Partner, locked his Arms in hers, and whisked her round cleverly above Ground in such manner, that I, who sat upon one of the lowest Benches, saw further above her Shoe than I can think[a] fit to acquaint you with. I could no longer endure these Enormities, wherefore just as my Girl was going to be made a Whirligig, I ran in, seized on the Child, and carried her home.

'Sir, I am not yet old enough to be a Fool. I suppose this Diversion might be at first invented to keep up a good Understanding between young Men and Women, and so far I am not against it; but I shall never allow of these things. I know not what you will say to this Case at present, but am sure that had you been with me you would have seen matter of great Speculation.

I am
Yours, &c.'

I must confess I am afraid that my Correspondent had too much Reason to be a little out of Humour at the Treatment of his Daughter, but I conclude that he would have been much more so, had he seen one of those *kissing Dances*[3] in which WILL. HONEYCOMB assures me

[a] I can think] I think *Fol*.

---

[1] To set is a term in dancing: 'to take up a position and perform a number of steps with one's face to one's partner or to the dancer on one's right or left' (*OED*).

[2] For the tune of this popular dance see William Chappell, *Popular Music of the Olden Time* (1855–9), i. 289–90.

[3] Another name for Cushion-dance, a round dance formerly danced at weddings, in which the men and women alternately knelt on a cushion to be kissed. According to an article in William King's *Useful Transactions in Philosophy*, no. iv (Jan.–Feb. 1708/9), the Greeks in the time of Pericles 'invented the Dances call'd *Ormoi*, by us kissing Dances: They had a brisk motion, which caus'd a great enlivening of the Faculties, and elevating of the Spirits, so that Kisses then taken seem'd to be out of Rapture and Extasie, more than out of the Contrivance and Design that was laid for 'em' (pp. 35–36).

they are obliged to dwell almost a Minute on the Fair One's Lips, or they will be too quick for the Musick, and dance quite out of Time.

I am not able however to give my final Sentence against this Diversion; and am of Mr. *Cowley*'s Opinion,[1] that so much of Dancing at least as belongs to the Behaviour and an handsom Carriage of the Body, is extreamly useful, if not absolutely necessary.

We generally form such Ideas of People at first Sight, as we are hardly ever persuaded to lay aside afterwards: For this Reason a Man would wish to have nothing disagreeable or uncomely in his Approaches, and to be able to enter a Room with a good Grace.

I might add, that a moderate Knowledge in the little Rules of Good-breeding gives a Man some Assurance, and makes him easie in all Companies. For Want of this, I have seen a Professor of a Liberal Science at a Loss to Salute a Lady; and a most excellent Mathematician not able to determine whether he should stand or sit while my Lord drank to him.

It is the proper Business of a Dancing Master to regulate these matters; tho' I take it to be a just Observation, that unless you add something of your own to what these fine Gentlemen teach you, and which they are wholly ignorant of themselves, you will much sooner get the Character of an Affected Fop, than of a Well-bred Man.

As for *Country Dancing*, it must indeed be confessed, that the great Familiarities between the two Sexes on this Occasion may sometimes produce very dangerous Consequences; and I have often thought that few Ladies Hearts are so obdurate as not to be melted by the Charms of Musick, the Force of Motion, and an handsom young Fellow who is continually playing before their Eyes, and convincing them that he has the perfect Use of all his Limbs.

But as this kind of Dance is the particular Invention of our own Country, and as every one is more or less a Proficient in it, I would not Discountenance it; but rather suppose it may be practised innocently by others, as well as my self, who am often Partner to my Landlady's Eldest Daughter.

[1] In 'A Proposition for the Advancement of Experimental Philosophy' (1661) Cowley describes the recreations of the pupils in his school: 'In foul weather it would not be amiss for them to learn to dance, that is, to learn just so much (for all beyond is superfluous, if not worse) as may give them a graceful comportment of their bodies' (*Essays*, ed. Waller, p. 257).

POSTSCRIPT.

Having heard a good Character of the Collection of Pictures which is to be Exposed to Sale on *Friday* next; and concluding from the following Letter, that the Person who Collected them is a Man of no unelegant Taste, I will be so much his Friend as to Publish it, provided the Reader will only look upon it as filling up the Place of an Advertisement.

From the Three Chairs in the Piazza Covent-Garden.

SIR,   *May* 16, 1711.

' AS you are SPECTATOR, I think we, who make it our Business to exhibit any thing to publick View, ought to apply our selves to you for your Approbation. I have travelled *Europe* to furnish out a Show for you, and have brought with me what has been admired in every Country through which I passed. You have declared in many Papers, that your greatest Delights are those of the Eye, which I do not doubt but I shall Gratifie with as Beautiful Objects as yours ever beheld. If Castles, Forests, Ruins, Fine Women, and Graceful Men, can please you, I dare promise you much Satisfaction, if you will appear at my Auction on *Friday* next. A Sight is, I suppose, as Grateful to a SPECTATOR, as a Treat to another Person, and therefore I hope you will Pardon this Invitation from,

SIR,

Your most Obedient
Humble Servant,
J. GRAHAM.'[1]

X[a]

---

[a] *No. 67 is signed R in Fol., X in 8vo and 12mo*

---

[1] The following advertisement appears in No. 64 and is repeated substantially in Nos. 65, 67, and 68:

A curious Collection of Italian Paintings (by Giacomo and Leandro Bassan, Schiavone, Tintoret, Spagnolet, Nicola, and Gaspar Poussin, Claude Lorain, Salvator Rosa, Fran. Bolognese, Mola, the Borgognon, Luca Jordano, Bourdon, and the Maltese; as also by Rubens and Vandyck, the Velvet Brueghel, Holben, Brouwer, Berchem, Schalken, Teniers, &c.) lately brought from beyond Sea: Will be sold by Auction on Friday the 18th Instant, at the three Chairs, the Corner House of the Little Piazza, Covent Garden; where Catalogues may be had, and the Pictures view'd to Day, to Morrow, and Thursday before the Sale; the House being taken up on Wednesday for an Annual Meeting.

Nos duo turba sumus . . .
Ovid.

ONE would think that the larger the Company is, in which we are engaged, the greater Variety of Thoughts and Subjects would be started in Discourse; but instead of this, we find that Conversation is never so much streightened and confined as in numerous Assemblies. When a Multitude meet together upon any Subject of Discourse, their Debates are taken up chiefly with Forms and general Positions; nay, if we come into a more contracted Assembly of Men and Women, the Talk generally runs upon the Weather, Fashions, News, and the like publick Topicks. In Proportion, as Conversation gets into Clubs and Knots of Friends, it descends into Particulars, and grows more free and communicative: But the most open, instructive, and unreserved Discourse, is that which passes between two Persons who are familiar and intimate Friends. On these Occasions, a Man gives a Loose to every Passion and every Thought that is uppermost, discovers his most retired[2] Opinions of Persons and Things, tries the Beauty and Strength of his Sentiments, and exposes his whole Soul to the Examination of his Friend.

Tully[3] was the first who observed, That Friendship improves Happiness and abates Misery, by the doubling of our Joy and dividing of our Grief; a Thought in which he hath been followed by all the Essayers[4] upon Friendship that have written since his Time. Sir *Francis Bacon*[5] has finely described other Advantages, or, as he calls them, Fruits of Friendship; and indeed there is no Subject of Morality which has been better handled and more exhausted than this. Among the several fine things which have been spoken of it, I shall beg Leave to quote some out of a very ancient Author, whose Book would be regarded by our Modern Wits[a] as one of the most shining Tracts of Morality that is extant, if it appeared under the Name of a *Confucius*, or of any celebrated *Grecian* Philosopher: I mean

---

^a by our Modern Wits] *om. in Fol.*

---

[1] *Motto.* Ovid, *Metamorphoses*, I. 355: We two are a multitude.
[2] Carried on in seclusion or quiet; private. *Obs.* (*OED*).
[3] Cicero, *De Amicitia*, 6. 22. Bacon repeats this in his essay on friendship.
[4] Essayer. The earlier and now obsolete form of 'essayist'.
[5] Essay 27, 'Of Friendship'.

the little Apocryphal Treatise entituled, *The Wisdom of the Son of Sirach*.[1] How finely has he described the Art of making Friends by an obliging and affable Behaviour? And laid down that Precept which a late excellent Author[2] has delivered as his own, 'That we should have many Well-wishers, but few Friends.' *Sweet Language will multiply Friends; and a fair speaking Tongue will encrease kind Greetings. Be in Peace with many, nevertheless have but one Counsellour of a Thousand.* With what Prudence does he caution us in the Choice of our Friends? And with what Strokes of Nature (I could almost say of Humour) has he described the Behaviour of a treacherous and self-interested Friend? *If thou would'st get a Friend prove him first, and be not hasty to credit him: For some Man is a Friend for his own Occasion, and will not abide in the Day of thy Trouble. And there is a Friend who being turned to Enmity and Strife will discover thy Reproach.* Again, *Some Friend is a Companion at the Table, and will not continue in the Day of thy Affliction: But in thy Prosperity he will be as thy self, and will be bold over thy Servants. If thou be brought low he will be against thee, and hide himself from thy Face.* What can be more strong and pointed than the following Verse? *Separate thy self from thine Enemies, and take Heed of thy Friends.* In the next Words he particularizes one of those Fruits of Friendship which is described at length by the two famous Authors above-mention'd, and falls into a general Elogium of Friendship, which is very just as well as very sublime. *A faithful Friend is a strong Defence; and he that hath found such an one, hath found a Treasure. Nothing doth countervail a faithful Friend, and his Excellency is unvaluable. A faithful Friend is the Medicine of Life; and they that fear the Lord shall find him. Whoso feareth the Lord shall direct his Friendship aright; for as he is, so shall his Neighbour* (that is his Friend) *be also.* I do not remember to have met with any Saying that has pleased me more than that of a Friend's being the Medicine of Life, to express the Efficacy of Friendship in healing the Pains and Anguish which[a] naturally cleave to our Existence in this World; and am wonderfully pleased with the Turn in the last Sentence, That a virtuous Man shall as a Blessing meet with a Friend who is as virtuous as himself. There is another Saying in the same Author which would have been very much admired in an Heathen Writer; *Forsake not an old Friend, for the new is*

---

[a] which] that *Fol.*

---

[1] Ecclesiasticus 6. 5–17.
[2] I have not discovered this author.

not comparable to him: A new Friend is as new Wine; when it is old thou shalt drink it with Pleasure.[1] With what Strength of Allusion and Force of Thought, has he described the Breaches and Violations of Friendship? *Whoso casteth a Stone at the Birds frayeth them away; and he that upbraideth his Friend, breaketh Friendship. Though thou drawest a Sword at a Friend yet despair not, for there may be a returning to Favour: If thou hast opened thy Mouth against thy Friend fear not, for there may be a Reconciliation; except for upbraiding, or Pride, or disclosing of Secrets, or a treacherous Wound; for, for these things every Friend will depart.*[2] We may observe in this and several other Precepts in this Author, those little familiar Instances and Illustrations which are so much admired in the moral Writings of *Horace* and *Epictetus.* There are very beautiful Instances of this Nature in the following Passages, which are likewise written upon the same Subject: *Whoso discovereth Secrets loseth his Credit, and shall never find a Friend to his Mind. Love thy Friend, and be faithful unto him; but if thou bewrayest his Secrets follow no more after him: For as a Man hath destroyed his Enemy, so hast thou lost the Love of thy Friend; as one that letteth a Bird go out of his Hand, so hast thou let thy Friend go, and shalt not get him again: Follow after him no more, for he is too far off; he is as a Roe escaped out of the Snare. As for a Wound, it may be bound up, and after reviling there may be Reconciliation; but he that bewrayeth Secrets, is without Hope.*[3]

Among the several Qualifications of a good Friend, this wise Man has very justly singled out Constancy and Faithfulness as the principal: To these others have added Virtue, Knowledge, Discretion, Equality in Age and Fortune, and, as *Cicero*[4] calls it, *Morum Comitas,* a Pleasantness of Temper. If I were to give my Opinion upon such an exhausted Subject, I should join to these other Qualifications a certain Æquability or Evenness of Behaviour. A Man often contracts a Friendship with one whom perhaps he does not find out till after a Year's Conversation; when on a Sudden some latent ill Humour breaks out upon him, which he never discovered or suspected at his first entering into an Intimacy with him. There are several Persons who in some certain Periods of their Lives are inexpressibly agreeable, and in others as odious and detestable. *Martial*[5]

---

[1] Ecclesiasticus 9. 10.
[2] Ibid. 22. 20–22 ('Though thou drewest a Sword at thy Friend . . .').
[3] Ibid. 27. 16–21 ('so hast thou lost the Love of thy Neighbour; . . . so hast thou let thy Neighbour go; . . . and after Reviling there may be Reconcilement').
[4] *De Amicitia,* 18. 66; 24. 89.
[5] *Epigrams,* 12. 47.

has given us a very pretty Picture of one of this Species in the following Epigram;

> *Difficilis, facilis, jucundus, acerbus es idem,*
> *Nec tecum possum vivere, nec sine te.*

> *In all thy Humours, whether grave or mellow,*
> *Thou'rt such a touchy, testy, pleasant Fellow;*
> *Hast so much Wit, and Mirth, and Spleen about thee,*
> *There is no living with thee, nor without thee.*

It is very unlucky for a Man to be entangled in a Friendship with one, who by these Changes and Vicissitudes of Humour is sometimes amiable and sometimes odious: And as most Men are at some Times in an admirable Frame and Disposition of Mind, it should be one of the greatest Tasks of Wisdom to keep our selves well when we are so, and never to go out of that which is the agreeable Part of our Character.   C[1]

No. 69   *Saturday, May* 19, 1711[2]
[ADDISON]

> *Hic segetes, illic veniunt felicius uvæ:*
> *Arborei fœtus alibi, atque injussa virescunt*
> *Gramina. Nonne vides, croceos ut Tmolus odores,*
> *India mittit ebur, molles sua thura Sabæi?*
> *At Chalybes nudi ferrum, virosaque Pontus*
> *Castorea, Eliadum palmas Epirus equarum?*
> *Continuo has leges æternaque fœdera certis*
> *Imposuit Natura locis . . .*
>
>   Vir.

THERE is no Place in the Town which I so much love to frequent as the *Royal-Exchange*.[3] It gives me a secret Satisfaction, and, in some measure, gratifies my Vanity, as I am an *Englishman*,

---

[1] A letter from B. B. dated 13 Aug. 1711 (Lillie, i. 274–5) praises 'your excellent spectator of the eighteenth of May last, upon friendship'.

[*For notes 2 and 3 see opposite page.*]

to see so rich an Assembly of Country-men and Foreigners[1] consulting together upon the private Business of Mankind, and making this Metropolis a kind of *Emporium* for the whole Earth. I must confess I look upon High-Change[2] to be a great Council, in which all considerable Nations have their Representatives. Factors in the Trading World are what Ambassadors are in the Politick World; they negotiate Affairs, conclude Treaties, and maintain a good Correspondence between those wealthy Societies of Men that are divided from one another by Seas and Oceans, or live on the different Extremities of a Continent. I have often been pleased to hear Disputes adjusted between an Inhabitant of *Japan* and an Alderman of *London*, or to see a Subject of the *Great Mogul* entering into a League with one of the *Czar* of *Muscovy*. I am infinitely delighted in mixing with these several Ministers of Commerce, as they are distinguished by their

---

[1] The visitor enters the square within the Exchange, says Koenig (pp. 240-1) 'by two sumptuous Gates, fronting North and South'. On the right of the south under the columns are the walks of the Spanish, French, Portuguese, Italian, and Jewish merchants, and on the left those of the English American plantations. At the north gate, the Irish; on the left, the Scotch and Germans; and in the middle of the open space, the citizens and brokers of London.

[2] The time of greatest activity on the 'Change.

[2] *Motto.* Virgil, *Georgics*, I. 54-61:

> This Ground with *Bacchus*, that with *Ceres* suits:
> That other loads the Trees with happy Fruits.
> A fourth with Grass, unbidden, decks the Ground:
> Thus *Tmolus* is with yellow Saffron crown'd:
> *India*, black Ebon and white Ivory bears:
> And soft *Idume* weeps her od'rous Tears.
> Thus *Pontus* sends her Beaver Stones from far;
> And naked *Spanyards* temper Steel for War.
> *Epirus* for th' *Elean* Chariot breeds,
> (In hopes of Palms,) a Race of running Steeds.
> This is the Orig'nal Contract; these the Laws
> Impos'd by Nature, and by Nature's Cause,
> On sundry Places. DRYDEN.

[3] The Royal Exchange, which Miege (p. 158) calls 'the noblest Building of this Kind in the Universe', was built in 1669, from designs by Edward Jarman, to replace the original building destroyed in the Great Fire. (It in turn was burnt down in 1838.) It was a large quadrangle structure of two stories, facing Cornhill on the south and Threadneedle Street on the north. (An illustration is given in Claud Golding, *London: the City* (Hale, 1951), facing p. 197.) Within was a paved court surrounded by arched galleries; and in niches the statues of the monarchs since the Norman conquest. In the middle of the court was a statue of Charles II by Grinling Gibbons, the king in the ancient habit of the Roman emperors, with a wreath of laurel on his head (Miège, p. 159). 'Above stairs there are *Walks*, with near 200 *Shops*, full of choice Commodities, especially for Mens and Womens Apparel, besides other *Shops* below along the Portico; and under Ground, great vaulted *Cellars*. The whole *Fabrick*, tho' standing upon less than an Acre of Ground, cost 50,000 *l.* building, and yields 4,000 *l.* yearly; Which makes it perhaps the richest Spot of Ground in the World, for the Bigness of it' (Miege, p. 159).

different Walks and different Languages: Sometimes I am justled among a Body of *Armenians*:[1] Sometimes I am lost in a Crowd of *Jews*, and sometimes make one in a Groupe of *Dutch-men*. I am a *Dane, Swede,* or *French-Man* at different times, or rather fancy my self like the old Philosopher, who upon being asked what Country-man he was, replied, That he was a Citizen of the World.[2]

Though I very frequently visit this busie Multitude of People, I am known to no Body there but my Friend, Sir ANDREW, who often smiles upon me as he sees me bustling in the Croud, but at the same time connives at my Presence without taking any further notice of me. There is indeed a Merchant of *Egypt*, who just knows me by sight, having formerly remitted me some Mony to *Grand Cairo*; but as I am not versed in the Modern *Coptick*, our Conferences go no further than a Bow and a Grimace.[3]

This grand Scene of Business gives me an infinite Variety of solid and substantial Entertainments. As I am a great Lover of Mankind, my Heart naturally overflows with Pleasure at the sight of a prosperous and happy Multitude, insomuch that at many publick Solemnities I cannot forbear expressing my Joy with Tears that have stolen down my Cheeks. For this reason I am wonderfully delighted to see such a Body of Men thriving in their own private Fortunes, and at the same time promoting the Publick Stock; or in other Words, raising Estates for their own Families, by bringing into their Country whatever is wanting, and carrying out of it whatever is superfluous.

Nature seems to have taken a particular Care to disseminate her Blessings among the different Regions of the World, with an Eye to this mutual Intercourse and Traffick among Mankind,[4] that the Natives of the several Parts of the Globe might have a kind of Dependance upon one another, and be united together by their

[1] According to a plan of the walks in the Royal Exchange in Hatton (p. 617), the Armenian Walk is on the east side facing Swithin's Alley.

[2] The old philosopher who gave this answer was Diogenes the Cynic, according to Diogenes Laertius (6. 63). Cicero (*Tusculan Disputations*, 5. 37. 108) attributes the reply to Socrates (cf. also Montaigne, *Essays*, I. xxv, 'Of the Education of Children', trans. Cotton, 1685, i. 262).

[3] 'Grimace, in our author's times meant, simply, such a turn of the countenance as expressed acquaintance, or civility: but, because this air of complaisance was assumed, or was taken by our surly countrymen, to be assumed, without meaning, the word came to be used (as it is now) in an ill sense, for any *affected distortion of features*' (Hurd).

[4] For similar statements see John Cary, *An Essay on the State of England in relation to its trade* (Bristol, 1695), pp. 49 ff., and John Pollexfen, *A Discourse of Trade, Coyn, and Paper Credit* (1697), pp. 83 ff.

common Interest. Almost every *Degree* produces something peculiar to it. The Food often grows in one Country, and the Sauce in another. The Fruits of *Portugal* are corrected by the Products of *Barbadoes*: The Infusion of a *China* Plant sweetned with the Pith of an *Indian* Cane: The *Philippick* Islands give a Flavour to our *European* Bowls. The single Dress[1] of a Woman of Quality is often the Product of an hundred Climates. The Muff and the Fan come together from the different Ends of the Earth. The Scarf is sent from the Torrid Zone, and the Tippet from beneath the Pole. The Brocade Petticoat rises out of the Mines of *Peru*, and the Diamond Necklace out of the Bowels of *Indostan*.

If we consider our own Country in its natural Prospect, without any of the Benefits and Advantages of Commerce, what a barren uncomfortable Spot of Earth falls to our Share! Natural Historians tell us, that no Fruit grows originally among us, besides Hips and Haws, Acorns and Pig-Nutts, with other Delicacies of the like Nature; That our Climate of it self, and without the Assistances of Art,[a] can make no further Advances towards a Plumb than to a Sloe, and carries an Apple to no greater a Perfection than a Crab: That our Melons,[b] our Peaches, our Figs, our Apricots, and Cherries, are Strangers among us, imported in different Ages, and naturalized in our *English* Gardens; and that they would all degenerate and fall away into the Trash of our own Country, if they were wholly neglected by the Planter, and left to the Mercy of our Sun and Soil. Nor has Traffick more enriched our Vegetable World, than it has improved the whole Face of Nature among us. Our Ships are laden[c] with the Harvest of every Climate: Our Tables are stored with Spices, and Oils, and Wines: Our Rooms are filled with Pyramids of *China*, and adorned with the Workmanship of *Japan*: Our Morning's-Draught comes to us from the remotest Corners of the Earth: We repair our Bodies by the Drugs of *America*, and repose our selves under *Indian* Canopies. My Friend Sir ANDREW calls the Vineyards

[a] and without the Assistances of Art,] *om. in Fol.*   [b] That our Melons,] That these Fruits, in their present State, as well as our Melons, *Fol.*   [c] laden] loaden *Fol.*

[1] Addison had written to similar effect in *Tatler* 116: 'I consider Woman as a beautiful Romantick Animal, that may be adorned with Furs and Feathers, Pearls and Diamonds, Ores and Silks. The Lynx shall cast its Skin at her Feet to make her a Tippet; the Peacock, Parrot, and Swan, shall pay Contributions to her Muff; the Sea shall be searched for Shells, and the Rocks for Gems; and every Part of Nature furnish out its Share towards the Embellishment of a Creature that is the most consummate Work of it.' Pope's account of Belinda's toilet in *The Rape of the Lock* (i. 129–36) may have been suggested by this passage.

of *France* our Gardens; the Spice-Islands our Hot-Beds; the *Persians* our Silk-Weavers, and the *Chinese* our Potters. Nature indeed furnishes us with the bare Necessaries of Life, but Traffick gives us a great Variety of what is Useful, and at the same time supplies us with every thing that is Convenient and Ornamental. Nor is it the least part of this our Happiness, that whilst we enjoy the remotest Products of the North and South, we are free from those Extremities of Weather which[a] give them Birth; That our Eyes are refreshed with the green Fields of *Britain*, at the same time that our Palates are feasted with Fruits that rise between the Tropicks.

For these Reasons there are not more useful Members in a Commonwealth than Merchants. They knit Mankind together in a mutual Intercourse of good Offices, distribute the Gifts of Nature, find Work for the Poor, add Wealth to the Rich, and Magnificence to the Great. Our *English* Merchant converts the Tin of his own Country into Gold, and exchanges his Wooll for Rubies. The *Mahometans* are cloathed in our *British* Manufacture, and the Inhabitants of the Frozen Zone warmed with the Fleeces of our Sheep.

When I have been upon the 'Change, I have often fancied one of our old Kings[1] standing in Person, where he is represented in Effigy, and looking down upon the[b] wealthy Concourse of People with which that Place is every Day filled. In this Case, how would he be surprized to hear all the Languages of *Europe* spoken in this little Spot of his former Dominions, and to see so many private Men, who in his Time would have been the Vassals of some powerful Baron, Negotiating like Princes for greater Sums of Mony than were formerly to be met with in the Royal Treasury! Trade, without enlarging the *British* Territories, has given us a kind of additional Empire: It has multiplied the Number of the Rich, made our Landed Estates infinitely more Valuable than they were formerly, and added to them an Accession of other Estates as Valuable as the Lands themselves.   C²

---

[a] which] that *Fol.*   [b] the] that *Fol.*

[1] See above. According to Koenig (p. 239) most of the statues were carved by Caius Gabriel Cibber.

[2] This essay becomes for eighteenth-century Whigs one of the classic expositions of the value of the merchant class to the nation. Steele quotes the two final paragraphs in *The Spinster* (1719), pp. 13–15. Addison's panegyric on trade may be contrasted with Swift's view in *Examiner* 21 (28 Dec. 1710) of the Whigs, who 'come with the Spirit of *Shop-keepers* to frame Rules for the Administration of Kingdoms; or, as if they thought the whole Art of Government consisted in the Importation of *Nutmegs*, and the Curing of *Herrings*' (*Prose Works*, ed. Davis, iii. 48).

Interdum vulgus rectum videt.

Hor.

WHEN I travelled, I took a particular Delight in hearing the Songs and Fables that are come from Father to Son, and are most in vogue among the common People of the Countries through which I passed; for it is impossible that any thing should be universally tasted and approved by a Multitude, tho' they are only the Rabble of a Nation, which hath not in it some peculiar Aptness to please and gratify the Mind of Man. Human Nature is the same in all reasonable Creatures; and whatever falls in with it, will meet with Admirers amongst Readers of all Qualities and Conditions. *Moliere*,[2] as we are told by Monsieur *Boileau*, used to read all his Comedies to an old Woman who[a] was his House-keeper, as she sat with him at her Work by the Chimney-Corner; and could foretell the Success of his Play in the Theatre, from the Reception it met at his Fire-Side: For he tells us the Audience always followed the old Woman, and never failed to laugh in the same Place.

I know nothing which[b] more shews the essential and inherent Perfection of Simplicity of Thought, above that which I call the Gothick Manner in Writing, than this, that the first pleases all Kinds of Palates, and the latter only such as have formed to themselves a wrong artificial Taste upon little fanciful Authors and Writers of Epigram. *Homer*, *Virgil*, or *Milton*, so far as the Language of their Poems is understood, will please a Reader of plain common Sense, who[c] would neither relish nor comprehend an Epigram of *Martial* or a Poem of *Cowley*: So, on the contrary, an ordinary Song or Ballad that is the Delight of the common People, cannot fail to please all such Readers as are not unqualified for the Entertainment by their Affectation or Ignorance; and the Reason is plain, because

---

[a] an old Woman who] a little old Woman that *Fol*.   [b] which] that *Fol*.
[c] who] that *Fol*.

---

[1] *Motto.* Horace, *Epistles*, 2. 1. 63: At times the public see and judge aright.
[2] See Boileau, 'Critical Reflections on . . . Longinus', i: "'Tis said, *Malherb* read his Verses to his Servant Maid; and I remember, *Moliere* has often shewn me an Old Maid of his, to whom, he told me, he read his Comedies; assuring me, that when any Part of the Pleasantry did not Strike her, he Corrected it; because he frequently found at his Theatre, that those very Places did not Succeed' (*Works*, 1711–12, ii. 89).

the same Paintings of Nature which recommend it to the most ordinary Reader, will appear beautiful to the most refined.

The old Song of *Chevy Chase*[1] is the favourite Ballad of the common People of *England*; and *Ben. Johnson*[2] used to say he had rather have been the Author of it than of all his Works. Sir *Philip Sidney*[3] in his Discourse of Poetry speaks of it in the following Words; *I never heard the old Song of* Piercy *and* Douglas, *that I found not my Heart more moved than with a Trumpet; and yet is sung by some blind Crowder with no rougher Voice than rude Stile; which being so evil apparelled in the Dust and Cobweb of that uncivil Age, what would it work trimmed in the gorgeous Eloquence of* Pindar? For my own Part, I am so professed an Admirer of this[a] antiquated Song, that I shall give my Reader a Critick[4] upon it, without any further Apology for so doing.

The greatest modern Criticks[5] have laid it down as a Rule, That

---

[a] this] that *Fol.*

---

[1] The ballad praised by Addison is a more polished version of the revised 'Hunting of the Cheviot', a broadside ballad frequently printed in song collections of the time, e.g. in *Mirth Diverts All Care*, published by Morphew in 1708. A Latin version is given in Henry Bold's *Latine Songs, with their English: and Poems* (1685). The text quoted by Addison is Version B in Child (iii. 303). The many allusions to the poem in contemporary literature show that it was by no means unknown, but that it was associated with an old-fashioned and rustic taste. In Shadwell's *Sullen Lovers* (II. i) Caroline says to Lovel: 'I had rather hear a silenc'd Parson preach Sedition, than you talk seriously of Love: . . . you look more Comically than an old-fashion'd Fellow singing of *Robin Hood* or *Chevy Chase*.' A letter signed Lucinda (Lillie, ii. 54–56) complains that her mother 'still persists in confining me to the dull reading of my prayers, with now and then the old ballads of Chivy-chace, the Children in the wood, and Fair Rosamond'. 'Chevy Chase' and 'The Children in the Wood' are two of the songs sung by Bowzybeus in Gay's *Shepherd's Week*, 'Saturday'. Thomas Hearne speculates on the historical facts behind the poem on 26 Oct. 1710 and 10 Aug. 1711 (*Remarks and Collections*, ed. C. E. Doble, iii. 73, 203–4). For other references to the ballad before Addison see Karl Nessler, *Geschichte der Ballade Chevy Chase* (Berlin, 1911), pp. 94–109.

[2] Jonson's conversations with Drummond were first printed in this year (1711) at Edinburgh, in the *Works* of William Drummond ed. by Bishop John Sage and Thomas Ruddiman (pp. 224–7), but this statement of Jonson does not occur in it. A transcript of the conversations, made by the Edinburgh antiquary, Sir Robert Sibbald, and preserved in the National Library of Scotland, contains a sentence about Southwell somewhat similar: 'That Southwell was hanged yett so he had written that piece of his ye burning babe he would have been content to destroy many of his' (*Works* of Jonson, ed. Herford and Simpson, i. 137). As Herford and Simpson suggest, Addison may be recalling this verdict of Jonson on Southwell and transferring it to 'Chevy Chase'.

[3] *Apology for Poetry* (*Elizabethan Critical Essays*, ed. G. Gregory Smith, i. 178).

[4] The old form of the word, now superseded by *critique*.

[5] Addison is right: the weight of seventeenth-century critical opinion was solidly in support of the view that art should serve the ends of morality (cf. René Bray, *La Formation de la doctrine classique en France*, 1927, pp. 63–84), but the formulations he makes and the examples he gives show that he is following the critic who gave the most extreme expression to the theory of heroic poetry as 'moral instruction disguised under the allegory of an action', viz. Le Bossu. Book i, chap. vii of the *Traité du poème*

an heroick Poem should be founded upon some important Precept of Morality, adapted to the Constitution of the Country in which the Poet writes. *Homer*[1] and *Virgil* have formed their Plans in this View. As *Greece* was a Collection of many Governments, who suffered very much among themselves, and gave the *Persian* Emperour, who was their common Enemy, many Advantages over them by their mutual Jealousies and Animosities, *Homer*, in order to establish among them an Union, which was so necessary for their Safety, grounds his Poem upon the Discords of the several *Grecian* Princes[2] who were engaged in a Confederacy against an *Asiatick* Prince, and the several Advantages which the Enemy gained by such their Discords. At the Time the Poem we are now treating of was written, the Dissentions of the Barons, who were then so many petty Princes, ran very high, whether they quarrell'd among themselves or with their Neighbours, and produced unspeakable Calamities to the Country: The Poet, to deter Men from such unnatural Contentions, describes a bloody Battle and dreadful Scene of Death, occasioned by the mutual Feuds which[a] reigned in the Families of an *English* and *Scotch* Nobleman. That he design'd this for the Instruction of his Poem, we may learn from his four last Lines, in which, after the Example of the modern Tragedians, he draws from it a Precept for the Benefit of his Readers.

> *God save the King and bless the Land*
> *In Plenty, Joy, and Peace;*
> *And grant henceforth that foul Debate*
> *'Twixt Noblemen may cease.*

[a] which] that *Fol.*

épique (1675) deals with the method of composing a fable. The first thing, says Le Bossu, is 'to chuse the Instruction, and the point of Morality, which is to serve as its Foundation . . .' (ed. 1719, i. 28–29). For the extraordinary reputation of Le Bossu at this period—from the time of Dryden through the greater part of the eighteenth century—see A. F. B. Clark, *Boileau and the French Classical Critics in England (1660–1830)* (Paris, 1925), pp. 243–61.

[1] Le Bossu (book i, chap. viii) makes this point about Homer.

He saw the *Grecians*, for whom he design'd his Poems, were divided into as many States as they had Capital Cities. Each was a Body Politick, and had its Form of Government independent from all the rest. And yet these distinct States were very often oblig'd to unite together in one Body against their common Enemies. . . . *Homer* then has taken for the Foundation of his *Fable* this great *Truth*; viz. *That a Misunderstanding between Princes is the Ruin of their own States* (ed. 1719, i. 34–35).

[2] This historical inaccuracy is refuted by Nichols, Chalmers, and other editors.

The next Point observed by the greatest Heroic Poets, hath been to celebrate Persons and Actions which do Honour to their Country: Thus *Virgil*'s Hero was the Founder of *Rome*, *Homer*'s a Prince of *Greece*; and for this Reason *Valerius Flaccus*[1] and *Statius*, who were both *Romans*, might be justly derided for having chosen the Expedition of the *Golden Fleece* and *the Wars of Thebes*, for the Subjects[a] of their Epic Writings.

The Poet before us, has not only found out an Hero in his own Country, but raises the Reputation of it by several beautiful Incidents. The *English* are the first who[b] take the Field, and the last who[c] quit it. The *English* bring only Fifteen hundred to the Battle, the *Scotch* Two thousand. The *English* keep the Field with Fifty three: The *Scotch* retire with Fifty five: All the rest on each Side being slain in Battle.[2] But the most remarkable Circumstance of this Kind, is the different Manner in which the *Scotch* and *English* Kings receive[d] the News of this Fight, and of the great Mens Deaths who commanded in it.

> *This News was brought to* Edinburgh,
>   *Where* Scotland'*s King did reign,*
> *That brave Earl* Douglas *suddenly*
>   *Was with an Arrow slain.*
>
> *O heavy News, King* James *did say,*
>   Scotland *can Witness be,*
> *I have not any Captain more*
>   *Of such Account as he.*
>
> *Like Tydings to King* Henry *came*
>   *Within as short a Space,*
> *That* Piercy *of* Northumberland
>   *Was slain in* Chevy-Chace.
>
> *Now God be with him, said our King,*
>   *Sith 'twill no better be,*
> *I trust I have within my Realm*
>   *Five hundred as good as he.*

[a] Subjects] Subject *Fol.*   [b] who] that *Fol.*   [c] who] that *Fol.*   [d] receive] received *Fol.*

---

[1] His epic poem, the *Argonautica*, was left unfinished at the time of his death (*c.* A.D. 90). The *Thebaid* of Statius was completed about A.D. 92.
[2] A letter signed P. L. and dated from Portsmouth, 31 May 1711 (Lillie, i. 276–9) corrects some of these statements, utilizing *The History of the House and Race of Douglas and Angus* by David Hume of Godscroft (1644).

Yet shall not Scot *nor* Scotland *say*
But I will Vengeance take,
And be revenged on them all
For brave Lord Piercy's *Sake.*

This Vow full well the King perform'd
After on Humble-down,
In one Day Fifty Knights were slain
With Lords of great Renown.

And of the rest of small Account
Did many Thousands dye, &c.

At the same Time that our Poet shews a laudable Partiality to his
Country-men, he represents the *Scots* after a Manner not unbecoming so bold and brave a People.

Earl Douglas *on a milk-white Steed,*
Most like a Baron bold,
Rode foremost of the Company
Whose Armour shone like Gold.

His Sentiments and Actions are every Way suitable to an Hero. One
of us two, says he, must dye: I am an Earl as well as your self, so that
you can have no Pretence for refusing the Combat: However, says
he, 'tis Pity, and indeed would be a Sin, that so many innocent Men
should perish for our Sakes; rather let you and I end our Quarrel in
single Fight.[a]

E'er thus I will out-braved be,
One of us two shall dye;
I know thee well, an Earl thou art,
Lord Piercy, *so am I.*

But trust me, Piercy, *Pity it were,*
And great Offence, to kill
Any of these our harmless Men,
For they have done no Ill.

Let thou and I the Battle try,
And set our Men aside;
Accurst be he, Lord Piercy *said,*
By whom this is deny'd.

[a] in single Fight.] by a single Combat. *Fol.*

When these brave Men had distinguished themselves in the Battle and in single Combat with each other, in the Midst of a generous Parly, full of heroic Sentiments, the *Scotch* Earl falls; and with his dying Words encourages his Men to revenge his Death, representing to them, as the most bitter Circumstance of it, that his Rival saw him fall.

> *With that there came an Arrow keen*
> *Out of an* English *bow,*
> *Which struck Earl* Douglas *to the Heart*
> *A deep and deadly Blow.*

> *Who never spoke more Words than these,*
> *Fight on my merry Men all;*
> *For why, my Life is at an End,*
> *Lord* Piercy *sees my Fall.*

Merry Men, in the Language of those Times, is no more than a chearful Word for Companions and Fellow-Soldiers. A Passage in the Eleventh Book of *Virgil's Æneids* is very much to be admired, where *Camilla* in her last Agonies, instead of weeping over the Wound she had received, as one might have expected from a Warriour of her Sex, considers only (like the Hero of whom we are now speaking) how the Battle should be continued after her Death.

> *Tum sic exspirans, &c.*[1]

> *A gathering Mist o'erclouds her chearful Eyes;*
> *And from her Cheeks the rosie Colour flies.*
> *Then, turns to her, whom, of her Female Train,*
> *She trusted most, and thus she speaks with Pain.*
> *Acca, 'tis past! He swims before my Sight,*
> *Inexorable Death; and claims his Right.*
> *Bear my last Words to* Turnus, *fly with Speed,*
> *And bid him timely to my Charge succeed:*
> *Repel the* Trojans, *and the Town relieve:*
> *Farewel. . . .*

Turnus did not die in so heroic a Manner; tho' our Poet seems to have had his Eye upon *Turnus's* Speech in the last Verse

---

[1] *Aeneid,* 11. 820. The English translation here, and below, is Dryden's.

Lord Piercy *sees my Fall.*
  . . . Vicisti, & victum tendere palmas
  Ausonii videre . . . .[1]

Earl *Piercy*'s Lamentation over his Enemy is generous, beautiful,
and passionate; I must only caution the Reader not to let the
Simplicity of the Stile, which one may well pardon in so old a Poet,
prejudice him against the Greatness of the Thought.

> *Then leaving Life Earl* Piercy *took*
>   *The dead Man by the Hand,*
> *And said Earl* Douglas *for thy Life*
>   *Would I had lost my Land.*

> *O* Christ*! my very Heart doth bleed*
>   *With Sorrow for thy Sake;*
> *For sure a more renowned Knight*
>   *Mischance did never take.*

That beautiful Line *Taking the dead Man by the Hand,* will put the
Reader in Mind of *Æneas*'s Behaviour towards *Lausus,* whom he himself had slain as he came to the Rescue of his aged Father.

> *At vero ut vultum vidit morientis, & ora,*
> *Ora modis Anchisiades, pallentia miris:*
> *Ingemuit, miserans graviter, dextramque tetendit, &c.*[2]

> *The pious Prince beheld young* Lausus *dead;*
> *He griev'd, he wept; then grasp'd his Hand, and said,*
> *Poor hapless Youth! What Praises can be paid*
> *To Worth so great . . . !*

I shall take another Opportunity to consider the other Parts of
this old Song.   C

---

[1] Thou hast conquered, and the Ausonians have seen me stretch forth my hands.
Aeneid, 12. 936–7.

[2] *Aeneid*, 10. 821–3.

No. 71

[STEELE]

Tuesday, May 22, 1711[1]

. . . *Scribere jussit amor.*
Ovid.

THE entire Conquest of our Passions is so difficult a Work, that they who despair of it should think of a less difficult Task, and only attempt to Regulate them. But there is a third thing which may contribute not only to the Ease, but also to the Pleasure[a] of our Life; and that is, refining our Passions to a greater Elegance, than we receive them from Nature. When the Passion is Love, this Work is performed in innocent, though rude and uncultivated Minds, by the mere Force and Dignity of the Object. There are Forms which naturally create Respect in the Beholders, and at once Inflame and Chastise the Imagination. Such an Impression as this gives an immediate Ambition to deserve, in order to please. This Cause and Effect are Beautifully described by Mr. *Dryden*[2] in the Fable of *Cymon* and *Iphigenia.* After he has represented *Cymon* so stupid, that

He Whistled as he went, for want of Thought,

he makes him fall into the following Scene, and shows its Influence upon him so excellently, that it appears as Natural as Wonderful.

> *It happen'd on a Summer's Holiday,*
> *That to the Greenwood-shade he took his way;*
> *His Quarter-Staff, which he cou'd ne'er forsake,*
> *Hung half before, and half behind his Back.*
> *He trudg'd along unknowing what he sought,*
> *And whistled as he went, for want of Thought.*
>
>   *By Chance conducted, or by Thirst constrain'd,*
> *The deep Recesses of the Grove he gain'd;*
> *Where in a Plain, defended by the Wood,*
> *Crept through the matted Grass a Crystal Flood,*
> *By which an Alablaster Fountain stood:*

---

[a] also to the Pleasure] also the Pleasure *Fol.*

---

[1] *Motto.* Ovid, *Heroides,* 4. 10: Love bade me write. Steele uses this motto also for No. 199 (vol. ii).

[2] 'Cymon and Iphigenia', 79–116. The story, 'from Boccace', is in the *Fables* of 1700. Steele omits line 81 ('For *Cymon* shunn'd the Church, and us'd not much to Pray') and lines 102–3 ('Where two beginning Paps were scarcely spy'd, | For yet their Places were but signify'd').

And on the Margin of the Fount was laid
(Attended by her Slaves) a sleeping Maid,
Like Dian, *and her Nymphs, when tir'd with Sport,*
To rest by cool Eurotas *they resort:*
The Dame her self the Goddess well express'd,
Not more distinguish'd by her Purple Vest,
Than by the charming Features of her Face,
And ev'n in Slumber a superior Grace:
Her comely Limbs compos'd with decent Care, ⎫
Her Body shaded with a slight Cymarr; ⎬
Her Bosom to the view was only bare: ⎭
The fanning Wind upon her Bosom blows, ⎫
To meet the fanning Wind the Bosom rose; ⎬
The fanning Wind, and purling Streams continue her Repose. ⎭
  The Fool of Nature, stood with stupid Eyes
And gaping Mouth, that testify'd Surprize,
Fix'd on her Face, nor cou'd remove his Sight,
New as he was to Love, and Novice in Delight:
Long mute he stood, and leaning on his Staff,
His Wonder witness'd with an Ideot Laugh;
Then would have spoke, but by his glimmering Sense
First found his want of Words, and fear'd Offence:
Doubted for what he was he should be known,
By his Clown-Accent, and his Country-Tone.

But lest this fine Description should be excepted against, as the Creation of that great Master Mr. *Dryden*, and not an Account of what has really ever happened in the World; I shall give you, *Verbatim*, the Epistle of an enamour'd Footman[1] in the Country, to his Mistress. Their Sirnames shall not be inserted, because their

---

[1] Nichols, followed by later editors, names James Hirst, Edward Wortley's servant, as the original. This suggestion seems to have been first made by a correspondent signing himself 'Crito', whose letter, without references, appeared in the *Gentleman's Magazine* (edited by Nichols), June 1780, p. 269.

The following anecdote may be added to the account of writers in the *Spectator*, given in your April Magazine, p. 174: 'James Hurst, in the year 1711, lived servant with the Hon. Edward Wortley. It happened one day, in re-delivering a parcel of letters to his master, by mistake he gave him one which he had written to his sweetheart, and kept back one of Mr. Wortley's. He soon discovered the mistake, and hurried back to his master; but, unfortunately for poor James, it happened to be the first that presented itself to Mr. W. and before James returned he had given way to a curiosity which led him to open it, and read the love-told story of an enamoured footman. It was in vain that James begged to have it returned. "No," says Mr. W. "James, you shall be a great man; this letter shall appear in the

Passion demands a greater Respect than is due to their Quality. *James* is Servant in a great Family, and *Elizabeth* waits upon the Daughter of one as numerous, some Miles off of her Lover. *James*, before he beheld *Betty*, was vain of his Strength, a rough Wrestler, and quarrelsom Cudgel Player; *Betty* a publick Dancer at Maypoles, a Romp at Stool-Ball.[1] He always following idle Women, she Playing among the Peasants: He a Country Bully, she a Country Coquette. But Love has made her constantly in her Mistress's Chamber, where the young Lady gratifies a secret Passion of her own, by making *Betty* talk of *James*; and *James* is become a constant Waiter near his Master's Apartment, in Reading, as well as he can, Romances. I cannot learn who *Molly* is, who it seems walked Ten Mile to carry the angry Message, which gave Occasion to what follows.

To Elizabeth ——

My Dear Betty,   *May* 14, 1711.

'REMEMBER your bleeding Lover, who Lyes bleeding at the Wounds *Cupid* made with the Arrows he borrowed at the Eyes of *Venus*, which is your sweet Person.

'Nay more, with the Token you sent me for my Love and Service offered to your sweet Person, which was your base Respects to my ill Conditions, when alas! there is no ill Conditions in me, but quite contrary; all Love and Purity, especially to your Sweet Person; but all this I take as a Jest.

'But the sad and dismal News which *Molly* brought me, struck me to the Heart, which was, it seems, and is your ill Conditions for my Love and Respects to you.

'For she told me, if I came Forty times to you, you would not speak with me, which Words I am sure is a great Grief to me.

'Now, my Dear, if I may not be permitted to your sweet Company, and to have the happiness of speaking with your sweet Person, I beg the Favour of you to accept of this my secret Mind and Thoughts,

Spectator." Mr. W. communicated the letter to his friend Sir Richard Steele. . . . James found means to remove that unkindness of which he complains in his letter; but, alas! before their wishes were completed, a speedy end was put to a passion which would not discredit much superior rank by the unexpected death of Betty. James, out of the great regard and love he bore to Betty, after her death married her sister. He died not many years since in the neighbourhood of Wortley, near Leeds, Yorkshire.'

[1] A *romp* was a new, and popular, word at this period for a play-loving, lively, merry girl. Stool-ball was 'an old country game somewhat resembling cricket, played chiefly by young women, or, as an Easter game, between men and women, for a "tansy" as the stake. The "stool" was the wicket' (*OED*).

which hath so long lodged in my Breast; the which, if you do not accept, I believe will go nigh to break my Heart.

'For indeed, my Dear, I Love you above all the Beauties I ever saw in all my Life.

'The young Gentleman, and my Master's Daughter, the *Londoner* that is come down to marry her, sate in the Arbour most part of last Night. Oh! dear *Betty*, must the Nightingales sing to those who marry for Mony, and not to us true Lovers! Oh my dear *Betty*, that we could meet this Night where we used to do in the Wood!

'Now, my Dear, if I may not have the Blessing of kissing your sweet Lips, I beg I may have the Happiness of kissing your fair Hand, with a few Lines from your dear self, Presented by whom you please or think fit. I believe, if Time would permit me, I could write all Day; but the Time being short, and Paper little, no more from your never-failing Lover till Death,

James ——— '

Poor *James!* Since his Time and Paper were so short; I, that have more than I can use well of both, will put the Sentiments of his kind Letter (the Stile of which seems to be confused with Scraps he had got in hearing and reading what he did not understand) into what he meant to express.

Dear Creature,

'CAN you then neglect him who has forgot all his Recreations and Enjoyments to pine away his Life in thinking of you? When I do so, you appear more amiable to me than *Venus* does in the most beautiful Description that was ever made of her. All this Kindness you return with an Accusation, that I do not love you: But the contrary is so manifest, that I cannot think you in earnest. But the Certainty given me in your Message by *Molly*, that you do not love me, is what robs me of all Comfort. She says you will not see me: If you can have so much Cruelty, at least write to me, that I may kiss the Impression made by your fair Hand. I love you above all Things, and, in my Condition, what you look upon with Indifference is to me the most exquisite Pleasure or Pain. Our Young Lady, and a Fine Gentleman from *London*, who are to Marry for mercenary Ends, walk about our Gardens, and hear the Voice of Evening Nightingales, as if for Fashion-sake they courted those Solitudes, because they have heard Lovers do so. Oh *Betty!* could I hear these Rivulets Murmur, and Birds Sing while you stood near me, how little sensible should I be that we are both Servants, that there is any thing on Earth above us. Oh! I could write to you as long as I love you, 'till Death it self.

James.'

N.B. By the Words *Ill Conditions*,[1] JAMES means, in a Woman *Coquetry*, in a Man *Inconstancy*. R

No. 72 *Wednesday, May 23, 1711*[2]
[ADDISON]

> . . . *Genus immortale manet, multosque per annos*
> *Stat fortuna Domus, & avi numerantur avorum.*
> Virg.

HAVING already given my Reader an Account of several extraordinary Clubs both ancient and modern, I did not design to have troubled him with any more Narratives of this Nature; but I have lately received Information of a Club which I can call neither ancient nor modern, that I dare say will be no less surprising to my Reader than it was to my self; for which Reason I shall communicate it to the Publick as one of the greatest Curiosities in its Kind.

A Friend of mine complaining of a Tradesman who is related to him, after having represented him as a very idle worthless Fellow, who[a] neglected his Family, and spent most of his Time over a Bottle, told me, to conclude his Character, that he was a Member of the EVERLASTING CLUB. So very odd a Title raised my Curiosity to enquire into the Nature of a Club that had such a sounding Name; upon which my Friend gave me the following Account.

The EVERLASTING CLUB consists of an hundred Members, who divide the whole twenty four Hours among them in such a Manner,

---

[a] who] that *Fol.*

---

[1] 'Conditions', an old word, now obsolete, for 'personal qualities; manners, morals, ways; behaviour, temper'. The last example in *OED* is dated 1830.
[2] *Motto.* Virgil, *Georgics,* 4. 208–9:
> Th' immortal Line in sure Succession reigns,
> The Fortune of the Family remains:
> And Grandsires Grandsons the long List contains. DRYDEN.

that the Club sits Day and Night from one End of the Year to an-other;[a] no Party presuming to rise till they are relieved by those who are in course to succeed them. By this Means a Member of the EVERLASTING CLUB never wants Company; for tho' he is not upon Duty himself, he is sure to find some who[b] are; so that if he be dis-posed to take a Whet,[1] a Nooning, an Evening's Draught, or a Bottle after Midnight, he goes to the Club and finds a Knot of Friends to his Mind.

It is a Maxim in this Club that the Steward never dies; for as they succeed one another by way of Rotation, no Man is to quit the great Elbow-chair which[c] stands at the upper End of the Table till his Successor is in a Readiness to fill it; insomuch that there has not been a *Sede vacante* in the Memory of Man.

This Club was instituted towards the End (or, as some of them say, about the Middle) of the Civil Wars, and continued without Interruption till the Time of the *Great Fire*, which burnt them out and dispersed them for several Weeks. The Steward at that Time maintained his Post till he had like to have been blown up with a neighbouring House, (which was demolished in order to stop the Fire;) and would not leave the Chair at last till he had emptied all the Bottles upon the Table, and received repeated Directions from the Club to withdraw himself. This Steward is frequently talked of in the Club, and looked upon by every Member of it as a greater Man, than the famous Captain[2] mentioned in my Lord *Clarendon*, who was burnt[d] in his Ship because he would not quit it without Orders. It is said that towards the Close of 1700, being the great Year of Jubilee, the Club had it under Consideration whether they should break up or continue their Session; but after many Speeches

---

---

[1] A small draught of liquor taken as an appetizer. The Whetters are described in *Tatler* 138: those 'who drink themselves into an intermediate State of being neither drunk or sober before the Hours of 'Change, or Business, and in that Condition buy and sell Stocks, discount Notes, and do many other Acts of well disposed Citizens'. They are discussed more fully in *Tatler* 141.

[2] The reference, which is not in Clarendon's *History*, is probably to Captain Archi-bald Douglas, who was burned with his ship, the *Royal Oak*, at the defence of Chatham in 1667. When advised to retire, he refused, saying, 'It shall never be told that a Douglas quitted his post without orders' (*DNB*). 'A fragment of a Poem on the death of Capt. Douglas, burnt on one of his Majesty's ships at Chatham' is printed in Lillie (i. 239–43). Or Addison may have in mind the first Earl of Sandwich, who died, prob-ably by drowning, at the Battle of Solebay in 1672, after his flagship the *Royal James* had been set on fire (G.E.C., *Complete Peerage*).

and Debates it was at length agreed to sit out the other Century. This Resolution passed in a general Club *Nemine Contradicente.*

Having given this short Account of the Institution and Continuation of the EVERLASTING CLUB, I should here endeavour to say something of the Manners and Characters of its several Members, which I shall do according to the best Lights I have received in this Matter.

It appears by their Books in general, that since their first Institution they have smoaked Fifty Tun of Tobacco; drank Thirty thousand Butts of Ale, One thousand Hogsheads of Red Port, Two hundred Barrels of Brandy, and a Kilderkin of small Beer: There has been likewise a great Consumption of Cards. It is also said, that they observe the Law in *Ben. Johnson's* Club, which orders the Fire to be always kept in (*focus perennis esto*)[1] as well for the Convenience of lighting their Pipes, as to cure the Dampness of the Club-Room. They have an old Woman in the Nature of a Vestal, whose Business it is to cherish and perpetuate the Fire, which[a] burns from Generation to Generation, and has seen the Glass-house Fires[2] in and out above an Hundred Times.

The EVERLASTING CLUB treats all other Clubs with an Eye of Contempt, and talks even of the *Kit-Cat* and *October*[b][3] as of a Couple of Upstarts. Their ordinary Discourse (as much as I have been able to learn of it) turns altogether upon such Adventures as have passed in their own Assembly; of Members who[c] have taken the Glass in their Turns for a Week together without stirring out of the Club; of others who[d] have smoaked an Hundred Pipes at a Sitting; of others who[e] have not missed their Morning's Draught for Twenty Years together: Sometimes they speak in Raptures of a Run of Ale in King *Charles's* Reign; and sometimes reflect with Astonishment upon Games at Whisk,[4] which[f] have been miraculously recovered by Members of the Society, when in all humane Probability the Case was desperate.

a which] that *Fol.*   b and *October*] and the *October Fol.*   c who] that *Fol.*
d who] that *Fol.*   e who] that *Fol.*   f which] that *Fol.*

---

[1] This comes at the end of the *Leges Convivales* (Jonson's *Works*, ed. Herford and Simpson, viii. 656).
[2] For glass manufacture see No. 509 (vol. iv).
[3] See No. 9.
[4] A variant spelling of Whist. Playing-cards, including 'Whisk, Basset, Picquet, Ombre, and ordinary Cards, bought before the Duty of 6d. a Pack was laid on', are advertised by John Cliff, Stationer, in Queen-street, Cheapside, in Nos. 252, 254–6, 521, and 522.

They delight in several old Catches, which they sing at all Hours to encourage one another to moisten their Clay, and grow immortal by drinking; with many other edifying Exhortations of the like Nature.

There are four general Clubs held in a Year, at which Times they fill up Vacancies, appoint Waiters, confirm the old Fire-Maker or elect a new one, settle Contributions for Coals, Pipes, Tobacco, and other Necessaries.

The Senior Member has out-lived the whole Club twice over, and has been drunk with the Grandfathers of some of the present sitting Members.   C

No. 73   *Thursday, May 24, 1711*[1]

[ADDISON]

. . . O Dea certè!
Virg.

IT is very strange to consider, that a Creature like Man, who is sensible of so many Weaknesses and Imperfections, should be actuated by a Love of Fame: That Vice and Ignorance, Imperfection and Misery should contend for Praise, and endeavour as much as possible to make themselves Objects of Admiration.

But notwithstanding Man's Essential Perfection is but very little, his Comparative Perfection may be very considerable. If he looks upon himself in an abstracted Light, he has not much to boast of; but if he considers himself with regard to others, he may find Occasion of glorying, if not in his own Virtues, at least in the Absence of another's Imperfections. This gives a different Turn to the Reflections of the Wise Man and the Fool. The first endeavours to shine in himself, and the last to outshine others. The first is humbled by the Sense of his own Infirmities, the last is lifted up by the Discovery of those which he observes in other Men. The Wise Man considers what he wants, and the Fool what he abounds in. The Wise Man is happy when he gains his own Approbation, and the Fool when he Recommends himself to the Applause of those about him.

---

[1] *Motto.* Virgil, *Aeneid*, 1. 328: O goddess surely!

But however unreasonable and absurd this Passion for Admiration may appear in such a Creature as Man, it is not wholly to be discouraged; since it often produces very good Effects, not only as it restrains him from doing any thing which[a] is mean and contemptible, but as it pushes him to Actions which[b] are great and glorious. The Principle may be defective or faulty, but the Consequences it produces are so good, that, for the benefit of Mankind, it ought not to be extinguished.

It is observed by *Cicero*,[1] that Men of the greatest and the most shining Parts are the most actuated by Ambition; and if we look into the two Sexes, I believe we shall find this Principle of Action stronger in Women than in Men.

The Passion for Praise, which is so very vehement in the fair Sex, produces excellent Effects in Women of Sense, who desire to be admired for that only which deserves Admiration: and I think we may observe, without a Compliment to them, that many of them do not only live in a more uniform Course of Virtue, but with an infinitely greater Regard to their Honour, than what we find in the Generality of our own Sex. How many Instances have we of Chastity, Fidelity, Devotion? How many Ladies distinguish themselves by the Education of their Children, Care of their Families, and Love of their Husbands, which are the great Qualities and Atchievements of Womankind: As the making of War, the carrying on of Traffick, the Administration of Justice, are those by which Men grow famous, and get themselves a Name.

But as this Passion for Admiration, when it works according to Reason, improves the beautiful Part of our Species in every thing that is Laudable; so nothing is more Destructive to them when it is governed by Vanity and Folly. What I have therefore here to say, only regards the vain Part of the Sex, whom for certain Reasons, which the Reader will hereafter see at large, I shall distinguish by the Name of *Idols*.[2] An *Idol* is wholly taken up in the Adorning of her

[a] which] that *Fol.*   [b] which] that *Fol.*

---

[1] *De Officiis*, 1. 8. 26; *Tusculan Disputations*, 5. 24. 68.

[2] The Turkish Spy had made a similar comparison (*Letters writ by a Turkish Spy*, vol. ii, book 1, letter xxiii):
But, that which is to be had in greatest Abomination, is that it is common for Men to make Love to the Women in *Churches*: They present themselves before the *Altars*, but, the *Saint* whom they Invocate, is some beautiful Female. She engrosses all their Devotions; to her they make their Vows. The amorous Youth adores his Mistress that kneels by him, laden perhaps with more Sins than himself. His Eyes may be fixed on the *Altar*, or, on the Pictures and Images, but his Tongue Addresses to the more Charming Idol near him (5th ed., 1702, ii. 59).

Person. You see in every Posture of her Body, Air of her Face, and Motion of her Head, that it is her Business and Employment to gain Adorers. For this Reason your *Idols* appear in all publick Places and Assemblies, in order to seduce Men to their Worship. The Playhouse is very frequently filled with *Idols*; several of them are carried in Procession every Evening about the Ring, and several of them set up their Worship even in Churches. They are to be accosted in the Language proper to the Deity. Life and Death are in their Power: Joys of Heaven and Pains of Hell are at their disposal: Paradise is in their Arms, and Eternity in every Moment that you are present with them. Raptures, Transports and Extasies are the Rewards which they confer: Sighs and Tears, Prayers and broken Hearts are the Offerings which[a] are paid to them. Their Smiles make Men happy; their Frowns drive them to Despair. I shall only add under this Head, that *Ovid*'s Book of the Art of Love[1] is a kind of Heathen Ritual, which contains all the Forms of Worship which[b] are made use of to an *Idol*.

It would be as difficult a Task to reckon up these different kinds of *Idols*, as *Milton*'s[2] was to number those that were known in *Canaan*, and the Lands adjoining. Most of them are Worshipped, like *Moloch*, in Fires and Flames. Some of them, like *Baal*, love to see their Votaries cut and slashed, and shedding their Blood for them. Some of them, like the *Idol* in the *Apocrypha*,[3] must have Treats and Collations prepared for them every Night. It has indeed been known, that some of them have been used by their incensed Worshippers like the *Chinese Idols*,[4] who are Whipped and Scourged when they refuse to comply with the Prayers that are offered to them.

I must here observe, that those Idolaters who devote themselves to the *Idols* I am here speaking of, differ very much from all other kinds of Idolaters. For as others fall out because they Worship

---

^a which] that *Fol.*   ^b which] that *Fol.*

---

[1] *Ovid's Art of Love, together with his Remedy of Love,* 'by several eminent hands' (Dryden, Congreve, and Nahum Tate), had been published in 1709.

[2] *Paradise Lost,* i. 376 ff.

[3] *History of the Destruction of Bel and the Dragon,* 5. 3 ff.

[4] Cf. Louis Le Comte, *Memoirs and Observations made in a late Journey through the Empire of China* (1697), p. 326:

It is true they sometimes do not pay to these Gods all that respect which seems due to their Quality. For it often happens that if the People after worshipping them a great while do not obtain what they desire, they turn them off, and look upon them as impotent Gods; others use them in the most reproachful manner: some load them with hard names, others with hard blows.

different *Idols*, these Idolaters quarrel because they Worship the same.

The Intention therefore of the *Idol* is quite contrary to the Wishes of the Idolater; as the one desires to confine the *Idol* to himself, the whole Business and Ambition of the other is to multiply Adorers. This Humour of an *Idol* is prettily described in a Tale of *Chaucer*:[1] He represents one of them sitting at a Table with three of her Votaries about her, who are all of them courting her Favour, and paying their Adorations: She smiled upon one, drank to another, and trod upon the other's Foot which was under the Table. Now which of these three, says the old Bard, do you think was the Favourite? In troth, says he, not one of all the three.

The Behaviour of this old *Idol* in *Chaucer*, puts me in mind of the Beautiful *Clarinda*, one of the greatest *Idols* among the Moderns. She is Worshipped once a Week by Candle-light in the midst of a large Congregation generally called an Assembly. Some of the gayest Youths in the Nation endeavour to plant themselves in her Eye, while she sits in form with multitudes of Tapers burning about her. To encourage the Zeal of her Idolaters, she bestows a Mark of her Favour upon every one of them before they go out of her Presence. She asks a Question of one, tells a Story to another, glances an Ogle upon a third, takes a Pinch of Snuff[2] from the fourth, lets her Fan

[1] From the pseudo-Chaucerian poem, 'The Remedie of Love', stanzas 8 and 9.

[2] Snuff-taking in England had been introduced only within the past few years. Charles Lillie, from whose shop the original *Spectators* were distributed, compiled a book of recipes and notes, the manuscript of which was sold with his business and eventually published, in 1822, under the title, *The British Perfumer, Snuff Manufacturer, and Colourman's Guide*, edited by Colin Mackenzie. Part III deals with snuff. According to Lillie (chap. lvi, 'Origin of Snuff-taking in England') it was the sailors in the fleet commanded by Sir George Rooke who, disembarking near Cadiz, plundered and brought on board several thousand barrels and casks of snuffs manufactured in Spain. With this plunder on board they stopped at Vigo, where they destroyed most of the Spanish shipping and plundered many of the galleons from the Havannah which were there and acquired large quantities of gross snuff. 'The fleet having returned to England, and the ships being ordered to be laid up in their several ports, the sea-officers and sailors brought their snuff (which was called, by way of victorious distinction, Vigo snuff) to a very quick and cheap market; waggon-loads of it being sold at Portsmouth, Plymouth, and Chatham, for not more than three or four pence per pound' (pp. 296–7). Steele ridicules the habit of snuff-taking by women in *Tatler* 35: 'But of all Things, commend me to the Ladies who are got into this pretty Help to Discourse.' This number describes Sagissa (Mrs. Manley?) as addicted to snuff; when her gallant snatched a kiss, 'being unused to Snuff, some Grains from off her upper Lip made him sneeze aloud'. When Isaac Bickerstaff's sister Jenny was about to be married, he 'made her resign her Snuff-Box for ever, and half drown her self with washing away the Stench of the Musty' (*Tatler* 79). Swift refers to Stella's taking snuff on 28 Apr. 1711. On 7 June he writes to her: 'And are you as vicious in snuff as ever? I believe, as you say, it does neither hurt nor good; but I have left it off, and when any body offers me their box, I take about a tenth part of what I used to do, and then just smell to it, and privately fling the rest away.'

drop by accident to give the fifth an occasion of taking it up. In short, every one goes away satisfied with his Success, and encouraged to renew his Devotions on the same Canonical Hour that Day Seven-night.

An *Idol* may be Undeified by many accidental Causes. Marriage in particular is a kind of Counter-*Apotheosis*, or a Deification inverted. When a Man becomes familiar with his Goddess, she quickly sinks into a Woman.

Old Age is likewise a great Decayer of your *Idol*: The truth of it is, there is not a more unhappy Being than a Superannuated *Idol*, especially when she has contracted such Airs and Behaviour as are only Graceful when her Worshippers are about her.

Considering therefore that in these and many other Cases the *Woman* generally outlives the *Idol*, I must return to the Moral of this Paper, and desire my fair Readers to give a proper Direction to their Passion for being admired: In order to which, they must endeavour to make themselves the Objects of a reasonable and lasting Admiration. This is not to be hoped for from Beauty, or Dress, or Fashion, but from those inward Ornaments which[a] are not to be defaced by Time or Sickness, and which[b] appear most amiable to those who are most acquainted with them.   C[I]

No. 74   *Friday, May 25, 1711*[2]
[ADDISON]

. . . Pendent opera interrupta . . .
Virg.

IN my last *Monday's* Paper I gave some general Instances of those beautiful Strokes which[c] please the Reader in the old Song of *Chevy-Chase*; I shall here, according to my Promise, be more particular, and shew that the Sentiments in that Ballad are extremely natural

---

a which] that *Fol.*   b which] that *Fol.*   c which] that *Fol.*

I A letter from Euphelia (Lillie, i. 291–2) dated 2 July 1711 comments on this number, and recommends a method 'to make the creatures you call idols change the care you so much blame of adorning their persons, into that more laudable one of improving their minds'.

2 *Motto.* Virgil, *Aeneid*, 4. 88: The works are broken off . . .

and poetical, and full of the[a] majestick Simplicity which we admire
in the greatest of the ancient Poets: For which Reason I shall quote
several Passages of it, in which the Thought is altogether the same
with what we meet in several Passages of the *Æneid*; not that I
would infer from thence, that the Poet (whoever he was) proposed
to himself any Imitation of those Passages, but that he was directed
to them in general by the same Kind of Poetical Genius, and by the
same Copyings after Nature.

Had this old Song been filled with Epigrammatical Turns and
Points of Wit, it might perhaps have pleased the wrong Taste of
some Readers; but it would never have become the Delight of the
common People, nor have warmed the Heart of Sir *Philip Sidney*[1] like
the Sound of a Trumpet; it is only Nature that can have this Effect,
and please those Tastes which are the most unprejudiced or the most
refined. I must however beg Leave to dissent from so great an
Authority as that of Sir *Philip Sidney*, in the Judgment which he has
passed as to the rude Stile[2] and evil Apparel of this antiquated Song;
for there are several Parts in it where not only the Thought but the
Language is majestick, and the Numbers sonorous;[b] at least, the
Apparel is much more *gorgeous* than many of the Poets made use of
in Queen *Elizabeth*'s Time, as the Reader will see in several of the
following Quotations.

What can be greater than either the Thought or the Expression
in that Stanza,

> To drive the Deer with Hound and Horn
> Earl Piercy took his Way;
> The Child may rue that was unborn
> The Hunting of that Day?

This Way of considering the Misfortunes which this Battle would
bring upon Posterity, not only on those who were born immediately
after the Battle and lost their Fathers in it, but on those also who
perished in future Battles which took their rise from this Quarrel[c]

---

[a] the] that *Fol.*   [b] sonorous;] very sonorous; *Fol.*   [c] those also . . .
Quarrel] those also who should perish in future Battles which should arise from this
Quarrel *Fol.*

---

[1] See No. 70.
[2] Karl Nessler (*Geschichte der Ballade Chevy Chase*, p. 110) compares Dryden's remarks
on the vulgar words and low expressions in Shakespeare (Ker, i. 227, 165, 172) which
may have influenced Addison.

of the two Earls, is wonderfully beautiful, and conformable to the
Way of Thinking among the ancient Poets.

> *Audiet pugnas vitio parentum*
> *Rara juventus.* Hor.[1]

What can be more sounding and poetical, or resemble more the
majestick Simplicity of the Ancients, than the following Stanzas?

> *The stout Earl of* Northumberland
> *A Vow to God did make,*
> *His Pleasure in the* Scottish *Woods*
> *Three Summer's Days to take.*

> *With fifteen hundred Bowmen bold,*
> *All chosen Men of Might,*
> *Who knew full well, in Time of Need,*
> *To aim their Shafts aright.*

> *The Hounds ran swiftly thro' the Woods*
> *The nimble Deer to take,*
> *And with their Cries the Hills and Dales*
> *An Eccho shrill did make.*

> . . . Vocat ingenti Clamore Cithæron
> Taygetique canes, domitrixque Epidaurus equorum:
> Et vox assensu nemorum ingeminata remugit.[2]

> *Lo, yonder doth Earl* Dowglas *come,*
> *His Men in Armour bright;*
> *Full twenty hundred* Scottish *Spears,*
> *All marching in our Sight.*

> *All Men of pleasant* Tividale,
> *Fast by the River* Tweed, &c.

[1] Horace, *Odes*, 1. 2. 23–24.
> The Youth shall hear that impious steel
> Against our selves we madly drew,
> Which better haughty *Medes* should feel,
> The Youth our faults have left but few. CREECH.

[2] Virgil, *Georgics*, 3. 43–45.
> *Cytheron* loudly calls me to my way;
> Thy Hounds, *Taygetus*, open and pursue their Prey.
> High *Epidaurus* urges on my speed,
> Fam'd for his Hills, and for his Horses breed:
> From Hills and Dales the chearful Cries rebound:
> For Eccho hunts along; and propagates the sound. DRYDEN.

The Country of the *Scotch* Warriours described in these two last Verses, has a fine romantick Situation, and affords a Couple of smooth Words for Verse. If the Reader compares the foregoing six Lines of the Song with the following *Latin* Verses, he will see how much they are written in the Spirit of *Virgil.*

> *Adversi campo apparent, hastasque reductis*
> *Protendunt longe dextris; & spicula vibrant:*
> *Quique altum Preneste viri, quique arva Gabinæ*
> *Junonis, gelidumque Anienem, & roscida rivis*
> *Hernica saxa colunt: . . . qui rosea rura Velini,*
> *Qui Tetricæ horrentes rupes, montemque Severum,*
> *Casperiamque colunt, Forulosque & flumen Himellæ:*
> *Qui Tiberim Fabarimque bibunt. . . .*[1]

But to proceed.

> *Earl* Dowglas *on a milk-white Steed,*
> *Most like a Baron bold,*
> *Rode foremost of the Company,*
> *Whose Armour shone like Gold.*

Turnus ut antevolans tardum precesserat agmen, &c.
Vidisti, quo Turnus equo, quibus ibat in armis
Aureus. . . .[2]

> *Our* English *Archers bent their Bows,*
> *Their Hearts were good and true;*
> *At the first Flight of Arrows sent,*
> *Full threescore* Scots *they slew.*

[1] *Aeneid*, 11. 605–6; 7. 682–4, 712–15.
> Advancing in a Line, they couch their Spears;
> And less and less the middle Space appears.
> His own *Praeneste* sends a chosen Band,
> With those who plough *Saturnia's Gabine* Land:
> Besides the Succour which cold *Anien* yields,
> The Rocks of *Hernicus,* and dewy Fields.
>   Besides a Band
> That follow'd from *Velinum's* dewy Land:
> And *Amiternian* Troops, of mighty Fame,
> And Mountaineers, that from *Severus* came.
> And from the craggy Cliffs of *Tetrica,* ⎫
> And those where yellow *Tyber* takes his way, ⎬
> And where *Himella's* wanton Waters play. ⎭
> *Casperia* sends her Arms, with those that lye
> By *Fabaris,* and fruitful *Foruli.* DRYDEN.

[2] *Aeneid*, 9. 47, 269–70.
> The fiery *Turnus* flew before the rest.
> Thou saw'st the Courser by proud *Turnus* press'd. DRYDEN.

They clos'd full fast on ev'ry Side,
No Slackness there was found;
And many a gallant Gentleman
Lay gasping on the Ground.

With that there came an Arrow keen
Out of an English Bow,
Which struck Earl Dowglas to the Heart
A deep and deadly Blow.

Æneas was wounded after the same Manner by an unknown Hand in the Midst of a Parly.

Has inter voces, media inter talia verba,
Ecce viro stridens alis allapsa sagitta est,
Incertum quâ pulsa manu. . . .[1]

But of all the descriptive Parts of this Song, there are none more beautiful than the four following Stanzas, which have a great Force and Spirit in them, and are filled with very natural Circumstances. The Thought in the third Stanza was never touched by any other Poet, and is such an one as would have shined in *Homer* or in *Virgil*.

So thus did both these Nobles dye
Whose Courage none could stain;
An English Archer then perceiv'd
The noble Earl was slain.

He had a Bow bent in his Hand,
Made of a trusty Tree,
An Arrow of a Cloath-yard long
Unto the Head drew he.

Against Sir Hugh Montgomery
So right his Shaft he set,
The Grey-goose Wing that was thereon
In his Heart-blood was wet.

---

[1] *Aeneid*, 12. 318-20.
Thus while he spoke, unmindful of Defence,
A winged Arrow struck the Pious Prince.
But whether from some Human Hand it came,
Or Hostile God, is left unknown by Fame. DRYDEN.

> *This Fight did last from Break of Day*
> *Till setting of the Sun.*
> *For when they rung the Evening Bell*
> *The Battle scarce was done.*

One may observe likewise, that in the Catalogue of the Slain the Author has followed the Example of the greatest ancient Poets, not only in giving a long List of the Dead, but by diversifying it with little Characters of particular Persons.

> *And with Earl* Douglas *there was slain*
> *Sir* Hugh Montgomery,
> *Sir* Charles Carrel, *that from the Field*
> *One Foot would never fly:*

> *Sir* Charles Murrel *of* Ratcliff *too,*
> *His Sister's Son was he,*
> *Sir* David Lamb, *so well esteem'd,*
> *Yet saved could not be.*

The familiar Sound in these Names destroys the Majesty of the Description; for this Reason I do not mention this Part of the Poem but to shew the natural Cast[a] of Thought which[b] appears in it, as the two last Verses look almost like a Translation of *Virgil*.

> *. . . Cadit & Ripheus justissimus unus*
> *Qui fuit in Teucris & servantissimus æqui,*
> *Diis aliter visum est. . . .*[1]

In the Catalogue of the *English* who[c] fell, *Witherington*'s Behaviour is in the same Manner particularized very artfully, as the Reader is prepared for it by that Account which is given of him in the Beginning of the Battle: though I am satisfied your little Buffoon Readers (who have seen that Passage ridiculed in *Hudibras*)[2] will not be able to take the Beauty of it: For which Reason I dare not so much as quote it.[d]

---

 [a] Cast] Turn *Fol.*   [b] which] that *Fol.*   [c] who] that *Fol.*   [d] though . . . quote it. *om. in Fol.*

---

[1] *Aeneid,* 2. 426–8.

> Then *Ripheus* follow'd, in th' unequal Fight;
> Just of his Word, observant of the right;
> Heav'n thought not so. DRYDEN.

[2] *Hudibras,* I. iii. 94–96:

> And being down still laid about;
> As *Widdrington* in doleful dumps
> Is said to fight upon his stumps.

> *Then stept a gallant Squire forth,*
> Witherington *was his Name,*
> *Who said, I would not have it told*
> *To* Henry *our King for Shame,*

> *That e'er my Captain fought on Foot*
> *And I stood looking on.*

We meet with the same Heroic Sentiment in *Virgil*.

> *Non pudet, O Rutuli, cunctis pro talibus unam*
> *Objectare animam? numerone an viribus æqui*
> *Non sumus? . . .*[1]

What can be more natural or more moving, than the Circumstances in which he describes the Behaviour of those Women who had lost their Husbands on this fatal Day?

> *Next Day did many Widows come*
> *Their Husbands to bewail,*
> *They wash'd their Wounds in brinish Tears,*
> *But all would not prevail.*

> *Their Bodies bath'd in purple Blood,*
> *They bore with them away;*
> *They kist them dead a thousand Times,*
> *When they were clad in Clay.*

Thus we see how the Thoughts of this Poem, which naturally arise from the Subject, are always simple, and sometimes exquisitely noble; that the Language is often very sounding, and that the whole is written with a true poetical Spirit.

If this Song had been written in the *Gothic* Manner, which is the Delight of all our little Wits, whether Writers or Readers, it would not have hit the Taste of so many Ages, and have pleased the Readers of all Ranks and Conditions. I shall only beg Pardon for such a Profusion of *Latin* Quotations; which I should not have made use of, but that I feared my own Judgment would have looked too

---

[1] *Aeneid*, 12. 229–31.
> For shame, *Rutulians*, can you bear the sight,
> Of one expos'd for all, in single Fight?
> Can we, before the Face of Heav'n, confess
> Our Courage colder, or our Numbers less? DRYDEN.

singular on such a Subject, had not I supported it by the Practice
and Authority of *Virgil*.   C¹

No. 75   *Saturday, May 26, 1711*²
[STEELE]

Omnis Aristippum decuit color & status & res.
Hor.

IT was with some Mortification that I suffered the Raillery of a
Fine Lady of my Acquaintance, for Calling, in one of my Papers,³
Dorimant a Clown. She was so unmerciful as to take Advantage of
my invincible Taciturnity, and on that occasion, with great Freedom to consider the Air, the Height, the Face, the Gesture of him
who could pretend to Judge so arrogantly of Gallantry. She is full
of Motion, Janty and lively in her Impertinence, and one of those
that commonly pass, among the Ignorant, for Persons who have a
great deal of Humour. She had the Play of Sir *Fopling* in her Hand,
and after she had said it was happy for her there was not so charming

¹ Addison's criticism of the ballads, in Nos. 70, 74, and 85, has sometimes been
taken as evidence of 'pre-romantic' tendencies in Augustan literature, and Addison
has in this sense been presented as a kind of forerunner of romanticism. Nothing
could be farther from the truth. While it is correct to say that Addison is a pioneer
in calling attention to a hitherto neglected class of literature—so much so as to evoke
several parodies of these papers—his praise of the ballads rests nevertheless squarely
on the neo-classic grounds of universality of appeal: they please 'all kinds of
palates' because they offer 'a plain, simple copy of nature'. They are true to nature
in the sense that Horace and Virgil appeal to the universal elements in human
experience. They are examples of true wit, as opposed to those poems in the 'Gothick'
manner, those poems dressed in 'the helps and ornaments of art', which Addison
(with Cowley and Martial in mind) holds up as instances of false or mixed wit.
The principal repercussions are William Wagstaffe's very popular parody, *A Comment upon the History of Tom Thumb*, 1711 (the 3rd edition is advertised by Morphew in
the *Examiner* of 28 Feb. 1712; the 5th edition is reprinted in *Miscellaneous Works of
Dr. William Wagstaffe* in 1726, pp. 3–36); John Dennis's letter 'To H[enry] C[romwell]
Esq; Of Simplicity in Poetical Compositions, in Remarks on the 70th Spectator', in
Dennis's *Original Letters* (1721), i. 166–93 (reprinted by Hooker, ii. 29–40); a comment on 'The Dragon of Wantley' in *Mist's Weekly Journal* of 2 Sept. 1721 (on this
see R. P. McCutcheon in *Studies in Philology*, xxiii (1921), 451–6); and two essays in
the same periodical, on 'Chevy Chase', 13 July 1728, and again on 'The Dragon of
Wantley', 21 Sept. 1728 (on these see A. Sanford Limouze in *Studies in Philology*, xlvii
(1950), 607–18). All of these parodies and most of the critical comments, it should be
noted, were inspired partly by personal animus—against Steele as the presumed author
of the *Spectator*—or political bias.
² *Motto*. Horace, *Epistles*, i. 17. 23:
In Aristippus every form of life was fitting, every condition and circumstance.
³ No. 65.

a Creature as *Dorimant* now living, she began with a Theatrical Air and Tone of Voice to read, by way of Triumph over me, some of his Speeches. *'Tis she, that lovely Hair, that easy Shape, those wanton Eyes, and all those melting Charms about her Mouth, which* Medley *spoke of; I'll follow the Lottery, and put in for a Prize with my Friend* Bell-air.[1]

> *In Love the Victors from the Vanquish'd fly;*
> *They fly that wound, and they pursue that dye.*

Then turning over the Leaves, she reads alternately, and speaks,

> *And you and* Loveit *to her Cost shall find,*
> *I fathom all the Depths of Womankind.*

Oh the Fine Gentleman! But here, continues she, is the Passage I admire most, where he begins to Teize *Loveit*, and Mimick Sir *Fopling*. Oh the pretty Satyr, in his resolving to be a Coxcomb to please, since Noise and Nonsense have such powerful Charms!

> *I, that I may Successful prove,*
> *Transform my self to what you love.*[2]

Then how like a Man of the Town, so Wild and Gay is that!

> *The Wise will find a Difference in our Fate,*
> *You Wed a Woman, I a good Estate.*[3]

It would have been a very wild Endeavour for a Man of my Temper to offer any Opposition to so nimble a Speaker as my Fair Enemy is, but her Discourse gave me very many Reflections, when I had left her Company. Among others, I could not but consider, with some Attention, the false Impressions the generality[4] (the Fair Sex more especially) have of what should be intended, when they say a *Fine Gentleman*; and could not help revolving that Subject in my Thoughts, and setling, as it were, an Idea of that Character in my own Imagination.

No Man ought to have the Esteem of the rest of the World, for any Actions which are disagreeable to those Maxims which prevail, as the Standards of Behaviour, in the Country wherein he lives. What is opposite to the eternal Rules of Reason and good Sense, must be excluded from any Place in the Carriage of a Well-bred Man. I did not, I confess, explain my self enough on this Subject, when I called *Dorimant* a Clown, and made it an Instance of it, that

---

[1] *The Man of Mode*, III. iii.   [2] Ibid. V. i.
[3] Ibid. IV. ii.   [4] People in general. Now obsolete.

he called the *Orange Wench*, *Double-Tripe*: I should have shewed, that Humanity obliges a Gentleman to give no Part of Humankind Reproach, for what they, whom they Reproach, may possibly have in Common with the most Virtuous and Worthy amongst us. When a Gentleman speaks Coarsly, he has dressed himself Clean to no purpose: The Cloathing of our Minds certainly ought to be regarded before that of our Bodies. To betray in a Man's Talk a corrupted Imagination, is a much greater Offence against the Conversation of Gentlemen, than any Negligence of Dress imaginable. But this Sense of the Matter is so far from being received among People even of Condition, that *Vocifer* passes for a Fine Gentleman. He is Loud, Haughty, Gentle, Soft, Lewd, and Obsequious by turns, just as a little Understanding and great Impudence prompt him at the present Moment. He passes among the Silly Part of our Women for a Man of Wit, because he is generally in Doubt. He Contradicts with a Shrug, and confutes with a certain Sufficiency, in professing such or such a Thing is above his Capacity. What makes his Character the pleasanter is, that he is a professed Deluder of Women; and because the empty Coxcomb has no Regard to any thing that is of it self Sacred and Inviolable, I have heard an unmarried Lady of Fortune say, it is a Pity so fine a Gentleman as *Vocifer* is so great an Atheist. The Crowds of such inconsiderable[1] Creatures that infest all Places of Assembling, every Reader will have in his Eye from his own Observation; but would it not be worth considering what Sort of Figure a Man who formed himself upon those Principles among us, which are agreeable to the Dictates of Honour and Religion, would make in the familiar and ordinary Occurrences of Life?

I hardly have observed any one fill his several Duties of Life better than *Ignotus*. All the Underparts[2] of his Behaviour, and such as are exposed to common Observation, have their rise in him from great and noble Motives. A firm and unshaken Expectation of another Life, makes him become this; Humanity and good Nature, fortified by the Sense of Virtue, has the same Effect upon him, as the Neglect of all Goodness has upon many others. Being firmly Established in all Matters of Importance, that certain Inattention which makes Mens Actions look easie, appears in him with greater Beauty: By a thorough Contempt of little Excellencies, he is perfectly Master

---

[1] Here in the obsolete sense of 'inconsiderate, thoughtless'. The latest example in *OED* is dated 1726.

[2] The meaning is obvious, but the word soon dropped out of usage. The latest example in *OED* is dated 1715.

of them. This Temper of Mind leaves him under no necessity of Studying his Air, and he has this peculiar distinction, that his Negligence is unaffected.

He that can work himself into a Pleasure in considering this Being as an uncertain one, and think to reap an Advantage by its Discontinuance, is in a fair way of doing all Things with a graceful Unconcern, and Gentleman-like Ease. Such a one does not behold his Life as a short, transient, perplexing State, made up of trifling Pleasures and great Anxieties, but sees it in quite another Light; his Griefs are Momentary, and his Joys Immortal. Reflection upon Death is not a gloomy and sad Thought of Resigning every Thing that he Delights in, but it is a short Night followed by an endless Day. What I would here contend for is, that the more Virtuous the Man is, the nearer he will naturally be to the Character of Gentile and Agreeable. A Man whose Fortune is Plentiful, shews an Ease in his Countenance, and Confidence in his Behaviour, which he that is under Wants and Difficulties cannot assume. It is thus with the State of the Mind; he that governs his Thoughts with the everlasting Rules of Reason and Sense, must have something so inexpressibly Graceful in his Words and Actions, that every Circumstance must become him. The Change of Persons or Things around him do not at all alter his Situation, but he looks disinterested in the Occurrences with which others are distracted, because the greatest purpose of his Life is to maintain an Indifference both to it and all its Enjoyments. In a word, to be a Fine Gentleman, is to be a Generous and a Brave Man. What can make a Man so much in constant good Humour and Shine,[1] as we call it, than to be Supported by what can never fail him, and to believe that whatever happens to him was the best thing that could possibly befal him, or else he on whom it depends would not have permitted it to have befallen him at all?

R

---

[1] 'Sunniness of disposition. *Obs.*' *OED*. This is the only quotation given in *OED* to illustrate this sense.

No. 76   *Monday, May 28, 1711*[1]
[STEELE]

Ut tu Fortunam, sic nos te, Celse, feremus.
Hor.

THERE is nothing so common, as to find a Man whom in the general Observation of his Carriage you take to be of an uniform Temper, subject to such unaccountable Starts of Humour and Passion, that he is as much unlike himself, and differs as much from the Man you at first thought him, as any two distinct Persons can differ from each other. This proceeds from the Want of forming some Law of Life to our selves, or fixing some Notion of things in general, which may affect us in such Manner, as to create proper Habits both in our Minds and Bodies. The Negligence of this, leaves us exposed not only to an unbecoming Levity in our usual Conversation,[2] but also to the same Instability in our Friendships, Interests, and Alliances. A Man who is but a mere Spectator of what passes around him, and not engaged in Commerces[3] of any Consideration, is but an ill Judge of the secret Motions of the Heart of Man, and by what Degrees it is actuated to make such visible Alterations in the same Person: But at the same Time, when a Man is no way concerned in the Effect of such Inconsistencies in the Behaviour of Men of the World, the Speculation must be in the utmost Degree both diverting and instructive; yet to enjoy such Observations in the highest Relish, he ought to be placed in a Post of Direction, and have the dealing of their Fortunes to them. I have therefore been wonderfully diverted with some Pieces of secret History, which an Antiquary, my very good Friend, lent me as a Curiosity. They are Memoirs of the private Life of *Pharamond*[4] of *France*. '*Pharamond,* says

---

[1] *Motto.* Horace, *Epistles,* 1. 8. 17:
As you bear your fortune, Celsus, so we shall bear with you. Steele had used this also as the motto for *Tatler* 203.

[2] 'The action of consorting or having dealings with others; living together; commerce, intercourse, society, intimacy. *Obs.*' (*OED*). The usual meaning of the word in the *Spectator.*

[3] A word with similar sense to the above—'intercourse in the affairs of life; dealings'. This quotation is the last example (in plural form) in *OED.*

[4] Pharamond, the legendary king of the Franks, supposed to have ruled from 418 to 428. Mézeray's *General Chronological History of France* translated by John Bulteel in 1683 has as its subtitle, 'beginning before the reign of King Pharamond, and ending with the reign of King Henry the Fourth'. 'It may be doubted', says Mézeray, 'whether *Pharamond* be a proper Name, or whether it be only an Epithet' (p. 6).

my Author, was a Prince of infinite Humanity and Generosity, and at the same time the most pleasant and facetious Companion of his Time. He had a peculiar Taste in him (which would have been unlucky in any Prince but himself,) he thought there could be no exquisite Pleasure in Conversation but among Equals; and would pleasantly bewail himself that he always lived in a Crowd, but was the only Man in *France* that could never get into Company. This Turn of Mind made him delight in Midnight Rambles, attended only with one Person of his Bed-chamber: He would in these Excursions get acquainted with Men (whose Temper he had a Mind to try) and recommend them privately to the particular Observation of his first Minister. He generally found himself neglected by his new Acquaintance assoon as they had Hopes of growing great; and used on such Occasions to remark, That it was a great Injustice to tax Princes of forgetting themselves in their high Fortunes, when there were so few that could with Constancy bear the Favour of their very Creatures.' My Author in these loose Hints has one Passage that gives us a very lively Idea of the uncommon Genius of *Pharamond*. He met with one Man whom he had put to all the usual Proofs he made of those he had a Mind to know thoroughly, and found him for his Purpose: In Discourse with him one Day, he gave him Opportunity of saying how much would satisfy all his Wishes. The Prince immediately revealed himself, doubled the Sum, and spoke to him in this Manner. 'Sir, *You have twice what you desired, by the Favour of* Pharamond; *but look to it that you are satisfied with it, for 'tis the last you shall ever receive. I from this Moment consider you as mine; and to make you truly so, I give you my royal Word you shall never be greater or*

La Calprenède's *Faramond* (1661–70) helped to popularize the character and actions of the legendary king. Cf. Morley, note to No. 84:

> Steele uses the suggestion of the Romance of *Pharamond* whose 'whole Person,' says the romancer, 'was of so excellent a composition, and his words so Great and so Noble that it was very difficult to deny him reverence,' to connect with a remote king his ideas of the duty of a Court. Pharamond's friend Eucrate, whose name means Power well used, is an invention of the Essayist, as well as the incident and dialogue here given, for an immediate good purpose of his own, which he pleasantly contrives in imitation of the style of the romance. In the original, Pharamond is said to be 'truly and wholly charming, as well for the vivacity and delicateness of his spirit, accompanied with a perfect knowledge of all Sciences, as for a sweetness which is wholly particular to him, and a complacence which &c. . . . All his inclinations are in such manner fixed upon virtue, that no consideration nor passion can disturb him; and in those extremities into which his ill fortune hath cast him, he hath never let pass any occasion to do good.' That is why Steele chose Pharamond for his king . ..

Steele's immediate source, however, may be Bayle, art. 'Haillan', Remark K, which quotes a long passage on Pharamond, from Sorel's *Bibliothèque Français*.

less than you are at present. Answer me not, (concluded the Prince smiling) *but enjoy the Fortune I have put you in, which is above my own Condition; for you have hereafter nothing to hope or to fear.'*

His Majesty having thus well chosen and bought a Friend and Companion, he enjoyed alternately all the Pleasures of an agreeable private Man and a great and powerful Monarch: He gave himself, with his Companion, the Name of the merry Tyrant; for he punished his Courtiers for their Insolence and Folly, not by any Act of publick Disfavour, but by humourously practising upon their Imaginations. If he observed a Man untractable to his Inferiours, he would find an Opportunity to take some favourable Notice of him, and render him insupportable. He knew all his own Looks, Words and Actions had their Interpretations; and his Friend Monsieur *Eucrate* (for so he was called) having a great Soul without Ambition, he could communicate all his Thoughts to him, and fear no artful Use would be made of that Freedom. It was no small Delight when they were in private, to reflect upon all which had passed in publick.

Pharamond would often, to satisfy a vain Fool of Power in his Country, talk to him in a full Court, and with one Whisper make him despise all his old Friends and Acquaintance. He was come to that Knowledge of Men by long Observation, that he would profess altering the whole Mass of Blood in some Tempers, by thrice speaking to them. As Fortune was in his Power, he gave himself constant Entertainment in managing the mere Followers of it with the Treatment they deserved. He would, by a skilful Cast of his Eye and half a Smile, make two Fellows who hated, embrace and fall upon each others Neck with as much Eagerness, as if they followed their real Inclinations, and intended to stifle one another. When he was in high good Humour, he would lay the Scene with *Eucrate*, and on a publick Night exercise the Passions of his whole Court. He was pleased to see an haughty Beauty watch the Looks of the Man she had long despised, from Observation of his being taken Notice of by *Pharamond*; and the Lover conceive higher Hopes, than to follow the Woman he was dying for the Day before. In a Court where Men speak Affection in the strongest Terms, and Dislike in the faintest, it was a comical Mixture of Incidents to see Disguises thrown aside in one Case and encreased on the other, according as Favour or Disgrace attended the respective Objects of Men's Approbation or Disesteem. *Pharamond* in his Mirth upon the Meanness of Mankind used to say, 'As he could take away a Man's Five Senses, he could give him an Hundred. The Man in Disgrace shall immediately lose all his natural Endowments, and he that finds Favour have the Attributes of an Angel.' He would carry it so far as to say, 'It should not be only so in the Opinion of the lower Part of his Court, but the Men themselves shall think thus meanly or greatly of themselves, as they are out or in the good Graces of a Court.'

A Monarch who had Wit and Humour like *Pharamond*, must have Pleasures which no Man else can ever have Opportunity of enjoying. He gave Fortune to none but those whom he knew could receive it without Transport; he made a noble and generous Use of his Observations; and did not regard his Ministers as they were agreeable to himself, but as they were useful to his Kingdom: By this Means the King appeared in every Officer of State; and no Man had a Participation of the Power, who had not a Similitude of the Virtue of *Pharamond*.   R

No. 77   *Tuesday, May* 29, 1711[1]
[BUDGELL]

Non convivere licet, nec Urbe tota
Quisquam est tam propè tam proculque nobis.
                                    Mart.

MY Friend WILL. HONEYCOMB is one of those Sort of Men who are very often absent in Conversation, and what the *French* call a *reveur* and a *distrait*.[2] A little before our Club-time last Night we were walking together in *Somerset* Garden,[3] where WILL. had picked up a small Pebble of so odd a make, that he said he would present it to a Friend of his, an eminent *Virtuoso*. After we had walked some time, I made a full stop with my Face towards the West, which WILL. knowing to be my usual Method of asking what's a Clock,

---

[1] *Motto.* Martial, *Epigrams*, 1. 86. 8–10:
We must not live together, nor is there one in the city so near and yet so far off.

[2] The first word is not in *OED*, and for the second this quotation is the first example given. The phrase is used earlier, however, by Swift in a letter to Ambrose Philips of 10 July 1708: 'Colonel Frowde is just as he was, very friendly and *grand rêveur et distrait*' (*Correspondence*, ed. Ball, i. 101).

[3] Somerset Garden, attached to Somerset House. Auctions of pictures 'at the Two Flower Pots in Somerset House Yard in the Strand' are advertised in Nos. 39, 41, 42, 81–85, 364, 365, 367, and 369–73.

in an Afternoon, immediately pulled out his Watch, and told me we had seven Minutes good. We took a turn or two more, when, to my great Surprize, I saw him squirr away[1] his Watch a considerable way into the *Thames*, and with great Sedateness in his Looks put up the Pebble, he had before found, in his Fob. As I have naturally an Aversion to much Speaking, and do not love to be the Messenger of ill News, especially when it comes too late to be useful, I left him to be convinced of his Mistake in due time, and continued my Walk, reflecting on these little Absences[2] and Distractions in Mankind, and resolving to make them the Subject of a future Speculation.

I was the more confirmed in my Design, when I considered that they were very often Blemishes in the Characters of Men of Excellent Sense; and helped to keep up the Reputation of that *Latin* Proverb,[3] which Mr. *Dryden* has Translated in the following Lines:

> *Great Wit to Madness sure is near ally'd,*
> *And thin Partitions do their Bounds divide.*

My Reader does, I hope, perceive, that I distinguish a Man who is *Absent*,[4] because he thinks of something else, from one who is *Absent*, because he thinks of nothing at all: The latter is too Innocent a Creature to be taken notice of; but the Distractions of the former may, I believe, be generally accounted for from one of these Reasons.

Either their Minds are wholly fixed on some particular Science, which is often the Case of Mathematicians[5] and other Learned Men; or are wholly taken up with some violent Passion, such as Anger, Fear, or Love, which ties the Mind to some distant Object; or, lastly, these Distractions proceed from a certain Vivacity and Fickleness in a Man's Temper, which while it raises up infinite Numbers of *Idea*'s in the Mind, is continually pushing it on, without allowing it to rest on any particular Image. Nothing therefore is more unnatural than the Thoughts and Conceptions of such a Man, which are seldom occasioned either by the Company he is in, or any of those Objects which are placed before him. While you fancy he is

[1] Cf. Addison's adventures of a shilling in *Tatler* 249: 'he squirred me away from him as far as he could fling me.'

[2] i.e. inattention to what is going on. This quotation is the earliest in *OED* for this meaning.

[3] 'Nullum magnum ingenium sine mixtura dementiae.' A commonplace from antiquity (Plato, *Phaedrus*, 245A; Aristotle, *Problemata*, 30. 1; Seneca, *Dialogues* 9. 17. 10) which is frequently quoted. Bayle (Cardan, Remark T; Heloisa, Remark M) quotes it from Seneca. Dryden's couplet is from *Absalom and Achitophel*, 163–4 ('Great wits are sure to madness near allied').

[4] See No. 30 for 'absent' in the sense of 'absent-minded'.

[5] Possibly an allusion to Sir Isaac Newton.

Admiring a Beautiful Woman, 'tis an even Wager that he is solving a Proposition in *Euclid*; and while you may imagine he is reading the *Paris Gazette*, 'tis far from being impossible that he is pulling down and rebuilding the Front of his Country-House.

At the same time that I am endeavouring to expose this Weakness in others, I shall readily confess that I once laboured under the same Infirmity my self. The Method I took to Conquer it was a firm Resolution to learn something from whatever I was obliged to see or hear. There is a way of Thinking, if a Man can attain to it, by which he may strike somewhat out of any thing. I can at present observe those Starts of good Sense and Struggles of unimproved Reason in the Conversation of a Clown, with as much Satisfaction as the most shining Periods of the most finished Orator; and can make a shift to command my Attention at a *Puppet-Show* or an *Opera*,[1] as well as at *Hamlet* or *Othello*.[2] I always make one of the Company I am in; for though I say little my self, my Attention to others, and those Nods of Approbation which I never bestow unmerited, sufficiently shew that I am among them. Whereas WILL. HONEYCOMB, tho' a Fellow of good Sense, is every Day doing and saying an hundred Things, which he afterwards confesses, with a well-bred Frankness, were somewhat *mal a propos*,[3] and undesigned.

I chanced the other Day to go into a Coffee-house, where WILL. was standing in the midst of several Auditors whom he had gathered round him, and was giving them an Account of the Person and Character of *Moll Hinton*.[4] My Appearance before him just put him in mind of me, without making him reflect that I was actually present. So that keeping his Eyes full upon me, to the great Surprize of his Audience, he broke off his first Harangue, and proceeded thus,—'Why now there's my Friend (mentioning me by Name) he is a Fellow that thinks a great deal, but never opens his Mouth; I warrant you he is now thrusting his short Face into some Coffee-house about 'Change. I was his Bail in the time of the *Popish-Plot*,

---

[1] Mr. Spectator usually couples these forms of 'idle' entertainment together.

[2] Both plays had been given recently at Drury Lane—*Hamlet* on 3 May, and *Othello* on 24 April.

[3] This is the earliest example of the phrase in *OED*.

[4] A well-known woman of the town. She is mentioned in Part I of Robert Gould's poem, 'The Play-house' (*Works*, 1709, ii. 235):

> In the *Side-Box Moll Hinton* You may see,
> Or *Howard Moll*, much wickeder than she;
> That is their Throne; for there they best Survey
> All the Young *Fops* that flutter to the Play.

when he was taken up for a Jesuit.'[1] If he had looked on me a little longer, he had certainly described me so particularly, without ever considering what led him into it, that the whole Company must necessarily have found me out; for which reason, remembring the old Proverb, *Out of Sight out of Mind*, I left the Room; and upon meeting him an Hour afterwards, was asked by him, with a great deal of good Humour, in what Part of the World I had lived, that he had not seen me these three Days.

Monsieur *Bruyere*[2] has given us the Character of *an absent Man*, with a great deal of Humour, which he has pushed to an agreeable Extravagance; with the Heads of it I shall conclude my present Paper.

'*Menalcas* (says that excellent Author) comes down in a Morning, opens his Door to go out, but shuts it again, because he perceives that he has his Night-cap on; and examining himself further finds that he is but half shaved, that he has stuck his Sword on his right side, that his Stockings are about his Heels, and that his Shirt is over his Breeches. When he is dress'd he goes to Court, comes into the Drawing-room, and walking bolt upright under a branch of Candlesticks his Wigg is caught up by one of them, and hangs dangling in the Air. All the Courtiers fall a laughing, but *Menalcas* laughs louder than any of them, and looks about for the Person that is the Jest of the Company. Coming down to the Court-gate, he finds a Coach, which taking for his own, he whips into it, and the Coachman drives off, not doubting but he carries his Master. As soon as he stops, *Menalcas* throws himself out of the Coach, crosses the Court, ascends the Stair-case, and runs thro' all the Chambers with the greatest Familiarity, reposes himself on a Couch, and fancies himself at home. The Master of the House at last comes in, *Menalcas* rises to receive him, and desires him to sit down; he talks, muses, and then talks again. The Gentleman of the House is tired and amazed; *Menalcas* is no less so, but is every Moment in hopes that his impertinent Guest will at last end his tedious Visit. Night comes on, when *Menalcas* is hardly undeceived.

[1] Cf. No. 1.
[2] 'Of Man', in *Characters* (3rd ed., 1702), pp. 212–19. In the description of Menalcas Budgell follows the English version fairly closely. Other details in this number of the *Spectator* show the influence of La Bruyère: 'He walks by the Water-side, asks what's a Clock; they shew him a Watch, he scarce looks on't before he forgets both the Hour and the Watch, and throws it into the River as a thing which troubles him' (p. 215). According to *Menagiana* (iv. 220) the character of Menalcas was said to be based on the Comte de Brancas.

'When he is playing at Backgammon, he calls for a full Glass of Wine and Water; 'tis his turn to throw, he has the Box in one Hand and his Glass in the other, and being extreamly dry, and unwilling to lose Time, he swallows down both the Dice, and at the same time throws his Wine into the Tables. He writes a Letter, and flings the Sand into the Ink-bottle; he writes a second, and mistakes the Super-scription: A Noble-man receives one of them, and upon opening it reads as follows. *I would have you, honest* Jack, *immediately upon the Receipt of this, take in Hay enough to serve me the Winter.* His Farmer receives the other, and is amazed to see in it, *My Lord, I received your Grace's Commands with an intire Submission to* —— If he is at an Entertainment, you may see the Pieces of Bread continually multi-plying round his Plate: 'Tis true, the rest of the Company want it, as well as their Knives and Forks, which *Menalcas* does not let them keep long. Sometimes in a Morning he puts his whole Family in an hurry, and at last goes out without being able to stay for his Coach or Dinner; and for that Day you may see him in every part of the Town, except the very Place where he had appointed to be upon a Business of Importance. You would often take him for every thing that he is not; for a Fellow quite Stupid, for he hears nothing; for a Fool, for he talks to himself, and has an hundred Grimaces and Motions with his Head, which are altogether involuntary; for a proud Man, for he looks full upon you, and takes no notice of your Saluting him: The Truth on't is, his Eyes are open, but he makes no use of them, and neither sees you, nor any Man, nor any thing else. He came once from his Country-house, and his own Footmen under-took to rob him, and succeeded: They held a Flambeau to his Throat, and bid him deliver his Purse; he did so, and coming home told his Friends he had been robbed; they desire to know the Particulars, Ask my Servants, says *Menalcas*, for they were with me.'

X

No. 78   *Wednesday, May* 30, 1711[1]
[STEELE]

Cum Talis sis, Utinam noster esses!

THE following Letters[2] are so pleasant, that I doubt not but the Reader will be as much diverted with them as I was. I have nothing to do in this Day's Entertainment, but taking the Sentence from the End of the *Cambridge* Letter and placing it at the Front of my Paper; to shew the Author I wish him my Companion with as much Earnestness as he invites me to be his.

SIR,

'I SEND you the inclosed, to be inserted (if you think them worthy of it) in your SPECTATORS; in which so surprizing a Genius appears, that it is no Wonder if all Mankind endeavours to get somewhat into a Paper which will always live.

'As to the *Cambridge* Affair, the Humour was really carried on in the Way I describe it. However, you have a full Commission to put out or in, and to do whatever you think fit with it. I have already had the Satisfaction of seeing you take that Liberty with some things I have before sent you.

'Go on, Sir, and prosper. You have the best Wishes of,

Sir,
*Your very affectionate
and obliged humble Servant.*'

---

[1] *Motto.* Since you are such, would that you were one of ours! As Steele says (in the second sentence) he is using the sentiment at the end of the Cambridge letter for his motto. The Latin, however, is from Bacon's *Advancement of Learning*, I. iii. 3: 'as Agesilaus said to his enemy Pharnabazus, "Talis quum sis, utinam noster esses".' The reply of Agesilaus, as recorded in Plutarch (*Life of Agesilaus*, 12) and Xenophon (*Hellenica*, 4. 1. 38), is not given in this form in the Latin versions, so that Bacon is apparently to be taken as the source of the phrase.

[2] Nichols, followed by later editors, suggested that 'this was a communication from Mr. Eusden, of Trinity College in Cambridge', and that the account of the Lowngers also received from Cambridge (in No. 54) was from the same hand 'and one of the things with which Steele took the liberty here mentioned'. Laurence Eusden (1688–1730), afterwards Poet Laureate, is named by Steele in No. 555 as a contributor. He was educated at Trinity College, Cambridge (B.A., 1708; M.A., 1712), and was a member of the Whig circle under the patronage of Lord Halifax. He was a contributor to Steele's *Poetic Miscellanies* of 1714. According to Bisset, 'He wrote several letters in the Spectator, which, though they do not discover great vigour of mind, are sensible and well written. A letter about *Idols*, in No. 87, is his; as also most of the letters from Cambridge' (i. 242). In *Guardian* 164 'Mr. Eusden of Cambridge' is acknowledged as the author of two translations from Claudian in *Guardians* 127 and 164.

Mr. SPECTATOR, *Cambridge.*

'YOU well know it is of great Consequence to clear Titles, and it is of Importance that it be done in the proper Season: On which Account this is to assure you, that the CLUB OF UGLY FACES was instituted originally at *CAMBRIDGE* in the merry Reign of K—g *Ch—les* II. As in great Bodies of Men it is not difficult to find Members enow for such a Club, so (I remember) it was then fear'd, upon their Intention of dining together, that the Hall belonging to *CLARE HALL*, (the ugliest *then* in the Town, tho' *now* the neatest) would not be large enough HANDSOMLY to hold the Company. Invitations were made to great Numbers, but very few accepted them without much Difficulty. ONE pleaded, that being at *London* in a Bookseller's Shop, a Lady going by with a great Belly long'd to kiss him. HE had certainly been excus'd, but that Evidence appear'd, That indeed one in *London* did pretend she long'd to kiss him, but that it was only a *Pickpocket*, who during his kissing her stole away all his Money. ANOTHER would have got off by a Dimple in his Chin; but it was prov'd upon *him*, that he had by coming into a Room made a Woman miscarry, and frighten'd two Children into Fits. A THIRD alledg'd, That he was taken by a Lady for another Gentleman, who was one of the handsomest in the University: But upon Enquiry it was found, That the Lady had actually lost one Eye, and the other was very much upon the Decline. A FOURTH produc'd Letters out of the Country in his Vindication, in which a Gentleman offer'd him his Daughter, who had lately fall'n in love with him, with a good Fortune: But it was made appear that the young Lady was amorous, and had like to have run away with her Father's Coachman; so that 'twas suppos'd, that her Pretence of falling in love with him was only in order to be well married. It was pleasant to hear the several Excuses which were made, insomuch that some made as much Interest to be excus'd as they would from serving Sheriff; however, at last the Society was form'd, and proper Officers were appointed; and the Day was fix'd for the Entertainment, which was in *Venison Season*. A pleasant *Fellow* of *King's Colledge* (commonly call'd CRAB from his sour Look, and the only Man who did not pretend to get off) was nominated for Chaplain; and nothing was wanting but some one to sit in the Elbow-Chair, by way of PRESIDENT, at the upper End of the Table; and there the Business stuck, for there was no Contention for Superiority *there*. This Affair made so great a Noise, that the K—g, who was then at *Newmarket*,

heard of it, and was pleas'd merrily and graciously to say, HE
COULD NOT BE THERE HIMSELF, BUT HE WOULD SEND THEM A
BRACE OF BUCKS.

'I would desire you, Sir, to set this Affair in a true Light, that
Posterity may not be misled in so important a Point: For when *the
wise Man who shall write your true History* shall acquaint the World,
That you had a DIPLOMA sent from the *Ugly Club at OXFORD*, and
That by vertue of it you were admitted into it; what a learned War
will there be among *future Criticks* about the Original of that Club
which both Universities will contend so warmly for? And perhaps
some hardy *Cantabrigian* Author may then boldly affirm, That the
Word *OXFORD* was an Interpolation of some *Oxonian* instead of
CAMBRIDGE. This Affair will be best adjusted in your Life-Time;
but I hope your Affection to your MOTHER will not make you
partial to your AUNT.

'To tell you, Sir, my own Opinion: Tho' I cannot find any ancient
Records of any Acts of the SOCIETY OF THE UGLY FACES, consider'd
in a *publick* Capacity; yet in a *private* one they have certainly Antiquity on their Side. I am perswaded they will hardly give Place to
the LOWNGERS,[1] and the LOWNGERS are of the same Standing with
the University it self.

'Tho' we well know, Sir, you want no Motives to do Justice, yet
I am commission'd to tell you, that you are invited to be admitted
ad eundem at *CAMBRIDGE*; and I believe I may venture safely to
deliver this as the Wish of our whole University.'

To Mr. SPECTATOR.

The humble Petition of WHO and WHICH,[2]

Sheweth,

'THAT your poor Petitioners being in a forlorn and destitute
Condition, know not to whom we should apply our selves for
Relief, because there is hardly any Man alive who has not injured
us. Nay, we speak it with Sorrow, even YOU your self, whom we
should suspect of such a Practice the last of all Mankind, can hardly
acquit your self of having given us some Cause of Complaint. We
are descended of ancient Families, and kept up our Dignity and

[1] No. 54.
[2] Many of the textual revisions in the *Spectator*, particularly in the essays by
Addison, consist of substitutions of *who* or *which* for *that*. See further No. 80 ('the just
remonstrance of affronted *that*'). Historically, the relative pronoun *that*, far from being
a 'jacksprat', is actually the older.

Honour many Years, till the Jacksprat THAT supplanted us. How often have we found our selves slighted by the Clergy in their Pulpits, and the Lawyers at the Bar? Nay, how often have we heard in one of the most polite and august Assemblies in the Universe, to our great Mortification, these Words, *That THAT that noble L—d urg'd*; which if one of us had had Justice done, would have sounded nobler thus, *That WHICH that noble L—d urg'd*. Senates themselves, the Guardians of *British* Liberty, have degraded us, and preferred THAT to us; and yet no Decree was ever given against us. In the very Acts of Parliament, in which the utmost Right should be done to every *Body*, *WORD* and *Thing*, we find our selves often either not used, or used one instead of another. In the first and best Prayer Children are taught they learn to misuse us: *Our Father WHICH art in Heaven*, should be, *Our Father WHO art in Heaven*; and even a CONVOCATION,[1] after long Debates, refused to consent to an Alteration of it. In our *general Confession* we say, — *Spare Thou them, O God, WHICH confess their Faults*; which ought to be, *WHO confess their Faults*. What Hopes then have we of having Justice done us, when the Makers of our very Prayers and Laws, and the most learned in all Faculties, seem to be in a Confederacy against us, and our Enemies themselves must be our Judges?

'The *Spanish* Proverb[2] says, *Il sabio muda conscio, il necio no*; i.e. *A wise Man changes his Mind, a Fool never will*. So that we think YOU, Sir, a very proper Person to address to, since we know you to be capable of being convinc'd, and changing your Judgment. You are well able to settle this Affair, and to you we submit our Cause. We desire you to assign the Butts and Bounds of each of us; and that for the Future we may both enjoy our own. We would desire to be heard by our Council, but that we fear in their very Pleadings they would betray our Cause: Besides, we have been oppress'd so many Years, that we can appear no other Way, but in *forma pauperis*. All which consider'd, we hope you will be pleased to do that which to Right and Justice shall appertain.

And your Petitioners, &c.'

R

---

[1] Apparently a reference to the 1661–2 revision of the Prayer Book (cf. *N & Q.*, 8th ser., v (1894), 465), although no record of an actual Convocation debate on this subject has been found. Dr. Norman Sykes kindly informed me that the proposed revision was not under consideration in 1689.

[2] The proverb also occurs in English in the seventeenth century (Tilley, M 420).

No. 79   *Thursday, May 31, 1711*[1]
[STEELE]

Oderunt peccare boni virtutis amore.

Hor.

I HAVE received very many Letters of late from my Female Correspondents, most of whom are very angry with me for Abridging
their Pleasures, and looking severely upon Things, in themselves,
indifferent. But I think they are extreamly Unjust to me in this
Imputation: All that I contend for is, that those Excellencies, which
are to be regarded but in the second Place, should not precede more
weighty Considerations. The Heart of Man deceives him in spite
of the Lectures of half a Life spent in Discourses on the Subjection
of Passion, and I do not know why one may not think the Heart of
Woman as Unfaithful to it self. If we grant an Equality in the Faculties of both Sexes, the Minds of Women are less Cultivated with
Precepts, and consequently may, without Disrespect to them, be
accounted more liable to Illusion in Cases wherein natural Inclination is out of the Interests of Virtue. I shall take up my present Time
in Commenting upon a Billet or two which came from Ladies, and
from thence leave the Reader to judge whether I am in the right or
not, in thinking it is possible Fine Women may be mistaken.

The following Address seems to have no other Design in it, but
to tell me the Writer will do what she pleases for all me.

Mr. SPECTATOR,

'I AM Young, and very much inclined to follow the Paths of
Innocence; but at the same time, as I have a plentiful Fortune,
and am of Quality, I am unwilling to resign the Pleasures of Distinction, some little Satisfaction in being Admired in general, and
much greater in being beloved by a Gentleman, whom I design to
make my Husband. But I have a mind to put off entring into
Matrimony 'till another Winter is over my Head, which (whatever,
musty Sir, you may think of the Matter) I design to pass away in
hearing Musick, going to Plays, Visiting, and all other Satisfactions
which Fortune and Youth, protected by Innocence and Virtue, can
procure for,

SIR,
Your most Humble Servant,
M. T.

[1] *Motto.* Horace, *Epistles,* I. 16. 52: The good for virtue's sake abhor to sin.

'My Lover does not know I like him, therefore having no Engagements upon me, I think to stay, and know whether I may not like
any one else better.'

I have heard WILL. HONEYCOMB say, *A Woman seldom writes her
Mind but in her Postscript.*[1] I think this Gentlewoman has sufficiently
discovered hers in this. I'll lay what Wager she pleases against her
present Favourite, and can tell her that she will Like Ten more
before she is fixed, and then will take the worst Man she ever liked
in her Life. There is no end of Affection taken in at the Eyes only;
and you may as well satisfie those Eyes with seeing, as controul any
Passion received by them only. It is from Loving by Sight that Coxcombs so frequently succeed with Women, and very often a Young
Lady is bestowed by her Parents to a Man who weds her (as
Innocence it self,) tho' she has, in her own Heart, given her Approbation of a different Man in every Assembly she was in the whole
Year before. What is wanting among Women, as well as among
Men, is the Love of laudable Things, and not to rest only in the
forbearance of such as are Reproachful.

How far removed from a Woman of this light Imagination is
Eudosia![2] *Eudosia* has all the Arts of Life and good Breeding with so
much ease, that the Virtue of her Conduct looks more like an
Instinct than Choice. It is as little difficult to her to think justly of
Persons and Things, as it is to a Woman of different Accomplishments, to move ill or look awkward. That which was, at first, the
effect of Instruction, is grown into an Habit; and it would be as hard
for *Eudosia* to indulge a wrong Suggestion of Thought, as it would
be to *Flavia*, the Fine Dancer, to come into a Room with an unbecoming Air.

But the Misapprehensions People themselves have of their own
State of Mind, is laid down with much discerning in the following
Letter, which is but an Extract of a kind Epistle from my Charming
Mistress *Hecatissa*,[3] who is above the Vanity of external Beauty, and
is the better Judge of the Perfections of the Mind.

---

[1] Cf. Bacon's essay 'Of Cunning': 'I knew one that when he wrote a letter he would
put that which was most material in the postscript, as if it had been a bymatter.'
[2] Gk., endowed with beautiful gifts. Eudocia is the heroine of Hughes's last play,
The Siege of Damascus (1720).
[3] No. 48.

Mr. SPECTATOR,

'I WRITE this to acquaint you, that very many Ladies, as well as my self, spend many Hours more than we used at the Glass, for want of the Female Library[1] of which you promised us a Catalogue. I hope, Sir, in the Choice of Authors for us, you will have a particular Regard to Books of Devotion. What they are, and how many, must be your chief Care; for upon the Propriety of such Writings depends a great deal. I have known those among us who think, if they every Morning and Evening spend an Hour in their Closet, and read over so many Prayers in Six or Seven Books of Devotion, all equally nonsensical, with a sort of Warmth, (that might as well be raised by a Glass of Wine, or a Drachm of Citron)[2] they may all the rest of their time go on in whatever their particular Passion leads them to. The Beauteous *Philautia*,[3] who is (in your Language) an *Idol*, is one of these Votaries; she has a very pretty furnished Closet, to which she retires at her appointed Hours: This is her Dressing-room, as well as Chappel; she has constantly before her a large Looking-glass, and upon the Table, according to a very Witty Author,

> *Together lye her Prayer-Book and Paint,*
> *At once t'improve the Sinner and the Saint.*[4]

'It must be a good Scene, if one could be present at it, to see this *Idol* by turns lift up her Eyes to Heav'n and steal Glances at her own Dear Person. It cannot but be a pleasant Conflict between Vanity

[1] No. 37.

[2] Short for citron-water (a liquor made from brandy flavoured with citron- or lemon-peel). This is the earliest quotation for this word in *OED*. In No. 128 is advertised:

> The remaining Part of the late Mrs. HUNT's Stock of Palsey Drops, Viper Water, Spirit of Lavender, Citron Water, Spirit of Oranges, Spirit of Clary, Mint, and Balm, Plague Water, Syrop of Lemons, Oyl of Lavender, prepar'd Ambergriece, with other Perfumes, Cordials, &c. are to be sold at the usual Rates, by Mrs. Susanna Jackson at the Unicorn in Newgate-street: Also a Quantity of pickled Broombuds.

[3] Gk., love of self. Burton's *Anatomy of Melancholy*, I. ii. iii. 14, deals with the causes of 'Philautia, or Self-love, Vain-glory, Praise'.

[4] These lines, which Johnson quotes in the *Dictionary* and marks *Anon.*, are attributed to the Earl of Halifax ('On the Countess Dowager of ★★★') in *Works of Celebrated Authors, of whose writings there are but small remains* (1750), i. 235. They appear earlier in *Miscellaneous Works, Written by His Grace, George, Late Duke of Buckingham. . . . Also State Poems on the Late Times, by Mr. Dryden, Sir George Etherege, Sir Fleetwood Shepherd, . . . &c. Never Before Printed*, published by J. Nutt in 1704. Here the lines form part of a poem 'Upon an old affected Court Lady' by Sir Fleetwood Shepherd (p. 83):

> Her watchful Maids prevent the Peep of Day,
> And all in order on her Toylet Lay
> Pray'r-Books and Patch-Box, Sermon-Notes and Paint,
> At once t'improve the Sinner and the Saint.

and Humiliation. When you are upon this Subject, chuse Books which elevate the Mind above the World, and give a pleasing Indifference to little things in it. For want of such Instructions, I am apt to believe so many People take it in their Heads to be sullen, cross and angry, under Pretence of being abstracted from the Affairs of this Life, when at the same time they betray their Fondness for them by doing their Duty as a Task, and Pouting and reading good Books for a Week together. Much of this I take to proceed from the Indiscretion of the Books themselves, whose very Titles of Weekly Preparations,[1] and such limited Godliness, lead People of ordinary Capacities into great Errors, and raise in them a Mechanical Religion, intirely distinct from Morality. I know a Lady so given up to this sort of Devotion, that tho' she Employs six or eight Hours of the twenty four at Cards, she never misses one constant Hour of Prayer, for which time another holds her Cards, to which she returns with no little Anxiousness till two or three in the Morning. All these Acts are but empty Shows, and, as it were, Compliments made to Virtue; the Mind is all the while untouched with any true Pleasure in the Pursuit of it. From hence I presume it arises that so many People call themselves Virtuous, from no other Pretence to it but an Absence of Ill. There is *Dulcianara* is the most insolent of all Creatures to her Friends and Domesticks, upon no other Pretence in Nature but that (as her silly Phrase is) no one can say Black is her Eye.[2] She has no Secrets, forsooth, which should make her afraid to speak her Mind, and therefore she is impertinently Blunt to all her Acquaintance, and unseasonably Imperious to all her Family. Dear Sir, be pleased to put such Books in our Hands, as may make our Virtue more inward, and convince some of us that in a Mind truly Virtuous the Scorn of Vice is always accompanied with the Pity of it. This, and other things, are impatiently expected from you by our whole Sex; among the rest by,

SIR,

Your most Humble Servant,

B. D.'

R

[1] This may refer to *A Week's Preparation towards a Worthy Receiving of the Lord's Supper* . . . by G. B., published in 1679. It reached an eleventh edition by 1686, and a second part, published in 1684, was also frequently reprinted. There were other works with similar titles, e.g. *Monthly Preparations for the Holy Communion*, by R. B. (1696).

[2] To say evil of or to impute blame to one. See Apperson, 'Eye', 23; and Tilley, E 252.

No. 80
[STEELE]

Friday, June 1, 1711[1]

Cœlum non animum mutant qui trans mare Currunt.

Hor.

IN the Year 1688, and on the same Day of that Year, were born in *Cheapside*,[2] *London*, two Females of exquisite Feature and Shape; the one we shall call *Brunetta*, the other *Phillis*.[3] A close Intimacy between their Parents made each of them the first Acquaintance the other knew in the World: They play'd, dressed Babies,[4] acted Visitings,[5] learned to Dance and make Curtesies, together. They were inseparable Companions in all the little Entertainments their tender Years were capable of: which innocent Happiness continued till the Beginning of their fifteenth Year, when it happened that Mrs. *Phillis* had an Head-dress on which became her so very well, that instead of being beheld any more with Pleasure for their Amity to each other, the Eyes of the Neighbourhood were turned to remark them with Comparison of their Beauty. They now no longer enjoyed the Ease of Mind and pleasing Indolence in which they were formerly happy, but all their Words and Actions were misinterpreted by

[1] *Motto*. Horace, *Epistles*, i. 11. 27:
Those who go across the sea change their climate only, not their mind.

[2] One of the prosperous business streets of the City, running east from Paternoster Row at St. Paul's to the Poultry. It contained shops of linen-drapers, goldsmiths, and milliners, with many taverns; above or behind them lived families mostly of the trading class and usually owners or proprietors of the nearby shops.

[3] N. Darnell Davis, *The 'Spectator's' Essays relating to the West Indies* (Demerara, British Guiana, 1885), pp. 10-11, pointed out a probable source for this incident in a letter from a Captain Walduck (dated Barbadoes, 12 Nov. 1710) to James Petiver, apothecary to the Charterhouse, from whom Steele may have heard it:

There are two gentlewomen in this Island of the best rank that have ever endeavoured to outvie one the other, as well in housekeeping as in housewifery, and above all in making a figure in this little world. One of these ladies bought her a charming manto and petticoat of bragade silk; the richest that ever came to this Island. This she appeared at a ball in, where the other lady was, with such a porte and air that increased envy in the other lady. The emulator went all over the Town and to every shop to furnish herself with as good a silk, but the country could not afford such another or come anything near it, but this lady learning where the other lady bought her silk, went there where there was a remnant left of some yards, which she bought with the same trimming that the other lady had, and with this she privately made a petticoat for her negro woman that waited on her, and contrived an entertainment for the other lady to appear at in all her glory, where she likewise came, waited upon by her negro woman with this petticoat on, which when the other lady saw she fell into a fit, went home and unrobed herself, and has appeared in Norwich stuffs ever since.

[4] The usual word at this time for dolls. See Nos. 478 and 500 (vol. iv), and *Tatler* 95.
[5] On 'visiting days' see No. 24.

each other, and every Excellence in their Speech and Behaviour was looked upon as an Act of Emulation to surpass the other. These Beginnings of Disinclination soon improved into a Formality of Behaviour, a general Coldness, and by natural Steps into an irreconcileable Hatred.

These two Rivals for the Reputation of Beauty, were in their Stature, Countenance and Mien so very much alike, that if you were speaking of them in their Absence, the Words in which you described the one must give you an Idea of the other. They were hardly distinguishable, you would think, when they were apart, tho' extremely different when together. What made their Enmity the more entertaining to all the rest of their Sex was, that in Detraction from each other neither could fall upon Terms which did not hit her self as much as her Adversary. Their Nights grew restless with Meditation of new Dresses to outvie each other, and inventing new Devices to recall Admirers, who observed the Charms of the one rather than those of the other on the last Meeting. Their Colours failed at each others Appearance, flushed with Pleasure at the Report of a Disadvantage, and their Countenances withered upon Instances of Applause. The Decencies to which Women are obliged, made these Virgins stifle their Resentment so far as not to break into open Violences, while they equally suffered the Torments of a regulated Anger. Their Mothers, as it is usual, engaged in the Quarrel, and supported the several Pretensions of the Daughters with all that ill-chosen Sort of Expence which is common with People of plentiful Fortunes and mean Taste. The Girls preceded their Parents like Queens of *May*, in all the gaudy Colours imaginable, on every *Sunday* to Church, and were exposed to the Examination of the Audience for Superiority of Beauty.

During this constant Struggle it happened, that *Phillis* one Day at publick Prayers smote the Heart of a gay *West-Indian*, who appeared in all the Colours which can affect an Eye that could not distinguish between being fine and tawdry. This *American* in a Summer-Island Suit was too shining and too gay to be resisted by *Phillis*, and too intent upon her Charms to be diverted by any of the laboured Attractions of *Brunetta*. Soon after, *Brunetta* had the Mortification to see her Rival disposed of in a wealthy Marriage, while she was only addressed to in a Manner that shewed she was the Admiration of all Men but the Choice of none. *Phillis* was carried to the Habitation of her Spouse in *Barbadoes*; *Brunetta* had the ill Nature to enquire for her by every Opportunity, and had the Misfortune to hear of her being attended by numerous Slaves, fanned into Slumbers by successive Hands of them, and carried from Place to Place in all the Pomp of barbarous Magnificence. *Brunetta* could not endure these repeated Advices, but employed all her Arts and Charms in laying Baits for any of Condition of the same Island, out of a mere Ambition to confront her once more before she died. She at last succeeded in her Design, and was taken to Wife by a Gentleman whose Estate was contiguous to that of her Enemy's Husband. It would be endless to enumerate the many Occasions on which these irreconcileable Beauties laboured to excell each other; but in Process of Time it happened, that a Ship put into the Island consigned to a Friend of *Phillis*, who had Directions to give her the Refusal of all Goods for Apparel before *Brunetta* could be alarmed of their Arrival. He did so, and *Phillis* was dressed in few Days in a Brocade more gorgeous and costly than had ever before appeared in that Latitude. *Brunetta* languished at the Sight, and could by no Means come up to the Bravery of her Antagonist. She communicated her Anguish of Mind to a faithful Friend, who by an Interest in the Wife of *Phillis*'s Merchant, procured a Remnant of the same Silk for *Brunetta*. *Phillis* took Pains to appear in all publick Places where she was sure to meet *Brunetta*; *Brunetta* was now prepared for the Insult, and came to a publick Ball in a plain black Silk Mantua,[1] attended by a beautiful Negro Girl in a Petticoat of the same Brocade with which *Phillis* was attired. This drew the Attention of the whole Company, upon which the unhappy *Phillis* swooned away, and was immediately conveyed to her House. As soon as she came to her self she fled from her Husband's House, went on board a Ship in the Road, and is now landed in inconsolable Despair at *Plymouth*.

POSTSCRIPT.

After the above melancholy Narration, it may perhaps be a Relief to the Reader to peruse the following Expostulation.

To Mr. SPECTATOR.

The just Remonstrance of affronted That.

'THO' I deny not the Petition of Mr. *Who* and *Which*,[2] yet You should not suffer them to be rude and to call honest People

---

[1] A loose upper garment for women (a corruption of *manteau*). Fine mantua silks are frequently advertised.   [2] No. 78.

Names: For that bears very hard on some of those Rules of Decency, which You are justly famous for establishing. They may find Fault, and correct Speeches in the Senate and at the Bar: But let them try to get *themselves* so *often* and with so much *Eloquence* repeated in a Sentence, as a great Orator doth frequently introduce me.

'My Lords! (says he) with humble Submission, *That* that I say is this: that, *That* that, that Gentleman has advanced, is not *That*, that he should have proved to your Lordships. Let those two questionary Petitioners try to do thus with their *Who's* and their *Whiches*.

'What great Advantage was I of to Mr. *Dryden* in his *Indian Emperour*,[1]

You force me still to answer You in *That*.

to furnish out a Rhime to *Morat*? And what a poor Figure would Mr. *Bayes* have made without his *Egad and all That*?[2] How can a judicious Man distinguish one thing from another, without saying *This here*, or, *That there*? And how can a sober Man, without using the *Expletives* of Oaths (in which indeed the Rakes and Bullies have a great Advantage over others) make a Discourse of any tolerable Length, without *That is*; and if he be a very grave Man indeed, without *That is to say*? And how instructive as well as entertaining are those usual Expressions in the Mouths of great Men, *Such things as That*, and *The like of That*.

'I am not against reforming the Corruptions of Speech You mention, and own there are proper Seasons for the Introduction of other Words besides *That*; but I scorn as much to supply the Place of a *Who* or a *Which* at every Turn, as they are *unequal* always to fill mine: And I expect good Language and civil Treatment, and hope to receive it for the future: *That*, that I shall only add is, that I am,

Yours

THAT.'

R[3]

---

[1] The reference is not to this play but to Dryden's *Aureng-Zebe* (IV. i. 434–6):

Morat, Morat, Morat! You love the name
So well, your ev'ry question ends in that;
You force me still to answer you—Morat!

[2] These favourite expressions of Dryden are ridiculed in the Duke of Buckingham's *Rehearsal* and in *The Hind and the Panther Transvers'd* by Prior and Charles Montagu.
[3] Among the *Original Letters* of Lillie are 'The humble petition of Quod, anglice That' (i. 308–11) and a letter signed WHAT (i. 311–13) apropos of the petition in No. 78 and the remonstrance in No. 80.

No. 81
[ADDISON]

Saturday, June 2, 1711[1]

> *Qualis ubi audito venantum murmure Tigris*
> *Horruit in maculas . . .*
>
> Statius.

ABOUT the middle of last Winter I went to see an *Opera* at the Theatre in the *Hay-Market*, where I could not but take notice of two Parties of very Fine Women, that had placed themselves in the opposite Side-Boxes,[2] and seemed drawn up in a kind of Battel Array one against another. After a short Survey of them, I found they were *Patched* differently; the[a] Faces, on one Hand, being Spotted on the Right Side of the Forehead, and those[b] upon the other on the Left. I quickly perceived that they cast Hostile Glances upon one another; and that their Patches were placed in those different Situations, as Party Signals[3] to distinguish Friends from

---

[a] the] their *Fol.*   [b] those] that *Fol.*

[1] *Motto.* Statius, *Thebaid*, 2. 128–9:

> As when the tigress hears the hunters' din,
> Dark angry spots distain her glossy skin.

[2] In general at this time the custom seems to have been for the men to occupy the side-boxes and the women the front or middle-boxes. In No. 88 'lovers and men of intrigue' are in the side-boxes, and in No. 311 'Suffenus has taken his Stand in a Side-Box'. In Vanbrugh's *Aesop*, part ii (1702), Aesop questions a Beau: Where do you live? He replies, 'In the Side-Box.' 'What do you do there?' 'I Ogle the Ladies' (p. 62). See also Steele's *Theatre* no. 3 (5 Jan. 1720), *Guardian* 67, and *The Rape of the Lock*, v. 14–17. In Shadwell's *Bury Fair* (III. i) there is a conversation between Gertrude and Wildish, in which the latter promises to 'stare, and goggle at you, and never have my Eyes off you, while I Side-box you in the Play-house'. John Macky's *Journey through England* (1714) describes the seating thus:

> The Theatres here differ from those abroad; in that those at *Venice*, *Paris*, *Brussels*, *Genoa*, and other Parts, you know, are composed of Rows of small Shut-Boxes, three or four Stories in a Semi-Circle, with a *Parterre* below; whereas here the *Parterre* (commonly call'd the *Pit*) contains the Gentlemen on Benches; and on the first Row of Boxes sit all the Ladies of Quality; in the second, the Citizens Wives and Daughters; and in the third, the common People and Footmen; so that between the Acts you are as much diverted by viewing the Beauties of the Audience, as while they act with the Subject of the Play; and the whole is illuminated to the greatest Advantage (2nd ed., 1722, pp. 170–1).

[3] The setting of patches and the selection of fans and snuff-boxes to indicate party principles are satirized in the *Freeholder* (especially Nos. 15 and 38). In *Examiner* 31 (8 Mar. 1711) Swift had taken the same position:

> As the Zealots among the *Jews* bound the Law about their Foreheads and Wrists, and Hems of their Garments; so the Women among us have got the distinguishing Marks of Party in their Muffs, their Fans, and their Furbelows. The *Whig* Ladies put on their Patches in a different Manner from the *Tories*. They have made *Schisms* in the *Play-House*, and each have their particular Sides at the *Opera* . . . (*Prose Works*, ed. H. Davis, iii. 102).

Foes. In the Middle-Boxes, between these two opposite Bodies, were several Ladies who Patched indifferently on both sides of their Faces, and seemed to sit there with no other Intention but to see the *Opera*. Upon Enquiry I found that the Body of *Amazons* on my Right Hand were Whigs, and those on my Left, Tories; and that those who had placed themselves in the Middle-Boxes were a Neutral Party, whose Faces had not yet declared themselves. These last however, as I afterwards found, diminished daily, and took their Party with one Side or the other, insomuch that I observed in several of them, the Patches which were before dispersed equally, are now all gone over to the Whig or Tory Side of the Face. The Censorious say, That the Men whose Hearts are aimed at are very often the Occasions that one part of the Face is thus Dishonoured, and lyes under a kind of Disgrace, while the other is so much Set off and Adorned by the Owner; and that the Patches turn to the Right or to the Left, according to the Principles of the Man who is most in Favour. But whatever may be the Motives of a few Fantastical Coquets, who do not Patch for the Publick Good, so much as for their own Private Advantage, it is certain that there are several Women of Honour who Patch out of Principle, and with an Eye to the Interest of their Country. Nay, I am informed, that some of them adhere so stedfastly to their Party, and are so far from Sacrificing their Zeal for the Publick to their Passion for any particular Person, that in a late Draught of Marriage Articles a Lady has stipulated with her Husband, That, whatever his Opinions are, she shall be at Liberty to Patch on which side she pleases.

I must here take notice, that *Rosalinda*, a Famous Whig Partizan, has most unfortunately a very beautiful Mole on the Tory part of her Forehead, which, being very conspicuous, has occasioned many Mistakes, and given an Handle to her Enemies to misrepresent her Face, as though it had Revolted from the Whig Interest. But whatever this natural Patch may seem to intimate, it is well known that her Notions of Government are still the same. This unlucky Mole however has mis-led several Coxcombs, and, like the hanging out of false Colours, made some of them Converse with *Rosalinda* in what they thought the Spirit of her Party, when on a sudden she has given them an unexpected Fire, that has sunk them all at once. If *Rosalinda* is unfortunate in her Mole, *Nigranilla* is as unhappy in a Pimple which forces her, against her Inclinations, to Patch on the Whig side.

I am told that many Virtuous Matrons, who formerly have been

taught to believe that this Artificial Spotting of the Face was unlawful, are now reconciled by a Zeal for their Cause, to what they
could not be prompted by a Concern for their Beauty. This way of
declaring War upon one another, puts me in mind of what is reported
of the Tigress, that several Spots rise in her Skin when she is angry;
or as Mr. *Cowley*[1] has imitated the Verses that stand as the Motto
of this Paper,

> —*She Swells with angry Pride,*
> *And calls forth all her Spots on every side.*

When I was in the Theatre the time above-mentioned, I had the
Curiosity to count the Patches on both Sides, and found the Tory
Patches to be about twenty Stronger than the Whig; but to make
amends for this small Inequality, I the next Morning found the
whole Puppet-show filled with Faces spotted after the Whiggish
manner. Whether or no the Ladies had retreated hither in order to
rally their Forces I cannot tell, but the next Night they came in so
great a Body to the Opera, that they out-numbered the Enemy.

This Account of Party-Patches will, I am afraid, appear improbable
to those who live at a distance from the fashionable World, but as it
is a Distinction of a very singular Nature, and what perhaps may
never meet with a Parallel, I think I should not have discharged the
Office of a faithful Spectator had I not recorded it.

I have, in former Papers,[2] endeavoured to expose this Party Rage
in Women, as it only serves to aggravate the Hatreds and Animosities that reign among Men, and in a great measure deprive the Fair
Sex of those peculiar Charms with which Nature has endowed them.

When the *Romans* and *Sabines*[3] were at War, and just upon the
point of giving Battel, the Women, who were allied to both of them,
interposed with so many Tears and Intreaties that they prevented
the mutual Slaughter which threatned both Parties, and united
them together in a firm and lasting Peace.

I would recommend this noble Example to our *British* Ladies,
at a time when their Country is torn with so many unnatural
Divisions, that if they continue, it will be a Misfortune to be born
in it. The *Greeks*[4] thought it so improper for Women to interest
themselves in Competitions and Contentions, that for this Reason,

---

[1] *Davideis*, iii. 403–4 (the male Scythian tiger).
[2] No. 57.
[3] Livy, *History of Rome*, 1. 13.
[4] Bayle, art. Berenice, Remark B.

among others, they forbad them, under Pain of Death, to be present at the *Olympick* Games, notwithstanding these were the Publick Diversions of all *Greece*.

As our *English* Women excell those of all Nations in Beauty, they should endeavour to outshine them in all other Accomplishments proper[a] to the Sex, and to distinguish themselves as tender Mothers and faithful Wives, rather than as furious Partizans. Female Virtues are of a Domestick turn. The Family is the proper Province for Private Women to Shine in. If they must be showing their Zeal for the Publick, let it not be against those who are perhaps of the same Family, or at least of the same Religion or Nation, but against those who are the open, professed, undoubted Enemies of their Faith, Liberty, and Country. When the *Romans* were pressed with a Foreign Enemy, the Ladies voluntarily contributed all their Rings and Jewels to assist the Government under a publick Exigence, which appeared so laudable an Action in the Eyes of their Country-men, that from thenceforth it was permitted by a Law to pronounce publick Orations at the Funeral of a Woman in Praise of the deceased Person, which till that time was peculiar to Men.[1] Would our *English* Ladies instead of sticking on a Patch against those of their own Country, show themselves so truly Publick-spirited as to Sacrifice every one her Necklace against the Common Enemy, what Decrees ought not to be made in favour of them?

Since I am recollecting upon this Subject such Passages as occur to my Memory out of ancient Authors, I cannot omit a Sentence in the Celebrated Funeral Oration of *Pericles*,[2] which he made in Honour of those brave *Athenians*, that were Slain in a Fight with the *Lacedemonians*. After having addressed himself to the several Ranks and Orders of his Countrymen, and shewn them how they should behave themselves in the Publick Cause, he turns to the Female part of his Audience; 'And as for you (says he) I shall advise you in very few Words; Aspire only to those Virtues that are peculiar to your Sex; follow your natural Modesty, and think it your greatest Commendation not to be talked of one way or other.'   C

---

[a] Accomplishments proper] Accomplishments that are proper *Fol.*

---

[1] Bayle, art. Camillus, Remark C.
[2] Thucydides, *History of the Peloponnesian War*, 2. 45.

No. 82

[STEELE]

Monday, June 4, 1711[1]

. . . Caput domina venale sub hasta.

Juv.

PASSING under *Ludgate*[2] the other Day I heard a Voice bawling
for Charity, which I thought I had somewhere heard before.
Coming near to the Grate the Prisoner called me by my Name, and
desired I would throw something into the Box: I was out of Countenance for him, and did as he bid me, by putting in half a Crown.
I went away reflecting upon the strange Constitution of some Men,
and how meanly they behave themselves in all Sorts of Conditions.
The Person who begged of me is now, as I take it, Fifty: I was well
acquainted with him till about the Age of Twenty five; at which
Time a good Estate fell to him, by the Death of a Relation. Upon
coming to this unexpected good Fortune, he ran into all the
Extravagancies imaginable; was frequently in drunken Disputes,
broke Drawers Heads, talked and swore loud; was unmannerly to
those above him, and insolent to those below him. I could not but
remark that it was the same Baseness of Spirit which worked in his
Behaviour in both Fortunes: The same little Mind was insolent in
Riches, and shameless in Poverty. This Accident made me muse
upon the Circumstance of being in Debt[3] in general, and solve in
my Mind what Tempers were most apt to fall into this Errour of
Life, as well as the Misfortune it must needs be to languish under
such Pressures. As for my self, my natural Aversion to that Sort of
Conversation which makes a Figure with the Generality of Man-

---

[1] *Motto.* Juvenal, *Satires,* 3. 33: Or put up slaves for sale under the authority of the
spear.

[2] Ludgate Prison, 'purely for Insolvent Citizens of *London,* Beneficed Clergy and
Attorneys at Law' (Hatton, p. 756), at the east of Ludgate Hill and opening into
Ludgate Street. In Ward's *London Spy,* part v, it is described as 'so Plentifully supply'd
with Provisions by the Gifts of Good People, and other certain Allowances, that many
live better in it, than ever they did out on't, and are so fallen in Love with their
Confinement, that they would not change it for *Liberty*' (p. 112).

[3] Arresting under pretence of debt, writes Macky (*Journey through England,* 1714),
is nowhere practised with such rigour as in England.

You know, that abroad, if you have a pretence upon any Gentleman, you sue
him before a Judge; who either, through the Justice of your Demand, or his not
appearing, gives you a power of his Person: But here you may Arrest a Man for
any Sum you please, without having any Thing to show for it; and if the poor
unfortunate Man cannot give Bail (which a Stranger is not to be supposed very
capable of) he must go to Prison, the only Place of Cruelty and Barbarity in *England,*
and more Brutal than any of their Kind abroad (2nd ed., 1722, pp. 318–19).

kind, exempts me from any Temptations to Expence; and all my
Business lies within a very narrow Compass, which is, only to give
an honest Man who takes care of my Estate proper Vouchers for his
quarterly Payments[a] to me, and observe what Linnen my Laundress
brings and takes away with her once a Week: My Steward brings
his Receipt ready for my signing, and I have a pretty Implement
with the respective Names of Shirts, Cravats, Handkerchiefs and
Stockings, with proper Numbers to know how to reckon with my
Laundress. This being almost all the Business I have in the World
for the Care of my own Affairs, I am at full Leisure to observe upon
what others do, with Relation to their Equipage and Oeconomy.

When I walk the Street, and observe the Hurry about me in this
Town,

> *Where with like Haste, tho' different Ways, they run,*
> *Some to undo, and some to be undone.*[1]

I say, when I behold this vast Variety of Persons and Humours, with
the Pains they both take for the Accomplishment of the Ends mentioned in the above Verses of *Denham*, I cannot much wonder at the
Endeavour after Gain; but am extremely astonished that Men can
be so insensible of the Danger of running into Debt. One would
think it impossible a Man who is given to contract Debts should
know, that his Creditor has from that Moment in which he trans-
gresses Payment, so much as that Demand comes to in his Debtor's
Honour, Liberty and Fortune. One would think he[b] did not know
that his Creditor can say the worst thing imaginable of him, to wit,
That he is unjust, without Defamation, and can sieze his Person without being guilty of an Assault. Yet such is the loose and abandoned
Turn of some Mens Minds, that they can live under these constant
Apprehensions, and still go on to encrease the Cause of them. Can
there be a more low and servile Condition, than to be ashamed, or
afraid, to see any one Man breathing? yet he that is much in debt,
is in that Condition with relation to twenty different People. There
are indeed Circumstances wherein Men of honest Natures may
become liable to Debts, by some unadvised Behaviour in any great
Point of their Life, or mortgaging a Man's Honesty as a Security
for that of another, and the like; but these Instances are so particular

---

a Payments] Payment *Fol.*   b think he] think that he *Fol.*

---

[1] Denham, 'Cooper's Hill', 31–32 ('though several ways').

and circumstantiated, that they cannot come within general Considerations: For one such Case as one of these, there are ten, where a Man, to keep up a Farce of Retinue and Grandeur within his own House, shall shrink at the Expectation of surly Demands at his Doors. The Debtor is the Creditor's Criminal, and all the Officers of Power and State whom we behold make so great a Figure, are no other than so many Persons in Authority to make good his Charge against him. Humane Society depends upon his having the Vengeance Law allots him; and the Debtor owes his Liberty to his Neighbour, as much as the Murderer does his Life to his Prince.

Our Gentry are, generally speaking, in debt; and many Families have put it into a kind of Method of being so from Generation to Generation. The Father mortgages when his Son is very young, and the Boy is to marry assoon as he is at Age, to redeem it, and find Portions for his Sisters. This, forsooth, is no great Inconvenience to him, for he may wench, keep a publick Table, or feed Dogs like a worthy *English* Gentleman, till he has outrun half his Estate, and leave the same Incumbrance upon his First-born, and so on, till one Man of more Vigour than ordinary goes quite thorough the Estate, or some Man of Sense comes into it, and scorns to have an Estate in Partnership, that is to say, liable to the Demand or Insult of any Man living. There is my Friend Sir ANDREW, tho' for many Years a great and general Trader, was never the Defendant in a Law Suit, in all the Perplexity of Business, and the Iniquity of Mankind at present: No one had any Colour for the least Complaint against his Dealings with him. This is certainly as uncommon, and in its Proportion as laudable in a Citizen, as it is in a General never to have suffered a Disadvantage in Fight. How different from this Gentleman is *Jack Truepenny*,[1] who has been an old Acquaintance of Sir ANDREW and my self from Boys, but could never learn our Caution. *Jack* has a whorish unresisting good Nature, which makes him incapable of having a Property in any thing. His Fortune, his Reputation, his Time, and his Capacity, are at any Man's Service that comes first. When he was at School he was whipp'd thrice a Week for Faults he took upon him to excuse others; since he came into the Business of the World, he has been arrested twice or thrice a Year for Debts he had nothing to do with but as Surety for others; and I remember when a Friend of his had suffered in the Vice of the

---

[1] In this character 'Steele, to some extent, intended to describe himself, if we may believe a note in the early editions, ascribed to Dr. John Hoadly . . .' (Dobson).

Town, all the Physick his Friend took was conveyed to him by *Jack*, and inscribed, 'A Bolus or an Electuary for Mr. *Truepenny.*' *Jack* had a good Estate left him, which came to nothing; because he believed all who pretended to Demands upon it. This Easiness and Credulity destroy all the other Merit he has; and he has all his Life been a Sacrifice to others, without ever receiving Thanks or doing one good Action.

I will end this Discourse with a Speech which I heard *Jack* make to one of his Creditors (of whom he deserved gentler Usage) after lying a whole Night in Custody at his Suit.

SIR,

'YOUR Ingratitude for the many Kindnesses I have done you, shall not make me unthankful for the Good you have done me, in letting me see there is such a Man as you in the World. I am obliged to you for the Diffidence I shall have all the rest of my Life: *I shall hereafter trust no Man so far as to be in his Debt.*'   R

No. 83   *Tuesday, June 5, 1711*[1]

[ADDISON]

. . . *Animum* picturâ *pascit* inani.
                                                          Vir.

WHEN the Weather hinders me from taking my Diversions without Doors, I frequently make a little Party with two or three select Friends, to visit any thing curious that may be seen under Covert: My Principal Entertainments of this Nature are Pictures, insomuch that when I have found the Weather set in to be very bad, I have taken a whole Day's Journey to see a Gallery that is furnished by the Hands of Great Masters. By this means, when the Heavens are filled with Clouds, when the Earth swims in Rain, and all Nature wears a lowring Countenance, I withdraw my self from these uncomfortable Scenes into the Visionary Worlds of Art, where I meet with shining Landskips, gilded Triumphs, beautiful Faces, and all those other Objects that fill the Mind with gay *Ideas*, and disperse that Gloominess which is apt to hang upon it in those dark disconsolate Seasons.

[1] *Motto.* Virgil, *Aeneid*, I. 464:
    And with an empty Picture fed his Mind. DRYDEN.

I was some Weeks ago in a Course of these Diversions, which had taken such an entire Possession of my Imagination, that they formed in it a short Morning's Dream, which I shall communicate to my Reader, rather as the first Sketch and Outlines of a Vision, than as a finished Piece.

I dreamt that I was admitted into a long spacious Gallery, which had one side covered with Pieces of all the Famous Painters who are now living, and the other with the Works of the greatest Masters that are dead.

On the side of the *Living* I saw several Persons busy in Drawing, Colouring, and Designing. On the side of the *Dead* Painters, I could not discover more than one Person at Work, who was exceeding slow in his Motions, and wonderfully nice in his Touches.

I was resolved to examine the several Artists that stood before me, and accordingly applied my self to the side of the *Living*: The first I[a] observed at Work in this Part of the Gallery was VANITY, with his Hair tied behind him in a Ribbon, and dressed like a *French-man*. All the Faces he drew were very remarkable for their Smiles, and a certain smirking Air which he bestowed indifferently on every Age and Degree of either Sex. The *Toujours Gai* appeared even in his Judges, Bishops and Privy-Counsellors: in a word, all his Men were *Petits Maitres*,[1] and all his Women *Coquets*. The Drapery of his Figures was extreamly well suited to his Faces, and was made up of all the glaring Colours that could be mixt together; every part of the Dress was in a Flutter, and endeavoured to distinguish it self above the rest.

On the Left-hand of VANITY stood a laborious Workman, who I found was his humble Admirer, and copied after him. He was dressed like a *German*, and had a very hard Name, that sounded something like STUPIDITY.

The third Artist that I looked over was FANTASQUE, dressed like a *Venetian* Scaramouch:[2] He had an excellent Hand at a *Chimera*, and dealt very much in Distortions and Grimaces: He would sometimes affright himself with the Phantoms that flowed from his Pencil. In short, the most Elaborate of his Pieces was at best but a terrifying Dream; and one could say nothing more of his finest Figures, than that they were agreeable Monsters.

[a] first I] first that I *Fol.*

[1] The earliest quotation of this word in *OED*.
[2] See No. 37.

The fourth Person I examined was very remarkable for his hasty Hand, which left his Pictures so unfinished, that the Beauty in the Picture (which was designed to continue as a Monument of it to Posterity) faded sooner than in the Person after whom it was drawn: He made so much haste to dispatch his Business, that he neither gave himself time to clean his Pencils, nor^a mix his Colours. The Name of this expeditious Workman was AVARICE.

Not far from this Artist I saw another of a quite different Nature, who was dressed in the Habit of a *Dutch* Man, and known by the Name of INDUSTRY. His Figures were wonderfully laboured; if he drew the Portraiture of a Man, he did not omit a single Hair in his Face; if the Figure of a Ship, there was not a Rope among the Tackle that escaped him. He had likewise hung a great part of the Wall with Night-Pieces, that seemed to shew themselves by the Candles which were lighted up in several Parts of them, and were so inflamed by the Sun-shine which accidentally fell upon them, that at first sight I could scarce forbear crying out *Fire*.

The Five foregoing Artists were the most considerable on this side the Gallery; there were indeed several others whom I had not time to look into. One of them however I could not forbear observing, who^b was very busie in re-touching the finest Pieces, though he produced no Originals of his own. His Pencil aggravated every Feature that was before over-charged, loaded every Defect, and poisoned every Colour it touched. Though this Workman did so much Mischief on^c the side of the Living, he never turned his Eye towards that of the Dead: His Name was ENVY.

Having taken a cursory View of one side of the Gallery, I turned my self to that which was filled by the Works of those great Masters that were dead, when immediately I fancied my self standing before a Multitude of Spectators, and Thousands of Eyes looking upon me at once. For all before me appeared so like Men and Women, that I almost forgot they were Pictures. *Raphael's* Figures[1] stood in one Row; *Titian's*[2] in another; *Guido Rheni's*[3] in a third. One part of the

---

^a nor] or *Fol.*   ^b observing, who] observing that *Fol.*   ^c on] in *Fol.*

---

[1] The cartoons of Raphael at Hampton Court are discussed in Nos. 226 and 244 (vol. ii).
[2] Titian's 'inimitable Sun-shine' is referred to in No. 292 (vol. iii).
[3] i.e. Guido Reni (1575–1642), the Italian painter.

Wall was peopled by *Hanibal Carrache*,[1] another by *Correggio*,[2] and another by *Rubens*.[3] To be short, there was not a[a] great Master among the Dead who had not contributed to the Embellishment of this side of the Gallery. The Persons that owed their Being to these several Masters appeared all of them to be real and alive, and differed among one another only in the variety of their Shapes, Complexions and Cloaths, so that they looked like different Nations of the same Species.

Observing an old Man[4] (who was the same Person I before mentioned, as the only Artist that was at Work on this side of the Gallery) creeping up and down from one Picture to another, and re-touching all the fine Pieces that stood before me, I could not but be very attentive to all his Motions. I found his Pencil was so very light that it worked imperceptibly, and, after a thousand Touches, scarce produced any visible effect in the Picture on which he was employ'd. However, as he busied himself incessantly, and repeated Touch after Touch without rest or intermission, he wore off insensibly every little disagreeable Gloss that hung upon a Figure. He also added such a beautiful Brown to the Shades, and Mellowness to the Colours, that he made every Picture appear more perfect than when it came fresh from the[b] Master's Pencil. I could not forbear looking upon the Face of this ancient Workman, and immediately by the long Lock of Hair upon his Forehead discovered him to be TIME.

Whether it were[c] because the Thread of my Dream was at an end, I cannot tell; but upon my taking a Survey of this Imaginary old Man, my Sleep left me. C

---

[a] a] one *Fol.*   [b] the] its *Fol.*   [c] were] was *Fol.*

---

[1] i.e. Annibale Carracci (1560-1609), one of three Italian painters of this name, best known for his frescoes in the Palazzo Farnese in Rome. See R. Wittkower, *The Drawings of the Carracci in the Collection of Her Majesty the Queen at Windsor Castle* (Phaidon Press, 1952).
[2] Antonio Allegri (1494-1534), known as Correggio from his birthplace. In the *Parallel of Poetry and Painting* (1695) Dryden names Titian and Correggio as the most famous for colouring among modern painters (*Essays*, ed. Ker, ii. 148).
[3] Peter Paul Rubens (1577-1640), the Flemish painter.
[4] Hogarth has satirized this image in his 'Time smoking a Picture' (1761) (Nichols). In *The Analysis of Beauty* Hogarth has a long footnote to chap. xiv, 'Of Colouring', attacking the popular notion that 'time is a great improver of good pictures'. In spite of 'Mr. Addison's beautiful description of time at work in the gallery of pictures' and Dryden's lines to Kneller, it is, he says, nevertheless an error (*Analysis of Beauty*, ed. Joseph Burke, Oxford, 1955, pp. 130-2).

> . . . *Quis talia fando*
> *Myrmidonum Dolopumve aut duri miles Ulyssei*
> *Temperet a Lachrymis.*
>
> Virg.

LOOKING over the old Manuscript wherein the private Actions of *Pharamond*[2] are set down by way of Table-book, I found many things which gave me great Delight; and as humane Life turns upon the same Principles and Passions in all Ages, I thought it very proper[a] to take Minutes of what passed in that Age for the Instruction of this. The Antiquary who lent me these Papers gave me a Character of *Eucrate*, the Favourite of *Pharamond*, extracted from an Author who lived in that Court. The Account he gives both of the Prince and this his faithful Friend will not be improper to insert here, because I may have Occasion to mention many of their Conversations, into which these Memorials of them may give Light.

'*Pharamond*, when he had a Mind to retire for an Hour or two from the Hurry of Business and Fatigue of Ceremony, made a Signal to *Eucrate* by putting his Hand to his Face, placing his Arm negligently on a Window, or some such Action as appeared indifferent to all the rest of the Company. Upon such Notice, unobserved by others, (for their entire Intimacy was always a Secret) *Eucrate* repaired to his own Apartment to receive the King. There was a secret Access to this Part of the Court, at which *Eucrate* used to admit many whose mean Appearance in the Eyes of the ordinary Waiters[3] and Door-keepers made them be repulsed from other Parts of the Palace. Such as these were let in here by order of *Eucrate*, and had Audiences of *Pharamond*. This Entrance *Pharamond* called the Gate of the Unhappy, and the Tears of the Afflicted who came before him he would say were Bribes received by *Eucrate*; for *Eucrate* had the most compassionate Spirit of all Men living, except his generous Master, who

---

[a] proper] instructive *Fol.*

---

[1] *Motto.* Virgil, *Aeneid*, 2. 6–8:
What Myrmidon or Dolopian, or soldier of stern Ulysses, could in telling such a tale refrain from tears?
[2] No. 76.
[3] Waiter, in the old meaning of 'a member of the retinue or household of a royal or noble personage'. The last quotation in *OED* in this sense is dated 1678–9.

was always kindled at the least Affliction which was communicated to him. In the Regard for the Miserable, *Eucrate* took particular Care that the common Forms of Distress, and the idle Pretenders to Sorrow about Courts, who wanted only Supplies to Luxury, should never obtain Favour by his Means; but the Distresses which arise from the many inexplicable Occurrences that happen among Men, the unaccountable Alienation of Parents from their Children, Cruelty of Husbands to Wives, Poverty occasioned from Shipwreck or Fire, the falling out of Friends, or such other terrible Disasters to which the Life of Man is exposed; In Cases of this Nature, *Eucrate* was the Patron; and enjoyed this Part of the royal Favour so much without being envied, that it was never enquired into by whose Means, what no one else cared for doing, was brought about.

'One Evening when *Pharamond* came into the Apartment of *Eucrate*, he found him extremely dejected; upon which he asked (with a Smile which was natural to him) "What, is there any one too miserable to be relieved by *Pharamond*, that *Eucrate* is melancholy? I fear there is, answered the Favourite; a Person without, of a good Air, well dressed, and tho' a Man in the Strength of his Life, seems to faint under some inconsolable Calamity: All his Features seem suffused with Agony of Mind; but I can observe in him, that it is more inclined to break away in Tears than Rage. I asked him what he would have; he said he would speak to *Pharamond*. I desired his Business; he could hardly say to me, *Eucrate*, carry me to the King, my Story is not to be told twice, I fear I shall not be able to speak it at all." *Pharamond* commanded *Eucrate* to let him enter; he did so, and the Gentleman approached the King with an Air which spoke him under the greatest concern in what manner to demean himself.[a] The King, who had a quick Discerning, relieved him from the Oppression he was under; and with the most beautiful Complacency said to him, "Sir, do not add to that Load of Sorrow I see in your Countenance, the Awe of my Presence: Think you are speaking to your Friend; if the Circumstances of your Distress will admit of it, you shall find me so." To whom the Stranger: "Oh excellent *Pharamond*, name not a Friend to the unfortunate *Spinamont*: I had one, but he is dead by my own Hand; but, oh *Pharamond*, tho' it was by the Hand of *Spinamont*, it was by the Guilt of *Pharamond*. I come not, oh excellent Prince, to implore your Pardon; I come to relate my Sorrow,

[a] which spoke . . . himself.] which spoke the utmost Sense of his Majesty without the Ability to express it. *Fol.*

a Sorrow too great for humane Life to support: From henceforth shall all Occurrences appear Dreams or short Intervals of Amusement, from this one Affliction which has siez'd my very Being. Pardon me, oh *Pharamond*, if my Griefs give[a] me Leave, that I lay before you, in the Anguish of a wounded Mind, that you, Good as you are, are guilty of the generous Blood spilt this Day by this unhappy Hand: Oh that it had perished before that Instant!" Here the Stranger paused, and recollecting his Mind after some little Meditation, he went on in a calmer Tone and Gesture as follows.

'"There is an Authority due to Distress; and as none of humane Race is above the Reach of Sorrow, none should be above the hearing the Voice of it: I am sure *Pharamond* is not. Know then, that I have this Morning unfortunately killed in a Duel the Man whom of all Men living I most loved. I command my self too much in your Royal Presence, to say *Pharamond* give me my Friend! *Pharamond* has taken him from me! I will not say, shall the merciful *Pharamond* destroy his own Subjects? Will the Father of his Country murder his People; but the merciful *Pharamond* does destroy his Subjects, the Father of his Country does murder his People. Fortune is so much the Pursuit of Mankind, that all Glory and Honour is in the Power of a Prince, because he has the Distribution of their Fortunes. It is therefore the Inadvertency, Negligence or Guilt of Princes, to let any thing grow into Custom which is against their Laws. A Court can make Fashion and Duty walk together; it can never, without the Guilt of a Court, happen, that it shall not be unfashionable to do what is unlawful. But alas! in the Dominions of *Pharamond*, by the Force of a Tyrant Custom, which is misnamed a Point of Honour, the Duellist[1] kills his Friend whom he loves; and the Judge con-

---

[a] give] will give *Fol.*

[1] In *Tatler* 25 Steele announced his intention of talking very freely 'on a Custom which all Men wish exploded, tho' no man has Courage enough to resist it', and he devoted several numbers in the summer of 1709 (Nos. 25, 26, 28, 29, 31, 38, and 39) to an examination of the false principle of honour and the effect of custom as seen in duelling, thus carrying on a campaign which he had initiated in his earlier writings. In the preface to the first collected edition of the *Tatler* Steele states that one of his consistent purposes in that journal was the extirpation of gamesters and duellists. For a number of contemporary references to duelling see Ashton, ii. 189–95. Spinamont's story almost certainly refers—as Nichols asserted—to the famous duel which took place about a month earlier (on 9 May) between Sir Cholmondeley Dering and Richard Thornhill. 'They fought at sword and pistol this morning in Tuttle-fields, their pistols so near, that the muzzles touched.' Thornhill discharged first, and Dering having received the shot, discharged his pistol as he was falling, so it went into the air' (Swift, *Journal to Stella*, 9 May 1711). See also Hearne, *Collections*, iii. 160, 163–4. On 20 May Hearne writes, 'Mr. Thornhill has been try'd for killing

demns the Duellist, while he approves his Behaviour. Shame is the greatest of all Evils; what avail Laws, when Death only attends the Breach of them, and Shame Obedience to them? As for me, oh *Pharamond*, were it possible to describe the nameless Kinds of Compunctions and Tendernesses I feel when I reflect upon the little Accidents in our former Familiarity, my Mind swells into Sorrow which cannot be resisted enough to be silent in the Presence of *Pharamond*." With that he fell into a Flood of Tears and wept aloud. "Why should not *Pharamond* hear the Anguish he only can relieve others from in Time to come? Let him hear from me, what they feel who have given Death by the false Mercy of his Administration, and form to himself the Vengeance called for by those who have perished by his Negligence." '

R

No. 85
[ADDISON]

Thursday, June 7, 1711[1]

Interdum speciosa locis, morataque rectè
Fabula nullius Veneris, sine pondere & Arte,
Valdiùs oblectat populum, meliusque moratur,
Quàm versus inopes rerum, nugæque canoræ.

Hor.

IT is the Custom of the *Mahometans*,[2] if they see any printed or written Paper upon the Ground, to take it up and lay it aside carefully, as not knowing but it may contain some Piece of their *Alcoran*. I must confess I have so much of the *Mussulman* in me, that

Sʳ Cholmley Deering, and 'twas brought in Chance-Medley. Upon this Accident the House of Commons have brought in a Bill to prevent Duelling and to make it Felony' (iii. 163). Three months later Thornhill was murdered by two men on Turnham-Green, who, as they stabbed him, bid him remember Sir Cholmley Dering (Swift, *Journal to Stella*, 21 Aug. 1711). *The Account at large of Mr. Thornhill's Tryal, indicted for the Murder of Sir Cholmley Deering, Bar.* (printed for E. Curll and R. Gosling, and sold by J. Morphew) is advertised as 'Just Publish'd' in No. 82.

¹ *Motto.* Horace, *Ars poetica*, 319–22:

Sometimes in rough and undigested Plays
We meet with such a lucky Character,
As being humor'd right and well persu'd,
Succeeds much better, than the shallow Verse,
And chiming Trifles, of more studious Pens. ROSCOMMON.

² The Turks 'are so careful in shewing their reverence to the Name of God, that if they find the least bit of Paper in the way, they take it up, and put it into some hole of a wall . . .' (Jean de Thévenot, *Travels into the Levant*, part i (1687), p. 43). Cf. also *Letters writ by a Turkish Spy*, vol. vi, book i, letter 7 (ed. 1702, vi. 25).

I cannot forbear looking into every Printed Paper which comes in my way, under whatsoever despicable Circumstances it may appear; for as no Mortal Author, in the ordinary Fate and Vicissitude of Things, knows to what use his Works may, some time or other, be applied, a Man may often[a] meet with very celebrated Names in a Paper of Tobacco. I have lighted my Pipe more than once with the Writings of a Prelate, and know a Friend of mine who, for these several Years, has converted the Essays of a Man of Quality into a kind of Fringe for his Candlesticks. I remember, in particular, after having read over a Poem of an Eminent Author on a Victory, I met with several Fragments of it upon the next Rejoycing-day, which had been employed in Squibs and Crackers, and by that means celebrated its Subject in a double Capacity. I once met with a Page of Mr. *Baxter*[1] under a *Christmas* Pye. Whether or no the Pastry-Cook had made use of it through Chance, or Waggery, for the defence of that Superstitious *Viande*, I know not; but, upon the Perusal of it, I conceived so good an Idea of the Author's Piety, that I bought the whole Book. I have often profited[b] by these accidental Readings, and have sometimes found very Curious Pieces that are either out of Print, or not to be met with in the Shops of our *London* Booksellers. For this Reason, when my Friends take a Survey of my Library, they are very much surprised to find,[c] upon the Shelf of Folio's, two long Band-boxes standing upright among my Books, till I let them see that they are both of them lined with deep Erudition and abstruse Literature. I might likewise mention a Paper Kite, from which I have received great Improvement; and a Hat-Case, which I would not exchange for all the Beavers in *Great Britain*. This my inquisitive Temper, or rather impertinent Humour of prying into all sorts of Writing, with my natural Aversion to Loquacity, give me a good deal of Employment when I enter any House in the Country; for I can't, for my Heart, leave a Room before I have thoroughly studied the Walls of it, and examined the several printed Papers[2] which are usually pasted upon them. The last Piece that

---

[a] often] oftentimes *Fol.*   [b] often profited] often very much profited *Fol.*
[c] find,] see, *Fol.*

[1] Richard Baxter (1615–91), the celebrated Puritan divine and controversialist (see Nos. 445 and 598 (vol. iv)).
[2] For the use of tapestry and wall-hangings see No. 142 (vol. ii). There is a reference to the use of printed papers on walls in Etherege's *Comical Revenge* (IV. iii): 'Thou shalt be witness . . . how many Bellmen I'le rob of their Verses, to furnish a little Appartment in the back side of my Lodging.'

I met with upon this Occasion, gave me a most exquisite Pleasure. My Reader will think I am not serious, when I acquaint him that the Piece I am going to speak of was the old Ballad of the *Two Children in the Wood*,[1] which is one of the Darling Songs of the Common People, and has been the Delight of most *Englishmen* in some Part of their Age.

This Song is a plain simple Copy of Nature, destitute of all the Helps and Ornaments of Art. The Tale of it is a pretty Tragical Story, and pleases[a] for no other Reason, but because it is a Copy of Nature. There is even a despicable Simplicity in the Verse; and yet, because the Sentiments appear genuine[b] and unaffected, they are able to move the Mind of the most polite Reader with inward Meltings of Humanity and Compassion. The Incidents grow out of the Subject, and are such as are the most proper to excite Pity.[c] For which Reason the whole Narration has something in it very moving; notwithstanding the Author of it (whoever he was) has delivered it in such an abject Phrase, and poorness of Expression, that the quoting any part of it would look like a Design of turning it into Ridicule. But though the Language is mean, the Thoughts, as I have before said, from one end to the other are natural;[d] and therefore cannot fail to please those who are not Judges of Language, or those who notwithstanding they are Judges of Language, have a true[e] and

---

^a and pleases] and therefore pleases *Fol.*　　^b appear genuine] are natural *Fol.*　　^c Subject, and . . . Pity.] Subject, and are such as *Virgil* himself would have touched upon, had the like Story been told by that Divine Poet. *Fol.*　　^d the Thoughts . . . natural;] the Thoughts from one end to the other are wonderfully natural, *Fol.*　　^e true] genuine *Fol.*

---

¹ Also known as *The Babes in the Wood*, this is one of the best-known broadside 'vulgar' ballads—those dealing not with a single situation but with a connected story of some length, often giving an account of a murder or some other sensational deed. It was registered in 1595 as 'The Norfolk Gentleman, his Will and Testament, and how he committed the keeping of his children to his own brother, who delte most wickedly with them and how God plagued him for it' (M. J. C. Hodgart, *The Ballads*, 1950, pp. 142–3). The chap-book story, dating from about 1700, with 'The Old Song upon the Same', is reprinted in John Ashton, *Chap-Books of the Eighteenth Century* (1882), pp. 369–75. In *A Collection of Old Ballads . . . with Introductions historical, critical, or humorous* (1723–5), probably by Ambrose Philips, 'The Children in the Wood: or, the *Norfolk* Gentleman's last Will and Testament. To the Tune of, *Rogero*, &c.', is printed in vol. i (3rd ed., 1727, pp. 221–6). It begins,

> Now ponder well you Parents dear,
> These Words which I shall write.

In the first edition of Percy's *Reliques* (1765) it appears at vol. i, pp. 170–7. The tune *Rogero* became, if possible, more popular because of its use by Gay for one of the most affecting songs in the first act of *The Beggar's Opera* (Air XII; Gay identifies it simply as *Now ponder well, ye parents dear*).

unprejudiced Taste of Nature. The Condition, Speech and Behaviour of the dying Parents, with the Age, Innocence and Distress of the Children, are set forth in such tender Circumstances, that it is impossible for a Reader of common Humanity[a] not to be affected with them. As for the Circumstance of the *Robin-red-breast*, it is indeed a little Poetical Ornament; and to shew the Genius of the Author[b] amidst all his Simplicity, it is just the same kind of Fiction which one of the greatest of the *Latin* Poets has made use of upon a Parallel Occasion; I mean that Passage in *Horace*, where he describes himself when he was a Child, fallen asleep in a Desart Wood, and covered with Leaves by the Turtles that took pity on him.

> *Me fabulosæ Vulture in Appulo,*
> *Altricis extra limen Apuliæ*
> *Ludo fatigatumque somno*
> *Fronde novâ puerum palumbes*
> *Texere . . .*[1]

I have heard that the late Lord DORSET,[2] who had the greatest Wit tempered with the greatest Candour,[c] and was one of the finest Criticks as well as the best Poets of his Age, had a numerous

---

[a] a Reader of common Humanity] a good-natured Reader *Fol.*   [b] to shew the Genius of the Author] to show what a Genius the Author was Master of *Fol.*
[c] Candour,] Humanity, *Fol.*

---

[1] Horace, *Odes*, 3. 4. 9–13.

> In lofty *Vultur*'s rising grounds
> Without my Nurse *Apulia*'s bounds
> When young, and tir'd with sport and play,
> And bound with pleasing sleep I lay,
> Doves cover'd me with myrtle boughs
> And with soft murmurs sweetned my repose. CREECH.

[2] Charles Sackville, sixth Earl of Dorset (1643–1706). Hearne wrote in his diary on 8 June, the day following the publication of this essay:

> The late Earl of Dorset had a very large Collection of Old Ballads, wch he us'd oftentimes to read, with very great Delight, much admiring the Simplicity and Nakedness of ye Style; & yet he was a Man of admirable Sense & Understanding. I heard the late Dean of X^t Church, Dr Aldrich say, the last time I was with him, that he would give a good Sum of Money for a Collection of such Ballads, whenever he could meet with one (*Collections*, ed. Doble, iii. 173).

Since this is probably based on Addison's essay it does not offer much confirmatory evidence, except that Hearne tends to take issue with the *Spectator* whenever possible. Mr. Brice Harris, in his *Charles Sackville, Sixth Earl of Dorset* (Univ. of Illinois Studies in Language and Literature, vol. xxvi, 1940, nos. 3–4), mentions Addison's statement and also Hearne's, and adds that 'nothing further is known' about 'this reputed collection' (pp. 31–32). The statement about Lord Dorset, as well as the one in the following sentence about Dryden and others, may well rest, as Addison says, on oral report.

Collection of old *English* Ballads, and took a particular Pleasure in the Reading of them. I can affirm the same of Mr. DRYDEN, and know several of the most refined Writers of our present Age, who are of the same Humour.

I might likewise refer my Reader to *Moliere*'s Thoughts[1] on this Subject, as he has expressed them in the Character of the *Misanthrope*; but those only who are endowed with a true Greatness of Soul and Genius, can divest themselves of the little Images of Ridicule, and admire Nature in her Simplicity and Nakedness. As for the little conceited Wits[2] of the Age, who can only show their Judgment by finding Fault, they cannot be supposed to admire these Productions which[a] have nothing to recommend them but the Beauties of Nature, when they do not know how to relish even those Compositions that, with all the Beauties of Nature, have also the additional Advantages of Art.   L

---

[a] Productions which] Productions, that *Fol.*

---

[1] In *Le Misanthrope* (I. ii) Alceste, after quoting an old song, declares its superiority to a new modish sonnet:

> La rime n'est pas riche, et le style en est vieux:
> Mais ne voyez-vous pas que cela vaut bien mieux
> Que ces colifichets dont le bon sens murmure,
> Et que la passion parle là toute pure? (401–4)

[2] As Gregory Smith suggests, Addison probably has in mind William Wagstaffe's *Comment upon the History of Tom Thumb*, a three-penny pamphlet issued in 1711 from the press of the Tory publisher John Morphew. After expressing surprise that in such a polite age as the present, 'some of the best things that are extant in our Language shou'd pass unobserv'd amidst a Croud of inferiour Productions', Wagstaffe notes the presence of 'an Enterprising Genius of late, that has thought fit to disclose the Beauties of some Pieces to the World, that might have been otherwise indiscernable, and believ'd to have been trifling and insipid, for no other Reason but their unpolish'd Homeliness of Dress'. To desert the classics for the ballads 'and other ingenious Composures' would make for a great improvement of wit in general and the art of poetry in particular:

> And certainly our Passions are describ'd in them so naturally, in such lively, tho' simple, Colours, that how far they may fall short of the Artfulness and Embellishments of the *Romans* in their Way of Writing, *yet cannot fail to please all such Readers as are not unqualify'd for the Entertainment by their Affectation or Ignorance* (p. 4).

Taking up the *History of Tom Thumb*, he finds that such incidents as the hero's falling into a pudding-bowl 'give an agreeable Delight and Surprise, *and are such as* Virgil *himself wou'd have touch'd upon, had the like Story been told by that Divine Poet*' (p. 5). After various quotations from the poem, with parallel lines from Virgil, and side-glances at Bentley (p. 14), he concludes (pp. 22–23):

> I know there are some People that cast an Odium on me, and others, for pointing out the Beauties of such Authors, as have, they say, been hitherto unknown . . . And however they may call me *second-sighted*, for discerning what they are Blind to, I must tell them this Poem has not been altogether so obscure, but that the most refin'd *Writers* of this Age have been delighted with the reading it. Mr. *Tho. D'Urfey*, I am told, is an Admirer, and Mr. *John Dunton* has been heard to say, more than once, he had rather be the Author of it than all his Works.

No. 86

No. 86   *Friday, June 8, 1711*[1]

[ADDISON]

Heu quam difficile est crimen non prodere vultu!
Ovid. *Met.*

THERE are several Arts which all Men are in some Measure
Masters of,[a] without having been at the Pains of learning them.
Every one that speaks or reasons is a Grammarian and a Logician,
though he may be wholly unacquainted with the Rules of Grammar
or Logick, as they are delivered in Books and Systems. In the same
Manner, every one is in some Degree a Master of that Art which is
generally distinguished by the Name of Physiognomy;[2] and naturally
forms to himself the Character or Fortune of a Stranger from the
Features and Lineaments of his Face. We are no sooner presented
to any one we[b] never saw before, but we are immediately struck
with the Idea of a proud, a reserved, an affable, or a good-natured
Man; and upon our first going into a Company of Strangers,[c] our
Benevolence or Aversion, Awe or Contempt, rises naturally towards[d] several particular Persons before we have heard them speak
a single Word, or so much as know who they are.

Every Passion gives a particular Cast to the Countenance, and is
apt to discover itself in some Feature or other. I have seen an Eye
curse for half an Hour together, and an Eye-brow call a Man
Scoundrel. Nothing is more common than for Lovers to complain,
resent, languish, despair and dye, in dumb Show. For my own Part,
I am so apt to frame a Notion of every Man's Humour or Circumstances by his Looks, that I have sometimes employed my self from
Charing-Cross to the *Royal-Exchange* in drawing the Characters of
those who have passed by me. When I see a Man with a sour

---

^a which all Men . . . Masters of,] which every Man is in some Measure Master of,
Fol.   ^b one we] one that we *Fol.*   ^c Strangers,] unknown Persons, *Fol.*
^d rises naturally towards] rises towards *Fol.*

---

¹ *Motto.* Ovid, *Metamorphoses*, 2. 447:
    How in the looks does conscious guilt appear. ADDISON.

² The sixteenth and seventeenth centuries had seen the publication of numerous
works on this supposed science, from the treatise attributed to Aristotle down to
John Evelyn's 'Digression concerning Physiognomy' printed in his *Numismatica*
(1697). The *Bibliotheca Britannica* of Watt lists over thirty such titles. Most of the
writers on the subject were interested in chiromancy, astrology, and fortune-telling
generally, but the interest evidenced in the subject in classical literature was sufficient
to attract a reader of Addison's tastes. The papers on the Ugly Club and the frequent
references to Mr. Spectator's 'short face' had earlier touched on the subject.

rivell'd[1] Face, I cannot forbear pittying his Wife; and when I meet with an open ingenuous Countenance, think on the Happiness of his Friends, his Family, and Relations.

I cannot recollect the Author of a famous Saying to a Stranger who[a] stood silent in his Company, *Speak that I may see thee:*[2] But with Submission, I think we may be better known by our Looks than by our Words; and that a Man's Speech is much more easily disguised than his Countenance. In this Case however, I think the Air of the whole Face is much more expressive than the Lines of it: The Truth of it is, the Air is generally nothing else but the inward Disposition of the Mind made visible.

Those who have established Physiognomy into an Art, and laid down Rules of judging Mens Tempers by their Faces, have regarded the Features much more than the Air. *Martial* has a pretty Epigram on this Subject.

> *Crine ruber, niger ore, brevis pede, lumine læsus,*
> *Rem magnam præstas, Zoile, si bonus es.*[3]

> *Thy Beard and Head are of a diff'rent Die;*
> *Short of one Foot, distorted in an Eye:*
> *With all these Tokens of a Knave compleat,*
> *Should'st thou be honest, thou'rt a dev'lish Cheat.*

I have seen a very ingenious Author[4] on this Subject, who[b] founds his Speculations on the Supposition, That as a Man hath in the Mould of his Face a remote Likeness to that of an Ox, a Sheep, a

---

^a who] that *Fol.*   ^b who] that *Fol.*

---

¹ i.e. wrinkled. Now *dial.* or *arch.* (*OED*).

² Attributed to Socrates by Apuleius (*Florida*, 2. 1).

³ Martial, *Epigrams*, 12. 54. Evelyn quotes this in his 'Digression concerning Physiognomy' (p. 299).

⁴ Addison probably refers (as Nichols suggested) to Giovanni Battista Della Porta's treatise, *De humana physiognomonia*, first published in 1591 and often reprinted. In the 1601 edition the heads of various animals—including all those mentioned in this essay—and the heads of various types of men are placed side by side. The comparison of human heads to those of animals is made in most of the books on physiognomy, from Aristotle on, and the idea had become commonplace in other literature. Cf. the popular *Letters writ by a Turkish Spy*: 'Surely, there is no Species of Four-footed Beasts . . . whose Nature is not found in Man. How exactly agreeable to the Fox are some Mens Tempers? Whilest others are perfect Bears in human Shape. . . . And 'tis not hard for an observing Mind to see their Natural Complexion, through the borrow'd Vizard. The Physiognomy of Vice and Virtue, are easily distinguish'd. There are some secret Characters in every Face, which speak the Nature of the Person' (ed. 1702, viii. 16–17). See also *Menagiana* (3rd ed. 1715), iv. 26, for a conversation on the subject.

Lyon, an Hog, or any other Creature; he hath the same Resemblance in the Frame of his Mind, and is subject to those Passions which are predominant in the Creature that appears in his Countenance.[a] Accordingly he gives the Prints of several Faces that are of a different Mould, and by a little overcharging[b] the Likeness, discovers the Figures of these several Kinds of brutal Faces in humane Features. I remember in the Life of the famous Prince of *Condé*[1] the Writer observes, the Face[c] of that Prince was like the Face of an Eagle, and that the Prince was very well pleased to be told so. In this Case therefore we may be sure, that he had in his Mind some general implicit Notion of this Art of Physiognomy which I have just now mentioned; and that when his Courtiers told him his Face was made like an Eagle's, he understood them in the same Manner as if they had told him, there was something in his Looks which shewed him to be strong, active, piercing, and of a royal Descent. Whether or no the different Motions of the Animal Spirits in different Passions, may have any Effect on the Mould of the Face when the Lineaments are pliable and tender, or whether the same Kind of Souls require the same Kind of Habitations, I shall leave to the Consideration of the Curious. In the mean Time I think nothing can be more glorious, than for a Man to give the Lie to his Face, and to be an honest, just, good-natured Man, in spite of all those Marks and Signatures which Nature seems to have set upon him for the Contrary. This very often happens among those, who instead of being exasperated by their own Looks, or envying the Looks of others, apply themselves entirely to the cultivating of their Minds, and getting those Beauties which are more lasting and more ornamental. I have seen many an amiable Piece of Deformity, and have observed a certain Chearful-ness in as bad a System of Features as ever was clap'd together, which hath appeared more lovely than all the blooming Charms of an insolent Beauty. There is a double Praise due to Virtue, when it is lodged in a Body that seems to have been prepared for the Recep-tion of Vice: In many such Cases the Soul and the Body do not seem to be Fellows.

[a] Countenance.] Face. *Fol.*   [b] by a little overcharging] by overcharging *Fol.*
[c] observes, the Face] observes, that the Face *Fol.*

[1] According to 'The Life of Lewis II, Prince of Conde', 'His Eyes were lively and piercing, and some have observ'd that his Physiognomy resembled an Eagle' (*Lives English and Foreign*, 1704, ii. 464).

Socrates[1] was an extraordinary Instance of this Nature. There chanced to be a great Physiognomist in his Time at *Athens*, who had made strange Discoveries of Mens Tempers and Inclinations by their outward Appearances. *Socrates*'s Disciples, that they might put this Artist to the Trial, carried him to their Master, whom he had never seen before, and did not know he was then in Company with him.[a] After a short Examination of his Face, the Physiognomist pronounced him the most lewd, libidinous, drunken old Fellow that he had ever met with in his whole Life.[b] Upon which the Disciples all burst out a laughing, as thinking they had detected the Falshood and Vanity of his Art: But *Socrates* told them, That the Principles of his Art might be very true, notwithstanding his present Mistake; for that he himself was naturally inclined to those particular Vices which the Physiognomist had discovered in his Countenance, but that he had conquered the strong Dispositions he was born with by the Dictates of Philosophy.

We are indeed told by an ancient Author, that *Socrates* very much resembled *Silenus*[2] in his Face; which we find to have been very rightly observed from the Statues and Busts of both, that[c] are still extant, as well as on several antique Seals and precious Stones, which are frequently enough to be met with in the Cabinets of the Curious. But however Observations of this Nature may sometimes hold, a wise Man should be particularly cautious how he gives Credit to a Man's outward Appearance. It is an irreparable Injustice we[d] are guilty of towards one another, when we are prejudiced by the Looks and Features of those whom we do not know. How often do we conceive Hatred against a Person of Worth, or fancy a Man to be proud and ill-natured by his Aspect, whom we think we cannot esteem too much when we are acquainted with his real Character? Dr. *Moore*,[3] in his admirable System of Ethicks, reckons this

---

a know . . . him.] know who he was. *Fol.*   b met with in his whole Life.] seen in his Life. *Fol.*   c that] which *Fol.*   d Injustice we] Injustice that we *Fol.*

---

1 The meeting with the physiognomist Zopyrus is related in Cicero's *De fato* (5. 10); Socrates' explanation of how he had conquered these strong dispositions is in Cicero's *Tusculan Disputations* (4. 37. 80).

2 Plato, *Symposium* 215A. This point, as well as the incident related by Cicero, is to be found in Stanley's *History of Philosophy* ('Socrates', chap. xv), the 1701 edition of which was in Addison's library.

3 Henry More, *Enchiridion ethicum*, lib. i, cap. 13: 'Prosopolepsia est Impressio corporea quâ abripitur animus ad amorem vel odium, ad existimationem vel despectum rei vel personae, ex leviculis quibusdam externisque circumstantiis' (2nd ed., 1669, p. 78). The English translation (*An Account of Virtue; or, Dr. Henry More's*

particular Inclination, to take a Prejudice against a Man for his
Looks, among the smaller Vices in Morality, and, if I remember,
gives it the Name of a *Prosopolepsia*.   L

No. 87   *Saturday, June* 9, 1711[1]
[STEELE]

. . . Nimium ne crede colori.
Virg.

IT has been the Purpose of several of my Speculations to bring
People to an unconcerned Behaviour, with relation to their Persons, whether Beautiful or Defective. As the Secrets of the Ugly
Club[2] were exposed to the Publick, that Men might see there were
some Noble Spirits in the Age who were not at all displeased with
themselves upon Considerations which they had no Choice in: So
the Discourse concerning *Idols*[3] tended to lessen the Value People
put upon themselves from personal Advantages, and Gifts of Nature.
As to the latter Species of Mankind, the Beauties, whether Male or
Female, they are generally the most untractable People of all others.
You are so excessively perplexed with the Particularities in their
Behaviour, that, to be at ease, one would be apt to wish there were
no such Creatures. They expect so great Allowances, and give so
little to others, that they who have to do with them find in the
main, a Man with a better Person than ordinary, and a Beautiful
Woman, might be very happily changed for such to whom Nature
has been less Liberal. The Handsome Fellow is usually so much a
Gentleman, and the Fine Woman has something so becoming, that
there is no enduring either of them. It has therefore been generally
my Choice to mix with chearful Ugly Creatures, rather than Gentlemen who are Graceful enough to omit or do what they please; or

---

Abridgment of Morals, 1701) does not use the word. The English form *prosopolepsy* is
found as early as 1646, according to the *OED*, which defines it as 'Acceptance or
"acception" of the face or person of any one; respect of persons, undue favour shown
to a particular person; partiality'.

  [1] *Motto.* Virgil, *Eclogues,* 2. 17:
        Trust not too much to that enchanting Face. DRYDEN.

  [2] No. 17.   [3] No. 73.

Beauties who have Charms enough to do and say what would be disobliging in any but themselves.

Diffidence and Presumption, upon account of Our Persons, are equally Faults; and both arise from the want of knowing, or rather endeavouring to know, our selves, and for what we ought to be valued or neglected. But indeed, I did not imagine these little Considerations and Coquettries could have the ill Consequence as I find they have by the following Letters of my Correspondents, where it seems Beauty is thrown into the Account, in Matters of Sale, to those who receive no Favour from the Charmers.

Mr. SPECTATOR, *June* 4.
' AFTER I have assured you I am in every respect one of the Handsomest young Girls about Town—I need be particular in nothing but the Make of my Face, which has the Misfortune to be exactly Oval. This I take to proceed from a Temper that naturally inclines me both to speak and to hear.

'With this Account you may wonder how I can have the Vanity to offer my self as a Candidate, which I now do, to a Society, where the *Spectator* and *Hecatissa*[1] have been admitted with so much Applause. I don't want to be put in mind how very Defective I am in every thing that is Ugly; I am too sensible of my own Unworthiness in this Particular, and therefore I only propose my self as a Foil to the Club.

'You see how honest I have been to confess all my Imperfections, which is a great deal to come from a Woman, and what, I hope, you will encourage with the Favour of your Interest.

'There can be no Objection made on the side of the Matchless *Hecatissa*, since it is certain I shall be in no danger of giving her the least occasion of Jealousie: And then, a Joint-Stool in the very lowest Place at the Table is all the Honour that is coveted by

> *Your most Humble*
> *and Obedient Servant,*
> ROSALINDA.[2]

'I have sacrificed my Necklace to put into the Publick Lottery against the Common Enemy. And last *Saturday*, about Three a Clock

---

[1] No. 48.
[2] Lillie prints a similar letter (i. 198–9) dated 11 June and signed Merry Sue, requesting to be admitted into the Ugly Club, 'my person being as ugly as possible, for my face is longer and broader by three inches each way, than any I can yet meet with'.

in the Afternoon, I began to Patch indifferently on both sides of my Face.'[1]

Mr. SPECTATOR, London, *June* 7, 1711.

'UPON reading your late Dissertation concerning *Idols*, I cannot but complain to you that there are, in six or seven Places of this City, Coffee-houses kept by Persons of that Sisterhood. These *Idols* sit and receive all day long the Adoration of the Youth within such and such Districts; I know, in particular, Goods are not entered as they ought to be at the Custom-house, nor Law-reports perused at the Temple, by reason of one Beauty who detains the young Merchants too long near Change, and another Fair one, who keeps the Students at her House when they should be at Study. It would be worth your while to see how the Idolaters alternately offer Incense to their *Idols*, and what Heartburnings arise in those who wait for their Turn to receive kind Aspects from those little Thrones, which all the Company, but these Lovers, call the Bars. I saw a Gentleman turn as pale as Ashes, because an *Idol* turned the Sugar in a Tea Dish for his Rival, and carelessly called the Boy to serve him, with a *Sirrah! Why don't you give the Gentleman the Box to please himself?* Certain it is, that a very hopeful young Man was taken with Leads in his Pockets below Bridge, where he intended to drown himself because his *Idol* would wash the Dish in which she had just before drank Tea, before she would let him use it.

'I am, Sir, a Person past being Amorous, and do not give this Information out of Envy or Jealousy, but I am a real Sufferer by it. These Lovers take any thing for Tea and Coffee; I saw one Yesterday surfeit to make his Court, and all his Rivals, at the same time, loud in the Commendation of Liquors that went against every body in the Room that was not in love. While these young Fellows resign their Stomachs with their Hearts, and drink at the *Idol* in this manner, we who come to do Business, or talk Politicks, are utterly Poisoned: They have also Drams for those who are more enamoured than ordinary; and it is very common for such as are too low in Constitution to Ogle the *Idol*, upon the strength of Tea, to fluster themselves with warmer Liquors: Thus all Pretenders advance, as fast as they can, to a Feaver or a Diabetes. I must repeat to you, that I do not look with an Evil Eye upon the Profit of the *Idols*, or the Diversions of the Lovers; what I hope from this Remonstrance, is

[1] The references in the postscript are to No. 81.

only that we plain People may not be served as if we were Idolaters, but that from the time of Publishing this in your Paper the *Idols* would mix Ratsbane only for their Admirers, and take more care of us who don't Love them.

I am,
SIR,
Yours,
T. T.'[1]

R

No. 88

[STEELE]

Quid Domini facient, audent cum talia Fures?
Virg.

Mr. SPECTATOR, *May* 30. 1711.

'I HAVE no small Value for your Endeavours to lay before the World what may escape their Observation, and yet highly conduces to their Service. You have, I think, succeeded very well on many Subjects; and seem to have been conversant in very different Scenes of Life. But in the Considerations of Mankind, as a SPECTATOR, you should not omit Circumstances which relate to the inferiour Part of the World, any more than those which concern the greater. There is one thing in particular which I wonder you have not touched upon, and that is, the general Corruption of Manners in the Servants[3] of *Great Britain*. I am a Man that have travelled and

---

[1] At the end of No. 87 in Folio is the following:

ADVERTISEMENT.

☞ *This is to give Notice, That the three Criticks who last* Sunday *settled the Characters of my Lord* Rochester *and* Boileau, *in the Yard of a Coffee-house in* Fuller's Rents, *will meet this next* Sunday *at the same Time and Place, to finish the Merits of several Dramatick Writers: And will also make an End of* the Nature of True Sublime.

'This Letter subscribed T. T. was written by Mr. Eusden, afterwards Poet Laureat. The Idol was a young widow, who kept the Widow's Coffee-House in Devereux Court; which stood opposite to the house so called now' (Nichols).

[2] *Motto.* Virgil, *Eclogues*, 3. 16:
What will the masters do, when thus the servants dare?

[3] The following advertisement appears in No. 16 and later numbers:

The Duty of Servants: Containing, I. Their Preparations for, and Choice of a Service. II. Their Duty in Service: Together with Prayers suited to each Duty. All which may be accommodated likewise, for the most Part, to Apprentices. To

seen many Nations, but have for seven Years last past resided constantly in *London* or within twenty Miles of it: In this Time I have contracted a numerous Acquaintance among the best Sort of People, and have hardly found one of them happy in their Servants. This is Matter of great Astonishment to Foreigners, and all such as have visited foreign Countries, especially since we cannot but observe, That there is no Part of the World where Servants have those Privileges and Advantages as in *England*: They have no where else such plentiful Diet, large Wages, or indulgent Liberty: There is no Place wherein they labour less, and yet where they are so little respectful, more wasteful, more negligent, or where they so frequently change their Masters. To this I attribute, in a great Measure, the frequent Robberies and Losses which we suffer on the high Road and in our own Houses. That indeed which gives me the present Thought of this Kind, is, that a careless Groom of mine has spoiled me the prettiest Pad in the World, with only riding him ten Miles; and I assure you, if I were to make a Register of all the Horses I have known thus abused by Negligence of Servants, the Number would mount a Regiment. I wish you would give us your Observations, that we may know how to treat these Rogues, or that we Masters may enter into Measures to reform them. Pray give us a Speculation in general about Servants, and you make me,

'Pray do not omit the	*Yours*,
Mention of Grooms[1] in	Philo-Britannicus.'
particular.'	

This honest Gentleman, who is so desirous that I should write a Satyr upon Grooms, has a great deal of Reason for his Resentment; and I know no Evil which touches all Mankind so much as this of the Misbehaviour of Servants.

The Complaint of this Letter runs wholly upon Men-Servants; and I can attribute the Licentiousness which has at present prevailed among them to nothing but what an hundred before me have ascribed it to, The Custom of giving Board-Wages:[2] This one

which is added, A Discourse of the Sacrament, suited peculiarly to Servants: Proper to be read in Charity-Schools. The 3d Edition, by Dr. [Richard] Lucas. Printed for William Innys at the Prince's Arms in St. Paul's Church-yard.

[1] A letter signed T. T., from Spalding, Lincolnshire, 20 June 1711 (Lillie, i. 316–20), comments on this. 'You have been already requested to observe the conduct of the grooms, I must beg of you to look into that of the coachmen. . . .' Another (i. 324–5) from Jack Livery, dated 25 June 1711, pleads that masters who have honest and faithful servants should give them 'a seasonable encouragement'.

[2] Wages allowed to servants to keep themselves in victual. In Thomas Baker's

Instance of false Oeconomy is sufficient to debauch the whole Nation of Servants, and makes them as it were but for some Part of their Time in that Quality. They are either attending in Places where they meet and run into Clubs, or else, if they wait at Taverns, they eat after their Masters, and reserve their Wages for other Occasions. From hence it arises, That they are but in a lower Degree what their Masters themselves are; and usually affect an Imitation of their Manners: And you have in Liveries Beaux, Fops, and Coxcombs in as high Perfection, as among People that keep Equipages. It is a common Humour among the Retinue of People of Quality, when they are in their Revels, that is when they are out of their Masters Sight, to assume in an humourous Way the Names and Titles of those whose Liveries they wear. By which Means Characters and Distinctions become so familiar to them, that it is to this, among other Causes, one may impute a certain Insolence among our Servants, that they take no Notice of any Gentleman though they know him ever so well, except he is an Acquaintance of their Masters.

My Obscurity and Taciturnity leave[a] me at Liberty, without Scandal, to dine, if I think fit, at a common Ordinary, in the meanest as well as the most sumptuous House of Entertainment. Falling in the other Day at a Victualling-house near the House of Peers, I heard the Maid come down and tell the Landlady at the Bar, That my Lord Bishop swore he would throw her out at Window[b] if she did not bring up more Mild-beer, and that my Lord Duke would have a double Mug of Purle.[1] My Surprise was encreased in hearing loud and rustick Voices speak and answer to each other upon the publick Affairs by the Names of the most Illustrious of our Nobility; till of a sudden one came running in, and cryed the House was rising. Down came all the Company together, and away: The Ale-house was immediately filled with Clamour, and scoring one Mug to the Marquis of such a Place, Oyl and Vinegar to such an Earl, three Quarts to my new Lord for wetting his Title, and so forth. It is a thing too notorious to mention the Crowds of Servants, and

---

The Fine Lady's Airs (1709) Sir Harry Sprightly's valet Shrimp says 'tho' our Masters mayn't want us, we that are at Board-wages love to smell out where they dine' (I. i).
    ¹ 'A liquor made by infusing wormwood or other bitter herbs in ale or beer; later, a mixture of hot beer with gin, sometimes also with ginger and sugar; in repute as a morning draught' (*OED*).

their Insolence, near the Courts of Justice, and the Stairs towards the supreme Assembly; where there is an universal Mockery of all Order, such riotous Clamour and licentious Confusion, that one would think the whole Nation lived in jest, and there were no such thing as Rule and Distinction among us.

The next Place of Resort, wherein the servile World are let loose, is at the Entrance of *Hide-Park*, while the Gentry are at the Ring.[1] Hither People bring their Lacqueys out of State, and here it is that all they say at their Tables and act in their Houses is communicated to the whole Town. There are Men of Wit in all Conditions of Life; and mixing with these People at their Diversions, I have heard Coquets and Prudes as well rallied, and Insolence and Pride exposed, (allowing for their want of Education,) with as much Humour and good Sense, as in the politest Companies. It is a general Observation, That all Dependants run in some Measure into the Manners and Behaviour of those whom they serve: You shall frequently meet with Lovers and Men of Intrigue among the Lacqueys, as well as at *White's*[2] or in the Side-boxes.[3] I remember some Years ago an Instance of this Kind. A Footman to a Captain of the Guard used frequently, when his Master was out of the Way, to carry on Amours and make Assignations in his Master's Cloaths. The Fellow had a very good Person, and there are very many Women that think no further than the Outside of a Gentleman; besides which he was almost as learned a Man as the Collonel himself. I say, thus qualified, the Fellow could scrawl *Billets doux* so well, and furnish a Conversation on the common Topicks, that he had, as they call it, a great deal of good Business on his Hands. It happened one Day, that coming down a Tavern-stairs in his Master's fine Guard-Coat, with a well-dressed Woman masked, he met the Collonel coming up with other Company; but with a ready Assurance he quitted his Lady, came up to him, and said, *Sir, I know you have too much Respect for your self to cane me in this honourable Habit: But you see there is a Lady in the Case,*[4] *and I hope on that Score also you will put off your Anger till I have told you all another Time.* After a little Pause the Collonel cleared up

---

[1] See No. 15.

[2] White's Chocolate-House 'was then lower down in St. James's Street than it is at present, and on the other side' (Nichols, note to *Tatler* 1). Francis White, the original owner, died in February 1711 (*DNB*).

[3] See No. 81.

[4] Aitken quotes Gay ('The Hare and Many Friends'), but it was a common expression. Cf. Shadwell, *The Humourists*, III. i. In *The Drummer* of Addison (IV. i) Fantom says, 'When a Lady's in the Case, I'm more afraid of one Fop than twenty Conjurers'.

his Countenance, and with an Air of Familiarity whispered his Man apart, *Sirrah, bring the Lady with you to ask Pardon for you*; then aloud *Look to it* Will. *I'll never forgive you else.* The Fellow went back to his Mistress, and telling her with a loud Voice and an Oath, That was the honestest Fellow in the World, conveyed her to an Hackney-Coach.

But the many Irregularities committed by Servants in the Places above-mentioned, as well as in the Theatres, of which Masters are generally the Occasions, are too various not to need being resumed on another Occasion.   R[1]

No. 89   *Tuesday, June* 12, 1711[2]
[ADDISON]

> *. . . Petite hinc Juvenesque senesque*
> *Finem animo certum, miserisque viatica canis.*
> *Cras hoc fiet. Idem cras fiet. Quid? quasi magnum*
> *Nempe diem donas; sed cum lux altera venit,*
> *Jam cras hesternum consumpsimus; ecce aliud cras*
> *Egerit hos annos, & semper paulum erit ultra.*
> *Nam quamvis prope te, quamvis temone sub uno*
> *Vertentem sese frustra sectabere canthum.*
>
>   Per.

[1] This paper, the first of several on the duties of servants (see Nos. 96, 107, and 137 (vol. ii)), shows admirably Steele's conception of the *Spectator* as an instrument of reformation of manners. Many of the details are paralleled in the plays. In the opening scene of *The Lying Lover* Latine remarks, 'Do but listen at the entrance of the Mall at noon, and you'll have all the ladies' characters in town among their lackeys. You know all fame begins from our domestics.' The conversation between Tom and Humphry in *The Conscious Lovers* (I. i) shows the servants of London imitating the dignities and titles of their masters.
[2] *Motto.* Persius, *Satires*, 5. 64–71 ('Petite hinc puerique senesque'):
>   PERSIUS. From thee both old and young, with profit, learn
>   The Bounds of Good and Evil to discern.
>   CORNUTUS. Unhappy he who does this Work adjourn,
>   And to to morrow wou'd the search delay:
>   His lazy morrow will be like to day.
>   PERSIUS. But is one Day of Ease too much to borrow?
>   CORNUTUS. Yes sure: For Yesterday was once To Morrow.
>   That Yesterday is gone, and nothing gain'd:
>   And all thy fruitless Days will thus be drain'd;
>   For thou hast more To Morrows yet to ask,
>   And wilt be ever to begin thy Task;
>   Who, like the hindmost Chariot-Wheels art curst,
>   Still to be near, but ne'er to reach the first. DRYDEN.

AS my Correspondents, upon the Subject of Love, are very numerous, it is my Design, if possible, to range them under several Heads, and address my self to them at different Times. The first Branch of them, to whose Service I shall Dedicate this Paper, are those that have to do with Women of Dilatory Tempers, who are for spinning out the Time of Courtship to an immoderate Length without being able either to close with their Lovers, or to dismiss them. I have many Letters by me filled with Complaints against this sort of Women. In one of them no less a Man than a Brother of the Coiff[1] tells me, that he began his Suit *Vicessimo nono Caroli secundi*, before he had been a Twelve-month at the *Temple*; that he prosecuted it for many Years after he was called to the Bar; that at present he is a Serjeant at Law; and notwithstanding he hoped that Matters would have been long since brought to an issue, the Fair One still *Demurrs*. I am so well pleased with this Gentleman's Phrase, that I shall distinguish this Sect of Women by the Title of *Demurrers*.[2] I find by another Letter from one who calls himself *Thirsis*, that his Mistress has been Demurring above these seven Years. But among all my Plaintiffs of this nature, I most pity the unfortunate *Philander*, a Man of a constant Passion and plentiful Fortune, who sets forth that the timorous and irresolute *Sylvia* has demurred till she is past Child-bearing. *Strephon* appears by his Letter to be a very Cholerick Lover, and irrevocably smitten with one that demurrs out of Self-interest. He tells me, with great Passion, that she has bubbled him out of his Youth; that she drilled[a] him on[3] to Five and Fifty, and that he verily believes she will drop him in his old Age, if she can find her account in another. I shall conclude this Narrative with a Letter from Honest SAM. HOPEWELL, a very pleasant Fellow, who it seems has, at last, married a *Demurrer*. I must only premise, that SAM. who is a very good Bottle-Companion, has been the Diversion of his Friends, upon account of his Passion, ever since the Year One thousand Six hundred and Eighty one.

Dear Sir,

'YOU know very well my Passion for Mrs. *Martha*, and what a Dance she has led me: She took me out at the Age of Two

---

 a she drilled] she has drilled *Fol.*

[1] A white cap formerly worn by lawyers; especially that worn by a serjeant-at-law as part of his official dress (*OED*).
[2] Demurrer. The first example of this word in *OED*.
[3] Drilled him on, i.e. led him on. Common in the Restoration and early eighteenth century; now dialectal.

and Twenty, and dodged with me above Thirty Years. I have loved her till she is grown as Grey as a Cat, and am with much ado become the Master of her Person, such as it is at present. She is however, in my Eye, a very charming old Woman. We often lament that we did not marry sooner, but she has no Body to blame for it but her self. You know very well that she would never think of me whilst she had a Tooth in her Head. I have put the Date of my Passion (*Anno Amoris Trigesimo primo*) instead of a Posie on my Wedding Ring. I expect you should send me a Congratulatory Letter; or, if you please, an *Epithalamium* upon this occasion.

Mrs. Martha's *and*
Yours Eternally,
SAM. HOPEWELL.'

In order to banish an Evil out of the World, that does not only produce great Uneasiness to private Persons, but has also a very bad Influence on the Publick, I shall endeavour to show the Folly of *Demurrage*,[1] from two or three Reflections, which I earnestly recommend to the Thoughts of my Fair Readers.

First of all I would have them seriously think on the Shortness of their Time. Life is not long enough for a Coquet to play all her Tricks in. A timorous Woman drops into her Grave before she has done deliberating. Were the Age of Man the same that it was before the Flood, a Lady might sacrifice half a Century to a Scruple, and be two or three Ages in demurring.[2] Had she Nine Hundred Years good, she might hold out to the Conversion of the *Jews*, before she thought fit to be prevailed upon. But, alas! she ought to play her Part in haste, when she considers that she is suddenly to quit the Stage, and make room for others.

In the second Place, I would desire my Female Readers to consider, that as the Term of Life is short, that of Beauty is much shorter. The finest Skin wrinkles in a few Years, and loses the Strength of its Colouring so soon, that we have scarce time to admire it. I might embellish this Subject with Roses and Rain-bows, and several other ingenious Conceits, which I may possibly reserve for another Opportunity.

There is a third Consideration, which I would likewise recom-

---

[1] Stay; delay; hesitation; pause. *Obs.* The latest example in *OED* is dated 1823.
[2] The reminiscences here of Marvell's poem 'To his Coy Mistress' have more than once been noted. See especially Pierre Legouis in *Review of English Studies*, x (1934), 447–50.

mend to a Demurrer, and that is the great Danger of her falling in Love when she is about Threescore, if she cannot satisfie her Doubts and Scruples before that time. There is a kind of *latter Spring*, that sometimes gets into the Blood of an old Woman, and turns her into a very odd sort of an Animal. I would therefore have the Demurrer consider what a strange Figure she will make, if she chances to get over all Difficulties, and comes to a final Resolution in that unseasonable part of her Life.

I would not however be understood, by any thing I have here said, to discourage that natural Modesty in the Sex, which renders a Retreat from the first Approaches of a Lover both fashionable and graceful: All that I intend is to advise them, when they are prompted by Reason and Inclination, to demurr only out of Form, and so far as Decency requires. A Virtuous Woman should reject the first Offer of Marriage, as a good Man does that of a Bishoprick; but I would advise neither the one nor the other to persist in refusing what they secretly approve.[1] I would, in this Particular, propose the Example of *Eve* to all her Daughters, as *Milton*[2] has represented her in the following Passage, which I cannot forbear transcribing entire, tho' only the twelve last Lines are to my present Purpose.

> *The Rib he form'd and fashion'd with his hands:*
> *Under his forming hands a Creature grew,*
> *Manlike, but diff'rent Sex, so lovely fair,*
> *That what seem'd fair in all the World, seem'd now*
> *Mean, or in her summ'd up, in her contain'd*
> *And in her looks, which from that time infus'd*
> *Sweetness into my heart, unfelt before,*
> *And into all things from her Air inspir'd*
> *The spirit of love and amorous delight.*
>   *She disappear'd, and left me dark, I wak'd*
> *To find her, or for ever to deplore*
> *Her Loss, and other pleasures all*[a] *abjure:*

---

[a] *all] to Fol.*

[1] A letter from Dulcemera dated 12 June 1711 (Lillie, i. 329) comments:

You write so well on the demurers, that I hope you will find leisure to say something of the deceivers (as I stile them) who make a sort of silent love with their eye, without other declarations; and what can a woman do in such a case but demurr? I suppose your Thirsis, Philander, and Strephon are of that sort, whose pride will not bear repulse, but would be sure of their prize before they address. It is a pleasure to perplex those sort of men, and it would be a greater if you will instruct what method to use on such occasions. . . .

[2] *Paradise Lost*, viii. 469–95, 500–11.

When out of hope, behold her, not far off,
Such as I saw her in my Dream, adorn'd
With what all Earth or Heaven could bestow
To make her amiable: On she came,
Led by her Heav'nly Maker, though unseen,
And guided by his Voice, nor uninform'd
Of nuptial Sanctity and marriage Rites:
Grace was in all her Steps, Heav'n in her Eye,
In every Gesture dignity and love.
I overjoy'd could not forbear aloud.

    This turn hath made amends; thou hast fulfill'd
Thy words, Creator bounteous and benign,
Giver of all things fair, but fairest this
Of all thy gifts, nor enviest. I now see
Bone of my Bone, Flesh of my Flesh, my Self . . . .

    She heard me thus, and tho' divinely brought,
Yet Innocence and Virgin Modesty,
Her virtue and the conscience of her worth,
That would be woo'd, and not unsought be won,
Not obvious, not obtrusive, but retir'd,
The more desirable, or to say all,
Nature her self, though pure of sinful thought,
Wrought in her so, that seeing me, she turn'd;[a]
I follow'd her, she what was Honour knew,
And with obsequious Majesty approv'd
My pleaded reason. To the Nuptial Bowr
I led her blushing like the Morn: . . .

                                             L

No. 90
[ADDISON]

                      Wednesday, June 13, 1711[1]

         . . . *Magnus sine viribus Ignis*
    Incassum furit.

                                Virg.

THERE is not, in my Opinion, a Consideration more effectual to extinguish inordinate Desires in the Soul of Man, than the

[a] *turn'd;*] *fled; Fol.*

[1] *Motto.* Virgil, *Georgics*, 3. 99–100:
    In vain he burns, like hasty Stubble Fires. DRYDEN.

Notions of *Plato*[1] and his Followers upon that Subject. They tell us, that every Passion which has been contracted by the Soul during her Residence in the Body, remains with her in her separate State; and that the Soul in the Body or out of the Body, differs no more than the Man does from himself when he is in his House or in open Air. When therefore the obscene Passions in particular have once taken Root and spread themselves in the Soul, they cleave to her inseparably, and remain in her for ever after the Body is cast off and thrown aside. As an Argument to confirm this their Doctrine they observe, that a lewd Youth who goes on in a continued Course of Voluptuousness, advances by Degrees into a libidinous old Man, and that the Passion survives in the Mind when it is altogether dead in the Body; nay, that the Desire grows more violent, and (like all other Habits) gathers Strength by Age, at the same Time that it has no Power of executing its own Purposes. If, say they, the Soul is the most subject to these Passions at a Time when it has the least Instigations from the Body, we may well suppose she will still retain them when she is entirely divested of it. The very Substance of the Soul is festered with them; the Gangrene is gone too far to be ever cured; the Inflammation will rage to all Eternity.

In this therefore (say the *Platonists*) consists the Punishment of a voluptuous Man after Death. He is tormented with Desires which it is impossible for him to gratify, sollicited by a Passion that has neither Objects nor Organs adapted to it. He lives in a State of invincible Desire and Impotence, and always burns in the Pursuit of what he always despairs to possess. It is for this Reason (says *Plato*) that the Souls of the Dead appear frequently in Cœmitaries, and hover about the Places where their Bodies are buried, as still hankering after their old brutal Pleasures, and desiring again to enter the Body that gave them an Opportunity of fulfilling them.

Some of our most eminent Divines have made use of this *Platonick* Notion, so far as it regards the Subsistence of our Passions after Death, with great Beauty and Strength of Reason. *Plato* indeed carries the Thought very far, when he grafts upon it his Opinion of Ghosts appearing in Places of Burial; though, I must confess, if one did believe that the departed Souls of Men and Women wandered up and down these lower Regions, and entertained themselves with the Sight of their Species, one could not devise a more proper Hell for an impure Spirit than that which *Plato* has touched upon.

[1] *Phaedo* 81.

The Ancients seem to have drawn such a State of Torments in the Description of *Tantalus*,[1] who was punished with the Rage of an eternal Thirst, and set up to the Chin in Water that fled from his Lips whenever he attempted to drink it.

Virgil, who has cast the whole System of *Platonick* Philosophy, so far as it relates to the Soul of Man, into beautiful Allegories; in the sixth Book of his *Æneid* gives us the Punishment of a Voluptuary after Death, not unlike that which we are here speaking of.

> *. . . Lucent genialibus altis*
> *Aurea fulcra toris, epulæque ante ora paratæ*
> *Regifico luxu: Furiarum maxima juxta*
> *Accubat, & manibus prohibet contingere mensas;*
> *Exurgitque facem attollens, atque intonat ore.*[2]

> *They lie below on Golden Beds display'd,*
> *And genial Feasts with regal Pomp are made.*
> *The Queen of Furies by their Side is set,*
> *And snatches from their Mouths th' untasted Meat;*
> *Which if they touch, her hissing Snakes she rears,*
> *Tossing her Torch, and thundring in their Ears.*   Dryd.

That I may a little alleviate the Severity of this my Speculation (which otherwise may lose me several of my polite Readers) I shall translate a Story that[a] has been quoted upon another Occasion by one of the most learned Men of the present Age, as I find it in the Original. The Reader will see it[b] is not foreign to my present Subject, and I dare say will think it a lively Representation of a Person lying under the Torments of such a Kind of Tantalism, or *Platonick* Hell, as that which we have now under Consideration. Monsieur *Pontignan*[3] speaking of a Love-Adventure that happened to him in the Country, gives the following Account of it:

'When I was in the Country last Summer, I was often in Company with a couple of charming Women who[c] had all the Wit and Beauty one could desire in Female Companions, with a Dash of Coquetry,

---

ᵃ that] which *Fol.*   ᵇ see it] see that it *Fol.*   ᶜ who] that *Fol.*

---

[1] See Ovid, *Metamorphoses*, 4. 458 ff.
[2] Virgil, *Aeneid*, 6. 603–7. Dryden's translation 6. 819–24 (in line 821, 'by their sides').
[3] The story is told in *L'Academie galante* (Paris, 1682), pp. 160–3, and in Bayle, art. Fontevraud, Remark LΔΔ. Addison's account is fuller, particularly in the details at the end, than either of these two sources.

that from time to time gave me a great many agreeable Torments. I was, after my Way, in love with both of them, and had such frequent Opportunities of pleading my Passion to them when they were asunder, that I had reason to hope for particular Favours from each of them. As I was walking one Evening in my Chamber with nothing about me but my Night-Gown, they both came[a] into my Room and told me, they had a very pleasant Trick to put upon a Gentleman that was in the same House, provided I would bear a Part in it. Upon this they told me such[b] a plausible Story, that I laughed at their Contrivance, and agreed to do whatever they should require of me: They immediately began to swaddle me up in my Night-Gown with long Pieces of Linnen, which they folded about me till they had wrapt me in[c] above an hundred Yards of Swathe: My Arms were pressed to my Sides, and my Legs closed together by so many Wrappers one over another, that I looked like an *Ægyptian* Mummy. As I stood bolt upright upon one End in this antique Figure, one of the Ladies burst out a Laughing, "And now *Pontignan*, says she, we intend to perform the Promise that we find you have extorted from each of us. You have often asked the Favour of us, and I dare say you are a better bred Cavalier than to refuse to go to Bed to Ladies that desire it of you." After having stood a Fit of Laughter, I begg'd them to uncase me, and do with me what they pleased. "No, no, say they, we like you very well as you are"; and upon that ordered me to be carried to one of their Houses, and put to Bed in all my Swaddles. The Room was lighted up on all Sides; and I was laid very decently between a Pair[d] of Sheets with my Head (which was indeed the only Part I could move) upon a very high Pillow: This was no sooner done, but my two Female Friends came into Bed to me in their finest Night-Clothes. You may easily guess at the Condition of a Man that saw a couple of the most beautiful Women in the World undrest and abed with him, without being able to stir Hand or Foot. I begged them to release me, and struggled all I could to get loose, which I did with so much Violence, that about Midnight they both leaped out of the Bed crying out they were undone: But seeing me safe they took their Posts again, and renewed their Raillery. Finding all my Prayers and Endeavours were lost, I compos'd my self as well as I could; and told them, that if they would not unbind me, I would fall asleep between them, and

---

[a] both came] both of them came *Fol.*   [b] told me such] told such *Fol.*
[c] wrapt me in] wrapt me up in *Fol.*   [d] Pair] couple *Fol.*

by that Means disgrace them for ever: But alas! this was impossible; could I have been disposed to it, they would have prevented me by several little ill-natured Caresses and Endearments which they bestow'd upon me. As much devoted as I am to Womankind, I would not pass such another Night to be Master of the whole Sex. My Reader will doubtless be curious to know what became of me the next Morning: Why truly my Bed-fellows left me about an Hour before Day, and told me if I would be good and lie still, they would send somebody to take me up as soon as it was Time for me to rise: Accordingly about Nine a Clock in the Morning an old Woman came to unswathe me. I bore all this very patiently, being resolved to take my Revenge of my Tormentors, and to keep no Measures with them as soon as I was at Liberty; but upon asking my old Woman what was become of the two Ladies, she told me she believ'd[a] they were by that Time within Sight of *Paris*, for that they went away in a Coach and six before five a Clock in the Morning.'   L

No. 91   *Thursday, June* 14, 1711[1]
[STEELE]

In furias ignemque ruunt. Amor omnibus Idem.
                                                    Virg.

THO' the Subject I am now going upon would be much more properly the Foundation of a Comedy, I cannot forbear inserting the Circumstances which pleased me in the Account a young Lady gave me of the Loves of a Family in Town, which shall be nameless, or rather for the better Sound, and Elevation of the History, instead of Mr. and Mrs. such a one, I shall call them by feigned Names. Without further Preface, you are to know that within the Liberties of the City of *Westminster* lives the Lady *Honoria*, a Widow about the Age of Forty, of a healthy Constitution, gay Temper, and elegant Person. She dresses a little too much like a Girl, affects a Childish Fondness in the Tone of her Voice, sometimes a pretty Sullenness in the leaning of her Head, and now and then a Downcast of her Eyes on her Fan: Neither her Imagination nor her Health

[a] told me she believ'd] told me that she believ'd *Fol.*

---

[1] *Motto.* Virgil, *Georgics,* 3. 244:
                They rush into the Flame;
    For Love is Lord of all; and is in all the same. DRYDEN.

would ever give her to know that she is turned of Twenty, but that in the midst of these pretty Softnesses, and Airs of Delicacy and Attraction, she has a tall Daughter within a Fortnight of Fifteen, who impertinently comes into the Room, and Towers so much towards Woman, that her Mother is always checked by her Presence, and every Charm of *Honoria* droops at the Entrance of *Flavia*. The agreeable *Flavia* would be what she is not, as well as her Mother *Honoria*, but all their Beholders are more partial to an Affectation of what a Person is growing up to, than of what has been already enjoyed, and is gone for ever. It is therefore allowed to *Flavia* to look forward, but not to *Honoria* to look back. *Flavia* is no way dependant on her Mother, with Relation to her Fortune, for which Reason they live almost upon an Equality in Conversation; and as *Honoria* has given *Flavia* to understand, that it is ill bred to be always calling Mother, *Flavia* is as well pleased never to be called Child. It happens, by this means, that these Ladies are generally Rivals in all Places where they appear, and the Words Mother and Daughter never pass between them, but out of Spite. *Flavia* one Night at a Play, observing *Honoria* draw the Eyes of several in the Pitt, called a Lady who sat by her, and bid her ask her Mother to lend her her Snuff-Box for one Moment. Another time, when a Lover of *Honoria* was on his Knees beseeching the Favour to Kiss her Hand, *Flavia* rushing into the Room kneeled down by him and asked Blessing. Several of these Contradictory Acts of Duty have raised between them such a Coldness, that they generally converse when they are in mixed Company, by way of Talking at one another, and not to one another. *Honoria* is ever complaining of a certain Sufficiency in the young Women of this Age, who assume to themselves an Authority of carrying all things before them, as if they were Possessers of the Esteem of Mankind; and all, who were but a Year before them in the World, were neglected or deceased. *Flavia*, upon such a Provocation, is sure to observe that there are People who can resign nothing, and know not how to give up what they know they cannot hold; that there are those who will not allow Youth their Follies, not because they are themselves past them, but because they love to continue in them. These Beauties Rival each other on all Occasions, not that they have always had the same Lovers, but each has kept up a Vanity to shew the other the Charms of her Lover. *Dick Crastin* and *Tom Tulip*, among many others, have of late been Pretenders in this Family: *Dick* to *Honoria*, *Tom* to *Flavia*. *Dick* is the only surviving Beau of the last Age, and *Tom* almost the only one that keeps up that Order of Men in this.

I wish I could repeat the little Circumstances of a Conversation of the four Lovers, with the Spirit in which the young Lady, I had my Account from, represented it at a Visit where I had the Honour to be present; but it seems *Dick Crastin* the Admirer of *Honoria*, and *Tom Tulip* the Pretender to *Flavia*, were purposely admitted together by the Ladies, that each might show the other that her Lover had the Superiority in the Accomplishments of that sort of Creature, whom the sillier part of Women call a Fine Gentleman. As this Age has a much more gross Taste in Courtship, as well as in every[a] thing else, than the last had, these Gentlemen are Instances of it in their different manner of Application. *Tulip* is ever making Allusions to the Vigour of his Person, the sinewy Force of his Make, while *Crastin* professes a wary Observation of the Turns of his Mistress's Mind. *Tulip* gives himself the Air of a resistless Ravisher, *Crastin* practises that of a skilful Lover. Poetry is the inseparable Property of every Man in Love; and as Men of Wit write Verses on those Occasions, the rest of the World repeat the Verses of others. These Servants of the Ladies were used to imitate their manner of Conversation, and allude to one another, rather than interchange Discourse in what they said when they met. *Tulip*, the other day, seized his Mistress's Hand, and repeated out of *Ovid's Art of Love*,[1]

> *'Tis I can in soft Battels pass the Night,*
> *Yet rise next Morning Vigorous for the Fight,*
> *Fresh as the Day, and active as the Light.*

Upon hearing this, *Crastin*, with an Air of Deference, played *Honoria's* Fan, and repeated,

> *Sidley has that prevailing gentle Art,*
> *That can, with a resistless Charm, impart*
> *The loosest Wishes to the chastest Heart,*
> *Raise such a Conflict, kindle such a Fire,*
> *Between declining Virtue and Desire,*

[a] as in every] as every *Fol.*

---

[1] The translation is that of John Oldham, 'Some Elegies out of Ovid's Amours, Imitated: Book II, Elegy x' (*Poems and Translations*, 1683, p. 112):
> Oft in soft Battles have I spent the Night,
> Yet rose next Morning vig'rous for the Fight,
> Fresh as the Day, and active as the Light.

Steele quotes from Oldham's version of Horace's *Satires* in *Tatler* 268.

Till the poor vanquish'd Maid dissolves away
In Dreams all Night, in Sighs and Tears all Day.[1]

When *Crastin* had uttered these Verses, with a Tenderness which at once spoke Passion and Respect, *Honoria* cast a Triumphant Glance at *Flavia*, as exulting in the Elegance of *Crastin's* Courtship, and upbraiding her with the Homeliness of *Tulip's. Tulip* understood the Reproach, and in return began to applaud the Wisdom of old amorous Gentlemen, who turned their Mistress's Imagination, as far as possible, from what they had long themselves forgot, and ended his Discourse with a sly Commendation of the Doctrine of *Platonick* Love; at the same time he ran[a] over, with a laughing Eye, *Crastin's* thin Leggs, meager Looks and spare Body. The old Gentleman immediately left the Room with some Disorder, and the Conversation fell upon untimely Passion, after Love, and unseasonable Youth. *Tulip* sung, danced, moved before the Glass, led his Mistress half a Minuet, humm'd

Celia the Fair,[2] *in the Bloom of fifteen,*

when there came a Servant with a Letter to him, which was as follows.

SIR,

'I UNDERSTAND very well what you meant by your Mention of *Platonick* Love. I shall be glad to meet you immediately in *Hide-Park,* or behind *Mountague-house,* or attend you to *Barn Elmes,*[3]

[a] time he ran] time run *Fol.*

---

[1] One of Rochester's best-known poems, the 'Allusion to the Tenth Satire of the First Book of Horace', 64–70. Steele quotes the same lines in No. 400 (vol. iii) and also in a letter to Pope of 1 June 1712 (*Correspondence,* ed. Blanchard, p. 54).
[2] Dryden, 'A New Song' (Sylvia the Fair), first published anonymously in *Sylvae* (the Second Miscellany), 1685.
[3] Favourite duelling-places. Montague House was near the north-west corner of Bloomsbury Square, now the site of the British Museum. Hatton (p. 627) describes it as 'an extraordinary noble and beautiful Palace, situate on the north side of Great Russel Street near Bloomsbury, in the Occupation of his Grace the Duke of Montague'. The palace, erected in 1677, was of brick and rustic work, forming three sides of a quadrangle; the fields toward the north contained a fountain, a terrace, and several statues. Cf. *Tatler* 31: 'I am forced to break off abruptly, being sent for in Hast, with my Rule, to measure the Degree of an Affront, before the two Gentlemen (who are now in their Breeches and Pumps ready to engage behind *Montague-House*) have made a Pass.' Barn Elms, near Barnes, contained among other houses the residence of Jacob Tonson, where the Kit Cat Club convened. John Hughes has a poem entitled 'Barn-Elms' (*Poems,* ed. Duncombe, 1735, i. 76–77).

or any other fashionable Place that's fit for a Gentleman to dye in, that you shall appoint for,

SIR,

Your most Humble Servant,
Richard Crastin.'

Tulip's Colour changed at the reading this Epistle, for which Reason his Mistress snatched it to read the Contents. While she was doing so *Tulip* went away, and the Ladies now agreeing in a Common Calamity, bewailed together the Danger of their Lovers. They immediately undressed to go out, and took[a] Hackneys to prevent Mischief; but, after alarming all Parts of the Town, *Crastin* was found by his Widow in his Pumps at *Hide-Park*, which Appointment *Tulip* never kept, but made his Escape into the Country. *Flavia* tears her Hair for his Inglorious Safety, curses and despises her Charmer, is fallen in Love with *Crastin*: Which is the first Part of the History of the *Rival Mother*.[1] R[2]

[a] took] take *Fol.*

[1] There were several Restoration plays with similar titles—*The Rival Queens* by Lee, *The Rival Ladies* by Dryden, *The Rival Kings* by John Banks, *The Rival Sisters* by Robert Gould, &c. *The Rival Ladies* of Dryden contains a character named Honoria. *The Rival-Mother: a late true history, digested into a Novel*, is advertised in the *Term Catalogues*, Trinity 1694 (Arber, ii. 510). Nicoll's *History of English Drama 1660–1900* (4th ed., 1952), i. 444, lists a comedy with the title *The Rival Mother* (? 8vo, 1678), and comments: 'Some early playlists, followed by a few more modern, confidently record this title, but no copy seems to have been authoritatively reported.'

[2] This paper, although signed R in all editions, is in Duncombe's list of Hughes's contributions (preface to Hughes's *Poems and Essays*, 1735, vol. i, pp. xxxiv–xxxv). It is assigned to him by Nichols, Chalmers, and Bisset. Morley, Aitken, and Gregory Smith attribute it to Steele. Additional evidence for Steele's authorship lies in the fact that the germ of the story is given in *Tatler* 206 by Steele, with Flavia as the mother, and in language close to the fuller story in the *Spectator*:

To follow Nature is the only agreeable Course; which is what I would fain inculcate to those jarring Companions, *Flavia* and *Lucia*. They are Mother and Daughter. *Flavia*, who is the Mamma, has all the Charms and Desires of Youth still about her, and not much turned of Thirty: *Lucia* is blooming and amorous, and but a little above Fifteen. The Mother looks very much younger than she is, the Girl very much elder. If it were possible to fix the Girl to her Sick-Bed, and preserve the Portion (the Use of which the Mother partakes), the good Widow *Flavia* would certainly do it. But for fear of *Lucia's* Escape, the Mother is forced to be constantly attended with a Rival, that explains her Age, and draws off the Eyes of her Admirers. The Jest is, they can never be together in Strangers Company, but *Lucy* is eternally reprimanded for something very particular in her Behaviour; for which she has the Malice to say, She hopes she shall always obey her Parents. She carried her Passion and Jealousy to that Height the other Day, that coming suddenly into the Room, and surprising Colonel *Lofty* speaking Rapture on one Knee to her Mother, she clapped down by him, and asked her Blessing.

. . . Convivæ prope dissentire videntur,
Poscentes vario multum diversa palato;
Quid dem? Quid non dem? . . .

Hor.

LOOKING over the late Packets of Letters which have been sent to me, I found the following one.

Mr. SPECTATOR,

'YOUR Paper is a Part of my Tea-Equipage;[2] and my Servant knows my Humour so well, that calling for my Breakfast this Morning (it being past my usual Hour) she answered, the SPECTATOR was not yet come in; but that the Tea-Kettle boiled, and she expected it every Moment. Having thus in Part signified to you the Esteem and Veneration which I have for you, I must put you in Mind of the Catalogue of Books[3] which you have promised to recommend to our Sex: For I have deferred furnishing my Closet with Authors, till I receive your Advice in this Particular; being your daily Disciple and humble Servant,

LEONORA.'[4]

In answer to my fair Disciple, whom I am very proud of, I must acquaint her and the rest of my Readers, that since I have called out for Help in my Catalogue of a Lady's Library, I have received many Letters upon that Head; some of which I shall give an Account of.

In the first Class I shall take Notice of those which come to me from eminent Booksellers, who every one of them mention with Respect the Authors they have printed; and consequently have an Eye to their own Advantage more than to that of the Ladies. One tells me, that he thinks it absolutely necessary for Women to have true Notions of Right and Equity, and that therefore they cannot peruse a better Book than *Dalton's Country Justice.*[5] Another thinks

---

[1] *Motto.* Horace, *Epistles*, 2. 2. 61–63:
It is much like guests who disagree; their tastes vary, and they call for widely different dishes. What am I to put before them? what not?
[2] No. 10.   [3] No. 37.
[4] For the supposed original of Leonora see No. 140 (vol. ii).
[5] By Michael Dalton, of Lincoln's Inn, first published in 1630. The most recent edition appears to be the one advertised in *Term Catalogues* in Trinity 1697 (Arber,

they cannot be without *The Compleat Jockey.*[1] A third observing the Curiosity and Desire of prying into Secrets, which he tells me is natural to the fair Sex, is of Opinion this Female Inclination, if well directed, might turn very much to their Advantage, and therefore recommends to me *Mr. Mede upon the Revelations.*[2] A fourth lays it down as an unquestioned Truth, that a Lady cannot be thoroughly accomplished who has not read *The Secret Treaties and Negotiations of the Marshal D'Estrades.*[3] Mr. *Jacob Tonson,* Junr. is of Opinion, that *Bayle's Dictionary*[4] might be of very great Use to the Ladies, in order to make them general Scholars. Another, whose Name I have forgotten, thinks it highly proper that every Woman with Child should read *Mr. Wall's History of Infant Baptism:*[5] As another is very impor-

---

iii. 28): *The Country Justice; containing the Practices of the Justices of the Peace out of their Sessions: gathered for the better help of such Justices of the Peace as have not been much conversant in the study of the Laws of this Realm.*

[1] Published in 1695 (Wing C 5642).

[2] The *Clavis Apocalyptica* (1627) of Joseph Mede was translated by Richard More in 1643 and became 'as popular in the pulpit as "The Country Justice" was on the Bench' (Morley).

[3] The following advertisement appears in No. 95:

This Day is publish'd, Letters and Negotiations of the Count D'Estrades, Ambassador from Lewis the Fourteenth to the States General of the United Provinces of the Low Countries: From the Year 1663 to the Year 1669. Consisting chiefly of Original Letters and Instructions from the French King and his Ministers, to the said Count: with his Answers. Wherein are several secret Transactions between the Courts of England and France during that time. Translated by Several Hands. In Three Volumes. Printed for D. Brown [and others].

[4] The *Dictionnaire historique et critique* of Pierre Bayle was published at Rotterdam in 1697. Proposals for an English version were advertised in the *Daily Courant,* 27 Feb. 1706:

The best hands have been employ'd, and their several Translations carefully revis'd, and compar'd with the Original, by Two Gentlemen appointed by Mr. Bayle for that purpose. The whole Work will contain near 1000 Sheets, and will be printed in 5 Volumes in Folio, price to Subscribers 5 l. 10 s. a Seventh gratis, 30 s. only to be paid in hand. Some will be printed on large Paper, price 8 l.

The English translation, published by Jacob Tonson and others, is in four volumes, folio, dated 1710, although the work is advertised as 'Just Published' in the London *Gazette* on 20 Sept. and 17 and 24 Nov. 1709. A copy of the 1710 English edition, as well as a copy of the French edition in 3 volumes (Amsterdam, 1702, folio), is in the Sale Catalogue of Addison's library. According to *Addisoniana,* 1803, i. 207, 'old Jacob Tonson used to tell, that he seldom called upon Addison when he did not see Bayle's Dictionary lying open upon his table'. Many of the historical anecdotes in the *Spectator* can in fact be traced to the *Dictionary.*

[5] W. Wall, vicar of Shoreham, Kent, published his *History of Infant Baptism* in 1705. It was in two parts: the first, 'an Impartial Collection of all such Passages in the Writers of the four first Centuries as do make For, or Against it'; the second, 'Containing several things that do illustrate the said History'. A second edition, 'with large Additions', appeared in 1707. John Gale's *Reflections on Mr. Wall's History of Infant-Baptism, in several Letters to a Friend,* is advertised as 'lately publish'd' in the *Post Boy,* 4 Dec. 1711.

tunate with me, to recommend to all my Female Readers, *The finishing Stroke: Being a Vindication of the Patriarchal Scheme, &c.*[1]

In the second Class I shall mention Books which are recommended by Husbands, if I may believe the Writers of them. Whether or no they are real Husbands or personated ones I cannot tell, but the Books they recommend are as follow. *A Paraphrase on the History of Susanna.*[2] *Rules to keep Lent.*[3] *The Christians Overthrow prevented.*[4] *A Dissuasive from the Play-house.*[5] *The Virtues of Camphire,*[6] *with Directions to make Camphire Tea. The Pleasures of a Country Life.*[7] *The Government of the Tongue.*[8] A Letter dated from *Cheapside* desires me that I would advise all young Wives to make themselves Mistresses of *Wingate's Arithmetick,*[9] and concludes with a Postscript, that he hopes I will not forget *The Countess of Kent's Receipts.*[10]

[1] *The Finishing Stroke, being a Vindication of the Patriarchal Scheme of Government*, was written by Charles Leslie, the nonjuror and Jacobite. The subtitle reads, 'Wherein Mr. Hoadly's Examination of this Scheme in his late Book of the Original and Institution of Civil Government, is fully consider'd. To which are added, Remarks on Dr. Higden's late Defence. . . .' Leslie's book had been published only a month before this essay appeared. It is advertised as 'this day published' in the *Daily Courant* of 17 May.

[2] One of Powell's puppet-shows was entitled 'The History of Chast Susannah, and the two wicked Elders: the Figures being drest in Hebrew and Babilonian Habits . . .' (advertised in *Post-Man*, 16 Nov. 1710). 'The Chast Susanna; or, The Court of Babylon' was also given by Powell in Dec. 1711 (advertisements in *Daily Courant*, 3 to 8 Dec.).

[3] This title would apply to many devotional works advertised as suitable for the period of Lent. One such popular book was *Enter into thy Closet: the Method and Order for Private Devotion*, the 7th edition of which is advertised in the *Daily Courant*, 8 Apr. 1712, under the head 'Proper for the Time of Lent'.

[4] *The Christian's Overthrow Prevented, and Conquest Gain'd* is the title of a sermon preached before the Queen at St. James's Chapel on 22 Apr. 1705, by Robert Moss, D.D. It was published on 9 May 1705 (*Daily Courant*). The British Museum has also a copy of the 3rd edition, 1707, and another edition dated 1710. Moss, who became Dean of Ely, was also author of the charity sermon published in 1708 under the title, *The Providential Division of Men into Rich and Poor*.

[5] Jeremy Collier's book, published in 1703; the subtitle reads: 'in a Letter to a Person of Quality, Occasion'd By the late Calamity of the Tempest.' An enlarged edition appeared in 1704.

[6] No separate publication with this title has been found, but there were various articles on camphor in the *Philosophical Transactions*.

[7] This work, if it refers to a separate publication, has not been identified.

[8] *The Government of the Tongue*, 'by that celebrated Author of The Whole Duty of Man', is mentioned in *Tatler* 74. Another work by Richard Allestree, *The Ladies Calling*, was in Leonora's library (No. 37). *The Government of the Tongue* was a popular work. The Newberry Library has a copy of the 3rd impression (Oxford, 1675) and the 5th impression (Oxford, 1677). Steele reprints passages from it (on detraction) in vol. i of *The Ladies Library* in 1714.

[9] Edmund Wingate's *Arithmetique made easie* was published in 1630 and was often reprinted. The 11th edition of *Mr. Wingate's Arithmetick . . .*, revised and improved by John Kersey, with a new supplement by George Shelley, writing-master, appeared in 1704. A 12th edition is advertised in the *Daily Courant* of 22 Apr. 1708.

[10] A very popular collection attributed to Elizabeth Grey (1581–1651), wife of the 7th Earl of Kent (see *DNB*). The 21st edition is advertised in the *Daily Courant*, 26 Aug. 1707, and is still being advertised in 1710: *The Countess of Kent's Choice Manual;*

I may reckon the Ladies themselves as a third Class among these my Correspondents and Privy-Counsellors. In a Letter from one of them, I am advised to place *Pharamond*[1] at the Head of my Catalogue, and, if I think proper, to give the second Place to *Cassandra*.[2] *Coquettilla* begs me not to think of nailing Women upon their Knees with Manuals of Devotion, nor of scorching their Faces with Books of Housewifery. *Florella* desires to know if there are any Books written against Prudes, and intreats me, if there are, to give them a Place in my Library. Plays of all Sorts have their several Advocates: *All for Love*[3] is mentioned in above fifteen Letters; *Sophonisba, or* Hannibal's *Overthrow*,[4] in a Dozen; the *Innocent Adultery*[5] is likewise highly approved of: Mithridates *King of* Pontus[6] has many Friends; Alexander *the Great*[7] and *Aurenzebe*[8] have the same Number of Voices; but Theodosius, *or the Force of Love*,[9] carries it from all the rest.

I should, in the last Place, mention such Books as have been proposed by Men of Learning, and those who appear competent Judges of this Matter; and must here take Occasion to thank *A. B.*[10] whoever it is that conceals himself under those two Letters, for his Advice upon this Subject: But as I find the Work I have undertaken to be very difficult, I shall defer the executing of it till I am further acquainted with the Thoughts of my judicious Contemporaries, and have Time to examine the several Books they offer to me; being resolved, in an Affair of this Moment, to proceed with the greatest Caution.

In the mean while, as I have taken the Ladies under my particular

---

or, *Rare and Select Secrets in Physick and Surgery; With exquisite Ways of Preserving, Conserving, Candying and Cookery* (*Daily Courant*, 11 Aug.).

[1] See No. 76.

[2] See No. 37.

[3] *All for Love*, Dryden's tragedy, had been revived at Drury Lane on 2 May 1709, with Thurmond and Mrs. Knight in the chief parts.

[4] *Sophonisba, or Hannibal's Overthrow*, by Nathaniel Lee, always appeared, according to Langbaine, 'with applause, especially from the fair sex'. It had been given most recently at Drury Lane on 31 Dec. 1709.

[5] The subtitle of *The Fatal Marriage*, by Thomas Southerne. It had been performed at the Haymarket on 14 Nov. 1710, and more recently at Drury Lane on 1 May 1711.

[6] *Mithridates King of Pontus*, another tragedy by Lee, was given at Drury Lane on 14 Feb. 1708, and at Penkethman's Theatre at Greenwich on 20 June 1709.

[7] *The Death of Alexander the Great* is the subtitle of *The Rival Queens*, also by Lee. See Nos. 31, 36, 39.

[8] *Aureng-Zebe*, Dryden's tragedy, had been played recently at Drury Lane, on 24 Feb.

[9] *Theodosius, or the Force of Love*, by Nathaniel Lee. It was given at the Haymarket on 3 Apr. 1707 ('never acted there before'), for the benefit of Booth.

[10] Aitken suggests that the initials may stand for Alexander Bayne (d. 1737), the professor of Scots Law at Edinburgh. At this time he was an advocate living in London, and his name is in the list of subscribers to the 8vo edition of the *Spectator*.

Care, I shall make it my Business to find out in the best Authors ancient and modern such Passages as may be for their use, and endeavour to accommodate them as well as I can to their Taste; not questioning but the valuable Part of the Sex will easily pardon me, if from Time to Time I laugh at those little Vanities and Follies which appear in the Behaviour of some of them, and which are more proper for Ridicule than a serious Censure. Most Books being calculated for Male Readers, and generally written with an Eye to Men of Learning, makes a Work of this Nature the more necessary; besides, I am the more encouraged, because I flatter my self that I see the Sex daily improving by these my Speculations. My fair Readers are already deeper Scholars than the Beaus: I could name some of them who[a] talk much better than several Gentlemen that make a Figure at *Will's*;[1] and as I frequently receive Letters from the *fine Ladies* and *pretty Fellows*,[2] I cannot but observe that the former are superior to the others not only in the Sense but in the Spelling. This cannot but have a good Effect upon the female World, and keep them from being charmed by those empty Coxcombs that have hitherto been admired among the Women, tho' laugh'd at among the Men.

I am credibly informed that *Tom Tattle* passes for an impertinent Fellow, that *Will Trippit* begins to be smoaked,[3] and that *Frank Smoothly* himself is within a Month of a Coxcomb, in case I think fit to continue this Paper. For my Part, as it is my Business in some Measure to detect such as would lead astray weak Minds by[b] their false Pretences to Wit and Judgment, Humour and Gallantry, I shall not fail to lend the best Lights I am able to the fair Sex for the Continuation of these their Discoveries.   L

a who] that *Fol.*   b by] with *Fol.*

---

[1] See No. 1.

[2] For 'that Animal we call a *Pretty Fellow*' see *Tatler* 21. 'The humble petition of the Beaus, Smarts, and Pretty-fellows, in and about London and Westminster' appears in Lillie (i. 345–6). 'There is some amongst us who are ready to testify under our hands, that they have not so much as taken up a fan, been offered a pinch of snuff, or received a smile from any lady ever since the 15th of June' (p. 345).

[3] The word had several meanings at this time, all marked *Arch.* by *OED*. Here it seems to mean simply 'to get an inkling of, to smell or suspect'.

No. 93   *Saturday, June 16, 1711*[1]

[ADDISON]

> . . . *Spatio brevi*
> *Spem longam reseces: dum loquimur, fugerit Invida*
> *Ætas: carpe Diem, quàm minimum credula postero.*
>   Hor.

WE all of us complain of the Shortness of Time,[a] saith *Seneca*,[2] and yet have much more than we know what to do with. Our Lives, says he, are spent either in doing nothing at all, or in doing nothing to the purpose, or in doing nothing that we ought to do: We are always Complaining our[b] Days are few, and Acting as though there would be no End of them. That noble Philosopher has described our Inconsistency with our selves in this Particular by all those various turns of Expression and Thought which are peculiar to his Writings.

I often consider Mankind as wholly inconsistent with it self in a Point that bears some Affinity to the former. Though we seem grieved at the Shortness of Life[3] in general, we are wishing every Period of it at an end. The Minor longs to be at Age, then to be a Man of Business, then to make up an Estate, then to arrive at Honours, then to retire. Thus although the whole of Life is allowed by every one to be short, the several Divisions of it appear long and tedious. We are for lengthening our Span in general, but would fain

---

[a] of Time,] of our Time, *Fol.*   [b] Complaining our] Complaining that our *Fol.*

Motto. Horace, *Odes*, I. 11. 6–8:
> . . . Cut off long Cares
> From thy contracted Span,
> Nor stretch extensive Hopes and Fears
> Beyond a Man:
> E'en whilst we speak, the envious Time
> Doth make swift haste away;
> Then seize the Present, use thy Prime,
> Nor trust another Day.   CREECH.

[2] *De brevitate vitae* (*Moral Essays*, 10. I. I). Cf. also Cowley's essay, 'Of Solitude'.
[3] A letter signed Clorinda (Lillie, i. 351–2), written apparently after the close of the first series of the *Spectator*, refers to this number: 'The promise you have made of appearing again in print makes us acknowledge ourselves, wishing to contract that period of time, and demonstrate to us what you have so excellently described in your late ingenious paper: viz. the inconsistency of ourselves, who are complaining of the shortness of life in general, and yet wishing each period at an end.'

contract the Parts of which it is composed. The Usurer would be very well satisfyed to have all the Time annihilated that lies between the present Moment and next Quarter-day. The Politician would be contented to lose three Years in his Life, could he place things in the Posture which he fancies they will stand in after such a Revolution of Time. The Lover would be glad to strike out of his Existence all the Moments that are to pass away before the happy Meeting. Thus, as fast as our Time runs, we should be very glad in most parts of our Lives that it ran much faster than it does. Several Hours of the Day hang upon our Hands, nay we wish away whole Years, and travel through Time as through a Country filled[a] with many wild and empty Wastes, which we would fain hurry over, that we may arrive at those several little Settlements or imaginary Points of Rest which are dispersed up and down in it.

If we divide the Life of most Men into twenty Parts, we shall find that at least nineteen of them are meer Gaps and Chasms, which are neither filled with Pleasure nor Business. I do not however include in this Calculation the Life of those Men who are in a perpetual Hurry of Affairs, but of those only who are not always engaged in Scenes of Action; and I hope I shall not do an unacceptable piece of Service to these Persons, if I point out to them certain Methods for the filling up their empty Spaces of Life. The[b] Methods I shall propose to them, are as follow.

The first is the Exercise of Virtue, in the most general Acceptation of the Word. That Particular Scheme which comprehends the Social Virtues may give Employment to the most industrious Temper, and find a Man in Business more than the most active Station of Life. To advise the Ignorant, relieve the Needy, comfort the Afflicted, are Duties that fall in our way almost every Day of our Lives. A Man has frequent Opportunities of mitigating the Fierceness of a Party; of doing Justice to the Character of a deserving Man; of softning the Envious, quieting the Angry, and rectifying the Prejudiced, which are all of them Employments suited to a reasonable Nature, and bring great Satisfaction to the Person who[c] can busy himself in them with Discretion.

There is another kind of Virtue that[d] may find Employment for those Retired Hours in which we are altogether left to our selves, and destitute of Company and Conversation; I mean, that Intercourse

---

[a] Country filled] Country that is filled *Fol.*   [b] The] These *Fol.*   [c] who that *Fol.*   [d] that] which *Fol.*

and Communication which every reasonable Creature ought to maintain with the great Author of his Being. The Man who lives under an habitual Sense of the Divine Presence keeps up a perpetual Cheerfulness of Temper, and enjoys every Moment the Satisfaction of thinking himself in Company with his dearest and best of Friends. The Time never lies heavy upon him: It is impossible for him to be alone. His Thoughts and Passions are the most busied at such Hours when those of other Men are the most unactive; he no sooner steps out of the World but his Heart burns with Devotion, swells with Hope, and triumphs in the Consciousness of that Presence which every where surrounds him; or, on the contrary, pours out its Fears, its Sorrows, its Apprehensions to the great Supporter of its Existence.

I have here only considered the Necessity of a Man's being Virtuous, that he may have something to do; but if we consider further that the Exercise of Virtue is not only an Amusement[1] for the time it lasts, but that its Influence extends to those Parts of our Existence which[a] lie beyond the Grave, and that our whole Eternity is to take its Colour from those Hours which we here employ in Virtue or in Vice, the Argument redoubles upon us for putting in Practice this Method of passing away our Time.

When a Man has but a little Stock to improve, and has Opportunities of turning it all to good Account, what shall we think of him if he suffers nineteen Parts of it to lie dead, and perhaps employs even the twentieth to his Ruin or Disadvantage? But because the Mind cannot be always in its Fervours, nor strained up to a pitch of Virtue, it is necessary to find out proper Employments for it in its Relaxations.

The next Method therefore that I would propose to fill up our Time should be useful and innocent Diversions. I must confess I think it is below reasonable Creatures to be altogether conversant in such Diversions as are meerly innocent, and have nothing else to recommend them, but that there is no hurt in them. Whether any kind of Gaming has even thus much to say for its self I shall not determine; but I think it is very wonderful to see Persons of the best Sense passing away a dozen Hours together in shuffling and dividing a Pack of Cards, with no other Conversation but what is made

---

[a] which] that *Fol.*

[1] The obsolete meaning of *amuse*, in the sense of engaging, arresting, or occupying the attention of.

up of a few Game Phrases, and[a] no other Ideas but those of black or red Spots ranged together in different Figures. Would not a Man laugh to hear any one of this Species complaining that Life is short?

The *Stage* might be made a perpetual Source of the most noble and useful Entertainments, were it under proper Regulations.

But the Mind never unbends it self so agreeably as in the Conversation of a well chosen Friend. There is indeed no Blessing of Life that is any way comparable to the Enjoyment of a discreet and virtuous Friend. It eases and unloads the Mind, clears and improves the Understanding, engenders Thoughts and Knowledge, animates Virtue and good Resolutions, sooths and allays the Passions, and finds Employment for most of the vacant Hours of Life.

Next to such an Intimacy with a particular Person, one would endeavour after a more general Conversation with such as are able to entertain and improve those with whom they converse, which are Qualifications that seldom go asunder.

There are many other useful Amusements of Life, which one would endeavour to multiply, that one might on all Occasions have Recourse to something, rather than suffer the Mind to lie idle, or run adrift with any Passion that chances to rise in it.

A Man that has a Taste of Musick, Painting, or Architecture, is like one that has another Sense, when compared with such as have no Relish of those Arts. The Florist, the Planter, the Gard'ner, the Husbandman,[1] when they are only as Accomplishments to the Man of Fortune, are great Reliefs to a Country Life, and many ways useful to those who are possessed of them.

But of all the Diversions of Life, there is none so proper to fill up its empty Spaces as the reading of useful and entertaining Authors.[2] But this I shall only touch upon, because it in some measure interferes with the third Method, which I shall propose in another Paper, for the Employment of our dead unactive Hours, and which I shall only mention in general to be the Pursuit of Knowledge.   L

[a] and] or *Fol.*

---

[1] The Florist . . ., i.e. the skill, the knowledge, or the industry of . . . .
[2] A letter signed M. J. in Lillie (i. 343–4) reminds Mr. Spectator of his promised discourse 'on the advantage of reading, towards filling up the empty spaces of life', and requests his opinion on men who spend their time at the booksellers' shops and spend money 'for the shining dawbing profusely spread on the back and leaves of an imperial folio'.

No. 94
[ADDISON]

Monday, June 18, 1711[1]

... *Hoc est*
Vivere bis, vita posse priore frui.
Mart.

THE last Method which I proposed in my *Saturday*'s Paper, for
filling up those empty Spaces of Life which are so tedious and
burthensome to idle People, is the employing our selves in the Pursuit of Knowledge. I remember Mr. *Boyle*,[2] speaking of a certain
Mineral, tells us, That a Man may consume his whole Life in the
Study of it, without arriving at the Knowledge of all its Qualities.
The Truth of it is, there is not a single Science, or any Branch of it,
that might not furnish a Man with Business for Life, though it were
much longer than it is.

I shall not here engage on those beaten Subjects of the Usefulness
of Knowledge, nor of the Pleasure and Perfection it[a] gives the Mind,
nor on the Methods of attaining it, nor recommend any particular
Branch of it, all which have been the Topicks of many other Writers;
but shall indulge my self in a Speculation that is more uncommon,
and may therefore perhaps be more entertaining.

I have before shewn how the unemployed Parts of Life appear long
and tedious, and shall here endeavour to shew how those Parts of
Life which[b] are exercised in Study, Reading, and the Pursuits of
Knowledge are long but not tedious; and by that Means discover
a Method of lengthening our Lives, and at the same Time of turning
all the Parts of them to our Advantage.

---

^a Perfection it] Perfection that it *Fol.*   ^b which] that *Fol.*

---

[1] *Motto.* Martial, *Epigrams*, 10. 23. 7–8: This it is to live twice, to be able to enjoy
life past.
[2] Robert Boyle, *Some Considerations touching the Usefulness of Experimental Naturall
Philosophy* (Oxford, 1664), pp. 12–13:

Basilius Valentinus . . . publisht long since an excellent Treatise of Antimony,
inscribed *Currus Triumphalis Antimonii.* . . . He gives this account of his leaving
many things unmention'd, *That the Shortness of Life makes it impossible for one man
thoroughly to learn Antimony, in which every Day something of new is discovered,* and so
pregnant is each of that vast multitude of Creatures, that make up the Naturalists
Theme, with usefull matter to employ Mens studie, that I dare say, that the whole
life of a Philosopher spent in that alone, would be too short to give a full and perfect account of the Natural Properties and Uses of any one of several Minerals,
Plants, or Animals, that I could name.

Mr. *Lock*[1] observes, 'That we get the Idea of Time, or Duration, by reflecting on that Train of Ideas which succeed one another in our Minds: That for this Reason, when we sleep soundly without dreaming, we have no Perception of Time, or the Length of it, whilst we sleep; and that the Moment wherein we leave off to think, till the Moment we begin to think again, seem to have no Distance.' To which the Author adds; 'And so, I doubt not, but it would be to a waking Man, if it were possible for him to keep only one *Idea* in his Mind, without Variation, and the Succession of others: And we see, that one who fixes his Thoughts very intently on one thing, so as to take but little Notice of the Succession of *Ideas* that pass in his Mind whilst he is taken up with that earnest Contemplation, lets slip out of his Account a good Part of that Duration, and thinks that Time shorter than it is.'

We might carry this Thought further, and consider a Man as, on one Side, shortening his Time by thinking on nothing, or but a few things; so, on the other, as lengthening it, by employing his Thoughts on many Subjects, or by entertaining a quick and constant Succession of Ideas. Accordingly Monsieur *Mallebranche*,[2] in his *Enquiry after Truth*, (which was published several Years before Mr. *Lock's Essay on Humane Understanding*) tells us, That it is possible some Creatures may think Half an Hour as long as we do a thousand Years; or look upon that Space of Duration which we call a Minute, as an Hour, a Week, a Month, or an whole Age.

This Notion of Monsieur *Mallebranche* is capable of some little Explanation from what I have quoted out of Mr. *Lock*; for if our Notion of Time is produced by our reflecting on the Succession of Ideas in our Mind, and this Succession may be infinitely accelerated or retarded, it will follow, that different Beings may have different Notions of the same Parts of Duration, according as their Ideas, which we suppose are equally distinct in each of them, follow one another in a greater or less Degree of Rapidity.

[1] *Essay concerning Humane Understanding*, II. xiv. 4. The first sentence is a paraphrase of Locke, the remainder a direct quotation. Addison characteristically 'carries this thought further' into more imaginative paths. Cf. Jean-Claude Sallé in *RES*, N.S., vi (1955), 180–2.

[2] *Father Malebranche His Treatise concerning the Search after Truth*, trans. T. Taylor, bk. i, chap. viii (2nd ed., 1700), p. 20:

> At certain times one Hour seems to us as long as four; and on the contrary at other times, four Hours slip insensibly away: When, for Instance, a Man's Mind is fill'd with Joy, Hours seem no longer than a Moment; because then the time passes away without thinking of it. But when a Man is dejected with Grief, and lies under some sensible Pain or Affliction, every day is thought an entire Year.

399

There is a famous Passage in the *Alcoran*[1] which looks as if *Mahomet* had been possessed of the Notion we are now speaking of. It is there said, That the Angel *Gabriel* took *Mahomet* out of his Bed one Morning to give him a Sight of all things in the seven Heavens, in Paradise, and in Hell, which the Prophet took a distinct View of; and after having held ninety thousand Conferences with God, was brought back again to his Bed. All this, says the *Alcoran*, was transacted in so small a Space of Time, that *Mahomet*, at his Return, found his Bed still warm, and took up an Earthen Pitcher (which was thrown down at the very Instant that the Angel *Gabriel* carried him away) before the Water was all spilt.

There is a very pretty Story[2] in the *Turkish* Tales which relates to this Passage of that famous Impostor, and bears some Affinity to the Subject we are now upon. A Sultan of *Ægypt*, who was an Infidel, used to laugh at this Circumstance in *Mahomet's* Life, as what was altogether impossible and absurd: But conversing one Day with a great Doctor in the Law, who had the Gift of working Miracles, the Doctor told him, he would quickly convince him of the Truth of this Passage in the History of *Mahomet*, if he would consent to do what he should desire of him. Upon this the Sultan was directed to place himself by an huge Tub of Water, which he did accordingly; and as he stood by the Tub amidst a Circle of his great Men, the holy Man bid him plunge his Head into the Water and draw it up again: The King accordingly thrust his Head into the Water, and at the same time found himself at the Foot of a Mountain on a Sea-shore. The King immediately began to rage against his Doctor for this Piece of Treachery and Witchcraft; but at length, knowing it was in vain to be angry, he set himself to think on proper Methods for getting a Livelihood in this strange Country: Accordingly he applied himself to some People whom he saw at work in a neighbouring Wood; these People conducted him to a Town that stood at a little Distance

---

[1] Although chap. xvii of the *Koran*, 'The Chapter of the Night Journey', refers to Mohammed's journey by night to Jerusalem, the story told here comes verbatim from *Turkish Tales; consisting of several extraordinary Adventures; with the History of the Sultaness of Persia and the Visier's. Written originally in the Turkish Language, by Chec Zade, for the Use of Amurath the Second: Now done into English* (printed for Jacob Tonson, 1708). It is advertised in the *Gazette* and *Post-Man* of 4 Dec. 1707 as 'this day published'. The French edition (*Histoire de la Sultane de Perse & des Visirs*, 1707) by Pétis de la Croix was reviewed in the *History of the Works of the Learned* in June 1707 (pp. 338-41). The passage quoted here is from 'The History of Chec Chahabeddin' (*Turkish Tales*, pp. 18-19).

[2] This too is from 'The History of Chec Chahabeddin' in the *Turkish Tales* (pp. 25-41).

from the Wood, where after some Adventures he married a Woman of great Beauty and Fortune. He lived with this Woman so long till he had by her seven Sons and seven Daughters: He was afterwards reduced to great Want, and forced to think of plying in the Streets as a Porter for his Livelihood. One Day as he was walking alone by the Sea-Side, being seized with many melancholy Reflections upon his former and his present State of Life, which had raised a Fit of Devotion in him, he threw off his Cloaths with a Design to wash himself, according to the Custom of the *Mahometans*, before he said his Prayers.

After his first Plunge into the Sea, he no sooner raised his Head above the Water, but he found himself standing by the Side of the Tub, with the great Men of his Court about him, and the holy Man at his Side: He immediately upbraided his Teacher for having sent him on such a Course of Adventures, and betray'd him into so long a State of Misery and Servitude; but was wonderfully surprized when he heard that the State he talked of was only a Dream and Delusion; that he had not stirred from the Place where he then stood; and that he had only dipped his Head into the Water, and immediately taken it out again.

The *Mahometan* Doctor took this Occasion of instructing the Sultan, that nothing was impossible with God; and that *He*, with whom a Thousand Years are but as one Day, can if he pleases make a single Day, nay a single Moment, appear to any of his Creatures as a thousand Years.

I shall leave my Reader to compare these Eastern Fables with the Notions of those two great Philosophers whom I have quoted in this Paper; and shall only, by way of Application, desire him to consider how we may extend Life beyond its natural Dimensions, by applying ourselves diligently to the Pursuits of Knowledge.

The Hours of a wise Man are lengthened by his Ideas, as those of a Fool are by his Passions: The Time of the one is long, because he does not know what to do with it; so is that[a] of the other, because he distinguishes every Moment of it with some useful or amusing Thought; or in other Words, because the one is always wishing it away, and the other always enjoying it.

How different is the View of past Life, in the Man who is grown old in Knowledge and Wisdom, from that of him who is grown old in Ignorance and Folly? The latter is like the Owner of a barren

---

[a] with it; so is that] with it; that *Fol.*

Country, that fills his Eye with the Prospect of naked Hills and Plains which produce nothing either[a] profitable or ornamental; the other beholds a beautiful and spacious Landskip divided into delightful Gardens, green Meadows, fruitful Fields, and can scarce cast his Eye on a single Spot of his Possessions, that is not covered with some beautiful Plant or Flower. L

No. 95
[STEELE]

Tuesday, June 19, 1711[1]

Curæ Leves loquuntur, Ingentes Stupent.

HAVING read the two following Letters with much Pleasure, I cannot but think the good Sense of them will be as agreeable to the Town as any thing I could say either on the Topicks they treat of, or any other. They both allude to former Papers of mine, and I do not question but the first, which is upon inward Mourning, will be thought the Production of a Man, who is well acquainted with the generous Earnings[2] of Distress in a Manly Temper, which is above the Relief of Tears. A Speculation of my own on that Subject I shall defer 'till another Occasion.

The second Letter is from a Lady of a Mind as great as her Understanding. There is, perhaps, something in the beginning of it, which I ought in Modesty to conceal; but I have so much Esteem for this Correspondent, that I will not alter a Tittle of what she writes, tho' I am thus Scrupulous at the Price of being Ridiculous.

Mr. SPECTATOR,

'I WAS very well pleased with your Discourse upon General Mourning,[3] and should be obliged to you, if you would enter into the Matter more deeply, and give us your Thoughts upon the common Sense the ordinary People have of the Demonstrations of Grief, who prescribe Rules and Fashions to the most solemn Afflic-

---

[a] nothing either] nothing that is either *Fol.*

---

[1] *Motto.* Seneca, *Hippolytus,* 607: Light cares speak, great ones are benumbed.
[2] The obsolete form of *yearnings.* This quotation is the last given in *OED* for this form of the word. Cf. No. 340 (vol. iii), where the *Folio* reads 'an earning Curiosity', the 8vo and 12mo 'a yearning Curiosity'.
[3] No. 64.

tion; such as the Loss of the nearest Relations and dearest Friends. You cannot go to visit a sick Friend, but some impertinent Waiter[1] about him observes the Muscles of your Face, as strictly as if they were Prognosticks of his Death or Recovery. If he happens to be taken from you, you are immediately surrounded with Numbers of these Spectators, who expect a melancholy Shrug of your Shoulders, a Pathetical Shake of your Head, and an Expressive Distortion of your Face, to measure your Affection and Value for the Deceased: But there is nothing, on these Occasions, so much in their Favour as immoderate Weeping. As all their Passions are superficial, they imagine the Seat of Love and Friendship to be placed visibly in the Eyes: They judge what Stock of Kindness you had for the Living, by the quantity of Tears you pour out for the Dead; so that if one Body wants that Quantity of Salt-water another abounds with, he is in great Danger of being thought insensible or ill-natured. They are Strangers to Friendship, whose Grief happens not to be moist enough to wet such a Parcel of Handkerchiefs. But Experience has told us nothing is so fallacious as this outward Sign of Sorrow; and the natural History of our Bodies will teach us, that this Flux of the Eyes, this Faculty of weeping is peculiar only to some Constitutions. We observe in the tender Bodies of Children, when crossed in their little Wills and Expectations, how dissolvable they are into Tears. If this were what Grief is in Men, Nature would not be able to support them in the Excess of it for one Moment. Add to this Observation, how quick is their Transition from this Passion to that of their Joy. I won't say we see often, in the next tender things to Children, Tears shed without much grieving. Thus it is common to shed Tears without much Sorrow, and as common to suffer much Sorrow without shedding Tears. Grief and Weeping are indeed frequent Companions, but, I believe, never in their highest Excesses. As Laughter does not proceed from profound Joy, so neither does Weeping from profound Sorrow. The Sorrow which appears so easily at the Eyes, cannot have pierced deeply into the Heart. The Heart, distended with Grief, stops all the Passages for Tears or Lamentations.

'Now, Sir, what I would incline you to in all this is, that you would inform the shallow Criticks and Observers upon Sorrow, that true Affliction labours to be invisible, that it is a Stranger to Ceremony, and that it bears in its own Nature a Dignity much above the

[1] See No. 84.

little Circumstances, which are affected under the Notion of Decency. You must know, Sir, I have lately lost a dear Friend, for whom I have not yet shed a Tear, and for that Reason your Animadversions on that Subject would be the more acceptable to,

SIR,

Your most Humble Servant,

B. D.'

Mr. SPECTATOR, June *the* 15*th*.

' AS I hope there are but few that have so little Gratitude as not to acknowledge the Usefulness of your Pen, and to esteem it a Publick Benefit, so I am sensible, be that as it will, you must nevertheless find the Secret and Incomparable Pleasure of doing Good, and be a great Sharer in the Entertainment you give. I acknowledge our Sex to be much obliged, and I hope improved, by your Labours, and even your Intentions more particularly for our Service. If it be true, as 'tis sometimes said, that our Sex have an Influence on the other, your Paper may be a yet more general Good. Your directing us to Reading is certainly the best Means to our Instruction; but I think, with you, Caution in that Particular very useful, since the Improvement of our Understandings may, or may not, be of Service to us, according as it is managed. It has been thought we are not generally so Ignorant as Ill-taught, or that our Sex does so often want Wit, Judgment, or Knowledge, as the right Application of them: You are so well-bred, as to say your fair Readers are already deeper Scholars[1] than the Beaus, and that you could name some of them that talk much better than several Gentlemen that make a Figure at *Will*'s: This may possibly be, and no great Compliment, in my Opinion, even supposing your Comparison to reach *Tom*'s,[2] and the *Grecian*: Sure you are too wise to think That a Real Commendation of a Woman. Were it not rather to be wished we improved in our own Sphere, and approved our selves better Daughters, Wives, Mothers and Friends?

'I can't but agree with the Judicious Trader in *Cheapside*[3] (though I am not at all prejudiced in his Favour) in recommending the Study of Arithmetick; and must dissent even from the Authority which you mention, when it advises the making our Sex Scholars. Indeed

[1] No. 92.
[2] There were several coffee-houses of this name. This probably refers to the one in Russell Street, Covent Garden (see Austin Dobson, 'The Tour of Covent Garden', *Eighteenth-century Vignettes*, iii. 340).
[3] No. 92.

a little more Philosophy, in order to the Subduing our Passions to our Reason, might be sometimes serviceable, and a Treatise of that Nature I should approve of, even in Exchange for *Theodosius, or the Force of Love*; but as I well know you want not Hints, I will proceed no further than to recommend the Bishop of *Cambray's*[1] Education of a Daughter, as 'tis Translated into the only Language I have any Knowledge of, tho' perhaps very much to its Disadvantage. I have heard it objected against that Piece, that its Instructions are not of General Use, but only fitted for a great Lady; but I confess I am not of that Opinion; for I don't remember that there are any Rules laid down for the Expences of a Woman, in which Particular only I think a Gentlewoman ought to differ from a Lady of the best Fortune, or Highest Quality, and not in their Principles of Justice, Gratitude, Sincerity, Prudence or Modesty. I ought perhaps to make an Apology for this long Epistle, but as I rather believe you a Friend to Sincerity, than Ceremony, shall only Assure you I am,

SIR,

Your Most Humble Servant,

Annabella.'[2]

T

No. 96   *Wednesday, June 20, 1711*[3]

STEELE]

. . . *amicum*

Mancipium domino, & frugi . . .

Hor.

Mr. SPECTATOR,

'I HAVE frequently read your Discourse upon Servants,[4] and, as I am one my self, have been much offended that in that Variety of

[1] Fénelon's treatise, *De l'éducation des filles* (1687), was in a sense 'only fitted for a great Lady', since it was written for the eight daughters of the Duchesse de Beau-villiers. It was translated into English and revised by Dr. George Hickes in 1707 as *Instructions for the Education of a Daughter, by the Author of Telemachus.* The 2nd edition (*A New Year's Gift for Young Ladies: being Instructions for the Education of a Daughter . . .*) is advertised in the *Daily Courant*, 1 Jan. 1711, as 'this day published'. Steele quotes extensively from it in *The Ladies Library.*

[2] Cf. No. 53.

[3] *Motto.* Horace. *Satires*, 2. 7. 2–3:
The faithful Servant and the true. CREECH.

[4] No. 88.

Forms wherein you considered the Bad, you found no Place to mention the Good. There is however one Observation of yours I approve, which is, That there are Men of Wit and good Sense among all Orders of Men; and that Servants report most of the Good or Ill which is spoken of their Masters. That there are Men of Sense who live in Servitude, I have the Vanity to say I have felt to my woful Experience. You attribute very justly the Source of our general Iniquity to Board-Wages, and the Manner of living out of a domestick Way: But I cannot give you my Thoughts on this Subject any Way so well, as by a short Account of my own Life to this the Forty fifth Year of my Age; that is to say, from my being first a Foot-boy at Fourteen, to my present Station of a Nobleman's Porter in the Year of my Age above-mentioned.

'Know then, that my Father was a poor Tenant to the Family of Sir *Stephen Rackrent*: Sir *Stephen* put me to School, or rather made me follow his Son *Harry* to School, from my Ninth Year; and there, though Sir *Stephen* paid something for my Learning, I was used like a Servant, and was forc'd to get what Scraps of Learning I could by my own Industry, for the Schoolmaster took very little Notice of me. My young Master was a Lad of very sprightly Parts, and my being constantly about him and loving him, was no small Advantage to me. My Master loved me extremely, and has often been whipped for not keeping me at a Distance. He used always to say, That when he came to his Estate I should have a Lease of my Father's Tenement for nothing. I came up to Town with him to *Westminster* School, at which Time he taught me, at Night, all he learnt; and put me to find out Words in the Dictionary when he was about his Exercise. It was the Will of Providence that Master *Harry* was taken very ill of a Fever, of which he dyed within Ten Days after his first falling sick. Here was the first Sorrow I ever knew; and I assure you, Mr. SPECTATOR, I remember the beautiful Action of the sweet Youth in his Fever, as fresh as if it were Yesterday. If he wanted any thing, it must be given him by *Tom*: When I let any thing fall through the Grief I was under, he would cry, Do not beat the poor Boy: Give him some more Julep for me, no Body else shall give it me. He would strive to hide his being so bad, when he saw I could not bear his being in so much Danger, and comforted me, saying, "*Tom, Tom*, have a good Heart." When I was holding a Cup at his Mouth he fell into Convulsions; and at this very Time I hear my dear Master's last Groan. I was quickly turned out of the Room, and left to sob and beat my Head against the Wall at my Leisure. The Grief I was in was inexpressible; and every Body thought it would have cost me my Life. In a few Days my old Lady, who was one of the Housewives of the World, thought of turning me out of Doors, because I put her in Mind of her Son. Sir *Stephen* proposed putting me to Prentice, but my Lady being an excellent Manager, would not let her Husband throw away his Money in Acts of Charity. I had Sense enough to be under the utmost Indignation, to see her discard with so little Concern one her Son had loved so much; and went out of the House to ramble wherever my Feet would carry me.

'The third Day after I left Sir *Stephen's* Family, I was strolling up and down the Walks in the *Temple*: A young Gentleman of the House, who (as I heard him say afterwards) seeing me half starved and well dressed, thought me an Equipage ready to his Hand, after very little Enquiry more than *did I want a Master?* bid me follow him: I did so, and in a very little while thought my self the happiest Creature in this World. My Time was taken up in carrying Letters to Wenches, or Messages to young Ladies of my Master's Acquaintance. We rambled from Tavern to Tavern, to the Play-house, the Mulberry-garden,[1] and all Places of Resort; where my Master engaged every Night in some new Amour, in which and drinking he spent all his Time when he had Money. During these Extravagancies I had the Pleasure of lying on the Stairs of a Tavern half a Night, playing at Dice with other Servants, and the like Idlenesses. When my Master was moneyless, I was generally employed in transcribing amorous Pieces of Poetry, old Songs, and new Lampoons. This Life held till my Master married, and he had then the Prudence to turn me off because I was in the Secret of his Intreagues.

'I was utterly at a Loss what Course to take next; when at last I applied my self to a Fellow-sufferer, one of his Mistresses, a Woman of the Town.[2] She happening at that Time to be pretty full of Money, cloathed me from Head to Foot, and knowing me to be a sharp Fellow, employed me accordingly. Sometimes I was to go

---

[1] At the north-west corner of St. James's Park, where Buckingham Palace now stands. Evelyn (10 May 1654) had described it as 'the onely place of refreshment about the Towne for persons of the best quality, to be exceedingly cheated at'. See also Sedley's play, *The Mulberry-Garden* (1668). In Shadwell's *Humourists* (Act III) Mrs. Striker, 'a vain fantastick Strumpet', describes a *divertissement* there: 'the Garden was very full, Madam, of Gentlemen and Ladies, that made love together 'till twelve a Clock at Night, the prettily'st: I vow 'twould do one's Heart good to see them.'
[2] The earliest quotation in *OED* is dated 1766.

abroad with her, and when she had pitched upon a young Fellow she thought for her Turn, I was to be dropped as one she could not trust. She would often cheapen Goods at the *New Exchange*,[1] and when she had a Mind to be attacked, she would send me away on an Errand. When an humble Servant and she were beginning a Parley, I came immediately, and told her Sir *John* was come home; then she would order another Coach to prevent being dogged. The Lover makes Signs to me as I get behind the Coach, I shake my Head it was impossible. I leave my Lady at the next Turning, and follow the Cully to know how to fall in his Way on another Occasion. Besides good Offices of this Nature, I writ all my Mistress's Love-letters; some from a Lady that saw such a Gentleman at such a Place in such a coloured Coat, some shewing the Terrour she was in of a jealous old Husband, others explaining that the Severity of her Parents was such (tho' her Fortune was settled) that she was willing to run away with such a one tho' she knew he was but a younger Brother. In a Word, my Half-Education and Love of idle Books, made me outwrite all that made Love to her by way of Epistle; and as she was extremely cunning, she did well enough in Company by a skillful Affectation of the greatest Modesty. In the Midst of all this I was surprised with a Letter from her and a ten Pound Note.

"*Honest* Tom.

"You will never see me more. I am married to a very cunning Country-Gentleman, who might possibly guess something if I kept you still; therefore farewell."

'When this Place was lost also in Marriage, I was resolved to go among quite another People for the Future, and got in Butler to one of those Families where there is a Coach kept, three or four Servants, a clean House and a good general Outside upon a small Estate. Here I lived very comfortably for some Time, till I unfortunately found my Master, the very gravest Man alive, in the Garret with the

---

[1] A bazaar on the south side of the Strand, near Durham Yard, over against the modern Bedford Street. 'It consists of two long *Walks* even with the Street, and two more above Stairs; each of 'em paved with free Stone, and having two *Rows* of *Shops*, in which Goods are sold as in the *Royal-Exchange*. Many Shop-Keepers have got fair Estates here, in their Way of Trade' (Miège, p. 159). According to Hatton (p. 612) it contained about 150 shops above and below stairs, 'about 76 of which are let out to several *Milleners* and some *Mercers*, &c.' Young Bookwit in Steele's *Lying Lover* (II. ii) calls it 'a seraglio, a living gallery of beauties'. Bishop Percy writing to Boswell (5 Mar. 1787) says that Dr. Johnson 'remembered to have once walked through the New Exchange in the Strand, among the milliners' shops mentioned in the Spectator, before that building was pulled down and converted into private houses' (Nichols, *Literary Illustrations*, vii. 307). It was pulled down in 1737.

Chambermaid. I knew the World too well to think of staying there; and the next Day pretended to have received a Letter out of the Country that my Father was dying, and got my Discharge with a Bounty for my Discretion.

'The next I lived with was a peevish single Man, whom I stay'd with for a Year and a Half. Most Part of the Time I passed very easily; for when I began to know him, I minded no more than he meant what he said; so that one Day in good Humour he said, *I was the best Man he ever had, by my want of Respect to him.*

'These, Sir, are the chief Occurrences of my Life; and I will not dwell upon very many other Places I have been in, where I have been the strangest Fellow in the World; where no Body in the World had such Servants as they; where sure they were the unluckiest People in the World in Servants; and so forth. All I mean by this Representation, is, To shew you that we poor Servants, are not (what you called us too generally) all Rogues; but that we are what we are, according to the Example of our Superiors. In the Family I am now in, I am guilty of no one Sin but Lying; which I do with a grave Face in my Gown and Staff every Day I live, and almost all Day long, in denying my Lord to impertinent Suitors, and my Lady to unwelcome Visitants. But, Sir, I am to let you know, that I am, when I can get abroad, a Leader of the Servants:[1] I am he that keep Time with beating my Cudgel against the Boards in the Gallery at an Opera: I am he that am touched so properly at a Tragedy, when the People of Quality are staring at one another during the most important Incidents: When you hear in a Crowd a Cry in the right Place, an Humm where the Point is touched in a Speech, or an Hussa set up where it is the Voice of the People; you may conclude it is begun, or joined by,

Sir,
Your more than humble Servant,
Thomas Trusty.'

T

---

[1] Aitken, in a note to No. 88, quotes the following notice in *The Female Tatler*, 9 Dec. 1709:

Dropt, near the playhouse in the Haymarket, a bundle of horse-whips, designed to belabour the footmen in the upper gallery, who almost every night this winter have made such an intolerable disturbance that the players could not be heard, and their masters were forced to hiss 'em into silence.

No. 97
[STEELE]

Thursday, June 21, 1711[1]

Projecere animas . . .
Virg.

AMONG the loose Papers which I have frequently spoken of here-tofore, I find a Conversation between *Pharamond* and *Eucrate* upon the Subject of Duels, and the Copy of an Edict[2] issued in consequence of that Discourse.

Eucrate argued, That nothing but the most severe and vindictive Punishments, such as placing the Bodies of the Offenders in Chains, and putting them to Death by the most Exquisite Torments, would be sufficient to extirpate a Crime which had so long prevailed, and was so firmly fixed in the Opinion of the World as great and laud-able; but the King answered, That indeed Instances of Ignominy were necessary in the Cure of this Evil, but considering that it pre-vailed only among such as had a Nicety in their Sense of Honour, and that it often happened that a Duel was fought (to save Appear-ances to the World) when both Parties were in their Hearts in Amity and Reconciliation to each other; it was evident, that Turning the Mode another way would effectually put a Stop to what had Being only as a Mode. That to such Persons, Poverty and Shame were Torments sufficient, That he would not go further in punishing in others Crimes which he was satisfied he himself was most Guilty of, in that he might have prevented them by speaking his Displeasure sooner. Besides which the King said, he was in general averse to Tortures, which was putting Human Nature it self, rather than the Criminal, to Disgrace, and that he would be sure not to use this Means where the Crime was but an ill Effect arising from a laudable Cause, the Fear of Shame. The King, at the same time, spoke with much Grace upon the Subject of Mercy, and repented of many Acts of that kind which had a magnificent Aspect in the doing, but dreadful Consequences in the Example. Mercy to Particulars,[3] he observed, was Cruelty in the General: That tho' a Prince could not

---

[1] *Motto.* Virgil, *Aeneid*, 6. 436:
    . . . prodigally throw their Souls away. DRYDEN.

[2] See No. 84.

[3] 'La pitié envers les méchans est une cruauté envers tous les hommes' is one of the 'sentences persanes' in Chardin's *Voyages en Perse, et autres lieux de l'Orient* (Amster-dam, 1711), v. 179.

revive a Dead Man by taking the Life of him who killed him, neither could he make Reparation to the next that should dye by the evil Example; or answer to himself for the Partiality, in not pardoning the next as well as the former Offender. 'As for me, says *Pharamond*, I have conquer'd *France*, and yet have given Laws to my People; the Laws are my Methods of Life, they are not a Diminution but a Direction to my Power. I am still absolute to distinguish the Innocent and the Virtuous, to give Honours to the Brave and Generous: I am absolute in my Good-will, none can oppose my Bounty, or prescribe Rules for my Favour. While I can, as I please, reward the Good, I am under no Pain that I cannot pardon the Wicked: For which Reason, continued *Pharamond*, I will effectually put a stop to this Evil, by exposing no more the Tenderness of my Nature to the Importunity of having the same Respect to those who are miserable by their Fault, and those who are so by their Misfortune. Flatterers (concluded the King smiling) repeat to us Princes, that we are Heaven's Vice-gerents; Let us be so, and let the only thing out of our Power be *to do Ill*.'

Soon after the Evening wherein *Pharamond* and *Eucrate* had this Conversation the following Edict was Publish'd.

Pharamond's Edict against Duels.[1]

Pharamond, *King of the* Gauls, *to all his Loving Subjects sendeth Greeting.*

'Whereas it has come to our Royal Notice and Observation, that in Contempt of all Laws, Divine and Human, it is of late become a Custom among the Nobility and Gentry of this our Kingdom, upon slight and trivial, as well as great and urgent Provocations, to invite each other into the Field, there by their own Hands, and of their own Authority, to decide their Controversies by Combat, we have thought fit to take the said Custom into our Royal Consideration, and find, upon Enquiry into the usual Causes whereon such fatal Decisions have arisen, that by this wicked Custom, maugre all the Precepts of our Holy Religion, and the Rules of right Reason, the greatest Act of the Human Mind, *Forgiveness of Injuries*, is become vile and shameful; that the Rules of Good Society and Virtuous Conversation are hereby inverted; that the Loose, the Vain and the Impudent insult the Careful, the Discreet and the Modest; that all Virtue is suppressed, and all Vice supported, in the one Act

---

[1] For the edicts issued by Louis XIV see No. 99.

of being capable to dare to the Death. We have also further, with great Sorrow of Mind, observed that this Dreadful Action, by long Impunity, (our Royal Attention being employed upon Matters of more general Concern) is become Honourable, and the Refusal to engage in it Ignominious. In these our Royal Cares and Enquiries we are yet farther made to understand, that the Persons of most Eminent Worth, and most Hopeful Abilities, accompanied with the strongest Passion for true Glory, are such as are most liable to be involved in the Dangers arising from this Licence. Now taking the said Premises into our serious Consideration, and well weighing that all such Emergencies (wherein the Mind is incapable of commanding it self, and where the Injury is too sudden or too exquisite to be born) are particularly provided for by Laws heretofore enacted, and that the Qualities of less Injuries, like those of Ingratitude, are too nice and delicate to come under General Rules, We do resolve to Blot this Fashion, or Wantonness of Anger, out of the Minds of our Subjects, by our Royal Resolutions declared in this Edict, as follow.

'No Person who either Sends or Accepts a Challenge, or the Posterity of either, tho' no Death ensues thereupon, shall be, after the Publication of this our Edict, capable of bearing Office in these our Dominions.

'The Person who shall prove the sending or receiving a Challenge, shall receive, to his own Use and Property, the whole Personal Estate of both Parties; and their Real Estate shall be immediately vested in the next Heir of the Offenders, in as ample manner as if the said Offenders were actually Deceased.

'In Cases where the Laws (which we have already granted to our Subjects) admit of an Appeal for Blood, when the Criminal is condemned by the said Appeal, he shall not only suffer Death, but his whole Estate, Real, Mixed and Personal, shall from the hour of his Death be vested in the next Heir of the Person whose Blood he spilt.

'That it shall not hereafter be in our Royal Power, or that of our Successors, to pardon the said Offences, or restore the Offenders[a] in their Estates, Honour, or Blood for ever.

'*Given at our Court at* Blois *the 8th of* February, 420. *In the Second Year of our Reign.*'

T

---

a the Offenders] them *Fol.*

[ADDISON]

> ... *Tanta est quærendi cura decoris.*
> Juv.

THERE is not so variable a thing in Nature as a Lady's Head-dress:[2] Within my own Memory I have known it rise and fall above thirty Degrees. About ten Years ago it shot up to a very great Height, insomuch that the Female Part of our Species were much taller than the Men. The Women were of such an enormous Stature, that *we appeared as Grass-hoppers before them*:[3] At present the whole Sex is in a Manner dwarfed and shrunk into a Race of Beauties that seems almost another Species. I remember several Ladies, who were once very near seven Foot high, that at present want some Inches of five: How they came to be thus curtailed I cannot learn; whether the whole Sex be at present under any Pennance which we know nothing of, or whether they have cast their Head-dresses in order to surprize us with something in that Kind which shall be entirely new; or whether some of the tallest of the Sex, being too cunning for the rest, have contrived this Method to make themselves appear sizeable, is still a Secret; tho' I find most are of Opinion, they are at present like Trees new lopped and pruned, that will certainly sprout up and flourish with greater Heads than before. For my own Part, as I do not love to be insulted by Women who are taller than my self, I admire the Sex much more in their present Humiliation, which has reduced them to their natural Dimensions, than when they had extended their Persons, and lengthened themselves out into formidable and gigantick Figures. I am not for adding to the beautiful Edifices of Nature, nor for raising any whimsical Superstructure upon her Plans: I must therefore repeat it, that I am

---

[1] *Motto.* Juvenal, *Satires*, 6. 501: So studiously their persons they adorn.

[2] 'This refers to the Commode (called by the French *Fontange*) a kind of Head-Dress worn by the ladies at the beginning of this century, which by means of wire bore up the hair and fore part of the cap, consisting of many folds of fine lace, to a prodigious height. The transition from this to the opposite extreme was very abrupt and sudden' (Nichols). See Ashton, i. 163–6, and the illustration there from a playing-card of 1707. It had formerly been much higher: Swift in the *Journal to Stella* (22 Nov. 1711) speaks of dining with Sir Thomas Hanmer and his wife, who 'wears a great high head-dress, such as was in fashion fifteen years ago, and looks like a madwoman in it'. The fontange reached its height in the time of William and Mary. See Francis M. Kelly and Randolph Schwabe, *A Short History of Costume . . .* (1931), ii. 45–46.

[3] Num. xiii. 33.

highly pleased with the Coiffure now in Fashion; and think it shews the good Sense which at present very much reigns among the valuable Part of the Sex. One may observe, that Women in all Ages have taken more Pains than Men to adorn the Outside of their Heads; and indeed I very much admire, that those Female Architects who raise such wonderful Structures out of Ribbands, Lace and Wire, have not been recorded for their respective Inventions. It is certain there has been as many Orders in these Kinds of Building, as in those which have been made of Marble: Sometimes they rise in the Shape of a Pyramid, sometimes like a Tower, and sometimes like a Steeple. In *Juvenal*'s Time the Building grew by several Orders and Stories, as he has very humorously described it.

> *Tot premit ordinibus, tot adhuc compagibus altum*
> *Ædificat caput: Andromachen á fronte videbis;*
> *Post minor est: Aliam credas.* Juv.[1]

But I do not remember, in any Part of my Reading, that the Headdress aspired to so great an Extravagance as in the fourteenth Century; when it was built up in a couple of Cones or Spires, which stood so excessively high on each Side of the Head, that a Woman who was but a *Pigmie* without her Head-dress, appeared like a *Colossus* upon putting it on. Monsieur *Paradin*[2] says, 'That these old fashioned Fontanges rose an Ell above the Head; that they were pointed like Steeples, and had long loose Pieces of Crape fastened to the Tops of them, which were curiously fringed and hung down their Backs like Streamers.'

The Women might possibly have carried this Gothick Building much higher, had not a famous Monk, *Thomas Conecte*[3] by Name, attacked it with great Zeal and Resolution. This holy Man travelled from Place to Place to preach down this monstrous Commode; and succeeded so well in it, that as the Magicians[4] sacrificed their Books to the Flames upon the preaching of an Apostle, many of the Women threw down their Head-dresses in the Middle of his Sermon, and made a Bonfire of them within Sight of the Pulpit. He was so re-

[1] *Satires* 6. 502–4 ('credas aliam'), the lines following the motto chosen for this paper. 'So numerous are the tiers and stories piled one upon another on her head! In front, you would take her for an Andromache; she is not so tall behind: you would not think it was the same person.'
[2] Guillaume Paradin, *Annales de Bourgongne* (Lyon, 1566), pp. 700–2.
[3] A Carmelite monk born in Brittany, who was burnt for heresy at Rome in 1434 by Pope Eugenius IV.
[4] Acts xix. 19.

nowned, as well for the Sanctity of his Life as his Manner of preaching, that he had often a Congregation of twenty thousand People; the Men placing themselves on the one Side of his Pulpit and the Women on the other, that appeared (to use the Similitude of an ingenious Writer) like a Forrest of Cedars with their Heads reaching to the Clouds. He so warmed and animated the People against this monstrous Ornament, that it lay under a kind of Persecution; and whenever it appeared in Publick was pelted down by the Rabble, who flung Stones at the Persons that wore it. But notwithstanding this Prodigy vanished while the Preacher was among them, it began to appear again some Months after his Departure, or, to tell it in Monsieur *Paradin*'s own Words, 'The Women that, like Snails in a Fright, had drawn in their Horns, shot them out again as soon as the Danger was over.' This Extravagance of the Womens Head-dresses in that Age, is taken Notice of by Monsieur *Argentré*[1] in his History of *Bretagne*, and by other Historians as well as the Person I have here quoted.

It is usually observed, That a good Reign is the only proper Time for the making of Laws against the Exorbitance of Power: In the same Manner an excessive Head-dress may be attacked the most effectually when the Fashion is against it. I do therefore recommend this Paper to my female Readers by way of Prevention.

I would desire the fair Sex to consider, how impossible it is for them to add any thing that can be ornamental to what is already the Masterpiece of Nature. The Head has the most beautiful Appearance, as well as the highest Station, in a humane Figure. Nature has laid out all her Art in beautifying the Face: She has touched it with Vermillion, planted in it a double Row of Ivory, made it the Seat of Smiles and Blushes, lighted it up and enlivened it with the Brightness of the Eyes, hung it on each Side with curious Organs of Sense, given it Airs and Graces that cannot be described, and surrounded it with such a flowing Shade of Hair as sets all its Beauties in the most agreeable Light: In short, she seems to have designed the Head as the Cupola to the most glorious of her Works; and when we load it with such a Pile of supernumerary Ornaments,

[1] Bertrand d'Argentré, author of an *Histoire de Bretagne,* published at Rennes in 1582. The references to Paradin and d'Argentré are taken from Bayle, whose article 'Conecte' is the source of the present essay. Bayle says of Conecte: 'He inveighed against the Vices of the Clergy, and against the Luxury of Women, especially against their Head-dresses, which were of such a prodigious height, that the highest Top-knots now are but Dwarfs to them.'

we destroy the Symmetry of the humane Figure, and foolishly contrive to call off the Eye from great and real Beauties, to childish Gew-gaws, Ribbands, and Bone-lace. L

No. 99   *Saturday, June 23, 1711*[1]

[ADDISON]

. . . Turpi secernis Honestum.

Hor.

THE Club, of which I have often declared my self a Member, were last Night engaged in a Discourse upon that which passes for the chief Point of Honour among Men and Women, and started a great many Hints upon the Subject which I thought were entirely new. I shall therefore methodize the several Reflections that arose upon this Occasion, and present my Reader with them for the Speculation of this Day; after having premised, that if there is any thing in this Paper which seems to differ with any Passage of last *Thursday*'s,[a] the Reader will consider this as the Sentiments of the Club, and the other as my own private Thoughts, or rather those of *Pharamond*.

The great Point of Honour[2] in Men is Courage, and in Women Chastity. If a Man loses his Honour in one Rencounter it is not impossible for him to regain it in another; a Slip in a Woman's Honour is irrecoverable. I can give no Reason for fixing the Point of Honour to these two Qualities, unless it be that each Sex sets the greatest Value on the Qualification which renders them the most amiable in the Eyes of the contrary Sex. Had Men chosen for themselves, without regard to the Opinions of the fair Sex, I should believe the Choice would have fallen on Wisdom or Virtue; or had Women determined their own point of Honour, it is probable that Wit or Good-Nature would have carried it against Chastity.

Nothing recommends a Man more to the Female Sex than

[a] of last *Thursday*'s,] of *Thursday*'s, Fol.

[1] *Motto.* Horace, *Satires*, I. 6. 63:

You, who know what's bad from good. CREECH.

[2] Cf. (with a different application!) La Rochefoucauld, *Moral Maxims and Reflections*, part iv, sect. xv: 'Courage in Men, and *Chastity* in Women, are esteemed the principal Vertues of each *Sex* ,because they are the hardest to practise . . .' (ed. 1694, p. 173).

Courage; whether it be that they are pleased to see one who is a
Terror to others fall like a Slave at their Feet, or that this Quality
supplies their own principal Defect, in guarding them from Insults
and avenging their Quarrels, or that Courage is a natural Indication
of a strong and sprightly Constitution. On the other side, nothing
makes a Woman more esteemed by the opposite Sex than Chastity,
whether it be that we always prize those most who are hardest to
come at, or that nothing besides Chastity, with its Collateral Attendants, Truth, Fidelity and Constancy, gives the Man a Property in
the Person he loves, and consequently endears her to him above all
things.

I am very much pleased with a Passage in the Inscription on
a Monument erected in *Westminster* Abby to the late Duke and
Dutchess of *Newcastle*.[1] 'Her Name was *Margaret Lucas*, youngest
Sister to the Lord *Lucas* of *Colchester*; *a noble Family, for all the Brothers
were valiant, and all the Sisters virtuous.*'

In Books of Chivalry, where the Point of Honour is strained to
Madness, the whole Story runs on Chastity and Courage. The
Damsel is mounted on a white Palfrey, as an Emblem of her Innocence; and, to avoid Scandal, must have a Dwarf for her Page. She
is not to think of a Man 'till some Misfortune has brought a Knight-
Errant to her Relief. The Knight falls in Love, and did not Gratitude
restrain her from murdering her Deliverer, would die at her Feet
by her Disdain. However he must waste many Years in the Desart
before her Virgin Heart can think of a Surrender. The Knight goes
off, attacks every thing he meets that is bigger and stronger than
himself, seeks all Opportunities of being knock'd on the Head, and
after seven Years rambling returns to his Mistress, whose Chastity
has been attacked in the mean time by Gyants and Tyrants, and
undergone as many Tryals as her Lover's Valour.

In *Spain*, where there are still great Remains of this Romantick
Humour, it is a transporting Favour for a Lady to cast an accidental
Glance on her Lover from a Window, tho' it be two or three Stories
high; as it is usual for the Lover to assert his Passion for his Mistress
in single Combat with a mad Bull.

[1] The monument is in the north transept. William Cavendish, Duke of Newcastle,
died in 1677; Margaret Lucas, his second wife, had died three years earlier. The lines
quoted resemble a sentence in Molière's *Georges Dandin* (1668), I. iv: 'Dans la maison
de Sotenville, on n'a jamais vu de coquette; et la bravoure n'y est pas plus héréditaire
aux mâles que la chasteté aux femelles' (A. P. Stanley, *Historical Memorials of Westminster Abbey*, chap. iv, ed. 1886, p. 217).

The great Violation of the Point of Honour from Man to Man is giving the Lie. One may tell another he Whores, Drinks, Blasphemes, and it may pass unresented, but to say he Lies, tho' but in Jest, is an Affront that nothing but Blood can expiate. The Reason perhaps may be, because no other Vice implies a want of Courage so much as the making of a Lie: And therefore telling a Man he Lies, is touching him in the most sensible part of Honour, and indirectly calling him a Coward. I cannot omit under this Head what *Herodotus*[1] tells us of the ancient *Persians*, That from the Age of five Years to twenty they instruct their Sons only in three things, to manage the Horse, to make use of the Bow, and to speak Truth.[a]

The placing the Point of Honour in this false kind of Courage, has given Occasion to the very Refuse of Mankind, who have neither Virtue nor common Sense, to set up for Men of Honour. An *English* Peer,[2] who has not been long dead, used to tell a pleasant Story of a *French* Gentleman that visited him early one Morning at *Paris*, and after great Professions of Respect, let him know that he had it in his Power to oblige him, which in short amounted to this, that he believed he could tell his Lordship the Person's Name who justled him as he came out from the Opera, but before he would proceed, he begged his Lordship that he would not deny him the Honour of making him his Second. The *English* Lord, to avoid being drawn into a very foolish Affair, told him that he was under Engagements for his two next Duels to a Couple of particular Friends. Upon which the Gentleman immediately withdrew, hoping his Lordship would not take it ill, if he medled no farther in an Affair from whence he himself was to receive no Advantage.

The beating down this false Notion of Honour, in so vain and

[a] I cannot ... Truth. *om. Fol.*

---

[1] *History*, I. 136.
[2] 'The Editor has been told this was William Cavendish, the first Duke of Devonshire, who died Aug. 18, 1707' (Nichols). (His grandfather was first cousin to the William Cavendish mentioned above.) When he was on an embassy in Paris in 1669 he was insulted on the stage of the Opera by three officers of the King's Guard, struck one of them, and in the ensuing swordplay barely escaped with his life. See White Kennet, *Memoirs of the Family of Cavendish* (1708), p. 17. He was not averse to duelling. In 1675 he was only prevented from challenging Thomas Howard by parliamentary intercession; he dangerously wounded Lord Mohun in 1675; and in 1680 served as second to Lord Plymouth in a duel with Sir G. Huet (*DNB*). A few years later he challenged Count Coningsmark in Paris, 'but his lordship refused it, sayeing he had considerable employ's under the French king, and the lawes were very severe against duelling in France' (Luttrell, i. 210). This, or the incident at the French opera mentioned above, may be the source of the legend.

lively a People as those of *France* is deservedly looked upon as one of the most glorious Parts of their present King's Reign.[1] It is pity but the Punishment of these mischievous Notions should have in it some particular Circumstances of Shame and Infamy, that those who are Slaves to them may see that instead of advancing their Reputations they lead them to Ignominy and Dishonour.

Death is not sufficient to deter Men, who make it their Glory to despise it, but if every one that fought a Duel were to stand in the Pillory it would quickly lessen the Number of these[a] imaginary Men of Honour, and put an end to so absurd a Practice.

When Honour is a Support to virtuous Principles, and runs parallel with the Laws of God and our Country, it cannot be too much cherished and encouraged. But when the Dictates of Honour are contrary to those of Religion and Equity, they are the greatest Depravations of human Nature, by giving wrong Ambitions and false Ideas of what is good and laudable, and should therefore be exploded by all Governments, and driven out as the Bane and Plague of Human Society.   L

No. 100   *Monday, June 25, 1711*[2]
STEELE]

Nil ego contulerim jucundo sanus amico.
                                        Hor.

A MAN advanced in Years that thinks fit to look back upon his former Life, and calls that only Life which was passed with Satisfaction and Enjoyment, excluding all Parts which were not pleasant to him, will find himself very young, if not in his Infancy.

---

[a] these] those *Fol.*

---

[1] On his first appearance before the Parlement after attaining his majority Louis XIV read an edict on the duel. During his reign he published six additional edicts, the most famous being the Édit des Duels of 1679. In the *Review* of 29 Apr. 1704 Defoe writes of the French king: 'he has made an Entire Conquest among his own Subjects, of the most prevailing, and deeplyest rooted Crime that ever Nation had so generally Espoused, I mean that of Duelling.' Sir Charles Grandison esteemed Louis XIV's edict against duelling 'the greatest glory of his reign' (Richardson, *Works*, 1884, ix. 318).

[2] *Motto.* Horace, *Satires*, I. 5. 44:
                            A pleasant Friend,
            The dearest thing a Man in health can have.

Sickness, ill Humour, and Idleness, will have robbed him of a great
Share of that Space we ordinarily call our Life. It is therefore the
Duty of every Man that would be true to himself, to obtain, if
possible, a Disposition to be pleased, and place himself in a constant
Aptitude for the Satisfactions of his Being. Instead of this, you
hardly see a Man who is not uneasy in proportion to his Advancement in the Arts of Life. An affected Delicacy is the common Improvement we meet with in those who pretend to be refined above
others: They do not aim at true Pleasures themselves, but turn their
Thoughts upon observing the false Pleasures of other Men. Such
People are Valetudinarians[1] in Society, and they should no more
come into Company than a sick Man should come into the Air: If
a Man is too weak to bear what is a Refreshment to Men in Health,
he must still keep his Chamber. When any one in Sir ROGER's
Company complains he is out of Order, he immediately calls for
some Posset-drink for him; for which Reason that Sort of People
who are ever bewailing their Constitution in other Places, are the
Chearfullest imaginable when he is present.

It is a wonderful thing, that so many, and they not reckoned
absurd, shall entertain those with whom they converse by giving
them the History of their Pains and Aches; and imagine such Narrations their Quota of the Conversation. This is of all other the meanest
Help to Discourse; and a Man must not think at all, or think himself very insignificant, when he finds an Account of his Head-ach
answered by another's asking what News in the last Mail? Mutual
good Humour is a Dress we ought to appear in wherever we meet,
and we should make[a] no Mention of what concerns our selves, without it be of Matters wherein our Friends ought to rejoyce: But
indeed there are Crowds of People who put themselves in no Method
of pleasing themselves or others; such are those whom we usually
call indolent Persons. Indolence is methinks an intermediate State
between Pleasure and Pain, and very much unbecoming any Part
of our Life after we are out of the Nurses Arms. Such an Aversion
to Labour creates a constant Weariness, and, one would think,
should make Existence it self a Burthen. The indolent Man descends
from the Dignity of his Nature, and makes that Being which was
Rational meerly Vegetative: His Life consists only in the meer
Encrease and Decay of a Body, which, with Relation to the rest of

 a and we should make] and make *Fol.*

 ¹ No. 25.

the World, might as well have been uninformed, as the Habitation of a reasonable Mind.

Of this Kind is the Life of that extraordinary Couple *Harry Tersett* and his Lady. *Harry* was in the Days of his Celibacy one of those pert Creatures who have much Vivacity and little Understanding; Mrs. *Rebecca Quickly,* whom he married, had all that the Fire of Youth and a lively Manner could do towards making an agreeable Woman. These two People of seeming Merit fell into each others Arms, and Passion being sated, and no Reason or good Sense in either to succeed it, their Life is now at a Stand; their Meals are insipid, and their Time tedious; their Fortune has placed them above Care, and their Loss of Taste reduced them below Diversion. When we talk of these as Instances of Inexistence, we do not mean, that in order to live it is necessary we should always be in jovial Crews, or crowned with Chaplets of Roses,[1] as the merry Fellows among the Antients are described; but it is intended by considering these Contraries to Pleasure, Indolence and too much Delicacy, to shew that it is Prudence to preserve a Disposition in our selves to receive a certain Delight in all we hear and see.

This portable Quality of good Humour seasons all the Parts and Occurrences we meet with in such a Manner, that there are no Moments lost; but they all pass with so much Satisfaction, that the heaviest of Loads (when it is a Load) that of Time, is never felt by us. *Varilas*[2] has this Quality to the highest Perfection, and communicates it wherever he appears: The Sad, the Merry, the Severe, the Melancholy shew a new Chearfulness when he comes amongst them. At the same time no one can repeat any thing that *Varilas* has ever said, that deserves Repetition; but the Man has that innate Goodness of Temper, that he is welcome to every Body, because every Man thinks he is so to him. He does not seem to contribute any thing to the Mirth of the Company; and yet upon Reflection you find it all happened by his being there. I thought it was whimsically said of a Gentleman, That if *Varilas* had Wit, it would be the best Wit in the World. It is certain, when a well corrected lively Imagination and good Breeding are added to a sweet Disposition, they qualify it to be one of the greatest Blessings, as well as Pleasures of Life.

[1] Cf. No. 143 (vol. ii): 'It is not here pretended, that we should be always sitting with Chaplets of Flowers round our Heads. . . .' The first paragraph of No. 143, also by Steele, repeats many of the ideas of this essay, and many of the same phrases.
[2] In *Tatler* 52 Steele portrays Varillus as the man of true modesty.

Men would come into Company with ten Times the Pleasure they do, if they were sure of hearing nothing which should shock them, as well as expected what would please them. When we know every Person that is spoken of is represented by one who has no ill Will, and every thing that is mentioned described by one that is apt to set it in the best Light, the Entertainment must be delicate; because the Cook has nothing brought to his Hand but what is the most excellent in its Kind. Beautiful Pictures are the Entertainments of pure Minds, and Deformities of the corrupted. It is a Degree towards the Life of Angels, when we enjoy Conversation wherein there is nothing presented but in its Excellence; and a Degree towards that of Dæmons, wherein nothing is shewn but in its Degeneracy.   T

No. 101   *Tuesday, June 26, 1711*[1]
[ADDISON]

> *Romulus, & Liber pater, & cum Castore Pollux,*
> *Post ingentia facta, Deorum in templa recepti,*
> *Dum terras hominumque colunt genus, aspera bella*
> *Componunt, agros assignant, oppida condunt;*
> *Ploravere suis non respondere favorem*
> *Speratum meritis: . . .*
>
> Hor.

*C*ENSURE, says a late ingenious Author, *is the Tax a Man pays to the Publick for being Eminent.*[2] It is a Folly for an eminent Man to think of escaping it, and a Weakness to be affected with it. All the illustrious Persons of Antiquity, and indeed of every Age in the World, have passed through this fiery Persecution. There is no

---

[1] *Motto.* Horace, *Epistles*, 2. 1. 5–10:

> The Ancient *Heroes*, though in the blest Abodes
> Receiv'd when dead, exalted into Gods;
> Yet whilst they liv'd with Men, and whilst bestow'd
> The greatest Cares, and did the greatest Good,
> Built Towns, made Laws, and brought delightful ease,
> And civiliz'd the Rational Savages;
> Complain'd that They ingrateful Masters serv'd,
> And met far less rewards than They deserv'd. CREECH.

[2] Swift, 'Thoughts on Various Subjects', 1706 (*Prose Works*, ed. Davis, i. 241).

Defence against Reproach, but Obscurity; it is a kind of Concomitant to Greatness, as Satyrs and Invectives were an essential Part of a *Roman* Triumph.

If Men of Eminence are exposed to Censure on one hand, they are as much liable to Flattery on the other. If they receive Reproaches which are not due to them, they likewise receive Praises which they do not deserve. In a word, the Man in a high Post is never regarded with an indifferent Eye, but always considered as a Friend or an Enemy. For this Reason Persons in great Stations have seldom their true Characters drawn, till several Years after their Deaths. Their personal Friendships and Enmities must cease, and the Parties they were engaged in be at an end, before their Faults or their Virtues can have Justice done them. When Writers have the least Opportunity of knowing the Truth, they are in the best Disposition to tell it.

It is therefore the Privilege of Posterity to adjust the Characters of Illustrious Persons, and to set matters right between those Antagonists who by their Rivalry for Greatness divided a whole Age into Factions. We can now allow *Cæsar* to be a great Man, without derogating from *Pompey*; and celebrate the Virtues of *Cato*, without detracting from those of *Cæsar*. Every one that has been long dead has a due Proportion of Praise allotted him, in which whilst he lived his Friends were too profuse and his Enemies too sparing.

According to Sir *Isaac Newton*'s Calculations, the last Comet that made its Appearance in 1680, imbibed so much Heat by its Approaches to the Sun, that it would have been two thousand times hotter than red hot Iron, had it been a Globe of that Metal; and that supposing it as big as the Earth, and at the same Distance from the Sun, it would be fifty thousand Years in cooling, before it recover'd its natural Temper.[1] In the like manner, if an *English* Man considers

---

[1] Newton, *Principia* (1687), says this to show that the nuclei of comets must consist of solid matter. Cf. Henry Pemberton, *A View of Sir Isaac Newton's Philosophy* (1728), p. 236:

[The] comet of 1680 descended so near the sun, as to come within a sixth part of the sun's diameter from the surface of it. In which situation it must have been exposed ... to a degree of heat exceeding the heat of the sun upon our earth no less than 28000 times; and therefore might have contracted a degree of heat 2000 times greater, than that of red hot iron. Now a substance, which could endure so intense a heat, without being dispersed in vapor, must needs be firm and solid.

Addison alludes to the comet of 1680 in *Guardian* 103: 'it travelled in a much greater degree of swiftness than a cannon ball, and drew after it a tail of fire that was fourscore millions of miles in length.'

the great Ferment into which our Political World is thrown at present, and how intensely it is heated in all its parts, he cannot suppose that it will cool again in less than three hundred Years. In such a Tract of Time it is possible that the Heats of the present Age may be extinguished, and our several Classes of great Men represented under their proper Characters. Some eminent Historian may then probably arise that will not write *recentibus odiis,* (as *Tacitus*[1] expresses it,) with the Passions and Prejudices of a Contemporary Author, but make an impartial Distribution of Fame among the Great Men of the present Age.

I cannot forbear entertaining my self very often with the Idea of such an Imaginary Historian describing the Reign of *ANNE* the First, and introducing it with a Preface to his Reader, that he is now entring upon the most shining Part of the *English* Story. The great Rivals in Fame will be then distinguished according to their respective Merits, and shine in their proper Points of Light. Such a one (says the Historian) though variously represented by the Writers of his own Age, appears to have been a Man of more than ordinary Abilities, great Application and uncommon Integrity: Nor was such an one (tho' of an opposite Party and Interest) inferior to him in any of these Respects. The several Antagonists who now endeavour to depreciate one another, and are celebrated or traduced by different Parties, will then have the same Body of Admirers, and appear Illustrious in the Opinion of the whole *British* Nation. The Deserving Man, who can now recommend himself to the Esteem of but half his Countrymen,[2] will then receive the Approbations and Applauses of a whole Age.

Among the several Persons that flourish in this Glorious Reign, there is no Question but such a future Historian as the Person of whom I am speaking, will make mention of the Men of Genius and Learning, who have now any Figure in the *British* Nation. For my own part, I often flatter my self with the honourable Mention which will then be made of me, and have drawn up a Paragraph in my own Imagination that I fancy will not be altogether unlike what will be found in some Page or other of this Imaginary Historian.

It was under this Reign, says he, that the SPECTATOR Published those little Diurnal Essays which are still extant. We know very

---

[1] *Annals,* I. I.
[2] Cf. No. 57 ('Camilla, who values herself more upon being the Virago of one Party . . .').

little of the Name or Person of this Author, except only that he was a Man of a very short Face, extreamly addicted to Silence, and so great a Lover of Knowledge that he made a Voyage to *Grand Cairo* for no other Reason but to take the Measure of a Pyramid. His chief Friend was one Sir ROGER DE COVERLY, a whimsical Country Knight, and a *Templar* whose Name he has not transmitted to us. He lived as a Lodger at a House of a Widow-Woman, and was a great Humourist in all parts[a] of his Life. This is all we can affirm with any Certainty of his Person and Character. As for his Speculations, notwithstanding the several obsolete Words and obscure Phrases of the Age in which he lived, we still understand enough of them to see the Diversions and Characters of the *English* Nation in his time: Not but that we are to make Allowance for the Mirth and Humour of the Author, who has doubtless strained many Representations of things beyond the Truth. For if we interpret his Words in their litteral Meaning, we must suppose that Women of the First Quality used to pass away whole Mornings at a Puppet-Show: That they attested their Principles by their *Patches*: That an Audience would sit out an Evening[b] to hear a Dramatical Performance written in a Language which they did not understand: That Chairs and Flower-Pots were introduced as Actors upon the *British* Stage: That a Promiscuous Assembly of Men and Women were allowed to meet at Midnight in Masques within the Verge of the Court, with many Improbabilities of the like Nature. We must therefore, in these and the like Cases, suppose that these remote Hints and Allusions aimed at some certain Follies which were then in Vogue, and which at present we have not any Notion of. We may guess by several Passages in the *Speculations*, that there were Writers who[c] endeavoured to detract from the Works of this Author, but as nothing of this nature is come down to us, we cannot guess at any Objections that could be made to his Paper. If we consider his Style with that Indulgence which we must shew to old *English* Writers, or if we look into the Variety of his Subjects, with those several Critical Dissertations, Moral Reflections, ★ ★ ★ ★ ★ ★ ★
★ ★ ★ ★ ★ ★ ★ ★ ★ ★ ★ ★ ★ ★ ★
★ ★ ★ ★ ★ ★ ★ ★ ★ ★ ★ ★ ★ ★
★ ★ ★ ★ ★ ★ ★ ★ ★ ★ ★ ★ ★ ★
★ ★ ★ ★ ★ ★ ★ ★ ★ ★ ★ ★ ★ ★

[a] all parts] all the parts *Fol.*   [b] an Evening] a whole Evening *Fol.*   [c] who] which *Fol.*

The following part of the Paragraph is so much to my Advantage, and beyond any thing I can pretend to, that I hope my Reader will excuse me for not inserting it. L

No. 102   *Wednesday, June 27, 1711*[1]
[ADDISON]

> *... Lusus animo debent aliquando dari*
> *Ad cogitandum melior ut redeat sibi.*
>   Phædr.

I DO not know whether to call the following Letter a Satyr upon Coquets, or a Representation of their several fantastical Accomplishments, or what other Title to give it; but as it is I shall communicate it to the Publick. It will sufficiently explain its own Intentions, so that I shall give it my Reader at length without either Preface or Postscript.

Mr. SPECTATOR,

'WOMEN are armed with Fans[2] as Men with Swords, and sometimes do more Execution with them: To the End therefore that Ladies may be entire Mistresses of the Weapon which they bear, I have erected an Academy for the training up of young Women in the *Exercise of the Fan,* according to the most fashionable Airs and Motions that are now practised at Court. The Ladies who *carry* Fans under me are drawn up twice a Day in my great Hall, where they are instructed in the Use of their Arms, and *exercised* by the following Words of Command,

> *Handle your Fans,*[3]
> *Unfurl your Fans,*

---

[1] *Motto.* Phaedrus, *Fables,* 3. 14. 12–13:
The mind ought sometimes to be diverted, that it may return to thinking the better.
[2] In *Tatler* 52 Delamira's advice on the conduct of the fan is given, and there are of course many references to the 'little modish machine' in the literature of the time, including Gay's delightful poem of 1714.
[3] A pamphlet entitled *The Discipline of the Eye,* advertised in the *Protestant Post-Boy* of 5 Jan. 1712, recalls in its title the language used here:
The Discipline of the Eye: as, Advancing the eye; grounding the eye; resting the eye; priming the eye; cocking the eye; and giving fire with the eye; also the uses and abuses of the melting, or languid eye; the brilliant, or sparkling eye; the

Discharge your Fans,
Ground your Fans,
Recover your Fans,
Flutter your Fans.

By the right Observation of these few plain Words of Command, a Woman of a tolerable Genius who[a] will apply her self diligently to her Exercise for the Space of but one half Year, shall be able to give her Fan all the Graces that can possibly enter into that little modish Machine.

'But to the End that my Readers may form to themselves a right Notion of this *Exercise*, I beg Leave to explain it to them in all its Parts. When my female Regiment is drawn up in Array with every one her Weapon in her Hand, upon my giving the Word to *handle their Fans*, each of them shakes her Fan at me with a Smile, then gives her Right-hand Woman a Tap upon the Shoulder, then presses her Lips with the Extremity of her Fan, then lets her Arms fall in an easy Motion, and stands in a Readiness to receive the next Word of Command. All this is done with a close Fan, and is generally learned in the first Week.

'The next Motion is that of *unfurling the Fan*, in which are[b] comprehended several little Flirts and Vibrations, as also gradual and deliberate Openings, with many voluntary Fallings asunder in the Fan it self, that are seldom learned under a Month's Practice. This Part of the *Exercise* pleases the Spectators more than any other, as it discovers on a Sudden an infinite Number of Cupids,[1] Garlands, Altars,[c] Birds, Beasts, Rainbows, and the like agreeable Figures, that display themselves to View, whilst every one in the Regiment holds a Picture in her Hand.

'Upon my giving the Word to *discharge their Fans*, they give one general Crack that may be heard at a considerable Distance when the Wind sits fair. This is one of the most difficult Parts of the *Exercise*; but I have several Ladies with me, who at their first Entrance could not give a Pop loud enough to be heard at the further

---

[a] who] that *Fol.*   [b] are] is *Fol.*   [c] Cupids, Garlands, Altars,] Cupids, Altars, *Fol.*

---

wanton, or loose eye; the leer, or artificial squint; the ogling eye; the disdainful eye; the devout eye; the rowling eye; the pinking winking eye; the majestick eye, inscrib'd to the ladies. Sold by J. Baker, in Pater-Noster-Row.

[1] In *Tatler* 52 Cupid is 'the principal Figure' painted on Delamira's fan.

End of a Room, who can now *discharge a Fan* in such a Manner, that it shall make a Report like a Pocket-Pistol. I have likewise taken Care (in order to hinder young Women from letting off their Fans in wrong Places or unsuitable Occasions) to shew upon what Subject the Crack of a Fan may come in properly: I have likewise invented a Fan, with which a Girl of Sixteen, by the Help of a little Wind which is enclosed about one of the largest Sticks, can make as loud a Crack as a Woman of Fifty with an ordinary Fan.

'When the Fans are thus *discharged*, the Word of Command in Course is to *ground their Fans*. This teaches a Lady to quit her Fan gracefully when she throws it aside in order to take up a Pack of Cards, adjust a Curl of Hair, replace a falling Pin, or apply herself to any other Matter of Importance. This Part of the *Exercise*, as it[a] only consists in tossing a Fan with an Air upon a long Table (which stands by for that Purpose,) may be learned in two Days Time as well as in a Twelvemonth.

'When my Female Regiment is thus disarmed, I generally let them walk about the Room for some Time; when on a sudden (like Ladies that look upon their Watches after a long Visit) they all of them hasten to their Arms, catch them up in a Hurry, and place themselves in their proper Stations upon my calling out *recover your Fans*. This Part of the *Exercise* is not difficult, provided a Woman applies her Thoughts to it.

'The *Fluttering of the Fan* is the last, and indeed the Master-piece of the whole *Exercise*; but if a Lady does not mispend her Time, she may make herself Mistress of it in three Months. I generally lay aside the Dog-days and the hot Time of the Summer for the teaching this Part of the *Exercise*; for as soon as ever I pronounce *Flutter your Fans*, the Place is filled with so many Zephirs and gentle Breezes as are very refreshing in that Season of the Year, though they might be dangerous to Ladies of a tender Constitution in any other.

'There is an infinite Variety of Motions to be made use of in the *Flutter of a Fan*: There is the angry Flutter, the modest Flutter, the timorous Flutter, the confused Flutter, the merry Flutter, and the amorous Flutter. Not to be tedious, there is scarce any Emotion in the Mind which[b] does not produce a suitable Agitation in the Fan; insomuch, that if I only see the Fan of a disciplin'd Lady, I know very well whether she laughs, frowns, or blushes. I have seen a Fan so very angry, that it would have been dangerous for the absent

___

[a] as it] which *Fol.*   [b] which] that *Fol.*

Lover who[a] provoked it to have come within the Wind of it; and at other Times so very languishing, that I have been glad for the Lady's Sake the Lover was at a sufficient Distance from it. I need not add, that a Fan is either a Prude or Coquet, according to the Nature of the Person who[b] bears it. To conclude my Letter, I must acquaint you that I have from my own Observations compiled a little Treatise for the Use of my Scholars, entituled, *The Passions of the Fan*; which I will communicate to you, if you think it may be of Use to the Publick. I shall have a general Review on *Thursday* next; to which you shall be very welcome if you will honour it with your Presence.

I am, &c.

'P. S. I teach young Gentlemen the whole Art of Gallanting a Fan.

'N. B. I have several little plain Fans made for this Use, to avoid Expence.'

L

No. 103

[STEELE]

Thursday, June 28, 1711[1]

> . . . *Sibi quivis*
> *Speret idem frustra sudet frustraque laboret*
> *Ausus idem* . . .
>
> Hor.

M Y Friend the Divine having been used with Words of Complaisance[2] (which he thinks could be properly applied to no one living, and I think could be only spoken of him, and that in his Absence) was so extreamly offended with the excessive way of speaking Civilities among us, that he made a Discourse against it at the Club, which he concluded with this Remark,[c] that he had not heard one Compliment made in our Society since its Commencement.

---

[a] who] that *Fol.*   [b] who] that *Fol.*   [c] Remark,] Argument, *Fol.*

[1] *Motto.* Horace, *Ars poetica*, 240–2 (altered):
> Tho' any Man may hope to do the same,
> Yet let him try, and he shall sweat in vain:
> Idle his Labour, fruitless all his Pain.

[2] The action or habit of making oneself agreeable; desire and care to please; compliance with, or deference to, the wishes of others; obligingness, courtesy, politeness (*OED*). Cf. *Complacency* in the Dedication to vol. i.

Every one was pleased with his Conclusion, and as each knew his good Will to the rest, he was convinced that the many Professions of Kindness and Service which we ordinarily meet with are not natural where the Heart is well inclined, but are a Prostitution of Speech seldom intended to mean Any Part of what they express, never to mean All they express. Our Reverend Friend, upon this Topick, pointed to us two or three Paragraphs on this Subject in the first Sermon of the first Volume of the late Arch-Bishop's Posthumous Works.[1] I do not know that I ever read any thing that pleased me more, and as it is the Praise of *Longinus*,[2] that he speaks of the Sublime in a Stile suitable to it, so one may say of this Author upon Sincerity, that he abhors any Pomp of Rhetorick on this Occasion, and treats it with a more than ordinary Simplicity, at once to be a Preacher and an Example. With what Command of himself does he lay before us, in the Language and Temper of his Profession, a Fault, which by the least Liberty and Warmth of Expression would be the most lively Wit and Satyr? But his Heart was better disposed, and the good Man chastised the great Wit in such a manner, that he was able to speak as follows.

'... Amongst too many other Instances of the great Corruption and Degeneracy of the Age wherein we live, the great and general want of Sincerity in Conversation is none of the least. The World is grown so full of Dissimulation and Compliment, that Mens Words are hardly any Signification of their Thoughts; and if any Man measure his Words by his Heart, and speak as he thinks, and do not express more Kindness to every Man, than Men usually have for any Man, he can hardly escape the Censure of want of Breeding. The old *English* Plainness and Sincerity, that generous Integrity of Nature, and Honesty of Disposition, which always argues true Greatness of Mind, and is usually accompany'd with undaunted Courage and Resolution, is in a great measure lost amongst us: There hath been a long Endeavour to transform us into Foreign Manners and Fashions, and to bring us to a servile Imitation of none of the best of our Neighbours, in some of the worst of their Qualities. The Dialect of Conversation is now-a-days so swell'd with Vanity and Compli-

---

[1] Archbishop Tillotson's sermon 'Of Sincerity towards God and Man', on John i. 47, preached at Kingston, 29 July 1694, 'the last his Grace preach'd'. The passages quoted here will be found in the 1728 edition of Tillotson's *Works*, ed. by Ralph Barker, ii. 6, 7, 8.
[2] Cf. Boileau, preface to his translation of Longinus: 'He often employs the *Figure* he teaches, and in talking of the *Sublime*, is himself most *Sublime*' (*Works*, 1711-12, vol. ii, part 2, p. 2).

ment, and so surfeited (as I may say) of Expressions of Kindness and Respect, that if a Man that lived an Age or two ago shou'd return into the World again, he would really want a Dictionary to help him to understand his own Language, and to know the true intrinsick Value of the Phrase in Fashion, and wou'd hardly at first believe at what a low Rate the highest Strains and Expressions of Kindness imaginable do commonly pass in current Payment; and when he shou'd come to understand it, it wou'd be a great while before he cou'd bring himself with a good Countenance and a good Conscience to converse with Men upon equal Terms, and in their own way.

'And in truth it is hard to say, whether it shou'd more provoke our Contempt or our Pity, to hear what solemn Expressions of Respect and Kindness will pass between Men, almost upon no Occasion, how great Honour and Esteem they will declare for one whom perhaps they never saw before, and how entirely they are all on the sudden devoted to his Service and Interest, for no Reason; how infinitely and eternally oblig'd to him for no Benefit, and how extreamly they will be concern'd for him, yea and afflicted too, for no Cause. I know it is said, in Justification of this hollow kind of Conversation, that there is no Harm no real Deceit in Compliment, but the matter is well enough, so long as we understand one another; *& Verba valent ut Nummi,*[1] *Words are like Mony*; and when the current Value of them is generally understood, no Man is cheated by them. This is something, if such Words were any thing; but being brought into the Account, they are meer Cyphers. However it is still a just Matter of Complaint, that Sincerity and Plainness are out of Fashion, and that our Language is running into a Lie; that Men have almost quite perverted the use of Speech, and made Words to signify nothing; that the greatest part of the Conversation of Mankind is little else but driving a Trade of Dissimulation; insomuch that it wou'd make a Man heartily sick and weary of the World, to see the little Sincerity that is in Use and Practice among Men.'

When the Vice is placed in this contemptible Light, he argues unanswerably against it in Words and Thoughts so natural, that any Man who reads them would imagine he himself could have been Author of them.

---

[1] Cf. Hobbes, *Leviathan*, I. iv: 'Words are wise men's counters, they do but reckon by them; but they are the money of fools.' I have not found the source of the Latin saying.

'If the Shew of any thing be good for any thing, I am sure Sincerity is better; for why does any Man dissemble, or seem to be that which he is not, but because he thinks it good to have such a Quality as he pretends to? For to counterfeit and dissemble, is to put on the Appearance of some real Excellency. Now the best Way in the World to seem to be any thing, is really to be what he would seem to be. Besides, that it is many times as troublesome to make good the Pretence of a good Quality, as to have it; and if a Man have it not, it is ten to one but he is discovered to want it, and then all his Pains and Labour to seem to have it is lost.'

In another Part of the same Discourse he goes on to shew, that all Artifice must naturally tend to the Disappointment of him that practises it.

'Whatsoever Convenience may be thought to be in Falshood and Dissimulation, it is soon over; but the Inconvenience of it is perpetual, because it brings a Man under an everlasting Jealousie and Suspicion, so that he is not believ'd when he speaks Truth, nor trusted when perhaps he means honestly: When a Man hath once forfeited the Reputation of his Integrity, he is set fast, and nothing will then serve his turn, neither Truth nor Falshood.'

R

No. 104   *Friday, June* 29, 1711[1]
[STEELE]

> . . . *Qualis equos Threissa fatigat*
> *Harpalyce* . . .
>
> Virg.

IT would be a noble Improvement, or rather a Recovery of what we call good Breeding, if nothing were to pass amongst us for agreeable which was the least Transgression against that Rule of Life called Decorum, or a Regard to Decency. This would command the Respect of Mankind, because it carries in it Deference to their good Opinion; as Humility lodged in a worthy Mind is always attended with a certain Homage, which no haughty Soul, with all

[1] *Motto.* Virgil, *Aeneid*, I. 316–17:
With such Array *Harpalice* bestrode
Her *Thracian* Courser . . . DRYDEN.

the Arts imaginable, will ever be able to purchase. *Tully*[1] says Virtue
and Decency are so nearly related, that it is difficult to separate
them from each other but in our Imagination. As the Beauty of the
Body always accompanies the Health of it, so certainly is Decency
Concomitant to Virtue: As Beauty of Body, with an agreeable
Carriage, pleases the Eye, and that Pleasure consists in that we
observe all the Parts with a certain Elegance are proportioned to
each other; so does Decency of Behaviour which appears in our
Lives obtain the Approbation of all with whom we converse, from
the Order, Constancy, and Moderation of our Words and Actions.
This flows from the Reverence we bear towards every good Man,
and to the World in general; for to be negligent of what any one
thinks of you, does not only shew you arrogant but abandoned.[2] In
all these Considerations we are to distinguish how one Virtue differs
from another: As it is the Part of Justice never to do Violence, it is
of Modesty never to commit Offence. In this last Particular lies the
whole Force of what is called Decency; to this Purpose that excellent
Moralist abovementioned talks of Decency; but this Quality is more
easily comprehended by an ordinary Capacity, than expressed with
all his Eloquence. This Decency of Behaviour is generally trans-
gressed among all Orders of Men; nay the very Women, tho' themselves created as it were[a] for Ornament, are often very much
mistaken in this ornamental Part of Life. It would methinks be a
short Rule for Behaviour, if every young Lady in her Dress, Words,
and Actions were only to recommend her self as a Sister, Daughter,
or Wife, and make her self the more esteemed in one of those
Characters. The Care of themselves, with Regard to the Families
in which Women are born, is the best Motive for their being courted
to come into the Alliance of other Houses. Nothing can promote
this End more than a strict Preservation of Decency. I should be
glad if a certain Equestrian Order[3] of Ladies, some of whom one

---

[a] created as it were] *M*; created it as it were *all edd.*

---

[1] *De Officiis*, 1. 27. 94. Steele uses this sentence from Cicero as the motto of
No. 259 (vol. ii).
[2] This sentence, which Professor Bonamy Dobrée places at the head of his study
of Addison (*Essays in Biography*, 1925), is Steele's quotation from *De Officiis*, 1. 28. 99:
'Neglegere, quid de se quisque sentiat, non solum arrogantis est, sed etiam omnino
dissoluti.'
[3] No. 79 advertises 'a Compleat Riding Suit for a Lady, of Blue Camlet, well
laced with Silver, being a Coat, Wastecoat, Petticoat, Hatt and Feather, never
worn but twice; to be seen at Mr. Harford's at the Acorn in York-street, Covent-
garden'.

meets in an Evening at every Outlet of the Town, would take this Subject into their serious Consideration: In order thereunto the following Letter may not be wholly unworthy their Perusal.

Mr. SPECTATOR,

'GOING lately to take the Air in one of the most beautiful Evenings this Season has produced, as I was admiring the Serenity of the Sky, the lively Colours of the Fields, and the Variety of the Landskip every Way around me, my Eyes were suddenly call'd off from these inanimate Objects by a little Party of Horsemen I saw passing the Road. The greater Part of them escap'd my particular Observation, by reason that my whole Attention was fix'd on a very fair Youth who rode in the Midst of them, and seemed to have been dress'd by some Description in a Romance. His Features, Complexion, and Habit had a remarkable Effeminacy, and a certain languishing Vanity appear'd in his Air: His Hair, well curl'd and powder'd, hung to a considerable Length on his Shoulders, and was wantonly ty'd, as if by the Hands of his Mistress, in a Scarlet Ribbon, which play'd like a Streamer behind him: He had a Coat and Wastcoat of blue Camlet[1] trimm'd and embroider'd with Silver, a Cravat of the finest Lace, and wore, in a smart Cock, a little Beaver Hat edg'd with Silver, and made more sprightly by a Feather. His Horse too, which was a Pacer, was adorn'd after the same airy Manner, and seem'd to share in the Vanity of the Rider. As I was pitying the Luxury of this young Person, who appear'd to me to have been educated only as an Object of Sight, I perceiv'd on my nearer Approach, and as I turned my Eyes downward, a Part of the Equipage I had not observ'd before, which was a Petticoat of the same with the Coat and Wastcoat. After this Discovery, I look'd again on the Face of the fair *Amazon* who had thus deceiv'd me, and thought those Features which had before offended me by their Softness, were now strengthen'd into as improper a Boldness; and tho' her Eyes, Nose and Mouth seem'd to be form'd with perfect Symmetry, I am

---

[1] A name originally for a costly eastern fabric, subsequently for substitutes, made of various combinations of wool, silk, hair, and latterly cotton or linen (*OED*). Gay (*Trivia*, i. 46) speaks of showers drenching 'the camlet's cockled grain'. The variety of cloths used at this time is indicated in the following advertisement in No. 65:

To be Sold, at a lower Rate than ordinary, at the Queen's Head, joining to the Church Gate in Bedford street, Covent-Garden, all Sorts of Druggets, Hair and Worsted Camlets, Sagathies, Duroys, Shagreens, Shalloons, Durants, Padua Serges, Shags, Serge de Nisms, Calamancoes, and all other Goods fit for Mens Apparel. The Persons who now keep the Shop designing to leave off the Trade, and the House and Shop to be Lett at Michaelmas next.

not certain whether she, who in Appearance was a very handsome Youth, may not be in Reality a very indifferent Woman.

'There is an Objection which naturally presents it self against these occasional Perplexities and Mixtures of Dress, which is, that they seem to break in upon that Propriety and Distinction of Appearance in which the Beauty of different Characters is preserv'd; and if they shou'd be more frequent than they are at present, wou'd look like turning our publick Assemblies into a general Masquerade. The Model of this *Amazonian* Hunting-Habit for Ladies, was, as I take it, first imported from *France*, and well enough expresses the Gayety of a People who are taught to do any thing so it be with an Assurance; but I cannot help thinking it sits awkardly yet on our *English* Modesty. The Petticoat is a kind of Incumbrance upon it; and if the *Amazons* should think fit to go on in this Plunder of our Sex's Ornaments, they ought to add to their Spoils, and compleat their Triumph over us, by wearing the Breeches.

'If it be natural to contract insensibly the Manners of those we imitate, the Ladies who are pleas'd with assuming our Dresses will do us more Honour than we deserve, but they will do it at their own Expence. Why should the lovely *Camilla* deceive us in more Shapes than her own, and affect to be represented in her Picture with a Gun and a Spaniel, while her elder Brother, the Heir of a worthy Family, is drawn in Silks like his Sister? The Dress and Air of a Man are not well to be divided; and those who would not be content with the Latter ought never to think of assuming the Former. There is so large a Portion of natural Agreeableness among the fair Sex of our Island, that they seem betray'd into these romantick Habits without having the same Occasion for them with their Inventors: All that needs to be desir'd of them is, that they wou'd *be themselves*, that is, what Nature design'd them; and to see their Mistake when they depart from this, let them look upon a Man who affects the Softness and Effeminacy of a Woman, to learn how their Sex must appear to us when approaching to the Resemblance of a Man.

> I *am*,
> SIR,
> *Your most humble Servant.*[1]

T

---

[1] The letter is by Hughes; it is in Duncombe's list, and Hughes acknowledges the authorship in a letter of 22 Aug. 1716.

No. 105   *Saturday, June 30, 1711*[1]
[ADDISON]

. . . Id arbitror
Adprime in vita esse utile, ne quid nimis.
Ter. *Andr.*

MY Friend, WILL. HONEYCOMB, values himself very much
upon what he calls the Knowledge of Mankind, which has
cost him many Disasters in his Youth; for WILL. reckons every
Misfortune that he has met with among the Women, and every
Rencounter among the Men, as Parts of his Education, and fancies
he should never have been the Man he is, had not he broke Windows,
knocked down Constables, disturbed honest People with his Midnight Serenades, and beat up a Lewd Woman's Quarters, when he
was a young Fellow.[2] The engaging in Adventures of this nature
WILL. calls the studying of Mankind, and terms this Knowledge
of the Town the Knowledge of the World. WILL. ingenuously confesses that for half his Life his Head ached every Morning with
reading of Men over-night, and at present Comforts himself under
certain Pains which he endures from time to time, that without
them he could not have been acquainted with the Gallantries of the
Age. This WILL. looks upon as the Learning of a Gentleman, and
regards all other kinds of Science as the Accomplishments of one
whom he calls a Scholar, a Bookish Man, or a Philosopher.

For these Reasons WILL. shines in mixt Company, where he has
the Discretion not to go out of his Depth, and has often a certain
way of making his real Ignorance appear a seeming one. Our Club
however has frequently caught him tripping, at which times they
never spare him. For as WILL. often insults us with the Knowledge
of the Town, we sometimes take our Revenge upon him by our
Knowledge of[a] Books.

----

[a] of] in *Fol.*

----

[1] *Motto.* Terence, *Andria*, 60–61 (altered):
Not to be addicted too much to any one thing, I take to be the most excellent rule
of life.
[2] The typical activities of the Restoration rake. Cf. the conversation in Shadwell's
Sullen Lovers, 1668 (II. i):

EMILIA. Now the Qualifications of fine Gentlemen are to eat A-la-mode, drink
Champaigne, dance Jiggs, and play at Tennis.
STANFORD. To love Dogs, Horses, Hawks, Dice and Wenches, scorn Wit, break
Windows, beat a Constable, lye with his Sempstress, and undo his Taylor. . . .

He was last Week[a] producing two or three Letters which he writ in his Youth to a Coquet Lady. The Raillery of them was natural, and well enough for a meer Man of the Town; but, very unluckily, several of the Words were wrong spelt. WILL. laught this off at first as well as he could, but finding himself pushed on all sides, and especially by the *Templar*, he told us, with a little Passion, that he never liked Pedantry in Spelling, and that he spelt like a Gentleman, and not like a Scholar: Upon this WILL. had Recourse to his old Topick of showing the narrow Spiritedness, the Pride and Ignorance of Pedants;[1] which he carried so far, that upon my retiring to my Lodgings, I could not forbear throwing together such Reflections as occurred to me upon that Subject.

A Man who[b] has been brought up among Books, and is able to talk of nothing else, is a very indifferent Companion, and what we call a Pedant. But, methinks, we should enlarge the Title, and give it every one that does not know how to think out of his Profession, and particular way of Life.

What is a greater Pedant than a meer Man of the Town? Barr him the Play-houses, a Catalogue of the reigning Beauties, and an Account of a few fashionable Distempers that have befallen him, and you strike him Dumb. How many a pretty Gentleman's Knowledge lies all within the Verge of the Court? He will tell you the Names of the Principal Favourites, repeat the shrewd Sayings of a Man of Quality, whisper an Intriegue that is not yet blown upon by common Fame; or, if the Sphere of his Observations is a little larger than ordinary, will perhaps enter into all the Incidents, Turns and Revolutions in a Game of Ombre.[2] When he has gone thus far he has shown you the whole Circle of his Accomplishments, his Parts are drained, and he is disabled from any further Conversation. What are these but rank Pedants? and yet these are the Men who[c] value themselves most on their Exemption from the Pedantry of Colleges.

[a] Week] Night *Fol. Corrected in Errata (No. 106)*   [b] who] that *Fol.*   [c] who] that *Fol.*

[1] Steele concludes *Tatler* 244:

Pedantry proceeds from much Reading and little Understanding. A Pedant among Men of Learning and Sense, is like an ignorant Servant giving an Account of a polite Conversation. You may find he has brought with him more than could have entered into his Head without being there, but still that he is not a bit wiser than if he had not been there at all.

See also Malebranche, *Treatise concerning the Search after Truth*, book ii, chap. v (1700), p. 96.

[2] For the history and the rules of playing this popular card game see Appendix C in Geoffrey Tillotson's edition of Pope's *Rape of the Lock* (Methuen, 1940), pp. 361–8.

I might here mention the Military Pedant, who always talks in a Camp, and is storming Towns, making Lodgments, and fighting Battels from one end of the Year to the other. Every thing he speaks smells of Gunpowder; if you take away his Artillery from him, he has not a Word to say for himself. I might likewise mention the Law Pedant, that is perpetually putting Cases, repeating the Transactions of *Westminster-Hall*, wrangling with you upon the most indifferent Circumstances of Life, and not to be convinced of the Distance of a Place, or of the most trivial Point in Conversation, but by dint of Argument. The State-Pedant is wrapt up in News, and lost in Politicks. If you mention either of the Kings of *Spain* or *Poland*, he talks very notably, but if you go out of the *Gazette* you drop him. In short, a meer Courtier, a meer Soldier, a meer Scholar, a meer any thing, is an insipid Pedantick Character, and equally ridiculous.

Of all the Species of Pedants, which I have mentioned,[a] the Book-Pedant is much the most supportable; he has at least an exercised Understanding, and a Head which is full though confused, so that a Man who converses with him may often receive from him hints of things that are worth knowing, and what he may possibly turn to his own Advantage, tho' they are of little use to the Owner. The worst kind of Pedants among Learned Men are such as are naturally endued with a very small Share of common Sense, and have read a great number of Books without Taste or Distinction.

The Truth of it is, Learning, like Travelling, and all other Methods of Improvement, as it finishes good Sense, so it makes a silly Man ten thousand times more insufferable, by supplying variety of Matter to his Impertinence, and giving him an Opportunity of abounding in Absurdities.

Shallow Pedants cry up one another much more than Men of solid and useful Learning. To read the Titles they give an Editor, of Collator of a Manuscript, you would take him for the Glory of the Common Wealth of Letters, and the Wonder of his Age; when perhaps upon Examination you find that he has only Rectify'd a *Greek* Particle, or laid out a whole Sentence in proper Comma's.

They are obliged indeed to be thus lavish of their Praises, that they may keep one another in Countenance; and it is no wonder if a great deal of Knowledge, which is not capable of making a Man Wise, has a natural Tendency to make him Vain and Arrogant.

L

[a] have mentioned,] have above mentioned, *Fol.*

> *. . . Hinc tibi Copia*
> *Manabit ad plenum, benigno*
> *Ruris honorum opulenta cornu.*
> Hor.

HAVING often received an Invitation from my Friend Sir ROGER DE COVERLY to pass away a Month with him in the Country, I last Week accompanied him thither, and am settled with him for some Time at his Country-house, where I intend to form several of my ensuing Speculations. Sir ROGER, who is very well acquainted with my Humour, lets me rise and go to bed when I please, dine at his own Table or in my Chamber as I think fit, sit still and say nothing without bidding me be merry. When the Gentlemen of the Country come to see him, he only shews me at a Distance: As I have been walking in his Fields I have observed them stealing a Sight of me over an Hedge, and have heard the Knight desiring them not to let me see them, for that I hated to be stared at.

I am the more at Ease in Sir ROGER's Family, because it consists of sober and staid Persons; for as the Knight is the best Master in the World, he seldom changes his Servants; and as he is beloved by all about him, his Servants never care for leaving him: By this Means his Domesticks are all in Years, and grown old with their Master. You would take his Valet de Chambre for his Brother, his Butler is grey-headed, his Groom is one of the gravest Men that I have ever seen, and his Coachman has the Looks of a Privy-Counsellor. You see the Goodness of the Master even in the old House-dog, and in a grey Pad that is kept in the Stable with great Care and Tenderness out of regard to his past Services, tho' he has been useless for several Years.

I could not but observe with a great deal of Pleasure the Joy that appeared in the Countenances of these ancient Domesticks upon my Friend's Arrival at his Country-Seat. Some of them could not refrain

---

[1] *Motto.* Horace, *Odes,* I. 17. 14–16:
> Here to thee shall Plenty flow,
> And all her Riches show,
> To raise the Honours of the quiet Plain. CREECH.

from Tears at the Sight of their old Master; every one of them press'd forward to do something for him, and seemed discouraged if they were not employed. At the same Time the good old Knight, with a Mixture of the Father and the Master of the Family, tempered the Enquiries after his own Affairs with several kind Questions relating to themselves. This Humanity and good Nature engages[1] every Body to him, so that when he is pleasant upon any of them, all his Family are in good Humour, and none so much as the Person whom he diverts himself with: On the Contrary, if he coughs or betrays any Infirmity of old Age, it is easy for a Stander-by to observe a secret Concern in the Looks of all his Servants.

My worthy Friend has put me under the particular Care of his Butler, who is a very prudent Man, and, as well as the rest of his Fellow-Servants, wonderfully desirous of pleasing me, because they have often heard their Master talk of me as of his particular Friend.

My chief Companion when Sir ROGER is diverting himself in the Woods or the Fields, is a very venerable Man, who is ever with Sir ROGER, and has lived at his House in the Nature[2] of a Chaplain above thirty Years. This Gentleman is a Person of good Sense and some Learning, of a very regular Life and obliging Conversation: He heartily loves Sir ROGER, and knows that he is very much in the old Knight's Esteem; so that he lives in the Family rather as a Relation than a Dependant.

I have observed in several of my Papers, that my Friend Sir ROGER amidst all his good Qualities, is something of an Humourist; and that his Virtues, as well as Imperfections, are as it were tinged by a certain Extravagance, which makes them particularly *his*, and distinguishes them from those of other Men. This Cast of Mind, as it is generally very innocent in itself, so it renders his Conversation highly agreeable, and more delightful than the same Degree of Sense and Virtue would appear in their common and ordinary Colours. As I was walking with him last Night, he ask'd me, How I liked the good Man whom I have just now mentioned? and without staying for my Answer, told me, That he was afraid of being insulted with *Latin* and *Greek* at his own Table; for which Reason, he desired a particular Friend of his at the University to find him out a Clergy-

---

[1] To attach by pleasing qualities. Now rare (*OED*). This is the first example of the word in this sense in *OED*.

[2] As Hurd noted, the word is employed here 'a little licentiously'. It was used in the seventeenth century in the sense of 'capacity' or 'function', and is marked by *OED* as obsolete and rare.

man rather of plain Sense than much Learning, of a good Aspect, a clear Voice, a sociable Temper, and, if possible, a Man that understood a little of Back-Gammon.[1] My Friend, says Sir ROGER, found me out this Gentleman, who, besides the Endowments required[a] of him, is, they tell me, a good Scholar though he does not shew it. I have given him the Parsonage of the Parish; and because I know his Value, have settled upon him a good Annuity for[b] Life. If he out-lives me, he shall find that he was higher in my Esteem than perhaps he thinks he is. He has now been with me thirty Years; and though he does not know I have taken Notice of it, has never in all that Time asked any thing of me for himself, tho' he is every Day solliciting me for something in Behalf of one or other of my Tenants his Parishioners. There has not been a Law-Suit in the Parish since he has lived among them: If any Dispute arises, they apply themselves to him for the Decision; if they do not acquiesce in his Judgment, which I think never happened above once or twice at most, they appeal to me. At his first settling with me, I made him a Present of all the good Sermons which[c] have been printed in *English*, and only begged of him that every *Sunday* he would pronounce one of them in the Pulpit. Accordingly, he has digested them into such a Series, that they follow one another naturally, and make a continued System of practical Divinity.

As Sir ROGER was going on in his Story, the Gentleman we were talking of came up to us; and upon the Knight's asking him who preached to Morrow (for it was *Saturday* Night) told us, the Bishop of St. *Asaph*[2] in the Morning, and Doctor *South*[3] in the Afternoon. He then shewed us his List of Preachers for the whole Year, where I saw with a great deal of Pleasure Archbishop *Tillotson*,[4] Bishop

---

[a] Endowments required] Endowments I required *Fol.*   [b] for] during his *Fol.*   [c] which] that *Fol.*

---

[1] Backgammon is mentioned in No. 77. Swift speaks in the *Journal to Stella* (23 Aug. 1711) of playing it with Dillon Ashe; see also his letters to Gay of 4 May and 12 Aug. 1732.

[2] William Fleetwood (1656–1723), the prominent Whig bishop who was also a favourite of Queen Anne, had been Bishop of St. Asaph since 1708. As Canon of Windsor he had been a very popular London preacher, at St. Dunstan's-in-the-West. See No. 384 (vol. iii).

[3] Dr. Robert South (1634–1716), the popular and witty preacher of the reign of Charles II. He is quoted in *Tatlers* 205 and 211.

[4] See No. 103.

Saunderson,[1] Doctor *Barrow*,[2] Doctor *Calamy*,[3] with several living Authors who have published Discourses of practical Divinity. I no sooner saw this venerable Man in the Pulpit, but I very much approved of my Friend's insisting upon the Qualifications of a good Aspect and a clear Voice; for I was so charmed with the Gracefulness of his Figure and Delivery, as well as with the Discourses he pronounced, that I think I never passed any Time more to my Satisfaction. A Sermon repeated after this Manner, is like the Composition of a Poet in the Mouth of a graceful Actor.

I could heartily wish that more of our Country-Clergy would follow this Example; and instead of wasting their Spirits in laborious Compositions of their own, would endeavour, after a handsome Elocution and all those other Talents that are proper to enforce what has been penn'd by greater Masters.[4] This would not only be more easy to themselves, but more edifying to the People.　　L[5]

[1] Robert Sanderson (1587–1663), Bishop of Lincoln, was often quoted by the Tories on the favourite topics of non-resistance and passive obedience. *Medley* 22 (26 Feb. 1711) calls him the Tories' 'Great Apostle'. See also *Medley* 27 (2 Apr. 1711) for quotations from him on these subjects.

[2] Doctor Isaac Barrow (1630–77), equally distinguished in the fields of mathematics and theology and author of several standard works on doctrine.

[3] Identified by Morley as Edmund Calamy, the noted Presbyterian divine. 'His name', says Morley, 'added to the other three, gives breadth to the suggestion of Sir Roger's orthodoxy.' It is much more likely that the preacher referred to is his second son, Benjamin Calamy, D.D. (1642–86), Prebendary of St. Paul's and a strong advocate for the Established Church. He published seven separate sermons (a list is given in *Biographia Britannica*), and after his death a collection of his sermons was published (1690), which went through several editions (*DNB*).

[4] Cf. *Tatler* 57: 'I have heard, it has been advis'd by a Diocesan to his inferior Clergy, that instead of broaching Opinions of their own, and uttering Doctrines which may lead themselves and Hearers into Errors, they would read some of the most celebrated Sermons printed by others for the Instruction of their Congregations.' The following 'Advertisement' appears in *Tatler* 269:

> Whereas *Plagius* has been told again and again, both in publick and private, That he preaches excellently well, and still goes on to preach as well as ever, and all this to a polite and learned Audience; This is to desire, That he would not hereafter be so eloquent, except to a Country Congregation, the Proprietors of *Tillotson*'s Works having consulted the Learned in the Law, whether preaching a Sermon they have purchased, is not to be construed publishing their Copy.

The practice of reading sermons seems to have been fairly common in the eighteenth century, especially in country churches. The late Dr. Norman Sykes wrote me that he had discovered that Anthony Hastwell in his two Yorkshire villages of Kildale and Great Ayton, as well as Parson Woodforde, delivered abbreviated versions of Tillotson's sermons.

[5] No. 106 begins the famous series of papers dealing with Sir Roger de Coverley, most of them written by Addison, who had apparently spent most of the preceding month in the country, after the rising of Parliament (Smithers, p. 224).

Æsopo ingentem statuam posuere Attici,
Servumque collocârunt Æterna in Basi,
Patere honoris scirent ut Cuncti viam.

Phæd.

THE Reception, manner of Attendance, undisturb'd Freedom and Quiet which I meet with here in the Country, has confirmed me in the Opinion I always had, that the general Corruption of Manners in Servants[2] is owing to the Conduct of Masters. The Aspect of every one in the Family carries so much Satisfaction, that it appears he knows the happy Lot which has befallen him in being a Member of it. There is one Particular which I have seldom seen but at Sir *Roger's*; it is usual in all other Places, that Servants fly from the parts of the House through which their Master is passing; on the contrary, here they industriously place themselves in his way, and it is on both sides, as it were, understood as a Visit when the Servants appear without calling. This proceeds from the Human and equal Temper of the Man of the House, who also perfectly well knows how to enjoy a great Estate, with such Oeconomy as ever to be much before Hand. This makes his own Mind untroubled, and consequently unapt to vent peevish Expressions, or give passionate or inconsistent Orders to those about him. Thus Respect and Love go together, and a certain Chearfulness in Performance of their Duty is the particular Distinction of the lower part of this Family. When a Servant is called before his Master, he does not come with an Expectation to hear himself rated for some trivial Fault, threatned to be stripp'd,[3] or used with any other unbecoming Language, which mean Masters often give to worthy Servants. But it is often to know, what Road he took that he came so readily back according to Order; whether he passed by such a Ground; if the old Man who rents it is in good Health; or whether he gave Sir *Roger's* Love to him, or the like.

[1] *Motto.* Phaedrus, *Fables*, 2. Epilogue 1–3:
The Athenians raised a noble statue to the memory of Æsop, and placed a slave on the pedestal, that all might know the way to honour was open to all.
[2] In this paper Steele continues the discussion started in Nos. 88 and 96 and shows what the ideal master–servant relationship can be.
[3] To strip, in the obsolete sense of discharging a liveried servant. The only example in *OED* is dated 1756.

A Man who preserves a Respect, founded on his Benevolence to his Dependants, lives rather like a Prince than a Master in his Family; his Orders are received as Favours, rather than Duties, and the Distinction of approaching him, is part of the Reward for executing what is commanded by him.

There is another Circumstance in which my Friend excells in his Management, which is the manner of rewarding his Servants: He has ever been of Opinion, that giving his cast Cloaths to be worn by Valets has a very ill Effect upon little Minds, and creates a silly Sense of Equality between the Parties, in Persons affected only with outward things. I have heard him often pleasant on this Occasion, and describe a young Gentleman abusing his Man in that Coat, which a Month or two before was the most pleasing Distinction he was conscious of in himself. He would turn his Discourse still more pleasantly upon the Ladies Bounties of this kind; and I have heard him say he knew a fine Woman, who distributed Rewards and Punishments in giving becoming or unbecoming Dresses to her Maids.

But my good Friend is above these little Instances of Good-will, in bestowing only Trifles on his Servants; a good Servant to him is sure of having it in his Choice very soon of being no Servant at all. As I before observed, he is so good an Husband,[1] and knows so thoroughly that the Skill of the Purse is the Cardinal Virtue of this Life; I say, he knows so well that Frugality is the Support of Generosity, that he can often spare a large Fine when a Tenement falls, and give that Settlement to a good Servant who has a mind to go into the World, or make a Stranger pay the Fine to that Servant, for his more comfortable Maintenance, if he stays in his Service.

A Man of Honour and Generosity considers, it would be miserable to himself to have no Will but that of another, tho' it were of the best Person breathing, and for that Reason goes on as fast as he is able to put his Servants into independent Livelihoods. The greatest part of Sir *Roger*'s Estate is tenanted by Persons who have served himself or his Ancestors. It was to me extreamly pleasant to observe the Visitants from several parts to Welcome his Arrival into the Country, and all the Difference that I could take notice of, between the late Servants who came to see him, and those who staid in the Family, was, that these latter were looked upon as finer Gentlemen and better Courtiers.

This Manumission and placing them in a way of Livelihood, I

[1] In the sense only of thrifty person.

look upon as only what is due to a good Servant, which Encouragement will make his Successor be as diligent, as humble, and as ready as he was. There is something wonderful in the Narrowness of those Minds which can be pleased, and be barren of Bounty to those who please them.

One might, on this occasion, recount the Sense that Great Persons in all Ages have had of the Merit of their Dependants, and the Heroick Services which Men have done their Masters in the Extremity of their Fortunes; and shown, to their undone Patrons, that Fortune was all the Difference between them. But as I design this my Speculation only as[a] a gentle Admonition to thankless Masters, I shall not go out of the Occurrences of common Life, but assert it as a general Observation, that I never saw, but in Sir *Roger*'s Family, and one or two more, good Servants treated as they ought to be. Sir *Roger*'s Kindness extends to their Children's Children, and this very Morning he sent his Coachman's Grandson to Prentice. I shall conclude this Paper with an Account of a Picture in his Gallery, where there are many which will deserve my future Observation.

At the very upper End of this handsome Structure I saw the Portraiture of two Young Men standing in a River, the one naked the other in a Livery. The Person supported seemed half Dead, but still so much alive as to show in his Face exquisite Joy and Love towards the other. I thought the fainting Figure resembled my Friend Sir *Roger*; and looking at the Butler, who stood by me, for an Account of it, he informed me that the Person in the Livery was a Servant of Sir *Roger*'s, who stood on the Shore while his Master was Swimming, and observing him taken with some sudden Illness, and sink under Water, jumped in and saved him. He told me Sir *Roger* took off the Dress he was in as soon as he came home, and by a Great Bounty at that time, follow'd by his Favour ever since, had made him Master of that pretty Seat which we saw at a distance as we came to this House. I remember'd indeed Sir *Roger* said there lived a very worthy Gentleman, to whom he was highly obliged, without mentioning any thing further. Upon my looking a little dissatisfyed at some part of the Picture, my Attendant informed me, that it was against Sir *Roger*'s Will, and at the earnest Request of the Gentleman himself, that he was Drawn in the Habit in which he had saved his Master. **R**[1]

[a] only as a] only a *Fol.*

[*For note 1 see following page.*

No. 108   *Wednesday, July 4, 1711*[1]
[ADDISON]

Gratìs anhelans, multa agendo nihil agens.
Phæd.

AS I was Yesterday Morning walking with Sir ROGER before his House, a Country-Fellow brought him a huge Fish, which, he told him, Mr. *William Wimble*[2] had caught that very Morning; and that he presented it, with his Service, to him, and intended to come and dine with him. At the same Time he delivered a Letter, which my Friend read to me assoon as the Messenger left him.

Sir ROGER,

I DESIRE you to accept of a Jack, which is the best I have caught this Season. I intend to come and stay with you a Week, and see how the Perch bite in the *Black River*. I observed, with some Concern, the last Time I saw you upon the Bowling-Green, that your Whip wanted a Lash to it: I will bring half a Dozen with me that I twisted last Week, which I hope will serve you all the Time you are in the Country. I have not been out of the Saddle for six Days

---

[1] *Motto*. Phaedrus, *Fables*, 2. 5. 3: Puffing hard, and making much to do about nothing.

[2] The supposed 'original' of this character was a certain Thomas Morecraft, who died at Dublin on 2 July 1741 and was at that time described in the *Gentleman's Magazine* as 'the Person mentioned by the Spectator in the Character of *Will. Wimble*' (xi. 387). There seems to be no evidence for Nichols's statement (in a note to No. 269 (vol. ii)) that 'Steele, who knew him very early in life, introduced him to Addison, by whose bounty he was for some years supported'. Like 'the Hon. Thomas Gules' of *Tatler* 256, Will Wimble embodies in himself all the traits of the idle younger son in an ancient family, 'bred to no Business and born to no Estate'. In *The Midwife, or the Old Woman's Magazine*, published by Newbery 1750-3 and edited mainly by Christopher Smart, is a sketch of Will Wimble, amplifying the account in the *Spectator* (*The Midwife*, no. vi, pp. 264-9).

---

[1] In No. 125 'the Quarterly Contribution for the Benefit of faithful Servants' is advertised 'at the Office in Ironmonger-lane'.

Which Method has hitherto had very good Effects; for the Benefits arising thereby not being to be received without a dutiful Behaviour in the Servants, and a good Character from their Masters, has frequently occasioned a stricter Observance of the Servant's Duty, and incited them to a more earnest Endeavour to deserve that Character on which they have such Dependance. N.B. One whole Year's faithful Service in one Place, gives a Title to a Claim.

In the first announcement of this plan, in No. 88, it is called a 'Mutual Contribution, . . . according to the Liberty given by a Clause in the late Lottery-Act'.

last past, having been at *Eaton* with Sir *John*'s eldest Son. He takes to his Learning hugely.

I am,

SIR,

Your humble Servant,

Will. Wimble.'

This extraordinary Letter, and Message that accompanied it, made me very curious to know the Character and Quality of the Gentleman who sent them; which I found to be as follows: *Will. Wimble* is younger Brother to a Baronet, and descended of the ancient Family of the *Wimbles*. He is now between Forty and Fifty; but being bred to no Business and born to no Estate, he generally lives with his elder Brother as Superintendant of his Game. He hunts a Pack of Dogs better than any Man in the Country, and is very famous for finding out a Hare. He is extremely well versed in all the little Handicrafts of an idle Man: He makes a *May*-fly to a Miracle; and furnishes the whole Country with Angle-Rods. As he is a good-natur'd officious[1] Fellow, and very much esteemed upon Account of his Family, he is a welcome Guest at every House, and keeps up a good Correspondence among all the Gentlemen about him. He carries a Tulip-Root[2] in his Pocket from one to another, or exchanges a Puppy between a couple of Friends that live perhaps in the opposite Sides of the County. *Will.* is a particular Favourite of all the young Heirs, whom he frequently obliges with a Net that he has weaved, or a Setting-dog that he has *made*[3] himself: He now and then presents a Pair of Garters of his own knitting to their Mothers or Sisters, and raises a great deal of Mirth among them, by enquiring as often as he meets them *how they wear*? These Gentleman-like Manufactures and obliging little Humours, make *Will.* the Darling of the Country.

Sir ROGER was proceeding in the Character of him, when we saw him make up to us, with two or three Hazle-twigs in his Hand that he had cut in Sir ROGER's Woods, as he came through them, in his

---

[1] 'Doing or ready to do kind offices; eager to serve or please; attentive, obliging, kind' (*OED*). The word is frequently used in this sense in the *Spectator*, now obsolete; the last quotation in *OED* is dated 1827.

[2] The tulip-mania of the late seventeenth century was still a subject of satire. In *Tatler* 218 Addison had described an enthusiast: 'He seemed a very plain honest Man, and a Person of good Sense, had not his Head been touched with that Distemper which *Hippocrates* calls the *Tulippo-Mania*, τυλιππομανία, insomuch that he would talk very rationally on any Subject in the World but a Tulip.'

[3] Used here in the specialized sense of *training*.

Way to the House. I was very much pleased to observe on one Side the hearty and sincere Welcome with which Sir ROGER received him, and on the other the secret Joy which his Guest discovered at Sight of the good old Knight. After the first Salutes were over, *Will.* desired Sir ROGER to lend him one of his Servants to carry a Set of Shuttle-cocks he had with him in a little Box to a Lady that liv'd about a Mile off, to whom it seems he had promised such a Present for above this half Year. Sir ROGER's Back was no sooner turn'd, but honest *Will.* begun to tell me of a large Cock-Pheasant that he had sprung in one of the neighbouring Woods, with two or three other Adventures of the same Nature. Odd and uncommon Characters are the Game that I look for, and most delight in; for which Reason I was as much pleased with the Novelty of the Person that talked to me, as he could be for his Life with the springing of a Pheasant, and therefore listned to him with more than ordinary Attention.

In the Midst of his Discourse the Bell rung to Dinner, where the Gentleman I have been speaking of had the Pleasure of seeing the huge Jack, he had caught, served up for the first Dish in a most sumptuous Manner. Upon our sitting down to it he gave us a long Account how he had hooked it, played with it, foiled it, and at length drew it out upon the Bank, with several other Particulars that lasted all the first Course. A Dish of Wild-fowl that came afterwards furnished Conversation for the rest of the Dinner, which concluded with a late Invention of *Will*'s for improving the Quail Pipe.

Upon withdrawing into my Room after Dinner, I was secretly touched with Compassion towards the honest Gentleman that had dined with us; and could not but consider with a great deal of Concern, how so good an Heart and such busy Hands were wholly employed in Trifles; that so much Humanity should be so little beneficial to others, and so much Industry so little advantageous to himself. The same Temper of Mind and Application to Affairs might have recommended him to the publick Esteem, and have raised his Fortune in another Station of Life. What Good to his Country or himself might not a Trader or Merchant have done with such useful tho' ordinary Qualifications?

Will. Wimble's is the Case of many a younger Brother of a great Family, who had rather see their Children starve like Gentlemen, than thrive in a Trade or Profession that is beneath their Quality.

This Humour fills several Parts of *Europe* with Pride and Beggary. It is the Happiness of a trading Nation, like ours, that the younger Sons, tho' uncapable of any liberal Art or Profession, may be placed in such a Way of Life, as may perhaps enable them to vie with the best of their Family: Accordingly we find several Citizens that were launched into the World with narrow Fortunes, rising by an honest Industry to greater Estates than those of their elder Brothers. It is not improbable but *Will.* was formerly tried at Divinity, Law, or Physick; and that finding his Genius did not lie that Way, his Parents gave him up at length to his own Inventions: But certainly, however improper he might have been for Studies of a higher Nature, he was perfectly well turned for the Occupations of Trade and Commerce. As I think this is a Point which cannot be too much inculcated, I shall desire my Reader to compare what I have here written with what I have said in my Twenty first Speculation.   L

No. 109   *Thursday, July 5, 1711*[1]

[STEELE]

>   *. . . Abnormis sapiens . . .*
>   Hor.

I WAS this Morning walking in the Gallery, when Sir ROGER enter'd at the end opposite to me, and advancing towards me, said, he was glad to meet me among his Relations the DE COVERLEYS, and hoped I liked the Conversation of so much good Company, who were as silent as my self. I knew he alluded to the Pictures, and as he is a Gentleman who does not a little value himself upon his ancient Descent, I expected he would give me some Account of them. We were now arrived at the upper End of the Gallery, when the Knight faced towards one of the Pictures, and as we stood before it, he entered into the Matter after his blunt way of saying things, as they occur to his Imagination, without regular Introduction, or Care to preserve the appearance of Chain of Thought.

'It is, said he, worth while to consider the Force of Dress, and how the Persons of one Age differ from those of another, merely by that only. One may observe also that the General Fashion of one Age has been follow'd by one particular Set of People in another, and by

---

[1] *Motto.* Horace, *Satires*, 2. 2. 3: Unlearned in schools.

them preserved from one Generation to another. Thus the vast Jetting[1] Coat and small Bonnet, which was the Habit in *Harry* the Seventh's time, is kept on in the Yeomen of the Guard, not without a good and Politick View, because they look a Foot taller, and a Foot and an half broader: Besides that the Cap leaves the Face expanded, and consequently more Terrible, and fitter to stand at the Entrance of Palaces.

'This Predecessor of ours, you see, is dressed after this manner, and his Cheeks would be no larger than mine were he in an Hat as I am. He was the last Man that won a Prize in the Tilt-Yard[2] (which is now a Common Street before *Whitehall.*) You see the broken Lance that lyes there by his right Foot; He shivered that Lance of his Adversary all to pieces; and bearing himself, look you Sir, in this manner, at the same time he came within the Target of the Gentleman who rode against him, and taking him with incredible Force before him on the Pummel of his Saddle, he in that manner rid the Turnament over, with an Air that shewed he did it rather to perform the Rule of the Lists, than Expose his Enemy; however it appeared, he knew how to make use of a Victory, and with a gentle Trot he marched up to a Gallery where their Mistress sate (for they were Rivals) and let him down with laudable Courtesy and pardonable Insolence. I don't know but it might be exactly where the Coffee-house is now.[3]

'You are to know this my Ancestor was not only of a military Genius but fit also for the Arts of Peace, for he play'd on the Base-viol as well as any Gentleman at Court; you see where his Viol hangs by his Basket-hilt Sword. The Action at the Tilt-yard you may be sure won the Fair Lady, who was a Maid of Honour, and the greatest Beauty of her time; here she stands, the next Picture. You see, Sir, my Great Great Great Grand-Mother has on the new-fashioned Petticoat, except that the Modern is gathered at the Waste; my Grandmother appears as if she stood in a large Drum,[4] whereas the

[1] i.e. jutting, protruding. Now obsolete; the last quotation in *OED* is dated 1812.
[2] The Tilt-Yard had formerly been in front of the old Banqueting-Hall, in Whitehall, towards Charing Cross.
[3] This was Jenny Man's Coffee-house (see Nos. 283 and 403 (vol. iii), and 550 (vol. iv)), popular as a meeting-place for soldiers. Tom Brown describes the behaviour of soldiers there in the essay 'Upon Old Man's and Young Man's Coffee-houses' in *A Walk round London and Westminster* (*Works*, 1715, iii. 299–306). The Tilt-Yard Coffee-house was 'still in being' in 1789 (Nichols).
[4] According to Planché (*History of British Costume*, 3rd ed., 1874, p. 351) 'the old lady was evidently in the wheel fardingale'. See the description of this costume in Planché.

Ladies now walk as if they were in a Go-cart. For all this Lady was bred at Court she became an Excellent Country-Wife, she brought ten Children, and when I show you the Library, you shall see in her own hand (allowing for the Difference of the Language,) the best Receipt now in *England* both for an Hasty-Pudding and a Whitepot.[1]

'If you please to fall back a little, because it is necessary to look at the three next Pictures at one View; these are three Sisters. She on the right Hand, who is so very beautiful, dyed a Maid; the next to her, still handsomer, had the same Fate against her Will; this homely thing in the middle had both their Portions added to her own, and was Stolen by a neighbouring Gentleman, a Man of Stratagem and Resolution, for he poisoned three Mastiffs to come at her, and knocked down two Deer-stealers in carrying her off: Misfortunes happen in all Families: The Theft of this Romp, and so much Mony, was no great matter to our Estate; but the next Heir that possessed it was this soft Gentleman, whom you see there; observe the small Buttons, the little Boots, the Laces, the Slashes about his Cloaths, and above all the Posture he is drawn in, (which to be sure was his own chusing;) you see he sits with one Hand on a Desk writing, and looking as it were another way, like an easie Writer,[2] or a Sonneteer: He was one of those that had too much Wit to know how to live in the World; he was a Man of no Justice, but great good Manners; he ruined every body that had any thing to do with him, but never said a rude thing in his Life; the most indolent Person in the World, he would sign a Deed that passed away half his Estate with his Gloves on, but would not put on his Hat before a Lady if it were to save his Country. He is said to be the first that made Love by squeezing the Hand. He left the Estate with ten thousand Pounds Debt upon it, but however by all Hands I have been informed that he was every way the finest Gentleman in the World. That Debt lay heavy on our House for one Generation, but it was retrieved by a Gift from that Honest Man you see there, a Citizen of our Name, but nothing at all a-kin to us. I know Sir *Andrew Freeport* has said behind my Back, that this Man was descended from one of the ten Children of the Maid of Honour

[1] A spiced dish of cream, sugar, rice, and cinnamon, popular in Devonshire. It is mentioned in Dr. King's *Art of Cookery* (Chalmers, ix. 254), in *Hudibras* (I. i. 297), and in Gay's *Shepherd's Week* (Monday, 92).

[2] Cf. *Tatler* 9: 'The Town has this half Age been tormented with Insects call'd *Easie Writers*, whose Abilities Mr. *Wycherly* one Day describ'd excellently well in one Word. *That*, said he, *among these Fellows is call'd* Easy Writing, *which any one may easily write.*'

I shewed you above. But it was never made out; we winked at the thing indeed, because Mony was wanting at that time.'

Here I saw my Friend a little embarrassed, and turned my Face to the next Portraiture.

Sir ROGER went on with his Account of the Gallery in the following manner. 'This Man (pointing to him I look'd at) I take to be the Honour of our House, Sir HUMPHREY DE COVERLEY; he was in his Dealings as punctual as a Tradesman, and as generous as a Gentleman. He would have thought himself as much undone by breaking his Word, as if it were to be followed by Bankruptcy. He served his Country as Knight of this Shire to his dying Day: He found it no easie matter to maintain an Integrity in his Words and Actions even in things that regarded the Offices which were incumbent upon him, in the care of his own Affairs and Relations of Life, and therefore dreaded (tho' he had great Talents) to go into Employments of State,[1] where he must be exposed to the Snares of Ambition. Innocence of Life and great Ability were the distinguishing Parts of his Character; the latter, he had often observed, had led to the Destruction of the former, and used frequently to lament that Great and Good had not the same Signification. He was an Excellent Husbandman, but had resolved not to exceed such a degree of Wealth, all above it he bestowed in secret Bounties many Years after the Sum he aimed at for his own use was attained. Yet he did not slacken his Industry, but to a decent old Age spent the Life and Fortune which was superfluous to himself in the Service of his Friends and Neighbours.'

Here we were called to Dinner, and Sir ROGER ended the Discourse of this Gentleman, by telling me, as we followed the Servant, that this his Ancestor was a Brave Man, and narrowly escaped being killed in the Civil Wars; 'for, said he, he was sent out of the Field upon a private Message the Day before the Battel of *Worcester*'.[2] The Whim of narrowly escaping, by having been within a Day of Danger, with other Matters above-mentioned, mixed with good Sense, left me at a Loss whether I was more delighted with my Friend's Wisdom or Simplicity.   R

[1] Two years later Addison was to expand this thought into a famous couplet of *Cato* (IV. iv. 141–2):

> When vice prevails, and impious men bear sway,
> The post of honour is a private station.

[2] In 1651, the scene of Charles II's defeat by Cromwell.

Horror ubique animos, simul ipsa silentia terrent.
Virg.

AT a little Distance from Sir ROGER's House, among the Ruins of an old Abby, there is a long Walk of aged Elms; which are shot up so very high, that when one passes under them, the Rooks and Crows that rest upon the Tops of them seem to be Cawing in another Region. I am very much delighted with this Sort of Noise, which I consider as a kind of natural Prayer to that Being who supplies the Wants of his whole Creation, and, who in[a] the beautiful Language of the *Psalms*, feedeth the young Ravens that call upon him.[2] I like this Retirement[b] the better, because of an ill Report it lies under of being *haunted*;[3] for which Reason (as I have been told in the Family) no living Creature ever walks in it besides the Chaplain. My good Friend the Butler desired me with a very grave Face not to venture myself in it after Sun-set, for that one of the Footmen had been almost frighted out of his Wits by a Spirit that appeared to him in the Shape of a black Horse without an Head; to which he added, that about a Month ago one of the Maids coming home late that Way with a Pail of Milk upon her Head, heard such a Rustling among the Bushes that she let it fall.

I was taking a Walk in this Place last Night between the Hours of Nine and Ten, and could not but fancy it one of the most proper Scenes in the World for a Ghost to appear in. The Ruins of the Abby are scattered up and down on every Side, and half covered with Ivy and Eldar-Bushes, the Harbours of several solitary Birds which seldom make their Appearance till the Dusk of the Evening. The Place was formerly a Church-yard, and has still several Marks in it of Graves and Burying-Places. There is such an Eccho among the old Ruins and Vaults, that if you stamp but a little louder than ordinary you hear the Sound repeated. At the same Time the Walk of Elms, with the Croaking of the Ravens which from time to time

[a] and, who in] and, in *Fol.*   [b] Retirement] Walk *Fol.*

[1] *Motto.* Virgil, *Aeneid*, 2. 755:
All things were full of Horrour and Affright,
And dreadful ev'n the silence of the Night. DRYDEN.
[2] Psalm cxlvii. 9.
[3] Addison's comedy, *The Drummer* (produced in 1716), dealt with the Mompesson house at Tidworth, haunted according to legend by the ghost of a drummer.

are heard from the Tops of them, looks exceeding solemn and venerable. These Objects naturally raise Seriousness and Attention; and
when Night heightens the Awfulness of the Place, and pours out
her supernumerary Horrours upon every thing in it, I do not at all
wonder that weak Minds fill it with Spectres and Apparitions.

Mr. *Lock*,[1] in his Chapter of the Association of Ideas, has very
curious Remarks to shew how by the Prejudice of Education one
Idea often introduces into the Mind a whole Set that bear no Resemblance to one another in the Nature of things. Among several
Examples of this Kind he produces the following Instance. *The Ideas
of Goblins and Sprights have really no more to do with Darkness than Light;
yet let but a foolish Maid inculcate these often on the Mind of a Child, and
raise them there together, possibly he shall never be able to separate them again
so long as he lives, but Darkness shall ever afterwards bring with it those
frightful Ideas, and they shall be so joyned, that he can no more bear the one
than the other.*

As I was walking in this Solitude, where the Dusk of the Evening
conspired with so many other Occasions of Terrour, I observed a
Cow grazing not far from me, which an Imagination that is apt to
startle might easily have construed into a black Horse without an
Head; and I dare say the poor Footman lost his Wits upon some
such trivial Occasion.

My Friend Sir ROGER has often told me with a great deal of
Mirth, that at his first coming to his Estate he found three Parts of
his House altogether useless; that the best Room in it had the
Reputation of being haunted, and by that Means was locked up;
that Noises had been heard in his long Gallery, so that he could not
get a Servant to enter it after eight a Clock at Night; that the Door
of one of his Chambers was nailed up, because there went a Story
in the Family that a Butler had formerly hanged himself in it; and
that his Mother, who lived to a great Age, had shut up half the
Rooms in the House, in which either her Husband, a Son,[a] or
Daughter had died.[2] The Knight seeing his Habitation reduced to[b]
so small a Compass, and himself in a Manner shut out of his own
House, upon the Death of his Mother ordered all the Apartments[c]

---

[a] a Son,] her Son, *Fol.*   [b] to] into *Fol.*   [c] all the Apartments]
the Rooms *Fol.*

---

[1] *Essay*, II. xxxiii. 10.
[2] For the persistence of this practice down to the end of the eighteenth century
see *N & Q*, 1st ser., iii (1851), 142-3.

to be flung open, and *exorcised* by his Chaplain, who lay in every Room one after another, and by that Means dissipated the Fears which had so long reigned in the Family.

I should not have been thus particular upon these ridiculous Horrours, did not I find them so very much prevail in all Parts of the Country. At the same Time I think a Person who is thus terrify'd with the Imagination of Ghosts and Spectres much more reasonable, than one who contrary to the Reports of all Historians sacred and prophane, ancient and modern, and to the Traditions of all Nations, thinks the Appearance of Spirits fabulous and groundless: Could not I give my self up to this general Testimony of Mankind, I should to the Relations of particular Persons who are now living, and whom I cannot distrust in other Matters of Fact. I might here add, that not only the Historians, to whom we may joyn the Poets, but likewise the Philosophers of Antiquity have favoured this Opinion. *Lucretius*[1] himself, though by the Course of his Philosophy he was obliged to maintain that the Soul did not exist separate from the Body, makes no Doubt of the Reality of Apparitions, and that Men have often appeared after their Death. This I think very remarkable; he was so pressed with the Matter of Fact which he could not have the Confidence to deny, that he was forced to account for it by one of the most absurd unphilosophical Notions that was ever started. He tells us, That the Surfaces of all Bodies are perpetually flying off from their respective Bodies, one after another; and that these Surfaces or thin Cases that included each other whilst they were joined in the Body like the Coats of an Onion, are sometimes seen entire when they are separated from it; by which Means we often behold the Shapes and Shadows of Persons who are either dead or absent.

I shall dismiss this Paper with a Story out of *Josephus*,[2] not so much for the Sake of the Story it self, as for the moral Reflections with which the Author concludes it, and which I shall here set down in his own Words. 'Glaphyra the Daughter of King *Archilaus*, after the Death of her two first Husbands (being married to a third, who was Brother to her first Husband, and so passionately in Love with her that he turn'd off his former Wife to make Room for this Marriage) had a very odd kind of Dream. She fancied that she saw her first Husband coming towards her, and that she embraced him with

---

[1] *De rerum natura*, 4. 26 ff.
[2] *Antiquities of the Jews*, 17. 13. 4–5. It is told also in Bayle, art. Glaphyra, Remark C.

great Tenderness; when in the Midst of the Pleasure which she expressed at the Sight of him, he reproached her after the following Manner: *Glaphyra*, says he, thou hast made good the old Saying, That Women are not to be trusted. Was not I the Husband of thy Virginity? have I not Children by thee? How couldst thou forget our Loves so far as to enter into a second Marriage, and after that into a third, nay to take for thy Husband a Man who has so shamelesly crept into the Bed of his Brother? However, for the Sake of our passed Loves, I shall free thee from thy present Reproach, and make thee mine for ever. *Glaphyra* told this Dream to several Women of her Acquaintance, and died soon after. I thought this Story might not be impertinent in this Place, wherein I speak of those Kings: Besides that, the Example deserves to be taken Notice of, as it contains a most certain Proof of the Immortality of the Soul, and of Divine Providence. If any Man thinks these Facts incredible, let him enjoy his Opinion to himself, but let him not endeavour to disturb the Belief of others, who by Instances of this Nature are excited to the Study of Virtue.'   L

No. III

[ADDISON]

Saturday, July 7, 1711[1]

> *. . . Inter Silvas Academi quærere Verum.*
>
> Hor.

THE Course of my last Speculation led me insensibly into a Subject upon which I always meditate with great Delight, I mean the Immortality of the Soul. I was Yesterday walking alone in one of my Friend's Woods, and lost my self in it very agreeably, as I was running over in my Mind the several Arguments that establish this great Point, which is the Basis of Morality, and the Source of all the pleasing Hopes and secret Joys that can arise in the Heart of a reasonable Creature. I considered those several Proofs drawn,

First, From the Nature of the Soul it self, and particularly its

[1] *Motto*. Horace, *Epistles*, 2. 2. 45: To search for truth in groves of Academe.

Immateriality; which tho' not absolutely necessary to the Eternity of its Duration, has, I think, been evinced to almost a Demonstration.

Secondly, From its Passions and Sentiments, as particularly from its Love of Existence, its Horrour of Annihilation, and its Hopes of Immortality, with that secret Satisfaction which it finds in the Practice of Virtue, and that Uneasiness which follows in it upon the Commission of Vice.

Thirdly, From the Nature of the Supreme Being, whose Justice, Goodness, Wisdom and Veracity are all concerned in this great Point.

But among these and other excellent Arguments for the Immortality of the Soul, there is one drawn from the perpetual Progress of the Soul[1] to its Perfection, without a Possibility of ever arriving at it; which is a Hint that I do not remember to have seen opened and improved by others who have written on this Subject, tho' it seems to me to carry a great Weight with it. How can it enter into the Thoughts of Man, that the Soul, which is capable of such immense Perfections, and of receiving new Improvements to all Eternity, shall fall away into nothing almost as soon as it is created? Are such Abilities made for no Purpose? A Brute arrives at a point of Perfection that he can never pass. In a few Years he has all the Endowments he is capable of, and were he to live ten thousand more, would be the same thing he is at present. Were a human Soul thus at a stand in her Accomplishments, were her Faculties to be full blown, and incapable of further Enlargements, I could imagine it might fall away insensibly, and drop at once into a State of Annihilation. But can we believe a thinking Being, that is in a perpetual Progress of Improvements, and travelling on from Perfection to Perfection, after having just looked abroad into the Works of its Creator, and made a few Discoveries of his infinite Goodness, Wisdom and Power, must perish at her first setting out, and in the very beginning of her Enquiries?

A Man, considered in his present State, seems only sent into the

---

[1] For the background of this idea and examples from earlier writers see A. O. Lovejoy, *The Great Chain of Being* (Harvard Univ. Press, 1936), chap. ix, especially pp. 244–8. Addison is also indebted in this essay to one of his favourite books, *The Christian Life*, by John Scott (praised in No. 447 (vol. iv)): see part ii, vol. i, chap. v, 'Proofs of a Future State'. 'No *wise* Man would build a House unless he meant it should be *inhabited*; and can we imagine that the *All-wise* God would ever have created in us such *vast* and *boundless* capacities of happiness, merely to *stand empty* and be for ever *uninhabited* . . .?' (ii. 302).

World to propagate his Kind. He provides himself[a] with a Successor, and immediately quits his Post to make room for him.

> . . . *haeres*
> *Haeredem alterius, velut unda supervenit undam.*[1]

He does not seem born to enjoy Life, but to deliver it down to others. This is not surprizing to consider in Animals, which are formed for our use, and can finish their Business in a short Life. The Silk-worm, after having spun her Task, lays her Eggs and dies. But a Man can never have taken in his full measure of Knowledge, has not time to subdue his Passions, establish his Soul in Virtue, and come up to the Perfection of his Nature, before he is hurried off the Stage. Would an infinitely wise Being make such glorious Creatures for so mean a Purpose? Can he delight in the Production of such abortive Intelligences, such short-lived reasonable Beings? Would he give us Talents that are not to be exerted? Capacities that are never to be gratified? How can we find that Wisdom, which shines through all his Works, in the Formation of Man, without looking on this World, as only a Nursery for the next, and believing that the several Generations of rational Creatures, which rise up and disappear in such quick Successions, are only to receive their first Rudiments of Existence here, and afterwards to be transplanted into a more friendly Climate, where they may spread and flourish to all Eternity?

There is not, in my Opinion, a more pleasing and triumphant Consideration in Religion than this of the perpetual Progress which the Soul makes towards the Perfection of its Nature, without ever arriving at a Period in it. To look upon the Soul as going on from Strength to Strength,[2] to consider that she is to shine for ever with new Accessions of Glory, and brighten to all Eternity: That she will be still adding Virtue to Virtue, and Knowledge to Knowledge, carries in it something wonderfully agreeable to that Ambition which is natural to the Mind of Man. Nay, it must be a Prospect pleasing to God himself, to see his Creation for ever beautifying[3] in his Eyes, and drawing nearer to him, by greater degrees of Resemblance.

[a] his Kind. He provides] his Kind, and provide *Fol.*

---

[1] Horace, *Epistles*, 2. 2. 175–6.
> But Heir crowds Heir, as in a rowling Flood
> Wave urges Wave.... CREECH.

[2] Psalm lxxxiv. 7.

[3] A rare use of the intransitive verb (the last example in *OED*).

Methinks this single Consideration, of the Progress of a finite Spirit to Perfection, will be sufficient to extinguish all Envy in inferior Natures, and all Contempt in superior. That Cherubim which now appears as a God to a human Soul, knows very well that the Period will come about in Eternity, when the Human Soul shall be as perfect as he himself now is. Nay, when she shall look down upon that degree of Perfection, as much as she now falls short of it. It is true, the higher Nature still advances, and by that means preserves his Distance and Superiority in the scale of Being; but he knows how high soever the Station is of which he stands possess'd at present, the inferior Nature will at length mount up to it, and shine forth in the same Degree of Glory.

With what Astonishment and Veneration may we look into our own Souls, where there are such hidden Stores of Virtue and Knowledge, such inexhausted Sources of Perfection? We know not yet what we shall be, nor will it ever enter into the Heart of Man to conceive the Glory that will be always in Reserve for him. The Soul considered with its Creator, is like one of those Mathematical Lines[1] that may draw nearer to another for all Eternity, without a Possibility of touching it: And can there be a Thought so transporting, as to consider our selves in these perpetual Approaches to him, who is not only the Standard of Perfection but of Happiness!

L

No. 112   *Monday, July 9, 1711*[2]
[ADDISON]

Ἀθανάτους μὲν πρῶτα θεοὺς, νόμῳ ὡς διάκειται,
τίμα.   Pyth.

I AM always very well pleased with a Country *Sunday*;[3] and think, if keeping holy the Seventh Day were[a] only a human Institution,

---

^a were] had been *Fol.*

[1] The figure of parallel lines running together infinitely but never meeting is common: cf. Montaigne, 'Apology for Raimond de Sebonde' (*Essays*, trans. Cotton, 1686, ii. 414); Marvell, 'The Definition of Love', 25–28; *Tatler* 7; John Scott, *The Christian Life*, part ii, vol. i, p. 364, &c. 'Those lines are what the Geometricians call the *Asymptotes* of the Herbola, and the allusion to them here, is perhaps one of the most beautiful that has ever been made' (Nichols).

[For notes 2 and 3 see following page.]

it would be[a] the best Method that could have been thought of for the polishing and civilizing of Mankind. It is certain the Country-People would soon degenerate into a kind of Savages and Barbarians, were there not such frequent Returns of a stated Time, in which the whole Village meet together with their best Faces, and in their cleanliest Habits,[b] to converse with one another upon indifferent Subjects, hear their Duties explained to them, and join together in Adoration of the supreme Being. *Sunday* clears away the Rust of the whole Week, not only as it refreshes in their Minds the Notions of Religion, but as it puts both the Sexes upon appearing in their most agreeable Forms, and exerting all such Qualities as are apt to give them a Figure in the Eye of the Village. A Country-Fellow distinguishes himself as much in the *Church-yard*, as a Citizen does upon the *Change*, the whole Parish-Politicks being generally discuss'd in that Place either after Sermon or before the Bell rings.

My Friend Sir ROGER being a good Churchman, has beautified the Inside of his Church with several Texts[1] of his own chusing: He has likewise given a handsome Pulpit-Cloth, and railed in the Communion-Table[2] at his own Expence. He has often told me that at his coming to his Estate he found his Parishioners[c] very irregular; and that in order to make them kneel and join in the Responses, he gave every one of them a Hassock[3] and a Common-prayer Book; and at

[a] would be] would have been *Fol.*   [b] Habits,] Dress, *Fol.*   [c] his Parishioners] the Parish *Fol.*

---

[1] Among the Canons of 1604, Canon 82 had required 'that the Ten Commandments be set upon the east end of every church and chapel, where the people may best see and read the same, and other chosen sentences written upon the walls of the said churches and chapels in places convenient' (quoted in Sykes, p. 234).

[2] During this period the Table was not always in the Sanctuary or railed, especially in the early years of the century, 'when the race of Church Puritans was not yet extinct' (Sykes, p. 235).

[3] On the condition of pews and pulpit and lack of hassocks at this time see Sykes, pp. 236–7.

---

[2] *Motto.* Pythagoras, *Carmina Aurea*, 1–2:

> First to the Gods thy humble Homage pay;
> The greatest this, and first of Laws, obey. ROWE.

[3] The best commentary on this number is Norman Sykes, *Church and State in England in the XVIIIth Century* (Cambridge, 1934), chap. vi, 'The Whole Duty of Man'. Dr. Sykes, after quoting the opening paragraph of this essay, writes:

> The social and religious significance of church attendance in the Hanoverian age could hardly secure more faithful delineation and interpretation than from the pen of the essayist who, though writing during the high church *régime* of Anne, discerned the features of rural religion which persisted throughout the greater part of the century. Both the strength and shortcomings of contemporary churchmanship were adumbrated in his picture . . . (p. 231).

the same Time employed an itinerant Singing-Master, who goes about the Country for that Purpose, to instruct them rightly in the Tunes of the Psalms; upon which they now very much value themselves, and indeed out-do most of the Country Churches that I have ever heard.

As Sir ROGER is Landlord to the whole Congregation, he keeps them in very good Order, and will suffer no Body to sleep in it besides himself; for if by Chance he has been surprized into a short Nap at Sermon, upon recovering out of it he stands up and looks about him, and if he sees any Body else nodding, either wakes them himself, or sends his Servant to them. Several other of the old Knight's Particularities break out upon these Occasions: Sometimes he will be lengthening out a Verse in the Singing-Psalms half a Minute after the rest of the Congregation have done with it; sometimes, when he is pleased with the Matter of his Devotion, he pronounces *Amen* three or four times to the same Prayer; and sometimes stands up when every Body else is upon their Knees, to count the Congregation, or see if any of his Tenants are missing.

I was Yesterday very much surprized to hear my old Friend, in the Midst of the Service, calling out to one *John Mathews* to mind what he was about, and not disturb the Congregation. This *John Mathews* it seems is remarkable for being an idle Fellow, and at that Time was kicking his Heels for his Diversion. This Authority of the Knight, though exerted in that odd Manner which accompanies him in all Circumstances of Life, has a very good Effect upon the Parish, who are not polite enough to see any thing ridiculous in his Behaviour; besides that, the general good Sense and Worthiness of his Character, make his Friends observe these little Singularities as Foils that rather set off than blemish his good Qualities.

Assoon as the Sermon is finished, no Body presumes to stir till Sir ROGER is gone out of the Church. The Knight walks down from[a] his Seat in the Chancel, between a double Row of his Tenants, that stand bowing to him on each Side; and every now and then inquires how such an one's Wife or Mother, or Son, or Father do whom he does not see at Church; which is understood as a secret Reprimand to the Person that is absent.

The Chaplain has often told me, that upon a Catechizing-day, when Sir ROGER has been pleased with a Boy that answers well, he has ordered a Bible to be given him next Day for his Encouragement;

[a] walks down from] walks from *Fol.*

and sometimes accompanies it with a Flitch of Bacon to his Mother. Sir ROGER has likewise added five Pounds a Year to the Clerk's Place;[1] and that he may encourage the young Fellows to make themselves perfect in the Church-Service, has promised upon the Death of the present Incumbent, who is very old, to bestow it according to Merit.

The fair Understanding between Sir ROGER and his Chaplain, and their mutual Concurrence in doing Good, is the more remarkable, because the very next Village is famous for the Differences and Contentions that rise between the Parson and the 'Squire, who live in a perpetual State of War. The Parson is always preaching at the 'Squire, and the 'Squire to be revenged on the Parson never comes to Church. The 'Squire has made all his Tenants Atheists and Tithe-Stealers; while the Parson instructs them every *Sunday* in the Dignity of his Order, and insinuates to them in almost every Sermon, that he is a better Man than his Patron. In short, Matters are come to such an Extremity, that the 'Squire has not said his Prayers either in publick or private this half Year; and that the Parson threatens him, if he does not mend his Manners, to pray for him in the Face of the whole Congregation.

Feuds of this Nature, though too frequent in the Country, are very fatal to the ordinary People; who are so used to be dazled with Riches, that they pay as much Deference to the Understanding of a Man of an Estate, as of a Man of Learning; and are very hardly brought to regard any Truth, how important soever it may be, that is preached to them, when they know there are several Men of five hundred a Year who do not believe it. L

No. 113
[STEELE]

Tuesday, *July* 10, 1711[2]

. . . *Hærent infixi Pectore vultus.*
Virg.

IN my first Description of the Company in which I pass most of my Time, it may be remembered that I mentioned a great Afflic-

---

[1] There is little contemporary evidence as to the clerk's salary. According to the late Dean Sykes, since curates' salaries usually ranged from about £20 to £30, the average clerk might perhaps get £5 or £7 (information in letter).

[*For note 2 see opposite page.*]

tion which my Friend Sir ROGER had met with in his Youth, which was no less than a Disappointment in Love. It happened this Evening, that we fell into a very pleasing Walk at a distance from his House; as soon as we came into it, 'It is, quoth the good Old Man, looking round him with a Smile, very hard that any part of my Land should be settled upon one who has used me so ill as the perverse Widow[1] did, and yet I am sure I could not see a Sprig of any Bough of this whole Walk of Trees, but I should reflect upon her and her Severity. She has certainly the finest Hand of any Woman in the World. You are to know this was the Place wherein I used to muse upon her, and by that Custom I can never come into it, but the same tender Sentiments revive in my Mind, as if I had actually walked with that Beautiful Creature under these Shades. I have been Fool enough to Carve her Name on the Bark of several of these Trees, so unhappy is the Condition of Men in Love to attempt the removing of their Passion by the Methods which serve only to imprint it deeper. She has certainly the finest Hand of any Woman in the World.'

Here followed a profound Silence, and I was not displeased to observe my Friend falling so naturally into a Discourse, which I had ever before taken notice he industriously avoided. After a very long Pause, he entered upon an Account of this great Circumstance in his Life, with an Air which I thought raised my *Idea* of him above what I had ever had before, and gave me the Picture of that chearful

---

[1] Mrs. Catherine Bovey (or Boevey), the supposed original of this character, became a widow in 1692, at the age of twenty-two, upon the death of her husband William Bovey. She thereupon lived in retirement in the Manor of Flaxley, near Gloucester, devoting herself to religious and charitable works, in company with a friend, Mrs. Mary Pope of Twickenham. The identification of Sir Roger's 'perverse widow' with Mrs. Bovey is involved in the equally elusive identification of Sir Roger with Sir John Packington, of Westwood, Worcestershire—or with William Walsh, of Abberley Lodge, also in Worcestershire. Mrs. Bovey had the reputation of being a learned lady and a lover of books, and Steele dedicated volume ii of *The Ladies Library* to her. She also was involved in some kind of lawsuit, threatening her dower, shortly after her husband's death, but she won the suit and remained in possession of Flaxley until her death on 21 Jan. 1726. Both Steele and Addison are said to have visited her in Worcestershire, and a shady terrace in the park at Flaxley was long known as 'Addison's Walk'. For a full account of the family history and traditions see Arthur W. Crawley-Boevey, *The 'Perverse Widow': being passages from the life of Catharina, wife of William Boevey, Esq., of Flaxley Abbey, in the county of Gloucester . . .* (1898), pp. 63–112.

---

[2] *Motto.* Virgil, *Aeneid*, 4. 4:

His Words, his Looks imprinted in her Heart,
Improve the Passion, and increase the Smart. DRYDEN.

Mind of his, before it received that Stroke which has ever since affected his Words and Actions. But he went on as follows.

'I came to my Estate in my Twenty Second Year, and resolved to follow the Steps of the most Worthy of my Ancestors, who have inhabited this spot of Earth before me, in all the Methods of Hospitality and good Neighbourhood, for the sake of my Fame, and in Country Sports and Recreations for the sake of my Health. In my Twenty Third Year I was obliged to serve as Sheriff of the County, and in my Servants, Officers, and whole Equipage indulged the Pleasure of a Young Man (who did not think ill of his own Person) in taking that publick Occasion of showing my Figure and Behaviour to Advantage. You may easily imagine to your self what Appearance I made, who am pretty tall, ride well, and was very well Dressed, at the Head of a whole County, with Musick before me, a Feather in my Hat, and my Horse well Bitted. I can assure you I was not a little pleas'd with the kind Looks and Glances I had from all the Balconies and Windows, as I rode to the Hall where the Assizes were held. But when I came there a Beautiful Creature in a Widow's Habit sate in Court, to hear the Event of a Cause concerning her Dower: This commanding Creature (who was born for Destruction of all who behold her) put on such a Resignation in her Countenance, and bore the Whispers of all around the Court with such a pretty Uneasiness, I warrant you, and then recovered her self from one Eye to another, till she was perfectly confused by meeting something so wistful in all she encountered, that at last, with a Murrain to her, she casts her bewitching Eye upon me. I no sooner met it but I bowed like a great surprized Booby, and knowing her Cause to be the first which came on, I cry'd like a Captivated Calf as I was, Make way for the Defendant's Witnesses. This sudden Partiality made all the County immediately see the Sheriff also was become a Slave to the Fine Widow. During the time her Cause was upon Tryal, she behaved her self, I warrant you, with such a deep Attention to her Business, took Opportunities to have little Billets handed to her Council, then would be in such a pretty Confusion, occasioned, you must know, by acting before so much Company, that not only I but the whole Court was prejudiced in her Favour, and all that the next Heir to her Husband had to urge was thought so groundless and frivolous, that when it came to her Council to reply, there was not half so much said as every one besides in the Court thought he could have urged to her Advantage. You must understand, Sir, this perverse Woman is one of those unaccountable Creatures that secretly rejoice in the Admiration of Men, but indulge themselves in no further Consequences. Hence it is that she has ever had a Train of Admirers, and she removes from her Slaves in Town, to those in the Country, according to the Seasons of the Year. She is a reading Lady, and far gone in the Pleasures of Friendship; she is always accompanied by a Confident, who is witness to her daily Protestations against our Sex, and consequently a Barr to her first Steps towards Love, upon the Strength of her own Maxims and Declarations.

'However, I must needs say this accomplished Mistress of mine has distinguished me above the rest, and has been known to declare Sir ROGER DE COVERLEY was the Tamest and most Human of all the Brutes in the Country. I was told she said so by one who thought he rallyed me, but upon the Strength of this slender Encouragement, of being thought least detestable, I made new Liveries, new paired my Coach-Horses, sent them all to Town to be bitted, and taught to throw their Legs well, and move all together, before I pretended to cross the Country and wait upon her. As soon as I thought my Retinue suitable to the Character of my Fortune and Youth, I set out from hence to make my Addresses. The particular Skill of this Lady has ever been to inflame your Wishes, and yet command Respect. To make her Mistress of this Art she has a greater Share of Knowledge, Wit and good Sense, than is usual even among Men of Merit. Then she is beautiful beyond the Race of Women; if you won't let her go on with a certain Artifice with her Eyes, and the Skill of Beauty, she will arm her self with her real Charms, and strike you with Admiration instead of Desire. It is certain that if you were to behold the whole Woman, there is that Dignity in her Aspect, that Composure in her Motion, that Complacency in her Manner, that if her Form makes you hope, her Merit makes you fear. But then again, she is such a desperate Scholar, that no Country Gentleman can approach her without being a Jest. As I was going to tell you, when I came to her House I was admitted to her Presence with great Civility; at the same time she placed her self to be first seen by me in such an Attitude, (as I think you call the Posture of a Picture) that she discovered new Charms, and I at last came towards her with such an Awe as made me Speechless. This she no sooner observed but she made her Advantage of it, and began a Discourse to me concerning Love and Honour, as they both are followed by Pretenders, and the real Votaries to them. When she Discussed these Points in a Discourse, which I verily believe was as Learned as the best Philosopher in *Europe* could possibly make, she asked me whether she was so happy as to fall in with my Sentiments on these important Particulars. Her Confident sate by her, and upon my being in the last Confusion and Silence, this malicious Aid of hers, turning to her, says, I am very glad to observe Sir ROGER pauses upon this Subject, and seems resolved to deliver all his Sentiments upon the Matter when he pleases to speak. They both kept their Countenances, and after I had sate half an Hour meditating how to behave before such profound Casuists, I rose up and took my Leave. Chance has since that time thrown me very often in her way, and she as often has directed a Discourse to me which I do not understand. This Barbarity has kept me ever at a Distance from the most beautiful Object my Eyes ever beheld. It is thus also she deals with all Mankind, and you must make Love to her, as you would conquer the Sphinx, by posing her. But were she like other Women, and that there were any talking to her, how constant must the Pleasure of that Man be, who could converse with a Creature—— But, after all, you may be sure her Heart is fixed on some one or other; and yet I have been credibly informed; but who can believe half that is said! After she had done speaking to me, she put her Hand to her Bosom, and adjusted her Tucker.[1] Then she cast her Eyes a little down, upon my beholding her too earnestly. They say she sings excellently, her Voice in her ordinary Speech has something in it inexpressibly sweet. You must know I dined with her at a publick Table the Day after I first saw her, and she helped me to some Tansy[2] in the Eye of all the Gentlemen in the Country: She has certainly the finest Hand of any Woman in the World. I can assure you, Sir, were you to behold her, you would be in the same Condition; for as her Speech is Musick, her Form is Angelick; but I find I grow irregular while I am talking of her, but indeed it would be Stupidity to be unconcerned at such Perfection. Oh the Excellent Creature, she is as inimitable to all Women, as she is inaccessible to all Men——'

I found my Friend begin to rave, and insensibly led him towards the House, that we might be joined by some other Company; and am convinced that the Widow is the secret Cause of all that Inconsistency which appears in some Parts of my Friend's Discourse; tho'

---

[1] See No. 38.   [2] A pudding or omelet flavoured with juice of tansy.

he has so much Command of himself, as not directly to mention her, yet according to that of *Martial*,[1] which one knows not how to render in English, *Dum Tacet hanc Loquitur*. I shall end this Paper with that whole Epigram, which represents with much Humour my honest Friend's Condition.

> *Quicquid agit Rufus, nihil est nisi Nævia Rufo.*
>   *Si gaudet, si flet, si tacet hanc loquitur:*
> *Cænat, propinat, poscit, negat, annuit, una est*
>   *Nævia: Si non sit Nævia mutus erit.*
> *Scriberet hesterna Patri cum Luce Salutem*
>   *Nævia lux, inquit, Nævia, lumen ave.*

> Let Rufus *weep, rejoice, stand, sit, or walk,*
> *Still he can nothing but of* Nævia *talk:*
> *Let him eat, drink, ask Questions, or dispute,*
> *Still he must speak of* Nævia, *or be mute.*
> *He writ to his Father, ending with this Line,*
> *I am, my Lovely* Nævia, *ever thine.*

R

No. 114   *Wednesday, July* 11, 1711[2]

[STEELE]

> . . . *Paupertatis pudor & fuga* . . .
> Hor.

OECONOMY in our Affairs, has the same Effect upon our Fortunes which good Breeding has upon our Conversations. There is a pretending Behaviour in both Cases, which instead of making Men esteemed, renders them both miserable and contemptible. We had Yesterday at Sir ROGER's a Set of Country Gentlemen who dined with him; and after Dinner the Glass was taken, by those who pleased, pretty plentifully. Among others I observed a Person of a tolerable good Aspect, who seemed to be more greedy of Liquor than any of the Company, and yet, methought, he did not taste it with Delight. As he grew warm, he was suspicious of every thing that was said; and as he advanced towards being fudled,

[1] *Epigrams*, 1. 68. 1–6.
[2] *Motto.* Horace, *Epistles*, 1. 18. 24: The shame and dread of being poor.

his Humour grew worse. At the same Time his Bitterness seemed to be rather an inward Dissatisfaction in his own Mind, than any Dislike he had taken at the Company. Upon hearing his Name, I knew him to be a Gentleman of a considerable Fortune in this County, but greatly in Debt. What gives the unhappy Man this Peevishness of Spirit, is, that his Estate is dipp'd,[1] and is eating out with Usury; and yet he has not the Heart to sell any Part of it. His proud Stomach, at the Cost of restless Nights, constant Inquietudes, Danger of Affronts, and a thousand nameless Inconveniences, preserves[a] this Canker in his Fortune, rather than it shall be said he is a Man of fewer Hundreds a Year than he has been commonly reputed. Thus he endures the Torment of Poverty, to avoid the Name of being less rich. If you go to his House you see great Plenty; but served in a Manner that shews it is all unnatural, and that the Master's Mind is not at home. There is a certain Waste and Carelesness in the Air of every thing, and the whole appears but a covered Indigence, a magnificent Poverty. That Neatness and Chearfulness which attends the Table of him who lives within Compass, is wanting, and exchanged for a libertine Way of Service in all about him.

This Gentleman's Conduct, tho' a very common way of Management, is as ridiculous as that Officer's would be, who had but few Men under his Command, and should take the Charge of an Extent of Country rather than of a small Pass. To pay for, personate, and keep in a Man's Hands, a greater Estate than he really has, is of all others the most unpardonable Vanity, and must in the End reduce the Man who is guilty of it to Dishonour. Yet if we look round us in any County of *Great-Britain*, we shall see many in this fatal Errour, if that may be call'd by so soft a Name, which proceeds from a false Shame of appearing what they really are, when the contrary Behaviour would in a short Time advance them to the Condition which they pretend to.

Laertes has fifteen hundred Pounds a Year, which is mortgaged for six thousand Pounds; but it is impossible to convince him, that if he sold as much as would pay off that Debt he would save four Shillings in the Pound,[2] which he gives for the Vanity of being the reputed Master of it. But if *Laertes* did this, he would, perhaps, be easier in

---

[a] preserves] preserve *Fol. (Corrected in Errata, No. 116)*

---

[1] i.e. mortgaged.   [2] The amount of the land-tax.

his own Fortune; but then *Irus*, a Fellow of Yesterday, who has but twelve hundred a Year, would be his Equal. Rather than this shall be, *Laertes* goes on to bring well-born Beggars into the World, and every Twelve-month charges his Estate with at least one Year's Rent more by the Birth of a Child.

Laertes and *Irus* are Neighbours, whose Way of living are an Abomination to each other. *Irus* is moved by the Fear of Poverty, and *Laertes* by the Shame of it. Though the Motive of Action is of so near Affinity in both, and may be resolved into this, 'That to each of them Poverty is the greatest of all Evils, yet are their Manners very widely different.' Shame of Poverty makes *Laertes* launch into unnecessary Equipage, vain Expence, and lavish Entertainments; Fear of Poverty makes *Irus* allow himself only plain Necessaries, appear without a Servant, sell his own Corn, attend his Labourers, and be himself a Labourer. Shame of Poverty makes *Laertes* go every Day a Step nearer to it; and Fear of Poverty stirs up *Irus*[a] to make every Day some further Progress from it.

These different Motives produce the Excesses which Men are guilty of in the Negligence of and Provision for themselves. Usury, Stock-Jobbing,[1] Extortion and Oppression, have their Seed in the Dread of Want; and Vanity, Riot and Prodigality from the Shame of it: But both these Excesses are infinitely below the Pursuit of a reasonable Creature. After we have taken Care to command so much as is necessary for maintaining our selves in the Order of Men suitable to our Character, the Care of Superfluities is a Vice no less extravagant, than the Neglect of Necessaries would have been before.

Certain it is that they are both out of Nature when she is followed with Reason and good Sense. It is from this Reflexion that I always read Mr. *Cowley* with the greatest Pleasure: His Magnanimity is as much above that of other considerable Men as his Understanding; and it is a true distinguishing Spirit in the elegant Author[2] who

---

[a] Shame of Poverty ... stirs up *Irus*] Fear of Poverty makes *Laertes* ... and Shame of Poverty stirs up *Irus* ... *Fol.* (*Corrected in Errata, No. 116*)

---

[1] Used here, and generally, for speculative dealing in stocks and shares.
[2] Thomas Sprat, who prefixed 'An Account of the Life and Writings of Mr. Abraham Cowley' to Cowley's *Works* (1668). 'Yet, notwithstanding the narrowness of his Income, he remained fixed to his resolution [of forgoing public employments], upon his confidence in the temper of his own mind, which he knew had contracted its desires into so small a compass that a very few things would supply them all' (Spingarn, ii. 127).

published his Works, to dwell so much upon the Temper of his Mind and the Moderation of his Desires: By this Means he has render'd his Friend as amiable as famous. That State of Life which bears the Face of Poverty with Mr. *Cowley's great Vulgar*,[1] is admirably described; and it is no small Satisfaction to those of the same Turn of Desire, that he produces the Authority of the wisest Men of the best Age of the World, to strengthen his Opinion of the ordinary Pursuits of Mankind.

It would methinks be no ill Maxim of Life, if, according to that Ancestor of Sir ROGER[2] whom I lately mentioned, every Man would point to himself what Sum he would resolve not to exceed. He might by this Means cheat himself into a Tranquility on this Side of that Expectation, or convert what he should get above it to nobler Uses than his own Pleasures or Necessities. This Temper of Mind would exempt a Man from an ignorant Envy of restless Men above him, and a more inexcusable Contempt of happy Men below him. This would be sailing by some Compass, living with some Design; but to be eternally bewildered in Prospects of future Gain, and putting on unnecessary Armour against improbable Blows of Fortune, is a Mechanick Being which has not good Sense for its Direction, but is carried on by a Sort of acquired Instinct towards things below our Consideration and unworthy our Esteem. It is possible that the Tranquility I now enjoy at Sir ROGER's may have created in me this Way of Thinking, which is so abstracted from the common Relish of the World: But as I am now in a pleasing Arbour surrounded with a beautiful Landskip, I find no Inclination so strong as to continue in these Mansions, so remote from the ostentatious Scenes of Life; and am at this present Writing Philosopher enough to conclude with Mr. *Cowley*;

> *If e'er Ambition did my Fancy cheat,*
> *With any Wish so mean as to be Great;*
> *Continue, Heav'n, still from me to remove,*
> *The humble Blessings of that Life I love.*[3] ·T

[1] From Cowley's imitation of Horace's *Odes* (III. i) at the conclusion of his essay 'Of Greatness' (*Essays*, ed. Waller, p. 434):
> Hence, ye Profane; I hate ye all;
> Both the Great, Vulgar, and the small.

[2] No. 109.

[3] From the opening paragraph of the essay 'Of Greatness' (*Essays*, ed. Waller, p. 428).

> . . . *Ut sit mens sana in Corpore sano.*
>
> Juv.

BODILY Labour is of two kinds, either that which a Man sub-mits to for his Livelihood, or that which he undergoes for his Pleasure. The latter of them generally changes the Name of Labour for that of Exercise, but differs only from ordinary Labour as it rises from another Motive.

A Country Life abounds in both these kinds of Labour, and for that Reason gives a Man a greater Stock of Health, and conse-quently a more perfect Enjoyment of himself, than any other way of Life. I consider the Body as a System of Tubes and Glands, or to use a more Rustick Phrase, a Bundle of Pipes and Strainers, fitted to one another after so wonderful a manner as to make a proper Engine for the Soul to work with. This Description does not only compre-hend the Bowels, Bones, Tendons, Veins, Nerves and Arteries, but every Muscle and every Ligature, which is a Composition of Fibres, that are so many imperceptible Tubes or Pipes interwoven on all sides with invisible Glands or Strainers.

This general Idea of a Human Body, without considering it in the Niceties of Anatomy, lets us see how absolutely necessary Labour is for the right Preservation of it. There must be frequent Motions and Agitations to mix, digest, and separate the Juices contained in it, as well as to clear and cleanse that Infinitude of Pipes and Strainers of which it is composed, and to give their solid Parts a more firm and lasting Tone. Labour or Exercise ferments the Humours, casts them into their proper Channels, throws off Redundancies, and helps Nature in those secret Distributions, without which the Body cannot subsist in its Vigour, nor the Soul act with Chearfulness.

I might here mention the Effects which this has upon all the Faculties of the Mind, by keeping the Understanding clear, the Ima-gination untroubled, and refining those Spirits that are necessary for the proper Exertion of our intellectual Faculties, during the pre-sent Laws of Union between Soul and Body. It is to a Neglect in this Particular that we must ascribe the Spleen, which is so frequent in

---

[1] *Motto.* Juvenal, *Satires*, 10. 356: Pray for a sound mind in a sound body.

Men of studious and sedentary Tempers, as well as the Vapours[1] to which those of the other Sex are so often subject.

Had not Exercise been absolutely necessary for our Well-being, Nature would not have made the Body so proper for it, by giving such an Activity to the Limbs, and such a Pliancy to every Part as necessarily produce those Compressions, Extentions, Contortions, Dilatations, and all other kinds of Motion that are necessary for the Preservation of such a System of Tubes and Glands as has been before mentioned. And that we might not want Inducements to engage us in such an Exercise of the Body as is proper for its Welfare, it is so ordered that nothing valuable can be procured without it. Not to mention Riches and Honour, even Food and Raiment are not to be come at without the Toil of the Hands and Sweat of the Brows. Providence furnishes Materials, but expects that we should work them up our selves. The Earth must be laboured before it gives its Encrease, and when it is forced into its several Products, how many Hands must they pass through before they are fit for Use? Manufactures, Trade and Agriculture naturally employ more than nineteen Parts of the Species in twenty; and as for those who are not obliged to Labour, by the Condition in which they are born, they are more miserable than the rest of Mankind, unless they indulge themselves in that voluntary Labour which goes by the Name of Exercise.

My Friend Sir ROGER has been an indefatigable Man in Business of this kind, and has hung several Parts of his House with the Trophies of his former Labours. The Walls of his great Hall are covered with the Horns of several kinds of Deer that he has killed in the Chace, which he thinks the most valuable Furniture of his House, as they afford him frequent Topicks of Discourse, and show that he has not been Idle. At the lower end of the Hall is a large Otter's Skin stuffed with Hay, which his Mother ordered to be hung up in that manner, and the Knight looks upon with great Satisfaction, because it seems he was but nine Years old when his Dog killed him. A little Room adjoining to the Hall is a kind of Arsenal filled with Guns of several Sizes and Inventions, with which the Knight has made great Havock in the Woods, and destroyed many thousands of Pheasants, Partridges and Wood-Cocks. His Stable Doors are patched with Noses that belonged to Foxes of the Knight's own hunting down. Sir ROGER showed me one of them

[1] Spleen . . . vapours. Nos. 3, 53.

that for Distinction sake has a Brass Nail struck through it, which cost him about fifteen Hours riding, carried him through half a dozen Counties, killed him a brace of Geldings, and lost above half his Dogs. This the Knight looks upon as one of the greatest Exploits of his Life. The perverse Widow,[1] whom I have given some account of, was the Death of several Foxes, for Sir ROGER has told me that in the Course of his Amours he patched the Western Door of his Stable. Whenever the Widow was cruel the Foxes were sure to pay for it. In proportion as his Passion for the Widow abated, and old Age came on, he left off Fox-hunting, but a Hare is not yet safe that Sits within ten Miles of his House.

There is no kind of Exercise which I would so recommend to my Readers of both Sexes as this of Riding, as there is none which so much conduces to Health, and is every way accommodated to the Body, according to the *Idea* which I have given of it. Doctor *Sydenham*[2] is very lavish in its Praises, and if the *English* Reader would see the Mechanical Effects of it described at length, he may find them in a Book published not many Years since, under the Title of the *Medicina Gymnastica*.[3] For my own part, when I am in Town, for Want of these Opportunities, I exercise my self an Hour every Morning upon a dumb Bell[4] that is placed in a Corner of my Room, and pleases me the more because it does every thing I require of it in the

[1] No. 113.

[2] No. 25.

[3] *Medicina Gymnastica: or, a treatise concerning the power of exercise, with respect to the animal oeconomy; and the great necessity of it in the cure of several distempers,* by Francis Fuller, M.A. (1705). The 4th edition, printed for R. Knaplock, is advertised in No. 86 ('This Week will be publish'd'). The section headed 'Of the Exercise of Riding' occupies pp. 165–206, and quotes Sydenham: 'Dr. *Sydenham* tells us . . . that he Cur'd some of his Relations of Consumptions, by putting 'em upon Riding much' (p. 196). Fuller concludes this section by citing 'the Opinion of one who is known to have been a very Ample Judge, of the Demands of Nature, I mean Dr. *Sydenham*, with whose Encomium on this very Exercise, as he has given it us in his *Dissertatio Epistolaris*, and his Treatise of the Gout, I shall conclude' (p. 204).

[4] Addison does not refer to dumb-bells in the modern sense (these are described in the next paragraph) but to an apparatus like that for swinging a church-bell, but without the bell itself. A correspondent in *N & Q,* 2nd ser., xii (1861), p. 45, describes it as

a machine consisting of a rough, heavy, wooden fly-wheel with a rope passing through and round a spindle, which projects from one side, the whole apparatus being secured by stanchions to the ceiling of a room, and set in motion like a church bell, till it acquired sufficient impetus to carry the gymnast up and down, and so bring the muscles of the arms into play. . . .

The *Critical Specimen* (by Pope?) in 1711 refers to 'the Dumb Bell, which is put in Motion with much labour, but makes no manner of *Musick*' (Pope, *Prose Works*, ed. Ault, i. 11). Although this sentence from the *Spectator* is the earliest example in *OED*, this kind of dumb bell probably dates back to the first part of the seventeenth century. See Strutt's *Sports and Pastimes*, ed. J. Charles Cox (1903), pp. 64–65.

most profound Silence. My Landlady and her Daughters are so well acquainted with my Hours of Exercise, that they never come into my Room to disturb me whilst I am ringing.

When I was some Years younger than I am at present I used to employ my self in a more laborious Diversion, which I learned from a *Latin* Treatise[1] of Exercises, that is written with great Erudition. It is there called the σκιομαχία, or the Fighting with a Man's own Shadow, and consists in the brandishing of two short Sticks grasped in each Hand, and loaden with Plugs of Lead at either end. This opens the Chest, exercises the Limbs, and gives a Man all the pleasure of Boxing, without the Blows. I could wish that several Learned Men would lay out that Time which they employ in Controversies and Disputes about nothing, in *this method* of fighting with their own Shadows. It might conduce very much to evaporate the Spleen, which makes them uneasy to the Publick as well as to themselves.

To conclude, As I am a Compound of Soul and Body, I consider my self as obliged to a double Scheme of Duties, and think I have not fulfilled the Business of the Day, when I do not thus employ the one in Labour and Exercise, as well as the other in Study and Contemplation.   L

[1] The treatise of Hieronymus Mercurialis, *De arte gymnastica libri sex*, originally published at Venice in 1569, and often reprinted. In the Amsterdam edition of 1672 σκιομαχία is mentioned briefly in book iii, chap. iv ('Alteram plerumque sine telis, quam σκιαμαχίαν Graeci, *umbratilem pugnam* vocarunt nostri'), p. 191; but the principal discussion comes at p. 345 (book vi, chap. ii) in the section 'De pugnarum effectibus'. Here Addison is describing exercise with what are now usually called dumb-bells (again, the earliest example in *OED*), i.e. short bars weighted at each end with a rounded knob and used in pairs which are grasped in the hands and swung for exercise. As the book by Hieronymus Mercurialis suggests, the ancients had a similar kind of exercise—in their use of 'jumping-weights' or *halteres*, which gave an impetus for the long jump. 'The jumping weights were in later times used much in the same way as dumbbells, and it seems not unlikely they were already so used even in the fifth century: for athletes are often seen swinging them in attitudes which can hardly have any connexion with jumping' (E. Norman Gardiner, *Athletics of the Ancient World*, Oxford, 1930, p. 92). The history of this kind of exercise in England awaits further investigation.

> *. . . Vocat ingenti clamore Cithæron,*
> *Taygetique canes . . .*
>
> Virg.

THOSE who have searched into human Nature observe, that nothing so much shews the Nobleness of the Soul, as that its Felicity consists in Action.[2] Every Man has such an active Principle in him, that he will find out something to employ himself upon in whatever Place or State of Life he is posted. I have heard of a Gentleman who was under close Confinement in the *Bastile* seven Years; during which Time he amused himself in scattering a few small Pins about his Chamber, gathering them up again, and placing them in different Figures on the Arm of a great Chair. He often told his Friends afterwards, that unless he had found out this Piece of Exercise, he verily believed he should have lost his Senses.[3]

After what has been said, I need not inform my Readers, that Sir *Roger*, with whose Character I hope they are at present pretty well acquainted, has in his Youth gone through the whole Course of those rural Diversions which the Country abounds in; and which seem to be extremely well suited to that laborious Industry a Man may observe here in a far greater Degree than in Towns and Cities. I have before hinted at some of my Friend's Exploits: He has in his youthful Days taken forty Coveys of Partridges in a Season; and tired many a Salmon with a Line consisting but of a single Hair. The constant Thanks and good Wishes of the Neighbourhood always attended him on Account of his remarkable Enmity towards Foxes; having destroy'd more of those Vermin in one Year, than it was thought the whole Country could have produced. Indeed the Knight does not scruple to own among his most intimate Friends, that in order to establish his Reputation this Way, he has secretly sent for great Numbers of them out of other Counties, which he used to turn loose about the Country by Night, that he might the better signalize himself in their Destruction the next Day. His Hunting-Horses

---

[1] *Motto.* Virgil, *Georgics*, 3. 43–44:
> *Cytheron* loudly calls me to my way;
> Thy Hounds, *Taygetus*, open and pursue their Prey. DRYDEN.

[2] Cf. Cicero, *De Officiis*, 1. 6. 19.
[3] I have not identified this anecdote.

were the finest and best managed in all these Parts: His Tenants are still full of the Praises of a grey Stone-horse[1] that unhappily staked himself several Years since, and was buried with great Solemnity in the Orchard.

Sir *Roger*, being at present too old for Fox-hunting, to keep himself in Action, has disposed of his Beagles and got a Pack of *Stop-Hounds*.[2] What these want in Speed, he endeavours to make Amends for by the Deepness of their Mouths and the Variety of their Notes, which are suited in such Manner to each other, that the whole Cry makes up a compleat Consort. He is so nice in this Particular, that a Gentleman having made him a Present of a very fine Hound the other Day, the Knight return'd it by the Servant with a great many Expressions of Civility, but desired him to tell his Master, that the Dog he had sent was indeed a most excellent *Base*, but that at present he only wanted a *Counter-Tenor*. Could I believe my Friend had ever read *Shakespear*, I should certainly conclude he had taken the Hint from *Theseus* in *The Midsummer-Night's Dream*.[3]

> My Hounds are bred out of the Spartan *Kind*,
> So flu'd, so sanded; and their Heads are hung
> With Ears that sweep away the Morning Dew.
> Crook-Knee'd and dew-lap'd like Thessalian *Bulls*;
> Slow in Pursuit, but match'd in Mouths like Bells,
> Each under each: A Cry more tuneable
> Was never hallow'd to, nor chear'd with Horn.

Sir *Roger* is so keen at this Sport, that he has been out almost every Day since I came down; and upon the Chaplain's offering to lend me his easy Pad, I was prevail'd on Yesterday Morning to make one of the Company. I was extremely pleas'd, as we rid along, to observe the general Benevolence of all the Neighbourhood towards my Friend. The Farmers Sons thought themselves happy if they could open a Gate for the good old Knight as he passed by; which he generally requited with a Nod or a Smile, and a kind Inquiry after their Fathers or Uncles.

After we had rid about a Mile from home, we came upon a large Heath, and the Sports-men began to beat. They had done so for

[1] i.e. stallion.
[2] Hounds trained to hunt slowly and to stop at a signal from the huntsman (the earliest example in *OED*). 'Mr. Budgell . . . has shown himself to be no sportsman, by fixing the date of his hunting party in the month of July; and by making Sir Roger hunt with Stop-hounds, which are, I believe, peculiar to stag-hunting' (Percy).
[3] *A Midsummer-Night's Dream*, IV. i. 123–9 ('match'd in mouth').

some time, when, as I was at a little Distance from the rest of the Company, I saw a Hare pop out from a small Furze-brake almost under my Horse's Feet. I marked the Way she took, which I endeavoured to make the Company sensible of by extending my Arm; but to no Purpose, till Sir *Roger*, who knows that none of my extraordinary Motions are insignificant, rode up to me, and asked me *if Puss was gone that Way?* Upon my answering *Yes* he immediately call'd in the Dogs, and put them upon the Scent. As they were going off, I heard one of the Country-Fellows muttering to his Companion, *That 'twas a Wonder they had not lost all their Sport, for want of the silent Gentleman's crying STOLE AWAY.*

This, with my Aversion to leaping Hedges, made me withdraw to a rising Ground, from whence I could have the Pleasure of the whole Chase, without the Fatigue of keeping in with the Hounds. The Hare immediately threw them above a Mile behind her; but I was pleas'd to find, that instead of running strait forwards, or, in Hunter's Language, *Flying the Country*, as I was afraid she might have done, she wheel'd about, and describ'd a sort of Circle round the Hill where I had taken my Station, in such Manner as gave me a very distinct View of the Sport. I could see her first pass by, and the Dogs some Time afterwards unravelling the whole Track she had made, and following her thro' all her Doubles. I was at the same Time delighted in observing that Deference which the rest of the Pack paid to each particular Hound, according to the Character he had acquired amongst them: If they were at a Fault, and an old Hound of good Reputation opened but once, he was immediately follow'd by the whole Cry; while a raw Dog, or one who was a noted *Liar*, might have yelped his Heart out, without being taken Notice of.

The Hare now, after having squatted two or three Times, and been put up again as often, came still nearer to the Place where she was at first started. The Dogs pursu'd her, and these were follow'd by the jolly Knight, who rode upon a white Gelding, encompass'd by his Tenants and Servants, and chearing his Hounds with all the Gaiety of Five and Twenty. One of the Sports-men rode up to me, and told me that he was sure the Chase was almost at an End, because the old Dogs, which had hitherto lain behind, now headed the Pack. The Fellow was in the Right. Our Hare took a large Field just under us, follow'd by the full Cry *in View*. I must confess the Brightness of the Weather, the Chearfulness of every thing around me, the *Chiding* of the Hounds, which was returned upon us in a double Eccho from two neighbouring Hills, with the Hallowing of the Sports-men, and the Sounding of the Horn, lifted my Spirits into a most lively Pleasure, which I freely indulged because I was sure it was *innocent*. If I was under any Concern, it was on the Account of the poor Hare, that was now quite spent, and almost within the Reach of her Enemies; when the Hunts-man getting forward, threw down his Pole before the Dogs. They were now within eight Yards of that Game, which they had been pursuing for almost as many Hours; yet on the Signal before-mentioned they all made a sudden Stand, and tho' they continued opening as much as before, durst not once attempt to pass beyond the Pole. At the same Time Sir *Roger* rode forward, and alighting, took up the Hare in his Arms; which he soon after delivered to one of his Servants, with an Order, if she could be kept alive, to let her go in his great Orchard, where, it seems, he has several of these Prisoners of War, who live together in a very comfortable Captivity. I was highly pleas'd to see the Discipline of the Pack, and the Good-nature of the Knight, who could not find in his Heart to murther a Creature that had given him so much Diversion.

As we were returning home, I remember'd that Monsieur *Paschal*,[1] in his most excellent Discourse on *the Misery of Man*, tells us, That *all our Endeavours after Greatness, proceed from nothing but a Desire of being surrounded by a Multitude of Persons and Affairs, that may hinder us from looking into our selves, which is a View we cannot bear*. He afterwards goes on to shew that our Love of Sports comes from the same Reason, and is particularly severe upon HUNTING. *What*, says he, *unless it be to drown Thought, can make Men throw away so much Time and Pains upon a silly Animal, which they might buy cheaper in the Market?* The foregoing Reflection is certainly just, when a Man suffers his whole Mind to be drawn into his Sports, and altogether loses himself in the Woods; but does not affect those who propose a far more laudable End from this Exercise, I mean, *The Preservation of Health, and keeping all the Organs of the Soul in a Condition to execute her Orders*. Had that incomparable Person whom I last quoted been a little more indulgent to himself in this Point, the World might probably have enjoyed him much longer; whereas, thro' too great an Application

---

[1] 'The Misery of Man' is the title of chap. xxvi in *Thoughts on Religion and other Subjects*, by Monsieur Pascal, translated from the French (1704). For the passages cited here see pp. 217–18, 224–5. (A copy of this edition of Pascal was in Addison's library.)

to his Studies in his Youth, he contracted that ill Habit of Body, which, after a tedious Sickness, carried him off in the fortieth Year of his Age;[1] and the whole History we have of his Life till that Time, is but one continued Account of the Behaviour of a noble Soul struggling under innumerable Pains and Distempers.

For my own Part, I intend to hunt twice a Week during my Stay with Sir *Roger*; and shall prescribe the moderate use of this Exercise to all my Country Friends, as the best Kind of Physick for mending a bad Constitution, and preserving a good one.

I cannot do this better, than in the following Lines out of Mr. *Dryden*.[2]

> *The first Physicians by Debauch were made,*
> *Excess began, and Sloth sustains the Trade.*
> *By Chace our long-liv'd Fathers earn'd their Food,*
> *Toil strung the Nerves, and purify'd the Blood:*
> *But we their Sons, a pamper'd Race of Men,*
> *Are dwindled down to threescore Years and ten.*
> *Better to hunt in Fields for Health unbought,*
> *Than fee the Doctor for a nauseous Draught.*
> *The Wise for Cure on Exercise depend,*
> *God never made his Work for Man to mend.*   X

No. 117
[ADDISON]

Saturday, July 14, 1711[3]

> . . . *Ipsi sibi somnia fingunt.*
> Virg.

THERE are some Opinions in which a Man should stand Neuter, without engaging his Assent to one side or the other. Such a hovering Faith as this, which refuses to settle upon any Determination, is absolutely necessary in a Mind that is carefull to avoid Errors and Prepossessions. When the Arguments press equally on both sides in matters that are indifferent to us, the safest Method is to give up our selves to neither.

[1] Pascal, who was born in 1623, died on 19 Aug. 1662, aged 39 years and 2 months.
[2] 'To my honor'd kinsman, John Driden of Chesterton, in the county of Huntingdon, Esquire', 73–74, 88–95.
[3] *Motto.* Virgil, *Eclogues*, 8. 108: They fashion their own dreams.

It is with this Temper of Mind that I consider the Subject of
Witch-craft.[1] When I hear the Relations that are made from all parts
of the World, not only from *Norway* and *Lapland*, from the *East* and
West Indies, but from every particular Nation in *Europe*, I cannot
forbear thinking that there is such an Intercourse and Commerce
with Evil Spirits, as that which we express by the name of Witchcraft. But when I consider that the ignorant and credulous Parts of
the World abound most in these Relations, and that the Persons
among us who are supposed to engage in such an Infernal Commerce
are People of a weak Understanding and crazed Imagination, and
at the same time reflect upon the many Impostures and Delusions
of this Nature that have been detected in all Ages, I endeavour to
suspend my Belief till I hear more certain Accounts than any which
have yet come to my Knowledge. In short, when I consider the
Question, Whether there are such Persons in the World as those
we call Witches? my Mind is divided between the two opposite
Opinions, or rather (to speak my Thoughts freely) I believe in
general that there is and has been such a thing as Witch-craft; but
at the same time can give no Credit to any Particular Instance of it.

I am engaged in this Speculation, by some Occurrences that I met
with Yesterday, which I shall give my Reader an Account of at
large. As I was walking with my Friend Sir ROGER by the side of
one of his Woods, an old Woman applied her self to me for my
Charity. Her Dress and Figure put me in mind of the following
Description in *Otway*.[a2]

---

[a] of the following Description in *Otway*.] of a Description in *Ottway*, which I could
not forbear repeating on this occasion. Fol.

[1] Addison's essay on witchcraft appeared shortly before the celebrated trial of Jane
Wenham at Hertford on 4 Mar. 1712—the last person in England to be condemned
to capital punishment for witchcraft, although she was eventually reprieved and
pardoned. See W. Notestein, *History of Witchcraft in England from 1558 to 1718*
(Washington, 1911), pp. 324–30. Shadwell's *Lancashire Witches* would be familiar to
Addison's readers, and the subject of witchcraft recurs in much of the religious
literature of the time. Accounts of witches and spirits are collected, e.g. in Henry
More's *Antidote against Atheism*, book iii (3rd ed., 1662, pp. 89–133). A flood of
pamphlets on the subject appeared in conjunction with the case of Jane Wenham, but
there seems always to have been a steady market for books dealing with the black
art. Addison's essay, moderately sceptical, illustrates admirably the point of view of
the intelligent, religious observer. Toward the end of the *Remarks on . . . Italy* (1705)
Addison had taken the same position on the subject of witchcraft in Switzerland
(pp. 508–10). In his *Commentaries* (book iv, chap. iv) the great Blackstone concludes
his discussion by citing with approval this essay: 'it seems to be the most eligible
way to conclude, with an ingenious writer of our own [country], that in general
there has been such a thing as witchcraft; though one cannot give credit to any
particular modern instance of it' (Oxford, 1769, iv. 60).
[2] *The Orphan*, Act II (*Works*, ed. Ghosh, ii. 27). Addison omits a line ('And meditated

In a close Lane as I pursu'd my Journey,
I spy'd a wrinkled Hag, with Age grown double,
Picking dry Sticks, and mumbling to her self.
Her Eyes with scalding Rheum were gall'd and red,
Cold Palsy shook her Head; her Hands seem'd wither'd;
And on her crooked Shoulders had she wrap'd
The tatter'd Remnants of an old striped Hanging,
Which serv'd to keep her Carcass from the Cold:
So there was nothing of a-piece about her.
Her lower Weeds were all o'er coarsly patch'd
With diff'rent-colour'd Rags, black, red, white, yellow,
And seem'd to speak Variety of Wretchedness.

As I was musing on this Description, and comparing it with the
Object before me, the Knight told me,[a] that this very old Woman
had the Reputation of a Witch all over the Country, that her Lips
were observed to be always in Motion, and that there was not a
Switch about her House which her Neighbours did not believe had
carried her several hundreds of Miles. If she chanced to stumble,
they always found Sticks or Straws that lay in the Figure of a Cross
before her. If she made any Mistake at Church, and cryed *Amen* in
a wrong place, they never failed to conclude that she was saying
her Prayers backwards. There was not a Maid in the Parish that
would take a Pinn of her, though she should offer a Bag of Mony
with it. She goes by the Name of *Moll White*, and has made the
Country ring with several imaginary Exploits which[b] are palmed
upon her. If the Dairy Maid does not make her Butter come so soon
as she would have it, *Moll White* is at the bottom of the Churne. If
a Horse sweats in the Stable, *Moll White* has been upon his Back.
If a Hare makes an unexpected Escape from the Hounds, the Huntsman curses *Moll White*. Nay, (says Sir ROGER) I have known the
Master of the Pack, upon such an Occasion, send one of his Servants
to see if *Moll White* had been out that Morning.

This Account raised my Curiosity so far, that I beg'd my Friend
Sir ROGER to go with me into her Hovel, which stood in a solitary
Corner[c] under the side of the Wood. Upon our first entering Sir

[a] As . . . told me,] The Knight told me, upon hearing the Description, *Fol.*
[b] which] that *Fol.*   [c] which stood . . . Corner] that stood by it self *Fol.*

---

on the last nights Vision') after the first; in Otway line 7 reads 'The tatter'd
Remnant . . .'.

ROGER winked to me, and pointed at something that stood behind the Door, which upon looking that way I found to be an old Broom-staff. At the same time he whispered me in the Ear to take notice of a Tabby Cat that sate in the Chimny-Corner, which, as the Knight told me, lay under as bad a Report as *Moll White* her self; for besides that *Moll* is said often to accompany her in the same Shape, the Cat is reported to have spoken twice or thrice in her Life, and to have played several Pranks above the Capacity of an ordinary Cat.

I was secretly concerned to see Human Nature in so much Wretchedness and Disgrace, but at the same time could not forbear smiling to hear Sir ROGER, who is a little puzzled about the old Woman, advising her as a Justice of Peace to avoid all Communication with the Devil, and never to hurt any of her Neighbours Cattle. We concluded our Visit with a Bounty, which was very acceptable.

In our Return home, Sir ROGER told me that old *Moll* had been often brought before him for making Children spit Pins, and giving Maids the Night-Mare; and that the Country People would be tossing her into a Pond, and trying Experiments with her every Day, if it was not for him and his Chaplain.

I have since found, upon Enquiry, that Sir ROGER was several times staggered with the Reports that had been brought him concerning this old Woman, and would frequently have bound her over to the County Sessions, had not his Chaplain with much ado perswaded him to the contrary.

I have been the more particular in this Account, because I hear there is scarce a Village in *England* that has not a *Moll White* in it. When an old Woman begins to doat, and grow chargeable to a Parish, she is generally turned into a Witch, and fills the whole Country with extravagant Fancies, imaginary Distempers, and terrifying Dreams. In the mean time, the poor Wretch that is the innocent Occasion of so many Evils begins to be frighted at her self, and sometimes confesses secret Commerces and Familiarities that her Imagination forms in a delirious old Age. This frequently cuts off Charity from the greatest Objects of Compassion, and inspires People with a Malevolence towards those poor decrepid Parts of our Species, in whom Human Nature is defaced by Infirmity and Dotage.

L

No. 118 Monday, July 16, 1711[1]
[STEELE]

> ... *Hæret lateri lethalis arundo.*
> Virg.

THIS agreeable Seat is surrounded with so many pleasing Walks, which are struck out of a Wood, in the Midst of which the House stands, that one can hardly ever be weary of rambling from one Labyrinth of Delight to another. To one used to live in a City the Charms of the Country are so exquisite, that the Mind is lost in a certain Transport which raises us above ordinary Life, and yet is not strong enough to be inconsistent with Tranquility. This State of Mind was I in, ravished with the Murmur of Waters, the Whisper of Breezes, the Singing of Birds; and whether I looked up to the Heavens, down on the Earth, or turned to the Prospects around me, still struck with new Sense of Pleasure; when I found by the Voice of my Friend who walked by me, that we had insensibly stroled into the Grove sacred to the Widow.[2] This Woman, says he, is of all others the most unintelligible; she either designs to marry, or she does not. What is the most perplexing of all, is, that she does not either say to her Lovers she has any Resolution against that Condition of Life in general, or that she banishes them; but conscious of her own Merit, she permits their Addresses without Fear of any ill Consequence, or want of Respect, from their Rage or Despair. She has that in her Aspect, against which it is impossible to offend. A Man whose Thoughts are constantly bent upon so agreeable an Object, must be excused if the ordinary Occurrences in Conversation are below his Attention. I call her indeed perverse; but, alass! why do I call her so? because her superior Merit is such, that I cannot approach her without Awe, that my Heart is checked by too much Esteem: I am angry that her Charms are not more accessible, that I am more inclined to worship than salute her: How often have I wished her unhappy, that I might have an Opportunity of serving her? and how often troubled in that very Imagination, at giving her the Pain of being obliged? Well, I have led a miserable Life in secret upon her Account; but fancy she would have

[1] *Motto.* Virgil, *Aeneid*, 4. 73:
    ... Still the fatal Dart
    Sticks in her side; and ranckles in her Heart. DRYDEN.
[2] No. 113.

condescended to have some Regard for me, if it had not been for that watchful Animal her Confident.

Of all Persons under the Sun (continued he, calling me by my Name) be sure to set a Mark upon Confidents: They are of all People the most impertinent. What is most pleasant to observe in them, is, that they assume to themselves the Merit of the Persons whom they have in their Custody. *Orestilla* is a great Fortune, and in wonderful Danger of Surprizes, therefore full of Suspicions of the least indifferent thing, particularly careful of new Acquaintance, and of growing too familiar with the old. *Themista*, her Favourite-Woman,[1] is every whit as careful of whom she speaks to, and what she says. Let the Ward be a Beauty, her Confident shall treat you with an Air of Distance; let her be a Fortune, and she assumes the suspicious Behaviour of her Friend and Patroness. Thus it is that very many of our unmarried Women of Distinction, are to all Intents and Purposes married, except the Consideration of different Sexes. They are directly under the Conduct of their Whisperer, and think they are in a State of Freedom while they can prate with one of these Attendants of all Men in general, and still avoid the Man they most like. You do not see one Heiress in a hundred whose Fate does not turn upon this Circumstance of chusing a Confident. Thus it is that the Lady is addressed to, presented, and flattered, only by Proxy, in her Woman. In my Case, how is it possible that— Sir ROGER was proceeding in his Harangue, when we heard the Voice of one speaking very importunately, and repeating these Words, 'What, not one Smile?' We followed the Sound till we came to a close Thicket, on the other Side of which we saw a young Woman sitting as it were in a personated Sullenness just over a transparent Fountain. Opposite to her stood Mr. *William*, Sir ROGER's Master of the Game. The Knight whispered me, 'Hist, these are Lovers.' The Huntsman looking earnestly at the Shadow of the young Maiden in the Stream, 'Oh thou dear Picture, if thou could'st remain there in the Absence of that fair Creature whom you represent in the Water, how willingly could I stand here satisfied for ever, without troubling my dear *Betty* herself with any Mention of her unfortunate *William*, whom she is angry with: But alas! when she pleases to be gone, thou wilt also vanish— Yet let me talk to thee while thou dost stay. Tell my dearest *Betty*, thou dost not more depend upon her, than does her *William*? Her Absence will make away with me,

[1] Not in *OED*.

as well as thee. If she offers to remove thee, I'll jump into these Waves to lay hold on thee; her herself, her own dear Person, I must never embrace again— Still do you hear me without one Smile— It is too much to bear—' He had no sooner spoke these Words, but he made an Offer of throwing himself into the Water: At which his Mistress started up, and at the next Instant he jumped across the Fountain and met her in an Embrace. She half recovering from her Fright, said, in the most charming Voice imaginable, and with a Tone of Complaint, 'I thought how well you would drown your self. No, no, you won't drown your self till you have taken your Leave of *Susan Holliday*.' The Huntsman, with a Tenderness that spoke the most passionate Love, and with his Cheek close to hers, whispered the softest Vows of Fidelity in her Ear; and cryed, 'Don't my Dear believe a Word *Kate Willow* says; she is spiteful and makes Stories, because she loves to hear me talk to herself for your Sake.' Look you there, quoth Sir ROGER, do you see there, all Mischief comes from Confidents? But let us not interrupt them; the Maid is honest, and the Man dare not be otherwise, for he knows I loved her Father: I will interpose in this Matter and hasten the Wedding. *Kate Willow* is a witty mischievous Wench in the Neighbourhood, who was a Beauty; and makes me hope I shall see the perverse Widow in her Condition. She was so flippant with her Answers to all the honest Fellows that came near her, and so very vain of her Beauty, that she has valued herself upon her Charms till they are ceased. She therefore now makes it her Business to prevent other young Women from being more Discreet than she was herself: However, the saucy Thing said the other Day well enough, 'Sir ROGER and I must make a Match; for we are both despised by those we loved:' The Hussy has a great Deal of Power wherever she comes, and has her Share of Cunning.

However, when I reflect upon this Woman, I do not know whether in the Main I am the worse for having loved her: Whenever she is recalled to my Imagination my Youth returns, and I feel a forgotten Warmth in my Veins. This Affliction in my Life has streaked all my Conduct with a Softness, of which I should otherwise have been incapable. It is, perhaps, to this dear Image in my Heart owing, that I am apt to relent, that I easily forgive, and that many desirable things are grown into my Temper, which I should not have arrived at by better Motives than the Thought of being one Day hers. I am pretty well satisfied such a Passion as I have had is never well cured;

and between you and me, I am often apt to imagine it has had some whimsical Effect upon my Brain: For I frequently find, that in my most serious Discourse I let fall some comical Familiarity of Speech or odd Phrase that makes the Company laugh: However I cannot but allow she is a most excellent Woman. When she is in the Country I warrant she does not run into Dairies, but reads upon the Nature of Plants; but has a Glass Hive, and comes into the Garden out of Books to see them work, and observe the Policies of their Commonwealth. She understands every thing. I'd give ten Pounds to hear her argue with my Friend Sir ANDREW FREEPORT about Trade. No, no, for all she looks so innocent as it were, take my Word for it she is no Fool.   T

No. 119   *Tuesday, July* 17, 1711[1]
[ADDISON]

> *Urbem quam dicunt Romam, Melibœe, putavi*
> *Stultus ego huic nostræ similem . . .*
>
> Virg.

THE first and most obvious Reflections which arise in a Man who changes the City for the Country, are upon the different Manners of the People whom he meets with in those two different Scenes of Life. By Manners I do not mean Morals, but Behaviour and Good Breeding, as they show themselves in the Town and in the Country.

And here, in the first place, I must observe a very great Revolution that has happened in this Article of Good Breeding. Several obliging Deferencies, Condescensions and Submissions, with many outward Forms and Ceremonies that accompany them, were first of all brought up among the politer Part of Mankind who lived in Courts and Cities, and distinguished themselves from the Rustick part of the Species (who on all Occasions acted bluntly and naturally) by such a mutual Complaisance and Intercourse of Civilities. These Forms of Conversation by degrees multiplied and grew trouble-

---

[1] *Motto.* Virgil, *Eclogues,* I. 19–20:
Fool that I was, I thought Imperial *Rome*
Like *Mantua.* DRYDEN.

some; the Modish World found too great a Constraint in them, and have therefore thrown most of them aside. Conversation, like the *Romish* Religion, was so encumbered with Show and Ceremony, that it stood in need of a Reformation to retrench its Superfluities, and restore it to its natural good Sense and Beauty. At present therefore an unconstrained Carriage, and a certain Openness of Behaviour are the height of Good Breeding. The Fashionable World is grown free and easie; our Manners, sit more loose upon us: Nothing is so modish[1] as an agreeable Negligence. In a word, Good Breeding shows it self most, where to an ordinary Eye it appears the least.

If after this we look on the People of Mode in the Country, we find in them the Manners of the last Age. They have no sooner fetched themselves up to the fashion of the Polite World, but the Town has dropped them, and are nearer to the first State of Nature than to those Refinements which formerly reigned in the Court, and still prevail in the Country. One may now know a Man that never conversed in the World by his Excess of Good Breeding. A Polite Country Squire shall make you as many Bows in half an Hour, as would serve a Courtier for a Week. There is infinitely more to do about Place and Precedency in a Meeting of Justices Wives, than in an Assembly of Dutchesses.

This Rural Politeness is very troublesome to a Man of my Temper, who generally take the Chair that is next me, and walk first or last, in the Front or in the Rear, as Chance directs. I have known[a] my Friend Sir ROGER's Dinner almost cold before the Company could adjust the Ceremonial, and be prevailed upon to sit down; and have heartily pitied my old Friend, when I have seen him forced to pick and cull his Guests, as they sat at the several Parts of his Table, that he might drink their Healths according to their respective Ranks and Qualities. Honest *Will. Wimble*, who I should have thought had been altogether uninfected with Ceremony, gives me abundance of Trouble in this Particular; though he has been fishing all the Morning, he will not help himself at Dinner 'till I am served. When we are going out of the Hall he runs behind me, and last Night, as we were walking in the Fields, stopped short at a Stile

---

[a] known] seen *Fol.*

---

[1] 'The vulgar use of this term, has, I suppose, disgraced it. It would not, now, be endured in polite conversation, much less in polite writing' (Hurd).

till I came up to it, and upon my making Signs to him to get over, told me, with a serious Smile, that sure I believed they had no Manners in the Country.

There has happened another Revolution in the Point of Good Breeding, which[a] relates to the Conversation among Men of Mode, and which[b] I cannot but look upon as very extraordinary. It was certainly one of the first Distinctions of a well-bred Man to express every thing that had the most remote Appearance of being obscene in modest Terms and distant Phrases; whilst the Clown, who had no such Delicacy of Conception and Expression, cloathed his *Ideas* in those plain homely Terms that are the most obvious and natural. This kind of Good Manners was perhaps carried to an Excess, so as to make Conversation too stiff, formal and precise; for which Reason (as Hypocrisy in one Age is generally succeeded by Atheism in another) Conversation is in a great measure relapsed into the first Extream; So that at present several of our Men of the Town, and particularly those who have been polished in *France*, make use of the most coarse uncivilized Words in our Language, and utter themselves often in such a manner as a Clown would blush to hear.

This infamous Piece of Good Breeding, which reigns among the Coxcombs of the Town, has not yet made its way into the Country; and as it is impossible for such an irrational way of Conversation to last long among a People that make any Profession of Religion, or Show of Modesty, if the Country Gentlemen get into it they will certainly be left in the Lurch; their Good Breeding will come too late to them, and they will be thought a parcel of lewd Clowns, while they fancy themselves talking together like Men of Wit and Pleasure.

As the two Points of Good Breeding, which I have hitherto insisted upon, regard Behaviour and Conversation, there is a third which turns upon Dress. In this too the Country are very much behind hand. The Rural Beaus are not yet got out of the Fashion that took place at the time of the Revolution, but ride about the Country in red Coats and laced Hats, while the Women in many Parts are still trying to outvie one another in the Height of their Head-Dresses.[1]

But a Friend[2] of mine, who is now upon the Western Circuit,

---

[a] which] that *Fol.*   [b] Mode, and which] Mode, which *Fol.*

[1] See No. 98.
[2] His letter is printed in No. 129 (vol. ii).

having promised to give me an Account of the several Modes and Fashions that prevail in the different Parts of the Nation through which he passes, I shall defer the enlarging upon this last Topick till I have received a Letter from him, which I expect every Post.

L

No. 120   *Wednesday, July 18, 1711*[1]
[ADDISON]

> ... *Equidem credo quia sit Divinitus illis*
> *Ingenium* ...
>
>   Virg.

MY Friend Sir ROGER is very often merry with me, upon my passing so much of my Time among his Poultry: He has caught me twice or thrice looking after a Bird's Nest, and several times sitting an Hour or two together near an Hen and Chicken. He tells me he believes I am personally acquainted with every Fowl about his House; calls such a particular Cock my Favourite; and frequently complains that his Ducks and Geese have more of my Company than himself.

I must confess I am infinitely delighted with those Speculations of Nature which are to be made in a Country-Life; and as my Reading has very much lain among Books of natural History, I cannot forbear recollecting upon this Occasion the several Remarks which I have met with in Authors, and comparing them with what falls under my own Observation. The Arguments for Providence drawn from the natural History of Animals, being in my Opinion demonstrative.

The Make of every Kind of Animal is different from that of every other Kind;[2] and yet there is not the least Turn in the Muscles or Twist in the Fibres of any one, which does not render them more proper for that particular Animal's Way of Life than any other Cast or Texture of them would have been.

The most violent Appetites in all Creatures are *Lust* and *Hunger*:[3]

[1] *Motto.* Virgil, *Georgics*, 1. 415-16:
>   ... I think their Breasts with Heav'nly Souls
>   Inspir'd. DRYDEN.

[2] Cicero, *De natura deorum*, 2. 47. 121.

[3] 'Nature has implanted in us Two very strong Desires, Hunger for the Preservation of the Individual, and Lust for the Support of the Species; or, to speak more

The first is a perpetual Call upon them to propagate their Kind; the latter, to preserve themselves.

It is astonishing to consider the different Degrees of Care that descend from the Parent to the Young, so far as is absolutely necessary for the leaving a Posterity.[1] Some Creatures cast their Eggs as Chance directs them, and think of them no farther, as Insects and several Kinds of Fish: Others of a nicer Frame, find out proper Beds to deposite[a] them in, and there leave them; as the Serpent, the Crocodile and Ostrich: Others hatch their Eggs and tend the Birth, till it is able to shift for its self.

What can we call the Principle which directs every different Kind of Bird to observe a particular Plan in the Structure of its Nest, and directs all of the same Species to work after the same Model? It cannot be *Imitation*; for though you hatch a Crow under a Hen and never let it see any of the Works of its own Kind, the Nest it makes shall be the same, to the laying of a Stick, with all the other Nests of the same Species. It cannot be *Reason*; for were Animals indued with it to as great a Degree as Man, their Buildings would be as different as ours, according to the different Conveniencies that they would propose to themselves.

Is it not remarkable, that the same Temper of Weather which raises this genial Warmth in Animals, should cover the Trees with Leaves and the Fields with Grass for their Security and Concealment, and produce such infinite Swarms of Insects for the Support and Sustenance of their respective Broods?

Is it not wonderful, that the Love of the Parent should be so violent while it lasts; and that it should last no longer than is necessary for the Preservation of the Young?

The Violence of this natural Love is exemplified by a very barbarous Experiment; which I shall quote at Length as I find it in an excellent Author, and hope my Readers will pardon the mentioning such an Instance of Cruelty, because there is nothing can so effectually shew the Strength of that Principle in Animals of which I am

---

[a] deposite] depose *Fol.*

---

intelligibly, the former to continue our own Persons, and the latter to introduce others into the World' (*Tatler* 205). John Scott, in enumerating the proofs of a Providence, describes the parts and members of the body, 'some to propagate the *Kind*, others to preserve the *Individual*' (*The Christian Life*, part ii, vol. i, p. 208). Cf. also Cicero, *De Officiis*, I. 4. 11.

[1] Many of the examples here and in the following paragraphs come from Cicero, *De natura deorum*, 2. 47-52.

here speaking. 'A Person who was well skilled in Dissections opened a Bitch, and as she lay in the most exquisite Tortures offered her one of her young Puppies, which she immediately fell a licking; and for the Time seemed insensible of her own Pain:[a] On the Removal, she kept her Eye fixt on it, and began a wailing sort of Cry which seemed rather to proceed from the Loss of her young one, than the Sense of her own Torments.'

But notwithstanding this natural Love in Brutes is much more violent and intense than in rational Creatures, Providence has taken Care that it should be no longer troublesome to the Parent than it is useful to the Young; for so soon as the Wants of the latter cease, the Mother withdraws her Fondness and leaves them to provide for themselves: And what is a very remarkable Circumstance in this Part of Instinct, we find that the Love of the Parent may be lengthened out beyond its usual Time if the Preservation of the Species requires it; as we may see in Birds that drive away their Young assoon as they are able to get their Livelihood, but continue to feed them if they are tied to the Nest or confined within a Cage, or by any other Means appear to be out of a Condition of supplying their own Necessities.

This natural Love is not observed in Animals to ascend from the Young to the Parent, which is not at all necessary for the Continuance of the Species: Nor indeed in reasonable Creatures does it rise in any Proportion, as it spreads it self downwards; for in all Family-Affection, we find Protection granted and Favours bestowed, are greater Motives to Love and Tenderness, than Safety, Benefits, or Life received.

One would wonder to hear Sceptical Men disputing for the Reason of Animals, and telling us it is only our Pride and Prejudices that will not allow them the Use of that Faculty.[1]

Reason shews it self in all Occurrences of Life; whereas the Brute makes no Discovery of such a Talent, but in what immediately regards his own Preservation, or the Continuance of his Species. Animals in their Generation are wiser than the Sons of Men;[2] but their Wisdom is confined to a few Particulars, and lies in a very narrow Compass. Take a Brute out of his Instinct, and you find

[a] Pain:] Pains: *Fol.*

[1] The arguments concerning the question of reason in animals are discussed at great length by Bayle, particularly in the articles Rorarius, Pereira, and (Daniel) Sennertus.   [2] A reminiscence of Luke xvi. 8.

him wholly deprived of Understanding. To use an Instance that comes often under Observation.

With what Caution does the Hen provide her self a Nest[a] in Places unfrequented, and free from Noise and Disturbance?[1] When she has laid her Eggs in such a Manner that she can cover them, what Care does she take in turning them frequently, that all Parts may partake of the vital Warmth? When she leaves them to provide for her necessary Sustenance, how punctually does she return before they have Time to cool, and become incapable of producing an Animal? In the Summer you see her giving her self greater Freedoms, and quitting her Care for above two Hours together; but in Winter, when the Rigour of the Season would chill the Principles of Life, and destroy the young one, she grows more assiduous in her Attendance, and stays away but half the Time. When the Birth approaches, with how much Nicety and Attention does she help the Chick to break its Prison? Not to take Notice of her covering it from the Injuries of the Weather, providing it proper Nourishment, and teaching it to help it self; nor to mention her forsaking the Nest, if after the usual Time of reckoning the young one does not make its Appearance. A Chymical Operation could not be followed with greater Art or Diligence, than is seen in the hatching of a Chick; tho' there are many other Birds that shew an infinitely greater Sagacity in all the forementioned Particulars.

But at the same Time the Hen, that has all this seeming Ingenuity, (which is indeed absolutely necessary for the Propagation of the Species) considered in other Respects, is without the least Glimmerings of Thought or common Sense. She mistakes a Piece of Chalk for an Egg, and sits upon it in the same Manner: She is insensible of any Increase or Diminution in the Number of those she lays: She does not distinguish between her own and those of another Species; and when the Birth appears of never so different a Bird, will cherish it for her own. In all these Circumstances, which do not carry an immediate Regard to the Subsistance of her self or her Species, she is a very Ideot.

There is not in my Opinion any thing more mysterious in Nature than this Instinct in Animals, which thus rises above Reason, and falls infinitely short of it. It cannot be accounted for by any Pro-

---

[a] a Nest] of a Nest *Fol.*

[1] Cicero, *De natura deorum*, 2. 52. 129; Scott, *The Christian Life*, part ii, vol. i, pp. 217–20.

perties in Matter, and at the same Time works after so odd a Manner, that one cannot think it the Faculty of an intellectual Being. For my own Part, I look upon it as upon the Principle of Gravitation in Bodies, which is not to be explained by any known Qualities inherent in the Bodies themselves, nor from any Laws of Mechanism, but, according to the best Notions of the greatest Philosophers, is an immediate Impression from the first Mover, and the Divine Energy acting in the Creatures.[1]   L

No. 121   *Thursday, July 19, 1711*[2]
[ADDISON]

. . . Jovis omnia plena.
Virg.

AS I was walking this Morning in the great Yard that belongs to my Friend's Country House, I was wonderfully pleased to see the different workings of Instinct in a Hen followed by a Brood of Ducks.[3] The Young, upon the sight of a Pond, immediately ran into it, while the Stepmother, with all imaginable Anxiety, hovered about the Borders of it, to call them out of an Element that appeared to her so dangerous and destructive. As the different Principle which acted in these different Animals cannot be termed Reason, so when we call it *Instinct* we mean something we have no Knowledge of. To me, as I hinted in my last Paper, it seems the immediate Direction of Providence, and such an Operation of the Supreme Being as that which determines all the Portions of Matter to their proper Centers. A modern Philosopher, quoted by Monsieur *Bayle* in his Learned Dissertation on the Souls of Brutes, delivers the same Opinion, tho' in a bolder form of words, where he says *Deus est Anima*

---

[1] Cf. William Derham, *Astro-Theology*, book vi, chap. i: 'In the Earth itself there is manifestly such a thing as *Gravity*, which might as well be the Natural Cause of the Sphericity of our Globe, as it is in that of lesser Masses, but then . . . it is also evident, that an over-ruling Power, and a wise Providence not only gave Matter this Gravitating power, but guided and managed it in the formation of the World' (ed. 1715, p. 137). Ray refers to Newton's *Opticks*, Quaest. 23, and his *Principia*, Lib. 3, Prop. 5, 6, 7.

[2] *Motto.* Virgil, *Eclogues*, 3. 60: For all is full of *Jove*. DRYDEN.

[3] Mr. Spectator, of course, may have witnessed such an incident, but the illustration occurs in Cicero, *De natura deorum* (2. 48. 124), the source for much of the material in this and the preceding essay.

Brutorum,[1] God himself is the Soul of Brutes. Who can tell what to call that seeming Sagacity in Animals, which directs them to such Food as is proper for them, and makes them naturally avoid whatever is noxious or unwholesome? *Tully* has observed that a Lamb no sooner falls from its Mother, but immediately and of its own accord applies it self to the Teat.[2] *Dampier*, in his Travels, tells us, that when Seamen are thrown upon any of the unknown Coasts of *America* they never venture upon the Fruit of any Tree, how tempting soever it may appear, unless they observe that it is marked with the Pecking of Birds, but fall on without any Fear or Apprehension where the Birds have been before them.[3]

But notwithstanding Animals have nothing like the use of Reason, we find in them all the lower parts of our Nature, the Passions and Senses in their greatest Strength and Perfection. And here it is worth our Observation, that all Beasts and Birds of Prey are wonderfully subject to Anger, Malice, Revenge, and all the other violent Passions that may animate them in search of their proper Food; as those that are incapable of defending themselves, or annoying others, or whose Safety lies chiefly in their Flight, are suspicious, fearful and apprehensive of every thing they see or hear; whilst others that are of Assistance and Use to Man have their Natures softned with something mild and tractable, and by that means are qualified for a Domestick Life. In this case the Passions generally correspond with the Make of the Body. We do not find the Fury of a Lion in so weak and defenceless an Animal as a Lamb, nor the Meekness of a Lamb in a Creature so armed for Battel and Assault as the Lion. In the same manner, we find that particular Animals have a more or less exquisite Sharpness and Sagacity in those particular Senses which most turn to their Advantage, and in which their Safety and Welfare is the most concerned.

---

[1] The phrase cited comes from the *Nouvelles de la République des Lettres*, Oct. 1700, pp. 419–20, quoted by Bayle, art. Rorarius, Remark K. In reviewing the *Discours philosophique sur la création & l'arrangement du monde* by J. F. Vallade (Amsterdam, 1700), the editor of the *Nouvelles*, Jacques Bernard, criticizes Vallade for regarding animals as pure machines, since there are many animal actions hard to explain as mere mechanism.

Il seroit beaucoup plus court de se contenter de dire en général, que Dieu qui vouloit que leur machine subsistât pendant quelque tems, a par sa sagesse infinie disposé leurs parties convénablement à cette intention. Il me semble d'avoir lu quelque part cette Thése, *Deus est anima brutorum*; l'expression est un peu dure; mais elle peut recevoir un fort bon sens.

[2] *De natura deorum*, 2. 51. 128.

[3] Sir William Dampier, *A New Voyage round the World* (5th ed., 1703), i. 39. A four-volume edition printed for James Knapton is advertised in No. 100.

Nor must we here omit that great Variety of Arms[1] with which Nature has differently fortifyed the Bodies of several kind of Animals, such as Claws, Hoofs and Horns, Teeth and Tusks, a Tail, a Sting, a Trunk, or a *Proboscis*. It is likewise observed by Naturalists, that it must be some hidden Principle, distinct from what we call Reason, which instructs Animals in the Use of these their Arms, and teaches them to manage 'em to the best Advantage, because they naturally defend themselves with that part in which their Strength lies, before the Weapon be formed in it, as is remarkable in Lambs, which tho' they are bred within Doors, and never saw the Actions of their own Species, push at those who approach them with their Fore-heads, before the first budding of a Horn appears.

I shall add to these general Observations, an Instance which Mr. *Lock*[2] has given us of Providence, even in the Imperfections of a Creature which seems the meanest and most despicable in the whole animal World. *We may*, says he, *from the Make of an Oyster, or Cockle, conclude, that it has not so many nor so quick Senses as a Man, or several other Animals: nor, if it had, would it, in that State and Incapacity of transferring its self from one Place to another, be bettered by them. What good would Sight and Hearing do to a Creature, that cannot move it self to, or from the Object, wherein at a distance it perceives Good or Evil? And would not Quickness of Sensation be an Inconvenience to an Animal, that must be still where Chance has once placed it; and there receive the Afflux of colder or warmer, clean or foul Water, as it happens to come to it?*

I shall add to this Instance out of Mr. *Lock*, another out of the learned Dr. *Moor*,[3] who cites it from *Cardan*, in relation to another Animal which Providence has left Defective, but at the same time has shown its Wisdom in the Formation of that Organ in which it seems chiefly to have failed. *What is more obvious and ordinary than a Mole? and yet what more palpable Argument of Providence than she? The Members of her Body are so exactly fitted to her Nature and Manner of Life: For her dwelling being under Ground, where nothing is to be seen, Nature has so obscurely fitted her with Eyes, that Naturalists can scarce agree whether she have any Sight at all or no. But for amends, what she is capable of for her Defence and warning of Danger, she has very eminently conferred upon her; for she is exceeding quick of Hearing. And then her short Tail and short Legs, but broad Fore-feet armed with sharp Claws, we see by the event*

---

[1] Cicero, *De natura deorum*, 2. 47. 121–3.
[2] *Essay*, II. ix. 13.
[3] Henry More, *An Antidote against Atheism* (1652), II. x. 5 (3rd ed., 1662, pp. 70–71).

to what purpose they are, she so swiftly working her self under Ground, and making her way so fast in the Earth, as they that behold it cannot but admire it. Her Legs therefore are short, that she need dig no more than will serve the mere Thickness of her Body; and her Fore-feet are broad that she may scoup away much Earth at a time; and little or no Tail she has, because she courses it not on the Ground, like the Rat or Mouse, of whose Kindred she is, but lives under the Earth, and is fain to dig her self a Dwelling there. And she making her way through so thick an Element, which will not yield easily, as the Air or the Water, it had been dangerous to have drawn so long a Train behind her, for her Enemy might fall upon her Rear, and fetch her out before she had compleated or got full possession of her Works.

I cannot forbear mentioning Mr. *Boyle*'s Remark upon this last Creature, who, I remember, some where in his Works observes, that though the Mole be not totally blind (as it is commonly thought) she has not Sight enough to distinguish particular Objects.[1] Her Eye is said to have but one Humour in it, which is supposed to give her the Idea of Light, but of nothing else, and is so formed that this Idea is probably painful to the Animal. Whenever she comes up into broad Day she might be in danger of being taken, unless she were thus affected by a Light striking upon her Eye and immediately warning her to bury her self in her proper Element. More Sight wou'd be useless to her, as none at all might be fatal.

I have only instanced such Animals as seem the most imperfect Works of Nature, and if Providence shows it self even in the Blemishes of these Creatures, how much more does it discover it self in the several Endowments which it has variously bestowed upon such Creatures as are more or less finished and compleated in their several Faculties, according to the Condition of Life in which they are posted.

I could wish our Royal Society[2] would compile a body of Natural History, the best that could be gathered together from Books and Observations. If the several Writers among them took each his particular Species, and gave us a distinct Account of its Original, Birth and Education; its Policies, Hostilities and Allyances, with the Frame and Texture of its inward and outward Parts, and particularly those that distinguish it from all other Animals, with their peculiar Aptitudes for the State of Being in which Providence has placed

[1] Robert Boyle, *A Disquisition about the Final Causes of Natural Things* (1688), pp. 60–61.
[2] Cf. No. 10.

them, it would be one of the best Services their Studies could do Mankind, and not a little redound to the Glory of the All-wise Contriver.

It is true, such a Natural History, after all the Disquisitions of the Learned, would be infinitely short and Defective. Seas and Desarts hide Millions of Animals from our Observation. Innumerable Artifices and Stratagems are acted in the *Howling Wilderness* and in the *Great Deep*,[1] that can never come to our Knowledge. Besides that there are infinitely more Species of Creatures which are not to be seen without, nor indeed with the help of the finest Glasses, than of such as are bulky enough for the naked Eye to take hold of. However from the Consideration of such Animals as lie within the Compass of our Knowledge, we might easily form a Conclusion of the rest, that the same variety of Wisdom and Goodness runs through the whole Creation, and puts every Creature in a condition to provide for its Safety and Subsistence in its proper Station.

Tully[2] has given us an admirable Sketch of Natural History, in his second Book concerning the Nature of the Gods, and that in a Stile so raised by Metaphors and Descriptions, that it lifts the Subject above Raillery and Ridicule, which frequently fall on such nice Observations, when they pass through the Hands of an ordinary Writer. L

No. 122

[ADDISON]

Friday, July 20, 1711[3]

Comes jucundus in via pro vehiculo est.
Publ. Syr. frag.

A MAN'S first Care should be to avoid the Reproaches of his own Heart; his next, to escape the Censures of the World: If the last interferes with the former, it ought to be entirely neglected; but otherwise, there cannot be a greater Satisfaction to an honest Mind, than to see those Approbations which it gives itself seconded

[1] The first phrase comes from Deut. xxxii. 10; the second occurs frequently in the Old Testament—Gen. vii. 11; Ps. xxxvi. 6; &c.

[2] *De natura deorum*, 2. 47–52.

[3] *Motto.* Publilius Syrus, *Sententiae* 116: A pleasant companion in a journey is as good as a coach.

by the Applauses of the Publick: A Man is more sure of his Conduct, when the Verdict which he passes upon his own Behaviour is thus warranted, and confirmed by the Opinion of all that know him.

My worthy Friend Sir ROGER is one of those who is not only at Peace within himself, but beloved and esteemed by all about him. He receives a suitable Tribute for his universal Benevolence to Mankind, in the Returns of Affection and Good-will, which are paid him by every one that lives within his Neighbourhood. I lately met with two or three odd Instances of that general Respect which is shewn to the good old Knight. He would needs carry *Will. Wimble* and my self with him to the County-Assizes: As we were upon the Road *Will. Wimble* joyned a couple of plain Men who rid before us, and conversed with them for some Time; during which my Friend Sir ROGER acquainted me with their Characters.

The first of them, says he, that has a Spaniel by his Side, is a Yeoman of about an hundred Pounds a Year, an honest Man: He is just within the Game-Act,[1] and qualified to kill an Hare or a Pheasant: He knocks down a Dinner with his Gun twice or thrice a Week; and by that Means lives much cheaper than those who have not so good an Estate as himself. He would be a good Neighbour if he did not destroy so many Partridges: In short, he is a very sensible Man; shoots flying;[2] and has been several Times Foreman of the Petty-Jury.

The other that rides along with him is *Tom Touchy*, a Fellow famous for *taking the Law* of every Body. There is not one in the Town where he lives that he has not sued at a Quarter-Sessions. The Rogue had once the Impudence to go to Law with the *Widow*. His Head is full of Costs, Damages, and Ejectments: He plagued a couple of honest Gentlemen so long for a Trespass in breaking one of his Hedges, till he was forced to sell the Ground it enclosed to defray the Charges of the Prosecution: His Father left him four-score Pounds a Year; but he has *cast* and been cast so often, that he is not now worth thirty. I suppose he is going upon the old Business of the Willow-Tree.

As Sir ROGER was giving me this Account of *Tom Touchy*, *Will.*

[1] See No. 2. On 16 May of this year the House of Commons took under considera-tion the Lords' amendment to a bill for making this Act more effectual (*Journals of the House of Commons*, xvi. 666).
[2] 'In Anne's reign it was already not unusual to "shoot flying." But it was re-garded as a difficult art, the more so as it was sometimes practised from horseback' (Trevelyan, i. 24).

Wimble and his two Companions stopped short till we came up to them. After having paid their Respects to Sir ROGER, *Will.* told him that Mr. *Touchy* and he must appeal to him upon a Dispute that arose between them. *Will.* it seems had been giving his Fellow Travellers an Account of his angling one Day in such a Hole; when *Tom Touchy*, instead of hearing out his Story, told him, that Mr. such an One, if he pleased, might *take the Law of him* for fishing in that Part of the River. My Friend Sir ROGER heard them both, upon a round Trot; and after having paused some Time told them, with the Air of a Man who would not give his Judgment rashly, that *much might be said on both Sides*. They were neither of them dissatisfied with the Knight's Determination, because neither of them found himself in the Wrong by it: Upon which we made the best of our Way to the Assizes.

The Court was sat before Sir ROGER came, but notwithstanding all the Justices had taken their Places upon the Bench, they made Room for the old Knight at the Head of them; who for his Reputation in the Country took Occasion to whisper in the Judge's Ear, That *he was glad his Lordship had met with so much good Weather in his Circuit*. I was listening to the Proceedings of the Court with much Attention, and infinitely pleased with that great Appearance and Solemnity which so properly accompanies such a publick Administration of our Laws; when, after about an Hour's Sitting, I observed to my great Surprize, in the Midst of a Trial, that my Friend Sir ROGER was getting up to speak. I was in some Pain for him, till I found he had acquitted himself of two or three Sentences, with a Look of much Business and great Intrepidity.

Upon his first Rising the Court was hushed, and a general Whisper ran among the Country-People that Sir ROGER *was up*. The Speech he made was so little to the Purpose, that I shall not trouble my Readers with an Account of it; and I believe was not so much designed by the Knight himself to inform the Court, as to give him a Figure in my Eye, and keep up his Credit in the Country.

I was highly delighted, when the Court rose, to see the Gentlemen of the Country gathering about my old Friend, and striving who should compliment him most; at the same Time that the ordinary People gazed upon him at a Distance, not a little admiring his Courage, that was not afraid to speak to the Judge.

In our Return home we met with a very odd Accident; which I cannot forbear relating, because it shews how desirous all who know

Sir ROGER are of giving him Marks of their Esteem. When we were arrived upon the Verge of his Estate, we stopped at a little Inn to rest our selves and our Horses. The Man of the House had it seems been formerly a Servant in the Knight's Family; and to do Honour to his old Master, had some Time since, unknown to Sir ROGER, put him up in a Sign-post before the[a] Door; so that *the Knight's Head*[1] had hung out upon the Road about a Week before he himself knew any thing of the Matter. As soon as Sir ROGER was acquainted with it, finding that his Servant's Indiscretion proceeded wholly from Affection and Good-will, he only told him that he had made him too high a Compliment; and when the Fellow seemed to think that could hardly be, added with a more decisive Look, That it was too great an Honour for any Man under a Duke; but told him at the same Time that it might be altered with a very few Touches, and that he himself would be at the Charge of it. Accordingly they got a Painter by the Knight's Directions to add a Pair of Whiskers to the Face, and by a little Aggravation of the Features to change it into the *Saracen's Head*. I should not have known this Story, had not the Inn-keeper upon Sir ROGER's alighting told him in my Hearing, That his Honour's Head was brought back last Night with the Alterations that he had ordered to be made in it. Upon this my Friend with his usual Chearfulness related the Particulars above-mentioned, and ordered the Head to be brought into the Room. I could not forbear discovering greater Expressions of Mirth than ordinary upon the Appearance of this monstrous Face, under which, notwithstanding it was made to frown and stare in a most extra-ordinary Manner, I could still discover a distant Resemblance of my old Friend. Sir ROGER, upon seeing me laugh, desired me to tell him truly if I thought it possible for People to know him in that Disguise. I at first kept my usual Silence; but upon the Knight's conjuring me to tell him whether it was not still more like himself than a *Saracen*, I composed my Countenance in the best Manner I could, and replied, *That much might be said on both Sides*.[2]

[a] the] his *Fol.*

[1] For portrait signs cf. *Tatler* 18.
[2] A phrase which seems to have attained some popularity at the time. *The Plain Dealer*, no. 1, of 12 Apr. 1712 (by William Wagstaffe), describes a scuffle in the lobby of the House of Commons, in which Abel Roper was attacked by L—d W—m P—t and some others of the Whiggish faction. "'Tis to be fear'd, Posterity may fall together by the Ears to decide the Masterpiece of his [Lordship's] Character, Whether he was the greater Orator or General? For, according to Sir *Roger*, *Much may be said on both Sides*' In the burlesque 'Notes upon Notes' in *Odes of Horace* (Lintott, 1712), part v,

These several Adventures, with the Knight's Behaviour in them, gave me as pleasant a Day[1] as ever I met with in any of my Travels.

L

No. 123

Saturday, July 21, 1711[2]

Doctrina sed vim promovet insitam,
Rectique cultus pectora roborant:
Utcunque defecere mores,
Dedecorant bene nata culpæ.

Hor.

AS I was Yesterday taking the Air with my Friend Sir ROGER, we were met by a fresh-coloured ruddy young Man, who rid by us full Speed, with a couple of Servants behind him. Upon my enquiry who he was, Sir ROGER told me that he was a young Gentleman of a considerable Estate, who had been educated by a tender Mother that liv'd not many Miles from the Place where we were. She is a very good Lady, says my Friend, but took so much Care of her Son's Health that she has made him good for nothing. She quickly found that Reading was bad for his Eyes, and that Writing made his Head ach. He was let loose among the Woods as soon as he was able to ride on Horse-back, or to carry a Gun upon his Shoulder. To be brief, I found, by my Friend's Account of him, that he had got a great Stock of Health, but nothing else; and that if it were a Man's Business only to live, there would not be a more accomplished young Fellow in the whole County.

The Truth of it is, since my residing in these Parts I have seen and heard innumerable Instances of young Heirs and elder Brothers, who either from their own reflecting upon the Estates they are born

p. 15, Bentley is accused of arguing elaborately about two different readings, only to conclude that we may read it which way we please: 'Sir *Roger de Coverly* passed the very same Judgment, but with much more Conciseness, *that much might be said on both sides.*'

[1] 'Mr. Addison could not help giving himself this little applause, for one of the most humourous papers that ever was written' (Hurd).

[2] *Motto.* Horace, *Odes,* 4. 4. 33–36:

> Yet the best Blood by Learning is refin'd,
> And Virtue arms the solid Mind;
> Whilst Vice, will stain the noblest Race,
> And the paternal Stamp efface. OLDISWORTH.

to, and therefore thinking all other Accomplishments unnecessary, or from hearing these Notions frequently inculcated to them by the Flattery of their Servants and Domesticks, or from the same foolish Thought prevailing in those who have the Care of their Education, are of no manner of use but to keep up their Families, and transmit their Lands and Houses in a Line to Posterity.

This makes me often think on a Story I have heard of two Friends, which I shall give my Reader at large, under feigned Names. The Moral of it may, I hope, be useful, though there are some Circumstances which make it rather appear like a Novel, than a true Story.

Eudoxus and *Leontine* begun the World with small Estates. They were both of them Men of good Sense and great Virtue. They prosecuted their Studies together in their earlier Years, and entered into such a Friendship as lasted to the End of their Lives. *Eudoxus*, at his first setting out in the World, threw himself into a Court, where by his natural Endowments and his acquired Abilities he made his way from one Post to another, till at length he had raised a very considerable Fortune. *Leontine* on the contrary sought all Opportunities of improving his Mind by Study, Conversation and Travel. He was not only acquainted with all the Sciences, but with the most eminent Professors of them throughout *Europe*. He knew perfectly well the Interests of its Princes, with the Customs and Fashions of their Courts, and could scarce meet with the Name of an extraordinary Person in the Gazette whom he had not either talked to or seen. In short, he had so well mixt and digested his Knowledge of Men and Books, that he made one of the most accomplished Persons of his Age. During the whole course of his Studies and Travels he kept up a punctual Correspondence with *Eudoxus*, who often made himself acceptable to the principal Men about Court by the Intelligence which he received from *Leontine*. When they were both turned of forty (an Age in which, according to Mr. *Cowley*,[1] *there is no dallying with Life*) they determined, pursuant to the Resolution they had taken in the beginning of their Lives, to retire, and pass the remainder of their Days in the Country. In order to this, they both of them married much about the same time. *Leontine*, with his own and his Wife's Fortune, bought a Farm of three hundred a Year, which lay within the Neighbourhood of his Friend *Eudoxus*, who had purchased an Estate of as many thousands. They

---

[1] Essay 10, 'The Danger of Procrastination'. 'But there's no fooling with Life when it is once turn'd beyond Forty.' *Essays*, ed. Waller, p. 452.

were both of them *Fathers* about the same time, *Eudoxus* having a Son born to him and *Leontine* a Daughter; but to the unspeakable Grief of the latter, his young Wife (in whom all his Happiness was wrapt up) died in a few days after the Birth of her Daughter. His Affliction would have been insupportable, had not he been comforted by the daily Visits and Conversations of his Friend. As they were one Day talking together with their usual Intimacy, *Leontine*, considering how incapable he was of giving his Daughter a proper Education in his own House, and *Eudoxus* reflecting on the ordinary Behaviour of a Son who knows himself to be the Heir of a great Estate, they both agreed upon an Exchange of Children, namely that the Boy should be bred up with *Leontine* as his Son, and that the Girl should live with *Eudoxus* as his Daughter, till they were each of them arrived at Years of Discretion. The Wife of *Eudoxus*, knowing that her Son could not be so advantagiously brought up as under the Care of *Leontine*, and considering at the same time that he would be perpetually under her own Eye, was by degrees prevailed upon to fall in with the Project. She therefore took *Leonilla*, for that was the Name of the Girl, and educated her as her own Daughter. The two Friends on each side had wrought themselves to such an habitual Tenderness for the Children who were under their Direction, that each of them had the real Passion of a Father, where the Title was but imaginary. *Florio*, the Name of the young Heir that lived with *Leontine*, though he had all the Duty and Affection imaginable for his[a] supposed Parent, was taught to rejoice at the Sight of *Eudoxus*, who visited his Friend very frequently, and was dictated[1] by his natural Affection, as well as by the Rules of Prudence, to make himself esteemed and beloved by *Florio*. The Boy was now old enough to know his supposed Father's Circumstances, and that therefore he was to make his way in the World by his own Industry. This Consideration grew stronger in him every Day, and produced so good an Effect, that he applyed himself with more than ordinary Attention to the Pursuit of every thing which *Leontine* recommended to him. His natural Abilities, which were very good, assisted by the Directions of so excellent a Councellor, enabled him to make a quicker Progress than ordinary through all the Parts of

[a] his] a *Fol.*

[1] Hurd objected to this usage as unidiomatic: 'it should be *dictated to*: but the proper word, in this place, is *carried*, or *led*.' Hurd's objection is correct according to the *OED*, but all the texts have the reading as given here.

his Education. Before he was twenty Years of Age, having finished his Studies and Exercises with great Applause, he was removed from the University to the Inns of Court, where there are very few that make themselves considerable Proficients in the Studies of the Place, who know they shall arrive at great Estates without them. This was not *Florio*'s Case, he found that three hundred a Year was but a poor Estate for *Leontine* and himself to live upon, so that he Studied without Intermission till he gained a very good Insight into the Constitution and Laws of his Country.

I should have told my Reader, that whilst *Florio* lived at the House of his Foster-father he was always an acceptable Guest in the Family of *Eudoxus*, where he became acquainted with *Leonilla* from her Infancy. His Acquaintance with her by degrees grew into Love, which in a Mind trained up in all the Sentiments of Honour and Virtue became a very uneasy Passion. He despaired of gaining an Heiress of so great a Fortune, and would rather have died than attempted it by any indirect Methods. *Leonilla*, who was a Woman of the greatest Beauty joined with the greatest Modesty, entertained at the same time a secret Passion for *Florio*, but conducted her self with so much Prudence that she never gave him the least Intimation of it. *Florio* was now engaged in all those Arts and Improvements that are proper to raise a Man's private Fortune, and give him a Figure in his Country, but secretly tormented with that Passion which burns with the greatest Fury in a virtuous and noble Heart, when he received a sudden Summons from *Leontine* to repair to him into the Country the next Day. For it seems *Eudoxus* was so filled with the Report of his Son's Reputation, that he could no longer with-hold making himself known to him. The Morning after his Arrival at the House of his supposed Father, *Leontine* told him that *Eudoxus* had something of great Importance to communicate to him; upon which the good Man embraced him, and wept. *Florio* was no sooner arrived at the great House that stood in his Neighbourhood, but *Eudoxus* took him by the Hand, after the first Salutes were over, and conducted him into his Closet. He there opened to him the whole Secret of his Parentage and Education, concluding after this manner. *I have no other way left of acknowledging my Gratitude to* Leontine *than by marrying you to his Daughter, he shall not lose the Pleasure of being your Father, by the discovery I have made to you.* Leonilla *too shall be still my Daughter; her filial Piety, though misplaced, has been so exemplary that it deserves the greatest Reward I can confer upon it. You shall have the Pleasure of seeing a great Estate fall to you, which you would* *have lost the Relish of had you known your self born to it.* Continue only to *deserve it in the same manner you did before you were possessed of it.* I have *left your Mother in the next Room. Her Heart yearns towards you. She is* *making the same Discoveries to* Leonilla *which I have made to your self.* Florio was so overwhelmed with this Profusion of Happiness, that he was not able to make a Reply, but threw himself down at his Father's Feet, and amidst a flood of Tears, kissed and embraced his Knees, asking his Blessing, and expressing in dumb show those Sentiments of Love, Duty and Gratitude that were too big for Utterance. To conclude, the happy Pair were married, and half *Eudoxus's* Estate settled upon them. *Leontine* and *Eudoxus* passed the Remainder of their Lives together, and received in the dutiful and affectionate Behaviour of *Florio* and *Leonilla* the just Recompence, as well as the natural Effects, of that Care which they had bestowed upon them in their Education. L[1]

No. 124

[ADDISON]

Monday, July 23, 1711[2]

Μέγα βιβλίον, μέγα κακόν.

A MAN who publishes his Works in a Volume, has an infinite Advantage over one who communicates his Writings to the World in loose Tracts and single Pieces. We do not expect to meet with any thing in a bulky Volume, till after some heavy Preamble, and several Words of Course, to prepare the Reader for what follows: Nay Authors have established it as a Kind of Rule, That a Man ought to be dull sometimes;[3] as the most severe Reader makes Allowances

---

[1] On the day of publication of this paper Addison wrote to his friend Edward Wortley: 'Being very well pleased with this day's Spectator, I can not forbear sending you one of them and desiring your opinion of the story in it. When you have a Son I shall be glad to be his Leontine as my Circumstances will probably be like His' (facsimile in *Addisoniana*). A somewhat different version of this letter will be found in Graham, pp. 263–4.

[2] *Motto*. Adapted from Callimachus, *Fragments* 359: A great book is a great evil.

[3] Mr. Spectator had earlier, in No. 19, announced that he would 'sometimes be dull'. In the *Review* of 18 Aug. 1711 Defoe made the point that dullness is often a matter of the reader rather than the writer.

It was but a few Days ago I came into a Coffee-House, and I saw a Gentleman nodding over the Spectator, What have you got there said I to him, after I had wak'd him; the *Spectator*, says he, he's Damnable DULL to Day; I went on to talk

505

for many Rests and Nodding-places in a voluminous Writer. This gave Occasion to the famous *Greek* Proverb which I have chosen for my Motto, *That a great Book is a great Evil.*

On the contrary, those who publish their Thoughts in distinct Sheets, and as it were by Piece-meal, have none of these Advantages. We must immediately fall into our Subject and treat every Part of it in a lively Manner, or our Papers are thrown by as dull and insipid: Our Matter must lie close together, and either be wholly new in itself, or in the Turn it receives from our Expressions. Were the Books of our best Authors thus to be retailed to the Publick, and every Page submitted to the Taste of forty or fifty thousand Readers,[1] I am afraid we should complain of many flat Expressions, trivial Observations, beaten Topicks, and common Thoughts, which go off very well in the Lump. At the same Time, notwithstanding some Papers may be made up of broken Hints and irregular Sketches, it is often expected that every Sheet should be a kind of Treatise, and make out in Thought what it wants in Bulk: That a Point of Humour should be worked up in all its Parts; and a Subject touched upon in its most essential Articles, without the Repetitions, Tautologies, and Enlargements that are indulg'd to longer Labours. The ordinary Writers of Morality prescribe to their Readers after the Galenick Way; their Medicines are made up in large Quantities. An Essay Writer must practise in the Chymical Method, and give the Virtue of a full Draught in a few Drops.[2] Were all Books reduced thus to their Quintessence, many a bulky Author would make his Appearance in a Penny Paper: There would be scarce such a thing in Nature as a Folio. The Works of an Age would be contained on a few

of other Business to him, and by and by I was for taking the *Spectator* out of his Hand to read it—Hold, says he, I han't read it myself—Yet he could tell it was very Dull—That is to say he was very sleepy, and could not relish what he read— Well, having had his nap out, he read it over, and I perceiv'd him laughing to himself—What tickles you now, says I, D—n him says he, this *Spectator* would make any Body laugh, he is a very witty Fellow.

[1] This is slightly smaller than the figure mentioned in No. 10, if we estimate 'twenty readers to every paper', but there is no evidence that circulation was falling off. Addison says below that the demand is increasing.

[2] Dryden uses the same figure to contrast tragedies (strong medicines in small doses) and epics (vegetable remedies in large quantities): 'Chymical medicines are observed to relieve oftener than to cure; for 'tis the nature of spirits to make swift impressions, but not deep. Galenical decoctions, to which I may properly compare an epic poem, have more of body in them; they work by their substance and their weight' (Dedication to *Aeneis*; *Essays*, ed. Ker, !ii. 158). Cf. also the opening scene of Shadwell's *Epsom Wells*, where young Bevil makes a similar comparison: 'We, like subtile Chymists, extract and refine our Pleasure; while they [the temperate ones], like fulsome Galenists, take it in Gross.'

Shelves; not to mention Millions of Volumes that would be utterly annihilated.

I cannot think that the Difficulty of furnishing out separate Papers of this Nature has hindered Authors from communicating their Thoughts to the World after such a Manner: Though I must confess I am amazed that the Press should be only made use of in this Way by News-Writers, and the Zealots of Parties; as if it were not more advantageous to Mankind to be instructed in Wisdom and Virtue, than in Politicks; and to be made good Fathers, Husbands, and Sons, than Counsellours and Statesmen. Had the Philosophers and great Men of Antiquity, who took so much Pains in order to instruct Mankind, and leave the World wiser and better than they found it; had they, I say, been possessed of the Art of Printing, there is no Question but they would have made such an Advantage of it, in dealing out their Lectures to the Publick. Our common Prints[1] would be of great Use were they thus calculated to diffuse good Sense through the Bulk of a People, to clear up their Understandings, animate their Minds with Virtue, dissipate the Sorrows of a heavy Heart, or unbend the Mind from its more severe Employments with innocent Amusements. When Knowledge, instead of being bound up in Books, and kept in Libraries and Retirements, is thus obtruded upon the Publick; when it is canvassed in every Assembly, and exposed upon every Table; I cannot forbear reflecting upon that Passage in the *Proverbs, Wisdom cryeth without, she uttereth her Voice in the Streets: She cryeth in the chief Place of Concourse, in the Openings of the Gates. In the City she uttereth her Words, saying, How long, ye simple ones, will ye love Simplicity? and the Scorners delight in their Scorning? and Fools hate Knowledge?*[2]

The many Letters which come to me from Persons of the best Sense in both Sexes, (for I may pronounce their Characters from[a] their Way of Writing) do not a little encourage me in the Prosecution of this my Undertaking: Besides that, my Bookseller tells me, the Demand for these my Papers increases daily. It is at his Instance that I shall continue my *rural Speculations* to the End of this Month; several having made up separate Sets of them, as they have done

[a] for I may pronounce their Characters from] if I may guess at their Characters by *Fol.*

---

[1] i.e. the newspapers.
[2] Prov. i. 20–22.

before of those relating to Wit, to Operas, to Points of Morality, or Subjects of Humour.

I am not at all mortified, when sometimes I see my Works thrown aside by Men of no Taste nor Learning. There is a kind of Heaviness and Ignorance that hangs upon the Minds of ordinary Men, which is too thick for Knowledge to break through: Their Souls are not to be enlightned.

> . . . *Nox atra cavâ circumvolat umbra.*[1]

To these I must apply the Fable of the Mole,[2] That after having consulted many Oculists for the bettering of his Sight, was at last provided with a good Pair of Spectacles; but upon his endeavouring to make use of them, his Mother told him very prudently, 'That Spectacles, though they might help the Eye of a Man, could be of no use to a Mole.' It is not therefore for the Benefit of Moles that I publish these my daily Essays.

But besides such as are Moles through Ignorance, there are others who are Moles through Envy. As it is said in the *Latin* Proverb,[3] 'That one Man is a Woolf to another;' so, generally speaking, one Author is a Mole to another Author. It is impossible for them to discover Beauties in one another's Works; they have Eyes only for Spots and Blemishes: They can indeed see the Light, as it is said of the Animals which are their Namesakes, but the Idea of it is painful to them; they immediately shut their Eyes upon it, and withdraw themselves into a wilful Obscurity. I have already caught[a] two or three of these dark undermining Vermin, and intend to make a String of them, in order to hang them up in one of my Papers as an Example to all such voluntary Moles.   C

---

[a] have already caught] have caught *Fol.*

---

[1] Virgil, *Aeneid*, 2. 360: Night was our Friend, our Leader was Despair. DRYDEN.
[2] No. 172 in L'Estrange, *Fables and Storyes Moralized* (1699), p. 162.
[3] 'Lupus est homo homini' (Plautus, *Asinaria*, 495). See Apperson and Tilley (M 245) for examples in English.

Ne pueri, ne tanta animis assuescite bella:
Neu patriæ validas in viscera vertite vires.
Vir.

M Y worthy Friend Sir ROGER, when we are talking of the Malice of Parties, very frequently tells us an Accident that happened to him when he was a School-boy, which was at a time[a] when the Feuds ran high between the Round-heads and Cavaliers. This worthy Knight being then but a Stripling, had Occasion to enquire which was the Way to St. *Ann*'s Lane,[2] upon which the Person whom he spoke to, instead of answering his Question, called him a young Popish Cur, and asked him who had made *Ann* a Saint? The Boy being in some Confusion, enquired of the next he met, which was the way to *Ann*'s Lane, but was called a Prick-eared Curr for his Pains, and instead of being shown the Way was told, that she had been a Saint before he was born, and would be one after he was hang'd. Upon this, says Sir ROGER, I did not think fit to repeat the former Question, but going into every Lane of the Neighbourhood, asked what they called the Name of that Lane. By which ingenious Artifice he found out the Place he enquired after, without giving Offence to any Party. Sir ROGER generally closes this Narrative with Reflections on the Mischief that Parties do in the Country; how they spoil good Neighbourhood, and make honest Gentlemen hate one another; besides that they manifestly tend to the Prejudice of the Land-Tax, and the Destruction of the Game.

There cannot a greater Judgment befall a Country than such a dreadful Spirit of Division as rends a Government into two distinct

a   at a time *12mo*] at the time *Fol.*, *8vo*

1   *Motto.* Virgil, *Aeneid*, 6. 832–3.
     Embrace again, my Sons, be Foes no more:
     Nor stain your Country with her Childrens Gore. DRYDEN.

2   St. Anne's Lane was 'on the South side of St. Martins le Grand' (Hatton, p. 128), i.e. between Newgate and Aldersgate, and is now called Gresham Street (Harben, *Dictionary of London*, 1918, p. 80). Edlin's Coffee-house was 'in St. Ann's Lane near Aldersgate' (*Daily Courant*, 17 Oct. 1705). On the Puritans' objection to 'making Anne a saint' cf. *Hudibras*, III. ii. 315–18:
            Others, to make all things recant
            The *Christian* or *Surname* of Saint;
            And force all *Churches*, *Streets*, and *Towns*,
            The *Holy Title* to renounce.

People, and makes them greater Strangers and more averse to one another, than if they were actually two different Nations. The Effects of such a Division are pernicious to the last degree, not only with regard to those Advantages which they give the Common Enemy, but to those private Evils which they produce in the Heart of almost every particular Person. This Influence is very fatal both to Mens Morals and their Understandings; It sinks the Virtue of a Nation, and not only so, but destroys even Common Sense.

A furious Party Spirit, when it rages in its full Violence, exerts it self in Civil War and Blood-shed; and when it is under its greatest Restraints naturally breaks out in Falshood, Detraction, Calumny, and a partial Administration of Justice. In a word, It fills a Nation with Spleen and Rancour, and extinguishes all the Seeds of Good-nature, Compassion and Humanity.

Plutarch[1] says very finely, that a Man should not allow himself to hate even his Enemies, because, says he, if you indulge this Passion in some Occasions, it will rise of it self in others; if you hate your Enemies, you will contract such a vicious Habit of Mind, as by Degrees will break out upon those who are your Friends, or those who are indifferent to you. I might here observe how admirably this Precept of Morality (which derives the Malignity of Hatred from the Passion it self, and not from its Object) answers to that great Rule[2] which was dictated to the World about an hundred years before this Philosopher wrote;[a] but instead of that, I shall only take notice, with a real Grief of Heart, that the Minds of many good Men among us appear sowered with Party-Principles, and alienated from one another in such a manner, as seems to me altogether inconsistent with the Dictates either of Reason or Religion. Zeal for a Publick Cause is apt to breed Passions in the Hearts of virtuous Persons, to which the Regard of their own private Interest would never have betrayed them.

If this Party Spirit has so ill an Effect on our Morals, it has like-wise a very great one upon our Judgments. We often hear a poor insipid Paper or Pamphlet cryed up, and sometimes a noble Piece

[a] wrote;] writ; *Fol.*

---

[1] 'How to Profit by One's Enemies', *Moralia*, 91C. See *Plutarch's Morals by way of Abstract* (1707), p. 53: 'unless we forbear the practice of these ill qualities to our Enemies, they'll become habitual to us, and we shall be apt to do them to our Friends.'
[2] Luke vi. 27.

depretiated by those who are of a different Principle from the Author. One who is actuated by this Spirit is almost under an Incapacity of discerning either real Blemishes or Beauties. A Man of Merit in a different Principle, is like an Object seen in two different Mediums, that appears crooked or broken,[a] however streight and entire it may be in it self. For this Reason there is scarce a Person of any Figure in *England* who does not go by two contrary Characters, as opposite[b] to one another as Light and Darkness. Knowledge and Learning suffer in a particular[c] manner from this strange Prejudice, which at present prevails amongst all Ranks and Degrees in the *British* Nation. As Men formerly became eminent in learned Societies by their Parts and Acquisitions, they now distinguish themselves by the Warmth and Violence with which they espouse their respective Parties. Books are valued upon the like Considerations: An Abusive, Scurrilous Style passes for Satyr, and a dull Scheme of Party Notions is called fine Writing.

There is one Piece of Sophistry practised by both Sides, and that is the taking any[d] scandalous Story that has been ever whispered or invented of a Private Man, for a known undoubted Truth, and raising suitable Speculations upon it. Calumnies that have been never proved, or have been often refuted, are the ordinary Postulatums of these infamous Scriblers, upon which they proceed as upon first Principles granted by all Men, though in their Hearts they know they are false, or at best very doubtful. When they have laid these Foundations of Scurrility, it is no wonder that their Superstructure is every way answerable to them. If this shameless Practice of the present Age endures much longer, Praise and Reproach will cease to be Motives of Action in good Men.

There are certain Periods of Time in all Governments when this inhuman Spirit prevails. *Italy* was long torn in pieces by the *Guelfes* and *Gibellines*,[1] and *France* by those who were for and against the League, but it is very unhappy for a Man to be born in such a stormy and tempestuous Season. It is the restless Ambition of Artful Men that thus breaks a People into Factions, and draws several

---

a is . . . broken,] like an Object seen in two different Mediums, appears crooked or broken, *Fol.*   b two contrary Characters, as opposite] two Characters altogether different, and as opposite *Fol.*   c in a particular] in a very particular *Fol.*   d any] every *Fol.*

---

1 The quarrels between the Guelfs and Ghibellines took place in the thirteenth to the fifteenth centuries. The League refers to the Catholic League, formed by the Duc de Guise in 1576, for the purpose of dethroning Henri III.

well-meaning Persons[a] to their Interest, by a Specious Concern for their Country. How many honest Minds are filled with uncharitable and barbarous Notions, out of their Zeal for the Publick Good? What Cruelties and Outrages would they not commit against Men of an adverse Party, whom they would honour and esteem, if instead of considering them as they are represented, they knew them as they are? Thus are Persons of the greatest Probity seduced into shameful Errors and Prejudices, and made bad Men even by that noblest of Principles, the Love of their Country. I cannot here forbear mentioning the Famous *Spanish* Proverb, *If there were neither Fools nor Knaves in the World, all People would be of one Mind.*[1]

For my own part, I could heartily wish that all Honest Men would enter into an Association, for the Support of one another against the Endeavours of those whom they ought to look upon as their common Enemies, whatsoever side they may belong to. Were there such an honest Body of Neutral Forces,[b] we should never see the worst of Men in great Figures of Life, because they are useful to a Party; nor the best unregarded, because they are above practising those Methods which would be grateful to their Faction. We should then single every Criminal out of the Herd, and hunt him down, however formidable and overgrown he might appear: On the contrary, we should shelter distressed Innocence, and defend Virtue, however beset with Contempt or Ridicule, Envy or Defamation. In short, we should not any longer regard our Fellow-Subjects as Whigs or Tories, but should make the Man of Merit our Friend, and the Villain our Enemy.   C

[a] Persons] People *Fol. Corrected in Errata* (*No. 127*)   [b] Body of Neutral Forces,] Neutral Body of Forces, *Fol. Corrected in Errata* (*No. 127*)

[1] The proverb is recorded in England from the mid-seventeenth century (Tilley, K144, and Apperson). Spanish proverbs, according to Samuel Palmer, 'are remarkable for *Gravity* and fine *Instruction*' (*Moral Essays on Proverbs*, 1710, p. vi).